Secret Trades, Porous Borders

Secret Trades, Porous Borders

Smuggling and States Along a Southeast Asian Frontier, 1865–1915

Eric Tagliacozzo

Yale University Press

New Haven & London

Published with assistance from the Mary Cady Tew Memorial Fund.

Portions of Section III appeared previously as "Kettle on a Slow Boil: Batavia's Threat Perceptions in the Indies' Outer Islands," *Journal of Southeast Asian Studies* 31, 1 (2000): 70–100. The author is grateful to JSEAS for permission to reprint these materials.

Set in Garamond and Stone Sans types by The Composing Room of Michigan, Inc. Printed in the United States of America.

The Library of Congress has cataloged the hardcover edition as follows:

Tagliacozzo, Eric.
  Secret trades, porous borders : smuggling and states along a Southeast Asian frontier, 1865–1915 / Eric Tagliacozzo.
      p. cm
  Includes bibliographical references and index.
    ISBN 0-300-08968-6 (alk. paper)
      1. Smuggling—Asia, Southeastern—History. 2. Drug traffic—Asia, Southeastern—History. 3. Counterfeits and counterfeiting—Asia, Southeastern—History. 4. Illegal arms tranfers—Asia, Southeastern—History. 5. Asia, Southeastern—Commerce—History. 6. Asia, Southeastern—Boundaries—History. 7. Great Britain—Colonies—Asia, Southeastern—History. 8. Netherlands—Colonies—Asia, Southeastern—History—19th century. I. Title.
HJ7049.8.Z5T34 2005
364.1'33—dc22

2004027957

ISBN 978-0-300-14330-0 (pbk. : alk. paper)

A catalogue record for this book is available from the British Library.

This paper meets the requirements of ANSI/NISO Z39.48-1992 (Permanence of Paper). It contains 30 percent postconsumer waste (PCW) and is certified by the Forest Stewardship Council (FSC).

10 9 8 7 6 5 4 3 2 1

In memory of my father, Angelo Tagliacozzo

Contents

A Note on Orthography and Usage

Tracing the intertwined histories of the many populations who lived and interacted on the Anglo/Dutch frontier of colonial Southeast Asia requires the use of many spelling systems and orthographies. Both the Dutch and the British had their own (often very imperfect) systems of rendering names, places, and concepts; many local actors (such as the Acehnese and Overseas Chinese, for example) had systems as well. Applying some kind of consistency to this bewildering array of names has proved to be a difficult challenge.

I have followed several conventions to simplify these diversities. In the notes, I have used original spellings of names and places, so that documents can be found directly and easily by subsequent researchers in the various archives used in this book. Therefore Malacca rather than Melaka and Billiton rather then Belitung. In my own text, I use contemporary designations when referring to places: Aceh rather than Atjeh, Bengkulu rather than Bencoolen. This is to help the modern reader navigate the history presented here through familiar, present-day geographies.

I have used period spellings of names in virtually all cases. Because almost all of the "smugglers" discussed in this book were of the middle or lower classes, their names are not preserved other than in the ways that colonial governments recorded them. Particularly with Chinese populations, this has led to the Romanization of Chinese names with Dutch and English designations side by side. These are the only renderings we have, however, so I have used names as they appear in the sources. Chinese subethnic groupings have been simplified to modern usage: Hainanese rather than Hailam and Hakka rather than Keh.

Chinese villages mentioned in the text are noted by period renderings, with the modern designation immediately following in parentheses so that the village can be found on modern maps. Chinese cities and ports, where well known, are kept in original forms, though with the modern spellings in parentheses following the first mention: Amoy, not Xiamen, and Peking, not Beijing. Chinese provinces follow this same usage.

Acknowledgments

No book is ever written alone, and this one required more help than most, perhaps. It has been a source of considerable amazement to me how willing many colleagues have been to discuss the ideas, people, and places in this manuscript. My three former teachers among this group deserve special mention: they taught me about life and not just about scholarship, and for this and everything else they have imparted to me, I will always be grateful. Several scholars read all or most of the manuscript in one form or another over the years, and I owe them a great debt for their timely critiques and advice. Barbara Watson Andaya, Robert Cribb, Robert Elson, Ben Kiernan, Paul Kratoska, Anthony Reid, James Rush, James Scott, Jonathan Spence, Heather Sutherland, and Jean Gelman Taylor all gave of their time freely, and never asked for anything in return. Several other scholars agreed to read chapters of the manuscript related to their own work; I am indebted to J. a Campo, Jeffrey Hadler, J. Thomas Lindblad, Mona Lohanda, Rudolf Mrazek, Dian Murray, Curtis Renoe, Laurie Sears, Jim Siegel, John Sidel, Djuliati Suroyo, Thongchai Winichakul, G. Teitler, and Carl Trocki for doing so.

A much larger group of people has helped shape the way I thought about this time and place, either through my readings of their published work or through a series of fortuitous conversations over the years. In this regard, I wish to thank Leonard Andaya, Benedict Anderson, Maitrii Aung-Thwin, Greg Bankoff, Tim Barnard, Leonard Blusse, Peter Boomgaard, Raj and Ian Brown, Chris Duncan, Michael Feener, Bill Frederick, Christophe Giebel, Tom Goodman, Frances Gouda, Valerie Hansen, Lotta Hedman, Tineke Hellwig, David Henley, Cathryn Houghton, Paul Hutchcroft, Noboru Ishikawa, Eric Jones, Michael Laffan, Steve Lee, Li Tana, Elsbeth Locher-Scholten, Celia Lowe, Alfred McCoy, Ruth McVey, Audrey Kahin, Michael Montesano, Ng Chin Keong, Henk Niemeijer, Stan O'Connor, Lorraine Paterson, Nancy Peluso, Remco Raben, Merle Ricklefs, Geoff Robinson, Noelle Rodriguez, Singgih Sulistiyono, Sun Lai Chen, Tan Tai Yong, Keith Taylor, Esther Velthoen, Reed Wadley, James Warren, Meredith Weiss, Charles Wheeler, Alex Woodside, David Wyatt, and Peter Zinoman. Kerry Ward, Ray Craib, and Andrew Willford have been particularly important intellectual touchstones for me; I am very grateful to all three of them.

The History Department at Cornell and the Southeast Asia Program at Cornell have nourished me both financially and intellectually over the past five years. Colleagues and friends in both places have made learning and life, respectively, both interesting and fun. If I do not thank the members of both McGraw and Rockefeller Halls individually here, I hope they will forgive me—it's a very long list. Yet I'm especially grateful to my three modern Asian history colleagues at Cornell, Sherman Cochran, J. Victor Koschmann, and Tamara Loos, each of whom read and critiqued sections of the manuscript related to their own expertise. They (more than most) have made teaching and researching Asian history at Cornell a very good experience for me. I've had the good fortune to serve on the committees of many excellent graduate students at Cornell; they have invariably taught me more then I have taught them, both in the classroom and through their written work. Many thanks, therefore, to Andrew Abalahin, Rick Ruth, Oiyan Liu, Chie Ikeya, Jason McCluskey, Soon Keong Ong, Tai Wei Lim, Doreen Lee, Jane Ferguson, Yew-Foong Hui, Yun-Wen Sung, Jennifer Foley, Sze Wei Ang, Arsenio Nicolas, Christian Lenz, Upik Djalins, Jason Cons, Richard Guy, Jacco van den Heuvel, Lorling Lee, and Ling Xiang Quek. Kay Mansfield, Kris Mooseker, Nancy Loncto, Jenn Evangelista, Katie Kristof, Barb Donnell, and especially Judy Burkhard fed me local knowledge in New Haven and Ithaca, and I'm grateful to all of them for looking after me for the past ten years.

I am very grateful to the many funding bodies at Yale, Cornell, nationally, and internationally who funded my work over a period of twelve years in researching and writing this book. The collection of additional materials and most revisions were undertaken in Europe, Southeast Asia, and Ithaca over many scattered months. The last few weeks of revisions were completed at the Asia Research Institute in Singapore, where I had the good fortune to be a Visiting Fellow in 2003–04. I learned an enormous amount from other Fellows there. In addition to several names already mentioned, I wish to thank John Miksic, Ed McKinnon, Jamie Davidson, Mark Frost, Khoo Gaik Cheng, Vatthana Pholsena, Xiang Biao, Mika Toyota, Resil Mojares, Joel Kahn, Maila Stivins, Chee Heng Leng, Tran Ky Phuong, Momoki Shiro, K. S. Jomo, Cherian George, David Lim, Guillaume Rozenberg, Li Tang, Jenny Lindsay, and especially Geoff Wade for their friendship and companionship. Lara Heimert, Molly Egland, and Lawrence Kenney at Yale University Press waited patiently as I tried to get it right during the revisions process, and I thank them for taking a chance on the manuscript.

I am very grateful for the help I received from librarians and archivists on several continents. Collectively they assisted me in finding materials and navigating a range of different systems over the past several years. Allen Riedy, formerly of Cornell's Kroch Asia Collections, was extremely helpful in this regard. In Holland, Sierk Plantinga of the national archives guided me through the massive amounts of material on the Dutch Indies in the nineteenth century, and was always on hand when I had questions about the miles of documents still hidden away in the vaults. He also taught me how to drink genever. In Singapore, Tim Yap Fuan has been exceedingly kind to me for many years now, alerting me to sources that he thought I should see even when I never asked for them. Vimala Nambiar was also very helpful at NUS. Mona Lohanda has helped me in the Arsip Nasional on several occasions; her warmth and knowledge always made sojourns to Jakarta well worth the trip.

Lee Li Kheng of the Geography Department of the National University of Singapore expertly drafted four maps that appear in this book. Seow Chye Seng cropped and digitized all of the images with almost biblical patience. I am grateful to the Koninklijke Instituut voor Taal, Land, en Volkenkunde (Leiden), the Algemeen Rijksarchief (Den Haag), the Public Records Office (London), and the Arsip Nasional (Jakarta) for permission to publish images in their respective collections. Howard Daniel, of the Southeast Asian Treasury, provided me with an exhaustive list of currency collectors in my search for old counterfeit. I'm grateful to Francis Wee of Singapore and to Rachmana Achmad of Jakarta for permission to reprint images of two of their period counterfeit notes and coins in this book. Geoff Wade and Liu Hong provided timely advice on Chinese orthographies, and Jenny Lindsay and Tinuk Yampolsky weighed in on one particularly difficult translation from antiquated Malay that gave me fits for a week. Alex Claver and Arjan Taselaar chased down fugitive Dutch citations for me. I am very grateful for all of their efforts.

Many friends have heard versions of this story for many years now. I wish to thank them all for listening, and (as earlier) if I don't mention them all by name here, I hope they too will forgive me. Three friends from university days deserve special mention, however, as they listened for a longer period. Morgan Hall, John Heller, and Michael Steinberger made a big difference in my life. A group of friends from an even longer *duree* also helped me in ways too numerous to list here, but they will know what I mean. Jon Auerbach, Tom Crowe, Marc DeLeeuw, Douglas Gonzales, Sang Ho Kim, Dick Lau, Mark Mokryn, James O'Shea, Peter Stefanopolous, Tom Stepniewski, and, most important of all, Robert Yacoub did *not* have a hand in writing this book. It would not have been written without them, however.

My sister has been a wonderful listener for many years now. She and her family are not only my relatives, but my friends as well—an unexpected, added bonus in life. My mother also deserves much credit for this book seeing the light of day. This is not only owing to her own authorial trailblazing; there are other reasons, which she knows. My wife, Katherine Peipu Lee, had more to do with this book than any other person. Her incredible patience in the face of years of lost weekends, lost vacations, and lost summers still astounds me. She managed to smile through all of this; "It's OK, you can go and keep working," was the usual refrain. If this book has any merit at all, much of this belongs to her. Clara Tagliacozzo-Lee, our baby daughter, was born just as this manuscript was leaving my hands for the last time. She has eyed it with complete disinterest, except possibly as something good to eat. That suits me just fine.

Finally, my father, Angelo Tagliacozzo, had nothing to do with the writing of this book. It grieves me that at the time this book goes to press, I have spent exactly as long without him in this world as I was able to spend with him while he was here. My father was an extremely decent and gentle man; he had a difficult beginning in life, and the poverty and dislocation he suffered as a boy in wartime Italy led him toward knowledge as an escape. He had always wanted to be an historian, though he eventually turned in a different direction in order to help feed his family. I suppose it is not actually true that he had nothing to do with this book; he was no longer alive when my interest in this topic (and this region) started to grow, but his imprint is still here, as it is on me. This book is dedicated to him in gratitude, love, and remembrance.

Abbreviations

ARA	Algemeen Rijksarchief, The Hague (Netherlands)
ANRI	Arsip Nasional Republik Indonesia, Jakarta, (Indonesia)
BKI	Bijdragen tot de Koloniaal Instituut
BNB	British North Borneo
CO	Colonial Office Correspondence
ENI	Encyclopaedie van Nederlandsch Indie
FO	Foreign Office Correspondence
GGNEI	Governor General, Netherlands East Indies
IG	Indische Gids
IMT	Indisch Militair Tijdschrift
JMBRAS	Journal of the Malayan Branch of the Royal Asiatic Society
JSBRAS	Journal of the Straits Branch of the Royal Asiatic Society
JSEAS	Journal of Southeast Asian Studies
IWvhR	Indische Weekblad van het Recht
KIT	Koninklijk Instituut voor de Tropen
KITLV	Koninklijk Instituut voor Taal-, Land-, en Volkenkunde
KV	Koloniaal Verslag

Kyshe	Kyshe's Law Reports, Straits Settlements
MMK	Memorie van Overgaven, Ministerie van Kolonien
MR	Mailrapport
MvBZ	Minister, Buitenlandse Zaken (Foreign Affairs, The Hague)
MvK	Minister, Kolonien (Colonies, The Hague)
MvM	Ministerie van Marine (Marine, The Hague)
NEI	Netherlands East Indies
PRO	Public Records Office, London, (England)
PVBB	Politieke Verslagen en Berigten, Buitengewesten (MvK)
RIMA	Review of Malaysian and Indonesian Affairs
SLJ	Straits Law Journal
SS	Straits Settlements
SSBB	Straits Settlements Blue Books
SSGG	Straits Settlements Government Gazette
SSLCP	Straits Settlements Legislative Council Proceedings
SSLR	Straits Settlements Legal Reports
SSMAR	Straits Settlements Municipal Administrative Reports
TAG	Tijdschrift voor Aardrijkskundige Genootschap
TBB	Tijdschrift voor het Binnenlandsch Bestuur
TITLV	Tijdschrift voor Indische Taal-, Land-, en Volkenkunde
TNI	Tijdschrift voor Nederlandsch Indie
TBG	Tijdschrift van het Bataviaasch Genootschap
VBG	Verhandelingen van het Bataviaasch Genootschap

Chapter 1 Introduction

I remember a night near Bahia, when I was enveloped in a firework display
of phosphorescent fireflies; their pale lights glowed, went out, shone
again, all without piercing the night with any true illumination. So it is
with events; beyond their glow, darkness prevails.
—Fernand Braudel, *On History* (1977)

On May 22, 1890, the ruler of a small state under Dutch control in
Aceh, North Sumatra, wrote a brief letter in Malay. The addressee was
a Chinese man named Baba Seng, who lived across the Straits of
Melaka in the British colonial possessions on the Malay Peninsula.
The Acehnese chief informed the Chinese trader that he was in need
of certain items: twenty breech-loading rifles, twenty Russian-made
shoulder straps, percussion caps, and rifle oil, among other objects. In
return the Acehnese leader promised a cargo of pepper from his own
agricultural supplies, which would have fetched Baba Seng a good
deal of money on the open market of Melaka. The letter was sent via
two couriers, both of whom were Acehnese women.[1] There is no surviving record of whether the transaction actually occurred, or whether
this journey to smuggle arms and ammunition into the Dutch

Indies—and pepper out of it—was foiled by the colonial authorities. Two things are known for certain, however. This sort of contrabanding happened often on the Anglo/Dutch frontier in colonial Southeast Asia, and much of the time—if not most of the time—these voyages were never caught. The development of a three-thousand-kilometer boundary between British and Dutch spheres, starting about 1865 and more or less finishing in 1915, was always a work in progress. During this fifty-year period smuggled goods continued to cross the frontier against the wishes of both colonial states.

This hundred-year-old letter to Baba Seng nicely frames some of the major questions asked in this book. First, what is the nature of goods in transit? Is there a fixed nature of commodities as they travel across unstable spaces such as international boundaries? How do time, geography, and other factors help determine when goods are considered to be contraband and when they are not? Second, what is the role of culture in "smuggling"? How and when are partnerships formed to undertake these activities? Who gets involved? What role do ethnicity, language, and class play in these deliberations? Third, how do states "see"? What factors contribute to the optics of states, especially along frontiers? What is the role of technology on both sides of the contrabanding fence? What avoidance mechanisms are used by "smugglers" to outwit what is in most cases the state's far superior resources?[2]

In this book I chronicle the nature, practice, and extent of various "secret trades" along the Anglo/Dutch frontier in five decades around the turn of the twentieth century. What were the dynamics of this contraband milieu? How did the system function—ethnically, geographically, and in terms of social classes? Why did Singapore and, to a lesser extent, the ports of Penang, Melaka, and Labuan emerge as ideal centers for this commerce, and how far did their economic tentacles extend across the border into the Netherlands Indies? These questions are answered below in five sections, divided into two roughly equal halves of this book. The first half has two parts. Section 1 examines how a border was constructed by the two colonial states between 1865 and 1915 through various mechanisms of surveillance, interdiction, and enforcement, such as mapping, exploration, and armed force. Section 2 then asks which groups and phenomena the colonial state found threatening along the frontier, especially in terms of the dangers posed by activities like cross-border smuggling and movement. The second half of the book asks how this boundary, while in the process of being created both physically and in the colonial imagination, was crossed by a variety of contrabanders, each with their own agendas and concerns. Section 3 discusses these crossings through the examples of three contraband commodities: narcotics, counterfeit currency, and trafficked human beings. Section 4 subsequently narrows the field of vision down to a single contrabanding line, the commerce across the border in illegal arms and ammunition. Finally, section 5 looks at many of these issues through the lens of a single case, that of the junk *Kim Ban An,* which was caught "smuggling" off the coast of Aceh in 1873. Over the course of the next twenty-five years, the court records of this case, including the statements of the participants themselves, open a unique window on the world of smuggling at this time.

I argue in this book that the development of a border between British and Dutch colonial regimes in Southeast Asia was intimately linked with the massive amounts of smuggling that passed across this frontier. Stated another way, this book shows two sides of the same coin: boundary production and the boundary transgression (through contrabanding) that accompanied it. European abilities to construct and maintain a border certainly grew during the period 1865–1915, largely because of advancements in applied technologies and organization, which I explore below. Yet Western fears, and particularly Dutch fears, of the "wild space" of the frontier regions never really waned over the course of this half century, as section 2 suggests. Smuggling in its many manifestations (of drugs, arms, people, and currency, the four principal examples presented here) had much to do with this paradoxical dynamic. Although these states waged fairly successful wars against some of these "secret trades" (such as counterfeit currency), other lines, such as narcotics, were never controlled during the half century under discussion. Still other contraband commodities, such as the various trades in human beings in the form of prostitutes, "coolies," and slaves, metamorphosed over time and went more or less underground. I chronicle in this book the various ways in which the Anglo/Dutch border was created, nourished, and strengthened by these modernizing colonial states, but also prodded and ultimately penetrated by smugglers at the same time.

Borders, frontiers, and boundaries are not precisely the same thing, as scholars such as J. V. Prescott have shown. Yet for the purposes of this book, I use the terms more or less interchangeably. This is because the divide between British and Dutch spheres in Asia over fifty years was changing and evolving continually, from a frontier to a border or boundary over time.[3] Some reaches of this space remained frontier zones long after Europeans had decided that such a thing as a border now existed in any particular place. Every boundary has two sides, and it is tempting to give equal weight to sources and perspectives on both sides of the Anglo/Dutch frontier. In studying the history of smuggling and its relationship to the emergence of a border in this arena, however, this would be a mistake. The Dutch in the Netherlands Indies were always far more worried about the boundary and those crossing it than were the British in their Southeast Asian possessions. There was good reason for this: the vast majority of smuggling, for a variety of economic and political reasons that will be made clear, was crossing the frontier into the Indies. Thus, although I use a large amount of archival and historiographical data from English sources of various provenances, the majority perspective in this book is Dutch.[4] It was the Dutch, with their monopolistic economic tendencies and their continuous struggles with indigenous polities along the border, who left the most by way of sources for studying the dynamics of this shared frontier. Wherever possible, indigenous perspectives on border construction and smuggling are also highlighted, though these kinds of documents were rarely produced and are often difficult to find.

The story of borders and smuggling in this particular place is outlined schematically, using data and correspondence from the Dutch and British residencies and territories lining this evolving border in Southeast Asia.[5] Statistics have been compiled and provided where I think they are reliable, and even at times where I think they are useful for what they do *not* tell us about particular lines of commerce or overall trading milieus. Yet the nature of information on smuggling, and perhaps particularly smuggling that was crossing a sensitive, evolving international border, is always going to be fragmentary at best. I have not relied solely on a large-scale economic and political narrative in telling this story, therefore. Rather, I also focus on many individual people and places to give an idea of how borders and smuggling actually were interacting on the ground. The Dutch counterfeit currency expert G. C. Bouwman is introduced, therefore, as is G. A. F. Molengraaf, the great colonial explorer of Borneo. Testimonials of Chinese woodcutters who were trafficked to coastal Sumatra are provided, alongside the witness statements of men whose ships were pirated off the shore of Aceh. The island of Bangka's waters are scrutinized as a window on changes in imperial hydrographic abilities along the frontier toward the turn of the twentieth century. Seizures of morphine in Penang in 1906 are analyzed. The physical locus of this study is the Anglo/Dutch boundary in Insular Southeast Asia, but radials of the story occasionally penetrate the border and reach lands at some distance from the frontier, such as Java, Timor, and even China, Arabia, and Japan. This particular border can be seen, therefore, as a swirling maelstrom of people, landscapes, and connections that both increasingly bound the region into a new grid and also maintained links outside of it at the same time.

SMUGGLING AND ITS CONTEXTS

Study of the movements of large amounts of contraband leads to certain conclusions about the nature and conduct of these systems. The entirety of this illicit commerce might be called "undertrading": the passage of goods underneath, or at the legal and geographic interstices of, the majority of items being traded in this arena. Undertrading seems to have had a phased existence in this region, with certain products and even some ports passing in and out of an undertrade category. No items in these waters were designated as contraband simply on ontological grounds. Rather, particular historical moments dictated to regional colonial governments whether or not it was in their self-interest to designate products as officially illegal. Thus while guns, unfarmed opium, and especially human beings, for example, prostitutes and slaves, were often demarcated as contraband, other commodities such as pepper, porcelain, and even bulk shipments of rice were only sometimes listed so. Likewise, specific ports could be declared to be open to trade or strictly off-limits, depending on a variety of factors that worked to the advantage of these same colonial governments. Both scenarios encouraged a brisk flow of officially illicit goods, either in newly illegal items or to newly illegal places.

Some spaces were judged to be better than others for smuggling on a consistent basis, however, so that favored geographies of contrabanding make themselves apparent in the records. Undertrading as a category in history happens most often in three places: at borders and peripheries, furthest from the vision and reach of the state; at natural choke points, such as mountain passes and narrow waterways, where trade is channeled because of geography; and in urban confusion, where the state is somewhat blinded by the frenzy of activity. Singapore, for example, was the perfect focal point for undertrading activities. Situated along the narrow waterway of the Straits, it also served as a maritime border town at the frontier of two evolving colonial states, Dutch and British Southeast Asia.[6] The city was a crucial haven for smugglers because of its size and chaotic complexity as well. Here the vision and reach of the state, supposedly at its strongest at the seat of regional imperial power, were actually diminished in its own backyard. There were never enough coast guard cutters or police; there were always too many sampans or dark alleys. This amaurosis was very dangerous from the perspective of area regimes. When the coercive power of government was brought down upon local smugglers to stop their illegal activities, these groups resisted domination in various ways. False shipping papers, false destinations, hidden cargo spaces, and small, fast sailing craft were all utilized alongside other means of avoidance, including loopholes in the law and the use of fall guys by well-organized syndicates.[7]

Smuggling also happens often in a fourth space, albeit an abstract one: in the networks of corruption and private interest that riddle the state in the form of its own civil servants. The collaboration and cooperation of such actors was often crucial to the success of contraband undertakings, as these men could ensure that the gaze of the state potentially rested elsewhere at the appropriate time. This certainly happened in both the Dutch and British spheres in nineteenth-century Southeast Asia, as will be seen in this book. Yet it is difficult to find abundant records of these liaisons, as both colonial powers had much invested in their regimes' supposed moral superiority, at least in the face of their subject populations. Documentation of corruption in the ranks, therefore, whether the officials were European or indigenous, is not always readily or willingly or quickly forthcoming. Nevertheless, this phenomenon was also an important part of the history of contrabanding in the region, as will be shown below.

Archival documentation by itself would not be sufficient to cover the full dimensions of this story, however. It has been said that the job of peasants is to keep themselves out of the archives; historians know something has gone wrong when the state starts to take an interest in the daily lives of the peasantry, as the reason usually involves protest or discontent. It is difficult to think of another group for whom this adage is truer than for smugglers. Most state records of smuggling are chronicles of failure, therefore: the specifics of many cases wind up being written down only when contrabanders have been caught. Nevertheless, clues about smuggling and its relationship with colonial border formation can be searched for in other places as well. Newspapers are very helpful in this regard, as are the field notes of early anthropologists and missionaries at the turn of the century. Travelers' tales, such as those of Joseph Conrad, have also been scrutinized to show how much factual information can be gleaned from contemporary eyewitness descriptions of places and events.[8] Court cases, witness testimonials, and captured letters allow us to hear the specifics of operations, sometimes in smugglers' own voices. When period photographs, shipping columns, and treaties are thrown into this mix, an idea of the range and depth of sources available for use emerges. Oral accounts which have been eventually catalogued and written down, as well as surviving material culture artifacts themselves, have also been extremely helpful stores of information.[9]

Who smuggled commodities in colonial Southeast Asia? It would not be an exaggeration to answer, "Just about everyone": Chinese populations of various subgroupings and linguistic affiliations, "Malays," Bugis, Dayaks, Japanese, and "Sea Gypsies" all took their turn. Europeans, as just stated, were involved in these transactions as well, sometimes running contraband against their own colonial administrations. Sarasin Viraphol has shown how many people it took to outfit a single ocean-going junk for trade journeys abroad; the numbers could reach into the hundreds, all with an investment in the cargo. He has also noted the convenient fictions used by merchants and corrupt civil servants to get commodities past monopolistic state systems, including disguising trade goods as ballast to evade legal restrictions.[10] The importance of redistributing commodities to subordinates as a mode of ensuring vassalage seems to have been a pan—Southeast Asian trait, shoring up status and bonding manpower to leaders throughout the region.[11] The stakes for trading—or smuggling—successfully, therefore, were rather high in this part of the world. Ensuring a flow of desired goods whose transit nevertheless was sometimes against government regulations could mean the difference between maintaining one's power or losing it to one's rivals. The fact that the overhead needed for smuggling operations was often very low—a boat, some provisions, and knowledge of local tides, sandbars, and winds—meant that many actors could participate in contrabanding.[12] With the imposition of powerful European states in the region in the late nineteenth century, many local peoples did indeed try to make money in this way.

Why? What were the reasons that could induce people to risk life and limb on journeys of this sort? The contrabander's calculus is a complicated one, but the rationales and decisions concerning these journeys likely circled around three major issues: power, revenue, and morality. From a government's point of view, the state cannot afford to share the means of physical coercion or of power with any other partners; this was why the illegal traffic in arms, for example, was so anxiety provoking to Batavia. Flip this equation, and the smuggler's vantage on the issue of power appears: arms are needed precisely to fend off the unwanted advances of the state, or even to compete with other armed competitors locally in Southeast Asia. From a revenue perspective, the modern state cannot afford to lose out on the monopoly and taxation regimes it has erected to ensure its financial survival. Opium, for example, was a state monopoly in both the Dutch and English spheres, providing up to half of both government's revenues. The massive commerce in illegal opium therefore was seen as very dangerous. Finally, the ostensible morality of the civilizing mission of colonial states was also an issue upon which the dynamics of contraband turned. Such trades as the trafficking of underage prostitutes or slaves could not be allowed to continue if the civilizing mission was to hold any legitimacy, at least from the perspective of the colonial state. Yet Southeast Asians often saw these proscriptions very differently, as their own moral hierarchies vis-à-vis the commerce in slaves and women were dissimilar to European ones. Decisions to smuggle or not to smuggle thus revolved around all three of these issues and took on different complexions in different situations.

Such forms of state-designated criminality and resistance against ruling regimes have taken on many guises in human history. If James Scott is right in saying the peasantry has had certain everyday ways of resisting state and elite exactions, then how much more so must this have been true for merchants and long-distance traders?[13] Possessing capital and distant contacts which the peasantry would have been denied, and a mobility that was a component part of their occupation, merchants and the corrupt officials who often were their allies resisted the tightening strictures of government in many ways, but especially by smuggling. Some of these traders were merely continuing age-old commodity lines that only now were designated as contrabanding by area governments. Others saw the new imposition of borders and rigid controls as an opportunity to make money from the changing political and economic circumstances. In all of these cases, however, such actors often passed from colonial compradors to outlaws, though many of the smartest ones seem to have been able to occupy both niches at once. Studies on the nature of criminality in the nineteenth century, from industrializing Western Europe to colonial Southeast Asia, help us understand these processes as they unfolded.[14] Yet because resistance against the colonial state was such a highly contextual decision, it remains to be seen when local populations decided to contraband and when they did not. Scholarly debates have often been instructive in this vein, outlining the parameters of decision making in so-called criminal acts against the state at various times, venues, and places.[15]

Smuggling is a small but growing topic in histories of the emerging global political economy. For colonial Southeast Asia, however, only historiographical fragments touch in some way upon these activities. Prostitution has been examined in colonial Singapore, for example, but the actual mechanisms of human trafficking usually have appeared only as prologue to studies of women's lives *inside* the colony.[16] Likewise, pepper and tin smuggling in South Sumatra and contraband rice and iron cargoes in northern Vietnam have been explored, but only as brief notes in works dealing with other topics.[17] Economic histories of the Straits Settlements and the Dutch Indies have also tantalized with their overviews of trade in the colonies, but there has been little attempt to quantify or critique the movement of contraband *beneath* the statistics.[18] None of these studies has set out to describe illegal trafficking as the *raison d'être* of inquiry. Each has been concerned primarily with a holistic examination of a particular phenomenon, such as prostitution, piracy, or the overarching flow of a colony's trade. Yet it is precisely this marginalization of smuggling to an economic aside that has led to a gap in our understanding of colonial Southeast Asia generally. Many of the same actors—ethnically, geographically, and socioeconomically—were involved in a variety of legal and illegal activities simultaneously. This book moves away from an approach that studies these phenomena in isolation and asks how smugglers and advancing borders interacted with the larger structures of colonial society as a whole.

THE EVOLVING SPATIAL GRID

The history of smuggling in this part of Southeast Asia and the attempts to stop it by various incarnations of states and protostate polities stretches back centuries into the region's past. Early civilizations in this part of the world did not evince clear-cut borders and boundaries that could be crossed illegally. Rather, they often existed, especially on the mainland, in the form of mandalas, a geographic core of strong authority which radiated outward in progressively weaker fashion until it ceased to command effective allegiance at all. In Insular Southeast Asia, a concomitant model saw petty kingdoms establishing themselves in the mouths of rivers; authority consisted of trying to establish control over trade, especially in the taxing of products that moved up and down river (*hulu* and *hilir, respectively*). Both of these organizational scenarios left room for the activities of smugglers. The first great maritime civilization of Southeast Asia, Srivijaya (seventh to twelfth centuries CE), built much of its prosperity on the monopoly of trade through the Straits of Melaka. The kingdom held outposts on both the Sumatran and Malay Peninsula sides of the Straits and thus was able to force shipping that was passing through to submit to coercive taxation, a policy that encouraged contrabanding by merchants who were able to avoid paying these dues.[19] The Melaka Sultanate, which succeeded Srivijaya as the paramount locus of authority in these waters several centuries later, learned from this experience and kept customs and port duties at much lower levels, trying to encourage a high volume of trade.[20] Yet because Melaka (in present-day Malaysia) became a famous transit point for the passage of goods with very high value-to-bulk/weight ratios, including gold dust, gems, spices, and medicinal "exotica", it can be assumed that a fair amount of smuggling of these items took place as well.

With the concerted appearance of the Dutch on the scene in the seventeenth century, however, some of these patterns began to change. The Vereenigde Oostindische Compagnie (VOC), or Dutch East Indies Company, tried to ensure profits in its conquest of parts of what it called the East Indies (modern-day Indonesia) by enacting draconian policies of enforced monopoly, especially on the production and transit of spices. In eastern Indonesia, particularly in Maluku (what used to be called the Spice Islands), these policies included wholesale murder of the inhabitants of certain clove- and nutmeg-producing islands, deportation, and armed surveillance over spice gardens to ensure that the commodities were not smuggled out to the financial detriment of the Dutch monopoly.[21] In western Indonesia during the eighteenth and nineteenth centuries, repressive measures were also taken against the free trade of tin from Bangka and Belitung islands, which induced the inhabitants to try to sell their ores on the sly to passing English merchantmen and Chinese junks.[22] Certain inlets and creeks outside Batavia, the Dutch Indies capital (contemporary Jakarta), were famed in eastern waters as rendezvous points for smugglers. Some of the primary actors in these midnight liaisons, of course, were underpaid VOC men themselves, who bargained within sight of their own capital.[23]

By the decades around the turn of the nineteenth century, some of the political geography that would become important in the period this book examines was already beginning to harden. In 1769, the British took Balambangan island, off the tip of North Borneo, and in 1786, Penang, at the northern terminus of the Straits of Melaka, was also annexed. Sir Stamford Raffles's famous acquisition of Singapore in 1819, bisecting these two earlier outposts, begins to show the outline of the "necklace" that would become the Anglo/Dutch boundary throughout insular Southeast Asia (see maps). An important treaty in 1824 split the Straits for the first time, exchanging British and Dutch territories on either side, but trade and influence across this burgeoning frontier of influence continued apace. In the early 1840s, James Brooke, an English adventurer, set up his own petty kingdom in western Borneo; this move was watched carefully by Batavia, with great unease as to its implications. The British Crown took Labuan island, further north off the coast of West Borneo, in the 1840s as well. Attempts by other adventurers such as the American Gibson in Jambi in 1851 to carve out niches of their own along this rapidly developing frontier were viewed

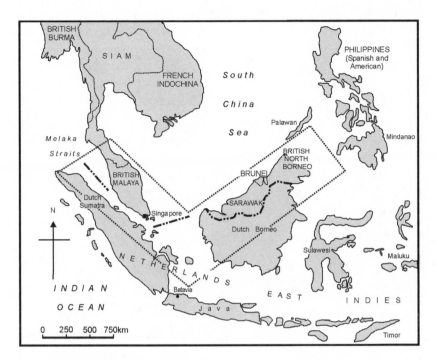

Lands and Seas of the Anglo/Dutch Frontier

with tremendous anxiety by the Dutch. Finally, in 1871, the two colonial powers came to the treaty table again to delineate their respective spheres. London acknowledged Sumatra as an entirely Dutch preserve, in exchange for guaranteed commercial rights across the newly stiffened maritime boundary. Two years later, the Dutch attacked and subsequently began the process of subjugating the Sultanate of Aceh, the last independent polity of any size along the length of the frontier. A year after that, in 1874, the British began their own Forward Movement on the Malay Peninsula, expanding their power and influence into Perak. This book examines cross-border smuggling in this region from the mid-1860s until around 1915, when the frontier took on the shape it predominantly has today.

Many processes were required to fashion this emerging Anglo/Dutch frontier in Southeast Asia. The various tasks of mapping the border, which included exploration, actual surveying, and then categorizing of the resulting data into forms the two colonial states could process and understand, proceeded throughout the period 1865–1915. Scholarly classics on the trajectories of imperialism have provided a broad conceptual framework for studying how these

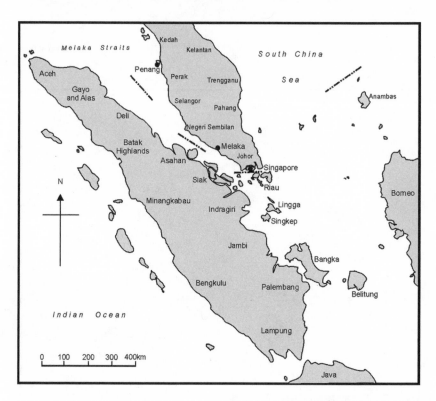

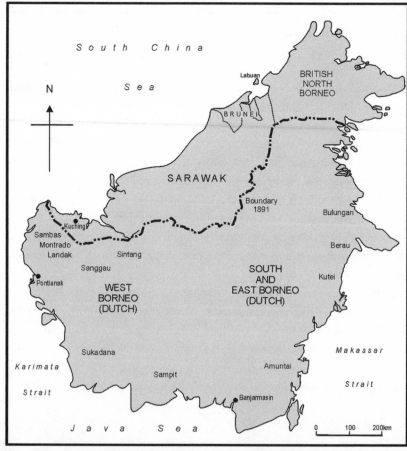

borders began to be enforced.[24] Analyses looking at the British side of this equation have been undertaken by comparatively few authors; India has always captured the attention of British imperial historiography much more than Southeast Asia.[25] Writings on Dutch imperialism in the Indies, on the whole, have been far more numerous and contentious. Some authors have questioned whether Dutch Imperialism has been qualitatively different from other imperial projects generally, a query that has generated fierce debate. Though this discussion started in earnest in the 1970s, in recent years some important studies have been added to the conversation, most notably new revisionist work on Dutch foreign policy. Much of the best of this scholarship, unfortunately for the incorporation of this topic into larger imperial themes, has been in Dutch.[26]

If border formation in Insular Southeast Asia was accomplished through programs of coercive European military force, it was also undertaken through sustained and complicated projects of mapping. Several important scholarly contributions have examined these processes in the region, though again much of the most detailed literature here is available only in Dutch.[27] The best work on the conceptual evolution of border formation in colonial Southeast Asia still remains outside of the Austronesian world, however, and is represented by Thongchai Winichakul's penetrating *Siam Mapped*.[28] The geographic and epistemological processes described in this book have not yet found an equivalent in the insular lands and seas of this region. Explanations of state formation in frontier areas along the lines of sophisticated recent studies of early modern Europe are also lacking. This is unfortunate, as the processes of state-sponsored violence described for European history were precursors for Western dynamics of expansion elsewhere in the world.[29] This has been true particularly in Southeast Asia, as this region, like Europe, consisted of many small to midsize polities with adjoining and sometimes overlapping border territories.

The conceptual study of how borders are actually formed has become a large and sophisticated field, as scholars have begun the task of showing how disparate regions experienced often similar processes in different ways. There are lessons to be learned for Southeast Asia in analyzing the history of the fur trade around the Canadian Great Lakes, for example, while St. Petersburg's push to the great timber reserves of the Russian far east is also instructive from a resource perspective.[30] In China, Xinjiang and Gansu provinces in the far west

The Malay Peninsula, Sumatra, and Borneo

were often used as places of exile by the Chinese imperium, while in the Amazon the Brazilian rubber frontier expanded until many local peoples had no choice but to become a part of regional economies.[31] In India, disease and its relationship with border regions have also been examined, as historians have tried to track the movement of pathogens into outlying populations.[32] All of these global frontier circumstances have had analogs on the emerging Anglo/Dutch boundary in Southeast Asia, whether resources, politics, or the incorporation of indigenous peoples is under discussion. Several scholars have made a start at comparing the experiences and circumstances of unrelated borderlands across time and space; their conclusions are interesting and surprising and span culture, politics, and rural economy.[33] Other authors have also weighed in on the debate, focusing on border villages in the Pyrenees, questions of identity on world frontiers, and revisions of the famous Turner Thesis of the American West as well its substantial intellectual heritage.[34]

Yet until recently the study of the emerging boundary between Dutch and British colonial spheres in Southeast Asia has lagged behind that of these other regions. In the late 1960s, solid work dealing with aspects of this frontier in Borneo and North Sumatra was published, but since then ideas of how to study borders have significantly changed.[35] Only in the past fifteen years have some studies looked at particular aspects of local boundary formation from a variety of new perspectives. Analyses of the nuanced, ever-changing relationship between regional indigenous powers and Batavia have been among these attempts, while exciting new work on the economy of the Indies' so-called Outer Islands also has been completed.[36] Other studies, particularly of the Koninklijke Paketvaart Maatschappij (Royal Dutch Packet Service) and of the Indonesian inter-island shipping industry, have shown how the maritime component of state formation in the periphery often brought the frontier much closer to the "center."[37] This was especially important in the Indies because most of the Anglo/Dutch frontier was water-, not land-based. Shallow, narrow, and separating lands claiming similar languages, ethnicities, and religions, the Straits of Melaka was not the ideal place to draw an international dividing line. The fact that trade and migration had filtered across and through the Straits for at least two thousand years also posed problems to anyone seeking to enforce boundary lines. These challenges to the fixity of borders and processes of boundary formation will be discussed in some detail in the pages that follow.

The economic world created by the political advances mentioned above was one of stark extremes and contrasts in the late nineteenth and early twentieth centuries. On the British side of the emerging boundary, the western coast of

Malaya was fast becoming a source of wealth through colonial plantations, especially for rubber and oil palms, and tin mining, which had a pedigree on the peninsula dating back to precolonial days.[38] Sarawak and British North Borneo, run by the Brookes and the North Borneo Company, respectively, ultimately became highly resource-driven enterprises as well, though at a later date than on the peninsula.[39] Yet there were still vast arboreous tracts of forest separating British and Dutch spheres along the border in Borneo, far from the burgeoning world of British mines and plantations. In the Indies, the economy of large parts of the border residencies classically has been described as evidence of a dual economy developing between Dutch capital-intensive agriculture and extraction and the village economy of local indigenous producers. In this depiction of the Outer Islands, there was little meeting between the economic world of indigenes and that of their colonial overlords.[40] Yet recent scholarship has suggested how complicated economic interactions and cross-fertilizations in the border residencies really were, in linking Dutch capital, local producers, and area ports such as Singapore into one convoluted web.[41] The economic bonds between colonizer and colonized on the border were extremely nuanced, therefore, and connections both to colonial centers such as Batavia and Surabaya and other colonial outposts like the Straits Settlements were various and complex.

COMMODITIES AND CHANGING WORLDS

The wide variety of sources that must be used to analyze border evolution opens a window on the equally wide variety of commodities that were smuggled across the Anglo/Dutch frontier. For the purposes of this book, several of these goods have been highlighted, so as to flesh out the specific details of these trades. As noted earlier, the commerce in illegal narcotics, counterfeit currency, and trafficked human beings makes up the content of section 3, while an examination of the illegal arms trade into the Indies constitutes the entirety of section 4. Section 5, where the details of a single junk caught contrabanding across the Straits of Melaka serves as the narrative, explores rice, pepper, and betel-nut smuggling as well as some of the items already mentioned above. Yet many other commodities could have been used to illustrate the patterns and trends explored in this book. The illegal transit of alcohol and spirits, printed matter, or a variety of other goods could also have been utilized to demonstrate these movements.

The quiet trade in spirits along this frontier is a good example. From as early as the 1850s, ports like Labuan, off the western coast of Borneo, farmed out licenses to sell spirits in order to raise revenues for the colony's exchequer. Almost as quickly, smuggling syndicates sprung up to challenge these monopolies, necessitating constant changes in the laws to fight these attacks on securing government profits.[42] Liquor was also contrabanded elsewhere in the British possessions, such as on the Malay Peninsula, while Malay-language newspapers from the 1890s make clear that even the seat of English power, Singapore, was never fully immune to these problems.[43] Gin, brandy, whisky, and even homemade arrack all poured across the border and into the Dutch Indies as well.[44] This happened in places like West Borneo, where smugglers brought small batches of European liquor in at a time to circumvent the regulations of the local monopoly, while the frontier-adjacent Dutch farms in Riau and Aceh also lost money.[45] Attempts to ban the transit of alcohol altogether to indigenous populations along the Dutch Indies border residencies (as part of a moral crusade) were doomed to failure because of the profits traders reaped by these sales. Only at the turn of the twentieth century were larger, more systemic efforts made to staunch these commodity flows, in places like Sulu where the cooperation of other colonial governments could be counted upon as well.[46]

The movement of certain types of print media is another case in point. Letters of certain types, such as those advocating conspiracy or revolt against the state, were also contrabanded across the frontier. In 1889, for example, a Dutch translator was sent to Sarawak to interpret thirty-eight Chinese letters linking secret society activities in Kuching with Chinese miners in Dutch Mandor and Montrado.[47] "Incendiary" letters between Muslims on both sides of the frontier seemed to be far more common, however. In between the two Dutch onslaughts on Aceh in 1873, reams of letters were sneaked across the Dutch border by members of the Acehnese war party in the Straits Settlements, linking Banjarmasin in southeastern Borneo, Padang in West Sumatra, and Cirebon and Banten, both in Java. Attempts like these to coordinate activities among Muslims frightened Batavia immensely, leading to the seizure of at least two hundred suspicious letters in 1881 alone. Some of the letters traveled from as far away as Arabia to get into the Indies, though they did not always reach their final destinations. The flow of radical Islamic newspapers from Ottoman Turkey and other locales also produced anxiety among Dutch policy planners in the Indies. The appearance of such agitprop periodicals in the archipelago led to seizures and bans on certain editions, as well as to jurisprudence being enacted which "protected" local peoples from such "evil" outside influences.[48]

Yet contraband could be just about anything else as well, so long as colonial governments in the region decided it was in their interests to call it that. The age-old trade in Sumatra gaharu-wood, dammar resins, and gold dust, therefore, was designated a contraband commerce during the Aceh War because the Dutch knew these products were valuable and easy to hide and would fetch the Acehnese high prices across the Straits in Penang.[49] Animal products from places under temporary quarantine for disease, such as offal, hooves, and manes from Bombay and Karachi, were also periodically banned but were brought quietly into the Indies anyway by those seeking a profit.[50] Salt was continuously contrabanded across the Dutch Indies frontier, largely because the prices for it were so variable from place to place and almost always cheaper on the British side of the border.[51] The list goes on and on, from high-quality cigars to stocks of cloth, coils of thin wire (considered to be dangerous during wartime) to uncopyrighted books.[52] Under the rain forest canopy in Borneo, a contraband trade developed in five-hundred-year-old Ming jars, which local Dayaks wanted to trade across the frontier but were told would now be taxed.[53] Even live orangutans were sometimes seized, such as one poor creature that was found in chains aboard a junk pulling out of Singapore harbor.[54] All of these commodities were transited across the border, at different times and at different places, but always against the will (moral, financial, or political) of at least one of the two European regimes.

Contrabanding was easier at some moments than at others in the period studied here. In the mid-1860s, the Anglo/Dutch frontier was already a continually evolving entity: the border was not fixed but was subtly changing shape in a variety of places. As new contracts were closed with area chieftains in Borneo and treaties were negotiated and renegotiated among other peoples on the frontier, the border continually undulated in its form on the ground. Dozens of small polities abutted the boundary in different places: in Dutch Borneo alone, Batavia had to compile comprehensive lists to keep track of such principalities. Chinese mining communities along the frontier also deepened this complexity, as did the presence of many nomadic peoples, who ignored the existence of a border altogether. The fact that area population statistics were changing rapidly lent even more instability to this equation, as migration and labor-based movements shifted people in all directions. Trying to carve a discrete, economically and politically enforceable frontier out of this sort of composite was very difficult, therefore. The resources available to the two colonial states rarely seemed sufficient for this task.

Nevertheless, around 1915 a very different picture of this three-thousand-kilometer-long space is evident. The complicated mix of micropolities, European states, freely wandering itinerant populations, and semi-independent mining communities no longer existed in the same form as a half century earlier. Though Dutch courts and even Dutch statesmen recognized that some Asian populations were still technically outside their direct supervision and control, the noose had tightened around these principalities at an increasingly rapid pace. Vassals who had formerly issued licenses to their own ships were no longer allowed to do so; even the word *vassal* was no longer used in Dutch dealings with these dominions, as *self-governing region* was thought to better convey the new "holistic" relationship.[55] Across the Straits in the British territories of Southeast Asia, matters were much the same. In 1909, the remaining Unfederated Malay States on the peninsula were incorporated to a position under British control. These administrative strengthenings by both colonial powers raised the level of enforcement each had on trade and movement in their respective spheres. Yet to survive, contrabanding needed to evolve as well. For this reason, smuggling, too, became more sophisticated by the decades around the turn of the century, matching the abilities of the state in many places along the length of the frontier.

One of the most important ways contrabanders were able to do this was by using local knowledge as an ally. The technological curve on surveillance, interdiction, and control capabilities was usually in the state's favor; to even the playing field somewhat, smugglers relied on their detailed knowledge of local conditions. The geography of the Straits of Melaka as an arena for smuggling is a case in point here. Five hundred miles long and with a width tapering from three hundred to only eight miles at its narrowest point, the Straits were a huge grid upon which to trade and travel, even when doing so was constricted by law. The depths of the Straits changed enormously from point to point, sometimes shrinking to only a few meters for the north-south passage, while the prevailing currents and wind conditions were also highly variable.[56] Contrabanders, from long experience trading across this shallow gulf, made the most of the speed and concealment possibilities offered by this domain to outwit the colonial state. A similar situation existed in overland Borneo, where local knowledge of the frontier manifested itself in the use of footpaths (*setapak*) and hidden tributaries, rather than of reefs and tiny waterways, which enabled one to hide. Much of the history of smuggling across the frontier was a game of knowledge of local conditions, therefore, a concept the colonial state came to learn over time, just as smugglers (conversely) learned to use the state's technologies.

A final note should be included here on geography and how it is used in this book, not just by smugglers and colonial states but conceptually as well. There has been an increasing awareness recently of the difficulties of studying regions by state-centered geographies, a concept that has received some attention in broader historiographical discussions of how historians write history.[57] In Southeast Asia and on the Anglo/Dutch colonial frontier in particular this movement has also gained momentum in recent years. Several scholars have begun to use this approach to great effect for the Early Modern period, while others have shown its implications in the study of economics, and still others for the analysis of culture patterns in the wider Java Sea.[58] For the study of smuggling and border-formation patterns in colonial-era Southeast Asia, such a perspective seems not only provocative and interesting, but also indispensable as a tool of analysis. The period 1865–1915 is interesting precisely because it was during this time that the building blocks of the nation-state were coming into being in this part of the world and were not yet taken for granted by colonial states or by their subjects. Hence patterning an examination around a wider, more inclusive geography—one that includes stretches of contemporary Malaysia, Singapore, Indonesia, Brunei, and the Philippines—seems only just. It was in the testing and contesting of these emerging boundaries that smuggling found its role, both as a profit-making enterprise and as a vigorous project of resistance.

NOTES

1. The letter, dated 2 Saawal 1307 A.H. (May 22, 1890), is enclosed in ARA, Dutch Consul, Singapore to Acting Colonial Secretary, Straits Settlements, 3 Nov. 1890, no. 1367, in (MvBZ/A Dossiers/Box 111/A.49ss).

2. I use the terms *smugglers* and *smuggling* in this book rather reluctantly because doing so immediately implies the perspective of the state. Obviously, one person's smuggling can be another's legitimate trade—and may have been so for a very long time.

3. Prescott says that "political frontiers and boundaries separate areas subject to different political control or sovereignty. Frontiers are zones of varying widths. . . . [B]y the beginning of the twentieth century most remaining frontiers had disappeared and had been replaced by boundaries which are lines. . . . Borderland refers to the transitional zone within which the boundary lies." This process was happening at different times and at different places in this book. See Prescott, *Political Frontiers and Boundaries* (1987), 1, 13.

4. Sources from the British side of the border include documents from the various colonial office series (144/Labuan; 273/Straits Settlements; 537/Colonies; and 882/Eastern Confidential Print); Foreign Office documents from British consulates in Borneo and Sumatra, as well as the Confidential Print series there; Federated Malay States documents from the various states under British administration, especially from the west coast of the

peninsula facing Sumatra; Board of Trade documents; Admiralty documents; *the Sarawak Gazette* and correspondence from the Brooke regime in Sarawak; papers from the British North Borneo Company; court cases from the Straits Settlements; and period newspapers, gazettes, official reports, and English books from the late nineteenth and early twentieth centuries.

5. Most of the evidence in this book comes from the Dutch residencies facing the Anglo/Dutch border (Aceh, the East Coast of Sumatra, Palembang, Jambi, Riau, Bangka, Belitung, West Borneo, and southeast Borneo), and from the British Straits Settlements, parts of British Malaya, Sarawak, and British North Borneo, which faced the boundary from the other side. The maps of Sumatra, the Malay Peninsula, and Borneo reproduced in the introduction predominantly give the local names for regions rather than colonial designations. This is because European residency and territorial boundaries changed over the period 1865–1915 and cannot be portrayed accurately in a single map.

6. For two good histories of Singapore, see Turnbull, *A History of Singapore* (1981), and Chew and Lee, *A History of Singapore* (1991).

7. Strangely, the urban literature on Southeast Asia makes almost no mention of contraband trading at all. Theoretical works by O'Connor and even quite specific, in-depth studies by Lockard (on Kuching) and Wheatley (on Melaka) problematize ethnicity in the cities but do not ask how these "market meetings" produced a culture of illicit trade. Similarly, the useful edited volumes on colonial Asian cities by Dilip Basu, Frank Broeze, John Villiers, and J. Kathirithamby-Wells provide much information on urban growth and morphogenesis but almost nothing on the "by-products" of growth into subterranean directions. See O'Connor, *Theory of Indigenous Southeast Asian Urbanism* (1983); Lockard, *From Kampung to City* (1987); Wheatley, ed., *Melaka: Transformation of a Malay Capital* (1983); Basu, ed., *Rise and Growth of the Colonial Port Cities* (1985); Broeze, ed., *Brides of the Sea* (1989); Villiers and Wells, eds., *The Southeast Asia Port and Polity* (1990).

8. Conrad was the most famous traveler in Southeast Asia at this time, but the narratives of many sojourners through the region, particularly those of Dutch explorers, are also filled with potentially useful information.

9. James Warren has reported that some Kenyah in Borneo remembered the historical Olmeijer (made famous in Joseph Conrad's stories) as late as the 1950s; they also still possessed some of the muzzle-loading rifles he had sold them. See Warren, "Joseph Conrad's Fiction as Southeast Asian History" (1987), 11.

10. See the fascinating discussion on this in the Sino/Siamese context in Viraphol, *Tribute and Profit* (1977), esp. 123.

11. This has been referenced generally by Reid in *Southeast Asia in the Age of Commerce* (1988) and in Warren *The Sulu Zone* (1981).

12. See Dian Murray's discussion on this in the Sino/Vietnamese context, in Murray, *Pirates of the South China Coast* (1987), esp. 27.

13. The argument is most fully articulated in Scott, *Weapons of the Weak* (1985), and in his *Domination and the Arts of Resistance* (1990).

14. See, for example, Cobb, *The Police and the People* (1970), and Jones, *Crime, Protest, Community, and Police* (1982); for Southeast Asia, see Schulte-Nordholt, "The Jago in the Shadow" (1991), and Bankoff, *Crime, Society, and the State* (1998).

15. See Hobsbawm, *Bandits* (1969); Blok, *The Mafia of a Sicilian Village* (1975); Scott, *The Moral Economy of the Peasant* (1976); and Popkin, *The Rational Peasant* (1979). Also useful in this regard are Hane, *Peasants, Rebels, and Outcastes* (1982); Cheah, *Peasant Robbers of Kedah* (1988); Nonini, *British Colonial Rule and the Resistance of the Malay Peasantry* (1992); and Wolf, *Peasant Wars of the Twentieth Century* (1973).

16. An exception is Warren, *Ah Ku and Karayuki-san* (1993), in which trafficking to Singapore is described in an early chapter in the book.

17. See Andaya, *To Live as Brothers* (1993) and Murray, *Pirates of the South China Coast*. Warren's *The Sulu Zone* also discusses the smuggling of forest products in North Borneo and the southern Philippines.

18. Chiang, *Straits Settlements Foreign Trade* (1978); Booth, ed., *Indonesian Economic History* (1990); Maddison, ed., *Economic Growth in Indonesia 1820–1940* (1989).

19. Wolters, *Early Indonesian Commerce* (1967), and Irfan, *Kerajaan Sriwijaya* (1983).

20. Hashim, *Kesultanan Melayu Melaka* (1990), 236–70.

21. Wertheim, *Indonesie van Vorstenrijk tot Neo-Kolonie* (1978), 22, for examples.

22. Locher-Scholten, *Sumatraans Sultanaat en Koloniale Staat* (1994), chap. 2; also Heidhues, *Bangka Tin and Mentok Pepper* (1992).

23. For some of the outlines of this trade, see Tagliacozzo, "A Necklace of Fins" (2004).

24. See Gallagher and Robinson, "The Imperialism of Free Trade" (1953); Schumpeter, *Imperialism and Social Classes* (1951); Arendt, *The Origins of Totalitarianism* (1958); and Brewer, ed., *Marxist Theories of Imperialism* (1989).

25. A few of the more important studies are Webster, *Gentlemen Capitalists* (1998); Tarling, *Imperialism in Southeast Asia* (2001), and Sardesai, *British Trade and Expansion in Southeast Asia* (1977).

26. Fasseur, "Een Koloniale Paradox" (1979); a Campo "Orde, Rust, en Welvaart" (1980); Schoffer, "Dutch 'Expansion' and Indonesian Reactions" (1978); van der Wal, "De Nederlandse Expansie in Indonesie" (1971); Voorhoeve, *Peace, Profits, and Principles* (1985); and Wesseling, "The Giant That Was a Dwarf" (1989). See also the best recent treatment of the subject, Kuitenbrouwer *The Netherlands and the Rise of Modern Imperialism* (1991).

27. Van Goor, ed., *Imperialisme in de Marge* (1986); Lindblad, ed., *Het Belang van de Buitengewesten* (1989); Cribb, ed., The *Late Colonial State in Indonesia* (1994).

28. Thongchai, *Siam Mapped* (1994).

29. One of the best monographs here is Thomson, *Mercenaries, Pirates, and Sovereigns* (1994). An exception to the Southeast Asian lacunae would be Warren's *Sulu Zone*, which describes these processes in the area bounded by the modern Philippines, Malaysia, and Indonesia.

30. See Eccles, *The Canadian Frontier* (1983), and Paine, *Imperial Rivals* (1996), for example.

31. Cohen, *Exile in Mid-Qing China* (1991); Murphy (1960).

32. See the fascinating works by Arnold, including *The Problem of Nature* (1996), and *Colonizing the Body* (1993).

33. The most important contribution here is van Schendel and Baud, "Towards a Comparative History of Borderlands" (1997).

34. Sahlin's *Boundaries* (1989) is a very sophisticated look at border and identity formation in

one locale in the Pyrenees; Wilson and Donnan also look at these questions in their *Border Identities: Nation and State at International Frontiers* (1998). One of the best recent books to examine how borders and boundaries are constructed (and deconstructed) is White, *The Middle Ground* (1991). The intellectual progenitor of many of these studies in Turner, *The Frontier in American History* (1920). See Faragher's critique of Turner and his critics as well in *Rereading Frederick Jackson Turner* (1994).

35. See Irwin, *Nineteenth Century Borneo* (1967); Reid, *The Contest for North Sumatra* (1969).

36. Locher-Scholten, *Sumatraans Sultanaat en Koloniale Staat;* Lindblad, "Economische Aspecten van de Nederlandse Expansie" (1986).

37. The "center," in this case, could be Batavia or even its later manifestation as Jakarta in postcolonial times. See a Campo, *Koninklijke Paketvaart Maatschappij* (1992); also see Dick, *The Indonesian Inter-Island Shipping Industry* (1987).

38. Drabble, *An Economic History of Malaysia* (2000), 32–41, and Courtenay, *A Geography of Trade and Development in Malaya* (1972).

39. See Ooi, *Of Free Trade and Native Interests* (1997), 120–67, and Kaur, *Economic Change in East Malaysia* (1998).

40. Boeke, *Economics and Economic Policy of Dual Societies* (1953); Boeke, *The Evolution of the Netherlands Indies Economy* (1946); and Boeke, *The Structure of the Netherlands Indies Economy* (1942). For a powerful critique of some of this scholarship, albeit in Java, see Elson, *Village Java Under the Cultivation System* (1994).

41. See Touwen, *Extremes in the Archipelago* (2001); Sulistiyono, *The Java Sea Network* (2003); Lindblad, "The Outer Islands in the Nineteenth Century" (2002), 82–110; Dick, "Interisland Trade" (1990), 296–321; Lindblad, "Economic Growth in the Outer Islands" (1993), 233–63; Ricklefs, *A History of Modern Indonesia* (2001), chap. 13; and for a regional overview, see Brown, *Economic Change in South-East Asia* (1997).

42. Officer of the Committee of the Privy Council for Trade to Herman Merivale, Esq., 17 June 1850, in CO 144/6; Extracts from the Minutes of the Legislative Council of Labuan, 3 Jan. 1853, in CO 144/11; Gov Labuan to CO, 9 Jan. 1872, no. 2, in CO 144/36; CO Jacket (Mr. Fairfield, and Mr. Wingfield), 21 May 1896, in CO 144/70; Gov Labuan to BNB HQ, London, 13 Nov. 1896, in CO 144/70.

43. See Enactment no. 6 of 1915, Malay States; also *Bintang Timor,* 6 Dec. 1894, 2.

44. *SSBB,* 1873, Spirit Imports and Exports, Singapore, p. 329, 379–80.

45. ANRI, Politiek Verslag Residentie West Borneo 1872 (no. 2/10); ARA, Extract Uit het Register der Besluiten, GGNEI, 2 Jan. 1881, no. 7, in 1881, MR no. 18.

46. ARA, First Government Secretary to Director of Finances, 6 Nov. 1889, no. 2585, in 1889, MR no. 773; also First Government Secretary to Resident Timor, 8 March 1892, no. 600, in 1892, MR no. 217; ARA, Dutch Consul, Manila to MvBZ, 5 April 1897, no. 32; MvBZ to MvK, 24 May 1897, no. 5768, both in (MvBZ/A Dossiers/223/A.111/"Verbod Invoer Wapens en Alcohol"); ARA, Dutch Consul, London to MvBZ, 28 Jan. 1893, no. 37, and GGNEI to MvK, 27 Nov. 1892, no. 2268/14, both in (MvBZ/A Dossiers/223/A.111/ "Still Zuidzee").

47. ARA, Resident West Borneo to GGNEI, 10 Oct. 1889, no. 93 Secret, in 1889, MR no. 730.

48. ARA, Dutch Consul, Singapore to GGNEI, 20 Sept. 1873, and Dutch Consul, Singa-

pore, to Gov Gen NEI, 23 Sept. 1873, both in (MvK, Verbaal 17 Dec. 1873, D33); ARA, Resident Surabaya to GGNEI, 30 Nov. 1881, no. 15258 Secret, in 1881, MR no. 1139; ARA, Dutch Consul, Djeddah to MvBZ, 30 Aug. 1883, no. 632, in 1883, MR no. 1075; ANRI, Dutch Consul, Singapore to GGNEI, 18 May 1876, in Kommissoriaal 20 June 1876, no. 469az, in Aceh no. 13, "Stukken Betreffende Atjehsche Oorlog (1876)"/no. 235–469; and Dutch Consul, Singapore to GGNEI, 7 Feb. 1876, in Kommissoriaal 25 Feb. 1876, no. 153az, in Aceh no. 12: "Stukken Betreffende Atjehsche Oorlog (1876)"/no. 4–234; and "Resume van Artikelen in de Turksche Bladen te Constantinopel over der Beweerde Slechte Behandeling van de Arabieren in NI en van de Beschermingen ter Zake van de Ned. Pers" *IG* (1898) no. 2, 1096–97; see also the laws enacted under Staatsblad 1900, nos. 317 and 318.

49. Kruijt, *Atjeh en de Atjehers* (1877), 130, 222; ARA, Dutch Consul, Penang to GGNEI, 19 Sept. 1873, no. 16, in (MvK, Verbaal 17 Dec. 1873, D33). Other kinds of biota, such as gutta-percha, were also declared to be contraband by the British on occasion; see *Federated Malay States Annual Report 1901* (Perak), 5.

50. ARA, 1898, MR no. 634.

51. ARA, Extract Uit het Register der Besluiten, GGNEI, in 1883, MR no. 24; ARA, 1892, MR no. 388; ARA, Memorie van Overgave van de Residentie Westerafdeeling van Borneo (MMK, 1912, no. 260), 34.

52. ARA, Dutch Consul, Singapore to GGNEI, 10 Dec. 1885, no. 986, in 1885, MR no. 807; *Utusan Malayu,* 9 Feb. 1909, 1; Gov. Straits to CO, 26 May 1900, Telegram, and Gov Straits to CO, 31 May 1900, Secret, both in CO 273/257; Longmans, Green, and Co., Publishers, to the Copyright Association, and forwarded to the CO, 15 Nov. 1888, in CO 273/157.

53. These types of *pusaka,* or heirlooms, were considered to be very valuable by various peoples living in the forest; a commerce in these products had been active for centuries. Jars were thought to have special attributes, such as being able to sing or cure diseases, while others served as canisters for burying the dead or as dowries. See Harrison, *Pusaka: Heirloom Jars of Borneo* (1986), 19–20; for jars across the frontier in Dutch Borneo, see Adhyatman, *Keramik Kuna* (1981).

54. Onreat, *Singapore: A Police Background* (n.d.), 30.

55. See *Geschiedenis van het Wetboek van Strafrecht voor Nederlandsch-Indië* (1918), 185; also van Kol, *De Bestuurstelsels der Hedendaagsche Koloniën* (1905), 71.

56. For dimensions and variabilities, see Kennedy, *Brief Geographical and Hydrographical Study of Straits* (1957), 40–41; see also Shaw and Thomson, *The Straits of Malacca* (1979).

57. See Lewis and Wiggen, *Myth of Continents* (1997), 189.

58. See, for example, Reid, *Southeast Asia in the Age of Commerce* (1998); Lindblad, "Between Singapore and Batavia" (1996); Dick, "Indonesian Economic History Inside Out" (1993); and van Dijk "Java, Indonesia and Southeast Asia" (1992).

Part I Creating the Frontier: Border Formation and the State

Section I Building the Frontier:
Drawing Lines in Physical Space

What engraves a frontier powerfully in the earth is not policemen or customs men or cannons drawn up behind ramparts. It is feelings, and exalted passions—and hatreds.
—Lucien Febvre in *Le Rhin* (1935), quoted in Schottler (1995), 84

Chapter 2 Mapping the
Frontier

The history of Western exploration, mapping, and concomitant categorization of the world is a huge subject, one that has fascinated scholars for a very long time. There is an almost Linnaean quality to the hunger for taxonomy that Europeans brought to this work: the world existed to be conquered, surely, but it also existed to be *known*. Explorers, cartographers, and statesmen carried out these projects, filing away newly "discovered" lands and seas into categories that could be interpreted by imperial concerns. In Southeast Asia, these dynamics were transregional in character, enveloping the length and breadth of this arena into a centuries-long embrace. Who were these new peoples? Where did they live, and what were their characteristics? By the mid—nineteenth century, the queries had become more covetous: Are the people on that bend of river part of your sphere of influence, or mine? How high are those mountains and do the minerals inside them fall into your dominion, or ours? Perhaps most important, the question began to be asked: How are the diverse economic and political realities of life in this region going to be interpreted and controlled? Lucien Febvre may have been right that policemen, customs agents, and cannons were not the only tools necessary for inscribing a new border in this region, but even the seeding of these initial aspects of imperial control seemed an enormous challenge to Europeans in the middle decades of the nineteenth century.

EXPLORING BOUNDARY LANDSCAPES

The political economies of the frontier areas between what was emerging as British and Dutch Southeast Asia were complex, and conceptually these spaces looked remarkably like a patchwork quilt in the decades leading up to 1900. By the Treaty of 1871, a line had been drawn bisecting the Straits of Melaka, separating the two colonial possessions by a shallow ribbon of water.[1] Yet on the ground, in the lands and seas adjoining the frontier regions, this picture was exceedingly more complicated. Chinese gold-mining cooperatives, or *kongsis,* in western Borneo, for example, and tin-mining cooperatives on islands like Bangka and Belitung in the South China Sea shared space along the boundary with burgeoning colonial cities such as Penang and Singapore. Nomadic peoples, both in the forests of Borneo and on the waters at the terminus of the Straits, moved back and forth across the border more or less at will. Massive plantations in Sumatra and Malaya also adjoined the frontier and often abutted independent sultanates, which were sometimes very powerful. Christian mission posts and government outstations watched Chinese miners, Malay traders, Japanese prostitutes, and transient sea peoples criss-crossing the boundary in both directions. A border may have existed as an aspiration in the minds of bureaucrats far away in Europe, but life on the ground in this part of Southeast Asia was much more nuanced and complex.

Despite the enormous diversity of ethnicities, power structures, and economic undertakings along this divide, both Batavia and Singapore had little knowledge of large parts of the frontier. From the 1860s until the early 1880s, new lands and peoples along the border were still being discovered quite frequently, as can be seen in period exploration and ethnological journals, examples of which will be referenced in a moment. By the later 1880s, however, and into the 1890s, the pace of exploration along the length of the frontier was starting to change. Discoveries were now more remote: highlands, tiny islands, and sources of rivers and lakes constituted the majority of geographical discoveries by this time. Exploration in and of itself was becoming harder to achieve; the remaining tracts of terra incognita were further and further afield and difficult to reach. By the first decade of the twentieth century, such regions had virtually disappeared. Exploration of the frontier by this time was of a completely different character, focusing on new oddities and small discoveries: unknown waterfalls, new and unused sailing routes, or even quiet valleys containing unknown insects and plants.

The exploration of the Anglo/Dutch frontier was a major undertaking, however, one which created, in a sense, an entity that had never previously existed: a line of lands and seas that separated two discrete colonial dominions. Exploration validated and described the limits of what had already been decided upon in European drawing rooms. The consequences of these explorations would be immense. Entire convoys of entrepreneurs, scientists, miners, and missionaries steamed to the Indies to take part in this process. Each came for his own reasons, including profit, knowledge, and soul saving, but all contributed to the opening of the new frontier. The publications of just a handful of these societies and institutions give an idea of how varied and enormous their impact would become. The Batavian Society for Arts and Sciences, the Royal Institute of Ethnology, the Royal Naturalists' Society in Batavia, the Society for the Furthering of Medical Knowledge in the Indies, the Indies Society for Industry, and the Royal Geographic Society all came or sent their representatives, men who took part in the "laying bare" of the unknown.[2] The frontier was to be explored and exploited, but mostly (in the colonial parlance of the day), in the interests of the local inhabitants themselves. "Toward this no force is necessary," one Indies publication intoned, "only the persuasion which the powerful, fatherly Indies government has in its possession. The peoples of our archipelago and the lands in which they live must in their own interests be made rich and prosperous."[3]

The realities of the opening of the frontier in this part of the world, of course, proceeded somewhat differently from this high-minded declaration. The exploration of Sumatra from the 1870s onward can serve as an example. Parts of this huge island had already been traversed by Dutch explorers and military columns earlier in the century; lowland Palembang from 1819 to 1824 and the Padri areas of West Sumatra, where a long, bloody war had been fought until 1837, had been claimed by the Dutch. Yet large parts of the island were still unknown in the 1870s and early 1880s or were only beginning to be explored. These included the river mouths of Jambi, Musi, Tonkal, Reteh, and Indragiri on the east coast, which began to be systematically surveyed only in the 1880s, as well as the higher reaches of the Kampar, which were described by J. B. Neumann's and J. Faes's extensive riverine expeditions (fig. 1).[4] In the interior of central Sumatra, J. C. Ploen was given permission to travel at government cost

Fig. 1. Exploration into the Jambi interior, Sumatra, 1879. (Photo courtesy KITLV, Leiden)

to several unknown and inaccessible areas, primarily to collect botanical and zoological specimens. Small polities in these interior regions were gradually contacted and annexed by Batavia, a fact that did not elude the attention of the British across the Straits, who busily translated these expedition reports to keep track of Dutch advances.[5] Yet the greatest attention in Sumatra exploration in these early years was reserved for Aceh, where war with that sultanate was raging unabated in the 1870s. Junghuhn's book of 1873 laid out some of the parameters of Acehnese geography in that year, but it would be the contributions of later explorers that showed where this interest was moving, especially in terms of resource exploitation.[6]

By the late 1880s and into the 1890s, the nature of these Sumatran frontier explorations was changing. The coasts and lowlands of the island were now fairly well known, leaving inland and upland areas as the major sites for new discoveries. One of those, for example, was Upper Jambi, where most exploration was still dependent on rivers for travel. Predictions declared that "it won't be long before the Dutch flag waves over all of Sumatra, as a symbol of peace and protection of the (local) inhabitants."[7] Universities and other institutions of higher learning in the Netherlands were also helping with the exploration process: the Rijkskunstnijverheidschool in Amsterdam, for example, volunteered to send a representative for frontier flora and fauna research, while a professor of zoology in Utrecht received forty-two hundred guilders in government funds to carry on state-sanctioned research expeditions. Lake Toba in North Sumatra also received renewed attention at this time, drawing explorers to the relatively unknown northern reaches of the lake, where the local Bataks were known to be unfriendly to the Dutch, and maps of the area still contained blank spaces. The search for bismuth and other minerals of potential value pushed these journeys forward.[8] Although Toba's existence had been known to European explorers and officials for some time, it was the further, distant reaches of the lake that attracted Dutch attention in the 1880s and 1890s.

By the turn of the century and into its first decades, the nature of these frontier explorations in Sumatra had changed once again. The biggest change was that there was no more true frontier, at least not in the traditional sense. Dutch maps of the island contained all of the major geographical landmarks and had catalogued Sumatra's peoples as well as their physical environments. What remained were explorations which filled in gaps in existing knowledge or took the process of discovery to a slower, more leisurely pace. The military apothecary W. G. Boorsma, for example, was given permission to set out on a chemical-pharmacological expedition, the special concern of which was to collect new plants that might be useful in the fabrication of medicines. J. T. Cremer set out for the Batak highlands in 1907 this time not with a column of laden-down coolies, but in an automobile, which could barely traverse the recently cut roads.[9] Not to be outdone, other explorers of the late period also ventured to the northern shores of Toba's great lake but did so by way of petrol-fueled motorboats. Even the coasts of Sumatra, which had been circumnavigated for years by Dutch traders, adventurers, and military men in various steamships, yielded up small discoveries, such as a waterfall at Mansalar, which could now be used as a navigation aide.[10] All of these voyages enhanced European knowledge of the "periphery," yet there was gradually a discernable slowing of the gathering of data as colonial explorers ran out of peoples and places to "discover."

Exploration on the frontier was not limited to Sumatra between 1865 and 1915. The maze of islands dotting the South China Sea also provided impetus for Dutch exploration around 1900, though these undertakings were more maritime in nature. Some of these islands had been known to the Dutch for a long time and had significant contacts with Malay politics and trade in the region. Barbara Watson Andaya has shown this for Bangka in the seventeenth and eighteenth centuries, and Carl Trocki for Riau, in the area just south of Singapore, in the eighteenth and nineteenth centuries. Other scholars have worked on the gradual incorporation of these islands into the regional web of trade and alliances through mining, through the Chinese presence, through local literature, and also through ethnolinguistic contacts.[11] Bangka and Belitung were, indeed, important centers of trade and production well before 1865, making explorations there essentially a matter of filling in already-known spaces.[12] Yet the island groups of Anambas, Natuna, and Tambelan, all in the lower reaches of the South China Sea, were much more distant from these crossroads and received only scant attention from Batavia at this stage. The Dutch knew these islands were populated by a mix of Malays, Orang Laut, Bugis, and Chinese but had little idea about everyday existence there, including the islands' trade contacts (legal or illegal) and other economic activities.[13]

By the late 1890s, this picture of benign neglect for the northernmost islands in the Dutch Indies' possessions was quickly changing. Ship captains' notations on the geography of the islands started to be compiled and collated, new bays and creeks were noted, depths in fathoms were presented, and drinking-water sources were all pointed out, rendering the islands more transparent to passing traders.[14] The exploration journeys of A. L. Van Hasselt between 1894 and 1896 especially broke new ground, showing that earlier maps of the area contained islands that did not exist or were drawn in the wrong place, to the detriment of travelers. Van Hasselt was straightforward in admitting the source of most of his information: English Admiralty charts, which had surveyed the area a few years earlier and had drawn excellent maps. Though these charts had been done with the permission of Batavia, Van Hasselt could not resist stating that Dutch explorers should have been the ones to make these measurements, as the islands (after all) were part of the Netherlands Indies. The vocabulary lists of area peoples, photographs of local topography, and ethnographic notes that followed in Van Hasselt's account brought Dutch knowledge of the archipelago to a new level. In the years around his voyages to the area, in fact, more general directives started to come down from Batavia, asking administrators of far-flung groups to send such ethnographic data to the capital. Important information could thus be systematized and reviewed.[15]

By the turn of the century, exploration of the South China Sea island groups had become part of a coherent program of development in the Indies. Mining interests took the lead in conducting new surveying operations and expeditions, mapping Bangka in incredible detail, and starting work on Belitung and even on the tiny islands off Belitung's coasts after 1894.[16] The island of Blakang Padang, facing Singapore in the Riau archipelago, was also extensively surveyed at this time. Though formerly it had been seen as a useless scrap of land with few natural resources and only a marginal population, by 1900 planners were seeing the island as a complementary port near Singapore, with coal sheds, docking complexes, and a series of interconnected lighthouses. This sort of exploration, indeed, with coherent and definitive development purposes in mind, was among the last stages of discovery along the length of the Anglo/ Dutch frontier. Even many of the myriad reefs and atolls which made up the maritime boundary of the Netherlands Indies, from Aceh eastward to coastal New Guinea, were explored and chronicled by Dutch oceanographers at this time.[17] Some of this interest was pure science or was fueled by the emerging nationalist impulse to mark the boundaries of the archipelago with Dutch flags. But a significant part of it was also economic and utilitarian, as exploration was bent to the service of the state to locate new resources and wealth.

The last section of the frontier that was targeted for exploration, outside of Sumatra and the islands of the South China Sea, was the vast forested wilderness of Borneo. Here too, as in Sumatra, initial contacts had already been made earlier in the century. The Dutch presence in Pontianak, West Borneo, for example, went back to the late eighteenth century.[18] Yet it was only in the 1870s and early 1880s that the Dutch started to explore inland areas in any more systematic fashion. Kater, Gerlach, and Bakker pushed the frontier of Dutch knowledge up the great rivers, for example, and into parts of the lake districts of internal West Borneo, while Dutch residents reached the high headwaters of the Mahakam, which eventually emptied out on the eastern half of the island.[19] The pace of exploration and the advancement of Dutch interests into the western half of the island was also the project of J. J. K. Enthoven, whose massive two-volume study became a landmark work on West Borneo. Like the British who carefully translated Dutch expedition accounts in Sumatra, however, the Dutch in Batavia also made sure to keep abreast of English stabs into the periphery on the other side of the Borneo frontier. Published accounts of British residents from the interior districts of Sarawak were translated into Dutch very quickly, so that the Dutch had an idea what their erstwhile allies (and competitors) were doing along the border.[20]

On the eastern half of the island, the pace of exploration also proceeded quickly, especially in the 1880s and 1890s. Carl Bock's famous journey into the interior of eastern Borneo was one of the first of these expeditions; the Norwegian received Batavia's blessing for the journey, despite the fate of several of his predecessors, who had been murdered when they proceeded inland along the great rivers.[21] The Royal Museum for Ethnology in Leiden sponsored further missions of this nature, and large government subsidies were made available to catalogue flora and fauna in unknown lands in the interior.[22] On the north-eastern coast, survey ships like the *Macassar* brought large stretches of the frontier into map form at the turn of the century, outlining coral reefs and stretches of shore where formerly piratical peoples had lived.[23] Across from the Dutch sphere of influence and in the territories of the British North Borneo Company, the nature of these activities was very similar. The diaries of Frank Hatton, one of the company's scientific officers in the 1880s, show how difficult expeditions into the unmarked interior were: armed guards had to stand by ready to shoot at crocodiles, and leeches crawled into sleeping men's ears, especially at night. Hatton's descriptions of the rigors of river travel in the interior, especially the forced pulling of equipment-laden craft in the face of fierce currents, show at what price knowledge of the frontier came to the men on these expeditions.[24]

Some of these explorers were more important than others, however, especially in the legacy they left for "opening up the frontier." One of the more noteworthy figures in this respect was Professor G. A. F. Molengraff, who led an expedition up the Kapuas into the center of Borneo in 1893–94. Molengraff's company consisted of four scientists, twenty soldiers, and one hundred Kayan porters and guides, all of whom disappeared into the forest canopy for a period of several months. The expedition halted short of its intended destination, however, when Molengraff, by now well into the interior, was warned their party was in danger of being attacked. Molengraff, his zoologist and botanist, and most of the others returned to the coast.[25] Yet the medic on this journey, A. W. Nieuwenhuis, went on to lead several other celebrated expeditions into the interior in the next few years and was actually the first explorer to cross Borneo from one side to the other. Nieuwenhuis's sojourns were undertaken with far fewer men than Molengraff's and included no soldiers, which was a precondition for their being allowed through. Many of the indigenous peoples of the interior were also impressed with Nieuwenhuis's medical skills as well as his language abilities, which he used to try to understand the varied people he met. Nevertheless, Nieuwenhuis was a man of his times, and the reason for his journey was not only pure science, but also to help establish a Dutch presence in the interior.[26] Because of this, Dutch residents in Borneo were apprised of his journeys by Batavia and asked to help troubleshoot problems, so that the expedition could be turned into a patriotic success.[27]

Yet especially after 1900, one concern drove exploration forward faster and with more energy than any other factor, and this was the search for natural resources. The case of Borneo can be taken again as an example here, to show how much the creation of the frontier owed to state and private interests racing to find ores throughout the entirety of the island. Applied geology drove empire forward in this sense; the geologist's shovel and the explorer's sextant were tools of equal importance in "opening" up the frontier. On the English side of the divide, this was happening very early: only a few years after the founding of British North Borneo, for example, the governor of that territory was calling weekly Gold Committee meetings, which involved state officials and several Chinese prospectors.[28] By the turn of the century, informal meetings within the company's dominions had given way to coded telegraph correspondences about potential diamond districts, as well as oil and mineral rights agreements being leased to various concerns.[29] In Brunei, which became a British protectorate, such dealings occurred even earlier, as the sultan there cut prospecting deals for antimony and tin with English speculators in the mid–nineteenth century.[30] Yet it was in Sarawak where the greatest amounts of minerals and ores were being found, pulling English officials deeper and deeper into the forest in search of raw materials and the profits they brought.[31] The resident of Bintulu, Sarawak, a man named A. Hart Everett, gives an idea of the kinds of resources being found in 1878: gold, iron, cobalt, and copper were all being discovered, as well as platinum, cats' eyes, and spinelle rubies. Diamonds were also turning up, like a huge stone of seventy-six carats that was slipped into Sarawak from across the Dutch border.[32]

Valuable stones and minerals may have leaked over the frontier into the English possessions, but there was no lack of material being found in Dutch West Borneo either. Chinese kongsis had long been active in the area, digging for gold in upriver regions near the Sarawak frontier. In the middle decades of the nineteenth century, however, the frequency and quality of resources found in West Borneo began to grow, partially as a result of more sophisticated prospecting techniques.[33] Coal, for example, was found in Sanggau in 1873 and was sent in small batches to Batavia for quality analysis.[34] Diamonds such as the one mentioned above were also occasionally to be found, and managed to quickly exit the Dutch dominions (avoiding Dutch taxes) while finding their way to Sarawak. Yet it was the possibility of large gold reserves, particularly in areas that had once been mined by the Chinese but had since fallen into disrepair, that really pushed Dutch interests forward into this periphery. By government decree no.15 of May 31, 1880, geological expeditions were sent to resurvey many of the Chinese areas between the Landak and Sambas rivers, all in search of gold.[35] Cinnabar and antimony were also being found in the far upper watershed of the Sekayam River at the same time.[36] By 1889, the fruit of these many expeditions trekking into the interior in search of natural resources was readily apparent: tellurium, selenium, and bismuth were all being uncovered, in addition to large caches of the precious metals mentioned previously.[37]

A final look at how the search for wealth propelled the Dutch forward can be taken on the eastern half of the island. Coal was one of the main products sought on this side of the island, and it was shipped to the Philippines, Australia, Japan, and even South Africa. More important, perhaps, was that it was desperately needed for the Indies' growing steam fleet, which sought as its highest priority coal reserves on Indies soil.[38] Yet the human price for this reliance was enormous. East Borneo coal mines, such as the Oranje Nassau vent, were often hells of sickness and maltreatment. This particular mine, which was run by 8 Europeans, 12 indigenous free laborers, 115 sailors, and 495 convicts in January 1870, routinely had one-sixth of its population in the hospital at any one time. Stomach ailments and fevers brought most of the men there, but fires in the coal magazines, not to mention suicides and suicide attempts, also increased their numbers.[39] In Kutei, further north along the coast toward the North Borneo border, asphalt, naphtha, and natural gas/petroleum contracts were also given out by Batavia, pushing the Dutch presence forward toward St. Lucia Bay.[40] Finally, the profits the Dutch state could make by farming out the rights to mine gold and diamonds also provided an extra incentive for expansion, as new tracts of resource-bearing lands came into use. Licenses for digging diamonds in Martapura brought 10,818 guilders to Batavia in the first three months of 1873 alone, while gold-washing permits given out in Tana Laut district increased Dutch revenues year after year.[41] Although these latter two sites were some distance from the evolving border, with revenues such as these pouring in Batavia had every incentive to explore the frontier as quickly and as aggressively as possible. The Brooke regime in Sarawak and Western speculators who were already eyeing the northern territories of Borneo were quick to follow suit.

MAPPING BY LAND, MAPPING BY SEA

As European explorers fanned out along the length of the frontier, pushing colonial knowledge and an imperial agenda far into the periphery, mapping of these areas became an important priority for both colonial states. In the British possessions, surveyors on government payrolls scattered to a variety of sites in order to bring the landscape into colonial knowledge. Geodesic measurements were taken under these auspices, and the results were sent back first to Singapore and then later to London. In the Netherlands Indies, the flagship institution for mapping Dutch expansion was the Topographische Dienst, which boasted six full brigades of cartographers by 1878.[42] The periodical *Tijdschrift voor de Aardrijkskundige Genootschap* (Journal of the geographical society) became the main disseminator of knowledge about these expeditions, chronicling the advance of Batavia's surveyors for a wider educated public. Projects such as the triangulation of Sumatra, which began in South Sumatra and slowly crept up the length of the enormous island, took decades to complete but showed how serious Dutch planners were about being able to accurately see their terrain in the late nineteenth century.[43] Yet concerted, centrally planned scientific expeditions like these were not the only impetus driving Dutch mapmaking forward. In West Borneo, for example, the lack of good maps during Chinese uprisings in the early 1880s led to new energy being invested in modern cartography, while in Sumatra the army and the Ministry for Education cooperated in outfitting expeditions, extending Batavia's reach by combining their resources.[44] On the British side of the frontier, no map of Labuan's topography existed even thirty years after the colony's founding. The island was mapped as part of the sea routes leading to China but not in its own local detail and context, an omission that limited British policing vision in Borneo waters.[45]

The crucial importance of the cartographic project to Dutch expansion can be seen best, however, in Aceh, where mapping was a matter of life and death for the invading Dutch armies. Reconnaissance voyages by the Dutch marine started triangulations of the coasts, while other ships steamed up Aceh's rivers to map the interior regions where the resistance forces were gathered.[46] Three maps from the Indonesian archives in Jakarta illustrate the progression of Dutch mapping in Aceh in consecutive years. The first map, from 1873, the year Batavia initially invaded, shows how haphazardly information had to be gathered: the vectors and distance measurements of the coast are taken from a ship, which could not gather more accurate data because of the threat of enemy fire. This "map," therefore, consists only of numerical notations, denoting azimuths and horizon lines at different distances as seen from the sea.[47] It does not look like a modern conception of a map at all. The second map, from only one year later and reproduced here, shows how Acehnese villages and rural areas now could be envisioned much more clearly, as the Dutch advance proceeded southward from the beachhead at Kota Raja.[48] The Acehnese and their physical environment were no longer abstract space, reduced to a sheaf of numbers; there is a visual element to European knowledge now, as local landscapes and people have been brought into the imperial optic (map 3). A third map from

1875, only two years after the initial attack, shows that a lighthouse had been erected at Pulau Bras, just off the coast of Aceh. This map allowed Batavia to grid whole sections of this particular coast from an aerial view (the lighthouse's tower) and map the local land to a high degree of accuracy.[49] These advances in mapping were crucial to eventual Dutch success in Aceh, where Batavia's abilities to deal with local conditions slowly caught up with those of local populations. By the first decade of the twentieth century, many parts of Aceh had been mapped down to minute detail, with hills, mountains, and other natural features carefully entered into Dutch military ledgers. The cartographic methodologies and processes of these expeditions, in fact, were eventually applied elsewhere in the Indies, as mapping in Aceh became a template for other border campaigns.[50]

By the twentieth century, cartography in the Indies had become a much more sophisticated science than in previous decades, its evolution being fueled by a variety of sources. One of these was popular interest and national pride. Dutch cartographers attended international congresses with their new data on the Indies, and the Dutch press back home picked up on their discoveries as well, spreading the new knowledge to a wider reading public.[51] The caliper and the sextant, therefore, became instruments not only for mapping, but also for fueling the burgeoning nationalist project back in the Netherlands. Perhaps more important, however, was the role industry and production were beginning to play, as mining and agricultural concerns mapped out huge tracts of land with potentially colossal profits in mind. This is seen in the detailed maps of the mining concession Karang Ringin in Palembang, for example, as well as in the Kahayan mine plots leased out by Batavia deep in eastern Borneo's interior.[52] The contentious nature of the border itself, however, was perhaps the main phenomenon advancing the mapping of the frontier, as the two European powers jockeyed over the laying of the boundary. As British cognizance of the region's topography increased, claims on territory became more specific, forcing the Dutch to catch up cartographically. This happened only slowly, however. An incident in 1909 in which the Dutch envoy to London seemed himself not to know the nature of Dutch claims in eastern Borneo alarmed The Hague and prompted it to acquaint all of its foreign service personnel with the Indies' "true boundaries."[53] Around this time, therefore, cartographers began producing maps which sketched the Dutch presence on the ground in hyperaccurate detail. One combined roads, railroad lines, toll offices, and garrisons, not to mention administrative divisions, mineral deposits, industrial centers, and lighthouses, all on one map.[54]

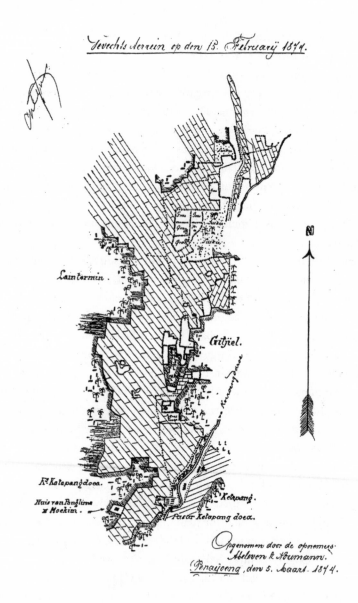

Dutch Mapping in Aceh, 1874. (Courtesy Arsip Nasional, Jakarta)

The mapping of the periphery did not take place only on land, however. The science of hydrography was also bent to empire's use in colonial Southeast Asia, and there were few places where it was more important than in the outstretched islands of the Dutch East Indies.[55] A Hydrographic Bureau set up in Batavia in 1860 was moved to the Netherlands in 1871 only to be brought back to the Indies four years later but then replanted yet again in Holland in 1894, this time for good. Such confusion and mismanagement seem to have typified Dutch hydrographic science in the Indies during the early period, as various notices of poorly mapped areas make clear. Yet in 1874 a steamer was specially built for hydrography in the Indies (the *Hydrograaf*), and by 1883, two sailing schooners had been added to carry out the necessary duties.[56] Funds were made available by the Ministry of Marine to translate English-language notations, so that Dutch mariners would have more up-to-date charts of the area.[57] By the early 1870s, hydrography was taking its place alongside cartographic measurements on land as a necessary component of Dutch expansion, even in the Aceh War. Batavia was even beginning to give out its own maritime notices to the British across the Straits, which then appeared as notifications and warnings in trade papers in the English possessions, such as the *Penang Guardian and Mercantile Advertiser*.[58]

Vast problems remained with Dutch hydrographical vision in the periphery, however, causing outcries and considerable losses in shipping among the fleets of many nations. The waters around Bangka, which sat astride the main sea route between China and India, can serve as an example. Dutch hydrographical drawings from the early 1860s show how primitive maritime knowledge of this frequently trafficked area really was: pencil sketches of hills, shorelines, and depth soundings offered very little help to the helmsmen of passing ships.[59] In the 1870s and early 1880s, the results of these inadequacies became clear: ship after ship went down in Bangka's waters, spilling cargoes and men at an alarming rate. The British bark *Blue Jacket* sank off Bangka in 1870, going down with a cargo of camphor and other goods, while German trading ships went down that same year as well as several years later. The American ship *Samuel Russel* experienced the same fate in 1870, and in the same decade French mail steamers routinely hit submerged rocks or had to be helped off shoals.[60] When the Dutch steamer *General Pel*, on its way from Batavia to the theater of war in Aceh, sprang a leak on rocks in the same area in 1878, many Dutchmen started to ask when Batavia would actually condescend to do something about the problem.[61] The complaints hit a crescendo in 1891, when the *Indische Gids* publicly chastised the government for overreliance on English sea measurements of the frontier and for not doing enough to ensure that Dutch crews were mapping these waters themselves.[62]

Around 1900, however, the Dutch vision of the intricacies of the maritime frontier had grown by leaps and bounds. The archives of the Hydrography Service show increasing numbers of maps being deposited into the central data files: Riau and Lingga, the mouths of the Asahan River, and various parts of the eastern Borneo coast were all mapped, sometimes down to extraordinary detail.[63] British maps of the maritime border region in northeastern Borneo and Dutch maps of the reefs and tiny islands separating Borneo from Sulawesi opened these states' vision onto the kinds of locales in which smugglers and pirates traditionally practiced their activities.[64] The older hydrographic schooners were retired and replaced with steamers that could undertake surveying under nearly any conditions.[65] There were still complaints in the late period of some areas being undersurveyed, such as the border waters between North Sulawesi and the southern Philippines and even certain channels south of Singapore; but the grumbling in both colonies' presses was now infrequent.[66] What emerges is a picture of the waters of the Anglo/Dutch frontier being almost entirely charted by 1915, when a useful map showing the dates of area surveys was published in the *Tijdschrift voor de Aardrijkskundige Genootschap* (map 4).[67] The enormous length and porosity of the frontier, which seemed endless and un-mappable in the 1870s, had become a fairly known quantity by the early twentieth century. Batavia and Singapore had committed these spaces to the archives now, where they could be studied and preserved to support the will of these two states.

CATEGORIZING THE FRONTIER

Lands and seas that had been explored and then mapped finally needed to be categorized and indexed by colonial states in the region. James Scott has called this process "seeing like a state": the propensity for governments to try to file local realities into a system understandable to policy planners, even if this has little to do with things as they are on the ground.[68] In the Indies, this took the form of several kinds of relationships between Batavia and area potentates, which N. J. Struijk concretized in 1881 into five types of obligation. First, there were local polities under no treaty with Batavia but still considered part of the Indies by virtue of their presence in the greater arc of the archipelago. Several small states in central Sumatra exemplify this kind of arrangement. Second, there were polities that were indeed under treaty with the Dutch but as yet had

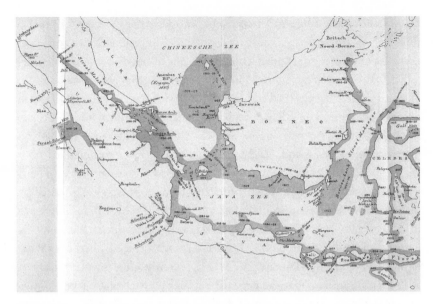

Hydrography of the Anglo/Dutch Frontier, 1910. (*Source:* Craandyk, "Het Werk Onzer Opnemings Vaartuigen" (1910) 27, p. 75)

received no formal representatives from Batavia; a few states in Borneo and Sulawesi could be counted as examples here. A third scenario was apparent in places such as Jambi and Indragiri in Sumatra where treaties had been concluded and there were Dutch envoys on the ground, but they held no power actually to order local life. A fourth type of obligation existed in parts of Riau, Siak, and Deli, where treaties put local peoples under the jurisdiction of Dutch courts and taxes were paid to Batavia, so that the fates of these polities were closely wound with Batavia's policies. The fifth and final possibility was a relationship of utter dependence and control between Indies potentates and the Dutch, which could be witnessed, for example, in several parts of West Borneo, such as Pontianak, Mempawah, and Sambas.[69]

This menu of gradations and possibilities blurred the simple fact that European power, especially in the 1860s and 1870s, was creeping forward everywhere on the ground. The Dutch, and the British as well, needed suzerainty over area potentates to work their will in many aspects of imperial expansion, the control of trade not least among them. Yet as European power was still comparatively underdeveloped, and suzerainty (vs. direct sovereignty) was often considered enough to preclude the claims of other European powers, complex arrangements were formulated to bind these relationships, regardless of conditions on the ground. Malay language letters from local sultans to the British in North Borneo show this very clearly from at least 1878.[70] In Jambi just two years later it was decided by contract that all opium revenue be handled through a farmer rather than by the sultan; at the same time, this sultan was also made responsible for the safety of shipwrecked Dutch seamen, who might occasionally wash up on his shores.[71] The sultan of Gunung Tabur was punished for his involvement in sponsoring piracy in East Borneo, while the sultan in Pontianak, on the other side of the island, was forced to allow Batavia's recommended coinages into circulation or face government censure.[72] European power edged forward, therefore, through a variety of means. Batavia, in fact, was required by the Treaty of 1824 to send copies of all agreements signed with local lords to Britain, so that Whitehall could be apprised of the nature of contacts along the border.[73] This did not stop both sides from maneuvering within these obligations, however, as London and The Hague responded late or sometimes not at all to new contracts that had been closed. Area potentates also paid close attention to the evasive possibilities of this complicated system, sometimes trying to play off one European power against the other to maintain their independence.[74]

The jockeying in and around the Riau archipelago, just south of Singapore in Dutch waters, is an example of the complexity of Batavia's dealings with local chiefs. Though Riau was technically self-governing in this period, the archipelago was in fact kept under stringent Dutch control through a broad spectrum of measures. The sultan of Riau and his underchiefs had to assent to continual readjustments in the lands kept in pepper and gambier cultivation, as well as to similar modifications to the borders of government-titled (as opposed to local) lands in the islands.[75] Malay letters also show how mapmaking expeditions were forced upon the local rulers, who had no say as to whether these nominally independent lands should be surveyed or not.[76] Visits from the British authorities in neighboring Singapore were closely watched and monitored, while payments to the indigenous rulers were withheld at government discretion to encourage desired behavior.[77] In 1888, Batavia decreed that anyone in Riau who was caught tampering with government telegraph wires, which passed through the islands on their way to Singapore, would be dealt with in Dutch courts, not through local judicial assemblies. The same trend is evident in mining concession policies: though Batavia allowed local decision making in the distribution of these licenses elsewhere, in Riau the privilege was to be shared with the state, as stipulated in Riau's revised contract.[78] The Dutch made sure, in other words, that frontier contact with local lords was modulated to Batavia's advantage. The porosity and development of the border were too important to let such matters evolve by chance.

By 1915, European relations with local lords in the periphery had been crafted down to more of an exact science. Formal contracts known as the *korte-verklaringen* and the *lange politieke contract* (short declaration and long political contract) were standardized to regulate Batavia's pull on states along the frontier. The system of reportage between Singapore and Batavia began to function on more regular lines as well, the two colonial powers sharing news of their relations with local states in a more timely and precise fashion. Advances in mapping and exploration helped this process along, as there were fewer unknown areas around 1900, and contracts were spelled out in considerably more detail.[79] Nevertheless, complications remained with the semi-independent local lords of the periphery, even after 1900. Compensation payments to rulers were repeatedly withheld to modulate behavior, while in some locales the government reserved the right to appoint its own civil functionaries, including port authorities and police in Riau.[80] In one revealing incident in 1907, the sultan of Sambas in West Borneo was admonished by Batavia for offering the king of England edible birds' nests as a gift. The action and Dutch response to this offer show how sensitive relations with these polities still were: a gift along these lines could be construed as form of vassalage, something Batavia would do anything to avoid.[81] Yet it also shows how short the leash was for these states as European power grew in the periphery into the twentieth century. Local lords were expected to adhere to a rigid code of rules and conduct, the outlines of which had been drawn by Batavia with painstaking detail.

This leaves the actual construction of the border itself as a last aspect of mapping the frontier, a process that also took place over the entire fifty-year period covered in this book. The treaties of 1824 and 1871, as noted earlier, and the work of the Boundary Commission of 1889 set the diplomatic parameters of the Anglo/Dutch frontier in Southeast Asia, drawing a fixed line between the two colonial spheres. Yet the small historiography touching on the border regions shows clearly that these lines were transgressed in a variety of ways. James Warren has shown, for example, how the historical Captain William Lingard (who would later become famous in Joseph Conrad's novels) traded opium, salt, and guns into the interior of East Borneo, setting off a "seepage effect" of movement and trade from the British North Borneo Company's territories south into the Dutch sphere.[82] Warren also has shown how Bugis trade settlements in eastern Borneo overlapped and complemented Taosug forts in the interior, connecting outstretched networking strands across the emerging frontier.[83] Daniel

Chew, working on the opposite side of the border in Sarawak, has deepened this picture by bringing to light the frontier-crossing activities of interior Chinese traders as well, who fled outstanding debts to larger Chinese merchants in the ports and disappeared silently across the Dutch boundary.[84] Other authors have illuminated how powerless the Dutch were to stop all of these transgressions in the 1860s and 1870s, as often Batavia was either unsure where spheres of influence precisely lay or had no civil servants on the ground to check on such movements.[85]

For our purposes, it is enough to note that such problems of enforcing the new geopolitical reality of the frontier existed even until the twentieth century. This is apparent nearly everywhere along the Anglo/Dutch frontier. In the Straits of Melaka in the 1880s, the sultan of Jambi's men continually were able to cross the maritime divide, bringing rice back from Singapore to feed the resistance against the Dutch. Matters were serious enough by 1887 that the Dutch consul in Penang asked Batavia to pull more of its diplomatic weight with Singapore and require passing traders to take an oath that they were not carrying any contraband to Sumatra.[86] Dutch attempts to concretize the imaginary line across the Straits eventually provoked a chorus of outrage from traders operating under the British flag, however, as they saw their economic freedom and opportunities being undercut by the stricter imposition of the frontier.[87] By the 1890s, when Dutch naval patrols were becoming better able to police the Straits against any and all trade movements passing across, this outrage had reached beyond the local authorities and was being heard even in London. Whitehall's policy by this time, however, was to let the Dutch win the peace in Sumatra, even if this meant a temporary decline in trade for London's own subjects in the Straits.[88] The maritime frontier, therefore, became more rigid over time, partially because of the growth of policing technologies and partially through the compliance of British diplomacy, which sought a long-term solution to the problem of trade instability in the region.

In Borneo, categorizing of the exact shape and nature of the frontier took longer, as the terrain was far more inaccessible than the shallow, navigable waters of the Straits. Dayak farming plots extended across the imaginary line between British and Dutch interests, and head-hunting in the interior made surveying expeditions both dangerous and costly in terms of protection.[89] In the 1870s and 1880s, such cross-border raids were exceedingly common, delaying the work of positioning teams and explorers who sought to map out the limits of the two colonial spheres.[90] By the late 1880s, however, there are indications that conditions were improving in this regard, though there was still a great degree of uncertainty as to where the respective colonial dominions actually merged into one another.[91] The Boundary Commission of 1889 settled these questions on the theoretical space of European maps and was legitimated by treaty in 1891, but on the ground of the actual frontier such deliberations continued to be problematic. No line of beacons and markers showed the interior populations of farmers, traders, and nomads which lands were English and which were Dutch, even at a comparatively late date. Though Batavia continually suggested the necessity of implementing this idea, the North Borneo Company balked at the costs of such a project, stating that armed escorts, medical personnel, and much money would be needed before such a scheme could be adopted.[92] It was only after 1910 that comparatively sophisticated work on delimiting the frontier's physical parameters began. At that time the resources of both states were bent toward marking a border that still existed more in the minds of European diplomats than of anyone living in the depths of the forest.[93]

Mapping the evolving boundary between emerging Dutch and British space in Southeast Asia was therefore a project of many decades. As an enterprise of colonial knowledge, exploration and mapping were accomplished by many people: professional explorers and surveyors as well as amateur adventurers whose interests were purely intellectual. Yet the state was never far removed from these journeys, and Batavia especially tabulated expedition results with voracious energy. Mensuration was a critical component of state expansion and backed up the processes of forward movement into the frontier in scientifically critical ways. Almost as soon as the various fiefdoms, principalities, and sultanates along the frontier were encountered, they were categorized under rubrics the state could understand. The acquiring of such knowledge was deemed crucial if these emerging boundary spaces ultimately were to be controlled. This was an uneven process, as has been shown in the preceding pages: colonial regimes understood some of these landscapes better than others and acquired this knowledge at different times. Yet most places that became known eventually became coveted. It would be the job of a different subset of state "servants" to enforce the claims and knowledge about the frontier that these governments already had won.

NOTES

1. As discussed in the introduction, this division of spheres had been attempted by treaty as early as 1824, when British Bengkulu and Dutch Melaka were swapped. Much of the tensile strength of the trade agreement was only really solidified in 1871, however.

2. A good contemporary overview is provided in Bakker, "Van Paradijs tot Plantage" (1998), 75–85; for a partial summary of these enterprises, see Kan, "De Belangrijkste Reizen" (1889), 530 passim.

3. "Een Wenk voor de Ontwikkeling" (1881), 318.

4. Faes, "Het Rijk Pelelawan" (1881), 491; also Neumann, "Reis Naar de Onafhankelijk Landschappen" (1883), 1, 38.

5. ARA, 1872, MR no. 632; "Annexatie's in Centraal Sumatra" (1880), 161; van Hasselt, "The Objects and Results of a Dutch Expedition" (1885), 39.

6. Junghuhn, *Atschin en Zijn Betrekkingen tot Nederland,* (1873); "Toekomst van Groot-Atjeh" (1880), 253.

7. Hellfrich, "Bijdrage tot de Kennis van Boven-Djambi" (1904), 973. See also the map preceding this page, which shows how the rivers were used by explorers to get to the upland regions.

8. See ARA, J. F. van Bemmelen to GGNEI, 23 Nov. 1890, in 1890, MR no. 1029; and ARA, Director of Onderwijs, Eeredienst, Nijverheid to GGNEI, 20 Dec. 1890, in 1890, MR no. 1039; Pleyte Wzn., "Geschiedenis der Ontdekking van het Toba-Meer" (1895), 740, and the map following page 740; d. M., "De Onafhankelijke Bataks" (1902), 246; and Djoko, "Si Singa Mangaraja Berjuang" (1973), 267–99.

9. ARA, 1897, MR no. 611; Cremer, "Per Automobiel naar de Battakvlakte" (1907), 245.

10. Meerwaldt, "Per Motorboat 'Tole' het Tobameer Rond" (1911), 63; "Waterval van Man-salar" (1911), 109.

11. Andaya, *To Live as Brothers* (1993); Trocki, *Prince of Pirates* (1979); Heidhues, *Bangka Tin and Mentok Pepper* (1992).

12. See, for example, Lange, *Het Eiland Banka en Zijn Aangelegenheden* (1850); van Dest, *Banka Beschreven in Reistochten* (1865); and de Groot, *Herinneringen aan Blitong* (1887).

13. Kroesen, "Aantekenningen over de Anambas-, Natuna-, en Tambelan Eilanden" (1875), 235 ff.; van Hasselt and Schwartz, "De Poelau Toedjoeh" (1898), 21–22.

14. "Chineesche Zee" (1896), 1–2.

15. Van Hasselt, "De Poelau Toedjoeh," 25–26. These directives had been issued for some time already but were particularly important around this time for the revision of de Hol-lander's "Handleiding voor de Beoefening der Land- en Volkenkunde." See ARA, Directeur van Onderwijs, Eeredienst, en Nijverheid to GGNEI, 21 March 1890, no. 2597, in 1890, MR no. 254.

16. The extensive surveying of Bangka began even earlier, in the 1870s. See ARA, 1894, MR no. 535; and Zondervan, "Bijdrage tot de Kennis der Eilanden Bangka en Blitong" (1900), 519.

17. "Balakang Padang" (1902), 1295; Niermeyer, "Barriere Riffen en Atollen" (1911), 877.

18. Van Goor, "A Madman in the City of Ghosts" (1985).

19. See Kater, "Dajaks van Sidin" (1867), 183–88; Gerlach, "Reis naar het Meergebied" (1881), 327; Bakker, "Rijk van Sanggau" (1884), 1 passim; ANRI, Algemeen Verslag Residentie West Borneo 1890 (no. 5/21).

20. Enthoven, *Bijdragen tot de Geographie van Borneo's Westerafdeeling* (1903); Perelaer, "Recensie over Jottings" (1881), 514–15; "Serawak en Noord Borneo" (1881), 1.

21. The explorer Muller had been killed inland from Kutei in 1825; in 1844 the Scotsman Er-

skine Murray was also slain along the Mahakam River, while a Dutch resident in the environs of Kutei had also been killed in the 1860s. See Bock, *The Headhunters of Borneo* (1881).

22. ARA, 1887, MR no. 531; ARA, Advies van Directeur van Onderwijs, Eeredienst, en Nijverheid to GGNEI, 18 June 1898, no. 10028, in ARA, 1898, MR no. 372.
23. "Noordoostkust Borneo" (1902).
24. PRO, Frank Hatton's Diary of His Last Expedition Up the Kinabatangan-Segama, vol. 76, 16 Jan. to 16 Feb. 1883, in CO 874/boxes 67–77, Resident's Diaries.
25. See Molengraaf, *Geologische Verkenningstochten* (1900).
26. Nieuwenhuis, *In Centraal Borneo* (1900); "Dr. Nieuwenhuis' Derde Tocht" (1901), 63. Dutch penetration of the interior followed Nieuwenhuis's journeys. See "Bij de Kaart van het Boven-Mahakam Gebied" (1902), 414.
27. ARA, Resident SE Borneo to GGNEI, 30 Dec. 1893, no. 7665/22, in 1894, MR no. 43; ARA, First Government Secretary to Resident West Borneo, 3 Feb. 1894, no. 337, in 1894, MR no. 141.
28. "Memorandum on Gold in North Borneo, 30 May 1934" in CO 874/996. This document gives a short history of gold prospecting in North Borneo's territory from the earlier period.
29. British Borneo Exploration Company, London, to R.W. Clarke, Telegraph, 29 Oct. 1908, in CO 874/350; see also the list of consignees in "Oil and Mineral Rights Agreements, 1905–1920," in CO 874/349.
30. "Sultan Omer Allie Sapprodin to Capt. Mason," 6 Dec. 1847; also "Sultan Omer Allie Sapprodin to William Glidden," 7 Dec. 1847, in CO 144/2.
31. See Everett, "Distribution of Minerals in Sarawak" (1878), 30.
32. Ibid., 28.
33. ARA, Directeur van Onderwijs, Eeredienst, en Nijverheid to GGNEI, 9 April 1873, no. 3364, in 1873, MR no. 285; Voute, "Goud-, Diamant-, en Tin-Houdende Alluviale Gronden" (1901), 116.
34. ANRI, Algemeen Administratieve Verslag Residentie West Borneo 1874 [no. 5/4].
35. Van Schelle, "Geologische Mijnbouwkundige Opneming" (1881) 1:263; "Metalen in Borneo's Westerafdeeling" (1883), 12–13.
36. Van Schelle, "Geologische Mijnbouwkundige Opneming" (1884), 123.
37. ANRI, Algemeen Verslag Residentie West Borneo 1889 [no. 5/20].
38. "Steenkolen en Brandstoffen" (1910), 66; "De Eerste Kamer over de Brandstof" (1910), 93.
39. ANRI, Maandrapport Residentie Borneo Z.O. 1870 [no. 10a/5 January; no. 10a/6 April.]
40. ARA, Extract Uit Het Besluiten, GGNEI, in 1902, MR no. 86.
41. ARA, 1874, MR no. 519; ARA, 1889, MR no. 720; ANRI, Maandrapport Residentie Borneo Z.O. 1873 [no. 10a/8 January].
42. For an overview, see Heslinga, "Colonial Geography in the Netherlands" (1996), 173–93, and van der Velde, "Van Koloniale Lobby naar Koloniale Hobby" (1988), 211–21; contemporary details can be found in *Koloniaal Verslag* (1878), Bijlage C, 36.
43. For the triangulation of Sumatra, see de Bas, *De Triangulatie van Sumatra* (1882).

44. ARA, 1872, MR no. 467; "Topographische Opneming" (1892), 1148.

45. Surveyor General R. Howard, Labuan, to Col. Secretary, Labuan, 6 May 1873, in CO 144/40.

46. Kruijt, *Twee Jaren Blokkade,* 169, 189.

47. See ANRI, Aceh no. 5; Stukken aan de Kommissie, Ingesteld bij het Gouvernement Besluit 18 Mei 1873, no. 1 te Batavia, Over de Expeditie 1873. Expeditie Tegen Atjeh, Topographische Dienst, Expeditionaire Brigade, Rapport Gb, Order no. 8, p. 11, 11a [April 1873; Bijlage K, Bundel Aa-Az; II].

48. ANRI, Aceh no. 8; Atjehsche Verslagen 1874–75; "Gevechts Terrein op den 15 Februarij 1874"; Behoort bij Missive van den Kommandant van het Leger, 25 Maart 1874, no. 18.

49. ANRI, Aceh no. 8: Lichttoren op Poeloe Bras, 23 Maart 1875.

50. Cornelis, "Een Poging tot Verbetering der Kaarten" (1907), 1042–47; Enthoven, *De Militaire Cartographie* (1905).

51. Kan, "Geographical Progress in the Dutch East Indies" (1904/5), 715; Oort, "Hoe een Groote Kaart tot Stand Komt" (1909), 363–65.

52. ARA, Bijzondere Voorwaarden der Mijnconcessie Karang Ringin (Afdeeling Moesi Ilir, Resident Palembang) under Besluit no. 30, 7 Feb. 1902, in 1902, MR no. 149; Bijzondere Voorwaarden der Mijnconcessie Kahajan (Dayaklanden, Borneo Z.O.) under Besluit no. 44, 27 Feb. 1902, in 1902, MR no. 204.

53. The Dutch ambassador in London, Baron Gericke, was confused as to the nature and extent of Dutch claims in East Borneo when a piratical act there necessitated Anglo/Dutch cooperation in 1909. In private correspondence between the Dutch ministers for the colonies and foreign affairs after this, both stressed the importance of having Dutch envoys familiar with the outlines of Dutch territory in the Indies. Atlases and maps were sent shortly thereafter to Dutch representatives in Berlin, London, Tokyo, Peking, Paris, Constantinople, Stockholm, St. Petersburg, Washington, and Bangkok. See ARA, MvK to MvBZ, 15 July 1909, no. I/14735; MvK 26 Nov 1909, no. I/23629, all in (MvBZ/A/ 277/A.134). Information on the nature and exact location of the frontier was also shared across the border: see ARA, First Government Secretary, Batavia, to Resident West Borneo, 20 Feb. 1891, no. 405, in 1891, MR no. 158, which ordered the resident there to send maps of the border and the road and river systems to the raja of Sarawak. These exercises in illuminating the frontier's exact contours sometimes surprised Batavia with their results. In 1894, the Dutch found out during surveying that the territory of the Indies was actually larger than had been previously thought, while in 1910 topographical expeditions in Borneo showed that some of the mountains along the frontier were smaller than originally indicated. See, respectively, "Herziening van de Areaal-Opgaven" (1894), 1734– 38; Rouffaer, "Foutive Vermelding van Berghoogten" (1910), 787–88.

54. "Nieuwe Kaart van Sumatra" (1908), 680.

55. For an overview, see Tagliacozzo, "Hydrography, Technology, Coercion" (2003), 89–107.

56. "Kaartbeschrijving: Zeekaarten" and "Hydrographie" (1918), 2403, 126–27.

57. ARA, 1871, MR no. 464.

58. See *Penang Guardian and Mercantile Advertiser,* 23 Oct. 1873, 4.

59. See ARA, Archief van de Dienst der Hydrografie (Ministerie van Marine), Doos 65: Journaal van Hoekmetingen en Peilingen Opname Straat Banka en N. Kust Banka,

1860–63 (IIIe 1c); see the crude drawings three pages before the end of the volume. For comparison, see in this same box, "Triangulatie Register Riouw en Lingga Archipel: Melville van Carnbee, 1894–99" (IIIb 1a), 58a, which shows how far hydrography had come just forty years later.

60. ANRI, Maandrapport Residentie Banka 1870 (no. 96, October, November); 1878 (no. 104, March); ANRI, Maandrapport Residentie Banka 1870 (no. 96, December); 1872 (no. 98, April); 1873 (no. 99, February).

61. ANRI, Maandrapport Residentie Banka 1878 (no. 104, September).

62. When Batavia allowed English surveying vessels to map parts of the Riau archipelago in 1891 and talked of sending Dutch vessels to do similar work off the coast of the Malay Peninsula that same year, the *Indische Gids* sneered at this as a face-saving gesture on the part of the Dutch. See "Engelands Hydrographische Opnemingen" (1891), 2013–15. Other articles in the Dutch press also criticized Batavia's hydrographic policy and prowess. See "Indische Hydrographie" (1882), 12–39; also "Naschrift van de Redactie" (1898), 1289.

63. See ARA, Archief van de Dienst der Hydrografie (Ministerie van Marine), box 9: Brievenboek no. 9, 1891–95, 35, 245, 285.

64. See the English map of northeastern Borneo, completed in the early twentieth century, which can be found in CO 531/20. Also see the Dutch map "Straat Makassar" reproduced in *Mededeelingen op Zeevaartkundig Gebied over Nederlandsch Oost-Indië* (1907), 1 May, no. 6. The penetration of state vision into the maritime periphery becomes more and more apparent in these maps as time passed.

65. See the photos in "Hydrographische Opname in Oost-Indië" (1907), 756–57. The surveying sailing craft *Bloemendaal* is in the foreground of a photograph in this article, beached and now removed from service. The survey steam vessel *Van Gogh,* meanwhile, continues to ply the seas in the background. The symbols the photographer is playing with are obvious: progress steams on, while the old science is left on the beach.

66. See PRO/Ministry of Trade 10/Harbour Department/no. 1031/File H/12434 "Alleged Uncharted Reef in the Middle Channel of the Singapore Straits, 1906"; Hickson, *Naturalist in North Celebes* (1889), 188–89; and Coops, "Nederlandsch Indies Zeekaarten" (1904), 129.

67. The shaded areas are those which have already been surveyed by the time of publication. The dates indicate the precise years in which the area was mapped. See Craandyk, "Het Werk Onzer Opnemings Vaartuigen" (1910), 75–76.

68. See Scott, *Seeing Like a State* (1998).

69. Struijk, "Toekomst der Inlandsche Vorsten" (1883), 451.

70. See Pangeran Jehudin to W. C. Cowie, Managing Director, BNB Co, 27 Aug. 1878, in PRO/CO/874/Box 186.

71. "Overeenkomsten met Inlandsche Vorsten: Djambi" (1882), 540; ARA, 1872, MR no. 170.

72. See ARA, 1872, MR no. 73, 229, and *Surat Surat Perdjandjian Bandjarmasin,* (1965), 258–67, for the oath of the sultan there to the Dutch, replete with promises of his future behavior. For Pontianak, see "Overeenkomsten met Inlandsche Vorsten: Pontianak" (1882), 549.

73. FO to CO, 29 Sept. 1871, in CO 273/53.

74. See the complaint of the sultan of Sulu to the British in Labuan, in which an alliance is

sought with the English to counteract the growing influence of Spain, in Gov Labuan to CO, 15 Aug. 1871, no. 33, in CO 144/34.

75. See ANRI, "Surat Perjanjian Sewah Tanah Atas Gambir dan Lada Hitam," 1893, in Archief Riouw, no. 225/5 (1893); also "Process Verbaal Tentang Perbatasan Tanah Gou-bernement Hindia Belanda di T. Pinang untuk Ditandangani oleh Raja Abdoel Rach-man dan Raja Abdoel Thalib" in Archief Riouw, no. 223/4 Stukken Sultan Lingga, 1899.

76. See ANRI, "Idzin Pembuatan Peta Baru Tentang Pulau Yang Mengililingi Sumatra," 1889, in Archief Riouw, no. 225/9 (1889).

77. ARA, 1890, MR no. 874; ARA, 1891, MR no. 395.

78. "Overeenkomsten met Inlandsche Vorsten: Lingga, Riouw" (1888), 163; "Het Eigendin-kelijke van Onze Behandeling der Inlandsche Vorsten" (1891), 73.

79. See PRO, Dutch Consul, London to FO, 20 Aug 1909, and FO to British Consul, Hague, 26 Aug. 1909, both in FO/Netherlands Files, "Treaties Concluded Between Hol-land and Native Princes of the Eastern Archipelago" (no. 31583). This was true not only between the British and Dutch in Southeast Asia, but also between British Malaya and Siam, for example. For the case of Perak and the Siamese dependencies of Kedah, Kelan-tan, and Trengganu, see *Perak Gov't Gazette*, 1900, "Agreements Between Her Britannic Majesty and His Siamese Majesty, 29 Nov. 1899," 350.

80. ARA, Kommissoriaal, Raad van NI, Advies van de Raad, 10 Jan. 1902, in 1902, MR no. 124a; and in 1902, MR no. 7; see also "Overeenkomsten met Inlandsche Vorsten: Lingga/ Riouw" (1907), 235.

81. "Aantword Namens de Soeltan van Sambas" (1907), 2.

82. Warren, "Joseph Conrad's Fiction as Southeast Asian History" (1987), 12.

83. Warren, *The Sulu Zone*, 83−84.

84. Chew, *Chinese Pioneers on the Sarawak Frontier* (1990), 115−17. The evolution of border demarcation between Sarawak and Dutch West Borneo, for example, can be seen in the *Sarawak Gazette*, 27 June 1876, 22 July 1884, and 1 June 1914.

85. Resink, "De Archipel voor Joseph Conrad" (1959), 192−208; Backer-Dirks, *Gouverne-ments Marine* (1985), 173.

86. ARA, Dutch Consul, Singapore to GGNEI, 26 Dec. 1885, no. 974 in 1885, MR no. 802.; ARA, Dutch Consul, Penang to GGNEI, 29 March 1887, no. 125, in 1887, MR no. 289.

87. ARA, 1894, MR no. 298.

88. See, for example, the plea by the Penang Chamber of Commerce to the English author-ities, 18 Aug. 1893, in PRO/FO Confidential Print Series no. 6584/16(i).

89. ANRI, Algemeen Administratieve Verslag Residentie West Borneo 1871 (no. 5/2); Alge-meen Verslag Residentie West Borneo 1874 (no. 5/4).

90. ARA, Resident, West Borneo to GGNEI, 8 June 1871, in 1871, MR no. 2804; Resident West Borneo to GGNEI, 18 April 1886, in 1886, MR no. 293.

91. ANRI, Algemeen Verslag Residentie West Borneo 1886 (no. 5/17); ARA, Asst. Resident Koetei to Resident Borneo Z.O., 25 Jan. 1883, in 1883, MR no. 368. For an account of this, see Wadley, "Warfare, Pacification, and Environment" (1999), 41−66.

92. FO to Dutch Consul, London, 2 Feb 1911, no. 392/11 in Co 531/3; and Dutch Chargé d'Affaires to FO, 19 Nov. 1910, in CO 531/2.

93. BNB Co. to CO, 2 May 1911, in CO 531/3.

Chapter 3 Enforcing the Frontier

As the Anglo/Dutch frontier was catalogued and mapped, it also was being progressively enforced by several institutions to ensure that the will of Batavia and Singapore was exercised on the ground. These institutions were the army, the navy, police forces, and the law. Each was bent to the service of the two colonial states in different ways, but they had the common purpose of being used as "tools of empire" to control a difficult and far-flung frontier. Lines delineated in space were fine for diplomats in the distant boardrooms of Europe, but local administrators in the region knew there needed to be mechanisms to enforce these agreements across the breadth of regional landscapes. The tensile strength of the boundary, therefore, continually was upgraded: guns, ships, and detectives were called upon to do this, as was the corpus of a new set of laws utilized to ensure the will of area regimes. Yet how were these institutions wielded? Did state capabilities universally improve? Or were some of these border tools more effective than others? How could the levers of coercive force be brought to bear along the outstretched domains of the frontier?

THE OVERLAND MILITARY

Raw armed force was always an option available to colonial regimes for the strengthening of a Western presence in the lands astride the border. The Dutch Indies army (KNIL) is a case in point here. An all-volunteer force, the KNIL had a Dutch and Eurasian officer corps, the rest of the units comprising men predominantly from the various indigenous groups of the archipelago. Two-thirds of the standing army was always stationed in the Outer Islands, away from the core of central authority in Java; by the turn of the century, this meant approximately fifteen thousand men in the Buitenbezittingen and a further seven thousand in Java, positioned away from the frontiers. One gets a sense of how small this force was when one considers the size of the population these twenty-two thousand men were patrolling: fifty million inhabitants, subsumed partially under direct Dutch authority and also under several hundred political contracts throughout the archipelago.[1] In frontier residencies, these arrangements meant Europeans often had very little control over daily affairs on the ground, depending on the nature of the agreements with local indigenous rulers. Especially in the 1860s and 1870s, these imbalances led to all kinds of problems for Europeans with regard to enforcing the border.

Perhaps the first and most important of these problems was the massive overextension of colonial military resources, and especially Dutch men and matériel. In 1872 alone, for example, disturbances were cropping up all along the Anglo/Dutch frontier, demanding a Dutch presence in arenas separated by thousands of nautical miles. The first of the Aceh expeditions was starting to be planned and outfitted for eventual war the following year, while further down the Sumatra coast in Deli requests for manpower were also being tendered, as local unrest spun out of centralized control.[2] On Sulawesi, troops were needed to deal with armed violence outside of Makassar, while in Borneo head-hunting in the interior of the western half of the island and piracy on the northeast coast also demanded precious resources.[3] Singapore was reporting similar overextension of its military at this time, though the territories involved here were quite a bit smaller.[4] Batavia's patchwork response to these flash points can be seen in the difficulties experienced in getting human and material resources to far-flung outposts along the border. Few ships were available for transport, so the army was forced to rent merchant shipping at exorbitant rates, totaling 5.7 million guilders for the second Aceh campaign alone.[5] A refined portage system was nonexistent in the KNIL, which necessitated forced laborers being co-opted from far and wide, all to carry the equipment of the Dutch army to the frontier. By 1875, radical plans to remedy this precarious situation were being studied, including trials with elephants as beasts of burden in the Aceh theater.[6]

Yet Dutch military problems in the middle decades of the nineteenth century were not limited to ineffective transport out to the expanding frontier. The very composition of the army itself caused difficulties with organization, especially in terms of recruitment and language. The KNIL was an army recruited from many sources, including Africa, Europe, and various parts of the Indies archipelago. Africans from the Guinea coast were in service, and attempts had been made to find recruits in Liberia as well, though these eventually ended in failure.[7] As for Europeans, Germans, Swiss, French, and Belgians were all represented, adding to the cacophony of languages and cultures stocking the KNIL corps.[8] By the 1880s, attempts were being made to add Persians (and even Japanese) to this list, contingent upon steam shipping lines being opened between the Indies and Hormuz.[9] This medley of ethnicities and languages leaves out entirely the varied nature of indigenes present: Madurese, Bugis, Sundanese, Malays, Javanese, Dayaks, Manadonese, and Ambonese were all recruited and served side by side. British forces in the Straits were also composed of soldiers from various ethnicities, but they were separated and organized better than on the Dutch side of the border.[10] Manpower problems forced Dutch decisions to recruit so widely, but the bottom line was that communications between members of the Indies army were often very difficult. This deficiency was understood by the Dutch command, but by the twentieth century European officers still received only a half hour's instruction in Malay per week.[11]

Poor transport and a Babel-esque compilation of languages were compounded by high desertion rates in the KNIL. In the 1870s, desertions were taking place not only in the Outer Islands—such as in Palembang in 1871, when a Dutch warship had to be sent to Sumatra to quell an armed uprising among indigenous soldiers—but also in Java, at the very center of Dutch rule.[12] Batavia saw the large foreign contingent in the KNIL as part of this problem: the central military administration kept statistics on desertions, which were organized by ethnic and subethnic groups in several categories.[13] Yet the ranks of the Dutch Indies army were constantly thinned by other causes as well, including prison sentences, dishonorable discharges, and financial abscondences. In many of the sources, therefore, one reads of soldiers being rattan-whipped back into formation or ridden down by cavalry in failed desertion attempts.[14] The army Batavia could field at any one time along the border residencies was considerably weakened by all of these issues, poking holes in the effectiveness with which it dealt with transgressive phenomena such as smuggling.

One index may show the jump in the army's efficacy from early to later periods better than any other, however, and that is the improving role of health. Until the turn of the century, the KNIL suffered some its worst systemic problems simply as a function of fielding unhealthy soldiers. The Geneeskundige Dienst (Medical service) in the army was continually reorganized in the 1870s but did not manage significantly to alter the health of Indies soldiers until several decades later. Beriberi was rampant among the rank and file, and at one point the disease had sent between 5 and 15 percent of all soldiers in Aceh to the hospital, killing hundreds every year.[15] Quinine was delivered to field apothecaries to forestall malaria, but the stricken—especially among conscripted laborers in many of the Dutch military campaigns—still tied up shipping lines with the size of their numbers.[16] The diet of KNIL soldiers was among the worst of all European-run armies. The Dutch were third from the bottom in terms of the amounts of animal protein dispensed to their men, for example, bettering only France and Italy in this respect.[17] Yet perhaps most serious of all was the persistent drunkenness among the soldiery, which reached enormous proportions in the years before 1900, appearing as a cause for complaint in literally dozens of articles in the Dutch press. Across the strait in the British garrisons, drunkenness was a huge problem as well.[18] British troops also developed *pamfagus* (blisters and sores) because their uniforms were much too bulky for the tropical climate, and every year soldiers died of ill health, even in Melaka, Penang, and Singapore.

Around the turn of the twentieth century, however, the KNIL gradually was becoming a more effective organization, both in Java and in the Outer Islands along the Anglo/Dutch frontier. An improvement in the health management of soldiers was one very important reason why. The Dutch military avidly read English and French medical journals, keeping up with the latest advances in knowledge of the tropics from places as far away as Madagascar and French Guyana. The Dutch also had started to build up a reservoir of practical knowledge themselves, having to do with clothing, food supplies, drinking water, and seasonal precautions. It was around this time that water-resistant clothing began to be studied in field tests in the Indies, as well as other kinds of fabrics that would be suitable for long expeditions in the border residencies.[19] Studies on boots also were commissioned, in trying to find the right kind of shoe for traction and insulation during monsoon campaigns.[20] Funds were set up to promote exercise and gymnastics among the troops, while detailed instructions were handed out on how to keep water fresh during prolonged periods in the bush.[21] By 1896, a whole range of conserved foods were available to sustain government troops far from any supply lines: Australian meats that had been cooked at over one hundred degrees Centigrade in chloro-calcium baths; dried fish; dried vegetables; and sardines were among these preserves.[22] Even drunkenness and beriberi were down, rendering the KNIL a more fit policing force by the early twentieth century.[23]

There were other reasons Europeans were better able to expand their armed presence into the broad spaces of the frontier by the early twentieth century. Some of these were organizational. In Sarawak, the Brookes built a network of forts up-country in order to establish a permanent presence in rural areas; these instillations could be found at Bentong, Kabong, Muka, Bintulu, and up the Baram and Trusan Rivers.[24] For the Dutch, a complex, accordionlike system in which the military and civil governments of the Outer Islands cooperated in trouble districts allowed for flexibility in watching over potentially rebellious populations. When circumstances were peaceful, many of the army units in these outlying residencies were reduced in size and reassigned to other areas. This happened in parts of Aceh and southeastern Borneo, two notorious flash points, around 1900.[25] In other districts, however, such as the Upper Dusun and Upper Kapuas regions of western Borneo, authority was maintained under a military umbrella at the expense of the civil administration. This often caused problems between the two branches of Dutch authority, as the administration saw its jurisdiction disappearing into the coercive powers of the military. From the standpoint of Batavia, however, concessions of this nature were almost always preferable to the opposite possibility, which was lack of control over local populations, especially in the border residencies. Batavia was only too happy, most of the time, to skimp on local administrative efficiency—that is, having civil servants in charge who knew the local customs and had long-standing ties with local peoples—if the military could ensure order in these newly conquered places.[26]

A last important aspect of military evolution concerned matériel, and how advances in technology allowed for quicker and more thorough state penetration into the periphery around the turn of the century Just as they perused foreign medical journals to keep pace with advances in medical technology, Batavia's military planners read foreign military journals to gain information on new weapons and materials, data that could be bent to the service of the expanding colonial state. Around the turn of the century, therefore, the KNIL took a keen interest in the development of aluminum for its lightweight properties in smaller field rifles, which allowed soldiers greater mobility in overgrown terrain. Trials with lighter-weight artillery were also being made, especially with a new Belgian model that could be assembled and disassembled in less than five minutes.[27] Automobiles were being studied for their military transport potential, and military airships—zeppelins—were also being discussed, especially for their surveillance and great water-crossing potential.[28] Nearly everywhere, in other words, the KNIL was looking for ways to enhance its speed and quick-strike capabilities in the periphery, especially in oft-troubled areas like the Anglo/Dutch frontier. By 1912, the Outer Islands were cut into military information grids, about which Batavia had instant information, no matter how distant the residency.[29] This information could then be used to quickly gauge dangerous situations as they developed, whether smuggling, rioting, or outright revolt was the potential difficulty at hand. Yet the army was not the only weapon at the disposal of these states to control order and movement along the border.

COERCIVE MEASURES BY SEA

The predominantly maritime nature of the Anglo/Dutch frontier also made the maintenance of a strong naval presence a high priority for Batavia. The British possessed the greatest navy the world had even seen by the late nineteenth century, yet the Dutch had fallen far behind their neighbors and erstwhile allies since the days of parity in the seventeenth century. Constant patrols were needed for several reasons, not least among which was surveillance of smugglers who were frequently penetrating into the Indies. To reach these ends, the Indies naval presence was divided into the following branches, each of which contributed to defense and interdiction in differing ways. The Gouvernements Marine, essentially the coast guard of the colony, was made up of a few steamers and smaller wooden craft that fulfilled a variety of functions. The Auxilliary Eskader was part of the Royal Dutch Navy and contributed a few larger ships to Indies service; these were controlled directly by the governor-general in Batavia and were under his command. The Indisch Militair Marine, the third component in this triad, was also part of the Royal Dutch Navy but was controlled directly from The Hague by the Ministry of the Colonies. By contrast with the servicemen in the Indies army, most of the men serving in these latter two marine services were Europeans, including all the officers and engineers on the fleet's ships. Sea power was understood to be vital to an effective Dutch presence in the Indies, which explains why more Europeans were filtered into this branch of the service than into the cavalry and infantry on land.[30]

Despite this understanding, in the 1860s and 1870s Batavia's marine presence in the Indies, like its overland component, was hopelessly overstretched. Border control was simply impossible on a daily practical basis: there were too few ships for the distances that needed to be covered, from the tip of North Sumatra to the open waters of the Sulu Sea and beyond. In western Borneo, the available marine presence was busy hunting down pirates from April to October and then acted as a government transport service the rest of the year, despite being short of effective ships.[31] Off the coast of eastern Borneo, the Dutch naval forces also had their hands full, predominantly chasing pirates from the northern mouth of the Makassar Straits.[32] Showing Batavia's flag in the upriver domains of this long, "anarchic" shoreline was also a responsibility of the Dutch marine forces, as was transporting vaccines and currency payments for troops and ferrying government passengers as well.[33] On the broad maritime littoral of Sumatra's Straits of Melaka coasts, the overextended nature of the Dutch marine was much the same. Piracy was rampant in the waters off Lampung, Bangka, and Palembang, while off Jambi cross-straits smuggling required concerted government surveillance.[34] Despite their global naval reach, the British faced similar maritime inadequacies locally in this region: ships stationed in Asia were described as being leaky or in dilapidated condition, while steam launches were desperately sought by Singapore to keep an eye on illegal trading in local waters.[35] With marine forces stretched to the limit and performing all sorts of tasks, including transport, lighthouse supply, beacon maintenance, and hydrography, precious little time was left for interdiction and control of smugglers operating on both sides of the strait.

One phenomenon took away more European maritime policing power than any other, though, and this was the constant drain on men and matériel posed by the Aceh War from 1873 onward. The British had to commit ships to the Straits of Melaka at this time to ensure their interests would be protected despite the outbreak of hostilities.[36] Yet the Dutch were hit much harder. A full twenty years after the start of the conflict, all but one of the Indies' regular warships were still in the North Sumatra theater: everywhere else, the Gouvernements Marine had to patrol the Indies as a makeshift force.[37] Documents from the blockading ships off Aceh show the limited efficacy of even the main ships of the line. Coal was in extremely short supply, so many of the vessels spent inordinate amounts of time convoying fuel from one ship to another, rather than carrying out their blockade duties.[38] Discipline was also faulty and unreliable, as constant notices of thievery, drunkenness, and sailors sleeping on duty make clear.[39] Sickness rates were high, and water-provisioning problems (most of the

Aceh shore was hostile and therefore out of bounds for freshwater collection) also took time away from surveillance and control. Perhaps most serious of all, however, was that often the blockading fleets could not get near enough to shore to enforce the blockade against smuggling. The main Dutch ships were too large to get in close, and coastal fire was too strong for the navy's sloops, which could be shot out of the water in trying to intercept blockade-running craft.[40]

These were not optimal conditions for Batavia to be able to keep a close eye, and a close rein, on the movement of various kinds of anxiety-provoking commodities across the outstretched regions of the Anglo/Dutch frontier. The 1880s and 1890s saw only limited improvements in these conditions. Much of the hydrography done in Indies waters was still being performed by the Gouvernements Marine, rather than by professionally trained surveyors; this retarded the state's vision of the maritime periphery significantly, as will be seen more definitively in the next chapter.[41] Budget shortfalls in the various marine exchequers necessitated the sale of many Indies vessels, which were too expensive to maintain along the entire length of the border.[42] When these realities are added to the fact that communication between the European officers and the mostly indigene crews was faulty at best—the Royal Marine Institute actually ended Malay-language instruction in favor of a Dutch-first policy by 1903/04—the pattern of difficulties in the Indies' naval ranks becomes clear.[43] Overextended and lacking a clear program for improvement, it would only be in the years around the turn of the century that Batavia would make serious inroads into improving control of the sea.

The seeds for this turnaround were sown as Dutch planners started to think more and more about how to protect the Indies' maritime borders in a variety of ways. One of the main forces behind this reappraisal was a fear that the Indies was overly vulnerable to external attack and that the colony could be easily cut off from the Netherlands. Batavia had been clipping articles from international military journals about the comparative naval strengths of the powers for some time, chronicling advances and deployments of the Chinese, Japanese, and various Western fleets since the mid-1870s.[44] Yet the revolutionary power of A. T. Mahan's *The Influence of Sea Power Upon History* (1890) and the defeat of the Russian Far Eastern fleet by the Japanese in 1904–05 lent new urgency to these deliberations in Dutch policy-planning circles.[45] In the first decade of the twentieth century, Royal Dutch decrees were setting the Indies' fleet strength at carefully monitored levels, stipulating parameters and tonnages of craft which should be present in the colonies at all times.[46] This had a positive effect on

Batavia's policing abilities along stretches of the Anglo/Dutch frontier, as more ships (and better quality ones) headed out to the Indies after 1900.

The pace of technological advances in naval capabilities was the spark that lit the fire in Dutch policy circles around this time. By 1895, urgent circulars were being sent out to Dutch envoys in many major capitals to find out how much the various powers were spending on their respective naval forces. These instructions went out to Dutch plenipotentiaries in London, Paris, Berlin, and Washington but also to less exalted powers such as Sweden, Norway, and especially minor colonial nations like Portugal and Spain). The goal was to determine how similarly small states were integrating the new changes into their navies.[47] From the Dutch envoy in Paris, Batavia learned that French fleet expansion was imminent, with improvement of colonial ports like Saigon, funding for colonial cable laying, and a colonial defense fund all on the table. From the Dutch representative in Berlin, information was received about German naval capabilities in the Pacific, which was important to Batavia because of Berlin's interests in telegraphs and shipping in the area.[48] Yet it was the obvious obsolescence of the Indies' marine in comparison to British naval strength in the Straits of Melaka that really gave Batavia cause for alarm. Clippings from the *Times* of London showed that English armor-plate experiments, steam trials, and shallow-draught construction were making Dutch ships obsolete in the archipelago, a tolerable situation while amity existed between the two powers but deemed undesirable for the long term.[49] The news in 1910 that Japan was planning to build ships of even greater technological advancement than Britain's deepened this anxiety, as the Dutch realized their naval presence in the region was inadequate compared with that of its neighbors.[50]

For internal purposes, however, such as the surveillance and interdiction of smugglers, the Indies' marine in the early twentieth century was now a much more effective force than it had been for the past several decades. The evidence of this improvement is nearly everywhere apparent. In Sumatra, more and more steamers were assigned now specifically for upriver patrols, traveling to formerly unreachable spaces where political resistance and "illegal" commerce had functioned almost at will.[51] Along the coast of East Borneo, a long stretch of shoreline seen as troublesome for decades for housing pirates, smugglers, and a variety of other people antithetical to Batavia's state-making project, improvements were also made, as ships were slotted into grids to patrol the entirety of the area.[52] Centralized control over many areas of the Outer Islands had improved so much that certain patrolling stations were actually relieved of ships.[53] This is not to say that the Indies' marine was now unassailable or that it did not continue to have some major problems, which certainly affected its abilities to patrol effectively against smugglers along the borders. Sanitation on board these ships, for instance, continued to be dismal, spawning disease and sickness among crews that often limited these vessels' practical effectiveness.[54] Yet the tide had turned against many structural problems that had curtailed Batavia's abilities in the periphery. By the early twentieth century, smugglers making their entrance into the Indies by sea had to evince considerably more ingenuity in doing so than at any time in the previous fifty years.

POLICING THE BORDER

The most important arms of colonial government charged with enforcing the physical restrictions of the border were the military and naval forces of both imperial powers. Yet beyond the assembled armies and flotillas on either side of the Straits, police forces of both the Dutch and British colonial governments also contributed to frontier surveillance. In the Indies, the police did not have its own separate administration as an organized institution per se. Rather, it was divided between the Ministry of the Interior, from which it received funding, and the Ministry of Justice, from which it received its rules and regulations. Special police subbranches also existed, including a forestry division, salt and coffee surveillance forces, and indigenous police belonging to various Outer Island potentates.[55] Each of these rubrics was concerned with the colonywide threat of smuggling. Across the Straits in Singapore, early police stations were established primarily on the coasts to deal with Chinese societies in the interior of the island as well as with pirates who frequently harbored in the island's small creeks. Various local rulers also maintained police forces in the British sphere as well, leading to a wide divergence in policing power across large tracts of territory.[56]

Like the other branches of state enforcement in the region, police forces on both sides of the Straits were inadequate to deal with the many tasks facing them in the 1860s and 1870s. The problems posed by smugglers and organized trafficking networks were certainly among these challenges. In Singapore, Ordinance no. 19 of 1869 had been specifically enacted for the "Suppression of Dangerous Societies"—the many triads and fraternal organizations that contested government authority among local populations. Throughout the 1870s, however, riots and factional fighting continued in the colony, showing that the police had only limited powers over these men, whatever the law might say. A realization of this state of affairs finally prompted the Straits Settlements to

consider drafting Chinese into the police force to use against the local population as potential allies and servants.[57] Further north in Penang, the island's
press complained that the police force was inadequate for local demands as
well, while spending on detectives and the secret service, for example, was piti-
fully low.[58] In Labuan, off the coast of Borneo, the situation was even more serious: the resident police population, mainly riflemen brought from Ceylon,
died by the dozens in the colony's terrible malarial climate. Pleas were circulated by the Labuan administration to remedy this state of affairs as soon as possible, as policing power was next to useless when half of the force was either in
the hospital or the cemetery.[59]

The prospects for exercising authoritarian control were little better in the
Dutch sphere. In western Borneo, the number of policemen was ludicrously
small for the needs of such a large residency, the resident himself commenting
that standards of discipline and professionalism left everything to be desired.[60]
In southeastern Borneo, the numbers of policemen were even lower, with most
of the available manpower clustered in and around the major towns on the
great rivers. This left plenty of room in the vast stretches of the interior for illegal trade and what was termed lawlessness, including numerous head-hunting
expeditions which claimed many lives.[61] Almost all of the state's police presence was concentrated in urban areas on Belitung and in Riau as well, leaving
large tracts of coastal space open to state-designated criminals of all descriptions.[62] In Riau, the result was a massive contraband commerce with Singapore, carried out especially by local Chinese who "spread left and right to live in
the forests and creeks."[63] The proximity of Singapore and the graft this near-
ness encouraged also affected Palembang, which had long stretches of empty
coast where smugglers could hide in the marshes. Complaints about the police's inability to make any inroads into crime along the borders eventually became a major newspaper topic, finally forcing Batavia to conduct an inquiry as
to why this was so.[64]

The 1880s and 1890s saw a continuation of many of these problems on both
sides of the Straits. In the Dutch sphere, cost cutting in Outer Island residencies such as Palembang deprived the state of many of its eyes and ears, bringing
already low levels of law enforcement down to barely serviceable numbers.[65] In
Riau, the problem was the same, maritime policing power being limited to a
paddleboat and two small surveillance craft, as steamers stationed in the region
were frequently off on other errands. A Dutch map of Riau in the 1890s shows
the maze of islands this undersized flotilla faced just south of Singapore: smuggling and cross-border movement were rife, with no relief in sight for govern-

ment forces (map 5).[66] The fractured nature of the police throughout the Buitenbezittingen made this state of affairs the rule rather than the exception, as different kinds of police presences were cobbled together as stopgap measures.[67] In the British dominions a similar landscape of functional inadequacy was apparent. In Singapore, the chief of detectives pronounced his division much too small to make a serious impact on organized crime on the island, while communications between departments was antiquated and slow.[68] Labuan's constabulary almost always declined to reenlist past their first term of service, a refusal the governor there attributed to the "Malay penchant for change" but which really signaled the dismal pay and conditions that persisted on the island.[69] In British North Borneo, the range of tasks required of the local police shows why they were often so hopeless at catching criminals: the constabulary there was expected to act as porters, letter carriers, boatmen, and revenue collectors in addition to their duties as policemen.[70] It was little wonder, therefore, that smuggling and related crimes flourished in this extended territory of forest, coastline, and wilderness.

Signs of improvement in this state of affairs did present themselves, however, in the years leading up to the turn of the twentieth century. Batavia and Singapore gradually were able to inject more manpower into surveillance and interdiction activities, with results paying off handsomely in the short term. The Dutch police presence was expanded in West Borneo, becoming a patchwork government force as the frontier was pushed inland toward the center of the island.[71] In southeastern Borneo as well, the police presence was extended to interior trading posts and also to coastal regions, which formerly had seen only temporary detachments.[72] More detectives were sent out from the Netherlands, and scientific advances in such fields as forensic chemistry research gave the police more of an arsenal with which to pursue serious criminals.[73] British gains were no less significant. Civil, criminal, and political intelligence branches were all set up after 1900 to track a variety of threats to the established colonial order.[74] The streets of the Straits Settlements were lit up by the addition of hundreds of electrical streetlamps, a civic improvement that gave Singapore the ability to see its subjects by night better than ever before, especially in alleys and on wharves by the docks.[75] This kind of state-sponsored luminescence had important consequences, not least of which was a reduction of darkened spaces where smugglers might operate. Ruling colonial regimes had literally begun to irradiate such spaces so that it became more and more difficult to carve out dissident economic and political geographies. Even popular consciousness recognized the broad changes, as Malay newspapers began speaking

Dutch Naval Complexities, Riau and Singapore, 1890s. (Courtesy KITLV Map Collection, Leiden)

of the *mata mata gelap* (eyes in the dark), that is, the British detective force or undercover police.[76] The police had started to make effective inroads into the workings of local society, and the indigenous populations of the Straits Settlements acknowledged this, even through changes in language.

Yet even by the early twentieth century, several aspects of policing along the lands and seas of this porous frontier still allowed for widespread distribution of goods away from the eyes of the state and against its explicit instructions. Policemen were regularly censured for graft and illegal practices, such as one member of the force in Singapore who was jailed for freeing an incarcerated suspect without any instructions to do so.[77] The police forces of large, difficult-to-govern residencies such as Dutch West Borneo may have increased in size but not necessarily in professionalism, if the reports of border administrators are to be believed.[78] When military units were withdrawn from the Buitenbezittingen upon pacification they were often replaced by an equal number of police officers, showing that a similar level of coercion was needed in the area, even if its composition or tactics had changed.[79] These kinds of signals reveal that "pacification" and policing along the frontier were still highly problematic, even into the early twentieth century. A total of 1,535 Indies policemen for all of the Outer Islands in 1896 was still a very small number; the extra 700 men who had joined this force by 1905 made hardly a dent in this problem.[80] By 1912, instructions were being promulgated to police about what commands they should shout in Malay to quell riots:

> *Djangan koempoel! Poelang! Kalo tida toeroet ini prentah, nanti dapat soesah!*
> *Kaloe tida lekas poelang, mahoe di pasang!*
> *Mahoe poelang atawa tidak? Nanti pasang betoel!*
> [Disperse! Go home! If you don't follow this order, you will be in trouble!
> If you don't go home at once, you'll get a good beating!
> Are you going or not? We mean it—you'll get a real beating!][81]

In the face of a huge mobile and multiracial population straddling both sides of the frontier, the police of neither colonial power was in a position to *fully* command the border at any time. This remains true, in some respects, even today.

THE REACH OF THE COURTS

A final category of border enforcement was the use of laws to "seal" the frontier, a program that was accomplished in a variety of ways, as the historiographical literature on colonial societies generally has shown.[82] The Dutch legal historian G. J. Resink has called attention to the haphazard manner in which this process was attempted in the Indies, from the late nineteenth into the early twentieth century. Resink showed how pirates, slavers, opium runners, and assorted other groups were gradually drawn into the legal jurisdiction of Dutch territorial waters, and how this concept of maritime ownership itself evolved over time. Though the Dutch set a three-mile limit in 1879 and extended it to six miles by 1883, these delineations were valid for only part of the Indies waters, especially when it came to the Outer Islands. Many Buitenbezittingen polities were acknowledged by Batavia to have their own territorial waters, which gave them certain rights off their own respective shorelines.[83] However, the approach of 1915 heralded an end to these independent privileges, as most Indies potentates lost these powers, along with all shreds of vestigial independence, after the first fifteen years of the new century.[84] The Dutch *corpus juris* had subsumed the entirety of the frontier by the dawn of World War I.

Early attempts at using legal codes to enforce the will of Singapore and Batavia on the frontier met with only limited success. Dutch Indies laws were

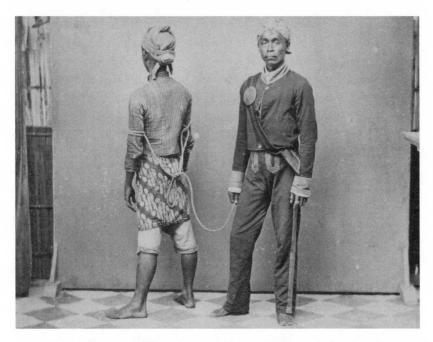

Fig. 2. Indies policeman and criminal, 1870. (Photo courtesy KITLV, Leiden)

translated into various archipelago languages and distributed among local populations, but it was the ability to expel troublemakers from the Dutch sphere that lent the most power to Batavia's plans in this regard (fig. 2).[85] Despite these powers of excision and deportation, Dutch laws in the Outer Islands were almost universally recognized as weak. This was so in Palembang, where the Dutch undertook comprehensive reviews to try to remedy the situation in 1874.[86] It was also true in Riau, where great distances separated the tiny numbers of judges and police, with Singapore beckoning as a convenient (and often-used) escape hatch for a variety of criminals, including smugglers.[87] The British in Borneo faced similar problems in their outpost at Labuan, realizing as far back as the 1850s that their legal powers over local populations were limited at best.[88] In Singapore, the seat of British power, state circumstances were better, with search warrants being available from judges and a smaller geography requiring policing.[89] Even here, however, enforcement and evasion went hand in hand, the latter often outmaneuvering the former for much of the 1860s.

Significant changes in this legal landscape were made in the late 1870s and into the 1880s, however, especially on the Dutch side of the frontier. A member of the powerful Council of the Indies, Th. der Kinderen, was charged with overhauling and reorganizing the judicature of the Outer Islands in 1876.[90] Der Kinderen roamed from residency to residency, examining problems of Buiten-bezittingen jurisprudence and suggesting improvements. In southeastern Borneo, the courts were brought under Surabaya's centralized jurisdiction, rather than Batavia's, which saved time and distance on consultations so that legal actions could be undertaken more quickly.[91] In Riau, the judiciary's procedural guidelines were revamped and realigned, so that there were fewer discrepancies with the contracts closed with local lords, which sometimes allowed criminals to escape punishment on technicalities.[92] On Sumatra's East Coast, the jurisdiction of courts was extended into the hinterland, and on Belitung new seats of law were promulgated to expedite the large numbers of cases yet to be tried.[93] Der Kinderen pushed ahead on Dutch efforts to reform the Outer Islands' legal structure with a vengeance, accomplishing in ten years what might have taken a much longer time to undertake under any other official.[94]

Yet perhaps the most formidable legal tool used to enforce the colonial frontier was extradition, a process that received impetus from both sides of the border. Though London and The Hague had signed an extradition treaty in 1874, the stipulations of the agreement were not legally binding on the two nations' colonies in Asia. Instead, Dutch and British administrators in the Straits relied on each other's friendly assistance in these matters, an arrangement that facilitated transfers on many occasions but also gave both colonial capitals rights of refusal in the absence of any law.[95] This system worked up to a point, but there were many civil servants (especially on the Dutch side of the frontier) who felt that the procedures in place were inadequate to deal with the rising number of cases.[96] Attempts were made, therefore, to solemnize these agreements into law with the Straits authorities, while further overtures were made to Britain's Australian colonies, Siam, and the French territories in mainland Southeast Asia. Batavia hoped to construct a "legal ring" around the Indies from which few criminals could escape and offered to extradite criminals to various administrations, such as the Malay States in Malaya, with which no treaties yet existed.[97] By the turn of the century, mechanisms were finally in place to assure many of these reciprocal agreements, including to the Straits Settlements.[98]

This important process and its implications can be examined usefully in more detail in one arena, from both sides of the evolving frontier. The case of Borneo is a useful example. In 1889, the Sarawak authorities extradited to Dutch West Borneo Tjang Tjon Foek, one of the principal organizers of the Chinese Mandor uprisings of 1884. The Dutch were delighted to receive this man back, as Tjang had been dealing in illegal arms shipments across the frontier and was considered very dangerous.[99] Two years later, five men escaped from British North Borneo in a boat and fled to Dutch eastern Borneo with a quantity of arms and ammunition. The British asked for the prompt return of the men, which the controleur of Bulungan, a neighboring Dutch territory, refused pending receipt of further instructions from his superiors. The governor of the British territory took a dim view of this noncompliance. He wrote to his own superiors that "as the southern boundary of this state is situated of no great distance from Boelangan, I can only anticipate that fugitive criminals from North Borneo will again fly to Boelangan in the future . . . unless an ample power be given to the controleur to make the arrests."[100] Despatches were exchanged between Singapore and Batavia, and, after a short series of wranglings, the British got their men. The *Sarawak Gazette* is filled with many similar cases crossing to West Borneo.[101] Arms traffickers and rebels were thus put on notice that the border would no longer be a divide behind which they could hide.

A formal agreement on extradition between British North Borneo and the Netherlands Indies did not take place until 1910. The establishment of coal mines on the frontier, with the attendant problem of runaway coolie labor, finally helped this "gentleman's agreement" to become codified into law.[102] Yet the informal channels that often characterized diplomacy in the region functioned well enough, for long enough, to convince many administrators on both sides of the frontier that existing agreements were sufficient as they stood. The time of gentlemen's agreements was fast drawing to a close, however. The rise of industry and capital-intensive enterprises in Borneo forced new legal structures into existence, especially as they related to movement across the frontier. British North Borneo eventually put into effect extradition ordinances for Labuan (1890), Sarawak (1891), and Hong Kong (1896), all at least partially as a result of these processes.[103] The agreement with Hong Kong, in fact, was predicated on the establishment of direct steam service between the two colonies. Laborers presently had an easy escape hatch, if they could get on returning ships, to quit their contracts and try to get back to villages in South China with their cash advances in hand.[104] Discussions on extradition with the Sultanate of Brunei also were eventually ratified into law, as Brunei had become a favorite place for counterfeiters as well as slave and coolie traffickers to flee to, away from British North Borneo.[105] Legal structures and the laying of legal connections between governments in the region were therefore two more ways to enforce frontiers in Southeast Asia, though these mechanisms were imperfect even after the turn of the century.

The process of enforcing the evolving boundary between British and Dutch colonial spheres was thus a difficult one. State resources rarely were what local administrators hoped they would be, and serious deficiencies existed in the coercive capabilities that either of the two regimes could call upon at any one time. Despite the shortcomings, however, the armed extension abilities of the Dutch, especially, radically improved along the frontier during the period 1865 to 1915. This was accomplished through waterproof clothing as it was through medicine, and through fingerprints as well as through evolving laws. It was not accomplished just at the point of a gun. Policing and legal enforcement were more difficult than the wholesale injection of new military technologies onto the border. These aspects of state coercion were less amenable to structural change, as they relied more on human beings than on the advances of hard steel and fast ships. Yet it is undeniable that the enforcement capabilities of area regimes on the border generally improved over the span of these fifty years. That which was being built needed to be maintained and strengthened, however, as a concomitant process of boundary formation.

NOTES

1. Wright, ed., *Twentieth-Century Impressions of Netherlands India* (1909), 277. Further information on the Indies' armed forces can be found in Heshusius, *KNIL van Tempo Doeloe* (1998); for the British presence in this part of the world, see Harfield, *British and Indian Armies* (1984).
2. ARA, 1872, MR no. 611, 685; ARA, Dutch Consul to Gov Gen NEI, 7 May 1872, Telegram no. 42, in 1872, MR no. 296. See also *Perang Kolonial Belanda di Aceh* (1997), and Napitupulu, *Perang Batak* (1971), 120–52.
3. ARA, Rapport, Stoomschip Suriname to Station Commandant, SE Borneo, 6 Aug. 1872, in 1872, MR no. 619; ARA, 1872, MR no. 499; ARA, Gov. Celebes to GGNEI, 8 March 1872, no. 166, in 1872, MR no. 203.
4. See Gov SS Diary, 7 Sept. 1868, no. 9812, National Library, Singapore.
5. "Transportschepen voor het Indische Leger" (1880), 36–55.
6. Philips, "De Transportdienst ten Velde" (1891), 46; "Olifanten voor het Transportwezen" (1880), 517.
7. ARA, 1871, MR no. 389; Nieuwenhuysen, "Negerelement bij het Indische Leger" (1899), 525.
8. "Geheimzinnige Werving van Neger Soldaten" (1892), 505–10; "Overzigt van een in het Berlijnsche Tijdschrift Opgenomen Artikel" (1882), 480–85, 681–85.
9. ARA, 1872, MR no. 47; "Eene Legerbelang" (1897), 44.
10. See Harfield, *British and Indian Armies* (1984), 388–89.
11. Nieuwenhuizen, "Beoefening der Inlandsche Talen" (1884), 335; Spat, "Welke Resultaten Mogen Verwacht Worden" (1899), 30–36. For an overview, see Bossenbroek, *Volk voor Indië* (1992).
12. ARA, 1871, MR no. 389; ARA, 1872, MR no. 47.

13. Panari, "Krijgstucht in het Indische Leger" (1881), 225–35; "Numerieke Opgave van Militairen" (1881), 286–325, 429–45.

14. "Militaire Administratie in Indië" (1887), 1883.; see also "Rietslagen en Discipline" (1883), 342, for example.

15. "Reorganisatie der Geneeskundige Dienst" (1880), 449, 596; Pekelharing, "Loop der Beri-Beri in Atjeh in de Jaren 1886–7" (1888), 305; ARA, 1885, MR no. 675. See also *Perang Kolonial Belanda di Aceh* (1997), 46.

16. ARA, Graphische Voorstelling van de 5 Daagsche Opgaven van Beri Beri Lyders, Oct. 1885-June 1886, in 1886, MR no. 497; ARA, 1885, MR no. 675.

17. "Een Enkel Woord Over de Voeding" (1883), 160.

18. Van Rijn, "Jenevermisbruik doer de Europeesche Fusiliers" (1902), 744; "Een Voorstel tot Beteugeling der Twee Hoofdzonden in het Leger" (1895), 540; Madras General Order, 15 Feb. 1864, National Library of Singapore Film no. 615, especially in Penang.

19. Van Haeften, "Voorkomen van Darmziekten Bij het Leger te Velde" (1895), 80; Vink, "Sprokkelingen Uit den Vreemde" (1899), 676; "Waterdichte Kleedingstuken" (1897), 224; van de Water "Doelmatige Kleeding" *IMT* 1 (1902): 230; and *IMT* 2 (1902): 212.

20. "Voor de Practijk" (1906), 669. For an account of the rigors of guerrilla warfare in the border residencies, see Gayo, *Perang Gayo-Alas* (1983), 217–35.

21. ARA, Rapport 29 March 1899, in 1899, MR no. 292; Cayaux "Voorschriften voor de Watervoorziening" (1906), 80.

22. "Verduurzaamde Levensmiddelen" (1896), 482.

23. ARA, Aantal Lijders aan Beri-Beri, Die op Ultimo November 1898 Onder Behandeling Zijn Gebleven, in 1899, MR no. 67; Koster, "Stem over de Drank Questie" (1902), 21.

24. See Harfield, *British and Indian Armies* (1984), 346.

25. ARA, 1899, MR no. 706; ARA, Commander, NEI Army to GGNEI, 10 Nov. 1888, no. 1022, in 1899, MR no. 94; ARA, 1899, MR no. 709.

26. Memorie van Overgave, Borneo Zuid-Oost, 1906 (MMK no. 270), 1; van den Doel, "Military Rule in the Netherlands Indies" (1994), 60–67.

27. Molenaar, "Aluminium en de Waarde van het Metal" (1895), 509; Nijland, "Repport Betreffende de Proef" (1903); Bombardier, "Een Nieuwe Vuurmond" (1895), 103; ARA, 1902, MR no. 206; ARA, 1902, MR no. 1062.

28. "Automobiel in Dienst van het Leger" (1906), 141, 179; de Fremery, "Militaire Luchtscheepvaart" (1907), no. 17.

29. See especially the Buitenbezittingen Military template fashioned for the Memorie van Overgave in 1912, "Schema van de Militaire Memorie in de Buitenbezittingen (1912)" in ARA, MvK, Inventaris van de Memories van Overgave 1849–1962, Den Haag, ARA, 1991.

30. Dyserinck, "Roeping van Zr. Ms. Zeemacht" (1886), 65.

31. ANRI, Algemeen Administratieve Verslag Residentie West Borneo 1872 (no. 5/3)

32. ARA, 1871, MR no. 301.

33. ANRI, Maandrapport Residentie Borneo Z.O. 1870 (no. 10a/5 January, July)

34. ARA, 1871, MR no. 425; ANRI, Algemeen Administratieve Verslag Residentie Palembang 1871 (no. 64/14); *Beschouwingen over de Zeemagt in Ned. Indië* (1875), 51–61. See also *Surat Surat Perdjandjian Riau* (1970), 207.

35. PRO/Admiralty, Vice Admiral Shadwell to Admiralty Secretary, 16 April 1872, no. 98, in no. 125/China Station Corrospondence/no. 21: ; Gov. SS to CO, 8 Jan. 1873, no. 2, in CO 273/65; Gov SS to CO, 14 Jan. 1875, no. 15, in CO 273/79; Gov SS to CO, 16 July 1881, no. 260, and CO to SS, 20 Aug. 1881, both in CO 273/109.

36. PRO/Admiralty, CO to Admiralty Secretary, 30 April 1873; Admiralty to Vice Admiral Shadwell, 1 May 1873, and same to same, 27 June 1873, all in no. 140/Straits of Malacca.

37. See the "Kwaartaalverslagen der Verrichtingen van Zr.Ms./Hr. Ms. Zeemacht in Oost-Indië 1884–92," as quoted in Backer-Dirks, *Gouvernements Marine* (1985), 215

38. See, for example, July shiplogs of the *Metalen Kruis,* stationed off Aceh, in ARA, MvK, Verbaal Geheim Kabinet 17 Dec. 1873, D33. There is constant mention of this problem in the blockade squadron sources.

39. ARA, Ministerie van Marine, Scheeps-Journalen [2.12.03]: see the shiplogs of the *Metalen Kruis* (Logbooks no. 3108–09, 3127, Friday, 27 June 1873, and Monday, 30 June 1873); the *Citadel van Antwerpen* (Logbooks no. 908, 914, Monday, 30 June 1873); and the *Maas en Waal* (Logbook no. 2755, Saturday, 28 June 1873).

40. ARA, MvK, Verbaal Geheim Kabinet 17 Dec. 1873, D33, *Coehoorn* to the Station Kommandant, East Coast Aceh, 13 Aug. 1873, no. 1004, 25 July 1873; ARA, MvK, Verbaal Geheim Kabinet 17 Dec. 1873, D33, "Telegraaf" to the Tijdelijke Kommandant der Maritieme Middelen in de Wateren van Atjeh, no. 11, July 22, 1873.

41. F. C. Backer-Dirks, *Gouvernements Marine,* 273.

42. ARA, Chief of Marine, NEI, to GGNEI, 10 April 1885, no. 3814 in 1885, MR no. 243; ARA, Chief of Marine, NEI, to GGNEI, 15 April 1885, no. 4034 in 1885, MR no. 264; ARA, 1885, MR no. 659; and ARA, Chief of Marine, NEI, to GGNEI, 7 Oct. 1885, no. 11346 in 1885, MR no. 707.

43. "Aankondiging door de Hollander" (1881), 810–11; Van der Star, "De Noodzakelijkheid voor de Inlandsche Scheepsonderofficieren" (1903/1904), 191.

44. For an overview, see Teitler, "Een Nieuwe en een Oud Richting" (1978), 165–86; see also "Marine Militaire du Japon," "Marine Militiare de la Chine," and "Station Anglaise de l'Inde" (1876), 536–38, 542.

45. Macleod, "Het Behoud Onzer O. I. Bezittingen" (1898), 755, 871.

46. "Koninklijke Besluit van den 18 Sept. 1909" (1908/1909), 401.

47. ARA, MvBZ Circulaire to the Dutch Envoys in London, Paris, Berlin, and Washington, 1 Feb. 1895, no. 1097; MvBZ Circulaire to Dutch Envoys in Austro-Hungary, Sweden, Norway, and Russia, 2 Nov. 1896, no. 11265; Dutch Consul, Lisbon to MvBZ, 18 April 1895, no. 59/38; Dutch Consul Madrid to MvBZ, 1 Feb. 1901, no. 36/10, all in (MvBZ/A/421/A.182).

48. ARA, Dutch Consul, Paris, to MvBZ, 14 Feb. 1900, no. 125/60, in (MvBZ/A/421/A.182); ARA, Dutch Consul, Berlin to MvBZ, 3 Aug. 1904; 22 May 1903; 5 April 1902; 6 July 1899; 17 June 1898; 13 July 1897; and 30 Nov. 1896, all in (MvBZ/A/421/A.182).

49. "The Navy Estimates" in *The Times* (of London), 3 March 1897, enclosed in ARA, Dutch Consul, London, to MvBZ, 5 March 1897, no. 113, in (MvBZ/A/421/A.182).

50. "The Destroyer Yamakaze" in *The Japan Times,* 4 June 1910, enclosed under ARA, Dutch Consul, Tokyo, to MvBZ, 13 June 1910, no. 560/159, in (MvBZ/A/421/A.182).

51. ARA, 1902, MR no. 25, 48, 92, 132.

52. ARA, Memorie van Overgave, Borneo Zuid-Oost, 1906 (MMK no. 270), 24.

53. ARA, 1899, MR no. 36.

54. Van Rossum, "Bezuiniginging bij de Zeemacht," *De Gids* 2 (1907): 274; *De Gids* 3 (1907): 287; "Schroefstoomschepen Vierde Klasse" (1880), 161–62.

55. Dekker, *De Politie in Nederlandsch-Indië* (1938); Wright, *Twentieth-Century Impressions of Netherlands India,* 285; see also Mrazek, "From Darkness into Light" (1999), 23–46; and Schulte-Nordholt, "Colonial Criminals" (1997), 47–69.

56. Onreat, *Singapore: A Police Background* (n.d), 72.

57. See Jackson, *Pickering: Protector of Chinese* (1965).

58. "The Penang Police," *Penang Argus and Mercantile Advertiser,* 16 June 1870, 2; "Expenditures," *SSBB,* 1873, 54.

59. War Office to CO, 12 March 1870; Army Medical Dept. to Quarter Master General, 2 March 1870; John Barry, Asst. Surgeon to Officer Commanding the Troops, Labuan, 4 Jan. 1870; CO to Ceylon Gov, 6 May 1870, Telegram no. 103; CO Minute Paper, 15 May 1870, all in CO 144/33.

60. ANRI, Algemeen Administratieve Verslag Residentie West Borneo 1872 (no. 5/3)

61. ANRI, Algemeen Verslag Residentie Borneo Z.O. 1871 (no. 9/2).

62. ARA, Plaatselijke Politieke Rapport, in ARA, 1877, MR no. 354. Partially as a result of this, the Dutch stipulated in their contracts with Riau that they should be allowed to begin policing in Riau's waters against pirates. See the contract of 30 Sept. 1868 in *Surat Surat Perdjandjian Riau* (1970), 183–84.

63. ANRI, Algemeen Administratieve Verslag Residentie Riouw 1871 (no. 63/2).

64. ANRI, Algemeen Administratieve Verslag Residentie Palembang 1874 (no. 64/17); ARA, 1869, MR no. 105.

65. ARA, Extract uit het Register der Besluiten van de GGNEI, 20 Jan. 1882, no. 8.

66. KITLV Map Collection, "Soematra, Banka, en de Riouw-Lingga Archipel," 1896, Blad 6 (by Dornseiffen); see also "Beschouwingen over de Toestand van Onveiligheid" (1887), 378.

67. "Iets over de Reorganisatie van het Politiewezen" (1888), 183.

68. See the police force report, Appendix 7, in *SSLCP,* 1890, C56–57.

69. Gov. Labuan to CO, 26 Aug. 1882, no. 52, in CO 144/56. The governor of the colony saw definitive reasons for the high state of crime, especially certain kinds of commercial crime: "There is, however, a certain amount of crime committed in connection with financial matters that I have reason to think remains undetected, and will continue to do so in the absence of a European at the head of the police force." See *Labuan Annual Report* 1887, 6.

70. Gov. Treacher to Capt. Harrington, 26 Nov. 1881, in CO 874/144.

71. ARA, Chart of Present and Soon-to-be-Modified Police Strengths in West Borneo, in 1891, MR no. 369.

72. Memorie van Overgave, Borneo Z.O. (MMK, 1906, no. 270), 12; ARA, Directeur Binnenlandsch Bestuur Rapport van 21 Nov. 1894, and Extract uit het Besluiten van de GGNEI, 10 Dec. 1894, no. 5, in 1894, MR no. 1131.

73. Van Dongen, "Gerechtelijk Scheikundige Onderzoekingen," 714; Cayaux "Gerechtelijk-Scheikundige Onderzoekingen in NI" (1908), 1.

74. See Gov SS to CO, 18 Oct. 1921, in Co 537/904; and Director of Criminal Intelligence, SS to Gov SS, 3 Oct. 1921, in CO 537/905.

75. "Appendix C: Singapore Municipality Expenditures, Comparative Statement," in *SS-MAR,* 1895. Street candles had been used previously, but they had never been as effective as the new lights.

76. "Seorang China telah ditangkap oleh mata-mata gelap di Anderson Road" [A Chinese was arrested by detectives on Anderson Road] *Utusan Malayu,* 16 Jan. 1908, 1; see also *Bintang Timor,* 13 Dec. 1894, 2. The term was already in use in Java in the later decades of the nineteenth century.

77. *Utusan Malayu,* 30 Jan. 1909, 1

78. Memorie van Overgave, West Borneo (MMK, 1912, no. 260), 43–44.

79. M. W. Sibelhoff "Gewapende Politiedienaran" (1907), 864–65; Memorie van Overgave, Billiton (MMK, 1907, no. 250), 32.

80. Ruitenbach, "Eenigen Beschouwingen" (1905), 1009.

81. ARA, Police Commissioner's Instructions, enclosure inside Asst Resident, Batavia, to Resident, Batavia, 26 Feb. 1912, no. 50, in MvBZ/A/40/A.29bisOK.

82. For an overview of Indies law, see Hooker, "Dutch Colonial Law" (1974), 250–300. For some of the wider implications as to how laws were used by states in colonial societies, see Comaroff, "Colonialism, Culture, and the Law" (2001), 305–11, and Cooper and Stoler, "Tensions of Empire" (1989), 609–21.

83. See Teitler, *Ambivalentie en Aarzeling* (1994), 37–54.

84. See Resink, "Onafhankelijke Vorsten" (1956); see also his "Conflichtenrecht" (1959), 1–39.

85. ARA, 1872, MR no. 604; ARA, Asst. Res. Siak to Asst. Res. Riouw, 2 May 1873, no. 585, in 1873, MR no. 419.

86. ANRI, Algemeen Administratieve Verslag Residentie Palembang 1874 (no. 64/17).

87. ANRI, Algemeen Administratieve Verslag Residentie Riouw 1871 (no. 63/2); Maandrapport Residentie Riouw 1875 (no. 66/2, November)

88. Memo by Mr. Scott, Lt. Gov. Labuan, 26 Dec. 1855, in Co 144/12.

89. See the examples reproduced in *SSGG,* 28 March 1873. The Malay Peninsula often served as an escape hatch, however.

90. "Eenige Opmerkingen over de Reorganisatie," (1882), 340.

91. "Vreemde Oosterlingen. Bevoegdheid" *IWvhR,* no. 1561, 29 May 1893, 86–87; "Circulaires van het Raadslid Mr. der Kinderen" (1880), 311.

92. "Opmerkingen en Mededeelingen" (1882), 333

93. Staatsblad 1887, no. 62; "Rechtswezen Billiton" *Bijblad Indische Staatsblad* (1894) no. 4813, 213.

94. ARA, 1887, MR no. 295.

95. ARA, Dutch Consul, Singapore to Col Sec, SS, 21 Sept. 1876, no. 531, in 1876, MR no. 792; ARA, Col. Sec., Singapore to Dutch Consul, 28 Sept. 1876, no. 5825/76, in 1876, MR no. 792.

96. "Circulaire van de Procureur Generaal 19 Juli 1884 Betreffende de Uitlevering naar de Straits-Settlements Gevluchte Misdadigers" *Bijblad Indische Staatsblad* 22 (1884): 198–200.

97. *Perak Gov't Gazette,* 1888, 160; ARA, 1876, MR no. 125; ARA, First Government Secretary, Batavia, to Dutch Consul, Singapore, 11 Jan. 1889, no. 75, in 1889, MR no. 37.

98. ARA, First Government Secretary to Dutch Consul, Penang, 1 Sept. 1899, no. 1947, in ARA, 1899, MR no. 624.

99. ANRI, Algemeen Administrative Verslag Residentie West Borneo 1889 (no. 5/20); see also "Reglement op het Rechtswezen in de Westerafdeeling van Borneo" *IWvhR,* no. 1376, 11 Nov. 1889, 178–79.

100. ARA, Gov. BNB to Controleur Boeloengan, Dutch East Borneo, 12 Sept. 1896, no. 255, in ARA, 1896, MR no. 86; ARA, Gov SE Borneo to Gov BNB, 26 Oct. 1896, no. 771/5, in 1896, MR no. 86; ARA, Gov BNB to Gov SS, 8 Dec. 1896, no. 344/96 in 1896, MR no. 86.

101. See, for example, *Sarawak Gazette,* 27 June 1876, 4 March 1879, 20 Dec. 1887, 2 March 1891, and 2 January 1892.

102. Gov BNB to BNB Co. Directorship, 21 Jan. 1908 in CO 531/1; FO Jacket, 25 Feb. 1910, in CO 531/2.

103. *BNB Official Gazette* no. 2, vol. 17, 1 Feb. 1906, in CO 874/800.

104. CO Jacket, 8 Dec. 1894, in CO 144/69.

105. "Draft Agreement Between Brunei and North Borneo for the Surrender of Fugitive Criminals," 19 March 1908, in CO 531/1.

Chapter 4 Strengthening the Frontier

As the Anglo/Dutch frontier in Southeast Asia was being mapped and enforced by arms of government such as the army, navy, police, and the courts, it was also being strengthened by a variety of forces at the disposal of these states. Communications, maritime technologies, economic policies, and human agents were all put into play to "domesticate" the border. This was a highly uneven project, only portions of which were ever fully coordinated from the center. Nevertheless, the gradual strengthening of the border regions eventually changed the nature of the divide between these colonial spheres and affected what smugglers could and could not accomplish in this broad, liminal space. Batavia and Singapore solidified their expansion in the periphery by using a range of institutions designed to bring the frontier itself closer to the reach of the state. How was this accomplished over fifty years and three thousand kilometers of expanding border space? Which tools of empire were utilized to strengthen the bonds between colonial centers and the landscapes and seascapes of the emerging international boundary? How could the link between ruling colonial elites and distant subject peoples be concretized in the outstretched spaces of the frontier?

THE EVOLVING COMMUNICATIONS GRID

Improved communication was one of the most important items on local impe-rial agendas. Communications were crucial for fulfilling the coercive processes noted earlier; no state could enforce its wishes along the border without quick and easy access to the frontier. Yet roads in the Outer Islands in the 1870s and early 1880s, for example, were extremely limited and poor, providing little ser-vice to the state even where they did exist. In western Borneo, a few roads had been constructed in the Chinese gold-mining districts, but most people trav-eled by water or by the few footpaths (*setapak*) known to local villagers. South-eastern Borneo also had few roads; a small number linked lands in the diamond districts of Bentok and Martapura, while most everywhere else locals traveled by riverboat or canoe. Dutch controleurs took note of these conditions and complained of the lack of available infrastructure, which hindered troop move-ments and the insertion of infantry into trouble spots in the periphery.[1] Rains periodically washed out the roads in Sumatra, making upland landscapes in Palembang, a particularly "recalcitrant" residency, according to the Dutch, un-reachable to the state for many months of the year. Batavia could not count on river transport to reach all interior residencies in the Buitenbezittingen; many of these rivers were impassable because of submerged tree trunks and low water tables, while others were populated by pirates, looking to pillage stranded way-farers.[2] Wild tigers made other routes into the interior extremely dangerous as well: one stretch of road in Palembang saw seventeen fatal attacks in 1869 alone. Where the Dutch authorities planned to build roads, doctors were standard members of research and clearance crews, on hand to deal with the many emer-gencies, including sickness, attacks, and injuries, attendant upon this kind of empire building.[3]

In contrast, road construction and the grid of paved thoroughfares available to the state around 1900 were much more extensive. Pleas to better this state of affairs date from at least the early 1880s, but only in the late 1890s do widespread concrete improvements in the Buitenbezittingen become apparent.[4] Many more construction surveys were being undertaken by this time, the objects of which were usually to extend Batavia's economic and policing power into the interior of Outer Island residencies.[5] Roads were being built, as in Aceh, to connect neighboring territories as well, often with the specific purpose of fun-neling troops more quickly and easily from one garrison to another.[6] In places such as southeastern Borneo, roads were widened to accommodate such move-ments, while on Sumatra's East Coast, they were hardened so they would not disappear with the onset of monsoon rains.[7] By 1906 there were over eight hundred miles of roads in Palembang alone, providing much more of a net for the state security apparatus than had ever existed before.[8] Lulofs captured the impetus behind these processes when he remarked that roads were often built over budget and without centralized permission but were tolerated as cost overruns because all knew their presence was so important.[9] This seems to have been true to some extent in British North Borneo as well.[10] By the early twentieth century, the results of this laissez-faire policy were clear. A map of Sumatra from 1915 shows the island's grid of public thoroughfares at this late date, available for quick use by Batavia and its soldiers (map 6).[11]

Yet roads were only part of the communications net developing in the border residencies. The development of the telegraph also enabled colonial states to strengthen their coercive presence in frontier areas. Early beginnings were made on the British side of the Straits in 1870, when Singapore was connected to Penang and, a year later, Penang to the British Raj in Madras.[12] A working connection was established between Singapore and Batavia in 1870 as well, bypassing an earlier attempt that ultimately had proven unreliable.[13] Surveillance and information processing could thus be exercised between ports and between colonial spheres now, but at a quickened pace, which had formerly been impossible. Batavia understood the importance of these connections immediately for their empire-building designs, and a cable across the narrow strait to South Sumatra soon followed.[14] Yet the Dutch had far fewer resources than the British for telegraphic expansion and often had to rely on British wires for their messages, especially in frontier landscapes. The Singapore–Penang cable was thus used extensively by Dutch civil servants, especially to report on Acehnese smuggling movements and intrigues during the war.[15] Problems with telegraph lines and resources dogged both colonial governments in the 1870s, however. Heavy rains often knocked down existing Dutch lines, and important British outposts such as Labuan were forced to do without telegraphic connections for many years.[16]

Toward the turn of the twentieth century, however, cable technologies gradually improved, costs came down, and both colonial powers saw the utility in expanding their web of communications. Much of the British North Borneo Company's acquisition of Sabah was undertaken via telegraphic communications, as the businessman Alfred Dent in London continually telegraphed his agents in Singapore, relaying instructions on how to proceed.[17] Ten years later, the company's officers in Borneo were trying to convince London to extend the imperial telegraphic net on to the island itself, using Dutch cable expansion on

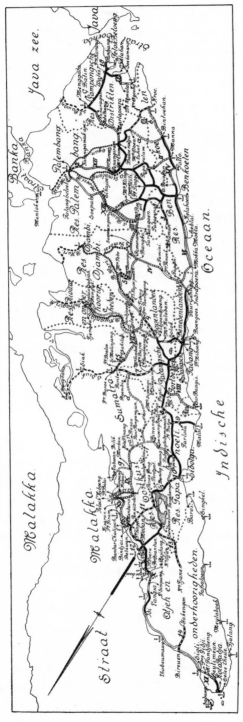

Strategic Roads, Sumatra, 1915. (*Source:* Borrel, *Mededeelingen Betreffende de Gewone Wegen* [1915])

the other side of the frontier as competitive bait before Whitehall's eyes.[18] The Dutch were indeed expanding: mineral acquisition and political instability prompted Batavia to invest in cables in Borneo, with an eye toward improving control of local conditions on the ground.[19] Yet the ratio of British to Dutch telegraph lines along the frontier was still heavily in British favor, as Dutch periodicals continually complained. Twenty of the twenty-three existing cable companies in the world were based in London at the beginning of the twentieth century. Geopolitically and strategically, this was simply unacceptable to many Dutchmen living in the Indies, though they could do little about it.[20]

Much of the reason for this distaste was nationalist pride—Batavia did not like depending on British wires for communication with the Netherlands, even in the face of the great costs they would have to incur to construct their own network. As one Dutch observer put it, however, Batavia could not afford to think like a "great power," and had to "piggy-back" messages home on other European lines.[21] Technological advances after the turn of the century, however, started to make the idea of wholly Dutch-run telegraphy in the Indies a potential reality, even along the outstretched frontier. The invention of wireless communication promised the advent of much cheaper and more mobile communications along the whole border in the second decade of the twentieth century. Wireless stations could be put on ships as well as on land; the comparative cheapness of the conduits meant that posts could be placed in remote areas and still report back swiftly to larger relay stations. The surveillance implications of this new technology were not lost on Batavia. Some policy planners drew up plans for a huge new grid of communications in the archipelago that would effectively unite Batavia with the entirety of its frontier.[22] The actual development of these apparatuses falls outside the time frame of this book, but these early developments were important in showing Europeans what could be accomplished. Both the British and Dutch eventually set up far-flung wireless stations connecting Mindanao in the Philippines, for example, with British North Borneo and Dutch southeast Borneo almost instantaneously.[23] Information on smugglers, piratical attacks, and suspicious movements could be tracked as never before, even in the most remote outlying areas of the region.

A final important aspect of land-based communications is the expansion of railroads into the periphery. Rail lines were crucial to the colonial project for several reasons. Not only did they enable the state to move men and matériel in large quantities, but they also acted as resources for long-term capital accumulation, once their initial costs had been paid off. The deliberations around the Ombilin coalfields in Sumatra can serve as an example here. In the early 1870s, concessions were given out for the laying of track between these fields and the port of Padang on Sumatra's West coast.[24] Preparations were made for exploitation, and studies were done on how much it would cost the government to put in rail lines from the coal-rich uplands to the steamship harbor below. The initial estimates were put at twenty-two thousand guilders per kilometer, but it was felt to be worth the price, as revenues would eventually pour in from the sale of coal.[25] Many of the planners argued—as they did about the telegraph lines going up at this time—that it was important to make sure that Batavia had its own sources of coal and that the Dutch colony was not overly reliant on foreign governments.[26] In 1890, the controleur of Indragiri, on the east coast of Sumatra, was sent out to neighboring self-ruled districts to see if the Dutch railway could pass through this territory on its way to the eastern seaboard as well.[27] In the process of trying to get coal cheaply and quickly from the interior to both coasts, therefore, Batavia was setting up rail lines which could be used for mineral exploitation, but also for any other kind of organized movement, across the width of this huge island.

The expansion of railroads in the plantation district of eastern Sumatra in the 1880s is also instructive. By 1880, the excitement over railway concessions in Dutch circles was so keen that "one could have gotten money to build a railway to the moon," the *Indische Mail* reported.[28] In 1881, a concession was given to the Deli Spoorwegmaatschappij (Deli Railroad Company) to connect some of the residency's growing areas to Belawan port; the primary concern was to get tobacco to market quicker and more cheaply, regardless of weather and surface conditions. In 1883, the resident of Sumatra's East Coast broke ground on the project himself, showing the intimate interconnection on this rail line between the government and private capital.[29] The cooperation did not stop here, however. Batavia allowed the Deli Company to ship freight on the lines even as the rail system was still being built, and it extended the contract time on finishing all building requirements when the company fell behind on construction.[30] Batavia even reserved the right to dictate the speeds at which Deli trains could travel—never more than thirty-five kilometers per hour—much like a parent might draw the line with a child and its new toy.[31] Railroads thus were intimately connected to state designs on peripheral expansion, even when the ownership and construction of these lines was managed by players other than the state.

By the early twentieth century, the ties between technology and state building were clearer than ever before. Rail construction was going on all along the frontier, in different guises but with unified effect. In Johor, the numbers of people using the expanding British railway jumped from 159,317 in 1912 to 418,047 just four years later, with net revenues for Federated Malay States railroads surpassing a million dollars just after the turn of the century.[32] In Aceh, the Dutch military built the first stages of a steam tram in 1876, one that eventually was expanded and taken over by the state in 1916. The goal of this line was to help with the pacification process, an aim that was met, but only after several decades of trying.[33] In South Sumatra, rail construction was tied to the idea of opening the region's fertile lands to Javanese transmigrants, who would come from overpopulated Java and make new lives there. This project too was only partially successful, expanding the state's presence in Lampung and elsewhere but never quite helping as many settlers as had been hoped.[34] In Borneo, some of the most dramatic plans ever for expansion were anticipated, one expert drawing up schemes for Borneo to be criss-crossed with rail lines in the space of only six years.[35] On the Dutch side of the Borneo border, this never really happened. Yet the British did indeed expand their rail net in Borneo (mostly on the coasts), though this was met almost everywhere with huge problems, such as floods, construction site collapses, and massive landslides.[36] Empire building via railroad technology, even at this late date, was still a very uncertain process in this part of the world. But the difficulties did not stop either colonial state from laying the groundwork for later decades, when such resources could be exploited more fully as tools for expanding the reach of the state.

STRENGTHENING A MARITIME DIVIDE

Alongside means of communication such as roads, telegraphs, and rail lines, Batavia and Singapore also strengthened the frontier through various maritime institutions. The majority of the evolving border lay over water, not land; these spaces included calm, shallow seas such as the Straits of Melaka and Sulu, and also the island-strewn seascapes of the southernmost South China Sea. Both of these marine spaces, based on winds, weather, and scattered island topographies, were ideal geographies for smugglers. One of the most important maritime institutions for strengthening a state presence in this arena was coast lighting, the beaconing of shores and harbor approaches through a variety of means. Lighthouses, gaslight buoys, and beacons of differing construction were all used to accomplish this end. If the state could see not only the periphery, but channel movements through these impressive devices, then the war against smuggling would be made that much easier, especially at night. Yet progress on this front, as with most other technological endeavors bent to the service of the state, came only slowly. State capabilities in the middle decades of the nineteenth century were ineffective and limited compared with widespread advances at the end of the century.

In 1859, there was only one working coastal light in the Dutch Indies, near Anjer, on the northwestern coast of Java. Batavia, and indeed even The Hague, knew this to be a perilous state of affairs, for the danger posed both to passing shipping in the Indies as well as to the limitations placed on the state's vision of its own archipelago. A twenty-five-year plan was decided upon, costing 6.5 million guilders and designed to expand Dutch coast lighting throughout the rest of the Indies.[37] Though only parts of the plan were ever instituted, beaconing and coast lighting in the archipelago were markedly better by 1870 than they had been ten years earlier. The tin-mining island of Bangka, for instance, was ringed with coastal lights, allowing the state much more vision in local waters than had previously been possible.[38] Yet there were still problems. Many beacons used by the Dutch marine were swept away by strong currents, as in South Borneo, where the approaches to Banjarmasin were unsafe even though this was the residency capital.[39] A steamer was put into service especially for beacon repair, but the ship was so old and so unsturdy it was in dry dock most of the time.[40] Across the strait, in the British possessions, Singapore was able to budget mere pittances for these functions as well. Penang, the second most important port in the Straits Settlements, had no lighting at all in 1873.[41]

The years toward the turn of the century saw only partial improvements in this situation. Lights were built off Lampung in South Sumatra, and also off Pekalongan and Bengkulu, ringing at least parts of Sumatra with light during nighttime hours. Harbors were better lit in Riau as well, with new funding becoming available for this in 1886, and older lights were replaced in some of the larger ports of those islands.[42] Indeed, in the 1880s, according to Dutch Ministry of Marine records, an unprecedented expansion of lighting began in the Buitenbezittingen, stretching from Sumatra in the west to territories in the comparatively little-explored eastern reaches of the archipelago.[43] Yet there were still serious problems. Major international waterways such as the eastern half of the Makassar Strait and even much of the maritime route between Singapore and Java still needed to be lit by the early twentieth century.[44] In British waters, the approach to Labuan remained "neither safe nor easy during the night," rocks and low shoals imperiling navigation.[45] In parts of Southeast Asia, the British simply could not see properly at night, and ships that sailed through their dominions were often invisible to the state. To make matters more complicated, the different administrative entities in British waters—the Straits government, the British North Borneo Company, the Raja of Sarawak, and the Federated Malay States—constantly quarreled over who should pay for necessary improvements.[46] In an atmosphere such as this, it was not difficult for smugglers to sail through the region without much interference at all.

Around 1900, however, the reach of the state in terms of coast lighting and the ability to see at night definitively improved. This was true in southeastern Borneo, where new lighthouses were being erected on coasts formerly frequented by pirates and smugglers.[47] It was also true off Sumatra's east coast, where decentralization policies put beaconing services in the hands of local officials, who knew where resources were needed most.[48] Even the construction of lighthouses, formerly a huge affair for which materials had to be dragged out all the way from Europe, was undergoing change. By the early twentieth century, the structures of the lights themselves, as well as many of the materials needed to light them, for example, mineral oil, now tapped at Langkat in Sumatra, were available in the Indies.[49] Lighthouses became imposing, efficient structures, floating panopticons where crews could remain self-sufficient for months at a time (fig. 3). It was much more difficult now for people to cross over unseen into the Indies, as a necklace of watchtowers—fully able to see, even at night—stretched all across the frontier. There were still problems, of course: outraged British marine reports occasionally spoke of dangerous lighting lacunae in some coasts, and diplomatic wranglings between the different British governments in the region continued to occur.[50] Yet even contested spots such as Aceh, which had caused so much grief to Batavia in the 1870s, had been more or less brought to heel by the early 1900s, at least partially because of the power of these beacons.[51] The spaces necessary to smuggle, or simply slip unnoticed across international frontiers, were quietly disappearing. By the early twentieth century, Batavia and Singapore had learned much more effectively how to see in the dark.

A second tool of maritime expansion used by the two states, beyond coast lighting and beaconing, was steam shipping. The advent of steam aided the imperial project immeasurably, not just in Southeast Asia but in the rest of the world as well. In the colonial Dutch Indies, the most important historian of these processes has been Joep a Campo, whose book on the Koninklijke Paketvaart Maatschappij (KPM, the Royal Dutch Packet Company) is a significant contribution to the literature. A Campo shows definitively how Batavia, and indeed even The Hague, used steam-shipping lines to push the state's agenda

Fig. 3. Dutch Indies lighthouse structure, Karimata Strait, 1909. (Photo courtesy KITLV, Leiden)

and presence into a huge maritime periphery. Because the resources for a project such as this were beyond the Batavia exchequer, however, expansion was carried out hand in hand with private capital, as in several other industries examined above. The KPM, founded in 1888 as a successor to earlier attempts to implement this program, quickly stretched its shipping lines into large parts of the Indies archipelago. Many of the most outlying areas, however, were not reached until the early twentieth century, leaving so-called mosquito fleets of Chinese and other shippers to continue plying these waters. A Campo argues that the KPM developed into an octopus under Batavia's control: its tentacles reached everywhere, and although it survived under a business-profit rationale, its resources were also made available to fulfill the wishes of the state.[52] The company's ships were used in the subjugation of various Outer Island polities, on Sulawesi, Lombok, and New Guinea, for example, while also taking part in the slow economic strangulation of the Acehnese resistance. A Campo posits that the KPM was therefore a critical tool of empire available to the Dutch, used as a revenue device and as a political apparatus in various contexts and at different times along the length of the border.

Batavia understood very clearly that shipping would be a key to expansion in the Dutch Indies. For this reason, a steady eye was kept on commercial shipping movements from a very early date, especially in the border residencies. This was true in places like southeastern Borneo, where maritime movements between coastal potentates and Singapore, for example, were watched very carefully. It was also true in western Borneo, where Chinese, Arab, and Bugis ships regularly sailed across the frontier to trade in Straits Settlements ports.[53] In the Riau archipelago, directly opposite Singapore, detailed statistics were compiled on types of goods and the ethnicities and flags of the ships trading them from a very early date.[54] On the other side of the Straits, the British in various locations were taking the same sets of notes. The loading and unloading of ships in Labuan, for example, were decried as unsatisfactory, as dispersed docking locations thwarted the state's limited policing powers. Furthermore, the lack of state steamship services between Singapore and Labuan at this early date also hindered the growth of trade, despite Labuan's many advantages. The governor of Labuan asked how it was possible that Labuan had no steam connection with Singapore, when the former colony had huge coal deposits to offer as well as a strategic location on the China routes and one of the best harbors in Eastern Seas.[55]

Steam shipping, therefore, presented two paradoxical phenomena. It could be used as an engine of growth and coercion by the state if harnessed, but it could also be used, especially in the Outer Islands, by those who wished to trade outside the state's vision. The 1880s and 1890s, therefore, saw a renewed effort on the part of the state to try to control these processes and to bend the rules toward the state's ends. The KPM was given its inaugural contract in 1891, with a license (and order) to expand its links to the rest of the archipelago over the next fifteen years.[56] A Campo has published a series of useful maps showing how KPM expansion slowly infiltrated up Borneo's and Sumatra's rivers and to some of the more distant coasts of the frontier region over the next several decades.[57] Yet this process was in concert with steamship additions to the Binnenlands Bestuur (Colonial Civil Service Department) as well, especially in outlying residencies such as Sumatra's East Coast, Lampung, and the coast of eastern Borneo.[58] British, French, Chinese, and German shipping continued to ply through the archipelago, connecting ports across the frontier and carrying a huge quantity of commodities, some of it illegal, of a great variety of descriptions.[59] Yet as the British consul in Aceh wrote in 1883, the Dutch also were using the advent of steam to get a better grip on maritime trade movements. Pointing to Dutch complaints about the levels of smuggling across the Straits, the British envoy suggested that many Dutchmen stood to lose money if steamshipping contracts were handed out fairly. Batavia limited certain forms of foreign participation in these steam-shipping trades, ostensibly (and perhaps even actually) because so much of the trade fell outside of legal channels.[60]

The maritime expansion of the state in these waters slowly evolved into a broad, interconnected grid. Although steam shipping outweighed sail in Singapore statistics shortly after the Suez Canal opened in 1869, it would not be until around 1900 that steam lines connected the vast reaches of the archipelago.[61] In Palembang, steam-shipping figures were up, as were Batavia's abilities to keep track of such movements; in Jambi this was also true, especially as clearance work on sandbars, projecting jungle, and shifting shoals proceeded on heavily trafficked rivers.[62] Makassar was budgeted huge new sums of money to make port improvements for steam facilities, and services in Borneo were expanded as well, both in the western and southeastern residencies of the island.[63] As perhaps the most signal indication of the expansion of these facilities, aims, and resources, however, part of Aceh was turned into a giant refueling station, based on the offshore island of Weh. By 1900, an immense dry dock had been installed on the island, complete with coal sheds, wharving facilities, and a Chinese work camp for repairs.[64] In this place, the formerly wildest of the "wild west" corners of the archipelago, a kind of maritime infrastructure and control had been established that formerly would have been impossible. KPM stations now stretched from the Weh docking station of Sabang to Merauke in New Guinea, on the opposite side of the Indies.[65] Batavia and Singapore were teaching themselves how to master the sea.

ECONOMIC PERSUASION AND ECONOMIC COERCION

State expansion into the periphery had much to do with these infrastructural improvements, but it also had to do with policy decisions, many of which were economic in nature. Strengthening the frontier, therefore, was the job of economic bureaucrats in Batavia as much as of marines and border guards. Each contributed to the solidification of the border as an enforceable entity. Indeed, in the 1860s and 1870s, many outlying parts of the Buitenbezittingen had extremely free trading relations with the outside world. Tariff regulations beginning to be imposed by Batavia held little force along vast stretches of the frontier. Yet a shifting cadence in the nature of global imperialism in the 1880s and 1890s, from free trade ideologies to a more hands-on, coercive approach to commerce, put pressure on this system in Southeast Asian seas. By the end of the nineteenth century, state-making projects everywhere in the region were trying to tax and control these trade flows as never before. In Sarawak, for example, the Brooke regime developed extensive regulations about who and what could go up and downstream, while upriver longhouses were subjected to spot checks and inspections.[66] In the Indies, the massive commerce in Outer Island forest products, long the preserve of small traders of various ethnicities, also came more and more under the eyes of the state.[67] Both sides of the Straits exercised this new grip—the expanding reach of coercive economic policies—directed outward from the two colonial capitals.

Notices from the 1870s on both sides of the frontier make this process clear. An extensive tariff law went into effect in the Netherlands Indies in 1873, seeking to control and tax a wide bandwidth of goods crossing the frontier. Yet the new law was working almost nowhere. The lead article of the *Bataviaasch Handelsblad* on June 10, 1875, told of massive transgressions against the spirit duties, as alcohol was ferried into the Indies by small boats, evading all import and export dues.[68] In Aceh, surveillance conditions were appalling, as no one trusted the official trade statistics at all, especially those monitoring movements across the Straits. The harbor master of Penang informed the Dutch consul there that a huge silent trade existed, which showed up nowhere in the state's books, let alone in those of the colonial exchequers.[69] Indeed, Dutch marine descriptions of toll stations being set up in the mouths of Sumatran rivers have an almost surreal quality to them, as sentinels had to be withdrawn at night for their own safety in hostile terrain, thereby giving free movement to any who might wish to trade.[70] Judicial returns from the British sphere show analogous patterns.

The numbers of arrests for transgressions of the Straits monopolies were in the hundreds every year, with detailed figures being kept for opium, spirits, and other valuable items.[71] The extensive duties placed on certain commodities in Labuan, for example, show the inducement to smuggle: why work within the system and pay the state's significant dues, when the policing powers of the colony were unable to detect fraud?[72]

The Dutch *tolgebied* (customs zone), which functioned in the core islands of Java and Madura as well as in large parts of the border residencies, tried to modulate these trading patterns to Dutch advantage. A complex and ever-changing slate of dues was delineated for all residencies in the Indies, regardless of their location. The import and export duties a trader could expect to pay varied: some items were taxed at 6 percent, while others were taxed at 8, 10, or 12 percent, depending on the regulations in force. Commodities like hides, earth oil, tin, and birds' nests were uniformly selected as items under this regime; other goods, such as many kinds of forest products, were taxed only in the Outer Islands.[73] Nevertheless, the range of identified items, including porcelain, beer, precious metals, tea, and zinc, was large enough that constant smuggling was apparent.[74] Contrabanding such goods, given the available means of surveillance in places, was simply too profitable to pass up. Even large commodities such as teak were spirited out of the Indies, and debates erupted in policy circles about how to best stop such cargoes. Some Outer Island administrators saw the situation as hopeless, pointing to all the revenue local chiefs would lose—revenue guaranteed to them by their contracts with the Dutch state—if such cargoes were preempted. Others tried to think of solutions, or at least of stopgap measures, as to how such journeys might be made more difficult.[75] Throughout the 1880s and 1890s, however, Batavia's import and export trade profits increased, both on the residency level and as a whole.[76] A certain amount of seepage seemed to have been deemed tolerable, so long as rising revenues were being accrued by the state.

The 1910s saw a continuation of this pattern. Export duties were still levied on a wide range of forest products which easily exited the Outer Islands, including bees' wax, benzoin, damar, rhino horn, and certain kinds of wood.[77] Tax revenues on trade items such as these brought larger and larger sums into Batavia every year.[78] When there were problems such as downturns in the market for forest products, Dutch civil servants wrote voluminously on how revenues might be raised, showing how important these taxation schemes had become to the central government.[79] Other actors also sought to make money from the taxation of such goods. Local chiefs, including several in Riau in 1897, also tried to take advantage of the upturn in general trade, taxing the transit of forest products from their own dominions, only without the permission of the state. This was not allowed, and such entrepreneurs were swiftly punished.[80] The important thing for Batavia was that greater peace in the Outer Islands brought greater means for enforcing taxation, as fewer regions still held the ability to evade state designs. By the early twentieth century, therefore, duties were levied on an entire range of new items: radium bromide and menthol eucalyptus throat drops, as well as steel ship masts, playing cards, and heavy gravel-breaking equipment.[81] The state could push the taxation of commodities crossing the frontier much further than ever before.

Import and export taxes were not the only economic means of border formation available to the colonial state, however. Blockades and shipping regulations (*scheepvaartregelingen*) were additional tools used to strengthen colonial borders and make money for the state at the same time. Since the early part of the nineteenth century, Batavia had been imposing rules on who could and could not trade between ports in the outstretched waters of the Indies archipelago. Foreign shipping had been forbidden to participate in the so-called coasting trade, or internal commerce between ports in the Indies, since 1825. This in itself was a form of border strengthening, as it gave Dutch vessels a huge advantage in local trade.[82] A phalanx of interests eventually came together to dispute this privilege, however, including Straits Settlements traders who were shut out from the coasting trade and large Dutch agricultural concerns, which wanted free competition to lower transport costs.[83] Only in 1912 was this form of boundary construction abandoned in Indies waters, and foreign competition let into the Indies for the internal port-to-port trade.

Blockades were a far more drastic measure taken to build—or preserve—the integrity of the state's maritime boundaries. Blockades were undertaken by several actors in several places along the Anglo/Dutch frontier in the late nineteenth and early twentieth centuries. Local polities sometimes blockaded one another to enforce dominance, for example, while the Spanish in Sulu and northern Borneo also instituted blockades, which were often broken by a variety of smuggling parties.[84] Yet the most important, and by far the largest, blockade in Indies waters during these years came at Aceh, and was exercised by the Dutch. The Aceh blockade stretched from the early 1870s well into the 1890s but was lifted and then reinstated on numerous occasions and in numerous places. Indeed, this was one of its main weaknesses: no one, including the Dutch, it seems, was ever quite sure where the blockade was operating or for what concrete reasons at any one time.[85] I discuss the Aceh blockade of the early 1870s in detail in chapters 13 and 14, but here it is useful simply to sketch out some of its basic dimensions. Designed to starve the Acehnese resistance into submission by cutting off its arms supplies as well as its means of making money through the sale of pepper, betel, and other valuable cash crops, the blockade never really worked, as several period comments below make clear.

Although Straits Settlements traders were among the most vociferous critics of the cordon drawn around Aceh from 1873 onward, as it cut off these traders' livelihoods and denied them access to a formerly open channel of trade, even internal Dutch commentary often disparaged the blockade as a useless waste of time. It was indeed useless for the first few years of its existence. There were never enough ships to seal off the vast coastline, and what ships there were had to spend inordinate amounts of time doing other tasks besides policing the shore. Some were detailed to carry Acehnese prisoners off to Batavia, for example, while others ran back and forth to Deli, miles down the coast, to provision the fleet with fresh water (almost all of North Sumatra was hostile, so going ashore for water was to court enemy fire). Telegrammed instructions from Batavia came rather frequently, but only to Penang, where there was a telegraph station, which drew off other ships.[86] Coaling took huge amounts of time and continually required vessels to be out of the theater of war. The coal had to be stockpiled in Deli; only later would coal ships be dragged up to Aceh to supply the squadron on the line. In the exasperated words of Lt. Commander Kruijt, the captain of one of the blockading vessels, oftentimes "ships remained worthless, and the blockade a dead phrase."[87]

Resistance to the exercise of blockades came in several forms. One was in the tactics of local rulers: many local potentates accepted Dutch terms by day, feigning an alliance with the occupying force so that their vessels could trade and their ports remain open, while at night they secretly supplied the resistance and even bragged of doing so. Other actors, such as many in the Straits Settlements trading community, simply smuggled across the Straits when they could, refusing to give up valuable commercial lines like textiles, gold, and other goods. The local people of Simpang Ulim, one of the most "recalcitrant" states in Dutch eyes, even dug interior canals out of reach of the Dutch, trying to connect internal river systems so they could exit Sumatra from legally approved river mouths.[88] The vagaries of the Dutch blockade, which stipulated and then continually changed provisions on ports, times, specific goods, and even the weights of allowed shipping, often necessitated such resistance.[89] It would only be toward the end of the nineteenth century, when the Dutch naval presence had grown significantly, both in number and sophistication, that the blockade became a more practical tool of regulating trade across the border. We know this from internal Dutch documents and the decline of Acehnese resistance, but also from British sources from across the Straits, as local traders there pressured their own government to work out an accommodation with the Dutch.[90] Even around the fin de siècle there was disillusionment, however: many Dutchmen understood that the blockade had been a failure for too long and that the state had miscalculated for years in its attempted program of submission. Critics railed against the waste, the lives lost, and the national prestige that had been dimmed in fighting an indecisive guerrilla action for twenty years.[91] Yet the truth was that the blockade finally did help the Dutch cause, but only when it was balanced and mature enough to really make a difference. Border strengthening in this economic sense took Batavia almost three decades to accomplish.

THE HUMAN FACTOR

A last tool at the disposal of the colonial state was the various human beings who were sent to the border for a variety of reasons. These men were missionaries and ethnographers, civil servants and administrators, and all were charged with studying the ways of the frontier. Their duty was to bring local populations into the realm of colonial understanding. Anthropologists, both amateur and, for the first time, professional, were among the most important of this group. Colonial states needed better information about the supposed peculiarities of border peoples, so that their reactions could be anticipated and expansion could proceed at pace. Yet the ethnographic reports being sent back from the lands ringing the Anglo/Dutch border in the 1860s and 1870s were anything but detailed. Instead, they were mostly broad-stroke descriptions of first-contact experiences, which could serve only as the barest of building blocks for the state's understanding. This is evident in anthropological journal articles of the time; "The Malays of Borneo's West Coast" and "The Malay Village" are examples of this kind.[92] The knowledge and experience of many of these peoples were simply not sophisticated enough yet to give colonial governments potentially useful kinds of information. Languages needed to be learned first, and schools set up to train expeditions; only then could the state hope to collect detailed data.[93]

By the turn of the century, however, a change was coming over these field reports, as ethnographers spent more and more time on the frontier and learned local circumstances and customs. Vague, generalized accounts of large culture areas started to be replaced with much more in-depth studies that chronicled local life to a degree never seen before. The details of real cultural values inside various local communities began to be much more seriously explored (fig. 4). Instead of thumbnail sketches of local groups, such as "The Punan," "The Melenau," "The Kelabit," or "The Bataks," articles with the following titles appeared: "The Tobacco Pipes of the Boven Musi Kubu," "Indigenous Pharmacoepia of the Padang Lowlands," and "Treatment of the Sick Among the Central Bornean Dayaks."[94] Certainly there was a high degree of scientific autonomy in these studies. Yet ethnography, self-consciously or not, was being used more and more by the state to identify aspects of material culture important to local peoples. Especially in the border residencies, these commodities might also be important enough to be traded across political boundaries. The Dutch collected these articles and indexed them in a central filing system called the Zaakelijk Aantekeningen, located in The Hague. When observers in the field noted that Dayaks in central Borneo, for example (straddling the Anglo/Dutch frontier), would "do anything for glazed corals," Batavia noted this in files.[95] Bugis, Chinese, and Malay traders, not to mention Europeans, made upriver journeys to trade in these items, selling them as ornaments. If such things were so valuable to interior populations, what might they give up for them? Birds' nests? Camphor crystals? Sheets of gutta-percha? Such forest products were supposed to be taxed, all the more so since they were so highly valuable.

During the first years of the twentieth century, ethnography was being used in another fashion to cement a border wall around the Indies. Cultural commonalities were being discovered among various Indies peoples. In an era of rising Dutch nationalism and increasing critique of the Dutch imperial project with the onset of the ethical period after 1900, anthropologists' assertions of cultural similarities between different Indies peoples helped to act as a rationale for expansion and pan-archipelago domination. Since vast tracts of the islands were said to have common culture traits, this legitimized, in the estimation of some Dutchmen at least, Batavia's push forward to unite all these lands under one umbrella. One can see these assertions of similarities between various peoples being promulgated in various arenas, from masks to aspects of marriage and love making in different parts of the Indies.[96] Exhibitions in Batavia brought together knowledge of practices from around the archipelago and exhibited these traits side by side in exhibition halls.[97] The burgeoning publications industry, especially volumes concerning "land and folk" collections, contributed to the development of this feeling as well.[98] *Onze Indië* (Our Indies) became a rallying cry to finish the *afronding* (rounding off) of the Dutch im-

Fig. 4. Anthropological photograph of a Dayak man, Dutch Borneo, 1890. (Photo courtesy KITLV, Leiden)

perium at its fullest possible limits. To assert these commonalities, Dutch ethnographers would eventually trek all the way out to New Guinea, a place where such culture traits were actually markedly different.[99] It did not matter. What did matter was that ethnography was brought into the service of the state—slowly, unevenly, but with important repercussions for the future of the frontier.

Missionaries were another class of servants available to help bring to fruition the state's agenda in the lands along the border. The spread of missionary societies in the Indies in the nineteenth century was phenomenal: the Ermeloosche Zending, the Java Comite, the Utrechtsche Zendingsvereeniging, the Nederlandsche Gereformeerde Zendingsvereeniging, the Christelijke Gereformeerde Kerk, the Luthersche Genootschap, and the Rijnsche Zendelinggenootschap all spread their messengers over the Indies during this time.[100] This initial presence was expanded further in the latter half of the century, pushing European servants of the church and often simultaneously of the state into almost every corner of the archipelago. Missionaries diffused into the interior of southeastern Borneo, to the various Batak lands in central Sumatra, and even to Aceh, though in smaller numbers.[101] Many of the indigenous peoples converted were of the lowest classes, such as debt-bonded retainers in parts of eastern Borneo.[102] Other residencies, such as Palembang, had little luck with the conversion of the local populace in the interior. Some missionaries were killed, meeting active antagonism from the people they were sent to "civilize."[103] More common was a delaying refusal in reluctant areas, as indigenes thought up many reasons they should not convert to Batavia's religions.[104] As quickly as some conversion schemes proceeded in the Outer Islands during the nineteenth century, both willing and less than fully willing, there were also enormous numbers of people who refused to adopt Christianity, whatever the pressures brought to bear.

Such pressures were not usually direct, as Batavia officially decreed that all religions were welcome in the Indies, even Islam. But many of Batavia's actions, and the writings of her servants as well, show that religion was often treated as one extra tool with which to subdue the Indies to Dutch rule. The minister for the colonies, L. W. Ch. Keuchenius, to the delight of many in the missionary community, declared this openly in 1888, stating it would be valued if the Dutch orders could work together in fighting the spread of Islam. His remarks led to an outcry, as there were still many in Dutch circles who felt the state should not be promoting any religion to its subjects.[105] Yet Keuchenius's remarks were not an isolated incident. The missionary societies actively lobbied

Batavia to expand their operations, pointing to the border residencies as huge domains where the word of Christ could be spread.[106] Some powerful administrators, such as the resident of southeastern Borneo, agreed. "When the Dayaks have turned in greater numbers to Christianity," he said in one report, "the government will find in these people a greater support toward the maintenance of Dutch authority."[107] The Dutch consul in Singapore echoed these sentiments and kept a vigilant eye on Muslim societies in the Outer Islands that might pose a threat to Dutch rule.[108] Others, such as the essayist L. W. C. van den Berg, saw no need to hide direct intentions: "The Christian religion is in my opinion . . . so unendingly above Islam, that an apology for evangelization in this regard is completely unnecessary."[109]

Yet with so many missionary orders crowding the frontier in their search for souls, sometimes this energy worked against any benefits the state might accrue. Missionaries expanded a European cultural presence along the border and gave the state extra sets of eyes. Yet they also competed with one another, and this sometimes caused significant problems. Tensions periodically erupted between Catholics and Protestants working in Minahasa, northern Sulawesi, occasionally prompting the state to deny permission to new missionaries seeking to enter the field.[110] In other places, each denomination accused the other of rebaptizing the other's converts, leading to quarrels that ultimately had to be arbitrated by the state.[111] Roman Catholics, as the minority Christian denomination in the Indies, suffered the brunt of these accusations, earning the title of propagandists for their faith in many blistering articles.[112] These were not the kinds of agents of the state, therefore, who might be associated with a concerted project of synchronized state expansion. Missionaries had their own agendas but were often used for their local knowledge by administrators in Batavia who needed data along the border. Catholics could provide this kind of information as well as Protestants, and as the civil service was of mixed denominations anyway, such frictions were allowed to stand. From 1865 until 1915, some information on the frontier was better than no information at all. Batavia allowed many sorts of missionaries into the periphery, therefore, regardless of sectarian affiliation.

A final category of important administrative strengthening was the increasing appearance of European civil servants sent out to rule the frontier.[113] These men, advance agents of the state, were injected into the border regions as representatives of centralized European authority. As such, they contributed in everyday ways to solidifying the presence of the boundary by collecting tolls, monitoring movements, and reporting back to regional centers with information about the frontier. Like almost all other aspects of colonial strengthening of the periphery, however, this process was uneven at best, succeeding in some geographic locales better than others and gaining momentum only over time. There was never any unity of state presence in the lands along the boundary, but rather pockets of effective governance and large swaths of territory in which centralized authority was much less reliable. Smugglers were dissuaded from crossing the frontier at a very early date in some landscapes, while nearby their movements continued unabated for much longer periods.

In general, the state's administrative presence on the frontier was thin at best in the 1860s and 1870s. Outer Island civil servants, regardless of residency, stress this again and again in the local records. In western Borneo, the chief administrator bemoaned the fact that he had only fifteen civil servants under his command, outfitted to govern a territory the size of Java and Madura combined.[114] Many such Outer Island administrators were periodically cut off from the capitals of their own residencies as well, as transport and communications with outlying stations were anything but effective. Roads, as already detailed, were often washed away in the rainy season, and rivers, the traditional transport arteries of much of Southeast Asia, were also unreliable, both during droughts and then during the monsoon. In the interior of these regions, therefore, "the old injustices continue," wrote this same resident, as the reach of the state was still too short to effect significant change.[115]

Nor was this the only challenge. Border residency administrators, both European and indigenous, were also notoriously underpaid, leading to serious governance problems of another kind. Graft was omnipresent. In British Borneo, corruption cases plagued English administration, while across the Dutch frontier civil servants also toyed with the law.[116] The problem, the Dutch resident of West Borneo said in a report, was that local officials were entirely dependent on their meager salaries; sometimes this remuneration was barely enough to live on. Matters became so serious in Palembang that the colonial administration there was forced to fine, and even sometimes jail, local administrators for persistent graft.[117] Court cases from various parts of the archipelago reveal that smuggling among many of these civil servants was rampant.[118] The Dutch Indies press also singled out officials for contrabanding and graft, asking if it wasn't natural for Indies subjects to smuggle if they saw their local officials doing so as well.[119] Especially along the border residencies, such self-interest on the part of colonial administrators did not bode well for border enforcement, as many such men enhanced their salaries precisely in this way.

Corruption was not taking place only in the residencies of Palembang and

Borneo and at other far-flung locales along the Anglo/Dutch frontier. It was also occurring quite close to, and sometimes directly inside, centers of European power. Perak was a notorious locality for these kinds of activities, and the *Penang Gazette* ran occasional stories on bribery and corruption that greased the wheels of local government.[120] In 1894, the brother-in-law of Frank Swettenham, one of the most powerful men in Malaya, was convicted of embezzling eight thousand dollars in Kuala Kangsar, and other Englishmen threatened to expose more examples of graft unless their own pending cases of wrongdoing were cleared.[121] These accusations sent the Colonial Office into periodic scrambles. Even in Singapore, the seat of British power, irregularities and "dark alliances" between officials and smugglers became clear. An anonymous indigenous petition in 1894 intoned that the "government servants of Singapore cheat the poor inhabitants. . . . they make their own laws." Specific cases of police demanding protection money were outlined, as were court cases being influenced by dealings behind the scenes. Among the accused were the colony's detective inspector, police superintendents, and the colonial surgeon, all of whom were identified as taking money on the sly.[122]

Perhaps just as important as the issue of corruption, however, was the fact that colonial states had little grasp in the early years about the actual dimensions of their territory and about who lived where inside it. A Dutch Indies cadastral bureau had existed since much earlier in the century, but was, for all intents and purposes, ineffective in mapping out state knowledge of local lands and conditions. By 1884, this situation was changing, as personnel and equipment were added to help the state see its dominions. Yet most of this activity was still taking place in the center, on the islands of Java and Madura.[123] In the periphery, especially in border residencies such as southeastern Borneo and Riau, administrators still had little idea of who lived where or of the extent of local landholdings. Local chiefs and Chinese leaders did hand in the required population data to the Dutch provincial administrations but often misreported populations so as to pay less tax to the central government in Batavia.[124] The Hague tried to strengthen this arm of Indies administration, but progress was painful and slow. Surveyors were sent out from the Netherlands and schools were set up to train new staff, but the results on these endeavors were considered unsatisfactory even into the early twentieth century.[125]

By that time, the state's human presence in the periphery still afforded serious problems to the center's abilities, but improvements were also being made. The dismal chances for promotion and even more dismal pay schemes for

Outer Islands administrators were being revamped. Batavia was trying to remove two of the primary causes of complaint that often led to bad government, including graft and smuggling in the periphery.[126] There were also attempts to redraw the political contracts with self-governing polities in the border residencies, which gave local rulers a little more room to earn a decent living, rather than having to resort to smuggling to maintain their status.[127] Yet problems persisted, often serious enough to impair government functioning in the outstretched borderlands where the state needed this presence most. Controleurs were still badly overworked and responsible for a huge variety of tasks: education, infrastructure, harbor control, and governance were among their duties. These burdens often overtaxed their effectiveness.[128] Authority in the self-governing areas remained broken and diffuse, with a variety of interests—sultans, their children, strongmen, and *orang kaya* (rich merchants)—all holding sway over different territories.[129] Some of Batavia's Dutch civil servants, such as one notorious womanizer in Manado, also exercised their authority in ways objectionable to the local populace, lowering the government's prestige in local eyes.[130] All of these phenomena happened at once and across the length of the Anglo/Dutch frontier. Their simultaneity shows better than any other index, perhaps, the somewhat broken nature of European authority on the border for most of the years discussed in this book.

The erection of a boundary between Western possessions in Southeast Asia required the utilization of many tools by these states. Roads, telegraphs, and railroads were constructed, to move men and matériel quickly to distant geographies. Lighthouses and steamships started to ensure more active control of the sea, as Batavia and Singapore tried to monitor the archipelagic spaces between them. Economic policies like the *tolgebied* and economic coercion, such as blockades, also targeted expanding control, though these measures were never as successful as European policy planners had hoped. Agents of Western influence were also deployed along the frontier, and whether there at state behest or following their own programs, their observations on the dynamics of the border were always tabulated carefully by the two imperial regimes. The boundary between the neighboring colonial projects gradually became a more physical construct between 1865 and 1915, therefore. What was only a notion in 1865 had become something very much more than that by 1915, though many local actors still would have had difficulty defining exactly what this was even after the turn of the twentieth century. Yet the building of this construct happened not only on the ground in physical space, but in the colonial imagination as well.

NOTES

1. ANRI, Algemeen Administratieve Verslag Residentie West Borneo 1872 (no. 5/3); ANRI, Algemeen Administratieve Verslag Residentie Borneo Z.O. 1871 (no. 9/2); "Bijzonderheden Omtrent Sommige Werken," *KV* (1871), 115.

2. ANRI, Maandrapport Residentie Palembang 1871 (no. 74/9); ANRI, Algemeen Administratieve Verslag Residentie Palembang 1870 (no. 64/13).

3. ARA, 1872, MR no. 624; ARA, 1872, MR no. 632; ANRI, Maandrapport Residentie Palembang 1870 (no. 74/8 September)

4. "Wegen op Sumatra," (1881), 921.

5. *Straits Maritime Journal* 4 Jan. 1896, 5.

6. *Singapore Free Press* 3 Nov. 1904, 3.

7. Memorie van Overgave, Borneo Z.O., 1906, (MMK no. 270), 21; Memorie van Overgave, Sumatra Oostkust, 1910 (MMK no. 182), 26–28.

8. Memorie van Overgave, Palembang, 1906 (MMK no. 206), 18.

9. Lulofs, "Wegen-Onderhoud," (1904), 31. By contrast, in Sarawak road building was deliberately neglected, not only because it was expensive, but also because it was thought that the traditional mode of river travel should be maintained.

10. See Kaur, "Hantu and Highway," (1994), 1–50.

11. From Borrel, *Mededeelingen Betreffende de Gewone Wegen in Nederlandsch-Indië*, (1915).

12. For an overview of the situation in the Indies generally, see G. C. Molewijk, "Telegraafverbinding Nederlands-Indië" (1990), 138–55; for the specifics of the 1870 connection, see "Telegraphie," *KV* (1871): 123–24.

13. ARA, 1870, MR no. 564, 574, 606, 622.

14. ARA, "Nota Voor Directeur der Burgerlijke Openbare Werken, van Ingenieur Chef Afdeling Telegrafie," in 1873, MR no. 490; also ARA, 1871, MR no. 648, 663, 672.

15. ANRI, Dutch Consul Singapore to GGNEI, 12 Jan. 1876, Confidential in Kommissoriaal, 10 Feb. 1876, no. 117az, in Aceh no. 12, "Stukken Betreffende Atjehsche Oorlog" (1876).

16. ANRI, Maandrapport Residentie Palembang 1871 (no. 74/9 October); Gov Labuan to CO, 14 Feb. 1871, no. 4, CO 144/34. The governor said he had received no dispatches from London since November 1870; some news received via French and English mails was accumulated in the Singapore post office, but these got to Labuan only very slowly.

17. See Dent (in London) to Read (in Singapore), 24 July 1880, in CO 874/112.

18. BNB Co HQ to CO, 18 Nov. 1889 Confidential, in CO 144/67; Gov Labuan to CO, 15 April 1894, in CO 144/69.

19. Memorie van Overgave, Borneo Z.O. (MMK no. 270), 23.

20. Le Roy, "Een Eigen Telegraafkabel," (1900), 287–95; "Nieuwe Kabelverbindingen in Ned. Oost-Indië," (1903/1904), 784. British wires in Kedah alone jumped from 508 miles in 1912 to 988 miles in 1916, with similar increases in other states. See *Kedah Annual Report*, 1916, 9.

21. Explanatory Memo Accompanying Bill Relating to German-Netherlands Cables Laid Before the General Session, 1901–02 (n.d), in PRO/Board of Trade/MT 10: Harbour Department, no. 943/H/3910.

22. ARA, 1902, MR no. 1049; "Recensie van "De Draadlooze Telegrafie," (1906), 936–39; "Draadlooze Telegrafie," (1903), 258.

23. BNB Gov. to BNB Co. HQ, 19 June 1917, in CO 531/11.

24. ARA, 1870, MR no. 177; ARA, 1872, MR no. 509, 533; ATA, A. S. Warmolts to GGNEI, 2 Nov. 1872, in 1873, MR no. 10.

25. Quarles van Ufford, "Koloniale Kronik," (1882), 260–72.

26. Kielstra, "Steenkolen en Spoorwegen," (1884), 1.

27. ANRI, Algemeen Verslag Residentie Riouw 1890 (no. 64/1–2).

28. Van Daalen, "Spoorwegen in Indië," (1886), 770.

29. "Deli-Spoorwegmaatschappij," (1884), 683–85.

30. ARA, Extract Uit het Register der Besluiten van de GGNEI, 30 Sept. 1885, no. 2/c, in 1885, MR no. 630; ARA, 1886, MR no. 703.

31. Batavia didn't want the trains moving too fast, as high speeds increased the possibility of expensive accidents. ARA, Extract Uit het Register der Besluiten van de GGNEI, 29 Oct. 1886, no. 1/C, in 1886, MR no. 705.

32. See *Johore Annual Report,* 1916, 23; *Perak Gov't Gazette,* 1902, 6; and *FMS Annual Report for 1901.*

33. De Krijthe, *'Bergkoningin'*, (1983); "Spoor- en Tramwegen," (1921), 69, passim; ARA, 1902, MR no. 117, 526; ARA, Extract Uit het Register der Besluiten van de GGNEI, 13 Dec. 1901, no. 272, 35, in 1902, MR no. 38; "Spoorweg-Aanleg op Noord-Sumatra" (1899), 817.

34. Memorie van Overgave, Palembang 1906 (MMK no. 206), 4; Memorie van Overgave, Lampongs 1913 (MMK no. 216), 110; ARA, 1902, MR no. 153; Van der Waerden, "Spoor-wegaanleg in Zuid-Sumatra," (1904), 175.

35. Eekhout, "Aanleg van Staatsspoorwegen," (1891), 955.

36. British Consul, Borneo to FO, 5 March 1904, in CO 144/78; BNB Co. HQ to CO, 19 Oct. 1910, Confidential in CO 531/2.

37. De Meijer, "Zeehavens en Kustverlichting," (1847–97), 304.

38. ARA, 1869, MR no. 99; ARA, 1870, MR no. 594; ANRI, Algemeen Verslag Residentie Banka 1872 (Banka no. 63).

39. ANRI, Algemeen Verslag Residentie Borneo Z.O. 1871 (no. 9/2).

40. Van Berckel, "De Bebakening en Kustverlichting" (1847–97), 308.

41. *SSBB,* 1873, "Expenditures," 55–56; see also the section "Lighthouses."

42. ARA, Extract Uit het Register der Besluiten GGNEI, 21 July 1885, no. 6, in 1885, MR no. 444; ARA, Extract Uit het Register der Besluiten GGNEI, 20 June 1886, no. 3/C, in 1885, MR no. 423.

43. See ARA, Ministerie van Marine, Plaatsinglijst van Archiefbescheiden Afkomstig van de Vierde Afdeling (Loodswezen), 1822–1928 (2.12.10). Series 321–32. Bijlage 3 is especially helpful for an overview of beaconing and coast lighting construction.

44. "Uitbreiding der Indische Kustverlichting," (1903), 1172.

45. Board of Trade to CO, 12 Jan. 1900, no. 16518, in CO 144/74.

46. BNB Co. HQ to CO, 26 Oct. 1899, in CO 144/73.

47. Memorie van Overgave, Borneo Z.O., 1906 (MMK no. 270), 19.

48. ARA, Commander, of the Marine to GGNEI, 24 Jan. 1899, no. 895, in 1899, MR no. 159.

49. *De Kustverlichting in Nederlandsch-Indië* (1913), 4.

50. Capt. E. Wrightson to Imperial Merchant Service Guild, (n.d), in CO 531/5; CO to Charles Brooke, 9 Jan. 1907, in CO 531/1. There were never enough lighthouses constructed, according to some British mariners.

51. "Kustverlichting in NI," (1906), 81.

52. See a Campo, *Koninklijke Paketvaart Maatschappij* (1992), and a Campo, "Steam Navigation and State Formation" (1994). A useful overview of shipping patterns for this period can be found in Huijts, "De Veranderende Scheepvaart" (1994), 57–73, and in the works of Lindblad, Dick, and Touwens, already cited in the introduction.

53. ANRI, Maandrapport Residentie Borneo Z.O 1872 (no. 10a/7), "Korte Overzigt van de Handel en Scheepvaart ter Koetei"; ANRI, Algemeen Administratieve Verslag Residentie West Borneo 1872 (no. 5/3).

54. ARA, 1870, MR no. 173; ANRI, Algemeen Administratieve Verslag Residentie Riouw 1871 (no. 63/2).

55. Gov Labuan to CO, 24 June 1876, no. 42, in CO 144/46; Gov Labuan to CO, 27 Nov. 1871, no. 17, in CO 144/35.

56. ARA, 1888, MR no. 461. Though the KPM was legislated into being in 1888, it did not start actual operations until three years later.

57. See the maps reproduced in his book.

58. ARA, Directeur van Binnenlandsch-Bestuur to GGNEI, 13 April 1888, in 1888, MR no. 483; ARA, Raad van NEI, Advies, in Kommissoriaal, 12 March 1888, no. 4340, in 1888, MR no. 483.

59. La Chapelle, "Bijdrage tot de Kennis van het Stoomvaartverkeer" (1885), 689–90.

60. British Consul, Oleh Oleh to Gov SS, 29 June 1883, no. 296, in "Traffic in Contraband," vol. ii, in PRO/FO/220/Oleh-Oleh Consulate (1882–85).

61. See Bogaars, "Effect of the Opening of the Suez Canal" (1955), 104, 117.

62. Memorie van Overgave, Palembang, 1906, (MMK no. 206), 4; ARA, 1902, MR no. 93; Memorie van Overgave, Jambi, 1908 (MMK no. 216), 47.

63. ARA, Directeur Burgerlijke Openbare Werken to GGNEI, 31 May 1902, no. 8564/A, in 1902/MR no. 542.

64. "Sabang-Baai," (1903), 237–38; Heldring, "Poeloe Weh," (1900), 630. For a useful analysis of the expansion of harbors generally in North Sumatra during this time, see Airress, "Port-Centered Transport Development," (1995), 65–92.

65. ARA, 1902, MR no. 402.

66. Chinese traders, for example, were forbidden to head upriver to certain places, as it was feared they would cheat Dayaks in the interior; see Chew, *Chinese Pioneers,* (1990), 130. The Brookes also began to carefully tax products coming across the border from Dutch Borneo; see *Sarawak Gazette,* 2 April 1893, 1 March 1894, and 1 Sept. 1900, and Cleary, "Indigenous Trade," (1996), 301–24.

67. See Resink, "De Archipel voor Joseph Conrad" (1959).

68. As reported in ARA, Directeur van Financien to GGNEI, 24 Aug. 1875, no. 11004, in 1875, MR no. 563.

69. ANRI, Dutch Consul Penang to GGNEI, 21 June 1876, no. 991G in Kommissoriaal, 14 July 1876, no. 522az in Aceh no. 14, Stukken Betreffende Atjehsche Oorlog (1876).

70. Kruijt, *Atjeh en de Atjehers,* 172.

71. *SSBB,* 1873, "Judicial Returns," 574; see also the statistics reported in subsequent years in the same volumes, especially 1874, 1875, and 1876.

72. Gov Labuan to CO, 17 Sept. 1872, no. 70, in CO 144/38. Duties were skimmed off brandy, spirits, arrack, wine, tobacco, beer, toddy, and even produce to be sold in the Labuan market.

73. Many regulations existed on the import and export of spirits, petroleum, matches, gold and silver, coffee, and rice, for example, instructions for which can be found in various Staatsbladen. See also "Belastingen" (1921), 255.

74. "Nieuwe Tarieven," (1886), 213.

75. ARA, Resident West Borneo to GGENI, 13 Aug. 1879, no. 4423 in 1880, MR no. 252; Van der Haas, "Belasting op het Vervoer van Djatihout," *IG* (1897): 416. Dutch courts in 1888 decided to give themselves competency to determine whether declarations of imported goods' values were purposefully written too low, so as to lower the amounts of tax that would have to be paid. See "In en Uitvoerregten" *IWvhR,* no. 1280, 9 January 1888, 5–6.

76. See, for example, ARA, Directeur van Financien to GGNEI, 18 Feb. 1881, no. 2959, in 1881, MR no. 161; ANRI, Algemeen Administratieve Verslag Residentie Palembang 1887 (no. 65/7).

77. *Review of the Netherlands Indian Tariff Law* (1921).

78. ARA, Directeur van Financien to GGENI, "Rapport van 5 Jan 1894, no. 15," in 1894, MR no. 32; Memorie van Overgave, Borneo Z. O, 1906 (MMK no. 270), 14.

79. Memorie van Overgave, Jambi, 1908 (MMK no. 216), 46.

80. ARA, 1897, MR no. 281; ARA, 1897, MR no. 527.

81. Of course, this opened up smuggling opportunities on a whole range of new items as well.

82. *Tractaat van Londen 1824; Tractaat van Sumatra 1872; Bepalingen Inzake Kustvaart Doorschoten, met Aantekeningen in Handschrift,* from Indische Staatsblad no. 477, 479, 1912; "Handel en Scheepvaart" (1921), 22.

83. "Het Voorstel tot Opheffing van het Verbod" (1887), 938–39.

84. Kruijt, *Atjeh en de Atjehers,* 18; *British North Borneo Herald,* 1 Oct. 1896, 284; Warren, *The Sulu Zone,* 117–18; British Consul, Oleh-Oleh to Gov SS, 18 June 1883, no. 283, in "Blockades of the Aceh Coast, 1883," in PRO/FO/220/Oleh-Oleh Consulate, 1883 Correspondence.

85. See Reid, *The Contest for North Sumatra,* on this; also a Campo *Koninklijke Paketvaart Maatschappij,* for details.

86. For a good overview of the blockade, see Ismail, *Seuneubok Lada* (1991), 101–15; for contemporary specifics, see ARA, "Citadel van Antwerpen" to Kommandant der Maritieme Middelen, Atjeh, 12 Aug. 1873, no. A/5; also Commander Zeemacht to GGNEI, 18 Sept. 1873, no. 9744, both in Verbaal Geheim Kabinet, 17 Dec. 1873, D33; ARA, "Zeeland" to Kommandant der Maritieme Middelen, Atjeh, 13–26 Aug. 1873, no. 92, in Verbaal Geheim Kabinet, 17 Dec. 1873, D33.

87. Kruijt, *Atjeh en de Atjehers,* 33.

88. ANRI, Dutch Consul Penang to GGNEI, 16 Aug. 1876, no. 103/G Confidential, in Kommissoriaal, 28 Sept. 1876, no. 719az, in Aceh no. 14 Stukken Betreffende Atjehsche

Oorlog, (1876); ANRI, Dutch Consul Penang to GGNEI, 11 May 1876 Confidential, in Kommissoriaal, 28 Sept. 1876, no. 719az, in Aceh no. 14 Stukken Betreffende Atjehsche Oorlog, (1876).

89. See British Consul, Oleh-Oleh, to Gov Aceh, 1 Sept. 1883, and 25 Sept. 1883 (no. 473, no. 534), both in PRO/FO/220/Oleh-Oleh Consulate (1882–85).

90. PRO/FO/Confidential Print Series, vol. 29: SE Asia, 1879–1905, 194, 196, 233, etc., in *British Documents on Foreign Affairs* (1995).

91. Kempe, "Scheepvaartregeling," (1893), 410; "Havens- en Scheepvaartregeling op Atjeh" (1907), 1079.

92. See Van Basel, "Maleyers van Borneo's Westkust" (1874), 196; Verkerk Pistorius, "Maleisch Dorp" (1869), 97.

93. ARA, 1873, MR no. 119; ARA, First Gov. Sec., Batavia, to Directeur Onderwijs, Eeredienst, Nijverheid, 18 May 1878, no. 793, in 1878, MR no. 583. For an overview of colonial Dutch anthropology in the Indies, see Ellen, "The Development of Anthropology" (1976), 303–24.

94. Snelleman, "Tabakspijpen van de Koeboe's," (1906); J. J. Kreemer, "Bijdrage tot de Volksgeneeskunde" (1907), 438; "Ziekenbehandeling onder de Dayaks" (1908), 99 passim.

95. "Ruilhandel bij de Bahau's" (1909/1910), 185.

96. Juynboll, "Mededeelingen omtrent Maskers" (1902), 28–29; Bezemer, "Van Vrijen en Trouwen" (1903), 3.

97. ARA, 1902, MR no. 501, 674.

98. "Beoordeling van het werk van Blink, "Nederlandsch Oost- en West-Indië," (1905/1907), 1102.

99. ARA, 1902, MR no. 173.

100. A book which gives an excellent idea of the width and breadth of these journeys is Boomgaard, ed., *God in Indië* (1997). For a contemporary rendering, see "Verschillende Zendelinggenootschappen" (1887), 1922.

101. ARA, 1899, MR no. 444; ARA, 1902, MR no. 950; ARA, First Gov. Sec. to Dir. Education and Industry, 17 March 1902, no. 954, in 1902, MR no. 242.

102. ANRI, Algemeen Verslag Residentie Borneo Z.O. 1874 (no. 9/5)

103. ANRI, Algemeen Administratieve Verslag Residentie Palembang 1874 (no. 64/17); ANRI, Politiek Verslag Residentie Borneo Z.O. 1871 (no. 4/1)

104. "Eenige Mededeelingen van de Zending" (1905), 1 passim. A missionary at Pangombusan reported that a powerful chief there, "an upright man who wants to become a Christian," could not do so; first, he had to give a burial feast for his mother, whose body was lying in a chest in his house. In the meantime, if other relatives of the chief died, he would have to do the same for them. Finally, the missionary said, the chief himself would die as a "heathen," and then his sons would have to give a death feast for him too. "Thus there is no end to these death feasts," he sighed.

105. "De Missive" (1889), 336.

106. ARA, 1889, MR no. 216.

107. ANRI, Algemeen Verslag Residentie Borneo Z.O. 1890 (no. 9a/11).

108. ARA, Dutch Consul, Singapore to GGNEI, 6 Dec. 1889, no. 1230, in 1899, MR no. 866.

109. Van den Berg, "Het Kruis Tegenover de Halve Maan" (1890), 68.

110. ARA, GGNEI to Titulair Apostolic Bishop, Batavia, 3 Oct. 1902, Kab. Geheim no. 29, in Extract Uit het Register der Besluiten van de GGNEI, 3 Oct. 1902, no. 29, in 1902, MR no. 905.

111. "Verdeeling van het Zendingsveld" (1889), 596–99.

112. See "Katholieke Propaganda" (1889), 69; "Roomsch-Katholiek Propoganda" (1902), 1407, for example.

113. For an interesting interpretation of Dutch colonial practice in the Indies via men such as these, see Gouda, *Dutch Culture Overseas* (1995), 39–74.

114. ANRI, Politiek Verslag Residentie West Borneo 1872 (no. 2/10).

115. Ibid.; ARA, Directeur van Binnenlandsch Bestuur to GGNEI, 23 May 1877, no. 5329, in 1877, MR no. 444. According to this letter, there were only 119 Dutch controleurs outside Java and Madura in all of the Netherlands Indies.

116. Gov Labuan to CO, 19 March 1883, no. 26, in CO 144/57; High Commissioner, SS to CO, 10 March 1910, no. 1, in CO 531/2; ANRI, Algemeen Verslag Residentie West Borneo 1874 (no. 5/4).

117. ANRI, Algemeen Administratieve Verslag Residentie Palembang 1887 (no. 65/7).

118. For one case of a clerk smuggling six hundred bottles of genever (Dutch gin), see "Vonnis in Zake Urbanus de Sha," *IwvhR*, 2 December 1872, no. 491, 492–93; see also "Poging tot Omkooping van een Openbaar Ambtenaar van de Rechterlijke Macht" *IWvhR*, no. 835 (1879), 103.

119. See "Aanslagbijletten" (1894), 151–52; "Controle op Inlandsche Hoofden" (1899), 218–20; Van Leeuwen, "Een Voorstel tot hervorming" (1906), 193–210, 321–23.

120. See Fred Toft to Sec. State Colonies, 31 May 1894, in CO 273/201; the *Penang Gazette*, 20 April 1894; and CO Jacket, 31 May 1894, in CO 273/201. Much of Perak was close to the major British outpost of Penang.

121. CO Jacket, 28 March 1894, and Fred Toft to Sec. State Colonies, 28 March 1894, both in CO 273/201.

122. See the Anonymous Petition under "Bribery of Government Officials" in CO 273/233. Part of the petition reads: "If your Honour wishes to find if this is true get missionaries who can talk and read Chinese to go into shops and look at the books. Hoping that your Honour could help the poor inhabitants of Singapore."

123. De Bas "Het Kadaster in Nederlandsch-Indië" (1884), 252 passim.

124. ANRI, Politiek Verslag Residentie Borneo Z.O. 1871 (no. 4/1); Algemeen Administratieve Verslag Residentie Riouw 1871 (no. 63/2).

125. "Versterking van het Indische Kadastrale" (1904), 187; "Iets Over het Kadaster" (1885), 1582.

126. ARA, Directeur Binnenlandsch Bestuur to GGNEI, 9 Feb. 1892, no. 834, in 1892, MR no. 634; "Het Corps Ambtenaren," (1887/1888), 286; "Kontroleurs op de Bezittingen Buiten Java" (1884), 14–15.

127. Memorie van Overgave, Sumatra Oostkust, 1910 (MMK no. 182), 7, 24.

128. "Controleur op de Buitenbezittingen" (1910), 2.

129. Memorie van Overgave, Riouw, 1908 (MMK no. 236), 1–2, 8.

130. ARA, Process Verbaal 4 April 1893, in 1893, MR no. 608. In this particular case the con-

troleur in Manado, J. H. Vermandel, was brought up on inquiry and questioned by the resident for his harassment of indigenous women working in his employ. He sometimes put flowers in their hair and (more seriously) occasionally entered their bedchambers at night, despite their shutting the doors to their rooms. The local populace unleashed an outcry over these transgressions; the story also eventually found its way back to the Dutch press, via the *Nieuwe Rotterdamsche Courant.*

Section II Imagining the Frontier: State Visions of Danger Along the Border

The government personnel here are under the best of circumstances insufficiently numerous, fifteen of them in an area greater than Java and Madura combined. Yet this is an area where there is also insufficient means of communication, where the climate is terrible for Europeans, and where a hugely scattered and warlike population live. . . . We've told the [local population] that henceforth slavery, the pawning of humans, forced trade, and head-hunting belong to the past; in the future these things will be punished by the police and by the judiciary. But this hasn't happened. Most of these promises I've had to completely give up . . . and the old injustices continue.
—Government Resident, Dutch West Borneo, ANRI, Politiek Verslag 1872 (#2/10)

Chapter 5 The Specter of Violence

The forging of a border between the emerging British and Dutch colonial spheres in Southeast Asia was a technological project. European regimes used a range of means at their disposal to accomplish this goal, pressing existing technologies into service and inventing new ones through systems of trial and error to better their chances at success. These processes were ongoing, and Western colonies throughout the world were seen in this respect as laboratories for developing new forms of control.[1] The border was not fabricated only in physical space, however; it was also a complex formation woven from imperial fears and ideologies. Despite the ongoing domestication of these lands and seas to European control, the frontier between British and Dutch Southeast Asia continually was seen as wild space needing to be tamed. Populations and "problems" along the border were targeted and identified; policy planners and the colonial public alike asked how these peripheries could be better controlled. Despite decades of coercive processes already creeping forward in the mid–nineteenth century, when European colonial regimes looked out upon the wide spaces of Insular Southeast Asia in the 1860s and 1870s, they often were dismayed by what they saw.[2]

MARITIME ANOMIE: THE THREAT OF PIRACY

Violence and the perceived damage it caused to any attempts to impose European "order" seemed to be everywhere. One of the foremost perceived threats to the viability of colonial border construction in the Indies archipelago during this time, in fact, was piracy: the looting, robbing, and violence practiced by various seafaring peoples in the region. Nineteenth-century British and Dutch treatments of the phenomenon of piracy were numerous and primarily policy grounded: such authors as the Dutchman H. P. E. Kniphorst and the much more famous Thomas Raffles and James Brooke saw piracy as a manifestation of cultural anomie and violence that needed to be stamped out if civilization was to come to the region.[3] The realities of what has loosely been called "piracy" in this period, however, were far more complicated, of course. Contemporary scholars have shown how maritime violence, slaving, and attacks on commercial shipping can often be much more accurately understood within the context of local political and economic systems, providing the necessary status and surplus that made whole societies run. Some of the best revisionist scholarship in this vein has focused on piracy in Borneo waters, though the contested areas often stretch further afield to include North Sulawesi and the Sulu basin as well.[4] Other scholars, working in different locales, have problematized the conception of piracy from other angles, showing how these depredations could be seasonal or temporary survival strategies which had little to do with any overt political challenge against any particular state.[5]

For Dutch and British writers and statesmen of the time, however, the threat of piracy was immediate and often functioned as a real impediment to programs of commerce and administrative stabilization in the periphery. This was particularly true in the decades leading up to 1865. Kniphorst referenced the example of the classical Mediterranean in voicing his frustrations over the continuation of piracy in Indies waters; he likened Dutch suppression difficulties to those of the Greeks in the Aegean, who could not curb piracy because of its sponsorship by many small, sovereign lords.[6] In his multichapter history of piracy in the Indies, Kniphorst searched for origins in the centuries predating European contact, pondering whether this sort of behavior might indeed be culturally endemic to the region.[7] The British at midcentury took less of a philosophical approach to the phenomenon and instead focused on means of suppression. Brooke repeatedly chronicled to London "the increasing boldness of the pirates, who now venture to cruise in large fleets."[8] Brooke's missives ultimately worked, as resolutions on piracy in the East Indies eventually circulated all the way up to the House of Commons, involving the metropole with adventurers like Brooke himself in distant Asian waters.[9] The British eventually were also able to enlist local rulers in the Indies to help them in their fight against piracy, though some of these potentates entered into these arrangements much more willingly than others.[10]

Piracy remained a threat to processes of Outer Island state formation in the 1860s and 1870s for several interconnected reasons. Perhaps first among these was the fact that the geography of the long frontier between Dutch and British interests lent itself admirably to concealment and evasion on the part of potential marauders. The writings of Dutch residents in the border residencies in the 1870s comment on this prolifically: the maze of tiny islands that make up the Riau archipelago opposite Singapore served as a natural choke point for these sorts of activities, as did the huge Gulf of Gorontalo in North Sulawesi, which became a pirate haven for *perahus* (ships) operating on the northern fringes of Dutch authority.[11] Yet the marshes and creeks of longer, more unprotected coastlines also served as natural refuges for pirates. Dutch and British administrators found this out in Aceh and the Malay Peninsula, respectively, when Malay potentates complained about the Straits' labyrinthine coastal swamps and the protection they offered to lurking Chinese corsairs.[12] Local geographies, therefore, were constantly bent toward practical advantage, though the physical circumstances of these geographies could cover a broad spectrum of possibilities. Men with guns seemed to be everywhere in the Straits of Melaka especially, a state of affairs noted on both sides of the international waterway.

The many rivers of the region also abetted piracy. Networks of rivers have been the traditional arteries of commerce and contact in much of Insular Southeast Asia for centuries. As early as 1849 the British were conducting expeditions to curtail piracy up the rivers of Borneo, while Dutch residents on the eastern coast of the island posted warnings that the mouths of the Berau and Barito (made famous in many of Joseph Conrad's stories) were unsafe because of high levels of piracy.[13] Yet the waters in and around Borneo were not the only sites of potential trouble for Europeans. Surviving letters between Malay sultans and Chinese mining chiefs in Malaya show how common piracy was in Malayan river mouths during troubled times in the early 1870s.[14] Even in Palembang, South Sumatra, which had been officially conquered by the Dutch for fifty years by the 1860s, the headwaters of the Musi River continued to pump out piracy, chaos, and violence into the sea lanes until after the end of the century. The rebellion of Taha in the Jambi uplands saw to this, as did the proximity of the flourishing harbor of Singapore, with all the rich maritime prizes this port offered.[15] One Dutch naval officer theorized that because the rivers of Sumatra connected in many places in the inaccessible interior, pirates could enter the Strait of Melaka at numerous points and exit, under European duress, just as quickly.[16]

Local maritime geographies, and the ways in which they were used by indigenes, rendered piracy a continual threat to the expansion of colonial states and the law-and-order policies they espoused. Yet at least in the early period under discussion here, the British and Dutch never really possessed the proper resources to dictate the terms of this enforcement. That European administrators and marine personnel in the region understood this is everywhere apparent in the sources. The governor of the Straits Settlements, William Ord, said as much when he asked the Colonial Office for more ships to fight piracy off Singapore in 1873. Off British Borneo, the governor of Labuan was also writing to London at this time, informing the Colonial Office that expeditions against certain corsairs were being postponed, as many pirate lairs were on coasts yet to be surveyed.[17] In the Dutch sphere, matters were even more complicated. Dutch territory stretched far further than the British settlements, and the Dutch possessed proportionally many fewer ships. This inverse ratio was an invitation to chaos, in the eyes of Batavia. When a Dutch ship, the *Susanna Cornelia,* was pirated by no fewer than twenty-seven *perahus* in the Makassar Strait at the end of 1870, a steamer was finally sent to perform station duty at that choke point; Palembang had no such luck and made a futile request for government ships from Bangka to give chase to pirates in 1871.[18] The lack of available ships was exacerbated by the constant naval drain of the Aceh War, which from 1873 onward became the focal point of Dutch marine resources in the region. If the Spanish had not started a new campaign at just this time to pacify the southern Philippines through the aggressive patrolling of steamships, piracy would have been even more rampant in the outer stretches of the Dutch Indies than it already was.[19]

Colonial European states knew very little, in the early period, about who area pirates actually were. Attempts were made to classify suspected culprits at sea based on the designs of sailing craft and sails, with Lingga, in Riau, being identified as one possible source of many pirates of the Outer Islands.[20] It is telling that when the Dutch did come across former captives or escapees of pirates, they interrogated such people relentlessly to find out as much as possible about pirate whereabouts and practices. One such escapee, a woman named Amina, was questioned as to how many weapons her captors had, how many ships, and even as to the men's customs and habits, all in an attempt to procure valuable information which was otherwise unavailable.[21] What Batavia and Singapore did come to know through experience was that they were often up against vessels that were only marginally inferior to their own, at least in the early decades. Piratical craft off the coast of the Malay Peninsula were mounted with swivel guns and manned by up to eighty men working sails and oars, so the British, in chases across the Straits of Melaka to Sumatra, often could not overtake them.[22] Towing cables and impressive stocks of firearms were also not uncommon on pirate ships, as were all sorts of planking and shielding devices to render boats impervious to cannon fire.[23] Where European ships could press technological advances, as they did, for example, with the gradual advent of steam in these waters after 1870, pirates learned to adapt. One account of an English warship tells of the ship's being unable to approach the Borneo shore in pursuit of some pirates because the low draught of the ship would have stranded it in tidal mudflats. The British had to content themselves with firing cannon shot at the pirates over a distance of nine hundred yards, as the pirates continually submerged their heads upon seeing the plume of approaching cannon fire.[24] Another account tells of pirates in Dutch waters learning that a light beacon near the Sumatra coast was an ideal place to trap passing ships of prey. Because all European craft naturally made for the lights to guide their passage toward the coast, the pirates would lie in wait nearby and come upon them unawares.[25] The new technologies of states along the border were thus also bent to local advantage, after indigenes undertook their own processes of piratical trial and error.

Yet perhaps the largest problem facing early colonial administrators in their battle against piracy was the fact that pirates seemed to be able to appear out of and disappear into thin air. Batavia and Singapore slowly came to understand that there was, in fact, no ontological category of pirates at all—the threat to law and order was by and large an unseen one, as such people often moved in and out of piracy even as they practiced other professions. Governor William Treacher of Labuan was among the first to state this explicitly, commenting in 1879 that "for a gunboat to cruise about, expecting to pick up pirates at sea would be of no avail, as they can quickly assume the appearance of quiet traders."[26] Off the western coast of Malaya the situation was even more complicated, as the competing sultans of Perak and Larut as well as various factions of Chinese miners in the area all possessed their own supporting fleets, which preyed on any craft they caught sailing in the area.[27] Chinese shrimping villages on the coast developed a particularly evil reputation for these chameleon-like qualities, though there is evidence of Chinese and Malay traders in Dutch Riau also fluctuating in and out of so-called legal occupations as opportunities arose.[28] Off the eastern coast of Borneo, it was no secret at all that the sultans of Berau and Gunung Tabur, among others, sponsored piracy, despite their official protestations to the contrary. In these waters and off neighboring Sulawesi, trepang fishers took on the notoriety of Chinese shrimpers further west. The sight of men collecting edible sea cucumbers was an immediate, internationally known sign for caution.[29]

Although both colonial states saw piracy as a threat, and later as a nuisance, to establishing and maintaining strong, workable authority in the region, the primary victims of such attacks were most often peaceful trading ships passing through these waters. The detailed testimony of a Chinese crew before the Penang superintendent of police in early 1876 gives us an idea of how such depredations could work: Joo In Tek and Too Ah On both barely escaped an attack off Aceh with their lives. Their vessel, the *Sin Soon Seng,* left South China in December 1875 with a cargo of livestock, immigrants, and tea for the Straits Settlements. The men of the *Sin Soon Seng* then transported other cargoes, including tiles and fine cloth, between ports in the region before heading to Aceh in early 1876. When the ship was off the coast of Pulau Weh, just north of the Aceh coast, the crew of sixteen split up to carry out different tasks: some were preparing bales of pepper for trade, while others were on the beach foraging for firewood. A pirate crew of Malays must have been watching from the coast and chosen this moment; before anyone knew what had happened, Joo In Tek said, the Malays had pulled out long knives and had killed several of the crew. Others jumped overboard but were hunted out of the water by these men. The crew on shore was able to return to their vessel only after the Malays had made off with everything of value. The surviving members of the *Sin Soon Seng* eventually were able to return to Penang to make their deposition. The sources are littered with accounts of traders barely escaping such attacks in one piece (table 1). Piracy was simply considered to be one of the calculated risks that merchants had to take if they wished to pursue commerce, licit or illicit, in large parts of the border arc.[30]

A second attack, this time on an Arab trading vessel in waters much closer to the center of Dutch administrative and naval surveillance in Java, is equally instructive. In March 1873 the *perahu Tjemplong,* captained by a man named To Mariam and carrying five crew members and three Arab merchants on board, was pirated off the northern coast (*pasisir*) of Java. The ship had been chartered by a wealthy Arab trader named Sech Achmat Bin Abdul Rachman Bin Sa'im,

Table 1. Testimonials of Crew Members of the Penang Junk *Sin Soon Seng* About an Act of Piracy Committed Against Their Craft in Acehnese Waters, 1876

After arriving there (Pulau Weh), some of the crew went to look for firewood, others to get cocoanuts, leaving six men on board, when a sampan with seven Malays came to the junk. They killed two of the crew and a nacodah and a carpenter. I was on shore and could see what took place. I also saw five Malays jump into the sampan alongside and pursue the men who were swimming, and cut one man on the face. He is in my junk now. Afterwards the Malays cut the cable, plundered the junk, and brought the things on shore. I was with the wood-cutting party. We had tried to find the party who had gone for cocoanuts. When we found them we got two sampans and went on board the junk which had drifted close in. The Malays had gone into the woods. At low water we found the dead bodies and buried them . . . . At midnight we sailed for Acheen, but not having a favorable wind we came to Penang.

— Testimony of Joo In Tek, 4 April 1876, Penang

At a place called Pulo Way (Pulau Weh), on the fourth day of the third Chinese month, we were getting pepper at half past one in the day, and twelve Malays came to the ship. There were only six of us on board. The Malays were all armed with long knives. One man cut me on my shoulder. Seven men came on board, five remained in the sampan. Two of our men were killed and three jumped in the water. The five men in sampans followed and cut me again badly. The Malays thought me dead and returned to the ship. After they had got all things they wanted they went away. I floated near the shore. My friends picked me up when the Malays had gone.

— Testimony of Foo Ah On, 5 April 1876, Penang

Source: ANRI, NEI Consul General to GGNEI, 13 April 1876, #921 G Confidential, in Kommissoriaal, 3 May 1876, #332az.

also of Java, and it was carrying 1,500 guilders in cash and 2,150 guilders' worth of trade goods at the time of its plundering. At 11:00 A.M. on the morning of March 14, five other *perahus* came upon the *Tejemplong* not far off the coast of Java and relieved the vessel of everything of value on board. The Arab trader who lost the entire worth of his trading venture was apoplectic at what happened next: the Dutch detective cutter that was stationed nearby could not give chase to the pirates as almost the whole crew of the vessel was down with fever.[31] Piratic elusion, therefore, was compounded by state ineptitude. The case clearly shows that Arabs were victims of crime and violence as well as racialized suspects of the colonial Dutch state, as will be examined later in this book. It also shows that even at the central locus of Dutch power in the Indies, in the relatively well-policed waters of the north Java coasts, piracy was possible even in broad daylight in the 1870s. The Dutch had laid claim to these stretches of the archipelago for many, many years by this time, so that piracy was a potential worry even in supposedly secure spaces, let alone in the less policed waters of the frontier.

Through the 1870s and into the 1890s, piracy continued in the waters of the border residencies in uneasy balance with expanding colonial power. Though Dutch legal codes started to become more sophisticated and direct in how to deal with the perpetrators of such actions, effectively enforcing these new realities on the ground was a whole other matter.[32] A range of Dutch legal cases from this period make this clear.[33] The historical Captain Lingard of Singapore, one of the chief personages upon whom Conrad's Eastern Waters stories was based, was attacked repeatedly by pirates off of eastern Borneo in the late 1870s, Malay informants stating that the corsairs were after Lingard's valuable holds of cloth.[34] When attacks on shipping in the Anambas islands in the South China Sea (the northernmost islands of Dutch control in the western archipelago) became prevalent, a steamer from Jambi in Sumatra was eventually sent. This worked for a while, but in the vacuum left behind Sumatran piracy soon picked up again, as evidenced by one famous bandit who robbed shipping in the area and burned coastal settlements to the ground.[35] In Borneo, the beginnings of oversight of the northern extremity of the island in 1878 by the British North Borneo Company allowed London to partially wash its hands of the piracy problem in these notorious waters, a fact that elicited some delight from Foreign Office officials who sneered that the violence and disorder were "now the Company's problem."[36] Batavia saw the expanding company as a potential new ally, however, in its own dealings with piracy and launched discussions with its directors on how the two regimes might deal with the problem together.[37]

By the first decade of the twentieth century, piracy was in retreat in most parts of the Outer Islands. The phenomenal growth of steam shipping and its incorporation into British and Dutch navies in the region had much to do with this, but the general "civilizing projects" of both states also played an important role. As people were forced into more sedentary lifestyles and the reach of these states into the periphery grew, less and less space was available for such free-wheeling forms of politicoeconomic activity. Not that piracy disappeared altogether. It just moved into the interstitial seams between the sinews of state power, seeking out places and moments in which such attacks had a chance of success. In 1910, for example, two Dutch traders were killed by seven *Moros* ("Moors") who had crossed from the southern Philippines into the Dutch waters of Sulawesi. The Dutch and American colonial regimes cooperated in sending out reconnaissance parties and naval forces, until the Filipino marauders, who had crossed back into Sulu waters to try to take advantage of the border as a buffer, were killed.[38] A second incident in 1909 further illustrates the shrinking spaces available to marauders on this frontier. When an American citizen was kidnapped in Dutch waters off Borneo, the British ship *Merlin* and nearby American forces were alerted by Batavia to help in the retrieval of the hostage. The pirates were eventually "annihilated," in the words of the British Foreign Office, but the incident managed to touch a raw nerve in Holland. The Dutch envoy to London wrote home of Anglo grumbling that the "Dutch territories in the East are too big for us," a seemingly offhand remark which nevertheless greatly concerned policymakers in The Hague.[39]

Although piracy, hounded from the seas of the archipelago, was no longer a real threat to either state by the turn of the twentieth century, it did remain a nuisance even beyond far-flung borders. If the interstitial spaces mentioned above allowed for the continuation of piracy owing to a lack of organized state presence, then some of the largest ports in the region continued to foster hazy, concentric rings of piratical opportunity which were still predicated on the density, not the sparsity, of valuable shipping in the area. These spheres of occasional maritime violence were evident not only around most of the ports of the Straits of Melaka and the western Java Sea, but also even near Singapore, the largest port in the entire region. Court cases like "The King vs. Chia Kuek Chin and Others," which dealt with a piratical act committed by Chinese marauders against other Chinese off the coast of Singapore in 1909, show that these waters were by no means totally safe at this late juncture.[40] The Johor Strait, in fact, seems to have been fertile ground for all sorts of corsairs even into the early twentieth century.[41] The relatively long, open coasts off of Singapore's Pasir Panjang were also still visited by pirates at this late date, as articles in the colony's Malay-language press make clear.[42] Piracy may have undergone a transformation between 1865 and 1915, from a phenomenon threatening to the lifeblood of colonial states to opportunistic anomaly of limited moments and places, but it never wholly disappeared. The sight of small local trading craft bearing down on trading ships in the region was a cause for anxiety in the early twentieth century and remains so even today.

LOW-LEVEL VIOLENCE ALONG THE BORDER

Piracy was not the only kind of uncontrolled violence that alarmed Singapore, and particularly Batavia, during the years around the turn of the twentieth century. General low-level violence was also seen to be pervasive throughout the Indies, as reports from the great majority of border residencies make clear. *Low-level violence* does not mean the fighting of wars against local rajas and sultans, which the colonial armed forces dealt with, more and more successfully as the century wore on. Neither does it mean urban crime, which police forces in the region began to tame more effectively toward the beginning of the twentieth century. The violence of the border arc under scrutiny here was of a more tenuous, chronic character than these forms of "disorder." The Dutch, in particular, did not seem to understand that their own state-making project in fact created much of this violence: in large parts of the Indies people were being asked to live under new sets of rules and under terms and conditions set by the colonial state. Naturally there was a certain amount of resistance to this evolving matrix of power, proscribed behavior, and hierarchy in the Indies. If conditions in the outer spaces of the archipelago were already seen as inherently unstable in the years before 1865, the imposition of European rule over large parts of the archipelago only exacerbated these conditions for the next several decades.[43]

It is with this dynamic in mind that the frontier residency reports coming into Batavia must be examined. At first glance, the reports seem to contradict an initial supposition of destabilizing, fractious conditions prevalent in the 1860s and 1870s. Almost all letters back to Batavia start with professions of peace and order in these far-flung border residencies. In Bangka, the resident informed the governor-general in 1870 that "the general situation was favorable, with things being peaceful"; the resident's counterparts in East and West Borneo, respectively, also intoned that "the peace left nothing to wish for" and "in general, the political situation of this residency is certainly not unfavorable."[44] Reports from Palembang and several other residencies along the border generally continue these mild appraisals.[45] Yet what these declarations seem to show more than anything else is that a certain level of systemic, low-level violence was thought to be unavoidable by rural administrators, at least in the period 1860–1880. In Bangka, only a few lines after declaring that life was peaceful in 1870, the resident admitted that uprisings had led several dozen people to be arrested and that eighteen ultimately had to be sentenced to hard, forced labor. Following the above statement of tranquility in western Borneo, the resident proceeded to outline a litany of low-level violence, including Dayak insurrections in the interior and, as in Bangka, revolts among Chinese miners resident in the region. The generally favorable political situation of southeastern Borneo was also contradicted by the lengthy revolt of the Chinese "river-rebel" Wangkang, which led to the taking of three hundred prisoners by the Dutch and the imprisonment of large numbers of these men after an inquiry had found them guilty of insurrection.

The disparities between these stated and actual levels of violence seem to show that violence and instability were still seen to be normal components of life in the border residencies, at least by certain people at this early date. This was largely true of the civil servants who wrote these reports and had to live in the outstations; they understood the limits of Dutch authority in the 1870s and 1880s. It was much less true of the government in Batavia, however, who with its own state-making project in mind received these reports and came to its own conclusions. The governor-general reported to the Ministry for the Colonies in The Hague that a worrying lack of safety prevailed in the Indies, and this state-ment, founded on the reports of residencies all along the border, was most probably correct.[46] Several kinds of spaces became zones in which chronic vio-lence and instability thrived in the Outer Islands. Areas along the Anglo/Dutch border were one of these places; the resident of western Borneo declared this openly, tying the frontier to robberies and murders that often occurred under his jurisdiction.[47] Truly outlying regions of only nominal Dutch authority, such as the long coasts off of New Guinea, were another of these spaces, as was reported when eighteen British subjects were mysteriously (and embarrass-ingly, to Batavia) killed there in early 1873.[48] Yet perhaps the most chronically violent space of all was not a space per se, but an occupation that existed in cer-tain spaces: mining. Mining colonies, whether Chinese gold-mining coopera-tives (*kongsis*) in Borneo or tin-mining cooperatives on Bangka and Belitung, were sites of continual trouble throughout the late nineteenth century. This was certainly true in the overextended Dutch sphere of influence and also true in British Malaya in the early 1870s. One need only read the frantic dispatches from Singapore to London in 1873, when heavily armed war junks from Macau were sailing all the way to Malaya to support rival Chinese tin-mining kongsis, to see the chaos mining caused nearby British administrators.[49]

Still more worrisome, from the vantage point of Batavia, especially, was that attacks and depredations in the Outer Islands were continually perpetrated against Europeans. The numbers of these attacks were never high. Yet a glance across many border residencies in the early 1870s shows their frequency: acts of defiance and violence were committed against Europeans fairly regularly, such depredations becoming known very quickly to the center. In Palembang in 1870, for example, wandering bands of men who had helped burn down a Dutch house at Muara Bliti were still at large, while in neighboring Jambi three years later a resident Sergeant Major van Kesteren was stabbed to death by a local man.[50] Further up the coast, in Asahan, a messenger sent by the local controleur into the interior was shot as he tried to deliver his letter; hit in the leg, he was left by the side of the road until he bled to death from his wounds.[51] Further east, a

European trader was murdered in Bali, also in 1873; here the perpetrators were Chinese, Buginese, and Balinese all working together, a fact that did not escape the notice of the resident of that place.[52] A European woman was killed on Banda, far to the east in the Dutch Indies possessions, while the assistant resident of Bengkulu, one of the most secure and long-standing areas of Dutch occupation in all of the Outer Islands, was nearly slain in the quiet dawn by people of his own regency. "I have the honor to report to Your Excellency," he said, "that at about 6 o'clock in the morning today an attempt was made—without favorable result—directly on my life." Though he had to flee his house in a nightrobe in disgrace, he eventually escaped unscathed—a condition, he noted in the postscript of his letter, that could not also be said for his belongings or his home.[53]

On the British side of the border in the early 1870s, conditions were little better. The vast complex of interests, actors, and profit that we have examined previously in the mining districts of the Malay Peninsula gave rise to continual instabilities in the 1860s and 70s, with all-out factional fighting over tin deposits and waterways finally serving as one of the excuses for the British Forward Movement in 1874. The Chinese dialect–groups that were so involved in these disputes and struggles for resources were also well connected with burgeoning British cities in the region, however, so that much of the violence spilled over into "secret society" fighting in the streets of Penang and Singapore.[54] Yet, as Cheah Boon Kheng has shown, banditry as a socioeconomic phenomenon was endemic and widespread in large parts of the peninsula, making travel and contact across open lands severely circumscribed, at times, by bands of men preying on anyone they could find.[55] The fact that most Malay males of the time did not leave home without having several weapons on their person is an indication of these instabilities, but often it was the agents of elites, like the *budak raja* bodyguards of local sultans and rajas, who inspired the most fear of so-called lawless behavior among peasants in the region.[56] When Wilfred Birch, the first British resident in Perak, was killed by local Malays in November of 1875, policymakers in the Straits decided they had seen enough. Expansion and England's own brand of compulsory exactions markedly increased after that.[57]

Across the southern terminus of the South China Sea in British Borneo, similar conditions of chronic violence were commonplace in the 1860s and 1870s. James Warren and Ulla Wagner have shown how various Bornean peoples acted and reacted within a radically changing forest landscape, as economic trade routes, interethnic rivalry for resources, and the expanding reach of colonial states combined to form a heightened landscape of competition in Borneo.[58] Culturally contested complexes around head-hunting and the protection of economically valuable resources such as birds' nest caves lay behind much of the shifting violence of the period, argue these two scholars. Low-level systemic violence could also be seen in other dimensions, however. Kidnapping and the "robbing of men" from their environs was one of these forms, as the slaving practices of various indigenous groups came under sharp attack by colonial authorities in the region.[59] Outright robbery and murder of traders laden down with commercial goods on the rivers of Borneo were other common occurrences, especially among Chinese merchants who were relatively powerless in the interior when faced with the threat of force. When the governor of Labuan was able to compel the sultan of Brunei to execute one of the worst perpetrators of this sort of crime against Chinese traders in 1871, it was the first time in over a century that one of the sultans there had agreed to such punishment, for the "mere crime" of killing a few innocent Chinese.[60] The archives are littered with instances of violence of this sort against Chinese traders, three heads taken here, four there, in various parts of British Borneo. In at least one of these cases the Malay perpetrators of such crimes claimed that rival Chinese factions to the Chinese who were murdered ordered the killings, though there is no way to prove if these assertions were correct.[61]

Last, Europeans were also common perpetrators of violence on a day-to-day basis, as the letters and depositions of various sultans and Chinese traders in the region reveal. Indeed, among the many ethnic actors in Borneo in the 1870s, the Spanish appear to have been among the most merciless in performing acts of violence against those who opposed them. In this case, the offending parties in Spanish eyes were smugglers, or anyone who tried to break their commercial blockades in the Sulu Sea north of Borneo. The ramming of innocent trading craft by Spanish steamers and their razing of coastal villages also contributed to a lawless atmosphere in the region, in this case perpetrated by one of the self-described guardians of law and public order.[62] The British and Dutch were also seen by local peoples as perpetrators of chronic, everyday violence in various parts of the archipelago. Statements about these depredations in the form of written records by local actors are relatively rare, however, and were not actively collected by either of the two powers. Yet it is clear that Europeans and Asians saw violent intent and violent action in each other, and that these conditions were viewed as commonplace and as part of the natural way of things. What had changed, however, was that by the middle decades of the nineteenth century Europeans were trying to change the underlying structures of politics and trade in the archipelago in ways that had never been attempted before. This was happening not only on the Anglo/Dutch frontier in the island world, but also on the mainland in various other parts of Southeast Asia as well.[63]

These conditions of systemic violence led both Singapore and especially Batavia to worry greatly about the effects of illegal trade, especially in commodities such as firearms. Batavia's concerns on this question were particularly pronounced, as even by the 1880s and 1890s random violence had not been eradicated from Java, let alone the border residencies. A series of articles in the *Indische Gids* makes this clear. Even in the 1880s, the Dutch were having trouble controlling the core areas of their authority on the island, as potential conflagrations sprung up all over Java, from Surabaya to Batavia. On the eastern third of the island in 1886, an armed band of seventy men set a district head's house on fire outside of Madiun, escaping into the night: the local police patrol of twelve men hid during the incident, and only a fraction of the perpetrators were eventually caught and brought to trial.[64] In central Java, "conspiratorial" religious and political meetings were taking place throughout various residencies in 1888, prompting police roundups and detentions of many Javanese, the leaders of whom were accused of inciting nativist rebellions to overthrow Dutch authority.[65] In western Java, around Banten, the violence and instability were far more serious in 1888. European hostages were taken by armed crowds of Muslim "radicals," and many of them, including an assistant resident, a salt caretaker, a town mayor, and members of their immediate families, were eventually killed. The *Indische Gids* furiously upbraided the government for not having an idea of what had caused these riots, as well as for Batavia's inability to deal with those involved in an organized (and efficacious) fashion.[66]

The violence practiced by Dutchmen against the local populations of the Indies far exceeded the reverse, of course. This is easily proven on a panarchipelago scale. Yet the border residencies were continually deemed unsafe by the Dutch, even if by the end of the century certain places began to exhibit less and less outright violent crime. In western Borneo attempts on the life of controleurs in outlying areas, like the one made upon E. F. G. Lorrain in Sanggau (1890), still occurred, while in eastern Borneo the "veiligheid van goederen en personen" (safety of goods and people) was still considered to be fairly poor by the resident, with head-hunting, robberies, and murder still existing in the lands not yet under direct control.[67] Across the border in the British possessions in Borneo, systemic low-level violence also continued in peripheral areas. Chinese sago collectors working in upriver Brunei preyed on Malay traders from Sarawak when they could, and armed bands from the British North Borneo Company's dominions attacked Brunei settlements on occasion, murdering Chinese villagers and Dayak policemen in the process.[68] It is apparent, therefore, that instability accompanied by armed violence was still fairly normal in large parts of the border arc, even in the last decades of the 1800s. Other residencies, however, saw some of the most serious sorts of crimes begin to diminish, as Dutch authority seeped into the villages and made a discernable impact on the ground. In Riau, for example, which included administratively not just the islands south of Singapore, but also wide swaths of the East Sumatra coast, murders and armed insurrection decreased over the course of the late 1880s. Killings, arson, and piracy were being replaced by the crimes of a more sedentary, effectively policed residency: petty theft, disorderly conduct, and the like.[69]

In keeping with the concept of certain spaces in which low-level violence was able to continue even after the turn of the twentieth century, however, it is important to note that the general trend of instability diminishing over time in the border arc did not reach all places equally or at the same time. Certain stretches of the frontier remained more troublesome than others, Batavia in particular singling out these places as areas where special surveillance should be employed against the importation of contraband such as illegal firearms (fig. 5). In Sumatra, unpacified uplands (*hulu*) were among these liminal spaces, as in the Gangsal area of Indragiri in 1905, where several policemen were murdered by roving bands from Jambi.[70] Acehnese resistance fighters also periodically attacked Sumatra's East Coast Residency in 1904, taking advantage of the relative quiet and lax security of that neighboring administration, while outlying villagers resisted heavy corvée duties in parts of Lampung by burning down the houses of local officials.[71] Other spaces of chronic violence existed besides the "untamed hills," borders of Aceh, and remote flatlands of Sumatra, however. On Belitung, Chinese miners fought raging battles among themselves even into the twentieth century, with the police often "not in a state to interfere" until reinforcements could be ordered from outside the regency.[72] And in Borneo, the boundary with British possessions was used as a buffer space for indigenous raiding parties, as Dayaks on both sides of the frontier made lightning stabs into Dutch and British territory and then beat a hasty retreat back across the border.[73] Low-level violence was able to survive well into the twentieth century, therefore, in certain generic spaces and places. Singapore and Batavia had laid claim to most of the lowlands and important waterways by 1915, but the hills, swamps, and forests continued to be sites in which guns, resistance, and dissenting ideas managed to continue circulating. The civilizing project of the state could still be challenged from afar.

Although it is tempting to believe much colonial literature of the period that described Southeast Asia as a domesticated paradise wholly under European control, the realities of the situation were usually more complicated. It certainly

Fig. 5. Dutch armed sloops heading upriver into Aceh, 1893. (Photo Courtesy KITLV, Leiden)

was true that Western telegraphs and steamships criss-crossed the border territories by 1915, linking Batavia and Singapore with their far-flung frontiers. It was also true there was quantitatively less piracy in these regions, and less of what the Dutch called systemic "uncontrolled violence," in the turn-of-the-century lands and seas of the border arc as well. Yet there remained unease among Europeans, and particularly among Dutchmen, about how stable and controlled the boundary zone really had become. Even after the fin de siècle, Batavia worried that violence was all too possible along the outstretched frontier and that this violence was abetted by the continuing movement of men and matériel across the border. Violence in these locales was real to some degree, as is shown by many acts and events in the historical record. Yet it was also always part of a Western narrative that was constructed about the frontier, one that saw such violence as a vestigial artifact of recently conquered space. The transgression of this frontier—that is, the survival of wild space—can be usefully examined through the lens of the most important single phenomenon challenging the integrity of the border: smuggling. A boundary had been built between local colonial spheres in Southeast Asia, but in the decades around the turn of the twentieth century, smuggling continually threatened to tear it down.

NOTES

1. See the arguments put forward in Rabinow, *French Modern* (1989).
2. Parts of this section have been condensed and previously argued in Tagliacozzo, "Kettle on a Slow Boil" (2000), 70–100.
3. See Kniphorst, multivolume, in *Tijdschrift Zeewezen* "Historische Schets van den Zee-rof" (1876) 3; "Inleiding" (1876), 48; "De Bewoners van den Oost-Indischen Archipel" (1876), 159; "Oorsprong and Ontwikkeling van den Zeeroof" (1876), 195, 283; "Philippij-nsche Eilanden en Noordelijk Borneo" (1876), 353, and (1877), 1; "De Moluksche Eilan-den en Nieuw-Guinea" (1877), 135, 237; "Timorsche Wateren" (1878), 1; "Celebes en On-derhoorigheden" (1878), 107, 213; "Sumatra" (1879), 1, 85; "Het Maleische Schiereiland" (1879), 173; "Riouw en Onderhoorigheden" (1880), 1; "Banka en Billiton" (1880), 89; "Borneo's Oost-, Zuid- en West-Kust" (1880); also Raffles, *Memoir of the Life* (1835), and Brooke, *Narrative of Events* (1848).
4. See Lapian, "The Sealords of Berau and Mindanao" (1974), 143–54; Trocki, *Prince of Pi-rates* (1979); Anderson, "Piracy in Eastern Seas" (1997), 87–115; and Gullick, "The Kuala Langkat Piracy Trial" (1996), 101–14. These somewhat supercede Tarling, *Piracy and Pol-itics in the Malay World* (1963), and Rutter, *The Pirate Wind* (1986), which has primary ac-counts of an earlier age. The best single study is still Warren, *The Sulu Zone* (1981).
5. See Dian Murray's work on the South China/Vietnamese coasts of the turn of the nine-teenth century, in her *Pirates of the South China Coast* (1987), esp. 17 passim; see also Rediker, "The Seaman as Pirate" (2001), 139–68; Starkey, "Pirates and Markets" (2001), 107–24; Anderson, "Piracy and World History" (2001), 82–106, and Nadal, "Corsairing as a Commercial System" (2001), 125–36. The activities of various European nations' shipping (English, Dutch, Spanish, etc.) can easily be described as being piratical during this time period as well. For an indigenous account of piracy in the region (albeit focus-ing primarily on the first half of the nineteenth century), see Matheson and Andaya, trans., *The Precious Gift (Tuhfat al-Nafis)* (1982).
6. Kniphorst, "Inleiding" (1876), 39–41.
7. Kniphorst, "Oorsprong and Ontwikkeling van den Zeeroof" (1876), 159 passim.
8. James Brooke to Viscount Palmerston, 13 Sept. 1848 and 6 March 1849, CO 144/3.
9. Herman Merivale to H. V. Addington, 16 Feb. 1850, CO 144/3.
10. Translation of letter by the Sultan of Sulu to Gov Pope Hennessey (Labuan), no date, CO 144/28; translation of letter by the Sultan of Brunei to Gov Pope Hennessey, 19 Sept. 1868, CO 144/28. The sultan of Brunei was much more willing to help in these projects of suppression, generally.
11. ANRI, Maandrapport der Residentie Riouw 1873 (Riouw no. 66/2: July); "Verslag Omtrent den Zeeroof" (1877), 475.
12. Kruijt, *Atjeh en de Atjehers* (1877); Captain Woolcombe to Vice Admiral Shadwell, China Station, 6 Sept. 1873, no. 38, PRO/Admiralty 125/140; "Rajah Abdulah Mohamat Shah ibn Almarhome Sulatan Japahar to the Chinese Chiefs of the Sening Tew Chew and the Tew Chew Factions of the Chinese at Larut," 8 Aug. 1873, PRO/Admiralty 125/140.
13. Rear Admiral Sir F. Collier to Secretary Admiralty, 4 Sept. 1849, CO 144/3; ANRI, Poli-tiek Verslag Residentie Borneo Zuid-Oost 1871 (no. 4/1).

14. See "Rajah Abdullah Muhammad Shah to the Chinese Chiefs of the Sening Tew Chew at Larut," 11 Aug. 1873, in PRO/Admiralty/125/no. 148.

15. ANRI, Maandrapport Residentie Banka 1871 (no. 97/4: April).

16. Kruijt, *Atjeh,* 169.

17. Gov. Ord, Straits, to Earl Kimberley, 9 May 1873, no. 253, PRO/Admiralty 125/148; Gov. Labuan to Earl of Kimberley, 6 Nov. 1872, no. 76, CO 144/38.

18. ARA, 1871, MR no. 301; ARNAS, Maandrapport der Residentie Palembang, 1871 (Palembang no. 74/9: April).

19. Kniphorst, "Vervolg der Historische Schets van den Zeerof" (1882), 340.

20. ANRI, Politiek Verslag Residentie Banka 1871 (no. 124).

21. ARA, Report of Marsaoleh Tenaloga, Chief of Bone, Including Transcript of his Interview with Amina, Woman Who Escaped Tobelo Pirates (18 March, 1876) in 1876, MR no. 624.

22. Capt. Woolcombe to Vice-Admiral Shadwell, China Station, 6 Sept. 1873, no. 38; Capt., HMS *Midge* to Capt. Woolcombe on the *Thalia,* 20 Aug 1873, both in PRO/Admiralty 125/148.

23. ANRI, Maandrapport Residentie Banka 1871 (no. 97/5: July); Parkinson, *Trade in the Eastern Seas* (1937), 348.

24. Statement of W. C. Cowie to Act. Gov. Treacher, 4 May 1879, CO 144/52.

25. ANRI, Maandrapport Residentie Banka 1871 (no. 97/5: July).

26. Gov Treacher to Senior Naval Officer, Straits, 12 June 1879, CO 144/52.

27. Woolcombe to Shadwell, 6 Sept. 1873, no. 38, PRO/Admiralty 125/148.

28. Capt. Grant of HMS *Midge* to Capt. Woolcombe on the *Thalia,* 11 Sept. 1873, PRO/Admiralty 125/148; Kniphorst, "Historische Schets van den Zeerof" (1879), 224.

29. ANRI, Politiek Verslag Residentie Borneo Zuid-Oost 1872 (no. 4/2); ANRI, Maandrapport Residentie Borneo Zuid-Oost 1871 (no. 10a/6: May).

30. See the testimonials of Joo In Tek and Too Ah On (4 and 5 April 1876) to the superintendent of police, Penang, in Consul Lavino to Governor General of the NEI, April 13, 1876, Confidential no. 921G, which is enclosed in Kommissoriaal, 3 May 1876, no. 332az. See also Lt. Gov. Anson (Penang) to Consul Lavino, 6 May 1876, no. 858/76 Police, which is enclosed in Kommissoriaal, 15 June 1976, no. 458az. Both in ANRI, no. 13 ("Stukken Betreffende Atjehsche Oorlog"), 1876, no. 235–469 series.

31. ARA, Resident Probolingo to GGNEI, 20 March 1873, #977, in MR #204.

32. For punishments against piracy, as well as legal competencies of Dutch captains against piratical craft, see *Indische Staatsblad* 1876, no. 279, and 1877, no. 181, respectively. See also the contract closed with the Sultanate of Riau about piracy on 26 Jan. 1888 in *Surat Surat Perdjandjian Riau* (1970), 205 passim.

33. See, for example, "Zeeroof," *IWvhR,* no. 1056, 24 Sept. 1883, 155–56; "Zeerof," *IWvhR,* no. 1609, 30 April 1894, 70–71; and "Zeerof," *IWvhR,* no. 1800, 27 Dec. 1897, 208.

34. See the statements of Dungin and Nauduah enclosed in W. C. Cowie to Act. Gov. Treacher, 2 June 1879, CO 144/52.

35. ARA, Resident Riouw to GGNEI (22 April 1881, no. 823) in 1881, MR no. 396; also Resident East Coast Sumatra to GGNEI (10 Aug. 1885, no. 523) in 1885, MR no. 523.

36. See Gov. Leys, Labuan to FO, 30 Jan. 1882, and the jacket enclosing this letter, CO 144/56. The Crown did not own these lands at any point previous to the company's title, but

London was constantly preoccupied with geostrategic considerations vis-à-vis Spain and Germany. The company's firm lease on the lands and the treaties signed between the European powers ended much of London's anxiety on the issue.

37. ARA, 1894, MR no. 289.

38. ARA, Executive Secretary Philippine Islands (Thomas Cary Welch) to Dutch Consul, Manila (PKA Meerkamp van Embden), 13 May 1910, Telegram (MvBZ/A/277/A.134).

39. ARA, Louis Mallet for Sir Edward Grey, FO to MvBZ, The Hague, 4 Nov. 1909, no. 1927; and Dutch Consul, London to MvBZ, The Hague, 6 July 1909, no. 1900/1203 (MvBZ/A/277/A.134).

40. For the Javanese case, see "Regeling van Rechtsgebied: Zeerof," *IWvhR*, no. 2030, 26 May 1902, 81–83; for the Singapore case, see "The King vs. Chia Kuek Chin and Others," *SSLR* 13, 1915, 1.

41. "Perompak-Perompak di Laut Johore," *Utusan Malayu*, 17 April 1909, no. 223, 3.

42. *Utusan Malayu*, 19 Dec. 1907, no. 19, p. 1–2.

43. For analogues of the kinds of violence under discussion here, see Abdullah, "Dari Sejarah Lokal" (1987), 232–55, but especially page 234 on Jambi and Sultan Taha; George, *Showing Signs of Violence* (1996) for western Sulawesi; Robinson, *The Dark Side of Paradise* (1995), chap. 2; and the essays in Hoskins, ed., *Headhunting and the Social Imagination* (1996), for headhunting and colonial control around the archipelago. For a comparison of these processes in India, see Irschick, "Order and Disorder in Colonial South India" (1989), 459–92.

44. ANRI, Politiek Verslag Residentie Banka 1870 (no. 123); ANRI, Politiek Verslag Residentie West Borneo 1870 (no. 2/8); ANRI, Politiek Verslag Residentie Borneo Zuid-Oost 1871 (no. 4/1).

45. ANRI, Maandrapport Residentie Palembang 1871 (no. 74/9: May). "Except for several irregularities of unclear origin . . . which are presently being looked into, peace and order were not disturbed in the past month."

46. ARA, 1872, MR no. 24.

47. ANRI, Algemeen Verslag Residentie West Borneo 1874 (no. 5/4).

48. ARA, 1873, "Kort Verslag van de Stand van Zaken, en van Personeel in de Residentie Ternate over de Maand Maart, 1873—Bijzondere Gebeurtenissen." in 1873, MR no. 257.

49. Gov. SS to Earl Kimberley, 24 July 1873, no. 216, PRO/Admiralty 125/148.

50. ANRI, Maandrapport Residentie Palembang 1870 (no. 74/8: May); ARA, Resident Palembang to GGNEI (5 April 1873, no. 1798/6) in 1873, MR no. 281.

51. ANRI, Maandrapport Residentie Riouw 1870 (no. 66/2: April).

52. ARA, Resident Banjoewangi to GGNEI (23 Feb. 1873, no. 20) in 1873, MR no. 138.

53. ARA, 1873, MR no. 337; and Asst. Res. Benkoelen to GGNEI (18 April 1873, no. 983) in 1873, MR no. 262. Accounts of violence against Europeans were given far more careful scrutiny and attention than "internecine" attacks between indigenes, so that the paper trail for the former is disproportionately large in the European historical record.

54. Gov SS to Earl Kimberley, 24 July 1873, no. 216, PRO/Admiralty 125/148.

55. See Cheah, *The Peasant Robbers of Kedah* (1988).

56. Swettenham, *The Real Malay: Pen Pictures* (1900), 24–25; Innes, *The Chersonese with the Gilding Off* (1885), 182.

57. Birch's journals of life in Perak have been published in Burns, ed., *The Journal of J. W. W. Birch* (1976).

58. See James Warren's *Sulu Zone,* esp. chap. 6; also Wagner, *Colonialism and Iban Warfare* (1972).

59. See, for example, FO to CO, 2 Aug. 1864, and CO to Gov Labuan, 4 Aug. 1864, both in CO 144/23.

60. Gov. Labuan to CO, 10 Aug. 1871, no. 29, CO 144/34. Also see the *Sarawak Gazette,* 4 March 1879 and 27 Sept. 1883, for notices of Sarawak subjects being killed in Dutch Sambas.

61. See the testimony provided in Report of Pangiran Anak Dampit, Pangiran Anak Besar, and Pangiran Mahomet Jappar, Ordered by the Sultan of Brunei, A.H. 1284, 14 Jamadawal, in CO 144/26.

62. The sultan of Sulu, in a neat piece of historiographic reversal, said of the Spanish, "They are more like pirates, stealing boats and men and spoiling the goods." See Sultan of Sulu to Gov Labuan, 26 Samadil Akhir 1290 A.M., CO 144/41; Testimony Before Gov. Treacher (Labuan) of Tong Kang, Former Supercargo of the *Sultana,* CO 144/45; and Señor Calderon Collantes to Mr. Layard, 4 Jan. 1877, CO 144/49. The Spanish Crown was only partially apologetic for such appropriations. Of course, there were also Spanish victims as well as perpetrators of this kind of violence.

63. For an analysis of these patterns in regard to Burma and Siam over the course of the nineteenth century, see Eric Tagliacozzo, "Ambiguous Commodities, Unstable Frontiers" (2004): 354–377.

64. "Poeloong-Zaak" (1886), 231.

65. "Officieel Relaas Omtrent Samenzweringen" (1888), 1992; "Officieele Relaas van de Ongeregelheden in Solo" (1889), 216.

66. "Onlusten in Bantam," *IG* (1888): 1122; "Officieel Relaas van de Onlusten te Tjilegon" (1889), 1768.

67. ANRI, Algemeen Verslag Residentie West Borneo 1890 (no. 5/21); ANRI, Algemeen Verslag Residentie Borneo Zuid-Oost 1890 (no. 9a/11).

68. Rajah Sarawak to Consul Trevenen (Brunei), 12 April 1892, CO 144/69.

69. ANRI, Algemeen Verslag Residentie Riouw 1890 (no. 64/1–2). This was also the case in Johor and Kelantan; see *Johore Annual Report,* 1916, 16, and *Kelantan Annual Report,* 1916, 9.

70. ARA, Asst. Res. Deli to GGNEI, 12 March 1904, Telegram no. 117 (Sumatra O.K., fiche no. 156) (MvK, PVBB).

71. ARA, 1906, MR no. 634, 711, 828 (Riouw, fiche no. 296) (MvK, PVBB); MR 1906/07, no. 1054, 1352, 1629 (Lampongs, fiche no. 386) (MvK, PVBB).

72. ARA, Asst. Resident Billiton to GGNEI, Feb. Verslag, 18 March 1911, (Banka, fiche no. 389) (MvK, PVBB).

73. ARA, NF Deshon (Officer Administering Sarawak Gov't in Absence of the Raja) to Resident, West Borneo, 21 April 1904, no. F 12/04 (no. 394); Resident, Borneo Southeast to GGNEI, 22 May 1909 (April 1909 Report) (Borneo Z.O., fiche no. 477) (MvK, PVBB).

Chapter 6 "Foreign Asians"
on the Frontier

Beyond the threats to Dutch legitimacy and "order" that piracy and uncontrolled violence presented on the frontier, Batavia worried about another potentially dangerous entity: Foreign Asians, or the *Vreemde Oosterlingen*. The Dutch Indies was home to a number of ethnic actors subsumed under this category. Chinese populations of various compositions, Japanese populations, and foreign Muslims, usually Arabs or Turks from the Persian Gulf or Middle East, were among the most important of these suspect peoples. Batavia and The Hague constantly worried about the potential disruption these Asians might cause by their smuggling of opium, counterfeit currency, and large quantities of illegal arms across the boundary. One of the main reasons for their concern was very straightforward: there were extremely few Dutchmen in the Indies compared to the combined populations of these ethnic groups, a ratio that was even more exaggerated outside Java, in the outlying lands of the border residencies. In western Borneo in 1870, for example, there were only 207 Europeans in the entire residency, 60 of whom were adult men, compared to 24,000 Chinese and a population of Dayaks approaching 250,000. In southeastern Borneo, the comparative numbers were even more lopsided, according to statistics reported by the resident there in 1871. On the islands of Bangka and in Riau, the figures were roughly similar for the early 1870s: 63 European men on Bangka compared to almost 19,000 Chinese and over 40,000 Malays; 123 Europeans on Riau, against a population of 25,000 Malays and over 30,000 Chinese.[1] Palembang in Sumatra and even Singapore itself reproduced these general ratios.[2] The Dutch, ostensible masters of a vastly overextended island colonial empire in 1865, gathered these statistics and were alarmed by what they saw. What were these Foreign Asians doing on the frontier? How were they to be controlled?

Batavia's worries are apparent in various legislative actions taken in the colony to try to neutralize the potential threat Foreign Asians represented. In general, Foreign Asians were conceptually grouped and then dealt with as a common problem. One of the most telling ways this was done was in the restrictions Batavia placed on the movements of these populations, what came to be broadly known as the Pass Laws. Chinese especially were assigned residence requirements in urban areas (*wijken*) and could not leave these domains without a pass. The idea was to keep tabs on their influence and movements in the Indies, with protection of the indigenous peoples of the archipelago a corollary part of the argument.[3] The pass system lasted in one form or another for almost a century (from 1816 to 1914), though its effectiveness varied from place to place. A second broad measure attempted by the Dutch had to do with bookkeeping. Vreemde Oosterlingen were told to keep copies of their commercial records in languages comprehensible to the state. Much of the impetus behind this move seems to have come from large Dutch financial concerns like the Javasche Bank and the Nederlandsch-Indische Handelsbank, institutions that were often on the losing end of Chinese bankruptcies that might have been avoided had debtors' books been examined and understood.[4] Yet the state saw its own interests involved in this issue as well, as there was a conviction that "the Foreign Asian is a master in hiding and obscuring goods; spouses, children, good friends and neighbors all work towards this, and it is extremely difficult for the European. . . . to control."[5] Carefully altered account books in languages that Batavia could barely understand were not compatible with the Dutch state-making project. This was especially so if the classes of goods being hidden included opium and currency, which threatened the colonial economy, or guns, which threatened the viability of the Dutch Indies, period. A decree of 1865 stated that Foreign Asian record keeping had to be in a European language or Rumi (Romanized Malay), besides the original language of use (Chinese,

Arabic, etc.). The Indies legal community in particular thought this to be crucial, or Batavia would be powerless in the face of such men.[6]

A last aspect of Foreign Asians as a conceptual category was how they were treated under Indies law. For several centuries before the middle of the nineteenth century, religion had been the hallmark upon which Dutch Indies law had been based: Christians were Christians in Dutch East India Company lands no matter what their ethnicity, and this categorization mattered more than anything else under existing legal codes. By 1854, however, this state of affairs no longer held: article no. 109 of the Regeeringsregelment (government stipulations) that year set up a new distinction based upon race, so that Europeans occupied one category under jurisprudence and "Natives" (that is, Malays, Buginese, Javanese, etc.), another.[7] Foreign Asians were equated under the law with "Natives," not Europeans. Yet in keeping with the policies of a government that wished to rule over these Asian populations, while at the same time using them to their advantage when it was convenient to do so, Foreign Asians were actually only grouped under the same *public* law as "Natives" (for example, criminal law). *Private* and *commercial* law saw Vreemde Oosterlingen as Europeans. The reason for the distinction was purely practical from Batavia's point of view: the Dutch found it much easier to do business with Foreign Asians under Dutch civil and commercial law than under a separate public law, which would have impeded efficiency.[8] I examine arrangements of this sort in chapters 8 and 10, where government relations with opium farmers and coolie brokers, respectively, are discussed. The decision to legally bifurcate the Vreemde Oosterlingen is interesting because it shows their dual nature in the eyes of the state: a population to be feared and controlled under one set of discriminatory laws, but to be engaged for commercial profit under another set altogether. This complex legal situation of Foreign Asians in the Indies seems to have mirrored their status in general. As both compradors and suspects of the state, Vreemde Oosterlingen were a people apart.[9]

CHINESE POPULATIONS IN COLONIAL MINDS

Far and away the largest population of Foreign Asians in the Indies were Chinese. Chinese migrants and settlers had been coming to Southeast Asia for centuries by the 1860s: Carl Trocki has proposed a periodization of these travels which starts in the early seventeenth century, when the first large-scale communities of Chinese settled in cities like Manila, Ayutthaya, and Batavia.[10] Many of the Chinese were involved in trade, and they became a crucial part of the fabric of colonial societies, driving both retail and wholesale commerce while integrating themselves into the burgeoning cities. The establishment of *kongsis* (Chinese cooperatives) based on mining and agriculture started soon after this; the late eighteenth and early nineteenth-centuries were the golden age of these semi-independent polities. By the middle third of the nineteenth century, however, multiplying European colonies were attracting more of the passengers of the junk trade, rivaling the kongsis as destinations for the majority of Chinese migrants. The kongsis, especially the powerful confederations in western Borneo that had built their own roads, defenses, waterworks, and foreign policies, eventually lost out to European power on both sides of the Straits.[11] Hokkien, Teochew, Hainanese, and Cantonese sojourners were still spread out all over the archipelago, but they increasingly came under the authority and auspices of expanding colonial states. Despite this, as late as 1891 the great Leiden Sinologist J. J. M. de Groot lamented the lack of European knowledge about the Chinese: "Their train of thought, their internal lives, their religion, morals, and customs, the ancestral practices which are the chief driving force of all they do—all of this is still a closed book for us."[12]

The Chinese were seen another way by a good deal of the local Dutch population. Unlike the professed ignorance of the Sinologist de Groot, popular attitudes about the Chinese and their place in the Indies were sometimes very fearful and were becoming more negative over time. Much of this had to do with the increasing flow of *singkeh* (newcomers, usually laborers) who began to stream down to Southeast Asia in large numbers in the latter decades of the nineteenth century. "Yellow Peril" sentiments that were slowly gaining credence across the Straits were mimicked by a similar term in Dutch, *Gele Gevaar* (the translation is approximately the same.) So-called experts such as the inspector of agriculture on Java spread venom about the role of Chinese in impoverishing the indigenous population, while other, more generalized accounts called the Indies Chinese "thieves, falsifiers, and the perpetrators of a thousand other dishonorable acts."[13] One journal spoke of the *Chineezenplaag,* or "Chinese plague," that was said to be afflicting the Indies, while others asserted that "the dangers [presented by the Chinese] are certainly not imaginary—already now men should be questioning what the future holds, and how to do something about it."[14] The "unwished-for interference" of China in the affairs of Chinese residents in the Indies formed part of the substrate to this debate, so that even Dutch papers back in the Netherlands fiercely declared, "It may not be tolerated that a foreign power on the grounds of fellowship of language or origin . . . comes meddling in our internal affairs."[15] The real basis of such contempt and negativity, however, seems above all to have been fear, as the Dutch worried where the evolution of China proper might lead. "It would be good for men to see China clearly" the *Algemeen Handelsblad* reported in 1907, "as it should be seen after several decades: as a more or less closed community of related people, which will have undergone a great change in the coming decades, now that the rivers and coasts of China have been opened to trade, and unity has been spoken of."[16]

Were these fears of the Chinese justified? Did Chinese populations in the Indies present a threat to the well-being of the state? While it was true that Chinese were disproportionately involved in trade and commerce in the Indies during these years, at least as compared to indigenous populations—a situation that was indeed legislated and partially brought about by the Dutch themselves—most Chinese lived under conditions that were anything but threatening to Batavia. In Java, many Chinese took on the occupation of *klontong,* or wandering itinerant merchants, selling small goods out of sacks slung over their shoulders. In western Borneo, as one chronicler reported, many Chinese simply led lives of fishing, trapping, and farming, more or less integrating themselves into local rural life.[17] Far less lucky in totality, according to reports in Chinese newspapers in Singapore like the *Nanyang Chung Wei Pao.* were Chinese working in the mines of border residency locales like Bangka.[18] Here, as revealed in letters to the editor by witnesses who observed the depredations, coolies were sometimes beaten to death and certainly exploited; even Dutch reports told of fires, floods, and suicides among the miners, who labored under such circumstances for years.[19] In the open landscapes of Borneo conditions were often not much better for the Chinese. The surviving testimonies of Chinese women tell of husbands being attacked and killed for their goods, while local Malays or Dayaks, if they thought they could get away with it, sometimes plundered whole villages comprised of these migrants.[20] Chinese in all of these contexts were clearly not a threat to the development of colonial states. In fact, many Chinese of the border residencies were too busy feuding and competing with each other to pay much attention to any project of concerted political subversion.[21]

Yet the state did not see all Chinese in this light. Certain categories of Chinese made Batavia nervous, for a variety of reasons. One of the foremost among these categories was secret societies, or *geheime genootschappen,* which were found throughout Malaya and the Indies but seemed to be particularly prevalent along the border. A report on a Chinese secret society document linking the east coast of Sumatra with Penang was published by the Sinologist M.

Schaalje in 1873: the diploma refers to Penang as the headquarters of the Sumatra society, a prospect of cross-Straits unity that alarmed Batavia greatly[22] (fig.
6, top). Ten years later, another article was published on secret society documents found in Borneo: at issue this time were a small book and a scroll of red
Chinese paper. The book was described as an extract from one of the standard
texts of the Heaven and Earth Society. It related how the sect had spread from
China to a place in Malay waters known as Baan-saan. The scroll, which was interpreted to be a Ghee Hin Kongsi contribution request from members, placed
the locality of the society at Sik-Ka-Iam, which was transcribed as being in all
probability Sekayam, a river in the subdistrict Sanggau of western Borneo (fig.
6, bottom).[23] The existence of such documents for West Borneo established
proof of what the Dutch were already noting in their residency reports. Chinese
secret societies were highly active in the residency, taking part, for example, in
such operations as smuggling opium back and forth across the Borneo border,
a contraband trade that deprived the Batavia exchequer of huge sums of
money.[24] For this reason, the Dutch kept an eye on developments across the
Straits of Melaka as well to see how the British were faring in their own struggles against Chinese secret societies in the Straits Settlements and in places such
as Perak.[25]

 Geheim genootschappen were not the only threat the Dutch perceived emanat-
ing from their Chinese populations. Also disturbing to Batavia were the ways in
which the Chinese navigated the Indies legal system as well as their status as potential subjects of a new and dynamic Chinese state after 1911. Maneuvering
within the restrictive Indies legal system was something the Chinese managed
to do throughout the period under discussion. Tricks like jumping between the
different legal spheres of Java and the border residencies to avoid prosecution in
the former and borrowing travel passes under assumed names to travel in the
latter were strategies Chinese employed for years.[26] Smugglers seem to have
been particularly adept at these plans. More disturbing, however, and potentially far more destructive in Batavia's view, were the increasing demands of
China and many Indies Chinese to be classified as Chinese subjects rather than
Dutch subjects. This was a question that occupied some of the best Dutch legal
minds of the late nineteenth century, including Siberius Trip, C. P. K. Winckel,
and G. von Faber.[27] When an official Chinese-language letter from Peking arrived in The Hague in 1886 informing the Dutch that Chinese in the Indies
should be considered Chinese subjects and not under Dutch jurisdiction, the
minister for the colonies was aghast.[28] He instructed the Dutch consul in
Peking to say nothing of the nationality of the Indies Chinese but only to refer

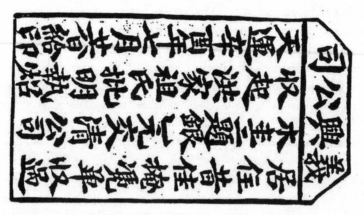

Fig. 6. Chinese secret society documents: Sumatra/Penang (top) and Borneo (bottom). (*Sources:* Schaalje, "Bijdrage tot de Kennis" (1873) 20, p. 1–6, and Young, "Bijdrage tot de Kennis" (1883) 28, pp. 547, 551–52, 574–77.

to them as subjects. By the early twentieth century, however, this question was becoming so urgent that Dutch consuls in Washington, Berlin, and London were being requested to report back to The Hague immediately on what efforts other Western governments were making in dealing with the problem.[29]

The fall of the Ch'ing Dynasty and the emergence of the Chinese Republic in 1911–12 brought matters to the boiling point in the space of a few months. Pressure had already been building in several forms. With Peking's direct assistance, Chinese Indies organizations started to pattern their schools on Chinese models, Chinese Chambers of Commerce were invited to take part in the electing of delegates to the Chinese Provincial Assemblies in 1910, and there were even Indies Chinese trying to raise the new Republican flag in the Indies, shortly after the revolution in 1912.[30] All of these moves were seen by many policymakers in Batavia as more or less direct challenges to Dutch rule. Matters got even more complicated when the Chinese envoy Chao Ch'ung Fan visited the Indies on what was called a study tour in 1911 and made several public speeches, including one to a Chinese organization in Surabaya. In the address, he informed the audience they could count on the Chinese government's protection and encouraged them to make as much money as possible, thereby contributing to the unifying cause of the Chinese motherland.[31] The officer for Chinese affairs in Surabaya, H. J. F. Borel, informed the Indies Ministry of Justice that despite pre-trip assurances to the contrary, Chao had delivered a royal message, and that the speech was not just to the trade body but was open to the Indies Chinese public at large, and was so advertised.[32] The governor-general was furious and wrote that Chao had hidden the true intentions of his visit, while proceeding to stir up Chinese sentiments toward greater racial unity.[33] Chinese-language newspapers in the Indies, however, saw the events leading up to and after 1911 as tokens of a new Golden Age. The Surabaya press, for example, reported excitedly on the pressures leading to the dismantling of the pass system for Chinese, letting its readers know they could soon travel unhindered through the length of the Dutch Indies.[34] The Batavia papers were even more provocative in their delight, joking that with the abolition of the pass system opium would be easier to smuggle and taxes more thoroughly evaded.[35] The combination of all of these issues—raised flags, schools being erected, Indies Chinese representation in Peking politics, and the visit of Chinese envoys to cheering crowds—laid the groundwork for increased paranoia. Batavia saw its grip loosening on a sizeable number of its Foreign Asian subjects.

Paranoia over the border residencies was even worse than that over the core, inner areas of Dutch authority like Java. One of the main reasons was that the

Chinese population was growing so quickly in the Buitenbezittingen, especially in areas close to the borders. In Bangka, for example, the Chinese population of miners grew by 50 percent between 1869 and 1873; the resident felt it necessary to add that these men were also among the "lowest of their race," as they were made up of the "worst elements of Chinese society back home."[36] In Riau, the government did not even possess accurate statistics on the numbers of Chinese, though the men here were also reckoned to be on the "low end of the moral scale," partly, said the resident, because of the lack of Chinese women to keep them occupied.[37] Continual reports of instabilities caused by the Chinese in these islands, from the robbing of passing ships to chronic, violent disturbances in the mines, accumulated in Batavia over the years.[38] In other residencies, such as the western half of Borneo, the threat of Chinese in the border residencies was more directly linked with their connections across the frontier. In 1870, a lively traffic of secret societies was already being spoken of that tied this region to Singapore, though by the late 1880s, such radials were also being traced across the land border to Sarawak. Pontianak, Mempawah, Montrado, and Mandor were all implicated as having Ghee Hin connections within the Brooke dominions, especially in the smuggling of vast quantities of illicit opium.[39] Dutch officials were sent across the border to consult with Brooke civil servants about the problem, and extradited Chinese "troublemakers" were sent in the opposite direction, but these illegalities and connections continued into the twentieth century.

Western Borneo is indeed a good case study in which to examine the dynamics and representations of Chinese on the frontier. West Borneo was often seen by Batavia as a microcosm of the diversity and potential chaos of the border regions, and this supposition may not have been entirely wrong on either count. Chinese mining camps dotted the interior, and though several of these mines were large in scale, with 30 to 50 men digging for gold or diamonds at any one time, the great majority were smaller and spread haphazardly throughout the residency. Bingkayang regency alone had a total of 44 mines and 524 men in 1871; Montrado had 57 mines, with a further population of 590 miners.[40] Chinese authority and manpower were thus diffuse and woven throughout the length of this forest landscape. The chronic instability of the mines, as in 1891 when work-stoppage protests and a turf war broke out between Hakka and Hoklo dialect groups,[41] happened frequently and violently in West Borneo: Batavia saw these types of conflagrations systematically every few years. Yet there were other spaces in the residency that also allowed Batavia to equate Chinese populations with violence, thereby alarming state sensibilities that disaster could be just around the corner. Chinese fought Malays periodically in the bazaars of the urban centers, and Chinese woodcutters caused unrest in the forests. Long stretches of unguarded coast, as in the northernmost reaches of the residency, were also known to be smuggling areas for Chinese boat trips across the border.[42] By 1913, Dutch legislation that attempted to limit the numbers of Foreign Asians moving into West Borneo was being labeled, correctly, as anti-Chinese by China's envoy to The Hague.[43] Two years later, however, Batavia's worst fears had come true: rifles had been buried underground and then exhumed in 1915, and Chinese revolted in the interior, burning a series of Dutch government buildings to the ground.

In Sumatra and the islands south of Singapore, Batavia saw similar problems that allowed the Dutch to conflate Chinese populations with their place on the border arc. If Chinese were already a "troublesome" minority based on their class, occupations, and cultural tendencies in Batavia's eyes, then the proximity of the border made these attributes only worse. Chinese woodcutters from Singapore, for example, often coasted down to Bangka to load up on timber stocks there. This in itself was not unusual, but police blotters from the island tell a steady tale of abuses and murders that accompanied these short-distance cruises. When Singaporean boat crews were caught stealing wood, their Chinese crews would often resist capture, sometimes killing local Malay officials whose job it was to enforce the regulations, and sometimes even taking on entire punitive expeditions with firearms and heavy axes.[44] Violence such as this engendered a steady stream of rumor about Chinese intentions to pillage the border residencies, but this was almost never true: a widespread military alert was posted in May 1879, for example, when it was thought that three hundred Chinese were en route from Singapore to plunder the Riau islands.[45] This rumor turned out to be completely false. Closer to the mark, however, was a chronic effort by Chinese on the frontier to use the demarcation as a competitive advantage, deriving full benefit from a split in local legal jurisdictions. The same boat crews in Bangka continually cut more wood than their licenses allowed and in officially forbidden places; bribes were also paid to coastal watchmen in Aceh, while extension agents in Sumatra skimmed profits whenever they could.[46] The Dutch often knew of these evasions of the law but were hampered by the sheer length of the frontier in their efforts toward prevention. Given the many Chinese villages dotting the width of the border, not to mention mining camps in Borneo and Chinese fishing enclaves in Sumatra, such as the famous Bagan Si Api-Api, Batavia often felt it lacked control along large parts of the border.

These fears were given concrete form in 1912 when violent unrest among Chinese Indies populations exploded throughout the archipelago. On the Anglo/Dutch frontier, events were particularly serious in Borneo, Bangka, and East Sumatra. In Balikpapan, East Borneo, a fight between two Chinese and some Malay men escalated into a pitched battle with knives and sharpened sticks; the police eventually fired on the Chinese as instigators, killing and wounding several, according to Chinese newspapers in Swatow.[47] In western Borneo, Chinese populations killed tax collectors in both Sambas and Mempawah; anonymous Chinese leaflets then circulated widely, threatening more violence if tax burdens were not lessened.[48] In Deli, East Sumatra, the *Pei Ching Chih Pao* reported the killing of Chinese coolies by police under suspicious circumstances,[49] and in Bangka, right off the coast, more than three hundred Chinese coolies were fired upon when they refused to be separated and taken to different mines.[50] Casualties in this last incident were nine dead and twenty wounded; a letter about the massacre indicated that the men had been "treated like horses and cows . . . their conditions are that of slaves."[51] All along the frontier, seemingly, the border arc had started to burn.

What made things more worrisome for the Dutch, however, was that the fires burned brightest not in the Outer Islands, but at home in Java during this year. The year 1912 saw massive Chinese disruptions in the two biggest cities of the island, Batavia and Surabaya: the cause was repression of celebrations of the new republic in which Indies Chinese set off fireworks and observed assorted stoppages of work. Hundreds of local Chinese were arrested and brought into protective custody, while Chinese shops were smashed and their stores thoroughly looted.[52] News of the riots spread immediately to China by telegram; more serious, from Batavia's point of view, was that the new government in Nanking was sending back telegrams in response to these Indies Chinese. One of the locals, a newspaperman named Ong Thiong Hoei from the Indies newspaper *Hok Tok,* informed local Chinese about the support they were receiving from Nanking:

> *Pada tanggal 22 Februari trima telegram dari Department van Buitenlandse Zaken de Nanking, boewat orang orang tjina jang ada di sini (poelo Jawa) terseboet. Hal jang terjadi di Batavia soedah mengerti, soedah manghadap pada oetoesan di oeroes dengan giat.*
> [On the 22d of February a telegram was received from the Department of Foreign Affairs in Nanking, with regard to Chinese who are here in Java. Matters as they have occurred in Batavia are understood; they have been brought before the Minister and will be dealt with energetically.][53]

Several Chinese newspapers in China offered cash rewards for reports on the incidents.[54] Others, such as the *Chung Kwo Jih Pao,* ran patriotic editorials on negotiations in The Hague.[55] Indeed, the ability to get information about the riots out of these two cities and into the hands of other Indies Chinese was one of the factors that concerned Batavia most. The Surabaya chapter of one Chinese organization contacted no fewer than twenty-six places around the archipelago, while messages were also sent to the Chinese consul in The Hague.[56] The fact that number-scripts were used in these telegraphic dispatches worried the Dutch; unless Batavia held the codes, the telegrams were difficult to translate.[57]

Batavia counted on their traditional channels of control—the Chinese *Kapitans*—to deal with the insurrections. Although it is clear from Malay-language documents that the Kapitans tried to restore order to placate the Dutch, these men were often termed "dogs" and "traitors" on Chinese placards.[58] Two signs found in Pancuran accused Chinese Kapitans of complicity with Dutch repression and threatened eventual retribution.[59] The Dutch response to these disturbances was predictable and swift: hundreds of Chinese were jailed, and the worst so-called rabble-rousers were deported. The minister for the colonies saw little choice in what he termed "a general Chinese movement against authority."[60] The chaos eventually died down, and the Chinese ultimately returned to their *wijken* (assigned neighborhoods). Yet police procedures on how to deal with such situations, including detailed instructions outlining what officers had to yell in Malay to try to stop such riots before they started, were recirculated and revamped.[61] The so-called Chinese problem, unlike piracy and low-level chronic violence, was an anxiety of the state that did not seem to be fading away.

JAPANESE POPULATIONS AND THE BORDER

A second group of Vreemde Oosterlingen who presented difficulties to the concept of European colonial security were the Japanese. Japanese populations presented quite a different kind of threat to policymakers in the Indies than the Chinese. Even in the 1880s and 1890s there were still few Japanese in Dutch waters, the majority of them being prostitutes from southern Kyushu.[62] Japanese started to filter into the Indies in greater numbers around 1900, however, with traders, pearlers, and shippers scattering into the Outer Islands in a variety of places. The Meiji Restoration (1868) and the concomitant industrialization of Japan pushed the Japanese southward. Some came as the agents of business and state development (the aforementioned shiphands, timber workers in Borneo, and small tramp-steamer companies, etc.), while others came as a result of the by-products these new changes engendered (poor women off the land as prostitutes, impoverished traders to Java and Singapore, etc.).[63] By the early decades of the twentieth century, Japanese were starting to make inroads into the Indies economy, and Batavia began to notice the phenomenon and keep tabs on its development. Their presence in the Indies, and particularly in the border residencies, was considered both economically useful and increasingly-politically sensitive. Geographically closer to the Indies than the Western nations that traded there, Japan forged ahead with its commercial ties to the islands, linking the two economies through export and the spread of steamship services.[64] Though Japanese in the Indies were only a tiny fraction of the Chinese at any given time, Batavia ultimately saw in Tokyo an expansionist power not discernable in China. If the multitudes of uncontrollable Chinese on the borders presented a threat to the colonial state, therefore, Japan's threat to the Indies was distant but deemed no less real.

The major reason for this appraisal was that Japan was developing politically and industrially by leaps and bounds at the end of the nineteenth century. The unequal treaties signed by the Japanese and European powers between 1856 and 1866, which had given Europe all sorts of rights and privileges at the expense of the island nation, were being reversed by the late 1890s. "Japan is moving quickly," one Dutch authority tersely pronounced, "in a certain direction these past few years."[65] Batavia's quarrel with this movement was that it seemed to be heading south. One Dutch expert, J. H. Engelbregt, asked his countrymen to regard the rise of the Japanese "with an eye toward the future of our East Indies possessions, from commercial as well as political and military standpoints."[66] He published data showing massive increases in the Japanese state budget, especially in departments such as the War, Trade, and Colonization divisions. New consulates were being earmarked for Hawaii, Sydney, Siam, and Manila, while hundreds of millions of yen were being set aside for military projects. According to Englebregt's calculations, "By 1906—and maybe much earlier—Japan will have in these waters a navy greater than those currently employed [in Asia] by all of the Western powers combined." All of this, he added, was coming from a nation that thirty years ago "was still in the Middle Ages."[67]

Such widespread changes in Japan's capabilities and international status, especially after its surprise rout of China in the Sino-Japanese War of 1894–95, led to a Dutch rethinking of Japanese status in the Indies as well. In 1897, a new treaty closed between Tokyo and The Hague gave full most-favored-nation rights to Japanese citizens in the Indies. Article no. 109 of 1854 was thus super-seded, and the Japanese were now considered equal under the law to all Euro-peans. Part of this reversal had to do with the facilitation of commerce, as al-ready seen. The legal revision, called *gelijkstellingen,* or equating, in Dutch, did not meet with unqualified approval in Dutch public opinion, however. The *Avondpost* in The Hague, under an article ominously titled *Waarschuwing* (Warning), categorically called the move a big mistake. Even Indies jurists such as J. A. Nederburgh, writing in the legal journal *Wet en Adat,* questioned the propriety of changing the classification: "As a rule, the most undeveloped and uncivilized components of Asians come to the Dutch Indies, a sort of folk with a dun Western varnish. . . . under which is hidden the real, unfalsified Asian."[68] Nederburgh went on to ask if there had really been a turn in the "morals and understanding, in the very nature of the people," implying that Japan's political and economic transformation meant little in terms of "civilizing" its people.[69] The juxtaposition in attitudes is paradoxical but clear: on the one hand, the Japanese were to be feared for their rising military might and expansionist poli-cies, while on the other they were held in contempt as barbarians in civilized dress. Several phenomena of the early twentieth century helped codify and en-force these opinions.

Perhaps the first was the growth of the Japanese population in the Indies, only portions of which were visible to the state. A list prepared by the Dutch envoy to Tokyo and mailed to the Ministry for Foreign Affairs in The Hague provided details to the Dutch government of how many Japanese were leaving the country's shores and where they were going: the figures included various Southeast Asian colonies, East Asia, and other destinations in the greater Pacific (table 2).[70] Because the United States and Canada had recently estab-lished laws limiting the number of Japanese immigrants, however, the minister of the colonies advised the Dutch government to examine very closely from now on the number of Japanese removing to the Indies.[71] Indeed, by 1908, Batavia's data on Japanese population diffusion into various parts of the Indies, especially the Outer Islands and border residencies, showed marked in-creases.[72] Japanese could be found everywhere, from the most isolated island chains where they conducted pearling expeditions to the heart of the Bornean rain forest, where they engaged in timber extraction. More alarming, from the Dutch standpoint, was that the numbers of immigrants Batavia and Tokyo each said had gone to the Indies did not nearly correspond. Even the Japanese press admitted that large numbers of Japanese were leaving for the archipelago, a statement that led the Dutch consul in Kobe to check matters further.[73]

Table 2. Japanese Population Movements to Southeast Asia from Dutch Colonial and Consular Records

Dutch Consular Statistics (Tokyo) on Japanese Immigration to SE Asia, 1905/6:

Select Destinations	1905 male	female	total	1906 male	female	total
Malay Islands	0	1	1	2	1	3
Singapore	23	11	34	10	19	29
Penang	0	0	0	5	2	7
Borneo	0	0	0	1	5	6
Java	0	0	0	1	0	1
Dutch Sumatra	12	14	26	14	26	40
East India Islands	27	0	27	2	0	2
Totals:	62	26	88	35	53	88

*** Note: The destinations for 1905/1906 also included statistics for Hong Kong, French Asia, Siam, the United States, Mexico, Peru, Hawaii, and the Philippines.

Japanese in Netherlands East Indies Border Residencies, 1908

Residency (Selected)	1st Half Year men	women	total	2nd Half Year men	women	total
Lampung	0	2	2	—	—	2
Palembang	2	15	17	0	14	14
Jambi	1	2	3	4	1	5
Sumatra, EC	24	65	89	19	65	84
Aceh	5	7	12	8	22	30
Riau	0	0	4	—	—	22
Bangka	—	—	16	—	—	22
Belitung	0	0	0	0	1	1
W. Borneo	17	16	33	12	17	29
SE. Borneo	2	4	6	9	5	14
Totals:	—	—	182	—	—	223

Sources: Adapted from ARA, Dutch Consul, Tokyo to Minister for Foreign Affairs (11 May 1908, #448/57–12128) in (MvBZ/A/589/A.209), and enclosure in Minister of the Colonies to Minister for Foreign Affairs (28 June 1909, Kab. Litt. Secret #13422) in (MvBZ/A/589/A.209).

What he found astonished him. Japanese were being smuggled into the Indies as fictitious boat crews, as stowaways, and even in small sailing craft.[74] Other ships were bypassing Dutch quarantine regulations and landing Japanese in the Indies via circuitous eastern routes.[75]

The fact that more and more Japanese seemed to be spilling into the Indies and that a certain number of these seemed to be unaccountable to the state worried Batavia greatly. Policymakers wondered about pan-Asian conspiracies, tracking leads extremely far afield to see if their suspicions were true. One such case in 1905 serves as a useful window on these anxieties. In October, the Dutch consul in Kobe wrote a letter to his superior in Tokyo relating intelligence about a certain Tan Hok Lok, a Chinese trader from Makassar who had recently arrived in Japan. According to the Kobe envoy's information, Tan had been very interested in the uprisings by indigenous chiefs in Sulawesi and had spoken to various people on the steamer to Japan about this. The consul theorized that Tan was in Japan to buy arms for the insurgents, as he seemed to have many contacts in Kobe, Nagoya, and Tokyo itself. His stated intention of exporting Japanese goods to South Sulawesi was highly suspicious, as there was little market for such commodities there. The Tokyo envoy had Tan followed by the Japanese police all over Japan and sent a translated Japanese police report back to The Hague to keep the minister for foreign affairs directly apprised of events.[76] Although nothing was ever proved in the case, and Tan eventually returned to Sulawesi, the resources marshaled by the state to track the possibility of an arms-running conspiracy involving Chinese, Japanese, and indigenous Indies peoples all acting together was impressive. Telegrams and letters shuttled back and forth between Kobe, Batavia, and The Hague every few days: several levels of government were involved, as were different administrative branches.[77] What is almost lost in the incident is that Tan seems to have been completely innocent of any charges, the scapegoat and target of Dutch anxieties about conspiracy.

If the Dutch government feared the Japanese as a potential threat to the Netherlands Indies, then newspaper presses in the region imagined these possibilities even more forcefully. A sample of Dutch feelings about the Japanese has been presented above, but Batavia also kept careful track of what other powers in the region were saying about Japan's evolution as well as of the statements in Japanese publications themselves. As early as 1895, as the Sino-Japanese War raged to the north, the Penang presses were already making judgments on these tumultuous events. The *Indo-Chinese Patriot,* for example, declared, "Japan aspires to play the part of Britain in the Far East," further declaring that "the rapid development of Japan as a nation powerful in war has come as a great surprise to the majority of people."[78] Where the British in Malaya saw a distant, expansionist threat modeled on imperial Britain itself, the Australian press saw Japanese armies potentially annexing islands off of its own shores. This was particularly so in the years following Japan's surprise victory over Russia in the Russo-Japanese War of 1905. The *Melbourne Herald* pointed out that thousands of Japanese were already resident in French New Caledonia and that "if the Japanese on the islands were to get it in their heads to rise tomorrow, the people of New Caledonia could no more stop them than they could stop the sun from rising."[79] Many of the Japanese in this French colony had fought in the Russo-Japanese War; a number of them still openly carried revolvers, the article continued. Another account reported that some of the Japanese in New Caledonia could also work wireless telegraph, while the expansion of Japanese sailing fleets in the South Pacific was also regarded with suspicion. Japanese magazines that complained of their countrymen's treatment in the East Indies only made the Dutch more nervous. As the numbers of articles piled up in Batavia's archives, the Dutch began to wonder seriously about Japan's intentions in the Indies.[80]

Events after the turn of the century consolidated and enforced these fears. In January 1908, the controleur of Sampit sent a letter to the resident of Southeastern Borneo; in it he enclosed a Malay-language letter that appeared to close a contract between a local lord and the Japanese government. The arrangement had been mediated by a Japanese middleman named K. Nonomura. The controleur ordered that if the man returned, he was not to be hindered, so that Batavia could figure out exactly what he was doing.[81] Shady dealings on the Borneo border were not the only circumstances worrying the Dutch, however. A new cause for concern developed right off the coasts of Batavia just a few years later, when a puzzling series of letters was received from the Dutch consul in Tokyo. The Netherlands' envoy reported that the embassy had been telephoned with queries about the Prinsen Islands, which lay scattered in the Sunda Strait between Java and Sumatra. The Sunda Strait was one of the major strategic waterways of the Indies and within close range of Batavia, the center of Dutch rule. The callers had asked for population figures on the islands and other information but were given no definite answers by the embassy staff. The Dutch envoy told his superiors that he did not wish to blow the incident out of proportion but thought it should be brought to their attention, especially as these particular islands, which served as an entryway into the greater Asian sea routes, were repeatedly mentioned in the Japanese press. Batavia and The Hague saw in both of the above events silent forces in motion.[82] A captured letter, anonymous phone calls, press clippings, and discrepancies on immigration figures eventually added up. Strategic planning in the Indies began to shift the axis of threat to possible invasions from the north.

British correspondence from across the Straits echoed these fears in the first decades of the twentieth century. The British chargé d'affaires in The Hague told London that the Dutch were extremely anxious about Japanese designs on the Netherlands Indies, but Singapore's own worries were no less real.[83] Exhaustive surveys were taken of the nature and extent of Japanese estates in the nearby Riau islands, using intelligence provided by one Kashio Hichitaro, a Japanese resident in the area. The results alarmed the British: Batam, Bintan, Lobam, Mamoi, Awi, and Kerimun islands all had Japanese plantations, several of which were more than ten thousand acres each and which could be used for staging attacks on Singapore.[84] The governor of the Straits Settlements also didn't like the fact that Japanese had acquired land on both sides of the railway in Johor, citing this as dangerous and counter to British interests. By late 1919, a case was being made in the Colonial Office to try to buy these nearby islands from the Dutch, as "in the event of temporary Japanese control of the Eastern Seas, they would be of great assistance to us in mining the Straits and keeping the Japanese at a distance from Singapore."[85] The Singapore armed forces espoused this idea vigorously. A potential scenario was sketched whereby Japan picked a quarrel with the Dutch Indies, forcing it to cede the islands in order to keep the peace. "Secretly," one of the army's planners concluded, "there is a strong desire among the Japanese to acquire by some means the Straits of Malacca and the Straits of Sunda. These aspirations have been voiced constantly by various writers in the Japanese language. There is no doubt that the Japanese covet the Dutch islands."[86]

The plan to buy the islands from Batavia never actually took place, and Japan did not invade the Indies until twenty-two years later, in the midst of the Second World War. However, aside from the increase of Japanese migrants to the Indies in the years following the turn of the century, there was one other aspect of Japanese penetration that concerned the Dutch. This was the entrance of Japanese capital, much of it entwined with Chinese banks. Batavia saw in this marriage two equal causes for concern. When a combined Sino-Japanese bank was set up in the Japanese colony of Taiwan in 1918 with the express purpose of uniting the capital of the two ethnic groups to further their combined business interests in the Indies, the Dutch took note immediately. Correspondence and translations of Japanese accounts of the merger were quickly sent back to The Hague.[87] The principals of the operation, four men designated as Rin Hei-sho, Wang Shin-ko, Rin Yu-cho, and Kuo Shu-rio by the Dutch, garnered official Japanese government support for the project. The bank, called the *Kwakyo,* or Colonists' Bank, was erected in Taiwan, however, so that "misunderstandings with the Netherlands Indies government can [therefore] be avoided."[88] The placing of the bank in an offshore site did not fool the Dutch: it was clear to everyone where the financing had come from. With a starting capital between five and ten million yen[89] and a manifesto to provide easier credit to East Asian traders in the Indies than they could get from Europeans, the banking venture was watched very carefully by the Dutch.[90] Holland's consul in Tokyo, aside from providing the above information, reported on the geographic spread of Japanese companies with investments in the Indies as well as the fact that the Dutch language was now being taught so as to "further the expansion of Japanese interests over-seas."[91] All of these facts helped create a psychology of fear and mistrust of the Japanese in the Indies, especially when it came to the borders. When a Japanese magazine said in April 1918 there were no "civilized Dutchmen any longer who are uneasy with the intentions of the Japanese," the words were more of a sales pitch to investors than a hard-boiled truth. Japan was perceived as a real threat in Insular Southeast Asia, on both sides of the Straits.

A LINK BASED ON FAITH: THE THREAT
OF PAN-ISLAM

The beginnings of a siege mentality visible in many of the above remarks developed slowly over the years. The Dutch were expanding their authority in the Indies' Outer Islands even as they were looking more and more over their shoulders at other populations who also criss-crossed the archipelago. While the assumed threat to established authority was often perceived in ethnic terms, it was also sometimes couched in religious ones. The Indies thinker J. P. Schoe-maker commented in 1878 that "jealousy of the great European powers in the Far East, and especially the giant progress of Japan, have in the last years focused more attention on Asian peoples, and it has not been absent . . . that the colonial states are now threatened by Islam and Buddhism."[92] The second part of the quote seems almost comical now: it was not Buddhism, but Fascism, a European import, that was at the bottom of any real threat from Japan. Yet the quotation is revealing because it provides a window on how some of these anxieties were seen in the Indies of the day. Schoemaker's take on Islam as a danger was much more widely current than his perception of Buddhism; many authors of the time commented on the threat of Islam, often with great gusto. Sometimes the lineage of this danger was traced all the way back to the Crusades, while commentators such as P. J. Veth harkened back to the days of the conversion of the Indies archipelago. Schoemaker himself pointed to the troubles Pan-Islam had caused the Dutch: the Padris in West Sumatra (1821–37), Abdul Wahib-bin Muhammad in Palembang (1881), and the revolt of 1888 in Banten. It still amazed him, Schoemaker said, that Batavia allowed the Muslim pilgrimage from the Indies to be undertaken at all: it was a ritual used by believers, he contended, only to sow seeds of discontent when the travelers returned to their homes.[93]

The hypothesized danger of Pan-Islam, or "the striving of Muslims toward political unity," as one Indies Islamic expert termed it, was indeed one of the most pressing topics among policymakers and administrators of the day.[94] Throughout the Indies archipelago and especially in the border residencies, where Batavia wielded far less control than in Java, the proselytization of militant Islam was looked upon with guarded and suspicious eyes. The Dutch kept a close watch on the movements of religious teachers from one residency to another. In Bangka, for example, the resident reported that famous Koranic teachers from Madura and the Padang Uplands visited the island in 1871 and 1872, respectively, filling mosques on both occasions. In western Borneo, the movements and population ratios of Arabs and Indian Muslims were also tracked, as there was a feeling that "Arabs can't be trusted, and Klings even less so."[95] Journeys into the interior by Arabs, Indian Muslims, and religious leaders were especially noted: the Dutch were concerned that here, as in other residencies where the local inhabitants were said to be "quiet and easy to lead," Muslim ideologies would make particular headway. In southeast Borneo, the more religious elements of the population had set themselves up as opponents to Dutch government, the resident said, a situation that was verified when the local Dutch military commander was stabbed repeatedly in the head by a "religious fanatic" in Amuntai.[96] The fact that Batavia knew various sultans of the Indies had regular contacts with each other through messengers made the state only more suspicious.[97] Islamic conspiracies were imagined around all corners, at different places and at different times (fig. 7).

The start of the long war against Aceh in North Sumatra, which began in 1873 and did not taper off until after the twentieth century had begun, increased these stakes enormously. Aceh was the religious rallying cry for Pan-Islam in the Indies: many local sultans and rajas watched the fortunes of this conflict extremely carefully, for omens as to their own impending fates under colonialism. It is interesting to see how the *categories* of residential reporting in the Outer Islands changed as soon as the war in Aceh had begun: from 1873/74 onward, new kinds of information were requested from the center regarding conditions in the periphery, much of it having to do with Islam. In Bangka, therefore, we see the resident being asked to describe for the first time the "Uitbreiding van het Mahomedanisme, en Invloed van de Hadjies op de Bevolking" (Expansion of Islam and Influence of Hajjis upon the Population); the

Fig. 7. Arab man in the Indies, 1870. (Photo courtesy KITLV, Leiden)

same category appears for the first time in Palembang, where the resident's answer pointed to Islamic gains in the interior.[98] In Borneo, the residents were very forthright in their appraisal of the situation. The director of the eastern portion of the island found that "the declaration of war against Aceh has woken discontent in the Muslim populations," while his counterpart in western Borneo described a steady crawl of Islam into the forest interior of his own residency.[99] That answers and new categories were being formulated in this general direction should not be surprising. Even a few years before the Aceh War had begun, commentators in the Indies were speaking of the ongoing dynamics of a Holy War in the archipelago. P. J. Veth went so far as to say that even the non-Muslim pirates of the Eastern Seas, including the "Sea-Dayaks" and the "Orang Laut," or "Sea Gypsies," were now part of this process, as they had been goaded into their depredations at the behest of Islamic corsairs.[100]

This last analysis was certainly far-fetched, but even by the 1880s and 1890s the spread of Islam was causing anxiety in Batavia and The Hague. This was not true in all places along the border, nor was Islam moving everywhere at the same speed. In Bangka in the mid-1880s, for example, the resident reported that Islam was not really expanding at all, probably because of the preponderance of Chinese miners on the island. In Riau, there was no more room for expansion, the resident there said, as almost everyone already had become Muslim long ago. The overall picture of the border residencies seems to be one of slow but steady growth, however, as Islam seeped into villages and interiors, often on the wings of trade. In Palembang, South Sumatra, this was certainly the case: the resident wrote that with the penetration of the coffee trade many villages were now seeing increases in Islam (and in the Hajj in particular, which will be discussed in the next chapter), as coffee merchants came up from lowland urban centers into the mountains. In southeast Borneo, trade seems to have been less responsible than political disaffection, as the followers of the Dutch-deposed sultan's party wandered the interior forests of the land converting Dayaks to Islam at quietly expanding rates.[101] Batavia asked its administrators in the Buitenbezittingen to keep an eye on these developments, as it was felt that only part of Islam's spread was a "natural, internal progression," the remainder having much more to do with concerted efforts orchestrated from abroad.[102] Such warnings and exhortations often stemmed from the combined surveillance of Dutch officials in many places: The Hague, Constantinople, Singapore, and in the Indies, all working together as a unit.[103]

Indeed, it is in the 1880s that a crescendo of activity in the state's supervision of Islam in the Indies can be seen. More and more attention was paid to the ways in which Islam entered the archipelago: Batavia wanted to know where, as well as how, militant Islamic doctrine entered its domains and how to stop this flow across the border. Although earlier legislation attempted to regulate the abilities of foreign Muslims to "infect" local populations to a degree, it was only in the 1880s that the state was able to act on these desires in a more concerted and effective fashion.[104] Arabs who had overstayed their permits in the Indies were carefully tracked down and evicted from the archipelago, while others who were about to enter the Indies were spied upon in offshore ports such as Singapore. By 1885, the Dutch consul in the Straits Settlements was keeping detailed statistics not only on how many Arabs crossed into the Dutch sphere, but also on the residencies, particularly those in the Outer Islands, to which they were heading.[105] Foreign Muslims bearing letters to their compatriots in the Indies, as seen previously, were zealously followed and risked having their packages confiscated whenever the state caught wind of such activities. Yet it was not only those Arabs legitimately suspected of fomenting religious rebellion who were watched and followed all along the border. Merely living in a frontier residency as an Arab meant that one's movements and daily activities were subject to examination. Batavia's vision of Pan-Islam as a movement of subversion left little room for Indies Arabs who might be quiet, loyal subjects. The explosion of the Krakatoa volcano off Java in 1883 provided an additional incentive for watchfulness on the part of the state: Batavia was furious that some Muslims were using the disaster as proof of the "impending end of the world," exhorting their fellows to rise as the end of subjugation was nigh.[106]

By the years around the turn of the century state anxieties about Pan-Islam, like those about Chinese and Japanese populations, had risen to uncomfortable levels. Two of the Indies' most famous Islamic scholars, L. W. C. van den Berg and C. Snouck Hurgronje, jousted in print about whose fault it was that Islamic brotherhoods had been overly ignored by the state. These societies were viewed as transmitters of militancy and rebellion, particularly in the various colonies of Africa and Asia.[107] Snouck, especially, had an almost hagiographical reputation as an expert on Islam by this time, and his pronouncements were taken very seriously by the Dutch public. The British also kept a finger on Islam's pulse across the Dutch frontier, worrying that instability and violence in the Indies could spell trouble among their own Muslim populations in the Straits.[108] Thousands of miles of permeable frontier shaped these anxieties, but strong ethnic and family ties stretching across it acted to solidify their fears. Batavia's response to outside stimuli of Pan-Islamic tension was usually swift and decisive. Supposed Islamic propaganda from abroad was routinely confiscated and banned, as in the case of a Turkish newspaper from Constantinople that had declared, "All Muslims around the world are brothers, and if one Muslim suffers an injustice, it is the duty of others to come to his aid."[109] The article dealt specifically with the treatment of Arabs in the Dutch colonies: rumors circulated that the Ottomans would come to the archipelago to free local peoples from the Dutch Christian yoke. What seems to have lain at the bottom of these discussions, however, was that Pan-Islam acknowledged only one master, God, and that this equation was untenable to the Netherlands Indies state. The idea that "Muslim chiefs do not belong to their sovereigns," as van den Berg put it, "has its roots in the teachings of orthodox Islamic law."[110] That this principle might be a subject of negotiation among Europeans was never even remotely considered. This was a proposition, ultimately, that the Dutch regime as well as other colonial states throughout the world simply could not abide.

If the threat of piracy and uncontrolled violence along the Anglo/Dutch frontier was seen to be diminishing in the decades after the turn of the twentieth century, the specter presented by Foreign Asians was moving in the opposite direction. Chinese populations were expanding enormously in the Outer Islands, and though much of this growth was sponsored by Europeans, the sheer size and purported proclivities of the Chinese community, in addition to the influences it was receiving from the turbulent birth of the Chinese Republic before and after 1912, rendered these increases dangerous to Dutch eyes. The Japanese in Southeast Asia were never as numerous as the Chinese, but behind the (sometimes unrecorded) sojourners who did make it down to the lands and seas of the frontier was seen to be the invisible hand of dubious Japanese military intentions. Muslim preachers and religious teachers from the Middle East also were judged to be a recurrent threat, especially as the "radical message" of Pan-Islam circled the world in the later decades of the nineteenth century. All of these populations posed problems to European conceptions of a controlled frontier; the actions and interactions of these Asian "Others" only became more threatening to Europeans after 1900. Yet there was deemed to be an even larger potential danger to the integrity of the border than these burgeoning populations, and this was the autochthonous peoples of the frontier themselves.

NOTES

1. ANRI, Politiek Verslag Residentie West Borneo 1870 (no. 2/8); ANRI, Politiek Verslag Residentie Borneo Zuid-Oost 1871 (no. 4/1); ANRI, Politiek Verslag Residentie Banka 1871 (no. 124); ANRI, Algemeen Administratie Verslag Riouw 1871 (no. 63/2).

2. ANRI, Algemeen Administratieve Verslag Residentie Palembang 1870 (no. 64/13); Saw, *Singapore Population in Transition* (1970), 11. The vast majority of Dutchmen in the Outer Islands were civil servants during this period. In Bangka in 1871, for example, all but three of the resident Europeans worked for the government; two of the remaining three were agents of the Nederlandsch-Indische Stoomvaart Maatschappij (Dutch Indies Steamship Company), while another had opened a bank. The balance of the non-European population (and thus the potential threat to the state) varied by residency: in some areas, like the East Coast of Sumatra, West Borneo, and the islands of Bangka and Belitung, the primary concern was the large numbers of Chinese; in other areas, as in Aceh and southeast Borneo, Arabs worried Batavia more comprehensively. Populations of Europeans did not change significantly in many Buitenbezittingen residencies until after the twentieth century; even in Singapore Europeans were only 2 percent of the population into the 1880s. See ANRI, Politiek Verslag der Residentie Banka 1871 (Banka no. 124), for more on Bangka.

3. Multavidi "Nieuwe Staatsinkomst" (1906), 340; Hulshoff, "Kaartsystem" (1910), 262 passim.

4. "Adres in Zake de Boekhouding" (1881), 948–49.

5. Ibid., 952–53.

6. "Boekhouding der Vreemde Oosterlingen" (1881), 7. See also "Koopmansboeken," *IWvhR*, no. 2005, 2 December 1901, 189–91.

7. Fasseur, "Cornerstone and Stumbling Block: Racial Classification" (1994), 35.

8. Keuchenius, *Handelingen van Regering*, (1857), 296.

9. For a good gloss on the different kinds of law to be found in the Indies by race, see Nederburgh, "Klassen der Bevolking van Nederlandsch-Indië" (1897), 79–80. These complexities were by no means only because of racial categories; even within European law in the colony, the legal landscape was extremely complicated and continually evolving. See "Invoering van het Nieuwe Strafwetboek" (1902), 1235 passim.

10. See Trocki, *Opium and Empire* (1987), 30. See also McKeown, "Conceptualizing Chinese Diasporas" (1999), 306–37; Skinner, "Creolized Chinese Societies" (1996), 51–93; Reid, "Flows and Seepages" (1996), 15–49; Salmon, "Taoke or Coolies?" (1983), 179–210; and Wang, *China and the Chinese Overseas*, (1991).

11. De Groot, *Het Kongsiwezen van Borneo* (1885). For more contemporary histories, see Heidhues, *Golddiggers, Farmers, and Traders* (2003), chaps. 3 and 4; Yuan, *Chinese Democracies* (2000), chap. 6; and Jackson, *Chinese in the West Borneo Goldfields* (1970).

12. De Groot cited in Nederburgh, "Klassen der Bevolking" (1897), 79.

13. See F. Fokken's Reports of 1896 and 1897, "Rapport Betreffende het Onderzoek Naar den Economische Toestand der Vreemde Oosterlingen op Java en Madoera en Voorstellen tot Verbetering" ARA, MvK, Verbaal, 17 April 1896, no. 27; also *Algemeen Handelsblad* 8 (April 1896).

14. Romer, "Chineezenvrees in Indië" (1897), 193; ARA, "De Chineesche Kwestie in Nederlandsch-Indië," *Nieuwe Rotterdamsche Courant,* 12 June 1907, 1–2 (MvBZ/A/43/A.29bis.OK).

15. ARA, "De Chineezen-Quaestie in Indië," *Nieuwe Courant,* 23 April 1907; *Nieuwe Rotterdamsche Courant,* 12 April 1907 (MvBZ/A/43/A.29bis OK).

16. ARA, "Het Chineezen Vraag-stuk in Indië," *Algemeen Handelsblad,* 3 April 1907 (MvBZ/A/43/A.29bis OK).

17. Suhartono "Cina Klonthong: Rural Peddlers" (1994), 181 passim; Senn van Basel, "De Chinezen op Borneo's Westkust" (1875), 59 passim.

18. *Nanyang Chung Wei Pao,* 30 Oct. 1906 and 11 Jan. 1907; in Dutch Consul, Singapore to GGNEI, (22 May 1907, no. 998) [transl.] in (MvBZ/A/246/A.119).

19. *Nanyang Chung Wei Pao,* 21 Aug. 1906 and 2 Aug. 1906; in Dutch Consul, Singapore to Gov Gen NEI, (22 May 1907, no. 998) [transl.] in (MvBZ/A/246/A.119). The Dutch reports are to be found in ANRI, Maandrapport Residentie Banka 1870 (no. 96), 1872 (no. 98), 1877 (no. 103) (December, July, and July, respectively).

20. One woman, Si Nia, recounted how two Malays came into her house and smoked opium with her husband; they then suddenly grabbed him, and proceeded to stab him until he was dead. A similar account is given by La Na, with the same result: both of the men's plaited hair were taken as trophies, and the houses later robbed. Testimony of Si Na, Wife of Shiong Shu, 8 Oct. 1867; Testimony of La Na, Wife of Ah Sing, 8 Oct. 1867; Gov Labuan to CO, 25 Oct. 1867, no. 37, all in CO 144/26; also ANRI, Algemeen Verslag Residentie West Borneo 1890 (no. 5/21).

21. ANRI, Politiek Verslag Residentie West Borneo 1870 (no. 2/8). For discussions of intra-Chinese competition in British Malaya and British Borneo, see, respectively, Trocki, *Opium and Empire* (1990), 4; and Chew, *Chinese Pioneers on the Sarawak Frontier* (1990), 130–31.

22. Schaalje, "Bijdrage tot de Kennis der Chinesche Geheime Genootschappen" (1873), 1–6. Schaalje gives a Dutch translation of part of the document as follows: "From the oldest times the existing traditions edify us with the secrets of the society; Our heart, in harmony with the sun and moon, make China and the foreigners tremble; Our unity and patriotism are evident to the entire world; Together in harmony we support our kingdom, making the royal heritage strong." Finding the correct sequence of the characters, Schaalje tells us, is difficult; based on the above translation, however, and in keeping with the peach tree emblem (which Schlegel had published on previously), it seems to be a document of the famous Hung League. Schaalje further hypothesized that other references in the text referred to Pulau Tikus, a village on Penang Island; the author thinks this is where inductions and meetings for the society probably took place. A Penang headquarters for a Chinese secret society stretching across the strait to Sumatra did not sit well with the Dutch; the document was found in Deli, on Sumatra's East Coast, and dates from 1861.

23. Young, "Bijdrage tot de Kennis der Chinesche Geheime Genootschappen" (1883), 547, 551–52, 574–77. The Sekajam document is a receipt-ticket stating that the sum of one dollar has been given to the kongsi. The date on the paper is the twenty-sixth day of the seventh month of the year Sin-joe, which Young posited was 1861 on the Western calendar.

24. ANRI, Algemeen Verslag Residentie West Borneo 1874 (no. 5/4); ANRI, Algemeen Verslag Residentie West Borneo 1889 (no. 5/20).

25. See ARA, Dutch Consul, Singapore to GGNEI (9 Jan. 1889, no. 37) in 1889, MR no. 38; also *Perak Gov't Gazette,* 1888, 32. British successes in dealing with Chinese secret soci-

eties went from "useless, for any practical purpose" in 1872 to significantly better after that; a whole codex of laws was drawn up to ensure that the state would win this battle. See "Report of the Inspector General of Police on the Working of Ordinance no. 19 of 1869, the "Dangerous Societies Suppression Ordinance," *SSLCP*1872, 98, for the inspector general of police's (Singapore) disparaging comment above; for the evolution of Straits laws on these societies, see Ordinance no. 19 of 1869, no. 4 of 1882, no. 4 of 1885, and no. 20 of 1909. By 1913, British North Borneo was adopting legislation that gave the state powers to enter meeting places, rights of seizure, and the power to photograph, fingerprint, and summon witnesses, all vis-à-vis secret societies. See Gov, BNB to Chairman, BNB Co., London, 31 Dec. 1913, no. 4066/13, in CO 874/803. The best general book dealing with these societies is Ownby and Heidhues, eds., *Secret Societies Reconsidered* (1993); for a more detailed picture in the Straits, see Fong, *The Sociology of Secret Societies* (1981).

26. "Privaatrechtelijke Toestand der Chineezen in Nederlandsch Indië" (1898), 210.

27. "Invloed der Vreemdelingschap op het Rechtswezen" (1897), 159–97. For an overview of some of the larger questions on how Chinese should be classified, both from their own vantage and from the vantage of others, see Salmon, "Ancestral Halls and Funeral Associations" (1996), 183–214, and Karl, "Creating Asia: China and the World" (1998), 1096–1117.

28. ARA, See the letter from the Chinese ambassador to the Netherlands authorities at The Hague, dated Guangxu twelfth year reign, seventh month, twenty-seventh day (1886), in Minister for the Colonies to Minister for Foreign Affairs (9 Nov. 1886, A3/21–9471) in (MvBZ/A/43/A.29bis OK). The ambassador makes the case for why Chinese in the Indies should be considered Chinese subjects only and not fall under Dutch jurisdiction; he references Chinese mixed marriages in the Indies, and also U.S. dealings with Chinese as examples.

29. ARA, MvK to MvBZ, 9 Nov. 1886, no. A3/21–9471 (MvBZ/A/43/A.29bis OK). The instructions were sent to Foreign Affairs first, then to be relayed to Peking; ARA, Dutch Consuls in Washington (14 May 1907, no. 294/120) and Berlin (5 June 1907, no. 2555/1011) as well as the Foreign Office, London (9 July 1909, no. 21833), all replying to MvBZ (MvBZ/A/43/A.29bis OK).

30. ARA, Dutch Consul, Singapore to GGNEI (6 Oct. 1910, no. 2563); Official for Chinese Affairs, Batavia to Dir. Justitie, NEI (19 Oct. 1909); and *Nieuwe Rotterdamsche Courant* (25 March 1912), all in (MvBZ/A/40/A.29bis OK).

31. ARA, Speech of Chao Ch'ung Fan, 24 April 1911 (translation by the Officer for Chinese Affairs, Surabaya) in (MvBZ/A/40/A.29bis OK).

32. ARA, Officer for Chinese Affairs, Surabaya to Dir. Justitie, NEI (27 April 1911, no. 55 Secret) in (MvBZ/A/40/A.29bis OK).

33. ARA, GGNEI to MvK (31 May 1911, Kab Geheim no. 50/1) in (MvBZ/A/40/A.29bis OK).

34. *Han Boen Sin Po* (19 Jan. 1911) (transl.) in (MvBZ/A/40/A.29bis OK).

35. *Hoa Tok Po* (30 Aug. 1909) in Office for Chinese Affairs, Batavia to Dir. Justitie (10 Sep 1909), [transl.] in (MvBZ/A/40/A.29bis OK).

36. ANRI, Politiek Verslag Residentie Banka 1871 (no. 124) and 1873 (no. 125).

37. ANRI, Algemeen Administratieve Verslag Residentie Riouw 1871 (no. 63/2).

38. ARA, 1873, MR no. 526; ANRI, Algemeen Verslag Residentie Banka 1888 (no. 79).

39. ARA, Resident Banka to GGNEI (14 Nov. 1876, no. 948) in 1876, MR no. 948; ANRI, Politiek Verslag Residentie West Borneo 1870 (no. 2/8); ANRI, Algemeen Verslag Residentie West Borneo 1886; 1889 (no. 5/17; 5/20).

40. ANRI, Algemeen Administratieve Verslag Residentie West Borneo 1871 (no. 5/2). The Bingkayang mines were divided into the following divisions: two mines of forty-eight men; one mine of thirty-four men; one of twenty-seven men; thirteen of ten to twenty men; twenty-five of five to ten men; and two mines of fewer than five men each. The enormous diffusion of Chinese miners in the periphery thus becomes clear.

41. "Europeesche Industrie in Borneo's Westerafdeeling" (1891), 2011.

42. ANRI, Politiek Verslag Residentie West Borneo 1870, 1872 (no. 2/8, 2/10); see also the *Sarawak Gazette*, 1 May 1885 and 1 March 1893, for notices of Chinese being arrested for illegal crossings across the border.

43. See Sun Chou Wei's letter of 3 Dec. 1913, no. 484 as referenced in ARA, MvK to MvBZ, 5 Dec. 1913 (A1/8-no. 24407) (MvBZ/A/246/A.119).

44. ARA, Resident Banka to GGNEI (14 Nov. 1876, no. 2348) in 1876, MR no. 948; ANRI, Maandrapport Residentie Banka 1876 (no. 102 Nov.).

45. ARA, Commander, Army to GGNEI (2 May 1879, no. 11) in 1879, MR no. 242.

46. See the Chinese testimonials inside ANRI, Surat Residen Riouw Kepada Sultan Lingga Mengenai Penebangan Kayu di Rantau Lingga Oleh Orang Cina Singapura (Archief Riouw), no. 223/18; British Consul, Oleh-Oleh to Gov Aceh, 8–10–1883, no. 408, FO 220/ Oleh-Oleh Consulate/General Correspondence, 1883; Memorandum on the Alleged Smuggling of War into Acheen by the Dutch Consul, 8–6/1883, FO 220/Oleh-Oleh Consulate/General Correspondence, 1883 Appendix. The consul said in the second dispatch, "It is too much to expect from a Chinaman that, however fit he may have hitherto proved for the post that he occupies, he will not take advantage of the position in which chance has placed him."

47. *Sun Chung Wa Po* (3 May 1912) in Dutch Consul, Peking to Minister for Foreign Affairs (20 May 1912, no. 954/176) [transl.] in (MvBZ/A/40/A.29bis OK).

48. ARA, Minister for the Colonies to Minister for Foreign Affairs (7 Nov. 1912, K16-no. 21448) (MvBZ/A/40/A.29bis OK).

49. *Pei Ching Jih Pao* (8 April 1914) in Dutch Consul, Peking to MvBZ, (9 Jan. 1914, no. 48/8) [transl.] in (MvBZ/A/40/A.29bis OK).

50. *Pei Ching Jih Pao* (5 Oct. 1912) [transl.] in (MvBZ/A/40/A.29bis OK).

51. *Pei Ching Jih Pao* (2 Aug. 1912) in ARA, Dutch Consul, Peking to MvBZ (25 Sept. 1912, no. 1611/291) [transl.] in (MvBZ/A/40/A.29bis OK).

52. *Chung Kwo Jih Pao* (7 April 1912) in Dutch Consul, Peking to MvBZ (11 April 1912, no. 717/132) (transl.) in (MvBZ/A/40/A.29bis OK).

53. The Malay-language note from Ong Thiong Hoei, of the Indies newspaper *Hok Tok,* can be found in ARA (MvBZ/A/40/A.29bis OK).

54. See, for example, the Dutch translation of an advertisement in a Swatow newspaper filed

away in Dutch Consul, Peking to MvBZ (22 April 1912, no. 785/142–8868) (MvBZ/A/
40/A.29bis OK). The rewards offered for information were $50 and $150 dollars, depending on the nature of the news.

55. *Chung Kwo Jih Pao* (28 April 1912) in Dutch Consul, Peking to MvBZ (30 April 1912, no.
824/150) [transl.] in (MvBZ/A/40/A.29bis OK).

56. ARA, Advisor for Chinese Affairs in Surabaya to Officer for Justice, Surabaya (2 March
1912, no. 34, Very Secret) in (MvBZ/A/40/A.29bis OK).

57. ARA, in Advisor for Chinese Affairs in Surabaya to Officer for Justice, Surabaya (20 Feb.
1912, no. 24) in (MvBZ/A/40/A.29bis OK). The telegram enclosed in this document is
one from a Surabaya Chinese organization (the Siang Hwee) to other Chinese organizations in the Indies. It reads, "The first can be done; the new Republican flag can be
hoisted, the Dutch authorities will not hinder; no leaflets spreading news and/or rumors;
special to Soe Po Sia and schools." (The Soe Po Sia was another Chinese organization,
with links to revolutionaries in China.) The telegram's message, that raising the new revolutionary Chinese flag in the Indies would be tolerated, was wrong—in several cities, the
minister for the colonies issued strict instructions that this was not to be allowed.

58. ARA, "Majoor der Chineezen Khouw Kim An to Kadjeng Toean Assistant Resident
Batavia" (14 Feb. 1912, no. 413/A Secret) in (MvBZ/A/40/A.29bis OK).

59. See the Dutch translations under cover of ARA, Resident Batavia to GGNEI (6 March
1912, no. 81/E Very Secret) in (MvBZ/A/40/A.29bis OK). One of the placards calls the
captain of Chinese a bastard and says he "cannot return to China, and cannot be termed
a European. He has no land to return to, only the land of the Hereafter." The other calls
him a tyrant of his own population and a wild dog.

60. ARA, MvK to MvBZ, (3 April 1912, no. A1/25–6828) in (MvBZ/A/40/A.29bis OK.)

61. See "High Commissioner of Police's Instructions to Follow in Case of Chinese Riots
Happening in Batavia (23 Feb. 1912) in Asst. Resident, Batavia to Resident of Batavia (26
Feb. 1912, no. 50) (MvBZ/A/40/A.29bis OK).

62. ARA, MvK, Verbaal, 16 April 1898/22. See also Post, "Japan and the Integration of the
Netherlands Indies" (1993), and Post, "Japanese Bedrijvigheid in Indonesie" (1991).

63. The best single book on both sides of this process is Hane, *Peasants, Rebels, and Outcasts*
(1982). See also Shimizu and Hirakawa, *Japan and Singapore in the World Economy,*
(1999), 19–61, and Shimizu, "Evolution of the Japanese Commercial Community"
(1991). For the case of Japanese prostitutes, see chapter 10 of this book.

64. Sugihara, "Japan as an Engine of the Asian International Economy, 1880–1930" (1990),
139; Hashiya, "The Pattern of Japanese Economic Penetration" (1993), 89–112.

65. "Tractaat van Handel en Scheepvaart" (1897), 351, 354.

66. Engelbregt, "Ontwikkeling van Japan" (1897), 800–03.

67. Ibid., 807–08, 814.

68. Piepers, "Waarschuwing," *De Avondpost* (den Haag) 21 Oct. 1898; Nederburgh,"Wijziging in Art. 109" (1898), 287.

69. Ibid., 287.

70. The destinations for 1905/1906 include Hong Kong, French Asia, Siam, the "Malay Islands," Singapore, Penang, the United States, Mexico, Peru, Hawaii, the Philippines,
Borneo, Java, Dutch Sumatra, and the "East-India Islands." See ARA, Dutch Consul,

Tokyo to Minister for Foreign Affairs (11 May 1908, no. 448/57–12128) in (MvBZ/A/ 589/A.209).

71. ARA, MvK to MvBZ (8 Jan. 1908, Kab. Litt Secret, no. 678) in (MvBZ/A/589/A.209).

72. The residencies reported on included "Tapaneoli, Benkoolen, Lampungs, Palembang, Djambi, Oostkust Sumatra, Atjeh, Riouw, Banka, Billiton, W. Afd. Borneo, Z.O. Afd. Borneo, Menado, Celebes, Amboina, Ternate, Bali en Lombok" (in other words, virtually all of the Outer Islands of the Dutch Indies). See enclosure in MvK to MvBZ (28 June 1909, Kab. Litt. Secret no. 13422) in (MvBZ/A/589/A.209).

73. "Japanese Immigration," *Kobe Herald* (27 July 1907) (in MvBZ/A/589/A.209).

74. The consul's observations were repeated in a circular, ARA, GGNEI to Regional Heads of Administration (3 Dec. 1907, no. 407 Very Secret) in (MvBZ/A/598/A.209). The mechanism of using a partially fictitious crew was emblematic of this process. Japanese coaling ships who put into Surabaya, for example, listed crews of sixty-five men; only half of these, the consul reported, might be legitimate crew members, while the rest were secret immigrants. Only thirty or thirty-five Japanese would thus leave with the boat at its sailing.

75. ARA, Dutch Consul, Kobe to GGNEI (12 Oct. 1907, no. 1209) in (MvBZ/A/589/ A.209).

76. ARA, Dutch Consul, Kobe to Dutch Consul, Tokyo (25 Oct. 1905, no. 911/95) in (MvBZ/A/43/A.29bis OK); ARA, Dutch Consul, Tokyo to MvBZ (10 Jan. 1906, no. 28/ 3–2629) in (MvBZ/A/43/A.29bis OK). Also see Tsuchiya, "The Colonial State as a Glass House" (1990), 67–76.

77. ARA, Dutch Consul, Tokyo to MvBZ (29 Nov. 1905, no. 1104/206–117) and MvK to MvBZ (27 Jan. 1906, A3/32-no. 1461), both in (MvBZ/A/43/A.29bis OK).

78. "The China-Japan War," *Indo-Chinese Patriot* (Penang), 1, no. 1, Feb. 1895, 21; "The China-Japan War," *Indo-Chinese Patriot* (Penang), 1, no. 2, March 1895, 15.

79. "Japanese Peril: Colony in New Caledonia," *Melbourne Herald* (17 March 1911); the copy of the article was sent by the Dutch consul in Melbourne to his counterpart in London, who then forwarded it to The Hague (ARA, Dutch Consul, London to MvBZ (29 April 1911, no. 1133/814–9201) in (MvBZ/A/589/A.209). Another triangulation of Dutch surveillance and information gathering is here at work, therefore: Australia/England/Holland, paralleling earlier examples of Dutch consuls fulfilling similar functions in China and Japan. These radials also stretched to the Middle East.

80. "Japanese Peril: Colony in New Caledonia—Rapid Advances," *Melbourne Herald* (21 March 1911); "Japanese Peril: New Caledonia as Base," *Melbourne Herald* (24 March 1911), both in (ARA, MvK/A/589/A.209); see also "The Semarang Exhibition," *Indo-Japanese Society Magazine* (August Issue, 1915) by Yoshio Noma, of the Japanese Dept. of Agriculture and Commerce, in (MvBZ/A/44/A.29bis OK).

81. Controleur, Sampit to Resident, Borneo Southeast, 2 June 1908, no. 2 (Borneo, Z.O., fiche no. 395) (MvK, PVBB).

82. ARA, Dutch Consul, Tokyo to GGNEI (28 Aug. 1916, no. 1268/97) in (MvBZ/A/589/ A.209); ARA, Dutch Consul, Tokyo to GGNEI (28 Aug. 1916, no. 1269/112); MvBZ to MvK (7 Nov. 1916, no. 48470), both in (MvBZ/A/589/A.209). See also Katayama, "The Japanese Maritime Surveys" (1985).

83. British Charge d' Affaires, The Hague to Foreign Office, 16 July 1919, CO 537/890.

84. "Memo Respecting the Acquisition of Dutch Islands Opposite Singapore, Annex 5: Japanese Estates in the Rhio Archipelago," 4 July 1921, Japan/Secret, F2840/23 no. 1, CO 537/903.

85. Gov, SS to CO, 16 Dec 1919, CO 537/890; CO Jacket, SS: Acquisition by Japanese of Properties in Strategic Positions, 16 Dec. 1919, CO 537/890.

86. Enclosure in Gov, SS to CO, 16 Dec. 1919, CO 537/890.

87. ARA, Dutch Consul, Tokyo to MvBZ (19 June 1918, no. 1012/89) in (MvBZ/A/43/A.29bis OK).

88. "Prognosis Concerning the Establishment of a Kwakyo Bank," *Tokyo Nichi Nichi* (9 May 1918), in Dutch Consul, Tokyo to Minister for GGNEI (18 May 1918, no. 836/60) [Dutch transl.] in (ARA, MvBZ/A/43/A.29bis OK).

89. *Osaka Mainichi* (11 June 1918) in Dutch Consul, Tokyo to MvBZ (19 June 1918, no. 1012/89) [Dutch transl.] in (ARA, MvBZ/A/43/A.29bis OK).

90. *Tokyo Asahi* (14 June 1918) in Dutch Consul, Tokyo to MvBZ (19 June 1918, no. 1012/89) [Dutch transl.] in (ARA, MvBZ/A/43/A.29bis OK).

91. Japanese concerns were well established in many Outer Island residencies by this time, including Sumatra, Borneo, the Aru Islands, and New Guinea. See ARA, Dutch Consul, Tokyo to GGNEI (10 June 1918, no. 956/72), and Dutch Consul, Tokyo to GGNEI (25 May 1918, no. 876/68), both in (MvBZ/A/43/A.29bis OK).

92. Schoemaker, "Het Mohammedaansche Fanatisme" (1898), 1517.

93. "Mohammedaansche Broederschappen" (1889), 189; Veth, "Heilige Oorlog" (1870), 169; Schoemaker, "Mohammedaansche Fanatisme" (1898), 1518.

94. Van den Berg, "Pan-Islamisme" (1900), 228. There is a growing literature of contemporary scholars' writings on this topic; see Reid, "Nineteenth-Century Pan-Islam in Indonesia and Malaysia" (1967), 267–83; Roff, "The Malayo-Muslim World of Singapore" (1964), 75–90; Van den Berge, "Indië, en de Panislamitische Pers" (1987), 15–24; Kaptein, "Meccan Fatwas" (1996), 141–60; Riddell, "Arab Migrants and Islamization" (2001), 113–28; Laffan, *Islamic Nationhood and Colonial Indonesia,* (2003); Clarence-Smith, "Hadhrami Entrepreneurs" (1997), 297–314; Mobini-Keseh, *The Hadrami Awakening* (1999); Van den Berg, *Hadramaut dan Koloni Arab* (1989); and De Jonge and Kaptein, eds., *Transcending Borders* (2002).

95. ANRI, Politiek Verslag Residentie Banka 1871 (no. 124); 1872 (no. 125); ANRI, Politiek Verslag Residentie Borneo West 1870, 1872 (no. 2/8, 2/10).

96. ANRI, Politiek Verslag Residentie Borneo Zuid-Oost 1871 no. 4/1); ANRI, Drie Maandelijkschrapport Residentie Borneo Zuid-Oost 1872 (no. 10a/7 [3rd quarter])

97. See Andaya, "Recreating a Vision" (1997), 483–508. Arabs in Palembang sent messengers to "notorious" Acehnese in Penang, for example; Singapore Arabs were also corresponding with the sultan of Sulu. See Consul Read (Singapore) to GGNEI, 12 Jan. 1876, Confidential; same to same, 7 Feb. 1876, both in ANRI, Atjeh no. 12: ("Stukken Betreffende Atjehsche Oorlog").

98. ANRI, Algemeen Verslag Residentie Banka 1874 (Banka no. 65); ANRI, Algemeen Administratieve Verslag Residentie Palembang 1874 (no. 64/17).

99. ANRI, Politiek Verslag Residentie Borneo Zuid-Oost 1873 (no. 4/3); ANRI, Algemeen Verslag Residentie West Borneo 1874 (no. 5/4).

100. Veth, "De Heilige Oorlog" (1870), 175.
101. ANRI, Algemeen Verslag Residentie Banka 1887 (no. 78); ANRI, Algemeen Verslag Residentie Riouw 1890 (no. 64/1–2); ANRI, Algemeen en Administratieve Verslag Residentie Palembang 1886, 1890 (no. 65/6; no. 65/10); ANRI, Algemeen Verslag Residentie Borneo Zuid-Oost 1888, 1890 (no. 9a/9, no. 9a/11).
102. ARA, 1879, MR no. 668.
103. ARA, Extract Uit het Register Besluiten, GGNEI (14 March 1881) in 1881, MR no. 259.
104. ARA, Resident West Borneo to GGNEI (8 July 1878, no. 78) in 1878, MR no. 474.
105. ARA, Resident Sumatra East Coast to Dutch Consul, Singapore (2 Oct. 1881, W/Secret) in 1881, MR no. 1107; Dutch Consul, Singapore to Resident Palembang (15 Sept. 1881, no. 541) in 1881, MR no. 860; ARA, Dutch Consul Singapore to GGNEI (28 Sept. 1885, no. 626) in 1885, MR no. 638. From March to August 1885, 295 Arabs crossed from Singapore into the Dutch Indies; the spread of Indies destinations included Palembang (34), Deli (30), Siak (17), Banjarmasin (13), Makassar (7), Pontianak (6), Mentok (2), Jambi (1), Indragiri (1).
106. ARA, Resident Surabaya to GGNEI (30 Nov. 1881, no. 15258) in 1881, MR no. 1139; also Dutch Consul Djeddah to MvBZ (30 Aug. 1883, no. 632 Very Secret) in 1883, MR no. 1075; ARA, Resident Sumatra East Coast to GGNEI (4 Sept. 1881, Secret); also Resident Madura to GGNEI (7 Sept. 1881, G/3 Secret), both in 1881, MR no. 839; ARA, Resident Bantam to GGNEI (18 Dec. 1883, R/1 Secret) in 1883, MR no. 1173.
107. "Mohammedaansche Broederschappen" (1889), 15–20; "Mohamedaansch-Godsdienstige Broederschappen" (1891), 189. For a good discussion of Hurgronje's role in policies geared toward Pan-Islam, see Algadri, *C. Snouck Hurgronje* (1884), 85–95, and Algadri, *Islam dan Keturunan Arab*, (1996), 43.
108. "The Dutch Government and Mohamedan Law in the Dutch East Indies," *Law Magazine and Review* (1895, February) N295, 183 passim.
109. "Resume van Artikelen in de Turksche Bladen" (1898), 1096–97.
110. Van den Berg, "Pan-Islamisme" (1900), 228. Legal aspects of this belonging were also discussed in the Indies courts; see "Bevoegdheid. Arabier of Europeaan?" *IWvhR,* no. 2323, 6 Jan. 1908, 3.

Chapter 7 The Indigenous Threat

A final broad category of border threat perceived especially by Batavia came not from low-level violence, and not from Vreemde Oosterlingen or Foreign Asians, but from the indigenous populations of the Indies. As we have seen, the Dutch were only a tiny minority compared to the assemblage of other ethnic groups in the Indies. This ratio was deemed to be unfavorable in comparison with Vreemde Oosterlingen, but when it came to the many populations native to the archipelago, Europeans were completely dwarfed numerically.[1]

Batavia used several methods to subjugate and control these much larger populations in advancing Dutch interests on the ground and expanding Batavia's authority into the periphery. One was to fight a series of wars with various sultanates and kingdoms in the archipelago. A second pacification method was to erect a body of laws that made indigenous peoples inferior to the Dutch within the confines of the Netherlands Indies state. This move also had the effect of rendering local peoples less threatening to established authority and to stability, as Indies jurisprudence leaned heavily in favor of Dutch policing power and control. Both of these programs were put in place to try to "capture" the autochthonous population of the Indies within forms of control that were favorable to the state.[2]

The two dynamics of state action and legislation in regard to local populations are explored below, alongside a third and final phenomenon which caused Batavia anxieties: the physical movement of indigenous peoples in certain places and contexts. The Hajj, or pilgrimage to Mecca, the cultural complex of wandering known as the Minangkabau *rantau*, and the nomadic wanderings of border peoples both in the forests and on the seas all posed serious problems to Dutch control of the border. This was especially so when such movements were accompanied, as they often were, by an increased access to contraband, such as opium sold outside state monopolies or the massive traffic in firearms. How were the many peoples of the Anglo/Dutch frontier to be ordered and controlled? What mechanisms were best for keeping these communities under the thumb of imperial designs? Perhaps most important, how could this be accomplished with minimum expenditure of resources and minimum loss of life? This complicated dialectic between European colonizers and colonized majority on the frontier ran continually just beneath the surface, as these expanding regimes sought to tilt the balance of surveillance, interdiction, and coercion in their favor over the space of half a century.

BORDER PACIFICATION AND THE REACH OF THE LAW

One of the main ways in which Batavia was able to strengthen its hold on far-flung indigenous populations in the Indies was through outright conquest. Dutch expansion in the archipelago was one of fits and starts, sometimes based on policy decisions, at other times reacting to events in various peripheries. There was no coherent program of expansion in its entirety, as many Indonesian historians have shown in an increasingly sophisticated historiographical literature based on regional conflicts.[3] At the turn of the nineteenth century, in fact, Dutch territorial control in the Indies held sway in little more than Java, parts of Sulawesi and Maluku, and a few scattered coastal settlements elsewhere in the islands. This was not so much an empire, as the VOC declined and then collapsed, as it was a colony of trade outposts, with the main nodes of importance widely scattered throughout the region. The middle years of the century saw little expansion, as Batavia saw any extension of existing possessions as costly and unlikely to pay for itself in future prospective revenues. This started to change in the 1860s, though it was the start of the Aceh War in 1873 that signaled the real beginnings of a sea change in Dutch policy.[4] Expansionism now became a vital part of government discourse, as the civilizing mission of the Netherlands was trumpeted with great fanfare and nationalism grew as a shaping force in politics and policy. Ironically, the demands this war made on Batavia proved so great that actual military expansion elsewhere in the archipelago took a back seat to Aceh until later in the nineteenth century. Yet by the mid-1890s, when the war in Aceh was going much better than it had in its first two decades, the tentacles of Dutch control had significantly spread. Lombok was overrun in 1894, while the remaining parts of Sumatra, Bali, Sulawesi, Borneo, Nusa Tenggara, Maluku, and New Guinea followed in the early twentieth century. Various interpretations have been forwarded to explain the guiding forces behind these wars, from economics and European competition to troubled peripheries and internal prestige, but the important fact is that almost all of the Indies was overrun in the space of a few decades.[5] By 1915, almost the entirety of the border arc was under various forms of Dutch control.

Two Outer Island confrontations are exemplary for this analysis. In southeastern Borneo, a war had been fought in 1860 to depose the sultan of Banjarmasin from his throne; the Dutch were able to claim control over the city and its coastal lowlands as a result, and the sultan and his party fled upriver into the interior. What happened next in this arena, however, as it did in many other places in the archipelago, showed the hazy nature of Dutch conquests and what they implied. The war continued in the periphery for the next several decades, pitting the original and rightful ruling dynasty against the forces of Dutch expansion and control. This can be seen in the reports of the local resident in the early 1870s: lands outside of immediate Dutch occupation were deemed completely unsafe, with resistance cropping up even in areas very close to Banjarmasin. Most of the danger, according to the resident, was attributable to bands of armed men who wanted to restore the sultan. The sultan himself was far away upriver converting various Dayak peoples, often with a great deal of success, the resident noted, to his cause of rebellion. Worst of all, from the perspective of the Dutch, was that the sultan was unreachable by law for all intents and purposes: the intersecting river systems in the interior meant he could appear at any moment, depending on which river he happened to traverse to get down to the lowlands.[6] Conquest in South Borneo, therefore, was contextual and ambivalent. The sultan's palace in Banjarmasin flew the Dutch flag, but meanwhile his followers traveled the length of the residency using rivers as their guides. Even into the early twentieth century, expeditions were being sent into the interior near the border to attempt to quell disturbances caused by remnants of the sultan's party.

A similarly fluid landscape of resistance is discernable in parts of South Sumatra. Here, Sultan Taha had been deposed by the Dutch in 1859; he fled with his followers to the Jambi uplands, where the sultan enjoyed "unlimited authority" ("onbeperkte gezag") even into the early twentieth century. This situation, lasting for several decades after the original war of conquest, sat very unfavorably with Batavia. "It is thus necessary," the first government secretary wrote in 1900, "to bring a change to this unacceptable state of affairs, and the resident of Palembang has already suggested means of force in order to accomplish this."[7] The resident had pointed out to Batavia that significant gains had been made both in Dutch weaponry and in Dutch tactics dealing with indigenous enemies—Aceh had taught this, if nothing else, to Indies military planners in Batavia. Yet the planned expedition into the interior took much longer than had been anticipated. The Dutch still had to wait for the water table to rise to get their ships upriver, and problems in supplying adequate stores of petrol further delayed the journey.[8] The next year Taha's insurgents were still being reported in upland positions, even as far inland as independent Kerinci, which they used as a safe haven.[9] The guerrilla war, which had started as a conventionally won conflict by the Dutch, would last until 1907. Using the rivers and hills as allies in insurrection, the sultan's forces were able to keep a much larger, technologically sophisticated enemy at bay for almost half a century. In South Borneo as in South Sumatra, therefore, there were ways to continue resistance against encroaching European authority all along the landscapes of the frontier.

These wars of conquest against "native enemies" are important in understanding how the state perceived threats at the turn of the twentieth century.[10] Though conventional conflicts against sultanates and petty kingdoms were invariably won by the Dutch, these conflicts rarely ended in neat demarcations of absolute Dutch control. Much more common was the scene that greeted Batavia's planners as they scanned their contemporary archipelago: low-level insurgencies were everywhere apparent, especially along the border arc (table 3). Such testings and proddings of authority were only exacerbated by the flow of illicit arms, which are examined later in this book. In western Borneo, numerous revolts against local Dutch proxies, almost always in the form of Malays ruling over Dayak populations, were reported in 1870; in southeastern Borneo, the aforementioned sultan's party was active, but so was the river rebel Wangkang, who at times amassed forces of one hundred perahus and five hundred men.[11] Insurrections had to be quelled in northern Sulawesi facing the southern Philippines and in Palembang and Jambi, where disturbances were only partially related to Taha's revolt further inland.[12] In Aceh, there was constant sniping at Dutch patrols well into the twentieth century.[13] Guns were available to indigenous peoples everywhere on the frontier, from North Sumatra to North Sulawesi and even in the heart of Borneo. They were used for hunting and for local squabbles but were also pointed at agents of the state by a range of indigenous actors all along the border.

A single incident from the eastern coast of Aceh in 1873 shows one of the reasons this state of affairs was so worrying to Batavia. In August, the Dutch steamship *Timor* was undertaking station duty on these coasts, checking passing craft for arms shipments and also enforcing the Netherlands' blockade against smuggling. Toward the end of the month, the *Timor* was off Idi, which of all the minor principalities in Aceh had always been the most favorable to the Dutch and in fact was considered a close ally in the struggle for North Sumatra. On the twenty-second, the *Timor* saw a small perahu advancing along Idi's coast; it was flying a red and white flag, Idi's colors, and moving toward the mouth of the Idi River. The captain of the *Timor,* C. Bogaart, sent an unarmed sloop to investigate. The small Dutch ship pulled near the perahu and then came skating back with the wind as fast as it could. The perahu, upon being approached, suddenly had bared cannon and invited the sloop to battle. The defenseless sloop returned to the *Timor,* while the perahu made for shore and her men disappeared into the forest. Bogaart was furious and took the matter up with the raja of Idi the next day. The raja's explanation was expected and understandable: he said the men must have been flying false colors, and the local peoples onshore who had helped them into the forest with their goods must also have been from a neighboring polity. When the perahu was brought to the Dutch as evidence, Bogaart commented that it was certainly a different craft from the one he had seen. He surmised what was later understood by the Dutch to be true everywhere on the frontier: almost all local rulers stood as Dutch allies only when it suited them. In this case, Idi acted as an ally only partially as a real policy: much of the rest of the time the polity, which counted no blockade on its coasts as part of its privilege of alliance, was funneling guns to the rest of the Acehnese.[14] The perahu of the day before undoubtedly had been involved in such activity. The Dutch learned quickly that even their purported local alliances on the frontier were not to be trusted.

Many indigenous peoples of the periphery, however, made no attempt to hide the nature of their insurgencies. Even into the early twentieth century,

Table 3. Armed Actions and Military Reporting in the Border Residencies of NEI, 1860–1916

Important Dutch Military Campaigns in the Border Residencies, Late Nineteenth and Early Twentieth Centuries	
Banjarmasin (South Borneo)	1860–65
Sedang and Asahan (East Coast Sumatra)	1864
Sintang (West Borneo)	1864
Deli (Sumatra East Coast)	1872
Aceh (North Sumatra)	1873–1913
Siak (East Coast Sumatra)	1876
Langasar (Aceh)	1877
Batak Regions (North Sumatra)	1878
Toba Regions (North Sumatra)	1883–87
Teunom (Aceh)	1884
Jambi (South Sumatra)	1885
Mandor (West Borneo)	1885
Trumon (Aceh)	1887
Sintang (West Borneo)	1896
Jambi (South Sumatra)	1901
Jambi (South Sumatra)	1916

NEI Military Reporting Template for the Outer Islands (1912):

Geographical Description of Region, to Include:
borders; mountain descriptions; hydrographic contours and monsoon particularities, landing places; rivers and their ability to be used as communications means; footpath connections to adjoining residencies; village terrain; vegetation and growth, and their effect on movement capabilities, etc.

Description of the Local Population, to Include:
relations of local people with adjoining residencies; total numbers and divisions thereunder; "fanaticism"; a dictionary of the local language; weaponing; experiences in former wars; local means of provisioning themselves; influence of "Foreign Asians"

Description of Transport Capabilities, to Include:
travel capabilities by land and sea; capabilities

Sources: Adapted from Heshusius (1986) and "Schema van de Militaire Memorie in de Buitenbezittingen, 1912"(in de Graaf and Tempelaars (1991))

Batavia was facing resistance to its state-making projects and was punishing "recalcitrant" populations who did not accept forms of central control. Instances of such suppression occurred over and over again on the border arc, albeit in different guises. A good source here is the *Indisch Militair Tijdschrift* (Military Journal of the Indies), which chronicled the penetration of the advancing Dutch frontier to its new eastern and western extremities. A Dutch expedition of 1889, for example, sent to explore tin mines in Flores, was attacked by local inhabitants there; in response, punitive strikes were sent by Batavia as late as 1907 in order to maintain Dutch access to the mines.[15] In Borneo and on Seram, in eastern Indonesia, head-hunting also served as a magnet for Dutch interference in the periphery, setting off small-scale insurgencies as local peoples fought Batavia's attempts to incorporate them into "civilized behavior."[16] In Halmahera, Maluku, the cause for resistance was tax evasion, as it was in South Sumatra, in the years surrounding 1908.[17] Finally, the twentieth century also saw insurrection in most central regions of North Sumatra, as Acehnese resistance spilled over into the Gayo and Batak regions, on the outskirts of the main theater of resistance.[18] Similar events were happening on the British side of the border. The Mat Salleh rebellion in North Borneo and periodic revolts against the Brooke regime in Sarawak also took place at this time.[19] All of these examples show variants of a common theme: expanding state control and local violent reactions to it along a wide section of the frontier. Insurgencies lasted until the early decades of the twentieth century. By the second decade of the new century, however, such resistance was increasingly futile, as the power of the state grew in new and unexpected directions.

Another important source for examining the marriage between political objectives and armed force in the frontier residencies is the *Politieken Verslagen Buitengewesten* (Outer Island Political Reports). The Political Reports are indeed political, but they are also profoundly military in nature as well: these two thrusts of Dutch expansion into the frontier could be separated only with difficulty until well after the turn of the twentieth century. The reports therefore chronicle the forward push of the Dutch colonial state in extraordinary detail, outlining how Batavia was able to subject the "peripheral" areas of the Indies archipelago to European rule in a variety of places and contexts. For the border landscapes facing the British imperium to the north, this meant a nearly endless program of contact and pacification, the latter often accomplished in fits and starts and only gradually achieving any real efficacy over long periods of time. This was the case on the eastern coast of Sumatra, where Batak populations continually resisted the imposition of tighter state controls on trade well into the 1900s.[20] This also happened further south in Sumatra in Jambi and in Lampung, with a continual state military presence proving necessary for far longer than Batavia's planners had hoped.[21] It was also true in both West and Southeast Borneo, two large residencies in which armed resistance to colonial programs of encroachment and governance continually took place into the early twentieth century.[22] Political maneuvering and military coercion therefore went hand in hand along the frontier, a state of affairs known to both colonizer and colonized alike.

A second way in which the Dutch Indies state tried to deal with potential threats from the indigenous population was through the codification of laws. We have seen how these laws were shaped by Europeans to fit concerns over the Vreemde Oosterlingen in the Netherlands Indies. Indigenous populations presented a different challenge to Batavia's policymakers because indigenes far outnumbered other populations, necessitating a different tactical approach under the law.[23] Indeed, for certain outlying areas of the archipelago, there was a cognizance that indigenes were outside of Dutch criminal jurisprudence altogether. The legal analyst C. W. Margadant commented on this in 1895, declaring that crimes committed by those peoples who had the right of self-government as part of their vassalage could not legally be punished by Batavia. J. W. G. Kruseman concurred in this opinion in 1902.[24] Such a state of affairs made the Dutch careful to control as thoroughly as possible those indigenes that were, indeed, directly under their jurisdiction. In 1873, a separate criminal code for local peoples was drawn up in the Indies, one that had none of the protections against government arbitrariness that European codes definitively espoused. Rights of the accused, custody, and protections against search warrants were all significantly less prominent than those outlined for Europeans. To make matters worse for the indigenous population, the court officers who sat in judgment upon them were very rarely trained jurists: more often than not, they were simply local civil servants. An effort to fix this less than fair situation was made in Java in the 1860s and 1870s, but in the Outer Islands it lasted far longer.[25] The result of these permutations was that the peoples native to the archipelago were kept under the thumb of Dutch law, in an effort to keep them pliant to Batavia's anxieties and wishes.

The fact that local peoples were judged in courts of law in the Outer Islands by Dutchmen only marginally prepared for the task caught the attention of the Indies press in the early twentieth century. Especially after the start of the ethical policy from 1900 onward, reformists asked how this could be allowed if there was a significant chance that indigenes received less than due process under the law as a result.[26] Lack of due process was not the only sign of a discriminatory judiciary in the Outer Islands, however. Other writers called attention to the fact that Dutch law and local practice in the border residencies often had little to do with each other, so that the indigenous population was often charged without due consideration for local constellations of culture. Snouck

Hurgronje was one of the most famous advocates of this position vis-à-vis Aceh in 1907, but similar calls were made to reconcile Dutch juridical theory and local practice in other areas of the frontier as well. A civil servant in Lampung, South Sumatra, phrased it this way: "Our judicature in the interest of the native population must be replaced by a practical, much quicker administration of justice, which fits local situations and conditions."[27] Still, evidence of state discomfiture in making these amendments lasted even to the turn of the century, as in one border residency case in which a suspect was held for fifteen months in preventive detention, the entire time without trial. Critics of the government asked if this sort of practice was at all defensible, from legal, political, or humanitarian vantage points.[28]

By the eve of the twentieth century, the entire corpus of discriminatory laws in the Indies that had been created to control the threat of local peoples was under assault in the Indies press. One of the first to be challenged was the law on preventive detention: the *Javasche Courant* of February 18, 1898, contained the new wording of the law on this issue, which now limited the powers of residents in their sentencing of indigenes to require probable cause.[29] Progress did not come without a price, however: the controlling interests behind these laws were still strong, and many critics of the legal structure vented their criticisms only anonymously. One such book made headlines in 1897, earning reviews by established scholars who were both sympathetic and angry.[30] Though Margadant lamented the fact that the author felt he could not use his name, other authorities reacted more conservatively: "I have become bitter. However much I continually have tried to keep this writer's good intentions in mind, it doesn't work. The further I read, the more I become convinced that his so-called revisions are merely an assault on the laws of the Indies."[31] The stakes of the argument were too high to forge a quick consensus: what was at issue was nothing less than how much representation local peoples would receive under the law and if they would continue to be treated as a threat. In the years leading up to 1915, there were further nods to the liberal spirit of the times; a commission was erected, for example, to study how greater numbers of the indigenes might be admitted to study the law.[32] The dawn of nationalism and nativist political entities in the Indies, however, effectively retarded these gains by the second decade of the twentieth century. As Takashi Shiraishi has shown, the years after 1910 often saw less, not more, political participation in Indies affairs by local peoples, as the state perfected repression as a tool against systemic change.[33]

Although the Indies legal structure treated indigenes as potentially dangerous to the power of the state, not all peoples of the border residencies were judged to be equally threatening within this rubric. Indigenous Christians, as we have seen, were equal to Europeans under the law until 1854: for civil, trade, and criminal matters up until that time, they were essentially reckoned with the power elite, though this changed with the new emphasis on race rather than religion after that date.[34] A significant proportion of Europeans in the Indies never liked this change, however, and continued to press for indigenous Christian rights under the laws. The spread of Christianity in the Indies certainly encouraged this lobby: Christian communities were to be found on most islands of the archipelago, though their concentration was larger in some places than in others.[35] These people had shed their blood for the Dutch for centuries in the Indies, and Christians were overrepresented in key institutions, most notably the Indies army. Many Dutchmen felt that their religion should make a difference in whether the state treated them as potentially threatening, as "conversion really does exercise a favorable influence on the natives' personal life. With Christianity come other thoughts to the forefront about law and justice, and these are the same ideas that Europeans hold as holy."[36] The government started to open this debate again in the 1890s, though there were still many who felt race, not religion, should determine Batavia's threat perception. "Men rightly hold the prospect of individual equality under the law with Europeans as a goad or stimulus; to spur the native forward toward development," said one commentator.[37] Indigenous Christians eventually remained where they were under these laws: racial perceptions and anxieties overrode all else in Batavia's eyes, even until the time of independence.

A last aspect of Dutch law and local practice pertaining to Batavia's control over indigenes and their activities on the border was the concept of *adat,* or traditional law. The Netherlands' expansion into the thousands of islands of the Indies brought the Dutch into contact with many diverse peoples and their customs. Adat was the Arabic-derived Malay term used to describe the many cultural practices encountered, practices that were only rarely codified into written compendiums of laws. As a colonial state with an allegedly civilizing, albeit repressing, agenda, the Netherlands Indies questioned whether Dutch law or local law held final sway in many conflicts and cases on the frontier. Batavia developed a piecemeal approach to this question in the late nineteenth and early twentieth centuries. Some peoples, like the Kubu, or forest dwellers, of inland Palembang residency, were left more or less alone to practice their own forms of jurisprudence, as they were seen to be marginal, "primitive" groups whose society was not really worth interference.[38] In other parts of the Outer Islands, however, indigenous criminal law as developed by local peoples was allowed to stand as it was, except for aspects that were deemed to be "incompatible with Western justice."[39] These practices included certain punishments and trials like maiming and torturing, which the Dutch found to be repugnant, at least when practiced by others rather than themselves. Still another option was the fusion of existing legal codes and Dutch law. Shipping contracts from Makassar, Southwest Sulawesi, show evidence of this variant, as trepang voyages to northern Australia were solemnized before the Dutch court even while containing many stipulations whose origins rested in older Makassar traditions.[40] The diversity of these practices in different border geographies shows the legal syncretism that held sway in these regions, often against Batavia's best efforts to the contrary.[41] Administrators in the field sometimes tested the rigidity of Dutch law by accommodating local practice, but many of Batavia's decision makers held onto the repressive force of Indies law for as long as they could. The Leiden professor C. van Vollenhoven became the great chronicler of adat traditions, but his adat project was conservative in orientation and ultimately helped keep indigenous communities firmly under Dutch legal jurisdiction.[42]

THE SPECTER OF MOVEMENT: HAJJIS, NOMADS, AND OTHERS IN MOTION

If outright conquest and a discriminatory legal structure were two ways in which Batavia tried to nullify the "threat" of local peoples to the state's authority, one phenomenon of indigenous life along the border presented more of a threat to these programs than any other: free and unrestricted movement. Though many peoples of the archipelago were more or less sedentary in the scope of their daily lives, certain groups moved in and out of the Dutch sphere—or simply through it—whenever and wherever they pleased. This was especially true of many nomadic and seminomadic groups like certain forest and sea peoples who inhabited areas of the frontier facing the Anglo/Dutch border. Yet it was also true of certain large-scale migrations such as the Hajj and the Minangkabau *rantau*. Free movements such as these subverted the controlling mechanisms of the state that had been erected to mediate contacts and commerce among locals. These movements also allowed passage through spaces where indigenes might or might not be able to get their hands on dangerous, border-crossing objects such as guns. Perhaps the single most important event within the greater scope of free movement in the Indies was the annual pilgrimage to Mecca. By the mid-1880s between forty thousand and fifty thousand Muslims from all over the world were undertaking the Hajj in any one year; the number of pilgrims from the Malay Archipelago, on both sides of the Straits, could comprise anywhere from 5 to 50 percent of this total, depending on the year.[43] Commentators on this grand, unifying event of the Muslim world wrote in awe of the scenes to be witnessed in Arabian cities during the pilgrimage time of year, as "Indians, Persians, Moors, Negroes from Niger, Malays from Java, Tartars from the Khanates, Arabs from the French Sahara, . . . and even Mussulmans from the interior of China" all descended upon Islam's holy cities.[44] Not all Europeans saw in these gatherings the makings of a grand spectacle, however, as the Hajj and its increasing influence on Islamic populations also elicited grave concern. A revival was said to be occurring, which was "difficult to believe had not received anxious consideration at the hands of those whose official responsibility lies chiefly in the direction of Asia."[45] Wilfred Blunt was wrong in this assessment. Colonial administrators in both Batavia and the Straits Settlements were already tracking radials of the Hajj and writing of their concerns to their respective metropolitan governments. By the early 1870s, for instance, a triangulation of Hajj surveillance had already been instituted by the Dutch in Asia, linking consuls in Jeddah and Singapore with supervising structures in Batavia.[46]

Surveillance was practiced on an internal level within the Indies as well. The movements of pilgrims who were undertaking or returning from the Hajj were routinely reported on, with particular interest lavished on the islands of the border arc. In South Sumatra, residents reported that the numbers of pilgrims were going up year by year; one of the three steamers which regularly plied the route between Palembang and Singapore, in fact, had now been converted to specially carry them back and forth.[47] In Bangka, the resident's figures also showed a rise in local people undertaking the Hajj over the long term, while in western Borneo, statistics were kept for the entire residency and also by individual *kampong* (village), with three times as many people leaving in 1878 as only five years previously (table 4).[48] In southeastern Borneo careful charts also were compiled, statistics which evidence a striking correlation between districts of high pilgrimage departure and those that received the largest assignments of Netherlands Indies soldiers.[49] Undertaking the Hajj was certainly not illegal, but it seems to have been equated in administrative discourse and procedure with areas of particular anxiety to the state.

Across the Straits of Melaka in the British dominions, many of these same concerns applied. Singapore was distressed in the 1860s that pilgrim ships often ignored regulations completely, stopping off at ports other than those on the

Table 4. Pilgrim Statistics to Mecca from the Dutch East Indies and Selected Border Residencies, 1873–1913

Pilgrims from the Netherlands East Indies to Mecca, 1881–1913

Year	Total Pilgrims from NEI	Total Pilgrims from Overseas	NEI as % of Total
1881	4,302	25,580	16.8
1883	4,540	31,157	14.6
1885	2,523	42,374	6.0
1887	4,328	50,221	8.6
1889	5,419	39,186	13.8
1891	6,841	54,491	12.6
1893	6,874	49,628	13.9
1895	11,78	862,726	18.8
1897	7,895	38,247	20.6
1899	5,068	unknown	unknown
1901	6,092	unknown	unknown
1903	9,481	74,344	12.8
1905	6,863	68,735	10.0
1907	9,319	91,142	10.2
1909	10,994	71,421	15.4
1911	24,025	83,749	28.7
1913	28,427	56,855	50.0

Pilgrims by Dutch East Indies Border Residency, 1873–1913

Year	1873	1878	1883	1888	1893	1898	1903	1908	1913
Lampung	105	54	139	26	114	197	268	95	593
Palembang	390	305	472	252	1100	800	436	310	1487
Jambi	nd	nd	nd	nd	nd	nd	nd	77	172
E Coast Sumatra	nd	51	259	210	322	413	274	137	638
Aceh	nd	nd	nd	3	17	73	79	30	308
Riau	4	17	3	31	218	24	nd	14	177
Bangka/Belitung	30	31	28	6	73	45	41	143	182
West Borneo	47	149	131	187	260	230	201	119	563
SE Borneo	209	184	241	173	644	603	716	668	1053

Source: Adapted from Vredenbregt (1962): 139–49.

manifest to pick up more people for the journey. A large number of these illegal stoppages occurred in Dutch border residencies, often in hostile territory in northeast Sumatra.[50] Statistics compiled and cross-checked in the Straits and Aden (Yemen) show how egregious these "secret pick-ups" could be: the numbers of pilgrims on a ship could often be off by literally hundreds of souls, as more and more devotees were picked up along the way.[51] This kind of loss of control over something as politically and religiously charged as Islamic journeying worried these states to no end. By the 1880s, a passport system had been developed to keep better track of these movements, but of the thousands of archipelago peoples who made the journey each year, only a tiny fraction ever applied for these documents, keeping area states blind in this regard.[52] Singapore and Batavia often had little idea of who was actually mixing on these ships, despite their carefully collected data at the source in each residency. Straits ordinances got tougher and tougher over the years in trying to redress this situation, with careful rules specified for sites and times of departure, powers of police inspection, and penalties for transgressions of the laws.[53] A part of the legislation was also intended to protect pilgrims as well as oversee them: sinkings, mal-treatment, and disease were all quite common, as outlined in period literature accounts like Conrad's *Lord Jim*.[54]

By the 1880s and 1890s, the numbers of archipelago peoples from the border residencies making the journey to Mecca were generally on the increase. This worried Batavia in particular because the Hajj was being blamed as a transmitter of militancy to other parts of the world (for example, to Sudan in northeast Africa) precisely at this time. In western Borneo, the number of pilgrims exceeded one hundred per annum for most of the late 1880s, while in southeastern Borneo, just to the east, the figures often doubled (and sometimes tripled) these totals into the 1890s.[55] Riau did not normally see significant increases in pilgrims, but Palembang reported that more and more were making the trip, especially in years of agricultural prosperity.[56] Such movements often led to the mixing of Arab and indigenous bloodlines, especially in residencies where Pan-Islam was deemed to be a recurring problem. In Jambi, for example, the "rebellious" Sultan Taha and his lineage had long-standing Arab ties; in western Borneo, especially among the former sultan of Pontianak's house, the Hajj had also woven Arab and indigenous bloodlines.[57] Batavia therefore saw in the passage of Islamic pilgrims the seeds of potential conspiracy and dissention, especially in the border residencies. This was stated explicitly in an Indies government pronouncement of 1883: the governor-general warned that Hajjis were using the Outer Islands as staging areas for insurrection, knowing that such places were still out of reach to the Dutch.[58]

By the turn of the twentieth century, statistics on pilgrimage source points and percentages in the Netherlands Indies were revealing an interesting trend: Hajj departures from the Outer Islands, especially from areas along the border arc, were absolutely smaller than departures from most parts of Java, but as a percentage of population they were often larger than the Javanese figures.[59] Put another way—a Muslim arc seemed to be becoming more and more discernable in the frontier residencies. When this trend was measured against much of the unrest already noted in the Outer Islands during these decades, Batavia started to pay even closer attention to such movements. Important Indies thinkers like P. J. Veth understood the connection between completing the Hajj and the resulting local prestige: returning pilgrims were treated with enormous respect, whether they came back to Java, Madura, or any of the border areas.[60] In the years after 1910, with the founding and growth of Islamic political organizations like Sarekat Islam and Muhammadiyah, vigilance of and uneasiness about the Hajj in Dutch policy circles only grew. Across the Straits in Singapore, legislation which kept both a suspicious eye on the pilgrimage and which also genuinely attempted to alleviate some of its abuses continued into the twentieth century.[61] Neither the British nor the Dutch disallowed their subjects to set out on the Hajj, but at best it was seen as a troublesome exercise to monitor. At worst, colonial administrators saw the pilgrimage as yet another threat to European rule: exposing local populations to material and ideas that all were far better off without.

The Hajj was only one, albeit the most important, of many aspects of indigenous movement that were seen to be potentially threatening to state making in the region. Nomadism, forays across the Indies borders, the Minangkabau *rantau*,[62] and even the state's own program of sponsored transmigration also elicited various levels of European concern. The relation of these phenomena to threat perception cannot be ignored (see below), but a linking factor in all of these movements was the rising power of the market in the Indies, which encouraged and enabled movement in the indigenous pursuit of profit. Many of these kinds of movement were of long standing: archipelago peoples had been accustomed to distant trade ventures for many centuries, and the idea of journeying in quest of commerce was by no means new. Yet the changing structural conditions brought about by European rule intensified the role of movement and the market in new ways. Daniel Chew has shown how rising demands for forest products drove many Iban to downgrade their own rice agriculture and concentrate instead on journeying to find such products, often as far away as Malaya, New Guinea, and the eastern coast of Sumatra.[63] James Warren has also commented on the effects of rising prices and competition for commodities such as these, showing how certain Bornean peoples began to move great distances to protect their access to birds' nest caves, as the nests themselves became tremendously valuable.[64] Descriptions of a vast array of goods in circulation even in the heart of Borneo should make the attractions of journeying clear: local peoples could obtain metals, textiles, salt, and dried fish, if they were willing to search out the markets that provided them.[65] If the market encouraged movement even in this forbidding terrain, it should come as no surprise that indigenes traveled in other locales too, where the Dutch state was building roads, steam connections, and later even rail lines. The problem from the Dutch vantage was that Batavia's infrastructure might ultimately be used against it: these same "blessings of modernity" could also be used to move arms, dissent, and dangerous ideas.

Western Borneo shows some of these dynamics in action, particularly as they relate to the frontier. Local peoples used the border as a tool, moving back and forth across it to their advantage in specific contexts. In the early 1870s, when the Dutch were acknowledging certain Malay chiefs as vassals in the Sintang interior, these men used their sponsorship to increase exactions on local Dayak populations, both for corvée duties and for forest product collection. Many Dayak groups responded by promptly picking up and relocating across the border, thereby revealing how shallowly Malay and, by extension, Dutch power had penetrated the area at this time.[66] By the mid—1880s and even into the 1890s, however, the problem had still not gone away. The Sarawak government was sending representatives to Pontianak asking for Dutch help in controlling the Batang Lupar Dayaks, who made continual incursions over the border into the British sphere. The Dutch resident responded by burning Dayak settlements on the frontier and forbidding further settlement there as well as by trying to force the Batang Lupar groups to settle permanently by lakes in the interior.[67] Dayaks in the region not only moved across international boundaries, however, to cause mayhem in both states. By the late 1880s they were also adeptly using Dutch administrative boundaries, realizing that European authority fractured along such lines, making punishment and enforcement more difficult. In 1888, a head-hunting expedition came from over the mountains in southeastern Borneo and took many heads in Bunut; Malays on the western side of the Borneo dividing line then organized a retaliatory raid, arming 150 men in the process.[68] The Dutch were unable to stop either action from developing. Even by the turn of the century such movements leading to disturbances in the state's peace were still fairly common. In 1905, Raja Brooke of Sarawak wrote that armed bands of Dayaks were still finding refuge on the Dutch side of the frontier, while four years later violence spilled over the other way, this time incensing Pontianak.[69] The movement of local populations across the border was the key: Dayaks realized they could ensure a better deal for themselves in terms of corvée, forest product collection, and tax obligations only if they maintained access to both sides of the frontier.

Such freedom of movement was the norm not only in the forest center of Borneo, however. It also was evident by sea. Indigenous peoples of the archipelago often moved great distances through the vast maritime spaces of the archipelago, causing Batavia and Singapore frequent anxieties as a result. In the first half of the nineteenth century, maritime slaving in Southeast Asia reached from the shores of southern Burma to Luzon in the Philippines, passing through the Indies in an arc of violence and despair. By the late nineteenth century, these sorts of expeditions were being stamped out by European steam power but were being replaced by lesser, lower-level movements that still demanded state surveillance and control. British scientific surveys on sea peoples in the area, such as the Cambridge expedition of the late 1890s, were eagerly read and filed by the Dutch Ministry for the Colonies: the Dutch wanted as much information as possible on the mobile populations inhabiting their frontier and used these data alongside their own.[70] Government residents in the Outer Islands also sent information on this subject to Batavia. The administrator for southeast Borneo reported that thousands of people were leaving his residency by boat, looking for work in Sumatra.[71] In western Borneo, it was the Bugis who were most active on the sea: the resident there cautioned Batavia of huge movements of Bugis migrants entering his residency, sometimes from the east in perahus from Sulawesi and other times from the west en route from Singapore.[72] Batavia undertook investigations of these maneuvers to decide which peoples in what contexts were dangerous and which were not. The primary concern of the state was to keep its own authority paramount on the frontier. This was a proposition that could be challenged if population balances radically changed or the sea lanes were threatened in any way.

It was indeed the specter of large-scale movements of specific ethnicities that made Batavia most nervous. Not all groups fit into this category: the Wood Age Kubu of South Sumatra, for example, were a predominantly migratory population, but their relative isolation and perceived "lower stage of development" did not render them as threatening to the state.[73] Other populations were seen in less benign terms. We have seen how the movement of ethnic Arabs, or people of mixed Arab and Malay descent, into the interior of Palembang and Lampung were frowned upon by the Dutch, mainly for proselytizing reasons. The movement of Bugis populations (as above), with their relatively strict traditions of Islam and formidable traditions of violence, also occasioned grave concern.

Yet there were other groups who also fit into this category. Acehnese traveling in other parts of the Indies were always watched after 1873, primarily because of the bitterness of the war. However, even Minangkabau travelers from West Sumatra undertaking the cultural complex of wandering known as *rantau* also elicited concern. Though Batavia had been aware of the existence of the *rantau* for quite some time by the late nineteenth century, the radials of this migration—throughout most of Sumatra and sometimes further afield—filled the Dutch with caution.[74] The fact that most Minangkabau were also fervent Muslims and that the region had a history of armed resistance to the Dutch helped these state anxieties along.

Even the state's own policies of planned movement, such as the transmigration program to ferry Javanese to South Sumatra, thereby relieving Java's crushing population problem, occasionally raised fears in Batavia. Not all Dutchmen saw the utility in these relocations, eyeing the benefits of population distribution less and the potential negative outcomes of state-sponsored migration, among which were chaos, instability, and ethnic rivalry, significantly more.[75] The extreme complexity of different kinds of population flows in the Outer Islands therefore produced varying narratives of how to deal with such movements in the center. What was generally agreed upon by all European parties, however, was that large movements of local peoples, in 1865 as in 1915, were always potentially dangerous to the stability of the colonial state. The border had been pacified for the most part by this later date, but it was still seen to be wild space in certain places and in certain contexts. Opportunities for smuggling and the transit of objects inimical to state interests were still very much possible along portions of the frontier. It is to the actual movement of a range of these dangerous commodities that we now turn.

NOTES

1. By the classification rubric *native* the Dutch (and British) in Southeast Asia meant Acehnese, Bataks, Boyanese, Bugis, Javanese, Malays, and a variety of other peoples indigenous to the region. Up until 1871 in Singapore, all of these groups were classified individually; after 1871, they were subsumed under the category Malay.
2. For the wider implications of an argument along these lines, see Tagliacozzo, "Finding Captivity Among the Peasantry" (2003), 203–32.
3. See Achmad et al., eds., *Sejarah Perlawanan* (1984); Napitupulu, *Perang Batak* (1971); and Gayo, *Perang Gayo* (1983).
4. See *Perang Kolonial Belanda di Aceh* (1977); and Van't Veer, *De Atjeh Oorlog* (1969).
5. See, in that order, Lindblad, "Economic Aspects of Dutch Expansion in Indonesia" (1989); Kuitenbrouwer, *Netherlands and the Rise of Modern Imperialism* (1991); Black,

"The 'Lastposten'" (1985); Hirosue, "The Batak Millenarian Response" (1994), 331–43; and Locher-Scholten, *Sumatraans Sultanaat en Koloniale Staat* (1994).

6. ANRI, Politiek Verslag Residentie Borneo Zuid-Oost 1872, 1873 (no. 4/2, no. 4/3); ANRI, Algemeen Verslag Residentie Borneo Zuid-Oost 1886, 1887 (no. 9a/7, no. 9a/8).

7. First Gov. Secretary, Batavia, to Commander, NEI Army, 18 April 1900, no. 120 Secret (Djambi, fiche no. 324–25) (MvK, PVBB).

8. Resident Palembang to GGNEI, 3–20–1900, no. 39 Very Secret, and same to same, 5–1–1900, no. 57 Very Secret (Djambi, fiche no. 324–25) (MvK, PVBB).

9. Van Tholen, "De Expeditie naar Korintji in 1902–1903: Imperialisme of Ethische Politiek?" (1989), 71–85.

10. Local polities looked for allies where they could against the Dutch. The Sultanate of Riau, for example, explored the possibilities of an alliance with Japan. See Andaya, "From Rum to Tokyo" (1977), 123–56.

11. ANRI, Politiek Verslag Residentie West Borneo 1870 (no. 2/8); ANRI, Maandrapport Residentie Borneo Zuid-Oost 1870 (no. 10a/5).

12. "Kraing Bonto-Bonto" (1872), 198–233; Gov. Heckler to GGNEI, 27 Sept. 1905, Telegram no. 554 (Riouw, fiche no. 294, 296) in (MvK, PVBB).

13. Van Daalen, Kotaradja to GGNEI, 20 Nov. 1905, Telegram no. 909; same to same, 16 Dec. 1905, Telegram no. 962, both in (Atjeh, fiche no. 10 (MvK, PVBB), for example. Many more citations exist on the phenomenon.

14. Report of Capt. C. Bogaart, "Timor," to Military Commander, Aceh, 23 Aug. 1873, inside August 26 jacket of same to same, ARA, MvK, V. Geheim Kabinet 17 Dec. 1873, D33 (no. 6042).

15. Schmidhamer, "Expeditie naar Zuid Flores" (1893), 101–15, 197–213; Tissot van Patot, "Kort Overzicht van de Gebeurtenissen op Flores" (1907), 762–72.

16. Troupier, "Borneo" (1909), 1046–51; "Kort Overzigt" (1906), 167–69.

17. "Kort Overzicht van de Ongeregeldheden" (1907), 328–31; see Young, *Islamic Peasants and the State* (1994).

18. Alting von Geusau, "Tocht van Overste Van Daalen" (1939), 593–613; Kempees, "Na Dertig Jaren" (1934), 111–16.

19. See Pringle, *Rajahs and Rebels* (1970), and Walker, *Power and Prowess* (2002).

20. See, for example, ARA, Assistant Resident of Batak Affairs to GGNEI, 14 April 1904, #1656/4 (Sumatra O.K., fiche no. 156) (MvK, PVBB).

21. ARA, First Gov't Secretary to Army Commander, 18 April 1900, Secret #120 (Djambi, fiche #324), and Resident, Lampongs, to GGNEI, 5 June 1906, #1221 (Lampongs, fiche #386) (MvK, PVBB).

22. ARA, Resident, West Borneo to Raja of Sarawak, 29 April 2005, #2320 (West Borneo fiche #394), and Resident Borneo, Southeast to GGNEI, 22 May 1909 (Borneo ZO, fiche #477), (MvK, PVBB).

23. For an overview, see Burns, "The Netherlands East Indies: Legal Policy" (1987), 147–297.

24. See Margadant in his *Verklaring van de Nederlandsch-Indische Strafwetboeken* (1895); Kruseman, *Beschouwingen over het Ontwerp-Wetboek* (1902), 61.

25. Fasseur, "Cornerstone and Stumbling Block," 34.

26. Kielstra, "Rechtspraak over de Inlandsche Bevolking" (1907), 1020.

27. Hurgronje, *Atjehers* (1893–94), 11; Kielstra, "Rechtspraak over de Inlandsche Bevolking" (1907), 165. The quote is from Perelaer, "Rechtspraak over de Inlandsche Bevolking" (1908), 422.

28. "Belangrijke Wijzigingen in de Rechts" (1898), 431.

29. The *Javasche Courant* (18 Feb. 1898) contains the modifications on the "Rules of the Exercise of the Police, Civil Administration of Justice, and Punishment of Natives and Those Legally Classified as Natives" (Ind. Staatsblad 1848, no. 16), as per the Koninklijke Besluit of 7 Oct. 1897.

30. Anonymous, *Rechtspraak in Nederlandsch-Indië,* (1896).

31. Margadant, "Beoordeling van het Geschrift "De Rechtspraak in NI" (1897), 1; see also Pieper's review in "Rechtspraak in Nederlandsch Indië" (1897), 298.

32. "Inlanders bij de Rechtelijke Macht" (1906), 432.

33. See Shiraishi, *An Age in Motion* (1990).

34. See Hekmeijer, *Rechtstoestand der Inlandsche Christanen* (1892).

35. Hekmeijer, writing to a legal audience in *Wet en Adat,* gave the numbers of indigenous Christians in the Indies around 1896 as follows: He counted approximately 26,500 indigenous Catholics, mainly in Minahasa and on Flores and Timor; around 212,000 indigenous Protestant church members, mostly in Maluku and parts of Java and Minahasa; and approximately 90,000 indigenous Christians not belonging to any single Christian denomination, who were primarily to be found on Java, Sumatra, Borneo, Nias, Savu, Sumba, and New Guinea. See Hekmeijer, "Inlandsche Christenen" (1896/1898), 31.

36. Schich, "Rechtstoestand der Inlandsche Christenen" (1892), 1532.

37. Rutte, "Is Gelijkstelling van den Christen-Inlander met den Europeaan Wenschelijk?" (1899), 56.

38. Gersen, "Oendang-Oendang of Verzameling van Voorschriften" (1873), 108.

39. "Hindoe-Strafrecht op Lombok" (1896), 166.

40. "Makassarsche Scheepvaart-Overeenkomsten" (1897), 48 passim.

41. For West Borneo alone, chronicling the *adat* of various groups can take up to six hundred pages; see Lontaan, *Sejarah Hukum Adat* (1975).

42. See his masterwork, Van Vollenhoven, *Het Adatrecht van Nederlandsch-Indië* (1906); see also Holleman, *Van Vollenhoven on Indonesian Adat Law* (1981).

43. Wolluston, "The Pilgrimage to Mecca" (1886), 408.

44. Blunt, *Future of Islam* (1882), 1–2; see also Hurgronje, *Mekka,* (1931), and Witlox, "Met Gevaar voor Lijf en Goed" (1991), 24–26.

45. Ibid., 3–4.

46. ARA, 1872, MR no. 820.

47. ANRI, Algemeen Administratieve Verslag Residentie Palembang 1874 (no. 64/17).

48. ANRI, Politiek Verslag Residentie West Borneo 1870 (no. 2/8).

49. ANRI, Algemeen Verslag Residentie Borneo Zuid-Oost 1871 (no. 9/2). See the statistics on Amuntai and Martapura in particular.

50. See *SSLCP,* 17–5-1869 on this common occurrence in Acehnese waters.

51. Gov SS to Secretary of State, Colonies, 18 Dec. 1873, no. 396, CO 273; on pilgrim ships leaving Singapore between 1870 and 1872, for example, the *Venus* had 582 people in ex-

cess of her registry by the time she landed in the Middle East, the *Fusiyama* was 267 over, the *Sun Foo* was 388 over, the *Ada* was 268 over, the *Rangoon* was 265 over, and the *Jedda* was 338 over.

52. Gov SS to Secretary of State, Colonies, 6 March 1889, CO 273/254. With 2,000–3,000 pilgrims leaving Singapore every year, the numbers of passports issued was next to use-less: one was issued in 1881, three in 1882, four in 1884, two in 1885, one in 1886, three in 1888, two in 1889, etc. The state had little real vision of who was undertaking this yearly journey. See Vredenbregt, "The Hadj: Some of its Features" (1962), 91–154, and Roff, "The Malayo-Muslim World of Singapore" (1964), 75–90.

53. See *SSGG,* Ordinance no. 16 of 1897, no. 9 of 1898, and no. 9 of 1899.

54. Conrad, *Lord Jim* (1968).

55. ANRI, Algemeen Verslag Residentie West Borneo 1886 (no. 517); ANRI, Algemeen Ver-slag Residentie Borneo Zuid-Oost 1886 (no. 9a/7).

56. ANRI, Algemeen Verslag Residentie Riouw 1890 (no. 64/1–2); ANRI, Algemeen Verslag Residentie Palembang 1886 (no. 65/6).

57. ARA, Resident Palembang to GGNEI (1 June 1881, Very Secret) in 1881, MR no. 563; see also Van Goor, "A Madman in the City of Ghosts" (1985).

58. ARA, Extract Uit het Register der Besluiten Gouverneur General, NI (8 March 1883, Very Secret no. 4) in 1883, MR no. 252.

59. "Bedevaart naar Mekka, 1909/1910" (1910), 1638.

60. Veth, *Java: Geographisch, Ethnologisch, Historisch* (1907), 128–67.

61. See *SSGG* Ordinances no. 12 (1901) and no. 3, no. 17 (1906) for amendments both on pil-grim ships and pilgrim brokers.

62. The *rantau* of the Minangkabau peoples of western Sumatra will be discussed further in the pages that follow. Here I briefly allude to the phenomenon as a culture-based migra-tion pattern that took young Minangkabau men away from their villages in western Sumatra, sometimes for long periods at a time. Other peoples of the archipelago also had rantau patterns of their own.

63. See Chew, *Chinese Pioneers,* 109.

64. See his discussion of the Segai-i and other peoples of the forest interior and littoral; com-petition was intense and spurred much violence (including head-hunting raids) over large parts of the island. Warren, *Sulu Zone,* 90 passim.

65. Some of the goods found traded in marketplaces in Borneo were guttah, rottan, iron, copper, textiles, tobacco, gambier, dried fish, timber, and rice; also much desired but in lower supply were glass, oil and salt, beads, and gold. See ANRI, Algemeen Adminis-tratieve Verslag Residentie West Borneo 1874 (no. 5/4).

66. ANRI, Politiek Verslag Residentie West Borneo 1870 (no. 2/8).

67. ANRI, Algemeen Verslag Residentie West Borneo 1886 (no. 5/17); *Sarawak Gazette,* 3 Jan. 1893.

68. ANRI, Algemeen Verslag Residentie West Borneo 1888 (no. 5/19).

69. Raja Sarawak to Resident West Borneo, 12 April 1905 and 16 May 1905 (West Borneo, fiche no. 394); Resident Southeast Borneo to GGNEI, 22 May 1909 (Borneo Z.O., fiche no. 477) both in (MvK, PVBB). For contemporary scholarship on this topic, see Pringle, *Rajahs and Rebels* (1970).

70. Skeat, "Orang Laut of Singapore" (1900), 248, referenced in the Ministry for the Colonies Archive, The Hague (ARA, MvK). The authors came to the conclusion that six of the eight ethnic stems of the then-contemporary Singapore Orang Laut were in fact piratical maritime peoples. The eight stems were Orang Tambus, Mantang, Galang, Pusek, Sekanak, Barok, Moro, and Sugi.

71. ANRI, Algemeen Verslag Residentie Borneo Zuid-Oost 1889(no. 9a/10). Most were searching for work on Sumatra's tobacco plantations.

72. ANRI, Algemeen Verslag Residentie West Borneo 1889, 1890 (no. 5/20, no. 5/21).

73. Verkerk Pistorius, "Palembangsche Schetsen" (1874), 150. This was the case more or less for the Orang Asli in Malaya as well; see Harper, "The Orang Asli" (1998), 936–66.

74. *Rantau* journeys could reach all the way north to the tip of Sumatra, up and down the west coast of the island, to parts of the east coast (including Jambi and almost to Medan) and even across the strait to Negeri Sembilan (a Minangkabau colony in Malaya). They sometimes stretched even further. See Naim, *Merantau: Pola Migrasi Suku Minangkabau* (1979), esp. 2–3 and the map on page 65. Period accounts of Minangkabau cultural practices can be found in Van Eerde, "De Adat Volgens Menangkabausche Bronnen" (1896), 209–20; and Klerk, "Geographische en Etnographische Opstel" (1897), 1–117. For a good discussion on the period under discussion, see Graves, *The Minangkabau Response to Dutch Colonial Rule* (1981), 19–21. Other archipelago peoples also undertook forms of *rantau;* the Minangkabau complex is only the most famous.

75. For an encapsulation of the debate on this issue and some of its history, see Ockerse, "Emigratie van Javanen naar de Buitenbezittingen" (1903), 1223; "Emigratie naar de Lampongsche Districten" (1906), 1734; Rouffaer, "Uitzwerving van Javanen Buiten Java" (1906), 1187–90; and Caron, "Immigratie en Irrigatie op de Buitenbezittingen" (1908), 707. A good contemporary treatment looking back historically is Tirtosudarmo, "Dari Emigratie ke Transmigrasie" (1996), 111–21.

Part II **Crossing the Frontier: Smuggling,**
Profit, and Resistance

Section III Secret Trades, Porous Borders

The influence of the criminal upon the development of the productive forces can be shown in detail. Would the locksmith's trade have attained its present perfection if there had been no thieves? Would the manufacture of banknotes have arrived at its present excellence if there had been no counterfeiters? Would the microscope have entered ordinary commercial life had there been no forgers?
—Karl Marx, "Theories of Surplus Value," in Bottomore (1964), 159

Chapter 8 The Smuggling of Narcotics

As the Anglo/Dutch border was being created, it simultaneously was being crossed by huge numbers of people carrying a wide range of commodities. Some of these sojourners were continuing trades that had been moving across local spaces for a very long time. Others were reacting to new economic opportunities created by the imposition of a bicephalous modernizing colonial state structure in the region. Still others traded in items that worried these regimes, either because the commodities were crucial to the governments' moral and economic underpinnings or because moving them constituted an act of political resistance. "Smugglers" fell into all three of these categories in interesting and innovative ways. The second half of this book analyzes a range of state-designated contraband trades to see how the border was penetrated by a variety of interested parties. How flexible was this evolving frontier? What were its strengths and its weaknesses? What mechanisms could be used to get contraband cargoes across the border, and how was porosity to be judged? What classes of commodities could be brought across the divide successfully, which items ultimately failed, and how was one to make decisions about the best items to traffic?

THE LURE OF OPIUM

Judging purely by the number of cases surviving in the records, no commodity was smuggled as often or to such profit in Insular Southeast Asia as opium. The illicit passage of several other narcotics, most notably morphine, cocaine, and marijuana, can be charted between 1865 and 1915 (see below), but for sheer volume and intensity opium was far and away the most important smuggled drug crossing the Anglo/Dutch frontier. Its transit both in Southeast Asia and in the wider orbit of Asian trade led to the publication of a substantial amount of period literature in which scholars and statesmen tried to figure out exactly what to do about the region's "opium problem."[1] Opium was a commodity of many contexts; as one recent historiographical contribution has stated, it was a "palliative medicine, an item of recreational consumption, an addictive drug food, a form in which capital could be stored, a sign of national and ethnic degradation, and a mechanism for transferring wealth and power between regions and nations."[2] The preeminence of opium as a border-crossing commodity of great value lasted throughout the period under discussion here. What can its polymorphous character tell us about the nature of local boundaries and smuggling?

Several hundred years of European occupation in Indonesia set the stage for the massive movements of this narcotic. While for centuries the Dutch brought thousands of kilos of raw opium to the Indies every year, their monopoly on the drug from 1677 onward never fully functioned. Dutch servants of the VOC, whether traders, administrators, or even armed soldiers out on patrol, made fortunes on smuggling, and in the process large quantities of opium were steadily siphoned off from the official channels for sale. The Amfioen (opium) Societeit, from 1741, and the Amfioen Directie, from 1792, institutions that inherited the VOC opium monopoly, could not curb smuggling either. There was simply too much profit to be made on the drug and too little strict control on its official distribution to enable these bodies to have a real impact on the illegal trade.[3] Indigenous rulers in the archipelago reacted to the expanding sales of opium in different ways. Some, like the sultan of Banten and the raja of Lombok, fought against its introduction but ultimately lost this battle. The first Dutch structure built in Aceh after conquest in the early 1870s, one scholar has claimed, was not a school or a church, but a Dutch-sanctioned opium den.[4] Other archipelago rulers, most notably those bordering the Sulu Sea, took the initiative and used opium to expand their own power bases, distributing the drug to vassals and potential clients.[5]

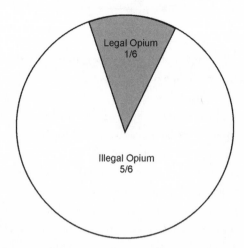

Fig. 8. Legal and illegal opium coming into the Dutch Indies, c. 1900. (*Source:* Scheltema, "The Opium Trade" [1907], p. 244)

By the late nineteenth century, however, most opium in Southeast Asia was portioned out by colonial states to Chinese revenue farmers, who paid huge sums for the privilege of retailing the drug to local populations. Eventually this system too was abolished, between 1894 and 1898 in the Dutch Indies and around 1910 in the British possessions. Chinese were thought to be too unreliable in stanching smuggling outside of the revenue farm; colonial states were also more fully taking over the reins of economic control in their respective colonies at this time.[6] The direct sale and supervision of the drug were ultimately adopted by the two colonial administrations, yet this did not stop opium smuggling on a massive scale either. Around the turn of the twentieth century, the Dutch consul in Singapore estimated from intelligence available to him that five times more illegal opium was in transit to the Indies than the legally moving supplies, a figure that probably increased after Batavia took over direct control of the retail trade (fig. 8).[7]

Studies on opium in the region have focused on several themes but are especially well represented in the pages of three important monographs. On the British side of the Straits, Carl Trocki's *Opium and Empire* has looked at opium as one of the lynchpins in class struggle in Singapore. As laboring and merchant classes of Chinese struggled for dominance in Straits society, opium was used as a tool by the British government to bond the latter group to its rule.[8] A predominantly Hokkien-speaking subset of merchants (*taukeh*) sold opium under the aegis of the state to rural Teochew laborers and later to an exploding population of urban workers as well. The urban proletariat of Singapore also forms the focus of James Warren's *Rickshaw Coolie,* which provides a bottom-up, subaltern perspective on opium use in the Straits. Warren examines how opium slowly destroyed the lives of many of the urban poor, consuming anywhere between 60 and 80 percent of their wages in a hopeless fight against drug addiction.[9] James Rush's *Opium to Java* examines opium as an institution in the Dutch East Indies, especially as it pertained to Chinese farms and Javanese customers in central and eastern Java.[10] Rush's study paints a portrait of how opium entered indigenous communities and of the efforts of the state to both modulate and make a profit on this enterprise at the same time. All three of these books have added enormously to an understanding of opium in the region, but the wider history of opium crossing this frontier—against the monopolies of the two colonial states and away from the centers of Singapore and Java—is not yet written. Though there are now several internationalist histories of opium in Asia generally, its role along the border arc (Aceh down to Riau and then up again to North Borneo) still needs exploration.[11]

Only a small start can be made toward that goal here, one that examines the breadth, not the depth, of smuggled narcotics. A more comprehensive study on this topic could consume an entire monograph. The first place to start in such an examination is the superstructure of laws created to modulate opium's transit across the border. On the Dutch side of the frontier, these regulations encompassed a variety of themes: from stipulations to prevent the medical misuse of opium by apothecaries and similar professions, to competencies granted to forest police to search for (and seize) opium in the course of their patrolling duties.[12] Dutch warships and the Indies coast guard were given legal authority to search passing ships for illicit opium, while research trips for detectives—all the way to Singapore and even South China—were authorized in order to track down smugglers in their home countries, before they could export to the Indies. Special laws enacted after the turn of the century show Batavia's concern that illicit opium was seeping into the armed forces as well as into the European community itself.[13] Yet most of the drug was always destined for Asians, whether they were from the various indigenous groups of the archipelago or Indies Chinese. A territorial limit of only a few miles beyond the coasts seriously impaired Dutch abilities to make seizures, however, as did the legal system itself, which allowed culprits access to the best Indies lawyers, if they could pay the fees.[14]

The legal edifice in the Straits Settlements, where most Indies-bound smuggled opium originated, at least in transit, also tried to enact an imposing superstructure to discourage the contraband trade by sea. Laws modulated the arrival and departure times of steamers known to be carrying opium to the colony, while also providing powers of search and forfeiture, in the hopes of discouraging smugglers from the outset. A five-thousand-dollar fine could be imposed for farmers illegally moving opium to another sovereign state, while opium warehouses were given specific instructions on how the drug was to be stored, watched, and entered in official ledgers.[15] *Chandu,* the retail, ready-to-use derivative of opium, was also given wide coverage in the legal apparatus, from laws enabling spot searches without any warrant to protection granted to informers in ultimately successful seizures.[16] Impressive as this edifice was, from 1865 to 1915 opium continued to stream into the Indies. It also continued to come into the British possessions as well.[17] As the inspector-general of finance in the Indies put it in 1872, few commodities provided better weight- or size-to-value ratios for smuggling than contraband opium.[18]

Even as early as the 1860s and 1870s opium smugglers were using the whole of the border to get their cargoes into the Indies. The Dutch consul in Singapore complained that trafficking was increasing exponentially in the 1870s, with the drug entering in all "forms and manners, in cases, bales, in tins of sardines, or preserved meat, in kegs and tins of butter, in wine casks, in bottles, in sausages," and in a variety of other casings, including fully assembled furniture.[19] The islands south of Singapore were among the primary destinations of these journeys: an inspection tour of Chinese villages on the Bangka coast, for example, revealed a huge smuggling trade to the Dutch, while statistics from Riau in 1871 show that fully a third of all court cases in the residency's capital district dealt with transgressions against the revenue farmers.[20] The authorities in Singapore were aware of these connections and attempted, with varying degrees of success during the nineteenth century, to keep the farms in Singapore and Dutch Riau in the same farmers' hands.[21] This deterred some opium smuggling some of the time, but often the drug simply found other routes. By the end of the 1870s, the Chinese farmer of Belitung was pleading with Batavia for more manpower in the form of opium agents, as a desperately phrased letter in Malay makes clear.[22]

The tiny inlets and intricate waterways south of Singapore were not the only passageways for the drug into the Indies. The entire length of the Straits of Melaka acted as a shallow sieve, one that leaked contraband opium onto the coasts of Sumatra, undermining the evolving monopoly of Batavia. Statistically, Singapore seems to have been the focus of this activity, though Penang also played a part and Melaka a much more minor role in the distribution of the drug.[23] By 1874, for example, large stretches of Palembang were being inundated with illicit opium, a situation the local resident attributed to insufficient policing power and the desire of village heads to supplement their meager incomes with the bribes smugglers could offer.[24] In Aceh, where the war raged unabated in the 1870s, contraband opium also found a ready market. The Netherlands-Indies marine officer A. J. Kruijt wrote about the inability of even Dutch-allied princes on the Aceh coast to stop their subjects from smuggling the drug to hostile Acehnese, while opium was also quietly transited in the holds of passing ships, including occasionally Dutch military supply boats calling from Penang.[25] The Dutch vice-consul in Penang reported in 1876 that according to his spies, opium was still available to the war party in Aceh at little more than prewar prices, despite official Dutch bans and the three-year blockade.[26]

The situation in the 1870s on the Borneo frontier was little different. Batavia's powers of surveillance and interdiction simply could not live up to the ideal of an indirectly controlled Dutch monopoly on opium. One reason for this was the existence of the entrepôt of Labuan in the British sphere, which in 1870 farmed out not only the rights to retail chandu, but also the import, export, and transport of the drug as a revenue device as well. A free port like Singapore, Labuan quickly became a regional center for opium smuggling to the surrounding territories, carried especially by small coasting craft that visited the colony's creeks and bays at night.[27] The extended and virtually unguarded border between Dutch West Borneo and Sarawak was also a hive of opium smuggling activity, however, as the drug crossed into the Dutch sphere mainly through the agency of the Chinese of Landak, earning them the epithet of "inveterate opium smugglers" from the government administrator there in 1872.[28] "The lying of this division on the coast nearby Singapore," he said, "and on the land side bordering Sarawak, gives plenty of opportunity to the clandestine import of opium, as the means toward watching the many entrance points by sea and by land are simply insufficient."[29] Here too, as in Riau, transgressions against the farm were by far the largest single crime statistic in local police ledgers.[30]

Corruption and what the Dutch saw as unholy alliances between smugglers, farmers, and officials greased the wheels of the massive amounts of illegal opium coming into the Indies. Many civil servants, one columnist wrote, helped along the contraband trade in opium by receiving payments for their intercessions. Some officials made a few hundred guilders a month in this manner, while the more audacious government functionaries could earn up to five hundred guilders a day for moving large quantities of the drug.[31] "The only thing that is certain," stated one other commentator, "is that such an enormous illegal trade in opium is only possible through the connivance of officials. . . . It is an open secret that the lower native civil servants and police enjoy huge sums from the farmers."[32] Court cases brought to light clear instances of graft caused by the huge profits of opium smuggling, while other cases brought before the judiciary had to be changed on appeal because of the influence of corruption.[33] The same exasperated observer above who quoted illicit prices received by officials for turning a blind eye to shipments estimated that the Indies bought fifty million guilders of opium per year, but that the government enjoyed revenue on less than 40 percent of this sum.[34]

By the 1880s and 1890s, certain patterns of ethnic participation in opium smuggling make themselves clear in the records. Chinese were among the most frequent offenders in these illicit transactions, appearing in Singapore, on the high seas, and in Dutch notices as well. The Malay-language press in Singapore is one place to search for these records, as often the subgroup of detained smugglers (they were usually Hainanese or Hokkien) is explicitly stated:

> *Ampat orang Hokien telah tangkap di Jalan Bencoolen Street, pada pukul 9 pagi, satu hari bulan ini, sebab membawa chandu gelap.*
> [Four Hokkien were arrested on Jalan Bencoolen Street at 9 in the morning one day this month because they possessed illegal opium.]

> *Chee Ah Jin, orang Hylam; adi tukang api di kapal di bawa ka Court smalam sebab dapat chandu falsu di dalam badan-nya yang harga $66, sudah di hukum ulih tuan Magistrate $100 atau 2 bulan jail.*[35]
> [The Hainanese Chee Ah Jin, ship's engineer, appeared before the court this evening for possessing illegal opium on his body worth $66, and has been judged by the magistrate with a fine of $100 or two months in jail.]

Charts kept by the Dutch consul in Singapore and by the administrators of Outer Island residencies in Sumatra show that Chinese were heavily involved, often appearing in over 50 percent of all compiled seizure records.[36] Yet Chinese syndicates and even individual, small-time operators looking to make some quick money were not alone in these ventures. Arabs were known to undertake smuggling journeys as well, sometimes making connections as they returned from the Hajj, and Armenians were large wholesale exporters of the drug too.[37] The local peoples of the archipelago also moved opium quietly when they could, often as crew members or passengers on steam vessels passing through the Indies (table 5).[38] Europeans, of course, also contrabanded the

Table 5. Dutch East Indies Illegal Opium Seizure Notices, Border Residencies, 1880s

Date	Residency	Circumstances
Aug 20, 1885	Bangka	Tongkang #1285, owned by the Arab Said Abdulrachman, was caught running a large amount of opium toward Palembang.
Oct 6, 1885	Indragiri	Opium smuggled to Indragiri by the super-cargo on the crew on the steamer *En Goean*
Oct 20, 1885	Bangka	Opium smuggled by the Chinese Lim Ah Kie and Tan Ah Soeie on tongkang #235 en route to Mentok.
Nov 21, 1885	West Borneo	The perahu *Tane Djelei* en route to Sukadana smuggled 3 cases of opium.
Nov 25, 1885	Bangka	Opium smuggled on board tongkang #236 en route to Mentok.
Feb 10, 1887	West Borneo	400 tahils of prepared opium smuggled on board the perahu *Phenis* declared for Kota Waringin January 28 and later en route to Sukadana February 5.
May 14, 1887	West Borneo	100 tahils of prepared opium smuggled on board the vessel *Loot Dazin* en route to Sambas.
Aug 4, 1887	East Borneo	One case of prepared opium and 300 tahils of unprepared opium smuggled on board the perahu *Phenis*.

Source: ARA, Dutch Consul, Singapore to GGNEI, 10 Dec 1885, #986 in 1185, MR #807; Dutch Vice-Consul to MvBZ, 30 Jan 1888, #106.

drug in large numbers. Ships' officers and engineers were among the most common culprits, like one Scottish boiler-room attendant caught on the Singapore/Batavia run in 1890.[39]

A glance at Belitung in the 1880s, one of the Dutch tin-mining islands south of Singapore, shows some of the reasons opium smuggling was so rampant. A letter from the Dutch-appointed opium farmer there, Ho Atjoen, to the governor-general of Batavia reveals several of the structural conditions that plagued the opium monopoly in a place like Belitung. Straddling the sea routes to Java, close to Singapore's port and supporting a large Chinese mining population, the island was a natural destination for opium smugglers setting out from the Straits.[40] Beyond Belitung's geography and population, general economic conditions during this period also made it an attractive haven for opium runners:

for example, the general falloff in trade in the late 1870s, which pushed many into smuggling to make a living, poor maritime policing in the area, and the willingness of local chiefs to engage in illicit transactions themselves.[41] In the second half of 1880, no fewer than fifty-five people in this small division were under suspicion of smuggling opium; the main routes of supply and distribution stretched both northwest to Singapore and northeast to Pontianak in Borneo, where the schooners of Chinese opium runners like Bong Kiesam and Ja Ji Tjong plied.[42] The Dutch tried to check the expansion of the trade, sometimes by extracting confessions from suspected miners and later by significantly strengthening their coast guard presence in the area.[43] By the end of the 1880s, a net of revenue cutters was cruising the Straits around Belitung, and spies had been inserted into the mines to report on any suspicious activities.[44]

The border residencies' proximity to Singapore and the influx of large numbers of Chinese there gave rise to some fascinating stories of opium smugglers out on the frontier. One of these was a man named by the Dutch A. Liang Ko. A. Liang Ko grew up by the side of a broad river in an undisclosed locale on the border that was visited by both small and large ships conducting commerce in the area. He went to Singapore with his father on trading expeditions, and by the age of eighteen he was a regular on these journeys. A few years later Liang became a captain on one of his father's trading ships. Singapore was an "outstanding learning place" for him, the journalist J. W. Young said, because there he became familiar with all of the ways and means of smugglers. Eventually he was noticed by the customs police, and things became more difficult for him. But the profits were too high for Liang to resist, and he got involved again in smuggling after some time off. Once he escaped a seizure action by jumping overboard, and he was followed by sharks and had to swim a considerable distance to escape the Dutch revenue cutters. Eventually he built a great house and became an important man in his local community. All of the ironies of the Dutch opium system were apparent in Young's account: huge opportunities existed for smugglers to the detriment of the opium farmers, and men such as Liang eventually became farmers themselves because their smuggling helped drive previous merchants out of business. Such tales are interesting because they show how for many years along the length of the Indies frontier commercial legitimacy and illegitimacy went hand in hand.[45]

Western Borneo also saw a continuous stream of incoming opium in the years leading up to the turn of the century. In the 1870s, as we have seen, much of the drug seems to have been moved by ethnic Chinese settlers on the Sarawak frontier. This pattern continued unabated into the 1880s and 1890s. By

1889, the resident had singled out the far-flung network of the Ngee Hin Kongsi as being primarily responsible for the traffic, as they bought and intimidated witnesses in West Borneo to ensure the arrival of their product.[46] Yet the routes into this residency were more circuitous as well. Islands some distance from the western Borneo coast, including Belitung, as we have seen, also served as supply centers. By the late 1880s, even the northernmost Dutch islands in the South China Sea, Natuna, Anambas, and the Tambelan groups, were also being used as transit points. An investigation conducted by the crew of the Dutch steamer *De Ruyter* in 1888 found that passing American ships (whose crews told the local inhabitants they were Russians) landed opium in the islands, which was then carried on to West Borneo. The ruse was discovered when the *De Ruyter's* crew asked villagers in South Natuna to describe the smuggling ship's flag—and were told it was thoroughly covered in stars and stripes.[47]

No matter how circuitous the route into the Indies, however, most contraband opium passed through Singapore before reaching its eventual destination across the Dutch border. The geography of the colony and of the surrounding areas facilitated this passage, according to the colonial engineer Major McCallum. "The very configuration of our settlements," he said, "lends itself to smuggling operations. A minimum of territory to the maximum of coastline, our bays, creeks, and rivers are full of junks passing incessantly to and from adjacent foreign states, which can be reached by them in smooth water and in a short time."[48] Of course, geography was only one part of this equation; Singapore's opium could almost always be bought cheaper than on the Dutch side of the border, and its enforcement mechanisms, though impressive on paper, were in reality riddled with weaknesses and loopholes. A great number of opium court cases tried before the Singapore magistrates make this fact clear; opium contrabanders used any one of a number of strategies to get out of trouble when they had been caught smuggling nearly red-handed.[49] These included questioning arrest procedures through their lawyers, using hiding places that were technically open and available to public passersby, and getting convictions overturned, often because several offenses had been lumped together in sentencing. Dutch court cases from the years around the turn of the twentieth century reveal the same dynamics in motion.[50] All through the 1880s literally thousands of opium seizures were made yearly by the Dutch, one source estimating that Singapore smuggled four thousand piculs of opium per annum, just to the Netherlands Indies alone.[51] Many in the Dutch press were disgusted with the way these figures were manipulated and "spun" by the Batavia administration, however. The *Indisch Gids* sneered that whether seizures went up or down, the government claimed victory: they quoted improved enforcement if the numbers rose, and smugglers' fear of continuing their criminal activities if the seizures declined.[52]

OTHER DRUGS AND LATE DEVELOPMENTS

Opium was not the only narcotic traveling across this porous frontier. Morphine, an alkaloid isolate of pure opium, cocaine, and marijuana also made the trip. The legal edifice around morphine was nearly as impressive as that around opium itself, with Dutch legislation on the drug starting in the early twentieth century and English laws a little earlier.[53] Morphine was defined as morphia or any salts or solutions of morphine, and special laws targeted chemists and other professionals who might have access to the drug and its transit.[54] Because morphine's introduction was much later than opium's, much of the legal architecture aimed at controlling it was borrowed from existing opium laws, with powers of search, witness protection, and procedure often largely transcribed from earlier laws.[55] Yet the later date also allowed for new ordinances to be passed, such as fingerprinting of suspects and more stringent controls on the passage of medical syringes.[56] Despite these advances, press reports on morphine smuggling regularly appeared in the Straits in the early twentieth century, both in Malay- and English-language newspapers.[57] Police accounts of this period also supply a fascinating window into morphine possession and its movement, especially evasion mechanisms and the various means used to hide the drug:

> It had taken us a little time to get into the house. We must have made more noise than we had first imagined, for we found no one in the room where the injections were reported to be given—no one except a Chinese woman with an infant on her knees. The child was a noisy child, it was lying on its stomach on a cushion, and the mother was patting its behind and crooning. We had been misinformed, so it seemed, and I was for leaving; but Ellis of the Malayan Civil Service . . . eyed the mother, the baby, the cushion, and stepping forward he lifted the infant. No wonder it had been crying; it must have been very uncomfortable, for under it and now lying exposed on the cushion were syringe, morphia phials and other paraphernalia! There was a large Chinese bed in the corner of the room, and from under it we pulled an incredible number of men who had lain there, piled on top of each other, as motionless as dead bodies.[58]

A series of large, interconnected morphine seizures in 1906 display some of these issues writ large. In January of that year, a case containing fifteen pounds of muriate of morphia was seized in the Penang jetty sheds of Messrs. A. Denys and Co.; the addressee, a Chinese company in Penang named Ho Guan, turned out to be a front. After persistent inquiries, the shipment was tied to a Chinese bill collector at Messrs. Huttenbach and Co., one of the suppliers of the Dutch army in Aceh, and to a Chinese subagent for the Langkat Oil Co., also on the northeast coast of Sumatra.[59] The shipper was a firm named Baiss Bros. and Stevenson in England. Subsequent correspondence dug up by the police revealed a chain of morphine orders and requests for discretion passing between Britain and several Chinese men in the Straits. Between January 1904 and February 1906, it turned out, twenty-eight shipments of morphine had passed between the two places, containing between 32 and 420 ounces of the drug per shipment.[60] The letters themselves are very revealing. One Chinese client pleaded, "I hope you will, however, not express my name," while the Baiss Brothers themselves assented to sending the morphine and all correspondence about it under separate covers (the morphine was marked "medicines" or "merchandise.")[61] The Colonial Office, in dealing with the correspondence, the seizures, and an evasive Baiss Brothers firm back in England, nevertheless was flustered by the inadequacies of the laws on morphine, which allowed the British firm to escape prosecution. The governor of the Straits Settlements, Sir John Anderson, was more direct; as a result of the case he wrote home to London that morphine smuggling in the colony was spinning out of control, and he requested stringent new laws to curb its burgeoning growth.[62]

Three years later, in 1910, Anderson was again writing to England, this time about cocaine. London's slow pace in enacting stricter legislation and the absence of complementary laws between Britain and the colonies (which allowed English smugglers to escape prosecution on technicalities), were causing more and more worries in the Straits. The governor wrote to the Colonial Office that "whatever may be the evils of opium smoking, the evils resulting from . . . cocaine injection are immeasurably greater in intensity and extent so far as the numbers physically and morally ruined by it are concerned. In spite of the activity of the police and revenue officers, and the systematic banishment of professional injectors and dealers in these drugs, we are, I regret, making no real progress toward an effective diminution in the evil."[63] By 1907, Straits law was officially including cocaine, salts of cocaine, and any "solutions thereof" in the Deleterious Drug Ordinances. By 1910, eucaine and its analogs were also listed as banned substances.[64] Legislation followed shortly thereafter on the Dutch side of the border, most notably by Government Bijblad no. 8253.[65]

Like the Baiss Brothers case in 1906, a major seizure of cocaine in Penang in 1914 reveals some of the parameters of the contraband cocaine trade. In March of that year three hundred ounces of the drug were seized in a sampan belonging to Lim Tsui Leng in Penang harbor. The cocaine had been sewn up in six bundles of sackcloth, each with an inner lining of the Copenhagen newspaper *Ekstrabladet.* The trail of the investigation eventually led to a shop called Sun Seng, where newspaper scraps of the same paper and same date were found. As the Penang police widened the inquiry and called in first the help of the London police force and then the Colonial and Foreign offices, it became apparent the captured shipment of cocaine was only one of many that had found its way down to the Straits. Here again false names were being used as addressees, though the trail this time led not only back to England, where the "British Iron and Enamel Works Co." of London was implicated, but also to Denmark, and to the offices of the worldwide German shipping concern, the Hamburg-America Line. Seven other shipments of similarly packed goods, addressed to the same consignee in Penang, were eventually discovered. In response to this large-scale European smuggling of cocaine, Governor Anderson's successor in the Straits, Governor Arthur Young, continued his predecessor's tradition of directing a plea for renewed action back to London. This was to little avail. On the eve of the First World War, Whitehall had more pressing concerns than the passage of drugs to England's far-flung colonies.[66]

The movement of marijuana, or *ganja* as it was called more commonly in the colonial records around the turn of the century, was also widespread. Marijuana's retail sale, like that of opium, was sometimes farmed out in the Straits, usually in a form called *bhang,* or paste, which could then be consumed in a variety of ways.[67] Toward the end of the century, however, this official allowance of marijuana (or ignorance of it, in the case of no action being taken at all) was no longer tolerated, and the British authorities in the region tried to clamp down on its use and sale. The Ganja Prohibition of 1898, which went into effect on January 1, 1899, effectively outlawed the sale, transport, or possession of marijuana in much of the Malay Peninsula and stipulated fines of up to one thousand dollars for repeat offenders or incarceration up to an entire year.[68] One problem with the new system, however, was that the new proscriptions did not come into force everywhere at the same time, so that Selangor, for example, possessed a bhang farm until 1899, while nearby Negeri Sembilan did not.[69] A second problem had to do with what ganja actually was taxonomically, as area peoples had been accustomed to using a variety of mind-altering plants since time immemorial. The 1898 prohibition, therefore, specifically had to define ganja as the "young flower, gum, stems, fruit, or leaves of the plant cannabis sativa, or the plant clerodendron siphonanthus."[70] The definition was provided by a botanical expert, L. Wray, curator of the Perak Museum. The Dutch took a similar interest in the quiet movement and cultivation of marijuana, especially in Aceh, where it became more commonly used during the war because of the ban on imported opium supplies.[71]

Yet even with the introduction of new narcotics and the new attention being paid to older ones like marijuana, opium remained the most common smuggled drug in the Straits in the years around the turn of the century. We can see this in the cities, overland in Borneo, and on the high seas. The maritime dimension of opium smuggling at the fin de siècle remained paramount: most of the contraband opium and chandu finding its way into the Indies arrived by water. The stress laid on sea routes can be seen not only in the grim attention Batavia paid to French mail steamers coming into Dutch waters, but also in Malay-language press reports of chandu being smuggled to major cities in the Indies (fig. 9).[72] Jambi, in Sumatra, facing a string of British ports on the Straits of Melaka, was still trying to get as many new police officers as it could and double its allotted interdiction expenditures for 1908, all in order to fight contraband opium coming across the Straits.[73] As early as 1892, Dutch policy planners were realizing that the water war against drug smugglers was being lost and that more drastic measures needed to be taken, including the recruitment of more spies.[74] In 1893/94, thousands of guilders were set aside to build steamers specifically for opium interdiction, which found form finally in the construction of the *Argus* and her sister ship, *Cyclops*. Built in Vlissingen for the Indische Gouvernements Marine, each was made of galvanized steel and could cruise at seventeen miles per hour with searchlights blazing for any unwanted intruders.[75]

The urban sprawl of Singapore directly across from the Indies remained the center of these illicit journeys even into the early twentieth century. One reason for this was that prices for chandu remained lower in Singapore than in the Dutch border residencies, especially after the introduction of Batavia's government-controlled opium *regie* in the mid-1890s.[76] Another, equally important reason, however, was that contraband syndicates in Singapore had built up a large stock of knowledge on how to beat existing systems of interdiction through artifice and loopholes in the law. Court cases in Singapore around the turn of the century show this incontrovertibly. Laws which protected ship owners and captains against ownerless seizures on board and proscriptions on when and how warrants needed to be served were all bent to the service of professional smugglers.[77] The deceptions on how to get opium into the Indies were known as far away as China, where the British inspector of imperial Chinese customs, Sir Robert Hart, was forced to get involved in matters.[78] Craft de-

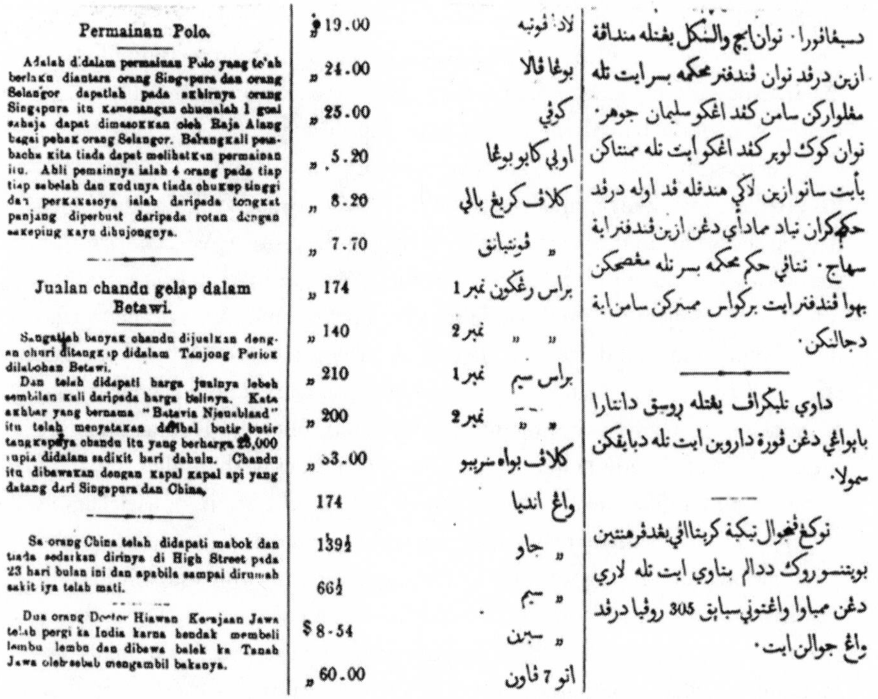

Permainan Polo.

Adalah didalam permainan Polo yang telah berlaku diantara orang Singapura dan orang Selangor dapatlah pada akhirnya orang Singapura itu kamenangan chumalah 1 goal sahaja dapat dimasokkan oleh Raja Alang bagai pehak orang Selangor. Barangkali pembacha kita tiada dapat melihatkan permainan itu. Ahli pemainnya ialah 4 orang pada tiap tiap sebelah dan kodanya tiada chukop tinggi dan perkakasnya ialah daripada tongkat panjang diperbuat daripada rotan dengan sakeping kayu dihujongnya.

Jualan chandu gelap dalam Betawi.

Sangatlah banyak chandu dijualkan dengan churi ditangkap didalam Tanjong Periok dilabohan Betawi.

Dan telah didapati harga jualnya lebeh sembilan kali daripada harga belinya. Kata akhbar yang bernama "Batavia Njeuwsblad" itu telah menyatakan dahal butir butir tangkapanya chandu itu yang berharga 25,000 rupia didalam sadikit hari dahulu. Chandu itu dibawakan dengan kapal kapal api yang datang dari Singapura dan China.

Sa orang China telah didapati mabok dan tiada sedarkan dirinya di High Street pada 23 hari bulan ini dan apabila sampai dirumah sakit iya telah mati.

Dua orang Doctor Hiawan Kerajaan Jawa telah pergi ka India karna hendak membeli lembu lembu dan dibawa balek ka Tanah Jawa oleh sebab mengambil bakanya.

Fig. 9. Opium smuggling into Batavia, 1909. (*Source: Utusan Malayu,* 2 Feb. 1909, p. 2)

clared they were en route to Hainan and South China with opium cargoes but then never showed up in these places at all, turning south instead into the Dutch sphere. Hart described a system in the waters of the South China Sea whereby only one-third of all junks with opium coming from Singapore actually were seen; two-thirds of the ships completely escaped inspection, and paid no duties. A complex system laid out by Singapore and China to telegraph arrivals never really worked. Strategies involving Portuguese Timor, on the distant eastern side of the Indies archipelago, were also utilized.[79] These journeys all had Singapore in common as a starting point for illicit movement. Reading the Straits presses around the turn of the century, in fact, is often akin to reading a police blotter: almost every day seizures were reported in both the Malay- and English-language editions.[80]

Aside from the maritime world of the Straits of Melaka and the urban milieu of Singapore, opium was still also transiting in the early twentieth century in and around Borneo. For various Dayak peoples on the Dutch side of the frontier, the attraction was obvious; long accustomed to trading and using opium, the indigenous peoples of the interior were now denied legal access to the drug as part of the Dutch "civilizing mission."[81] Yet the enforcing of these bans and of similar restrictions on the British side of the border that stipulated exactly when and where chandu was allowed to be bought proved to be more difficult in reality than on paper. The opium farms in various British—but legally autonomous—regions like Sarawak, Brunei, and North Borneo ended at different times, giving windows of opportunity to smugglers before the respective states took on direct responsibility for sales.[82] Prices also varied across these administrative frontiers. Sarawak under the Brookes proved particularly reluctant to bring retail levels up to parity with its neighbors' prices, as doing so would have lost the "White Rajas" business on their cheap opium.[83] Sandakan, in northern Borneo, became a famed haven for smuggling vast quantities of opium to non-British territories, usually in the hulls of small boats. "*Moro*" crews, who often represented Chinese interests, regularly took one hundred to five hundred tins of opium on these voyages, sailing with known winds and tides to rendezvous points.[84] The tentacles of the state may have been ever extending their reach in early twentieth-century Borneo, but there were still many places the British and Dutch alike could not begin to reach.

The composite picture, therefore, of how narcotics smuggling worked at the end of the century is a complex one. Both colonial states on either side of the Straits had taken direct measures to control the opium trade in particular, yet with only ambiguous results at best vis-à-vis smuggling. Top Dutch officials acknowledged as much in reports back to Batavia.[85] Critics of the Indies administration were less circumspect in their appraisals, however, and asked how the government could believe that disinterested civil servants would strive harder to curb smuggling than Chinese farmers whose livelihoods had depended on it.[86] Smuggling does indeed seem to have risen, partially because prices on legalized chandu were raised and partially because the now out-of-work farmers often used their specialized knowledge of smuggling mechanisms to practice it themselves.[87] On the British side of the frontier, Byzantine narcotics legislation and its uneven application in various territories and among various peoples also ensured continuity in smuggling. As already demonstrated, in the second decade of the twentieth century rules were drawn up for various British dependencies in the area, but these regulations were also written internally, within each polity. In the Federated Malay States, for example, legislation drew distinctions by race, occupation, and even coastal versus interior habitation as to whether narcotics use was acceptable. In the Unfederated Malay States also, prices, permits, and import/export rights varied from state to state.[88] The sheer complexity of the system on both sides of the border and the colonial states' inabilities to enforce the convoluted laws evenly across both of their dominions guaranteed that narcotics contrabanding would continue to thrive along the frontier well into the early twentieth century. Yet the British and Dutch regimes fared moderately better against other lines of illegal commerce. Among them, as we shall see, was the passage of counterfeit currency.

NOTES

1. See Turner, *British Opium Policy* (1876), and *Report of the International Opium Commission* (1909), for two important studies.
2. See Brook and Wakabayashi, eds., "Introduction" (2000), 24.
3. "Amfioen" translates roughly to "opium." For an interesting contemporary history of opium use in the Dutch-dominated Indies, see Baud, "Geschiedenis van den Handel en het Verbruik van Opium" (1853), 79–220. A useful modern history can be found in Vanvugt, *Wettig Opium* (1985).
4. See Scheltema, "The Opium Trade in the East Indies" (1907), 80–81. I have not been able to confirm if Scheltema's information on Aceh was correct; the Banten example dates from the seventeenth century, while the Lombok citation was late nineteenth century.
5. See, for example, Warren, *The Sulu Zone* (1981), which describes the circulation of opium as a way that sultans and datus ensured fealty with their subordinates.
6. See Trocki, "Drugs, Taxes, and Chinese Capitalism" (2000), 79–104. Also see Butcher and Dick, eds., *The Rise and Fall of Revenue Farming* (1993), an excellent edited volume on revenue farming in Southeast Asia with many important contributions.
7. Scheltema, "The Opium Trade," 244.
8. Trocki, *Opium and Empire* (1990). Trocki makes brief mention of the smuggling of opium outside of Singapore's borders, especially to Johor and Riau.
9. Warren, *Rickshaw Coolie* (1986).
10. Rush, *Opium to Java* (1990). Rush also deals peripherally with issues of movement and international contraband; his study is primarily concerned with Java (and to a lesser extent, Bali.)
11. Trocki's study on Singapore, as stated, includes a small discussion on Johor and Riau vis-à-vis the Singapore farms, and Rush incorporates Bali into his examination of opium smuggling into East and Central Java. No present work examines the Anglo-Dutch frontier, however, in regard to opium smuggling between the two colonial spheres. For new transregional histories of opium in Asia, detailing sourcing from India and Turkey and the involvement of other empires in this commerce (such as the Japanese), see Trocki, *Opium, Empire, and the Global Political Economy* (1999), Meyer and Parssinen, eds., *Webs of Smoke* (1998), and Jennings, *The Opium Empire* (1997).
12. See Staatsblad 1890, no. 149, and Bijblad no. 4428; for forest police regulations, see Staatsblad 1899, no. 122.
13. Staatsblad 1882, no. 115; for detective interdiction journeys see Bijblad no. 7462, and no. 8198; Staatsblad 1911, no. 644, and Staatsblad 1911, no. 494, respectively.

14. "Opium-Smokkelhandel op Zee" (1884), 30–32.

15. *Straits Settlements Ordinance* 1894, no. 9, articles 5, 45, 13; *Straits Settlements Ordinance* 1902, no. 36; for warehouses, see *Straits Settlements Ordinance* 1903, no. 19, articles 5, 8c, 9a.

16. *Straits Settlements Ordinance* 1909, no. 21, articles 28, 38.

17. See, for example, the *Perak Gov't Gazette,* 1893, 258.

18. ARA, Inspecteur Generaal van Financien to GGNEI, 31 May 1872, no. 10A, in (MvK, Verbaal 20 Aug 1872, no. 37).

19. ARA, Dutch Consul, Singapore to Secretary General, Batavia, (7 May 1877, no. 239) in 1877, MR no. 317.

20. ANRI, Maandrapport Residentie Banka, 1879 (no. 105/6 June); ANRI, Algemeen Administratieve Verslag Residentie Riouw 1871 (no. 63/2). The Bangka inspection party under inspector of finances Dr. de Roo visited Tanjung Tedung, which was "famed as a place of smuggling," and also Penagan, two centers for the illegal trade.

21. *SSLCP,* 21 Aug. 1873, 123–25. See the governor's discussion in the Legislative Council Meeting of that week.

22. ARA, Letter from Ho Atjoen, Opium Farmer in Belitung, to GGNEI (22 Dec. 1880) in 1881, MR no. 828. Ho Atjoen was the Chinese kapitan and opium farmer for 1880–82. He also had the farm for the next three years after that and complained bitterly of all the illegal opium trafficking taking place between the island and Singapore.

23. See the opium statistics produced in *SSBB,* 1873, 369–70 for Singapore, 444 for Penang, and 478 for Melaka.

24. ANRI, Algemeen Administratieve Verslag Residentie Palembang 1874 (no. 64/16). Specifically singled out were Rejang, Lebong, Sindang, Ampat, Lawang, and Ranom.

25. J. A. Kruijt, *Atjeh en de Atjehers* (1877); also Dutch Consul Penang to GGNEI, 30 March 1876, no. 91, G/Confidential, in ANRI, Aceh no. 13, Kommissoriaal, 13 May 1876, no. 326az. On the *Devonhurst,* a steamer contracted by Messrs. Katz Bros., Penang agents of the government contractors in Aceh, a Chinese man was caught trying to smuggle opium into Aceh.

26. ANRI, Aceh no. 12, Dutch Consul Penang to GGNEI, 7 Jan. 1876, no. 83, G/Confidential, in Dept. van Oorlog VII, no. 192, 31 Jan. 1876.

27. Governor Labuan to CO, 6 Jan. 1874, no. 1, CO 144/42; Governor Labuan to CO, 28 Jan. 1870, no. 55, CO 144/32. The governor remarked that the crafts entering and exiting Labuan for these purposes were small enough that they used oars when the wind failed. They carried no manifests or cargoes other than opium.

28. ANRI, Politiek Verslag Residentie West Borneo 1870 (no. 2/8); ANRI, Politiek Verslag Residentie West Borneo 1872 (no. 2/10).

29. Ibid., "Bijzonderheden Verpachten Montrado."

30. ANRI, Algemeen Administratieve Verslag Residentie West Borneo 1871 (no. 5/2); ANRI, Algemeen Verslag Residentie West Borneo 1874 (no. 5/4). The crime statistics mentioned are for Montrado only.

31. "Onze Opium Politiek" (1884), 406–07.

32. "Atavisme der O.I. Compagnie" (1884), 427.

33. "Opium Reglement. Openbaar Ambtenaar. Omkooping," *IWvhR,* no. 846, 1879, 147–

48; "Nog Eenige Opmerkingen over Amfioen-Overtredingzaken," *IWvhR*, no. 520, 16 June 1873, 96.

34. "Onze Opium Politiek" (1884), 409.

35. See *Bintang Timor*, 4 Jan. 1895, 2; *Bintang Timor*, 28 May 1895, 2.

36. See ARA, Dutch Consul Singapore to GGNEI, 10 Dec. 1885, no. 986, in 1885, MR no. 807. This is an extraordinary cross-sectional document which shows the extent and directions of opium smuggling for a single year. Chinese were caught running contraband opium to, among other places, Deli, Indragiri, Bangka, Belitung, and several places in Java; ARA, Governor of Sumatra's West Coast to Director of Finance, 1 Dec. 1883, no. 8762, in 1883, MR no. 1174. In his residency during 1882–83, forty-six opium seizures were made; thirty-one of the cases involved Chinese, twelve Malays, two Javanese, and one a native of Nias.

37. See "Overtreding van Art. 20 Amfioenpacht-Reglement. Vrijspraak," *IWvhR*, no. 613, 30 March 1875, 613; and ANRI, Politiek Verslag Residentie Banka 1870 (no. 123); also ARA, Dutch Consul Singapore to Secretary General Batavia, 7 May 1877, no. 239, in 1877, MR no. 317.

38. ARA, Dutch Consul Singapore to Secretary General, Batavia, 9 July 1877, no. 339, in 1877, MR no. 410; see also "Opium. Invoer van Opium," *IWvhR*, no. 1946, 15 October 1900, 166–67.

39. "Smokkelen van Opium" (1891), 2015–16.

40. ARA, Ho Atjoen to GGNEI, 22 Dec. 1880, in 1881, MR no. 828.

41. ARA, Dept. of Finance Kommissoriaal, 2 March 1881, no. 3616, in 1881, MR no. 828.

42. ARA, Asst. Resident Billiton to Director of Finance, 24 Nov. 1880, no. 1070, in 1881, MR no. 828.

43. ARA, Administrator Begerman to Asst. Res. Billiton, 8 Nov. 1881, no. 218, in 1882, MR no. 402. The Chinese mineworker Tjong Atjap, worker no. 1483 from mine no. 30, was arrested on November 5 near the capital; he was suspected of opium smuggling, but the accusation turned out to be false. The administrator reported he was still in the hospital as a result of the arrest, however.

44. ARA, Director of Finance to GGNEI, 6 Nov. 1889, no. 16728, in 1889, MR no. 858.

45. See Young, "A. Liang-Ko: Opiumsluiken en Weldoen" (1894), 1–29.

46. ANRI, Algemeen Verslag Residentie West Borneo 1889 (no. 5/20).

47. ARA, First Gov't Secretary to the Commander, NEI Navy, 7 Feb. 1888, no. 183 in 1888, MR no. 104; and Commander of *de Ruyter* to the Commander, NEI Navy, 3 March 1888, no. 888, in 1888, MR no. 201.

48. Memorandum on the Opium Traffic by the Colonial Engineer (Major McCallum), enclosed in Gov, SS to CO, 27 Feb. 1893, no. 60, CO 273/186.

49. See *Regina vs. Wee Kim Chuan and Pong Yow Kiat, SLJ* (1890): 3 69; Kim Seng vs. The Opium Farmer, *SSLR* (1892) p. 66, and (1893), p. 115; The Opium Farm Respondent vs. Chin Ah Quee-Appellant, *SLJ* (1891) IV, p. 33; Chua Ah Tong, Appellant, vs. Opium Farmers, Malacca, Respondents, *SLJ* (1890) II, p. 92; Regina vs. Tan Seang Leng, *SLJ*, (1889) II, p. 69.

50. See, for example, "Verbeurdverklaring van Clandestine Opium, Waarvan de Eigenaars of Bezitters Onbekend Zijn," *IWvhR*, no. 533, 15 September 1873, p. 146–7; "Opiu-

movertreding" *IWvhR* no. 657, 31 January 1876, p. 19–20; "Opiumreglement. Getuigen-bewijs," *IWvhR,* no. 658, 1876, 22–24; "Scheikundig Onderzoek van Achterhaalde Zoogenaamde Opium," Raad van Justitie te Batavia, 10 June 1876; "Opiumovertreding. Acte van Beschuldiging," *IWvhR,* no. 752, 1877, 192.

51. "Opium Aanhalingen" (1888), 474; "Opium Smokkelhandel Op Zee" (1884), 29.
52. "Smokkelen van Opium" (1891), 2016.
53. See Staatsblad 1911, no. 485; also Staatsblad 1914, no. 563, and 1917, no. 11, no. 497, for morphine legislation; Straits Settlements legislation on morphine started in 1896.
54. Straits Settlements Ordinance 1896, no. 7, article 2; and Ordinance 1903 no. 15, article 9.
55. Straits Settlements Ordinance 1903, no. 15, articles 3, 7; Ordinance 1904, no. 14, articles 5, 6; and Ordinance 1910, no. 27, articles 11, 12, 26, 34.
56. Straits Settlements Ordinance 1910, no. 27, articles 19, 21.
57. See, for example, *Utusan Malayu,* 25 Jan. 1908, 1, and *Straits Maritime Journal,* 4 Jan. 1896, 4.
58. See the period eyewitness account given by the author in Onreat, *Singapore: A Police Background* (n.d.), 144–45.
59. Chief of Police, Penang to Resident Councilor, 3 March 1906, no. 558/06 in CO 273/317.
60. See City of London Police Report, John Ottaway, Detective Inspector, 11 June 1906, in CO 273/322. A list of Chinese companies in Penang and Ipoh who were involved was finally quietly handed over by Baiss Bros. and Stevenson in London: Swee Guan and Co., Tan Eng Ching and Co., Ho Guan and Co., Kheng Ho and Co., and Poon Guan and Co.
61. Perak Dispensary, Ipoh to Baiss Bros. and Stevenson, 2 Jan. 1906; Baiss Bros. and Stevenson to Eu Poon Guan, 7 Dec. 1905, both in CO 273/317.
62. City of London Police Report, John Stark, Superintendent, 22 May 1906, in CO 273/322; and CO Jacket, 6 July 1906, Mr. Lucas, in CO 273/324. The police report sadly stated, "I do not know any law under which they could be punished here for sending the morphia in the way they have done," while the Colonial Office commented, "It is perfectly clear from their letter of 7 December that they knew there was something wrong." Both comments refer to Baiss Bros. and Co.
63. Governor Anderson, Straits, to CO, 30 March 1910, Confidential, in CO 273/357.
64. See Straits Settlements Ordinance 1907, no. 14, article 2; and Ordinance 1910, no. 27, Schedule, section 2.
65. Bijblad no. 8253; see also de Kort, "Doctors, Diplomats, and Businessmen" (1999), 123–45.
66. All of this information comes from the remarkable document "Memorandum on Seizures of Drugs and Opium in Penang, March and April, 1914, by Superintendent of Monopolies, Straits," enclosure in Gov. Young, Straits, to CO, 7 May 1914, Confidential, in CO 273/407.
67. For farming notices on ganja, see the *Perak Gov't Gazette,* 1888, 161. The notice that Koo-tien Chetty of Penang has been given the farm for Larut is posted in English and then translated into Tamil and Chinese.
68. Federated Malay States, 1898, no number, "Ganja Prohibition" (for Perak, June 1, 1899; for Negeri Sembilan, Effective after Expiration of One Month After Publication of the "Gazette"; for Pahang, date of publication of the "Gazette."

69. Gov, SS to CO, 29 Dec. 1898, no. 221, in CO 273/241.

70. FMS, 1898, "Ganja Prohibition"; Gov, SS to CO, 29 Dec. 1898, no. 221, in CO 273/241.

71. ARA, Dutch Consul Penang to Dutch Consul Singapore, 19 Sept. 1873, no. 16, in Verbaal Geheim Kabinet 17 Dec. 1873, D33 (no. 6042.)

72. ARA, 1885, MR no. 521; "Jualan Chandu Gelap Dalam Betawi," *Utusan Malayu,* 2 Feb. 1909, 2. The text of the article describes large quantities of contraband opium being found in Batavia's port. It sells there for nine times the price that was originally paid for it in Singapore. The newspaper *Batavia Nieuwsblad* is quoted as saying that a huge quantity of chandu has been captured; the chandu comes on steamers from Singapore and China. For another seizure, this time fifty katis of contraband chandu which arrived in Surabaya from Singapore on the steamer *Van den Bosch,* see *Utusan Malayu,* 4 Feb. 1909, 1.

73. Memorie van Overgave, Djambi, 1908 (MMK no. 216), 62.

74. ARA, Director of Finances to GGNEI, 29 March 1892, no. 4430 in 1892, MR no. 366; "Opium, Praktijken van Deskundigen," *IWvhR,* no. 879, 3 May 1880, 71–72.

75. ARA, 1894, MR no. 210; "Beschrijving van de Argus en de Cyclops" (1893), 382.

76. Huizer, "Opium-Regie in Nederlandsch-Indië" (1906), 363.

77. See *Attorney General v. Lim Ho Puah, SSLR* (1905), 9, 13; and *The Crown on Complaint of the Opium Farmers v. Lim Chiat" SSLR* (1904), 38. See also *Ing Ah Meng v. The Opium Farmer* (1890), *Kyshe,* vol. 4, 627.

78. See "1892: Singapore Opium, Report by Sir Robert Hart, Imperial Chinese Customs, China, 20 Feb. 1892," in CO 273/188, enclosed in Gov, SS to CO, 10 June 1893, no. 181, CO 273/188. Robert Hart's letter to Governor Mitchell of the Straits is also interesting for its descriptions of deceptions, 3 March 1894, in CO 273/194.

79. See Gov, SS to CO, 12 Nov. 1917, Confidential, in CO 273/458.

80. *Utusan Malayu,* 11 Feb. 1909, 1; *Utusan Malayu,* 13 Feb. 1909, 1; *Utusan Malayu,* 4 March 1909, 3, "Chandu Didalam Kapal Hong Bee"; *Utusan Malayu,* 11 March 1909, 3, "Chandu Didalam Kapal Hong Bee Lagi"; also *Singapore Free Press,* 1 Nov. 1904, 2.

81. Memorie van Overgave, West Borneo, 1912 (MMK no. 260), 35.

82. CO to British North Borneo Headquarters, 17 May 1911, CO 531/3; CO to BNB Headquarters, 20 Sept. 1911, CO 531/3; and CO to BNB Secretary, 10 June 1915, no. 25039, CO 874/914. The farms ended on January 1, 1910, in the Straits, on January 1, 1913, in Labuan, and on January 1, 1915, in British North Borneo.

83. The result of this, of course, was massive smuggling across Sarawak's land and sea borders with other polities in Southeast Asia. See Charles Brooke to Gov, SS, 7 May 1913, in CO 531/5; Gov, SS to Charles Brooke, 20 Jan 1913, CO 531/5; see also CO Jacket, 15 Jan. 1913, CO 531/5.

84. See Governor BNB to Directors BNB, 15 July 1913; BNB Co. Chairman to BNB Gov., 20 Aug. 1913; and BNB Gov to BNB Chairman, 3 Nov. 1913, all in CO 874/914. The opium farmer for British North Borneo himself, Chee Swee Cheng, was implicated in these smuggling ventures.

85. ARA, Chief Inspector, Opium Regie to GGNEI, 30 Oct. 1903, no. 3017/R, in Verbaal 13 Jan. 1904, no. 34.

86. Scheltema, "The Opium Trade in the East Indies," 240.

87. To discourage opium abuse, prices were raised as part of the moral argument for the government taking over the trade. In Trengganu, the opium farm was terminated in early 1917; the British took over after that, selling directly to the populace. Prices immediately rose from $5.50 per tahil to $6.50 per tahil. In Perlis, the price of chandu rose from $6 per tahil to $8 per tahil in 1916, when the farm was abolished there. See Trengganu Annual Report, 1916, 3, and Perlis Annual Report, 1916, 30. On Chinese farmers continuing on as smugglers, see Scheltema, "The Opium Trade in the East Indies," 241.
88. See CO/882 Eastern, 9, no. 114, which gives some of these stipulations for the Malay Peninsula. There were different laws depending on whether coastal or inland areas were in question, while racially only male Chinese over the age of twenty-one were allowed to smoke opium on licensed premises, etc. This document gives a good overview of the scope and complexity of narcotics legislation in the early twentieth century.

Chapter 9 Counterfeiters

Across the Frontier

Drugs were not the only commodities smuggled across the Anglo—Dutch frontier. Many other goods also made the trip, passing silently in boats or overland between the two developing spheres. Counterfeit currency in the form of government-issued bills and minted coins was another highly profitable type of contraband, one that traveled throughout the period 1865–1915. How did counterfeiting and the movement of "false money" leak across the length of this frontier? The range of actors, geographies, and strategies that developed around this secret trade was as complex as that of opium. Coiners, as counterfeiters often were called, hailed from a variety of ethnic groups, and the radials of their travels spanned not only the lands and seas of the border, but locales significantly further away. These journeys went as far as South China and western India, where counterfeit Dutch Indies currency was made in village workshops. What was the juridical, ethnic, and geographic milieu of counterfeiting in this arena? What were the mechanics involved in getting large sums of money across an increasingly stiffening border? Most important, how far did these practices extend? How serious a threat was the smuggling of counterfeit currency to the functioning of local colonial economies?

BURGEONING TRANSGRESSIONS

That money should be a highly desired good in and of itself is not surprising. Counterfeiting of currency, in this sense, has always been one of the most profitable kinds of smuggling, simply because the end product is by its nature a socially sanctioned item of value. Yet in nineteenth-century Southeast Asia means of exchange were highly varied, making the calculus of currency smuggling exceedingly complex. In the early years of the century, for example, barter was a common form of exchange in the ports of the region, despite many prices being quoted in Mexican dollars; this continued in many places through the 1870s, as in Dutch West Borneo, for example.[1] Certain items—various types of cloth, for example, and, as late as the waning years of the century, brass guns— were more commonly valued and exchanged in these barter circuits than others.[2] When currency, especially coinage, was involved in transactions, it was not always employed in the manner in which government minting facilities originally intended. Silver coins, both in Sumatra and in Borneo, for example, were often desired more for their ornamental value than for any exchange value dictated by colonial states.[3] Nevertheless, by 1865, Mexican dollars were the official coin of the realm in the Straits Settlements, and guilders served this function in most areas in the Dutch East Indies.[4] Yet how strictly was this system enforced?

The answer to this question, in the 1860s and 1870s, was not very strictly at all. The resident of West Borneo reported in 1872 that copper duiten, copper pasmunt, Mexican dollars, Dutch guilders, and raw gold were all in circulation at the same time. In southeastern Borneo, also Dutch territory, the resident there added that paper money was also in use in urban areas, though it lost its value as an exchange medium as one worked one's way further into the forest. This urban/periphery dichotomy on paper currency also held in Palembang, South Sumatra, while in neighboring Jambi both Dutch and Mexican coin was used side by side.[5] Further north in the Straits, on the coasts of wartime Aceh, *rijksdaalders* could be used in the ports, but Dutch copper coin had not yet penetrated into the villages. Across this narrow ribbon of water in British Singapore, Dutch currency was more than welcome and was held in comparatively high esteem, too.[6] The Riau Islands, just south of Singapore, had perhaps the most confusing blend of exchange media of all: Straits coin, Dutch currency, and Sarawak money were all accepted in turn, though the availability (and de-sirability) of each coinage depended on which part of the residency one was in.[7]

This diversity and complexity of currency systems on the long, outstretched frontier is important because it shows the opportunities available to counter-feiters on both sides of the border. Fabricating coin or paper was not just a profit-making venture in one's own settlement or colony; the money could also be passed off to neighboring lands and islands because the movement of cur-rency was so fluid. For this reason there are notices of Dutch fifty-guilder notes being refused in Palembang by local peoples, for example, because enough counterfeit was coming across the Straits in 1871 to make such items a risky speculation. Counterfeit also was showing up in the early 1870s in Bangka as well as in Bengkulu in West Sumatra and as far away as central Java.[8] Straits newspapers give one an idea of the mechanics of these early forgeries. Chinese apprentices in carriage-making workshops in Singapore were caught pilfering metal scraps, and later, coin molds matching extant counterfeit specimens were found in their homes. Penang also served as a haven for smugglers who under-took long voyages to unload these particular goods.[9] The *Straits Observer* re-marked in 1874 that "bad money is said to be a plague very prevalent just now" and warned the public to be on their guard against such objects in the pur-suance of everyday exchange.[10]

At this time the amount of counterfeit currency actually coming into the In-dies still appears to have been comparatively small. Court cases show suspects being followed for passing a single counterfeit rijksdaalder, and many of the early attempts to smuggle these items into Dutch territory appear to have had Java as an end destination.[11] Yet there were more and more cases appearing in the Outer Islands, and by the mid-1870s counterfeiting and more violent crimes, including murder, were sometimes intertwined.[12] Passing false coin was becoming a more serious business in the border residencies, being pursued by criminal syndicates, not just lone confidence men. Only a few years later the Dutch began to notice the quality in arriving fakes improving. Coins made of copper started to come in, but they were deceptively covered over in a very thin, well-worked casing of silver.[13] This trend was remarked upon and noted in ledgers by several low-level officials in various places along the length of the In-dies' border arc.

Yet the problem of smuggled counterfeit currency was still not seen to be se-rious in the upper echelons of the Dutch administration in the 1870s, as a prog-nosis of the Indies director of finance makes clear. In a letter to the governor-general in 1877, the director reported that the counterfeiting of rijksdaalders or guilders was probably not going to happen on a large scale for a variety of reasons. Counterfeiters more likely would concentrate on a currency that had a wider circulation than Dutch money, he thought, while the technological craft of producing such coins was beyond contemporary Asian manufacturing capabilities. A report on the same scenario in the subcontinent written by a colonel in the British Indian army was also cited, emerging as backup proof that such criminal possibilities seemed distant at best: "Thus we perceive that the temptation to unlawful coinage of genuine rupees could not apply to the solitary forger with his few rude implements, but to be of any benefit, must be undertaken on a large scale, and with good machinery. This could not occur in India without detection, nor could they be imported from abroad, subject as they would be to discovery and confiscation at the Custom House. Nor could any native state in friendly relations with our government permit or countenance a fraudulent imitation of our coins in a way that we could not immediately and for ever put a stop to."[14] The director of finance said tersely in his report that this evaluation of the state of affairs in British India summed up a similarly enforceable situation in the Dutch East Indies. This report typified official thinking in the 1870s.

The complex interchangeability of currencies on the border was beginning to erode at this time, the guilder and Straits dollar slowly emerging as paramount currencies on their respective sides of the frontier. While British money was still preferred as a more international currency in many boundary areas until quite late, the rising power of Dutch colonialism was increasingly able to promote the guilder as the only legitimate means of exchange. Hong Kong dollars, Medan tobacco notes, Mexican dollars, and Japanese yen—both real and counterfeit—slowly began to disappear from this region over the decades (fig. 10).[15] In 1904, Aceh was legally "cleansed" of Straits dollars, while in 1906 West Borneo and in 1908 the East Coast of Sumatra followed suit.[16] Realities on the ground, of course, made enforcement of these new economic, political, and policy imperatives lag behind the passage of these juridical benchmarks. Joseph Conrad's memorable short story "Because of the Dollars" recalls vividly the long, arduous work implied in what was called currency cleansing. Lonely inspectors traveled quietly from border isle to border isle collecting old dollars along the length of the frontier and exchanging them for shiny new guilders.[17]

The director of finance's optimistic projections from the 1870s, in the end, could not have been more wrong. By the late 1880s and into the 1890s, counterfeit Dutch coins were turning up all over the Indies—particularly in the Outer Islands—and fake money was even more common in the residencies fac-

Fig. 10. Counterfeit samples: Border coins and notes, 1868 (top) and 1899 (bottom). (Photos courtesy of Francis Wee and Rachmana Achmad)

ing the British border than in most other places. Huge statistical charts compiled by Batavia show this in detail: literally every frontier residency along the eastern coast of Sumatra, stretching through the islands south of Singapore and both divisions of Borneo, received counterfeit currency from across the border.[18] False rijksdaalders were seized on many occasions in southeastern Borneo, for example, while in Belitung customs authorities were also kept busy with this traffic, particularly in Tanjung Padang.[19] Counterfeit coins were also manufactured on the frontier arc in small workshops found outside Pontianak in West Borneo, and production centers were discovered in Bangka and coastal Palembang, Sumatra.[20] The penetrating routes of shipping companies made it easy to perforate the frontier and distribute counterfeit coins deep in the interior of the Indies as well. Chinese tramp steamers which linked Singapore to Surabaya and the islands of Nusa Tenggara apparently did a good business in smuggling false coin; the supercargo of the *Ban Hin Guan* was one notorious participant in these voyages, ferrying rijksdaalders from Hong Kong to the small islands east of Java.[21]

The scale and size of some of these counterfeiting networks show that the Indies were only part of a much larger circuit of illegal currency exchange at the turn of the century. Throughout Asia, false coins and bills were being made at an accelerating rate, often for export. This was certainly the case in East Asia, the Japanese minister Baron Hayashi bitterly complaining that his country's and Korea's treaty ports were overflowing with counterfeit silver yen.[22] Silver coins were also being manufactured outside the Canton mint, depriving the government of China of a "large portion of its legitimate profits," according to the British minister in Peking.[23] At the same time, counterfeit currency was also leaving Asia in the form of fabricated shillings, which were turning up as bank deposits by Chinese tea merchants in places like Melbourne and Vancouver.[24] These patterns did not escape the watchful eye of the viceroy of India and his staff. The secretary of the government there begged British consular officers in Asia to exhibit vigilance "in respect of attempts to export illicit rupees" back to India.[25] False rupees were turning up more and more often, in fact, by the late 1890s, despite the fact profit on their illegal manufacture was falling behind that of other counterfeited currencies.[26]

In the Straits, legal lacunae allowed such counterfeiting and currency smuggling to proceed fairly unchecked until a comparatively late date. In 1868, the Law Offices of the Crown were advising Singapore to deal with these defects as soon as possible, while in 1873, the Treasury Department approved a draft proclamation to carry out the changes immediately.[27] The laws that followed prohibited the importation and circulation of certain foreign coins, doled out six-month sentences for bringing in Japanese yen, and sentenced culprits caught with currency-manufacturing materials to a maximum five years in prison. Those caught redhanded forging notes faced ten years behind bars.[28] The Federated Malay States followed with their own laws on counterfeiting in 1912, which added more geographic coverage to the proscriptions on the open coasts of the peninsula.[29] Notices of problems with counterfeiting appear as late as 1916, despite the evolution of legislation.[30] Across the Straits in the Dutch East Indies, similar laws offered rewards for the discovery of counterfeiters as well as providing instructions to officers of the law on how to proceed in such cases.[31] By 1907, there were detailed regulations on the books about how to fight against the introduction of printing presses, excess metals, and other objects that could conceivably be used to manufacture Dutch bills.[32]

Counterfeiters came in many guises, however, and crossed ethnic and national boundaries in their efforts to make profits on the passage of bad money. Hindu moneychangers in Singapore were a class of people who occasionally turn up in the records, one such being Naga Pillay, who was caught, in conjunction with a Chinese colleague, trying to ship five hundred false rijksdaalders into the Netherlands Indies in 1897. His sentence was six months of hard labor as ordered by the magistrate of the colony; he was given away by a tiny mark appearing near the ear of the Dutch queen, which government analysts had seen before on other counterfeit coins.[33] Indian Muslims, or "Klings," also appear in the records as being counterfeiters of Dutch currency, as in the cases of a Singapore man who was caught smuggling rijksdaalders into Riau, and of another Indian Muslim involved in the passage of five hundred false rijksdaalders en route to Bali.[34] People of indeterminate origin, possibly Arab, Indian Muslim, "Malay," or some mixture of the three, also were caught counterfeiting on occasion. In 1898, a Sultan Meidin managed to get acquitted on appeal, as the witness in his case had died and was no longer available for questioning during the appeals proceedings.[35]

The large and economically powerful Arab community in Singapore was also involved in counterfeiting, especially across the border into the Indies. Yet as with the transit of opium across the frontier, it was the prospect of cooperation across racial boundaries that truly worried the state. The *Straits Times* of July 4, 1888, carried one such notice from the Surabaya papers: "At Surabaya, Singapore has come under suspicion as a coining center ... so says the *Surabaya Courant*, that Singapore is the chief seat of the coining industry. From thence the coins are exported to Java and other islands around. Some European mercantile firms at Surabaya are said to have a hand in the business, and to help certain Arabs, who have invested largely in the base coin enterprise. Through these European intermediaries, they get the raw material cheap."[36] Europeans, too, aside from acting as suppliers, carried illicit currency across frontiers themselves, especially men working as ships' engineers. These men seemed to make such sidelines a routine part of many of their voyages in Asia.[37] Nest eggs could be developed in this way, in preparation for eventual travels home when one's tour of duty on the local shipping concerns was finally over.

Yet as in the case of narcotics, the majority of counterfeit currency being smuggled across Southeast Asian frontiers seems to have come via Chinese populations. As early as 1868, a Chinese man was arrested in Singapore for possessing dies used to make Siamese currency, an act which caught the attention of the Foreign Office in London.[38] The Dutch, in reports from the Ministry for the Colonies in The Hague, also took great interest in these affairs, carefully noting court cases against suspected Chinese smugglers in Singapore and the occupations of culprits (especially of men like the trader Tong Tik Tong, one of the most important apothecaries in the colony.)[39] As it did in stories about the narcotics trade, the Malay-language press revealed subethnicities of currency counterfeiters and smugglers, spelling out specific Chinese dialect groups and the native places of apprehended transgressors.[40] Yet, again as in the underground narcotics trade, Chinese suspects often managed to escape punishment by achieving acquittals in the courts for lack of proof, or by jumping bail into Singapore' s narrow streets, never again to be found by the law.[41] In the Indies even Chinese k*apitans,* who were supposed to be the arm of the Dutch state in the Chinese communities, were apprehended running false banknotes, like the headman of the Surabaya Chinese who was arrested for currency smuggling in 1896.[42] This pattern has been seen before, when Chinese opium farmers, usually men of very high standing in local communities, were identified as being among the biggest opium smugglers in the region.

The arms of Chinese counterfeiting operations reached across the British dominions and deep into the Dutch Indies, sometimes puncturing the border into the very heart of the latter colony. A case in 1895 showed how far these radials could reach, transiting illegal currency all the way to the central and eastern islands of the Dutch imperium. Rumors of heightened Chinese counterfeiting had reached the chief agent of the KPM in that year, with the intelligence suggesting that Chinese smugglers were shipping coins from Singapore to Surabaya and from there to Bali and Sumbawa.[43] The currency traveled on a Chinese steamer that plied this long route once every twenty-two to twenty-three days. The Chinese supercargo on this ship, called the *Ban Hin Guan,* was very friendly with the local rajas in the latter two places and used his connections to distribute the coins from those locales to other places in the Indies. The captain of a ship who plied a similar route, the *van Goens,* had alerted the KPM with this news and said his story had been corroborated by one of his passengers, a water buffalo shipper named Haji Ali. The supercargo of the *Ban Hin Guan* was evidently using some of the counterfeit currency to buy bulk shipments of coffee as well, so that he spread his risk by offloading some of the coins before they even reached their end-destinations.[44] Stories such as these, common in the archives, show how normal Chinese commercial networks were sometimes used to distribute illegal cargoes alongside legal ones, and on long-standing Chinese trade routes as well.

COUNTERFEITING AT CENTURY'S END

By the late 1880s and into the 1890s, colonial authorities in Southeast Asia were able to plot on maps where such widespread counterfeiting physically was taking place. Many of these inquiries led to the South China coasts. In correspondence between the governor of Kwangtung and Kwanghsi (Guangdong and Guangxi provinces) and the Dutch ambassador in China, as well as between this same official and the Tsung-li Yamen (the Chinese equivalent to a Ministry of Foreign Affairs, or Zungli-Yamen), provinces, prefectures, and even towns and villages were described as origin points for the distribution of these currencies. Kwangtung and Fukien (Fujian) provinces on the southern seaboard were both centers of this production. Tatshan (Taishan) near Canton, Hingning and Lung Chwo (Xingning and Longchuan) near Swatow (Shantou), and Chang Chow (Zhangzhou) near Amoy (Xiamen) are all mentioned as production centers.[45] Many of the counterfeiters evidently got their stamping tools from Japan to make the coins, which then found their way down predominantly to Singapore, before crossing the border into the Indies.[46] Seizures on the South China coast were sometimes spectacular, as in one instance in 1895 when several chests "overflowing with false rijksdaalders" were found near Amoy.[47] Yet the Indies press did not take much comfort in these hauls, saying that although attempts would be made at discovery and control, production sites would inevitably be moved, with coolies being prosecuted while the "chief players remain in the wings."[48] The Dutch consul in Hong Kong agreed with this assessment and told the governor-general of the Indies that Chinese law enforcement was no doubt getting a cut of counterfeiting profits.[49]

It was indeed the constant threat of corruption on the China coasts that propelled the Dutch leadership forward in the search for workable solutions. In February 1895 an Indies Department of Finance missive was sent around the border residencies informing regional administrators that new counterfeit coins were en route; these reproductions were so skillfully wrought that Batavia had to give a list of tiny, almost imperceptible attributes of the coins so that lo-cal officials might check for them.[50] By August of that year the Dutch consul in Amoy was also writing to the acting commissioner of customs in that city ask-ing that impounded coins be given back to the Dutch for transit to Batavia, rather than to Chinese banks. The Dutch would then notch the coins, thereby rendering them useless; the implication was that the Chinese banks would sim-ply recirculate them because of corruption, thus prolonging Batavia's prob-lems.[51] Finally, in September 1895, the Raad van Nederlandsch-Indie (Indies Council) advised the governor-general that rewards should be commissioned for any information given on the China coasts about movement of counterfeit currency into the Indies. The suggested rate was 50 percent of the worth of any seizures, an enormous sum to any local Chinese who would be willing to in-form on his fellows.[52]

Two Chinese language letters seized in a raid on the house of one Lie Thoa Ho, in Mojokerto, East Java, provide a fascinating window on these activities at the turn of the century.[53] The author of the first letter, a man named Tjioe Kang Han, wrote to Lie on the fourteenth day of the ninth month of the year Kah (October 19, 1894). In his letter he stated that he had gone from Surabaya to Amoy to check on the manufacture of some false guilders, which had not yet been fabricated. An ironworker whom they were expecting had arrived, how-ever, and all of their shipment of counterfeit coins would be ready to travel in three to five days. The particular batch of coins being made was worth three to four thousand dollars, but Tjioe told Lie that altogether around ten thousand dollars worth of currency would be traveling, including both old and new de-signs of Dutch guilders. He asked for payment to be made to his address on Porcelain Street. He then asked Lie to look after his sons, as they were "young and ignorant." "Please be their compass," he said, and do not "treat them as strangers, which will make my heart glad."[54]

The second letter, also written by Tjioe nine days later, reported that the ship-ment finally was ready and would come over to the Indies on the first or second of November. Eighteen hundred to two thousand dollars would be brought in this batch, and the shipment was to be carried by brothers of both Tjioe and Lie, one from each side. Tjioe counseled that the money should be brought either by way of Makassar or Bali, with a preference for Bali because of its relative prox-imity to Probolinggo, a transit point for the operation. A discussion then ensued of who should invest what amount of money into the venture, and what every-one's profit percentages would be.[55] Tjioe advised that the capital actually should be doubled, each party putting in five to six thousand dollars. The letters are extraordinary in that they show clearly the concerns of counterfeiters at the turn of the century. Kinship—uncles, nephews, brothers, and sons all seem to be involved, both in China and in the Indies—preferred routes, fabrication techniques, and profit ratios are all discussed. Up until the very end of the venture, too, Tjioe was confident he was going to succeed: on the eve of the journey, as noted, he was counseling that all capital should be increased. He apparently never had any idea the authorities were on his trail, until it was too late.

Fighting against schemes and networks as organized as these, foreign governments whose currencies were suffering at the hands of Chinese counterfeiters finally decided their best hope was in joint action. The Dutch representative in London, Baron W. von Goltstein, asked the British Foreign Office if any overtures had been made to China about the counterfeiting problem in 1895, and when he was told the answer was no, a program of collective engagement was decided upon.[56] A telegram approving Britain's participation was sent from London to the British consul in Peking in early 1896; both the Dutch and Japanese would be signing the letters of protest as well, which it was hoped would strengthen the power of the appeal.[57] Nevertheless, the British envoy in Peking saw only limited potential in using diplomatic channels, reporting back to his superiors, "I am not sanguine of much practical result from these representations, but it is hoped that something will be done towards stopping the illegal traffic in question."[58] In a letter he wrote to the Tsungli Yamen on January 7, 1896, Ambassador Beauclerk tried to appeal to China's own sentiments for financial self-preservation, pointing out that Chinese currency also was being counterfeited in Southeast China and that Peking herself had much to lose by taking no action.[59] The Tsungli Yamen thanked the ambassador for his letter a week later and said that the appropriate instructions would be sent to the governors of the southern provinces to make "full enquiries" into the matter.[60] Nothing ever came of these investigations, however, leaving the Dutch press to continue wondering how many false rijksdaalders had transited even all the way back to The Hague.[61]

The illegal traffic was so heavy by the mid-1890s, in fact, that the Dutch began to consider sending a civil servant over to China expressly to deal with the rampant counterfeiting.[62] The problem now, however, was that the Dutchman who had put himself forward for the job, a man named G. C. Bouwman, had a dubious record at best. He had been dismissed by the Imperial Maritime Customs Service in China for striking a superior officer, and Sir Robert Hart had written to the Dutch in confidence that he felt Bouwman would be unsuitable for the job.[63] Nevertheless, as the Dutch consul in South China put it, Bouwman's familiarity with the lower strata of Chinese society and his ideas on how to launch a campaign against currency smuggling to the Indies (such as dividing ships up into eighty to one hundred sections and then having them searched by squads of Chinese detectives under his employ) might make him useful. Besides, added the consul, the problem on currency contraband had become so acute that Bouwman was worth the risk.[64] The monthly salary he asked for was negotiated down to a fifteen-hundred-dollar advance to use at his discretion, and at the end of January 1896 the Raad van Nederlandsch-Indie approved his employ.[65] Bouwman never really made a dent in the passage of false money to the Indies, and his men, despite their considerable experience in the Chinese underworld, never turned up any definitive proof against major contrabanders. The result of the Bouwman adventure in currency-smuggling control was ultimately a disappointment for Batavia, though different parties attributed the failure to different reasons.[66]

Despite the overall failure of Bouwman as the Dutch point man in South China, he did know quite a bit about some of the mechanisms currency smugglers used to get their product out of Chinese ports and into the Indies. Bouwman told the Dutch consul that the rings which kept sailcloths together on ships were one of the primary hiding places for false rijksdaalders; the rings, which kept the canvases straight and stiff, were ideal for hiding the bulk of many coins pressed against each other, which Bouwman then illustrated with rudimentary drawings.[67] It was small tricks of the trade like these that Bouwman brought to the attention of the Dutch authorities, alongside other potential maritime hiding places, like coal bunkers, bilges, shaft tunnels, and chain lockers.[68] Yet the strategies for moving these cargoes were wide and varied, ensuring that large numbers of rijksdaalders always got through. The French mailboat *Gadavery,* for example, was caught in Tanjung Priok harbor in Batavia with several thousand spurious rijksdaalders that had ingeniously been packed in the middle of condensed milk cases.[69] Chinese steamers were also caught making these journeys, one of which was searched in a Balinese port and found to contain boxes with false compartments literally brimming with Dutch coins.[70] The Hong Kong chief of police surmised that most of the currency had to be leaving as cargo, not personal baggage, because legally a ship's cargo could be ransacked by the police only on cause of suspicion, a state of affairs well known to local Chinese.[71] Yet the British representative in Peking was not so sure, deciding rather that false currency was leaving China in a variety of ways, including as hand baggage, in cargo, and via Chinese crews of ships, as well as through many well-placed merchants.[72]

As the concealment mechanisms for getting counterfeit money down to Southeast Asia became more sophisticated over time, the actual craft of fabricating false currency also progressed. As early as 1883 the first really good imitations of rijksdaalders were turning up in the Indies, although a hierarchy of competence was making itself immediately apparent. Locally made coins evinced the least skill in manufacture and technique, while foreign-made coins being turned into Indies banks and government institutions showed the most exactitude and craft. Counterfeit specimens were sent off to Utrecht to be examined by experts, who found they were made of silver, quicksilver, copper, zinc, and lead.[73] By the late 1880s, these coins were of nearly the exact size and weight of real rijksdaalders, though many still had the tendency to tarnish too quickly.[74] Seven or eight years later, however, in the mid-1890s, currency seizures of false coin were being described as perfect, with few people being in a position to judge if the coins actually were real or not.[75] Coins calibrated to 96/100 fineness were still barely detectable in the early 1890s; by August 1895, though, counterfeiters had gotten the silver ratio down to the exact purity of real rijksdaalders, that being .945 silver composition to each real coin.[76] The detection of counterfeit currency, therefore, was becoming more and more difficult to attain by servants of the colonial state. Glyptic techniques as well as the science of fabrication were both becoming more sophisticated on the part of counterfeiters in various places.

The Straits Settlements were the main distribution centers for counterfeiting activities. Though counterfeit currency was coming from China and even from as far away as India, almost all shipments transited through the British possessions in Southeast Asia.[77] Penang was one of these centers; hundreds of false guilders were being seized there in the 1880s and 1890s, the Dutch consul requesting all sorts of supplementary powers to fight the smugglers, including expanded telegraphic privileges, legal help, and the right to hire additional detectives.[78] Judgments were also continually passed against counterfeiters in Singapore as well, where men repeatedly tried to get rijksdaalders into boats heading into the neighboring Dutch Indies.[79] Rewards were posted in Straits newspapers for information leading to the arrest of currency smugglers in Dutch waters, and the Java Bank as well as the Dutch diplomatic service was mobilized to help staunch the flow of false money across the border.[80] The efficacy of these tactics, however, was decidedly mixed. Between October 1897 and August 1898, forty-six convictions of "moving prohibited currencies" through the Straits were handed down by the courts. Though this was a fairly large number, it could have been only a fraction of the actual amount of cash traveling.[81] The Straits were also only one of several conduits available to get counterfeit currency down to Southeast Asia, as is made clear in an 1896 extradition treaty between British North Borneo and Hong Kong that explicitly included counterfeiters in its text.[82]

Although the British dominions served as funnels for the passage of counterfeit Dutch coinage into the Indies, the British also had many problems in dealing with the trafficking of their own local currencies. The fragmented nature of British authority in the region, with entities as diverse as the Straits Settlements, British North Borneo, Sarawak, and Brunei all pursuing coordinated but nevertheless semi-independent monetary policies, gave tremendous impetus to smugglers to move currencies into areas where profits could be made. The British North Borneo Company was particularly notorious in this regard, emerging as a major contrabanding entity itself. The company exported large quantities of its own coin into neighboring Sarawak, Brunei, and Labuan at a discount in an attempt to expand its own circulation; Sarawak fought against these movements but ultimately to little avail.[83] Profiteers and smugglers of the company's coin also made Borneo's ports into forward bases for getting this particular currency into Singapore, where accomplices bought the coins at a discount and then shipped them illegally to the Straits.[84] The sultan of Sulu, the *Straits Times* reported, was one of the "wily traders" who practiced this ploy.[85] An examination of the North Borneo Company's rising production on coinage in the mid-1880s shows how aggressive these policies could be. A state agenda of quick expansion, coupled with the financial instincts of many astute traders in the region who saw that through favorable exchange rates they could make quick money on the passage of coin from one British dominion to another, ensured that coins were smuggled around Southeast Asia at an increasing rate.[86] Illegal paper money, especially in the form of counterfeit Hong Kong and Shanghai bank bills, were also passed into Singapore, as in one 1898 shipment worth $22,100.[87] Labuan was a particularly important port in channeling these illegal currency movements. An exhaustive record exists describing the headaches the administrators of this small island colony experienced over the problem of counterfeiting: there are literally scores of letters, memos, and telegrams on the topic. Some British civil servants blamed the situation on the "large area of savage or semi-civilized countries in immediate proximity to the colony," while others lamented that "the coins were easily imitated by private individuals," so that counterfeiting and coin smuggling were just unfortunate facts of life in Labuan.[88] Yet Labuan seems to have acted as a crossroads of sorts for the wide and wild waters around Borneo, routing and rerouting false currency in a variety of directions as circumstances and market opportunities permitted. Because it was a free port, and technically part of the Straits Settlements, its free trade market structure lent itself admirably to the kinds of kinetic evasion and subterranean commerce that flourished elsewhere in the Straits Settlements. Labuan was closer to the more economically controlled regimes of Sarawak and British North Borneo, however, and this meant that it was viewed as a convenient neighborhood outlet for those who wished to trade and market currency under the sight of local ruling regimes. The government apparatus in Labuan was also nowhere near as sophisticated or as capable as the ones in Singapore and Penang, and this also translated into gains for counterfeiters and those who associated with them. Organized crime syndicates recognized that Labuan had these strategic advantages of geography and limited state coercive capabilities on their side, and used the colony as a forward base for counterfeiting in the eastern stretches of Britain's South China Sea possessions.[89]

Yet it was the Dutch who suffered most from the counterfeiting and smuggling of currencies across borders in Southeast Asia at the turn of the twentieth century. A statistical reading is difficult to produce here; only a fraction of all the coinage and bills counterfeited and eventually sold ever found their way into government ledger accounts, on both sides of the border. Tabulations are further complicated by the fact that money traveled under many names in the statistics, including silver coin, specie, treasure, dollars, and sometimes, especially in the case of Dutch currency in the Straits, even as "merchandise for trans-shipment."[90] Yet some statistics on what was then called the counterfeiting plague were kept, and they provide clues as to the scope of the problem (table 6). One trend that stands out from these figures is that over time the denominations of Dutch coin being smuggled were steadily decreasing, as the authorities concentrated first on detection and prevention techniques of the more valuable bills and coins.[91] A second interesting statistic in the hundreds of counterfeiting cases processed each year has to do with the rates of convictions and acquittals, which remained approximately the same from year to year around the turn of the century. This suggests that although techniques for detecting whether currency specimens were false improved over time, smugglers were still able to make use of loopholes in the law to escape punishment until the late 1890s.[92]

The authorities definitely had need of these expanded capabilities of detection. In a shipment of nearly five thousand dubious rijksdaalders sent back to Holland for examination in 1897, only thirty-nine turned out to be genuine.[93]

Table 6. Reports on Cases Before NEI Judges of Consciously Distributing False Currency

Year	Guilty	Acquittals	Dismissed	Verdicts	Total Cases	Selected Seizure Sites
1900	174	152	65	326	391	
1899	165	164	153	329	482	Palembang, Celebes, Java
1898	190	158	46	348	394	
1897	241	210	68	451	519	Belitung, Bali, Lombok
1896	177	224	83	401	484	SE Borneo, Batavia
1895	113	113	127	226	353	
1894	139	126	86	265	351	Padang, Aceh, Palembang
1893	149	175	47	324	371	
1892	95	187	13	282	295	
1891	72	10	3	82	85	
1890	50	4	1	54	55	East Coast Sumatra

Source: Adapted from Koloniaal Verslagen (various), 1890–1900, Appx. C.

The former chief secretary of the Java Bank, in fact, postulated at the height of the troubles that according to his research anywhere between one in six to one in twelve Indies rijksdaalders were counterfeit in 1899. His statement showed how far the problem had come before it started to trail off in the early twentieth century[94] (fig. 11). By that time intergovernmental cooperation between the Dutch Indies, British India, the Straits Settlements, and China was improving—it had been nearly nonexistent up until the late 1890s—and was making the transit of counterfeit currency a much more difficult task.[95] Workshops where the coins and notes were fabricated began to be discovered and shut down. One important reason for this was that the physical circumstances needed to produce this kind of contraband commodity were much more elaborate than in the buying and selling of illegal drugs, for example. Telegraphs shuttled back and forth between the various Asian coasts, and paid informants eventually kept the governments fairly up to date. Counterfeiting did not disappear, but its seriousness as an economic problem of great financial consequence gradually diminished. This waning came only after several decades, however, when the counterfeiting and the smuggling of manipulated currency became a huge transnational business in the region.

The massive production and distribution of counterfeit money in late nineteenth-century Southeast Asia taught colonial regimes how cross-border smuggling might be stopped in the case of one particular contraband line. Access to the actual sites of illegal production was one key. This could be accomplished in

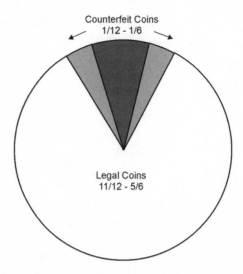

Fig. 11. Legal and counterfeit coins in Indies circulation, c. 1899. (*Source:* Rooseboom, "Valsche Rijksdaalders" (1899) 1, p. 393.

the case of coin and bank note fabrication, because the tools needed to fashion fakes usually were bulky and difficult to conceal. The network of spies and informants at imperial command was growing around the turn of the century, and more and more reporting reached the ears of Europeans about production factories located in China, India, or Southeast Asia itself. As the coasts, towns, and cities of all three of these regions came under tightening European control after 1900, counterfeiting became increasingly difficult, though it was never fully eradicated. In this particular arena, too, state capabilities to stay one step ahead of "coiners" was enabled through evolving technologies of legal currency production that were difficult for criminals to reproduce. State abilities to stay ahead of the technology curve ultimately started to work, for the most part, in regard to safeguarding colonial monetary systems in early twentieth-century Southeast Asia, but this slow success proved impossible to duplicate in the case of narcotics. The transit of illicit human cargoes across area frontiers would provide yet another serious challenge to imperial hegemony in the region.

NOTES

1. See Trocki, *Opium and Empire,* 58; ANRI, Algemeen Administratieve Verslag Residentie West Borneo, 1870 (no. 5/1).
2. Governor Labuan to CO, 24 July 1877, no. 68, in CO 144/48; Acting Consul General Treacher to FO, 29 April 1884, no. 14, in CO 144/58.

3. ANRI, Dutch Consul, Penang, to GGNEI, 21 June 1876, no. 991G Confidential, in Kommissoriaal, 14 July 1876, no. 522az, in Aceh no. 14, "Stukken Betreffende Atjehsche Oorlog (1876)"; ANRI, Algemeen Administratieve Verslag Residentie West Borneo 1874 (no. 5/4).

4. The literature on currency in this colonial Southeast Asian arena is mostly numismatic; few critical studies on the history of transaction regimes and modalities exist. For an overview of many of the coins and notes involved in the decades around the turn of the twentieth century, see Pridmore, *Notes and Coins* (1955), 77–84. For the British side of the Straits, see Pope, "The P & O and the Asian Specie Network" (1996), 145–72. For the Netherlands Indies, see Bakker, *Eenige Beschouwingen over het Geldverkeer* (1936); Scholten, *De Munten van de Nederlandsche Gebiedsdeelen Overzee* (1951), 113–16; Vissering, *Muntwezen en Circulatie-Banken in Nederlandsche-Indië* (1920), 70–78; Van den Berg, *De Muntquaestie* (1874), 177–284; Van den Berg, *Currency and the Economy of Netherlands India* (1895; 1996 reprint); and Mevius, *Catalogue of Paper Money* (1981), 24–29.

5. ANRI, Algemeen Administratieve Verslag Residentie West Borneo 1872 (no. 5/3); ANRI, Algemeen Verslag Residentie Borneo Z.O. 1872 (no. 9/2); ANRI, Algemeen Administratieve Verslag Residentie Palembang 1870 (no. 64/13); ANRI, Algemeen Administratieve Verslag Residentie Palembang 1871 (no. 64/14).

6. ANRI, Dutch Consul, Penang, to GGNEI, 21 June 1876, no. 991G Confidential, in Kommissoriaal, 14 July 1876, no. 522az, in Aceh no. 14 "Stukken Betreffende Atjehsche Oorlog (1876)"; Kruijt, *Twee Jaren Blokkade,* 179.

7. ANRI, Algemeen Administratieve Verslag Residentie Riouw 1871 (no. 63/2).

8. ANRI, Algemeen Administratieve Verslag Residentie Palembang 1871 (no. 64/14); ANRI, Algemeen Verslag Residentie Banka 1872 (Banka no. 63); ARA, 1875, MR no. 532; ARA, 1874, MR no. 15, 27.

9. "Counterfeit Cents," *Penang Argus and Mercantile Adviser,* 3 Feb. 1870, 3; "A Well Known Coiner at Large," *Penang Argus and Mercantile Adviser,* 14 Feb. 1873, 3; "Bad Money," *Penang Argus and Mercantile Adviser,* 10 Feb. 1870, 3. Of course, the forging of counterfeit coin also existed in VOC times; it was not new to the nineteenth century.

10. *Straits Observer,* 11 Nov. 1874, 3.

11. See "In Omloop Brengen van Valsch Geld," *IwvhR,* no. 609, 1 March 1875, 35; "Medepligtigheid aan het Maken van Valsch Zilvergeld," *IWvhR,* no. 306, 10 May 1869, 84; "Namaker van Zilveren Muntspecieen, Wettig Gangbaar in Nederlandsch-Indië," *IWvhR,* no. 291, 25 January 1869, 17.

12. "Strafzaken," *IWvhR,* no. 569, 25 May 1874, 83–84.

13. "Information Concerning the Circulation of False Silver Coins in Netherlands India," in Baron de Lynden to Henry Howard, 23 June 1903, CO 273/296.

14. For the minister's letter, see ARA, Director of Finance to GGNEI, 15 June 1877, La Qi Secret, in 1877, MR no. 416.

15. Colijn, ed., *Nederlands Indië, Land en Volk* (1913–14), 2:199–253, esp. 242. It took longer for plantation currencies to be phased out than the various means of exchange of other nations. This was part of the nationalist project in the Indies; internal Dutch company currencies were never as threatening to colonial prestige as business continuing in another power's notes and coins. Both of the samples produced here, a Hong Kong silver

dollar from 1868 and a Medan Company Tobacco note from 1899, were counterfeits found on the frontier.

16. See Resink's article "De Archipel voor Joseph Conrad" (1959) for details. The situation on the East Coast of Sumatra was particularly complicated; see also Potting, *De Ontwik-keling van het Geldverkeer*, (1997), esp. 288, which unfortunately devotes only one page to matters pertaining to counterfeiting.

17. Conrad, "Because of the Dollars," *Within the Tides: Tales* (1950), 172–73.

18. See the large charts under the name of "Vergelijkend Overzicht van hetgeen luidens de ingevolge de Geheime Circulaire van den Directeur van Financien van 13 October 1898, no. 109 ingediende Kwartaalstaten in Nederlandsch-Indië is Aangehouden aan Valsche Zilveren Munt," which can be found in 23 March 1903, CO 273/296. The statistics show seized false currency turning up in Banka, Lampung, Palembang, Sumatra East and West Coasts, Aceh, Riau, Bangka, Belitung, West and Southeast Borneo, and Sulawesi, as well as other residencies of the Dutch Indies.

19. See *KV* (1896), 188–89, and (1897), 191–92, respectively.

20. ANRI, Algemeen Administratieve Verslag Residentie Palembang 1887, 1888 (no. 65/7 and 65/8); ANRI, Algemeen Verslag Residentie Banka 1889 (no. 80); ANRI, Algemeen Verslag Residentie West Borneo 1888 and 1889 (no. 5/20 and 5/21).

21. See the fascinating report from the chief agent, KPM to the Director of Finances, 23 Feb. 1895, no. 2048, in 1895, MR no. 239.

22. Baron Hayashi to the Tsungli Yamen, Undated (1896), in CO 273/221.

23. Minister Beauclerk to the Tsungli Yamen, 7 Jan. 1896, in CO 273/221.

24. Treasury Department to CO, 14 Oct. 1895, no. 13911, CO 273/208.

25. Secretary, Government of India to British Minister in Peking, 1 Oct. 1895, no. 1833E, in CO 273/221.

26. Gov, SS to CO, 28 July 1898, no. 223, in CO 273/237.

27. Law Offices of the Crown to FO, 8 July 1868, in CO 273/23; Treasury to CO, 11 Oct. 1873, no. 14823, in CO 273/72.

28. See *Straits Settlements Ordinances* 1891 no. 2, 1898 no. 11, and 1897 no. 8, respectively.

29. Federated Malay States Enactment no. 10 of 1912.

30. See *Trengganu Annual Report*, 1916, 4.

31. See *Bijblad van het Staatsblad van Nederlandsch-Indië*, no. 1238, 3046, and 1277, respectively.

32. See *Indische Staatsblad* 1907, no. 465.

33. See Baron von Goltstein (Dutch Envoy in London) to FO, 14 June 1898, in CO 273/243; also Dutch Consul, Singapore to GGNEI, 13 Sep 1897, no. 845 Secret, in ARA, MvK, Verbaal 22 Oct. 1897, no. 8.

34. ARA, Directeur van Financien to GGNEI, 19 Feb. 1896, no. H; and Dept. of Finance to "Algemeene Ontvangers van 's Lands Kassen in Nederlandsch-Indie," 19 Feb. 1895, Letter Y, both in (MvK, Verbaal 28 March 1895, no. 44.)

35. See the court case of "Sultan Meidin and Meidin v. Regina," *SSLR* (1898–99), 5:67–70.

36. *Straits Times*, 4 July 1888, 3.

37. ARA, Dutch Consul, South China/Hong Kong to GGNEI, 14 Dec. 1895, no. 698, in (MvK, Verbaal 31 March 1896, no. 24.)

38. FO to CO, 10 July 1868, in CO 273/23.

39. ARA, Dutch Vice-Consul, Singapore to GGNEI, 7 Feb. 1895, no. 109, in (MvK, Verbaal 22 March 1895, no. 25), and Directeur van Financien to GGNEI, 19 Feb. 1895, no. H, in (MvK, Verbaal 28 March 1895 no. 44.)

40. See, for example, *Bintang Timor,* 7 Dec. 1894, 2: "Satu orang Macau nama-nya Ung Pueh, telah kena tangkap sebab membuat ringgit tembaga di Jalan South Bridge Road."

41. ARA, Dutch Consul Singapore to GGENI, 18 May 1895, no. 387, in 1895, MR no. 450; see also *Singapore Free Press,* 1 Nov. 1904, 5.

42. *Straits Maritime Journal,* 4 Nov. 1896, 5.

43. ARA, Chief Agent of the KPM to Director of Finances, 23 Feb. 1895, #2048, in 1895, MR #239.

44. ARA, Director of Finances to Governors of Celebes and Bali and Lombok, 8 March, 1895, #11 Secret, in 1895, MR #239.

45. See ARA, Dutch Minister Resident to China, to GGNEI, 16 Aug. 1888, no. 51, and Secretary of Translation, Canton, to Dutch Minister Resident in China, 4 July 1888 (twenty-fifth day of the fifth month of the Kwang Su (Guangxu) reign), both in 1888, MR no. 631; Minister Beauclerk to Tsungli Yamen, 7 Jan. 1896, in CO 273/221; and "Information Concerning the Circulation of False Silver Coins in Netherlands India," in Baron de Lynden to Henry Howard, 23 June 1903, CO 273/296.

46. Dutch Consul, Hong Kong to GGNEI, 6 Aug. 1895, no. 232, in ARA, MvK, Verbaal 4 Nov. 1895, no. 45.

47. Dutch Consul, Hong Kong to GGNEI, 8 Aug. 1895, no. 250, in ARA, MvK, Verbaal 4 Nov. 1895, no. 45.

48. "Overzicht van Artikelen van Notaris Vellema" (1896), 1252–55.

49. Dutch Consul, Hong Kong to GGNEI, 6 Aug. 1895, no. 232, in ARA, MvK, Verbaal 4 Nov. 1895, no. 45.

50. ARA, Dept. of Finance to "Algemeene Ontvangers van 's Lands Kassen in NI," 19 Feb. 1895, Letter Y, in MvK, Verbaal 28 March 1895, no. 44.

51. ARA, Acting Dutch Consul, Amoy, to Acting Commissioner of Customs, Amoy, 6 Aug. 1895, Confidential, in MvK, Verbaal 4 Nov. 1895, no. 45.

52. ARA, Advies van de Raad van NI, 9 Sept. 1895, in MvK, Verbaal 4 Nov. 1895, no. 45.

53. Directeur van Financien to Procureur Generaal, 5 Sept. 1895, no. H/6 Secret, in ARA, MvK, Verbaal 4 Nov. 1895, no. 45.

54. ARA, Nederlandse Vertaling van de Chineeschen Brief (no. 2) [forwarded by the Resident of Surabaya in his 23 Dec. 1894, no. 395], in (MvK, Verbaal 28 March 1895, no. 44.)

55. ARA, Nederlandse Vertaling van de Chineeschen Brief (no. 1) [forwarded by the Resident of Surabaya in his 23 Dec. 1894, no. 395], in (MvK, Verbaal 28 March 1895, no. 44.)

56. Baron von Goltstein, Dutch Consul, London, to FO, 15 May 1895, and FO to CO, 18 May 1895, both in CO 273/209.

57. FO to British Ambassador in Peking, 11 Jan. 1896, Telegram, in CO 273/221, and Minister Beauclerk to FO, 9 Jan. 1896, no. 16, in CO 273/221.

58. Minister Beauclerk to FO, 9 Jan. 1896, no. 16, in CO 273/221.

59. Minister Beauclerk to Tsungli Yamen, 7 Jan. 1896, in CO 273/221.

60. Tsungli Yamen to Beauclerk, 15 Jan. 1896, in CO 273/221.

61. "Overzicht van Artikelen van Notaris Vellema" (1896), 1254.

62. ARA, Government Secretary to Director of Finance, 15 Jan. 1894, no. 18, in 1894, MR no. 56.

63. See the situation as outlined in ARA, Dutch Consul South China/Hong Kong to GGNEI, 15 Nov. 1895, no. 549, in (MvK, Verbaal 31 March 1896, no. 24.)

64. ARA, Dutch Consul South China/Hong Kong to GGNEI, 12 Oct. 1895, no. 429, and same to same, 14 Dec. 1895, no. 698 in (MvK, Verbaal 31 March 1896, no. 24.)

65. ARA, Dutch Consul South China/Hong Kong to GGNEI, 18 Dec. 1895, no. 728 Secret, and Advies van den Raad van Nederlandsch-Indië, 31 Jan. 1896, both in (MvK, Verbaal 31 March 1896, no. 24.)

66. "Information Concerning the Circulation of False Silver Coins in Netherlands India," in Baron de Lynden to Henry Howard, 23 June 1903, CO 273/296.

67. ARA, Dutch Consul, South China/Hong Kong to GGNEI, 14 Dec. 1895, no. 698, in (MvK, Verbaal 31 March 1896, no. 24.)

68. J. C. Bouwamn, Late Chinese Imperial Maritime Customs Service, South China, to Dutch Consul Hong Kong, 16 Dec. 1895, in ARA, MvK, Verbaal 31 March 1896, no. 24.

69. *Straits Maritime Journal,* 4 Jan. 1896, 5; see also *KV* (1896), 188–89.

70. See *KV* (1897), 191–92.

71. ARA, Dutch Consul, Hong Kong to GGNEI, 6 Aug. 1895, no. 232, in (MvK, Verbaal 4 Nov. 1895, no. 45.)

72. Beauclerk to Tsungli Yamen, 7 Jan. 1896, in CO 273/221.

73. "Information Concerning the Circulation of False Silver Coins in Netherlands India," in Baron de Lynden to Henry Howard, 23 June 1903, CO 273/296.

74. ARA, Dutch Consul, Singapore to GGNEI, 8 Jan. 1894, no. 28, in 1894, MR no. 56; *Straits Times,* 18 July 1888, 3.

75. "Overzicht van Artikelen van Notaris Vellema" (1896), 1254; *Straits Maritime Journal,* 19 Feb. 1896, 6.

76. Gov, SS to CO, 7 Aug. 1895, no. 319, in CO 273/205.

77. ARA, 1894, MR no. 665. Correspondence between the Dutch consul in Bombay and the governor-general in the Indies revealed that false rijksdaalders were produced in India as well as in China.

78. ARA, 1888, MR no. 83; ARA, 1894, MR no. 316; Dutch Consul Penang to GGNEI, 9 July 1894, no. 412; and ARA, Directeur van Financien to GGNEI, 19 Feb. 1895, no. Z, both in (MvK, Verbaal 28 March 1895, no. 44.)

79. ARA, Judgement on *Chong See and Chong Ng vs. the Queen,* 5 Feb. 1895, Singapore Assize, in (MvK, Verbaal 28 March 1895, no. 44); and ARA, Dutch Vice Consul, Singapore to GGNEI, 7 Feb. 1895, no. 109, in (MvK, Verbaal 22 March 1895, no. 25.)

80. ARA, Directeur van Financien to Procureur Generaal, 5 Sept. 1895, no. H6 Secret, in (MvK, Verbaal 4 Nov. 1895, no. 45); *KV* (1896), 188–89); *KV* (1895), 207.

81. Gov, SS to CO, 20 Oct. 1898, no. 327, in CO 273/238.

82. *British North Borneo Herald,* 1 Sept. 1896, 79. See "Proclamation II of 1896, to Provide for the Extradition of Fugitive Criminals from the Colony to Hong Kong."

83. Charles Brooke to Consul General to Brunei and Sarawak, 18 Sept. 1886, in CO 144/62.

84. Gov. Labuan to CO, 28 Sept. 1886, no. 80, in CO 144/61; Gov. Labuan to CO, 3 Jan. 1887, no. 2, in CO 144/63.

85. *Straits Times,* 3 July 1888, 2.

86. CO Jacket (Mr. Branton) in 18 Sept. 1886, Co 144/62; Gov. Straits to CO, 24 May 1906, no. 185, in CO 273/317.

87. Gov. Straits to CO, 9 June 1898, no. 175, in CO 273/236.

88. Jacket Cover, Treasury Department to CO, 21 October 1873, in CO 144/41; Acting Consul General Treacher to FO, 29 April 1884, #14, in CO 144/58.

89. For some of the more important correspondence on this topic, see Gov. Labuan to CO, 12 April 1886, #37, and CO to BNB Co. HQ, London, 26 Nov. 1886, both in CO 144/61; also Gov Labuan to FO, 6 Oct 1887, #49, in CO 144/64, Gov Labuan to CO, 9 Oct 1888, #39, in CO 144/65, and Gov Labuan to FO, 14 Jan 1888, #1, in CO 144/66.

90. ARA, Dutch Consul, Singapore to GGNEI, 18 Dec. 1893, no. 1347, in 1893, MR no. 1427.

91. The numbers on seized rijksdaalders went steadily down between 1896 and 1897; numbers of seized quarter guilders, and "dubbeltjes," however, continually went up during this period. See "Information Concerning the Circulation of False Silver Coins in Netherlands India," in Baron de Lynden to Henry Howard, 23 June 1903, CO 273/296.

92. See the assembled statistics in the *Kolonial Verslagen* between 1895 and 1901. Both acquittals and convictions were in the hundreds every year.

93. "Valsche Rijksdaalders in Indië" (1899), 952.

94. Rooseboom, "Valsche Rijksdaalders in Nederlandsch-Indie" (1899), 393.

95. "Information Concerning the Circulation of False Silver Coins in Netherlands India," in Baron de Lynden to Henry Howard, 23 June 1903, CO 273/296.

Chapter 10 Illicit Human

Cargoes

Narcotics and counterfeit currency crossed the Anglo–Dutch border in Southeast Asia in many places over the entire half century covered in this book. The fact that both of these commodities were generally light in weight and easy to hide certainly helped in their illegal transmission across the frontier. Opium and chandu were stored in the holds of ships and in the baggage of passengers and crews; counterfeit coins traveled in sail rigging and in all kinds of false compartments in belongings. Yet not all contraband items were so easy to conceal. An extensive traffic in human beings also developed in the years around the turn of the twentieth century, one that ferried men and women to a variety of places for a variety of purposes against the wishes of the two colonial states. The victims were women and girls being sold as concubines and prostitutes, slaves, and undocumented labor referred to as "coolies."[1] These "human trades" were objectionable to Singapore and Batavia because their continued passage against government proscriptions made a mockery of the ostensible civilizing mission of colonial Europeans. How were these people trafficked? Where did they come from and how were they moved? Taken together, the movement of these three classes of human beings reveals the wide networks and geo-graphic dispersion of trafficking at the turn of the century, especially along the unstable, changing space of the Anglo/Dutch frontier.

THE TRAFFIC IN WOMEN

One of the most important subsets of people smuggled into and around South-east Asia at the turn of the century were women to be used for sexual purposes. A small historiography has started to document the passage of women for sex, but almost all of it has dealt with the legal, sanctioned aspects of these women's passage, not with the more subterranean facets of their movement. Women were transited into the Indies and the Straits from a variety of places. Sachiko Sone has estimated that nearly half a million Japanese women went or were brought to Southeast Asia for these purposes between 1868 and 1918. Some of them were under the age of eighteen, misled as to the purpose of their voyage, or unregistered, making their passage technically illegal.[2] Hiroshi Shimizu has added that by 1909, most of the *karayuki-san* (Japanese prostitutes) in Sumatra were deemed illegal, as that country's power and national prestige increased and laws to protect its "honor" abroad (by recalling all such women who had origi-nally left in poverty) were instituted.[3] The practice of selling Chinese women for sex in places as far away from their homes as possible was also widespread, argues Gail Hershatter, as by doing so traffickers diminished their ability to es-cape and limited the opportunities for their families to interfere.[4] In British and Dutch Southeast Asia, several other authors have shown how plantations, cities, and barracks, especially in Dutch Sumatra, served as sites for the large-scale movement and prostitution of Asian women.[5] The best-documented study is James Warren's *Ah Ku and Karuyuki-san,* which documents the whole edifice of prostitution in Singapore between 1880 and 1940, including an initial chapter on trafficking.[6]

Colonial states were deeply implicated in the movement of these women through the region. One reason Singapore and Batavia tolerated and encour-aged prostitution before changes swept over the region was that sex ratios for many groups made some system of prostitution necessary, in the eyes of many administrators. Prior to the nineteenth century, foreigners coming to Southeast Asia had been able to engage in sexual liaisons with local women via traditional regional practices of temporary marriage, concubinage, and female slavery, to a degree. These unions were considered normal and were not stigmatized in the Early Modern era. As the expansion of coolie labor proceeded, women were soon outnumbered by men, especially in certain populations such as the Chinese in the Straits, where in 1870 the ratio of men to women was six to one. After the founding of Labuan in the 1840s, London took an active role in trying to provide Asian women for the burgeoning colony's working population, a policy continued by the Eastern Archipelago Company, the major coal-producing concern there.[7] As Labuan became an important naval base for the British in the 1880s, the state tightened medical supervision on prostitutes there, trying to ensure that sailors would have the "necessary outlet" but not contract debilitating venereal diseases at the same time. In the Straits even Protector of Chinese William Pickering, whose job it was to fight against abuses in the system of prostitution, felt the overall institution was necessary, so long as the women coming into the colony for the purpose were willing.[8] Dutch policymakers also winked at the contrivance of the system, pointing out that young estate employees could not marry because they were often too poor, and a danger therefore existed that white women might fall into the vice trade themselves.[9] Many in the Indies press staunchly defended the system of concubinage and prostitution, saying that it fit the particular circumstances of the East and that moralists back home had no idea what they were talking about.[10]

The problem was that many women were, in fact, unwilling or underage participants in the colonial system of sanctioned prostitution. They were smuggled alongside the legally moving women-for-sale and crossed the region's borders in a variety of directions. In the late 1860s, it became clear that Batak women from Asahan, Sumatra, were being trafficked across the Straits to Melaka and landed at night. The customers who bought them included the son of the local Chinese *kapitan* and one of the wealthiest merchants in the colony, a *taukeh* named Tek Chang. Because these women were "heathens," not Muslim, the resident councilor of Melaka explained, the Chinese buyers could import and use them without fear of having to convert or of suffering any neighborhood repercussions.[11] Two Malay Hajjis also gave testimony to the authorities that Batak women were furtively being shipped inland to Malaya's tin mines, where Chinese and Malay buyers purchased them from Penang traders.[12] Into the 1870s and 1880s, women were also quietly smuggled into Singapore from China and also from Borneo and other neighboring islands stretching across the Dutch dominions.[13] Bugis shippers seem to have been particularly involved in these latter voyages, using their perahus to great effect in Riau's local shallow waters.[14] By the early 1880s the reports also singled out Annam (Vietnam) and Siam as source countries, with the purchasers of these women being Singapore Arabs and Chinese.[15]

A large legal structure was eventually set up to try to deal with the worst abuses of the organized system of prostitution in the region, but to relatively little effect for the welfare of trafficked women. James Warren has a long discussion of the legal apparatus and evolution in the Straits Settlements regarding prostitution. The Contagious Disease Ordinances (CDOs) of 1870 mark the start of this legislation, as Singapore decided to register and inspect brothels from this time forward. By 1887, passage of the Women's and Girls' Protection Ordinance gave the state the right to search ships and buildings in which they thought underage or unwilling prostitutes might be held. It also required suspected traffickers to give a security if girls were being brought into the colony.[16] A year later, however, the CDO's were repealed as a result of a vociferous campaign against state involvement in prostitution back in England, and many of the checks against abuse were lost. Across the Straits in the Indies, laws were also enacted to try to fight the *Handel in Vrouwen en Meisjes* (trade in women and girls), though the Dutch were also losing the war against the smuggling of underage and unwilling women.[17] There were simply too many ruses to get these classes of women into the colonial dominions for the states to really prevent abuse. Aside from outright smuggling, young girls were told under threat to pretend they were the daughters of traffickers or willing inmates, which very often they simply were not.[18] The culturally different nature of Asian marriages compared to Western unions, as in one fascinating case of a Chinese man from Singapore and his second wife, also acted to confuse matters, as sometimes these arrangements were only covers for trafficking.[19] Malay traffickers also made use of the hiding properties of the veil as well as the Muslim allowance for four wives to spirit women across frontiers and into prostitution.[20] By the turn of the twentieth century, lawmakers had to take into account all of these cultural divergences in order to keep some control on what the authorities themselves were unsure was trafficking of women or not.[21]

As in the case of narcotics and counterfeit currency, the Straits Settlements often served as clearinghouses for the passage of smuggled women. Though several laws remained on the books to try to stop the flow of underage or unwilling women through the colony (despite CDO repeal in 1888), results were decidedly unsatisfactory until a very late date. In 1891, the case of two Hainanese women who were discovered in a Johor brothel and who had passed through both the Hong Kong and Singapore customs without being detected underlined this failure; the Colonial Office asked how their passage had been possible, if so many checks had been set up precisely to stop this trade.[22] Another case in 1898 in which an Acehnese brothel-keeper arrived in Penang to buy ten girls between nine and fifteen years of age was thrown out of court by the magistrate. Despite the discovery of the girls in a place known to be used for prostitution, there was no direct proof that they were being trained or used for the purpose, so the matter had to be dropped.[23] Failures such as these enraged the Protector of Chinese, who said that most of the colony's main traffickers were well known to him but untouchable under law unless he could get direct proof of their involvement. This meant finding proof of underage status, false pretense, false representation, fraud, or deceitful means of entrance into prostitution.[24] The Colonial Office itself declared that "the extreme cleverness of these Chinese procurers, who have for years past succeeded in dodging the Ordinance for the Protection of Women and Girls both in Hong Kong and the Straits, necessitate an amendment of law every two or three years in order to frustrate their knavish tricks."[25]

Traffickers and smugglers of women and girls for prostitution were not only ethnically Chinese, however. Chinese did indeed make up the majority of these cases, from small-time Teochew dealers implicated in the Malay-language press to women who trafficked their own "daughters" into the colony, but they were not the only people carrying on this trade.[26] Bugis shippers, as noted, were involved in this commerce, and court cases implicate various people in Sumatra, even beyond the aforementioned Batak-sellers in the late 1860s. Malays also seem to have occasionally acted as traffickers and movers of human beings, as a representative court case from Singapore makes clear.[27] Indians regularly lent money to various Chinese brothel owners in the Straits, probably financing some of these investments indirectly, and Europeans, too, were sometimes brought before the courts for making money off prostitution.[28] Warren has published data on one Japanese trafficker, Muraoka Iheiji, who claimed to have brought over thirty-two hundred women from Japan in four years, a number which may not be too much of an exaggeration, considering the expansion of shipping lines at the time.[29] Certainly an examination of official lists and charts, such as the Licensed Brothel Registry for Singapore in 1877, shows the ethnic sweep of people responsible for the movement of women down to the Straits. Of the hundreds of names listed on that document, most are of Chinese madams and pimps, while others are Malays and Tamils. Yet there are other names on the document as well, such as Rosalie Brown and Utily Schwartz of 548 Victoria Street[30] (table 7).

By the early twentieth century, more and more voices were being raised against the system of prostitution that still manifested itself on both sides of the Straits. This was true in the Dutch East Indies, where several branches of gov-

Table 7. Partial List of Brothel-Keepers in Singapore, February 1877

Address	Keeper of Brothel	Number of Girls
230 New Bridge Road	Chow Ah See	14
234 New Bridge Road	Chow Ah Kiew	15
241 New Bridge Road	Wong Toi Jouh	13
4 Hong Kong Street	Yee Sam	13
7 Hong Kong Street	Chow Ah Toi	16
16 Hong Kong Street	Chow Ah Sam	11
39 Hong Kong Street	Soo Soh	18
12 Merchant Road	Sam Soh	11
16 Chin Hin Street	Ah Kum	8
21 Chin Hin Street	Lee Ah Sam	5
22 North Canal Road	Lam See Soh	6
35b North Canal Road	Ah Qui	9
40 North Canal Road	Choi Soon	4
2 Synagogue Street	Tow Ah Soh	1
186 South Bridge Road	Koh Soh	6
4 Hokien Street	Lee Lin Moi	13
6 Hokien Street	Cheong Ah Roi	14
35 Hokien Street	Leong Pah Hee	13
64 Chin Chew Street	Chow Ah Yee	15
67 Chin Chew Street	Leong Ah Voon	10
68 Chin Chew Street	Ong Ah Chop	10
26 Cross Street	Mumgodoh	1
27 Cross Street	Manjoor	2
35 Cross Street	Etam	1
104 Victoria Street	Toong Hoh	4
116 Victoria Street	Rosalie Brown	2
119 Victoria Street	Ah Ma	2
124 Victoria Street	Jerribah	3
5 Victoria Street	Adella	1
548 Victoria Street	Utily Schwartz	2
544 Victoria Street	Ah Hee	3
514 Victoria Street	Omelia Green	2
97 North Bridge Road	Ah Choi	3
99 North Bridge Road	Tow Kim Oo	2
487 North Bridge Road	Leong Ah Foo	9
489 North Bridge Road	Wong Ah Kum	6
52 Rochore Road	Morsenah	1
7 Shaik Medersah Lane	Katijah	1
12 Malay Street	Mariam	1
199 Arab Street	Sorintan	1

Source: Adapted from SSLCP, 1877, Appendix M, lxi.

ernment had been asked to deliberate changes to the prevailing structure of vice.[31] It was also true in the British possessions, where an anonymous letter to Straits authorities had detailed the purchase and sale of illegal female cargoes every day in Singapore, implicating twenty to thirty traffickers in these dealings. The petition also accused the Chinese Protectorate and the Poh Leung Kok (Office for protecting virtue) of taking bribes and looking the other way in some cases, charges that were never proved.[32] Yet the charges of corruption and official complicity in the smuggling of women were detailed enough, reaching even to the highest ranks of the office of the Protector of Chinese, that the issue could no longer be ignored by the British regime. As the Boxer rebellion in China and bad harvests in both China and Japan drove more women and girls to board steamships heading for the Straits, and as popular knowledge about Singapore's system of vice spread in Europe, embarrassing the colonial government, the authorities finally started to take more concrete measures.[33]

The British government did not sign the White Slave Traffic Agreement in Paris in 1904, which dealt with Japanese women, among others, in the Straits, but Singapore did agree to help out in uncovering these cargoes, though this was far short of a ringing government endorsement.[34] In the Dutch sphere, Javanese women continued to be sent to Singapore for sex, transiting from Semarang and Deli, while others were tricked into prostitution in the plantation sector of Sumatra, while Dutch policymakers debated.[35] Yet both colonial governments officially ended their involvement with tolerated prostitution around the end period of this book. Dutch regulation of prostitution ended finally in 1913; in the British possessions, prostitution was tolerated until 1927, when a three-year grace period spelled the end of the former system.[36] Yet for the *illegally* moved women in these trades, those who were smuggled into the region as underage or unwilling participants in prostitution, these changes meant very little. They were still caught in lives of grim servitude and exploitation, and the legislative modifications of Batavia and Singapore did little to alleviate their lot.

THE TRAFFIC IN SLAVES

Prostitutes were not the only human beings continually trafficked throughout the region. Slaving was still practiced in Insular Southeast Asia as well, despite the many edicts promulgated against the practice by regional colonial powers. Forms of slavery and debt-bondage have existed in Southeast Asia from time immemorial. Anthony Reid has outlined some of the structural reasons why this has been so, pointing to low population densities, cultural tendencies toward vertical bonding, and little extant wage labor as primary reasons for slavery's presence.[37] B. J. Terwiel and Gordon Means have shown that these were attributes of mainland polities, and by the late eighteenth and early nineteenth centuries, massive slaving expeditions scoured almost all of maritime Southeast Asia as well, moving vast quantities of men and matériel from the Bay of Bengal eastward to New Guinea and as far north as coastal Luzon. By the later nineteenth century, however, these massive movements were halting, partially because slavers were now keeping their human cargoes for themselves to use in the collection of marine and jungle products. European navies were now cruising more effectively as well.[38] Even after the high point of this phenomenon, however, certain regions continued to export slaves more than others. In the archipelago Bali, Nias, southern Sulawesi, and the Batak highlands in Sumatra were some of these places. Though slavery had first been banned in the Dutch dominions in 1818, and the ban was renewed with more force in 1860, it was not until 1874 that Batavia started to force indigenous chiefs also to give up their slaves, though these men were compensated for their losses.[39]

The 1860 renewal of the ban on slavery in the Dutch Indies abolished not only the right of Europeans and Chinese to own slaves, but also slave trading, although these proscriptions were really enforceable only in Java, not in the Outer Islands. There, debt-bondage for children was outlawed, and the movement of pawned people across borders was also legislated against, but the realities of Dutch power at this juncture prevented any more serious steps being undertaken in the border residencies.[40] As the Dutch legal edifice built on these laws evolved, however, Batavia's reach into the Outer Islands grew: competencies given to the Gouvernements Marine, especially, started to give the Dutch a longer arm against slave trafficking in the scattered seas of the archipelago. Staatsblad 1877 nos. 180 and 181, for example, gave the Dutch marine boarding rights on any ship flying the flag of indigenous states (or no flag at all), while other laws tried to push against slavery by various other means.[41] Across the Straits in the English possessions, the British also were moving against slave trafficking, though the process here, as in Batavia, was an uneven one. A treaty between Singapore and Selangor, for example, specifically mentioned that Selangor could not enslave Britons or British subjects, but this still gave Selangor plenty of room to deal in other archipelago peoples, notably Bataks from Sumatra.[42] By 1874, the Asian stations of the Royal Navy were receiving specific instructions on how to spot and deal with suspected slaving craft. The booklets reveal the legal preoccupations of London in searching out ways to head off lawsuits for seizures, while also revealing London's financial acumen in trying to skim tax off these same actions.[43]

Despite these efforts in both colonial camps, slaving was alive and well in Insular Southeast Asia in the middle decades of the nineteenth century, especially in many areas along the length of the frontier. Batavia saw the large scale of the slave trade between North Sumatra and the Malay Peninsula as a good reason— or excuse, depending on whose letters one reads—for expanding into this region in the late 1860s: eight to ten thousand slaves were said to pass across the Melaka Straits every year, though the British disputed this number[44] (fig. 12). The British did not dispute, however, that some slaving was indeed happening across the maritime divide, as correspondence from the resident councilor in Melaka makes clear. In his own jurisdiction, he wrote to the governor of Singapore in mid-1866, slaves were being landed in small boats at night, sometimes onto Melaka rice merchants' own perahus far out at sea and other times at the back porches of stilt-houses by the beach.[45] In Singapore, further down the coast, Bugis craft brought human cargoes to Kampung Gelam during the east monsoon, a phenomenon reported by men of both Dutch and English nationality. Many of these same Bugis shippers also had interests in slaving further east, as a huge traffic in humans still managed to take place between Sulawesi and East Borneo throughout the 1870s.[46] The perpetrators of most of these sales were Arabs who sailed from Pontianak in West Borneo and had networks and outposts stretching from Sulawesi to Singapore. Further north, near the terminus of North Borneo and the Sulu Sea, there were also traffickers, some of whom were native to this arena, while others, like the German captain of the steamer *Tony* named Sachsze, were European.[47]

As early as the 1870s Batavia was trying to turn its rhetoric of emancipation in the Outer Islands into a more coherent reality. One of the ways to do this was to offer money to local chiefs for every slave or pawned person who was freed. This, in conjunction with more coercive representations, did eventually lead to the freeing of large numbers of bonded people. The first place this was tried was in Sumatra, where by the mid-1870s twenty thousand people had gained their freedom as a result of these inducements.[48] On the east coast, slaves could buy their freedom in Deli, Langkat, and Serdang by 1879, though there still were bonded people ten years after that, probably because Batavia did not inject the finances to fully support the program.[49] In Deli, where there were more pawned people than outright slaves, subjects could buy their freedom from the sultan for between thirty two and sixty-four dollars.[50] The practice of keeping such bonded people does seem to have receded over time, though, especially (as

Fig. 12. Batak slave girl, nineteenth century. (Photo courtesy KITLV, Leiden)

the resident of Palembang noted further down the coast) as inspection tours penetrated further into the interior.[51] Nevertheless, in some places, such as southeastern Borneo in the early 1870s, the numbers of pawned people were actually rising, in this case among the residency's Chinese population.[52] Pawning and the "restocking" of these populations also took place through Bugis devices on the western half of the island, as a report in the *Tijdschrift voor Nederlandsch-Indie* makes clear.[53]

Yet large stretches of the border residencies still remained out of the reach of these programs and supposed colonial civilizing projects, especially in Borneo. Borneo remained an open field for the trade in slaves, even until a comparatively late date. On the British side of the frontier, the fragmented nature of English authority—split between the raja of Sarawak, the British North Borneo Company, the sultan of Brunei, who had a British advisor, and Labuan island—encouraged the continuity of trafficking for many years. In Sarawak, the Brookes tried to legislate the terms of slavery and bondage to their advantage, by fining any human transfers done outside the jurisdiction of the court. In such a scenario, not only would the masters lose money for dealing outside the purview of the state, but the slave would also go free.[54] In the company's dominions on the northern half of the island, however, diaries of company residents in the periphery show how slowly changes in attitude could be expected to transpire. William Pretyman's diary at Tempasuk in 1880 described armed combat between parties over stolen slaves, while Resident Everett at Papar made clear that area *datus* (rulers) were smuggling Bajaus wherever they wished, in defiance of company proscriptions.[55] In Brunei, London's representative also had his hands full, as area *pangerans* (princes) raided the company's territory for slaves and then attacked British police units sent out to arrest the perpetrators.[56] The British consul in Brunei sighed upon hearing news of these depredations, saying, "Slave-dealing and kidnapping are a part of Bornean traditions, which must be dealt with by degrees."[57] Even the Straits press expected only slow progress in the matter, intoning that it had taken the Dutch one hundred years to deal with the problem in Java, and that Brooke still could not abolish it after decades in Sarawak.[58]

On the Dutch side of the enormous land divide, progress was little quicker. In western Borneo, in areas far outside of any real Dutch jurisdiction, slavery and slave trafficking went on as they always had, despite local chiefs' signatures on contracts to the contrary.[59] Yet it was primarily in eastern Borneo, along the coast and in the interior just away from these coasts, that slave trafficking managed to survive with greatest tenacity. In 1876, the small polities of Kutei, Pasir,

Bulungan, Sambaling, and Pegatan committed themselves on paper against the long-standing area trade in humans. Yet only a few years later, in data collected by the Dutch administration, it became apparent these sultanates were not living up to their promises.[60] Some Dutchmen felt this was not for want of trying; the sultans themselves, these authors wrote, could not control their subjects or hinterlands, which essentially allowed trafficking free reign.[61] By 1883, the *Straits Times Overland Journal* was describing whole villages of slaves on the east coast near Berau, despite the Dutch regulations; many of these people worked in area mines and led particularly harsh, troglodytic existences underground. Three hundred of these slaves were said to be sold every year at Gunung Tabor, where they were shipped in from the southern Philippines, the result of barter transactions for opium, cloth, and guns.[62] By 1889, the Dutch station commander in East Borneo waters was still cruising outside the Berau and Bulungan river mouths, continually on the lookout for more perahus carrying slaves.[63]

Yet the remote border forests of Borneo were only one location where forms of slavery and slave trafficking managed to hold on, even until the end of the nineteenth century. Singapore, the central node of all commerce in Insular Southeast Asia and the seat of British power in the region, was another. Dutch consuls in Singapore were particularly incensed at the Straits authorities' lack of action on slave dealing through the colony—this despite a wide compendium of laws which had been legislated to prevent such abuses. All of this trafficking was on the sly and came in several forms. One manifestation was in the indebtedness some pilgrims managed to find themselves in while trying to undertake the Hajj. Many of these pilgrims, particularly Javanese and Boyanese ones, never got further than Singapore but had bonded themselves for several years to pay their passage to Arabia. The 117 houses of pilgrimage middlemen, known variously as sheikhs or *juragans,* frequently took advantage of the ten thousand archipelago pilgrims who passed through Singapore every year and enlisted them in multiyear contracts to pay off their trips. These contracts consigned the pilgrims to lives which were little better than slavery. Dutch representatives described the arrangements as remarkably similar to what had befallen "Africans of old," a complaint the British authorities said was an exaggeration or merely a difference in opinion.[64] There was less of a difference of opinion on other forms of trafficking which passed through the colony, such as Bugis shippers selling slaves from New Guinea in the back streets of Singapore, and Javanese females being sold as housekeepers and servants, both to Singapore and Melaka.[65]

It was this latter traffic, the selling of Indies women to rich Chinese merchants and Arabs in Singapore as domestic servants, which caused the Dutch
consul to write a letter of protest to the colonial secretary in May 1882. Four
women had just sought the protection of the consul on the eighth of that
month; three of them, named Poele, Masmirah, and Karimah, were from
Surabaya residency and had been induced by one Babah Sroening, the supercargo of the steamer *Rosa,* to come with him to Singapore. He had promised to
marry all of them, which as a Muslim he could legally do, and give them jewels;
instead, they were brought to the house of a partner in the *Rosa,* Lee Sing Wah,
on Telok Air Street and sold into domestic slavery. They were never paid a cent
for their work and were not allowed to ever leave their master's house. Finally
they were able to run away, after another inmate in the house had taken sick
and had been beaten for laziness until she died. It was cases like this one that induced the Dutch consul William Read to bring the matter up again and again
with the British, as there were other women, some of them Javanese, others
Bugis, who were brought to the Straits against their will and sold into servitude.
A final case mentioned by the consul was that of a woman who as a child in the
Netherlands Indies had been walking down a road when an Arab man had kidnapped and brought her to Singapore in a steamer. Some of the women had
been in Singapore for years; they had no way to get back home and did not
know whom to turn to for help.[66]

Forms of slavery and bondage lived on in Southeast Asia in manifestations
such as this for some time and can even be found today in some circumstances.[67] Most slave trafficking in the classic sense, however, of ships with
hostages chained to the floor, were becoming obsolete by the turn of the twentieth century. Pontianak in West Borneo, for example, which had been mentioned as a center for slaving in the 1870s, was free of such activities by the early
1890s; in Palembang and Jambi, too, such forms of servitude were no longer
practiced in 1891, except far inside the interior regions.[68] In Sulawesi there was
still pawning of slaves in 1897, while even after the turn of the century scattered
Arabs like the notorious Said Ali in Toraja could be found hunting for human
cargoes.[69] In most parts of the archipelago, however, even in areas that had formerly been slaving centers (for example, Bali, Lombok, Kutei, and Aceh), slave
trafficking had been pushed back by century's end, although in a few places
such as New Guinea and small parts of the rest of the islands it endured.[70] In-
terestingly, the Netherlands Indies state, while in the process of abolishing the
trade in humans as it expanded into the periphery, was the closest institution
left to practicing slavery as the twentieth century dawned. Reid has drawn at-

tention to the huge size and brutality of Dutch corvée labor in the Outer Islands, not to mention the massive coolie system, which in its own contracts and conditions often treated workers worse than any native master ever dared.[71] It was in these circumstances, in which slavery was being abolished under one rubric and more or less continued unofficially under another, that the practice of mass movements of human cargoes continued well into the years of the twentieth century.

THE TRAFFIC IN HUMAN LABOR

Although Batavia and Singapore tried to monopolize not only the passage of coolies from South India and South China down to the Straits, but also their subsequent movements, a significant traffic in human labor existed outside of the power of Europeans in Southeast Asia. Lynn Pann has shown how wide the state-sponsored trade in Chinese labor was at the turn of the century, funneling coolies as far as Cuba (for sugar plantations), Australia (for mining), and New Guinea (for copra) as well as to many other destinations.[72] In Southeast Asia, many planters, mining concerns, and merchants had agents in China and India to secure their necessary labor, which was only sometimes free, and often indentured, under the grimmest of circumstances. Millions of poor laborers passed in these semiofficial ways down to Southeast Asia, though others, most notably in China, were kidnapped (especially farmers and coastal fishermen), sold (including prisoners taken in interclan battles), or simply duped by traveling recruiters, who then trafficked such men into waiting boats.[73] The explosion in prosperity and building in the archipelago, especially in plantations and urban infrastructure projects such as wharves, rail-lines, and tobacco and rubber concerns, made the demand for labor so acute that many were willing to search outside the sanctioned system for the cheap workers they required. This was especially true in places such as Dutch Sumatra and British North Borneo, which had particularly evil reputations as to how coolies there were treated.[74] Yet massive disturbances such as the Taiping Rebellion and overpopulation in both China and India often made these concerns irrelevant to hungry multitudes. Several years' worth of laboring, even under the worst of circumstances, was seen as at least an opportunity to eat.[75]

As they did in the contraband trades examined above, colonial states in the region tried to combat the illegal passage of people by legislating juridical infrastructures that could combat these flows on the ground. In the Dutch Indies, this meant proclamations, for example, such as Staatsblad nos. 8 and 9 of 1887, which enacted a complete ban on the travel of Indies "natives" to any foreign place for the purpose of laboring. Surveillance on such movements and Batavia's abilities to ensure that her own subjects were not being trafficked or mistreated were considered inadequate, even by the state itself. Yet only a few years after these regulations were proclaimed, the demands of overpopulation, especially in Java, overrode such concerns, and the passage of indigenous coolies out of the Indies was again allowed.[76] In the British Settlements, the legal edifice built to deal with the smuggling of unwilling or mistreated labor was even larger. Laws regulated the hours and circumstances of passenger ships' departures, and stipulated special instructions and guidelines for the movement of indigenous perahus as well as Chinese junks and sampans.[77] Crimping, or impressment, was legally banned in 1877 in the seminal Crimping Ordinance of that year, while other legislation made special stipulations for the conduct of Chinese and Indian labor through the colony to bordering colonies.[78] It was only around the turn of the twentieth century, however, that strictures addressed the actual mechanisms of the dreaded "lodging houses" and the plight of Netherlands Indies coolies in the Straits Settlements in particular.[79] Yet as in the case of the movement of illegal narcotics and counterfeit currency, the laws and regulations always managed to be more impressive on paper than they ever were in reality, as Labor Commission Reports from both sides of the Straits make clear.

The Labor Commission Report of 1891 in Singapore and similar lengthy documents from the Dutch Indies government show how egregiously standing labor and recruitment practices were breached in the years around the turn of the twentieth century. One of the main reasons this could happen was that so many coolies of various ethnicities were being transited around Southeast Asia during this time. Javanese, Boyanese, Banjarese, Dayaks, Kelantanese, Tamils, and Chinese were all in motion, sometimes as bonded labor, sometimes as free immigrants.[80] There was much room in this human maelstrom to take advantage of the system, which many brokers and *barracoons* (labor contractors) figured out all too quickly. The English report, through expert witness testimonies, shows explicitly how secret societies had penetrated the movement of coolies to an enormous degree, transiting southern Chinese immigrants from place to place and often under abominable conditions outside the supervision of the state. It also shows how overseers specifically tried to get labor from more distant locations, so that inducements and opportunities to abscond would be minimized.[81] Human beings were graded into hierarchies under these conditions, northern Chinese receiving high marks of desirability from labor supervisors and southern Chinese, "Hailams" and "Macaos," for example, costing much less per head than their northern cousins.[82] Dutch reports also tallied wide abuses of the system, from people being moved under the guise of pilgrimage but really destined for plantations and mines to others being spirited out of the Indies, ostensibly as "folk life examples" for exhibitions in Europe. The residents of many places along the north coast of Java and from southeastern Borneo as well were told to be watchful for attempts to smuggle laborers to the neighboring English possessions.[83]

One of the main sites for this kind of human labor trafficking outside of the surveillance of the state was the plantation and mining district of East Sumatra. Huge numbers of Chinese coolies went to Deli and its environs to work on tobacco plantations and in the neighboring tin mines of Siak to the south, as charts kept by the Dutch consul in South China and by the Sumatra Planters' Committee make clear[84] (table 8). The system used to get them there was despised by both the Chinese laborers and the Dutch agricultural enterprises, however, as it relied on coolie-broking middlemen in the Straits and Hong Kong. These agents were quite often less than scrupulous in their procurement methods. Court cases from the Straits, such as *Ramsamy v. Lowe* (1888) and *Apolingam v. E.A.B. Brown* (1893), show how labor traffickers tried to get Straits coolies down to Deli against British laws; other cases show that these illicit movements happened entirely within the English sphere as well, as crimping secreted away immigrants from their true destinations and off to other places, usually locales of grim repute.[85] In January 1890 a riot broke out on the German steamer *Chow Foo,* which was carrying a huge number of Chinese coolies down to the Straits from South China; the men on board had found out they were actually being taken to Deli, not to the Straits as had been promised. Thirteen of the men were shot to keep the others in line.[86] Crimping in Penang, also in order to get Chinese coolies to East Sumatra, was just as bad, as Chinese witness statements given to the Straits authorities show in some detail:

Cheah Sin Ng: I am manager to Mr. Hermann, a proprietor of tin mines at Siak . . . I had chartered three *tongkangs* to take the coolies to Siak as my boat is undergoing repairs. This morning about 9:30 . . . 18 coolies had gone on board, the remainder said, "We won't go . . . you will sell us as little pigs to another country."

Lim Shit: I am from the . . . province of Canton, and am a farm labour (*sic*): I was induced . . . to leave my home, they told me that if I would follow them to Singapore, they would find me good employment as a sawyer or brickmaker. . . . From our village, 9 men besides me were induced to come away, and on the 15th of the 12th moon we were put on a Hainan junk . . . this morning I asked Chin-Sam for money to send to China, but he said we should get no money till we arrived at the place we were go-ing to. Hearing that we were being taken away from his country, we refused to go on board the boat; Hiap-tye's man attempted to force me, so I ran away, as I had seen others beaten.

Chew Ah Nyee: Chaing-See and Kuai-leong told me they could get me plenty of work at Singapore as a clerk, and that wages here were very good; I believed them, and was put on board a junk and brought to this place, where I was sold to a shop. . . . there were 90 men from my district, the strong men were sent to saw-yards I believe, but I was sold as a "little pig," being weak. This morning I was being taken to a boat with many others. I don't know where they were taking us to, but we heard that the place is 11 or 12 days' sail from this end, and that we had to work in tin-mines.

Hang Ship Ug: We were all locked up within three doors, and never allowed to go out—we were told that we should be locked up in the timber-yards.

Leong Ship Sam: We were kept in ignorance and could not see the sky, until to-day (sic), when we were told that we must work in some tin mines. . . . I and fourteen others were sent on board a boat, and if the gentlemen had not come and delivered me, I should have been stolen away in ignorance.

Lew Ship Yit: I was being taken on board a boat with a lot of others, and if any re-fused to go they were beaten by the Kheh-tows, there was a row and I got a blow dur-ing the struggle. I don't wish to go past Singapore, this is the place I agreed to come to.[87]

Indian Muslim men were sometimes employed in small sailing craft to pilot these journeys, with the coolies going for thirty-five dollars a head to Chinese subagents waiting in Sumatra.[88] These men were eventually ferried to a large vessel off the coast of Pulau Hantu (Ghost Island), and from there they were transported across the maritime border to the Dutch possessions. Chinese protest petitions were circulated in the Straits when the abuses became espe-cially bad, and many of the local Chinese accused British police of looking the other way or of being complicit and receiving kickbacks to get the men to the Indies.[89] There is good reason to believe there was a great deal of truth to these assertions, as seen already in regard to opium and several other contraband trades. Even some Straits administrators admitted the colony was being used to "entrap coolies for slavery in the neighboring Dutch settlements."[90] With the moral climate changing about issues such as slavery and coolie labor in the last decades of the nineteenth century, these kinds of abuses increasingly were an embarrassment to the Straits government in the larger international arena of Asia.

Reports and Chinese witness statements from Tebing Tinggi, also on the

Table 8. Statistics on Coolie Labor, Composition, and Transit in Dutch East Indies Border Residencies

Registered Contract Coolies in the Border Residencies, 1906–08			
	1906	1907	1908
Lampung	611	659	644
Palembang	615	812	843
E Coast Sumatra	71882	78361	79579
Aceh	858	839	851
Riau	2803	2399	1543
Belitung	1964	5053	4037
W Borneo	529	937	206
SE Borneo	2834	4062	4985

East Coast Sumatra: Ethnicities of Coolies, 1906–08			
	1906	1907	1908
Indigenous	65	270	75
Javanese	23500	28229	29322
Sundanese	2217	2205	2399
Madurese	59	19	45
Bawaenese	279	148	91
Malays	5	9	2
Banjarese	326	235	308
Buginese	4	0	0
"Klings"	1455	1349	1728
Chinese	43969	45897	45606
Other Foreign Asians	3	0	3
Total	71882	78361	79579

Coolies Departed from Swatow, South China, to Southeast Asia		
Straits (as Depot)	Sumatra (East Coast)	Year
46,710	—	1886
46,667	—	1887
40,066	1,222	1888
44,258	3,825	1889
35,570	5,066	1890
27,742	3,912	1891
30,728	2,991	1892
48,601	5,930	1893
33,146	5,882	1894
45,915	8,342	1895
49,918	7,194	1896

Sources: Adapted from ARA, Min van BZ, "A" Dossiers, Box 245, and *Koloniaal Verslag* 1909, Appx D, p. 22–3.

coast of Sumatra, show why it often took artifice to induce coolies to come to these areas to work. Chinese wood cutting concerns in this area made a huge business yearly cutting down logs and shipping them back to Singapore for export; one trunk of the timber went for approximately twenty dollars, more than the price of a coolie.[91] Yet the treatment these laborers received, mostly Chinese men funneled in from the Straits, was terrifyingly harsh. A report compiled by the Dutch resident of the East Coast of Sumatra took witness statements of various Chinese working in the kongsi; all complained of being beaten with fists, sticks, and thick cudgels and of being prevented from complaining to the police.[92] Yong Siu's testimony of November 13, 1908, told of coolies being denied medicine and forced to undertake labor despite illnesses; four men in his work gang hanged themselves, and he pointed to the photo of a man who was beaten to death. Yong himself finally made his way to a vessel lying at anchor in a neighboring stream and escaped to the Straits, where he told his tale to the authorities.[93] His account was corroborated by other court cases brought before the magistrate in the Straits, cases which also painted a picture of a porous maritime border being crossed by duped or unwilling coolies in one direction and a few lucky escapees in the other.[94]

Further down in the Straits, opposite Singapore in the islands of Dutch Riau, the situation was much the same. A Chinese sampan caught trying to land Chinese coolies there in 1904 illuminated the larger pattern; this particular craft had 161 Hainanese laborers huddled in the belly of the craft, all of whom had been loaded in Kwangtung (Guangdong), southern China. The officer of Chinese Affairs in Tanjung Pinang, Riau, reported the ship had false papers and a false destination; it was supposed to have been en route to the Bangka tin mines further south in the Straits, but had tried to land the coolies in Riau instead. The laborers, most of them men in their teens from the interior of Guangdong, had been lied to and given false promises. No passengers had been mentioned on the vessel's manifest either, though the captain eventually told the Dutch that the workers had been brought from Annam (Vietnam). This the officer of Chinese Affairs did not believe, as the entire documentation of the craft seemed to have been forged. The papers called the ship the *Khing Tu Li,* but by looking at the small altar to the God of the Sea inside the captain's quarters, where the *wangkang's* name had to be inscribed, the officer found it was actually the *Khing Goan Hin.* The shippers had tried to decoy the Dutch into thinking they were another craft already on colonial record, but the purpose of the voyage all along was to get the coolies to a secret work site in Riau. The Dutch consul in Hong Kong agreed. He pointed out that the Chinese authorities often saw coolie movements as a way to rid China of "bad elements" and that they didn't care much about illegal passages.[95] Twenty years earlier a similar case was documented in the region, when another unregistered junk was shipwrecked in local waters and most of the coolies on board drowned.[96]

The Dutch eventually made much more stringent efforts to get coolies directly from China themselves, a strategy which worked (mainly because of the Deli Planters Lobby's money and influence in Dutch diplomatic circles) after 1890. Yet getting enough labor through legitimate means still remained a problem, even after this date. This can be seen through the maneuverings of the Singkep Tin Company, a Dutch concern on the island of Singkep just south of the Riau archipelago, in the mid-1890s. The Singkep company's attempts to recruit labor in the Chinese countryside, outside of the recently established direct South-China-to-Deli funnel, aroused the concern of the Dutch authorities. The Hague's consul in Swatow, for example, told his superiors that any transgressions of the present system of labor procurement might make the Chinese nervous and endanger the much larger flows to Sumatra.[97] Yet the company pressed forward with its aggressive program, sending Chinese miners already working for them into the Guangdong periphery in search of able-bodied men to bring down to the Straits. The Malay-language letter of two of these Chinese, Thoe Nam Sin and Tjoa Eng Hay, survives: it shows the conditions the company imposed on labor procurement, which included a ban on men from Macao or Chuan-chou (Quanzhou) and the proviso that the coolies be brought directly down to Singkep and nowhere near Singapore.[98] This last stipulation was the more earnest of the two: bringing Chinese laborers near Singapore brought them into contact with coolie brokers and the official system, which allowed the workers opportunities to escape and the brokers opportunities to cheat the company. This particular trip to get coolies down to Singkep ultimately failed owing to too much resistance, both from entrenched Dutch interests and the protective policies of the Chinese.[99] Yet it was only one attempt among many to move men outside of the officially sanctioned channels and into lives of labor in Southeast Asia, hidden from the eyes of local colonial states.

Conditions in the Dutch tin mines on Bangka and Belitung, two islands further south in the Straits, eventually became so bad that the Chinese government lodged complaints on behalf of Chinese subjects working there. These islands, two thousand miles away from China and eight to ten days by steamer, had a resident population in 1905 of approximately 250 Europeans and 250 Arabs alongside 40,000 Chinese.[100] Many of the Chinese worked in mines that were to some extent self-governing but ultimately responsible to larger Dutch mining companies or the Netherlands Indies state.[101] By 1906, however, the stealthy transport of coolies down to these mines and the abominable treatment they received there were arousing the indignation of the provincial Chinese authorities. The viceroy of Guangdong and Guangxi wrote to the Dutch consul in Hong Kong that year that he knew of such secret enlistments; he warned the consul that this kind of recruitment was forbidden and asked him to work to forbid it.[102] The Chinese press, especially in Hong Kong, was less mild in its condemnation. An article published in December 1905 told of brandings on the coolies' thighs and hands and asked why the lives of Chinese were treated as being of no value.[103] The Dutch were quick to respond; under the cover of the name of a Mr. Kien of the Holland/China Trade Company, an article was inserted in the same paper two weeks later denying the validity of the stories.[104] Further protest articles were published in Chinese papers in the Straits, mirroring the earlier complaints.[105] The entire matter shows, however, that both the Chinese government in China and the Dutch authorities in Batavia were well aware of the secret transport of labor across the frontier but were more or less powerless to stop it. Though the viceroy banned the passage of more Chinese coolies down to Bangka in March 1906, there were always other ways to get labor through subterranean channels.[106]

In Borneo, finally, human beings were also trafficked for labor purposes, especially into the domains of the British North Borneo Company on the northern part of the island. Dutch surveillance reports on labor practices in the archipelago singled out North Borneo as a terminus for these sorts of activities, declaring that the company's territory was used repeatedly as work sites for illegally transited labor. Indies coolies who were en route to Sumatra's East Coast were sometimes decoyed away to the Borneo plantations by corrupt labor-foremen; the Dutch consul in Singapore reported in 1888 that forty coolies were duped in this way by one Hadji Taip, who landed them on the company's lands instead.[107] The North Borneo Company knew its territory held an evil reputation as a graveyard for laboring coolies and made sure to sign extradition treaties with neighboring polities to ensure that escapees would be brought back to its shores. Sarawak instituted similar practices throughout the years around the turn of the century.[108] This left to nearby ports like Labuan the unenviable task of constantly having to be on the lookout for absconding workers, who often dropped over the side of massive ships like ants in their eagerness to escape.[109] Eventually the company turned to labor sources as far away as southern India for its required manpower, though even other outposts of the extended British Empire in Asia were loathe to send their subjects to North Borneo. In 1913, China relented after many long years of complaints and allowed the movement of more settlers to the northern half of the island, though a Chinese supervisor, Dr. T. B. Sia, was required by treaty to accompany the workers to check on their conditions.[110] By the first decades of the twentieth century, nationalist awakenings in several parts of Asia made such scrutiny highly desirable. Even previously unwilling colonial regimes began to realize the consequences of not improving a system based on mistreatment and near slavery. The traffic in human labor had been going on long enough and had such a grim reputation that almost all parties involved now said coolies needed the protection of emerging international law.

This concern was a shared sentiment about all three of the human "secret trades" examined in this chapter. By the early twentieth century, most metropolitan Europeans saw the illegal traffic in human beings as morally indefensible; this was a far cry from the 1860s and 1870s, when the passage of categories of human "cargo" was more or less viewed as inevitable in places like Southeast Asia. Yet metropolitan concerns and colonial abilities to enforce change on the ground in the region were often two separate things. Counterfeiters were increasingly unsuccessful against the coercive powers of the colonial state, yet opium flourished across the Anglo/Dutch border between 1865 and 1915. The trade in human beings continued throughout these fifty years, but was pushed further and further underground by the imperial authorities. Prostitutes often became "taxi-dancers"; coolies were still exploited, but were no longer trafficked outside of existing systems as openly as before. Slavery did disappear, for the most part, along the length of the border, though this had less to do with interdiction and more to do with a concerted European administrative presence on the frontier. As a broad conceptual category, therefore, the commerce in humans shows the variability of the dance between smugglers and states. Some of these transited peoples found their lives to have improved immeasurably by the early twentieth century, while others still toiled grimly in various kinds of human bondage.

NOTES

1. As with the terms *smuggling* and *smugglers,* I use the term *coolie* with caution here; it has a demeaning connotation to some modern ears. This was the term in use at the time, however, and utilizing it seems to make more sense than the term *laborer,* which does not necessarily have the same implication of movement to foreign shores in this context.
2. See Sone, "The Karayuki-san of Asia" (1992), 46.

3. Shimizu, "The Rise and Fall of the Karayuki-san" (1992), 20. See also Mihalopoulos's interesting article, "The Making of Prostitutes" (1993).

4. See Hershatter, "The Hierarchy of Shanghai Prostitution" (1989), 471. See also Jaschok, *Concubines and Bondservants* (1988), and Hershatter, "Modernizing Sex, Sexing Modernity" (1994), 147–74.

5. Ming, "Barracks-Concubinage in the Indies" (1983); Christanty, "Nyai dan Masyarakat Kolonial" (1994), 21–36; Hesselink, "Prostitution: A Necessary Evil" (1987); Ingleson, "Prostitution in Colonial Java" (1986). For analogs in the colonial Philippines, see Dery, "Prostitution in Colonial Manila" (1991), 475–89, and Terami-Wada, "Karayuki-san of Manila 1880–1920" (1986), 287–316.

6. Warren, *Ah Ku and Karayuki-san* (1993), see esp. chap. 4. See also a new dissertation on the topic, Abalahin, "Prostitution Policy and the Project of Modernity" (2003).

7. Many of the coal miners purchased Kling (Indian) women as concubines. FO to Spenser St. John, British Consul in Borneo, 4 July 1856, in CO 144/13; also Eastern Archipelago Co. to Colonial Land and Immigration Office, 28 May 1856, and Eastern Archipelago Co. to Radford, Esq., 23 May 1856, both in CO 144/13.

8. Gov. Labuan to CO, 16 June 1880, no. 52, in CO 144/53; Gov Straits to CO, 27 June 1883, no. 274, in CO 273/121.

9. Hesselink, "Prostitution: A Necessary Evil," 211.

10. See "Indische Concubinaat en Prostitutie" (1899), 1380. Also see Adelante, "Concubinaat" (1898), 304–14, 610–17.

11. The women were landed at the backs of houses at night and were kept as concubines after that at a price of fifty to seventy dollars per head. See Resident Councilor, Malacca to Sec. of Gov't, Straits, 10 April 1866, in CO 273/9.

12. Testimony of Hadji Abdul Raman and of Hadji Abdullah bin Batu, both given to Major Burns, 10 April 1866, in CO 273/9. See also Resident Councilor, Penang, to Sec. of Gov't., Straits, 24 April 1866, and May 30, 1866, both in CO 273/9. The Resident Councillor said that the women were generally only sold in times of distress, when they would be taken down to the coasts. After the turn of the century, miners received prostitutes who had been warded by the state as brides; see *Perak Gov't Gazette*, 1902, extract following page 336.

13. "Persons, chiefly women and children, are bought in China, Borneo, and the islands adjacent to Singapore and brought here as prostitutes and servants. It is quite possible that these persons change hands here, but this is not done openly. . . . It is an offense punishable with seven years of imprisonment." Captain Dunlop, Inspector General of Police, Straits, to Acting Colonial Secretary, 4 April 1874, in CO 273/79.

14. Quahe, *We Remember: Cameos of Pioneer Life* (1986), 80.

15. Gov, SS to CO, 11 Aug. 1882, no. 290, in CO 273/115. Governor Weld stated that the chief traffickers of women into the colony were perahus and junks, many of which came from across the Dutch frontier.

16. See Ordinance no. 23 of 1870, "An Ordinance to Prevent the Spread of Certain Contagious Diseases," as published in the *SSGG*, 9 Dec. 1870, and Ordinance no. 1 of 1887, "An Ordinance to Make Further Provision for the Protection of Women and Girls," in *SSGG*, 13 May 1887. In Perak any woman wanting to leave a brothel legally could not be prevented from doing so; see *Perak Gov't Gazette*, 1890, 3.

17. For the provisions that stood on this topic in the early twentieth century, see Staatsblad 1907, nos. 278, 279; Staatsblad 1916, no. 199; and Bijblad nos. 347, 7332.

18. For the full range of mechanisms used to get females into the colony, see the reports under the rubric *League of Nations: Commission of Inquiry into the Traffic in Women,* multivolume (1932–38).

19. See "In the Matter of the Estate of Choo Eng Choon, Deceased, and Choo Ang Chee vs. Neo Chan Neo (et al.), Singapore" in *SSLR* 12 (1911): 120 passim. The contours of this case show how unsure the authorities were about the nature of Chinese marriages—whether, for example, Chinese were monogamous or polygamous. The result of this debate, obviously, could affect trafficking very much. In this particular case, to get to the roots of what Chinese marriages actually might be, Mencius, the translator James Legge, and Cochin-Chinese laws on Chinese marriages were all invoked, in an effort to make a judgment. The court found that Chinese were indeed polygamous.

20. *League of Nations: Commission of Inquiry* (1932), 81.

21. See Ordinance no. 13 of 1894, *SSGG,* 7 Sept 1894; Ordinance no. 5, 1880, *SSGG,* 27 Aug. 1880; and Ordinance no. 25 of 1908; see also the *Sarawak Gazette,* 12 May 1871.

22. Gov. Straits to CO, 20 Jan. 1892, no. 31, in CO 273/179; CO Jacket, Mr. Elders, 20 Jan. 1892, in CO 273/179.

23. Report of Mr. Firmstone, Acting Assistant Protector of Chinese, Penang, 11 Nov. 1899, in CO 273/249. See also FMS Enactment no. 7, 1902, in the FMS Annual Report of 1901, in the *Perak Gov't Gazette,* 1902, 624, which describes age limits.

24. CO Jacket, 21 Nov. 1894, in CO 273/201.

25. CO Jacket, Mr. Cox, 16 Nov. 1899, no. 426, in CO 273/249.

26. See *Bintang Timor,* 10 Dec. 1894, 2: "Satu orang Teo-chew nama-nya Tang Ah Moey sudah kenah tangkap smalang petang di Johor, sebab menchuri dan bawa lari satu budak perampuan, umor-nya 10 tahun, nama-nya Ung Eng Neo, deri Jawa Road dia bawa pergi budak itu di Johor dan jual-kan dia disana" [A Teochew named Tang Ah Moey has been arrested in Johore, because he stole and then brought there a girl of ten years of age named Ung Eng Neo, from Java Road; he brought her to Johor and then sold her]. See also *Regina v. Quah Ah So,* in *ST,* 18 July 1883, 3.

27. See "In re Lam Tai Ying" in *Kyshe* 4:685 passim, and "Regina v. Rajaya and Anor." in *Kyshe,* 2:112 passim.

28. See "Ahvena Ravena Mana Aroomoogim Chitty v. Lim Ah Hang, Ah Gee, and Chop Lee Whatt," *SSLR* 2 (1894): 80 passim; "Moothoo Raman Chetty v. Aik Kah Pay and Another," *SSLR* 9 (1905): 115 passim; "Joseph Scher, Appelent, v. Regina, On the Prosecution of Henry Perrett, Respondent," *SSLR* 4 (1900–01): 84 passim; "Martin Mosesko, Appellant, v. the Queen. On the Prosecution of William Evans, Respondent," SSLR 6 (1900–01): 69 passim.

29. See Warren, *Ah Ku and Karayuki-san,* 82.

30. "Appendix M: Contagious Diseases Ordinance: List of Licensed Brothels for the Month of February, 1877," in "Report of the Committee Appointed to Enquire into the Working of Ordinance no. 23 of 1870," *SSLCP,* 2 April 1877.

31. See ARA, 1889, MR no. 439; ARA, 1889, MR no. 766; ARA, 1891, MR no. 688; ARA, 1891, MR no. 211; and especially, for the Buitenbezittingen, ARA, 1890, MR no. 228.

32. Anonymous Petition on Bribery of Government Officers, 26 March 1897, in CO 273/233. Tan Yang Fook, Tse Chye Wong, and several other prominent Singapore subjects were implicated in these schemes.

33. See *SSLCP,* 1903, C165; *Annual Report of the Chinese Protectorate, Straits Settlements* (1907), 38; see also Alistair Duncan to CO, 29 Dec. 1913, in CO 273/404, and Gov, SS to CO, 5 Sept., 1912, Confidential, in CO 273/383.

34. Gov, SS to CO, 15 March 1905, no. 95, in CO 273/308; also CO Cover Jacket, Mr. Johnson, 15 March 1905, in CO 273/308.

35. See J. Kohlbrugge's article, "Prostitutie in Nederlandsch-Indië" (1901), 1736; see also van Kol, "Het Lot der Vrouw in Onze Oost-Indische Koloniën" *Koloniaal Weekblad* (25 Dec. 1902), 5. Kol describes a Javanese woman who had been tricked into a life of prostitution on Sumatra's East Coast, servicing Chinese and Javanese coolies there; she went mad eventually and was transported back to Java in a sack, her hands and feet tied to a bamboo pole.

36. Concubinage, which had been tolerated as a "moral compromise" in both the Indies and the British possessions for quite some time, also came under censure after the turn of the century. Victorian moralities and the presence of larger numbers of European women in Southeast Asia helped cause these changes. See Kern, "De Controleurs en 't Concubinaat" (1905), 250–52, and Hyam, "Concubinage and the Colonial Service" (1986), 170.

37. Reid, "Decline of Slavery in Nineteenth-Century Indonesia" (1993), 64–65, and Reid, "Introduction: Slavery and Bondage" (1983), 1–43.

38. See Terweil, "Bondage and Slavery" (1983), 118–39; Means, "Human Sacrifice and Slavery" (2000), 188–89; Warren *The Sulu Zone* (1981), 147, 14; see also Scwalbenberg, "The Economics of Pre-Hispanic Slave Raiding" (1994), 376–84.

39. Reid, "The Decline of Slavery," 69, 77; see also van Balen, "De Afschaffing van Slavenhandel" (1987), 83–96.

40. Backer-Dirks, *Gouvernements Marine* (1985), 57.

41. Staatsblad 1877, nos. 180, 181; see also Staatsblad 1876, nos. 35, 166, 246; Staatsblad 1877, nos. 89, 90; Staatsblad 1880, nos. 21, 114; Staatsblad 1883, no. 40; Staatsblad 1884, no. 162; and Staatsblad 1901, nos. 286, 287.

42. Gov, SS to Sec. State India, London, 21 May 1866, no. 587, in CO 273/9.

43. The instruction booklet for 1869 let naval commanders know that "slavery as a legal institution exists in several states with which Great Britain has treaties for the suppression of the slave trade. The mere finding therefore of slaves on board a vessel will not justify an officer in detaining her." Officers who seized ships suspected of slaving under the wrong set of circumstances, therefore, were liable themselves for any damages or legal actions against the Crown—and would incur the Admiralty's "serious displeasure" as well. Nonroyal naval ships that seized slavers on the high seas were entitled to a bounty from the Crown, but this sum, equal to two-thirds of the ship's value, was also considered as taxable income. See Vice-Admiral Shadwell Circulaire to Ship Commanders, China-Station, 2 April 1874, no. 86; "Admiralty Instructions for the Guidance of Naval Officers Employed in the Suppression of the Slave Trade," 11 June 1869; and "An Act for Consolidating with Amendments the Acts for Carrying into Effect Treaties for the More Effectual Suppression of the Slave Trade, and for Other Purposes Connected with the Slave

Trade," 5 Aug. 1873, all in PRO/Admiralty/125/no. 20, China Station General Correspondence (1871–74.)

44. See British Envoy, The Hague to FO, 1 Feb. 1866, no. 20, and Gov, SS to Sec. of State for India, London, 6 April, no. 406, both in CO 273/9.

45. Resident Councillor, Malacca, to Sec. of Gov't, Straits, 10 April 1866, in CO 273/9.

46. ARA, Resident West Borneo to GGNEI, 11 April 1871, no. 32, Secret, in 1871, MR no. 522; Dutch Consul, Singapore to Col. Secretary, Straits, 6 Nov. 1874, in CO 273/79; ARA, 1870, MR no. 633; Berigt van de Resident der Zuider en Ooster Afdeeling van Borneo, 22 July 1875, no. 37, in 1875, MR no. 655.

47. ARA, Resident West Borneo to GGNEI, 11 April 1871, no. 32, Secret, in 1871, MR no. 522; ARA, Extract Uit het Register der Besluiten, GGNEI, 16 Aug. 1879, no. 1, in 1879, MR no. 476; also British Consul, Brunei to FO, 13 March 1877, no. 5 Political, in CO 144/48. Captain Sachsze was well known in local waters as a slaver; he was also sentenced in Singapore at one time for shooting one of his crew members.

48. *EvNI* 3 (1928): 806.

49. Ch. Kerckhoff, "Eenige Mededeelingen en Opmerkingen Betreffende de Slavernij" (1891), 757.

50. ARA, Resident Sumatra Oostkust to GGNEI, 3 Aug. 1875, no. 1037/10, in 1875, MR no. 655.

51. ANRI, Algemeen Administratieve Verslag Residentie Palembang 1871 (no. 64/14).

52. ANRI, Algemeen Verslag Residentie Borneo Z.O. 1871 (no. 9/2).

53. Kater, "Iets over de Pandelingschap" (1871), 296–305.

54. British Consul, Borneo to FO, 5 Feb. 1883, Consular no. 7, in CO 144/57.

55. See William Pretyman's Diary at Tempasuk (vol. 72, 17 May 1880), and Everett's Diary at Papar (vol. 73, 22 April 1880), both in PRO/CO/874/British North Borneo, boxes 67–77, Resident's Diaries (1878–98).

56. See especially Gov. BNB to Consul Trevenen, 3 March 1891, in CO 144/68. As a result of British pressure, the sultan of Brunei was forced to issue a ban on slaving, which particularly mentioned that the company's subjects were now off-limits. Sultan of Brunei Proclamation, 26 Rejab, 1308 A.H., in CO 144/68.

57. Consul Trevenen to Marquis of Salisbury (FO), 31 March 1891, no. 2 Confidential, in CO 144/68.

58. *Singapore Daily Times*, 4 Jan. 1882, 2.

59. ARA, 1877, MRno. 423.

60. See the *Koloniaal Verslagen* cites in Kerkhoff, "Eenige Mededeelingen en Opmerkingen Betreffende de Slavernij," 756.

61. "Varia" (1880), 481–83.

62. See the *Straits Times Overland Journal*, 26 March 1883, for example.

63. ARA, Stations-Commandant Oosterafdeeling van Borneo to Commander, NEI Navy, 28 Nov. 1889, no. 898, in 1889, MR no. 149. See also "Slavenhandel. Slavernij." *IWvhR*, no. 1655, 18 March 1895, 42.

64. Some members of the Colonial Office, in hearing more about the systematic oppression of pilgrims in Singapore, disagreed with the Singapore administration in its dismissal of the Dutch consul's claims. "I feel some doubt whether this question should be allowed to re-

main uninvestigated," wrote Mr. Meade in the C.O. in early 1875. "The present 'investiga-tion' is next to none at all. Mr. Read (the Dutch consul) may have overstated his case in calling the position of these Hajjis 'slavery.' But it seems to me not very far removed from it." See CO Jacket, Mr. Meade, 2 Feb. 1875; Gov, SS to CO, 2 Feb. 1875, no. 26; Dutch Consul, Singapore, in "Letter to the Editor," *Singapore Daily Times,* 21 Sept. 1873; and Capt. Dunlop and Allan Skinner to Col. Secretary, SS, 12 Sept. 1874, all in CO 273/79.

65. See *Straits Times Overland Journal,* 5 May 1882, in CO 273/118. The newspaper was glib in its disapproval of the Straits government's efforts to deal with such abuses: "It is very generally believed that the Bugis do a little 'in ebony' from New Guinea on the sly, and that women are frequently brought up from Java and disposed of, at a price, to some of the rich towkays. Of course, our government knows nothing of this. Why should it?" Various other sources confirm both of these transactions.

66. See the details in the fascinating letter by Read, Dutch Consul, Singapore to Col. Sec., Singapore, 8 May 1882, no. 243, in CO 273/115.

67. See Tagliacozzo, "Smuggling in Southeast Asia" (2002), 193–220.

68. ARA, "Verslag Omtrent de Slavernij en den Slavenhandel in de Residentie Westerafdeel-ing van Borneo over het Jaar 1889" 17 July 1890, in 1890, MR no. 530; also "Verslag Be-treffende Slavernij door de Resident van Palembang" (1891), in 1891, MR no. 194.

69. ARA, Controleur of the North coast to Resident, Manado, 5 Oct. 1896, no. 202, in 1897, MR no. 438; also ARA, 1902, MR no. 877.

70. "Slavernij in Nederlandsch-Indië" (1907), 425–26.

71. Reid, "Decline of Slavery," 74–77. For an interesting debate on just how much slavery, whether this was traditional slavery, or forced and unwilling corvée labor, was left in the Outer Islands around the turn of the century, see Rookmaaker, "Heerendiensten" (1902), 278–82, and van Sluijs, "Heerendiensten in de Buitenbezittingen" (1903), 282–87.

72. Pan, *Sons of the Yellow Emperor* (1990), 47.

73. See especially Eunice Thio's article on the mechanisms of labor trafficking; "The Chinese Protectorate" (1960), and Blusse, "China Overzee: Aard en Omvang" (1998), 34–50. Ja-vanese labor was also utilized and exploited in similar ways; see Houben, "Nyabrang/Overzee Gaan: Javaanse Emigratie" (1998), 51–65.

74. For particularly good critiques of the Dutch labor regime in Sumatra, see Breman, *Koelies, Planters, en Koloniale Politiek* (1992); Breman, *Labour Migration and Rural Transformation"* (1990); Breman, *Taming the Coolie Beast* (1989); Stoler, *Capitalism and Confrontation* (1985), and Usman et al., eds., *Sejarah Sosial Daerah Sumatra Utara* (1984), 8–9. For the situation in the South China Sea islands of Bangka, Belitung, and Singkep, see Heidhues, *Bangka Tin and Mentok Pepper* (1992), chap. 3, and Kaur, "Tin Mines and Tin Mining" (1996), 95–120. For a good case study on Malaya, see Loh, *Beyond the Tin Mines* (1988), 7–54.

75. "Overzicht van eene Voordracht" (1891), 305–11.

76. *Nota Over de Uitoefening van Staatstoezicht op de Werving* (1907), 3–4.

77. See *Straits Settlements Ordinances* 1867, no. 31; 1890, no. 7; 1868, no. 14; 1870, no. 6; and 1883, no. 5, for example.

78. Crimping was defined as the unlawful sale of laborers for profit. *Straits Settlements Ordi-nances* 1873, no. 10; 1877, no. 2; 1880, no. 4; 1902, no. 9; 1910, no. 30; 1876, no. 1; 1884, no. 4; 1877, no. 3; 1892, no. 14; 1896, no. 21; and 1891, no. 8. Chinese coolies had to be pho-

tographed by law in Perak as of 1888, as a protection against smuggling. See *Perak Gov't Gazette,* 1888, 74.

79. *Straits Settlements Ordinances* 1896, no. 18; 1897, no. 18; and 1908, no. 21.

80. *Labour Commission: Glossary of Words and Names in the Report of the Commissioners"* (1891).

81. "Evidence of Tun Kua Hee, a Depot Keeper, 29 Oct. 1890 Sitting" in the *Labour Commission Report,* Singapore, 1891; and *The Labour Commission Glossary,* Singapore, 1891 under "Javanese and Native Labor," especially the accounts of Mr. Halloway, Mr. Gunn, Count D'Elsloo, Mr. Patterson, Mr. Wittholft, and Mr. Reimer. Indian coolies on estates in Perak in 1870 were absconding (or fleeing) at very high rates—over 20 percent of the total workforce, in some instances. See *Perak Gov't Gazette,* 1890, 572.

82. See "Evidence of D. W. Patterson, Shipping Clerk in Messrs. Guthrie and Co., 27 Oct. 1890 Sitting," in *The Labour Commission Report,* Singapore, 1891.

83. "Nota Over de Uitoeffening van Staatstoezicht op de Werving" (1907), 9–12.

84. See ARA, Dutch Consul for South China to Chairman of the Planters' Committee, Medan, 27 March 1909, no. 213, Appx. 1, in (MvBZ/A/245/A.119). The numbers for a range of border residencies are presented and then are blown up for East Sumatra, the main destination for these laborers.

85. For the Deli cases, see "Apolingam v. E.A.B. Brown," *SSLR* (1893): 69 passim; "Ramsamy v. Lowe" *Kyshe* 4 (1888): 396 passim. For internal transiting of coolies inside British territory and against the law, see "Brown v. Vengadashellum" *Kyshe* 4 (1889): 524, and "Tio Ang Boi v. Hia Ma Lai" *Kyshe* 4 (1887): 230 passim.

86. See the version as printed in the Amsterdam newspaper *De Standaard,* 11 April 1890. See ARA, Dutch Consul Hong Kong to Gov Gen NEI, 22 Dec. 1905, no. 1153, in (MvBZ/A/246/A.119).

87. See the official statements provided by "Cheah Sin Ng, Lim Shit, Chew Ah Nyee, Hang Ship Ug, Leong Ship Sam, and Lew Ship Yit," in "Paper Laid Before the Legislative Commission, Friday 23 Feb. 1877; Report by Mr. Pickering on Kidnapping Sinkehs" in *SSLCP* 1877, 4 of the report.

88. Ibid., 2–3.

89. See the "Proclamation by the People of Canton and Hokkien Province" in the *Straits Observer* (Penang), 14 Dec. 1874, 2.

90. "Report by Mr. Pickering on Kidnapped Sinkehs" *SSLCP* 1877, 3.

91. ARA, "Chuk Fu's Statement" [3 Feb 1909, Contract no. 17596] in Resident East Coast of Sumatra Report on the Mishandeling of Workers at Tebing Tinggi Woodcutting Kongsi (n.d.) in (MvBZ/A/246/A.119). See also *Surat Surat Perdjandjian Riau"* (1970), 215.

92. ARA, Resident East Coast of Sumatra Report on the Mishandeling of Workers at Tebingtinggi Woodcutting Kongsi (n.d.) in (MvBZ/A/246/A.119).

93. ARA, "Yong Siu's Statement" [13 Nov. 1908, Contract no. 17593] in Resident East Coast of Sumatra Report on the Mishandeling of Workers at Tebingtinggi Woodcutting Kongsi (n.d.) in (MvBZ/A/246/A.119).

94. See for Tebingtinggi especially "Attorney General v. Wong Yew," *SSLR* 10 (1908): 44; and "Rex v. Koh Chin, Ang Tap, and Ang Chuan," *SSLR* 10 (1908): 48. The mortality rates among coolies in Sumatra were horrific; see van Klaveren, "Death Among Coolies" (1997), 111–25, and Emmer, "Mortality and the Javanese Diaspora" (1997), 125–36. For

an overview of woodcutting, coolie labor, and migration in Riau and coastal Sumatra, see Erman, "Tauke, Kuli, dan Penguasa" (1994), 20–33.

95. ARA, Dutch Consul, Peking to MvBZ, 22 May 1905, no. 593/79; Dutch Consul Hong Kong to Dutch Consul Peking, 9 May 1905, no. 474/35; GGNEI to Dutch Consul Peking, 18 Nov. 1904, Kab. no. 48; and Officer for Chinese Affairs in Tandjong Pinang to Resident of Riau, March 1904, no. 4, all in (MvBZ/A/246/A.119).

96. ANRI, Maandrapport Residentie Banka 1872 (no. 98, December).

97. ARA, Dutch Acting Consul, Swatow to Dutch Minister for China, Peking, 20 June 1894, no. 41, in (MvBZ/A/245/A.119).

98. The miners were trying to recruit thirty or forty men according to the letter; they were to be brought directly to the mines in Singkep. Macao and Quanzhou men were considered physically weak; they were also often considered to be troublemakers. See Thoe Nam Sin and Tjoa Eng Hay's letter, enclosed in ARA, Dutch Consul Hong Kong to New Chief Administrator of the Singkep Tin Co, 31 Dec. 1895, no. 759, in (MvBZ/A/245/A.119).

99. ARA, Dutch Consul, London to MvBZ, 19 Oct 1896, no. 43, in (MvBZ/A/245/A.119).

100. ARA, Dutch Consul Hong Kong to MvBZ, 25 Dec. 1905, no. 1156/86 in (MvBZ/A/246/A.119).

101. "Nijverheid en Technische Kunsten," *Nieuwe Rotterdamsche Courant,* 12 Feb. 1911.

102. ARA, Viceroy Guangdong and Guangxi to Acting Dutch Consul, Hong Kong, 24th Day, 11th Moon, 32nd Year Guangxu Reign, in (MvBZ/A/246/A.119).

103. *Sai Kai Kung Yik Po,* 11 Dec. 1905. The article particularly lays blame upon Chinese who are used as henchmen by the Dutch in the mines. The Dutch themselves also participate in the injustices, leaving the Chinese workers in terrible shape, their bodies and spirits broken by their labors and by the cruelty of their oppressors. The author of the piece then warns that if China were powerful, no one would dare to heap such abuses upon her subjects. In ARA (MvBZ/A/246/A.119).

104. *Sai Kai Kung Yik Po,* 25 Dec. 1905. The rebuttal says there are untrue statements in the former article; Chinese, rather, have come down to the Dutch Indies for centuries to try to make their fortunes there. Some eventually become wealthy and are able to return home for visits. The article also points out that Chinese foremen supervise the labor, and that these men would never allow the inhuman treatments complained of above. In ARA (MvBZ/A/246/A.119).

105. See *Nanyang Chung Wei Pao,* 21 Aug. 1906; 2 Aug. 1906; 30 Oct. 1906; 11 Jan. 1907; 21 Jan. 1907. In ARA (MvBZ/A/246/A.119).

106. ARA, Dutch Consul Hong Kong to MvBZ, 25 Dec. 1905, no. 1156/86, in (MvBZ/A/246/A.119).

107. "Nota Over de Uitoeffening van Staatstoezicht op de Werving" (1907), 8.

108. See the *Sarawak Gazette,* 1 April 1891, 1 Dec. 1893, 2 April 1894, and 20 Sept. 1895.

109. See CO to BNB Co. HQ, London, 18 Jan. 1889, in CO 144/66 and Act. Gov. Labuan to CO, 6 June 1889, in CO 144/67; also Gov. BNB to BNB Co. HQ, London, 18 June 1912, in CO 531/4.

110. See Gov. Sec. Madras to Gov. Sec. BNB, 3 July 1912, and CO Jacket, 2 Oct. 1912, both in CO 531/4; BNB Co. HQ, London to CO, 3 Jan. 1913, in CO 531/5; BNB Co HQ, London, to CO, 22 June 1915, in CO 531/9.

Section IV The Illegal
Weapons Trade Across the
Anglo/Dutch Frontier

However active the vigilance of the Government may be, the innumerable islands of this archipelago offer so many opportunities for smuggling that it is vain to hope that this illicit traffic can be effectually checked, as long as the trade in implements of war can supply itself from ports situated in the immediate vicinity of Netherlands India, where every occasion to import them into this colony is eagerly watched for and speedily seized. . . . But there are higher and more general interests at stake. Your Excellency is aware that among the Mahomedans considerable agitation has lately been observed. . . . Your Excellency will, I am sure, agree with me that the interests of powers ruling Mussulman subjects peremptorily require at the present moment that they should support one another to the utmost and join in maintaining peace and order."
—ARA, Governor-General, Netherlands East Indies to Governor, Labuan, 11 December 1882, #41, in 1882 MR #1222

Chapter 11 Munitions and Borders: Arms in Context

Illegal drugs, counterfeit currency, and trafficked human beings passed across the Anglo/Dutch frontier in large quantities in the years around the turn of the twentieth century. Each of these "commodities" presented challenges and opportunities to colonial states and their subjects. The diffusion of contraband weapons in the region mirrored some of these dynamics, yet the perceived dangers posed by an unchecked flow of arms made this passage arguably the most important "secret trade" to area regimes and of greater concern than all the others. Surveillance and interdiction of the transit of weapons became a full-time occupation for local colonial states and a matter of increasing political importance, especially to Batavia. How did arms travel across borders? Where did these transactions take place? These movements are examined in several spaces along the frontier, from the ongoing conflict in Aceh, south to the weapons emporium of Singapore and north again to the unstable arena of Sulu and North Borneo. I also explore the subject of illegal arms topically. Who was involved in moving these commodities? Which legal structures were employed by smugglers and area states in their battle with one another? What avoidance mechanisms were utilized by contrabanders to keep themselves out of jail? The illegal arms trade speaks to smuggling patterns generally in Southeast Asia, primarily because the passage of guns was so important to colonial states. The voluminous archival record that records this trade provides clues as to the mechanics of contrabanding across borders in the region. Arms smuggling became a massive commerce in the decades around the turn of the twentieth century, before mutating qualitatively and quantitatively on the eve of World War I.

CHARTING DIRECTIONS

The transit of arms through Southeast Asia has a long historical pedigree, reaching back even before the early decades of European contact in the sixteenth century. Local societies were quick to understand the importance of firearms for survival and geopolitical maneuvering in the region. Scholars have pointed out that the learning curve on new forms of weaponry and their acquisition seems to have been shorter (by necessity of survival) than that on any other commodity.[1] In Southeast Asia this dialectic was evident very quickly, as arms-production centers appeared in seventeenth-century Aceh and even in areas as comparatively remote from large-scale commerce as upriver Borneo.[2] Muskets and well-forged blades traveled to Maluku as well as into distribution networks in highland New Guinea, while other firearms penetrated into Mindanao. One old VOC cannon was even worshiped as a totem by indigenes in western Borneo.[3] Surviving manuscripts in Southeast Asian languages give an idea of how these commodities were integrated into local societies. Bugis sources passed on the knowledge of how to handle and use various firearms, including information on gunnery, ballistics, and pyrotechnics, while Malay-language documents show that requests for gunpowder and firearms quite often crossed the Straits of Melaka, connecting Sumatra and the Malay peninsula.[4] Batak bone carvings were worn as amulets against the penetration of bullets; inscribed on these objects were incantations of protection similar to those used against traditional Batak dangers, such as poison, rheumatism, and leeches.[5]

Europeans took careful notes on the penetration of firearms into various Southeast Asian societies. In large parts of Borneo, brass guns were sold not only as trade items, but as units of currency as well; a picul, or 133 pounds' worth of brass guns in 1865 was considered the equivalent of thirty silver dollars.[6] Cast cannons of five to ten feet in length were also sold and marketed, particularly into upriver regions of Sarawak, while gunpowder was acquired and fired off on "every possible occasion of family sorrow or rejoicing, such as Fast days and feast days, at births, marriages, and deaths."[7] In Aceh, as on the Malay peninsula, European travelers noted that men went about their daily business heavily armed, usually with three or more arms on their person at all times, and more if they were traveling abroad. Some of these personal weapons were firearms, such as Lefaucheux hunting rifles and revolvers.[8] Women too were often skilled in the use of firearms, as contemporary and later observers would attest.[9] The huge profits to be made on the sale of firearms in the region, often in excess of 100 percent per purchase, enabled these commodities to diffuse into local societies on a large commercial scale and to the widest possible geography by the mid—nineteenth century. Bugis, Malays, Taosug, Chinese, Americans, and various Europeans were all involved in this transit, while customers, even until the early 1900s, remained scattered across nearly all ethnic categories.[10] By the early twentieth century, when colonial governments were trying to maintain a much more strict control on such items, firearms were to be found hidden away nearly everywhere in the region. A police inspector in Singapore told of arms searches going on day and night in the colony: in tenements, in brothels, in opium dens, and across a "sea of junks" in the harbor.[11]

As early as the 1860s, European administrations were trying to undo the legacy of centuries of free arms trading by progressively legislating against the transit in firearms. This was an extremely uneven process, however, with national policies and even personal predilections heavily influencing the speed and depth of enforcement. In 1863, for example, the Straits Settlements temporarily banned arms exports out of the colony, seemingly out of a concern that too many guns were finding their way from Singapore to Taiping-ravaged China. The decision was reversed shortly thereafter, though, the port regaining its former status as a weapons emporium frequented by all manner of perahus and junks in search of such goods.[12] If Singapore was the central node of arms purchases in the archipelago, Labuan was not too far behind, a fact that distressed many in the Colonial Office back in London.[13] Yet it was the start of the Aceh War in 1873 which gave new impetus to arms control measures in Insular Southeast Asia, as the Dutch immediately banned weapons imports to North Sumatra and asked the Straits Settlements to do the same. The governor of Singapore, Sir Harry Ord, was hawkish on this matter and only too glad to oblige his Dutch neighbors; a British ban on arms to Aceh was enacted only a few days after this request. Ord's decision stood until the turn of the twentieth century, but not without huge opposition from the various powerful forces of British Free Trade, both in the Straits and home in England.[14] The free passage of arms, and how this issue intertwined with both politics and economics in the region, would become a major issue in Southeast Asia for the next several decades.

The immediate fallout of the Straits arms ban to North Sumatra was financial; Singapore's reported arms exports to the Netherlands Indies fell from $13,211 in 1873 to less than $4,000 in 1874, and ammunition revenues fell from $14,331 to $6,202 in the same period.[15] Though these are only the above-board figures, the real numbers almost certainly being quite a bit higher, the hue and cry that arose from the Straits trading community about these losses was loud and rancorous. Yet as the war in Aceh progressed, with few concrete advancements in the first few years of the conflict from Batavia's point of view, the Dutch decided that nothing short of a total arms ban into the Indies would suit their purposes. In 1876, Batavia instituted such a ban, declaring all arms and ammunition exports into the Indies unlawful, and asked Singapore to do the same. Governor Ord was no longer in office, however, and the new governor was not as obliging. In 1877, the Dutch banned weapons exports into the Indies from Portuguese Timor as well, the Straits Settlements again declining to follow suit, despite great exertions from The Hague. It was only in 1879, after long internal wrangling in both London and the Straits, that Singapore assented to a uniform arms export ban to the entirety of the Dutch Indies. A year later Labuan followed suit, and all weapons movements into Dutch territory (no longer just to North Sumatra) became illegal from the perspective of both sides of the Straits.[16]

Once these basic parameters were in place, little changed over the next two decades with regard to arms legislation. The emergence of separate spheres of British authority in the various dominions of Southeast Asia—the Straits Settlements, the North Borneo Company, Sarawak, and the Federated Malay States—saw different rules and regulations applied to the particulars of movement, but state aims were primarily the same, namely, to keep guns out of the hands of local peoples.[17] In 1897, a new Sulu accord banned arms trafficking in that maritime domain, but only in 1900 did the Dutch finally see fit to ask Singapore for the rescinding of its general export ban into the Indies.[18] The situation in Aceh was safer now, and legislation across the Dutch archipelago universally condemned arms imports, except in highly controlled circumstances. Yet what was really different was that both of the colonial states were much more powerful now than they had been in the 1860s, and they could oversee such matters as illegal arms trafficking more effectively than ever before. Even the British, who had been so unsteady in charting their own arms-trafficking policies in Southeast Asia for so long, shuttling constantly between diplomatic and Free Trade initiatives, were firmly in the camp of international arms control by the early twentieth century. The imperial powers now saw such policies as being in their definite long-term interests and had come to more of an understanding that they needed to cooperate to keep such commodities out of the hands of subject populations.[19] By the decade of 1910, therefore, the transit in illegal arms in Southeast Asia was no longer the weighty issue it had been for so long. Nineteen fourteen and the outbreak of World War I would again push this dynamic into a new crisis mode for colonial regimes.

This late state of affairs should not detract from an understanding of how bitter the battle often was between the British and the Dutch, precisely over the issue of arms contraband, in the years before the turn of the twentieth century. Though supporters of free trade and stricter arms control existed on both sides of the Straits, each European power saw in the other a significant rival when it came to matters of arms trafficking in the region. Straits Settlements merchants lodged an avalanche of complaints about the treatment of British ships crossing into the Indies, alleging that Batavia was using arms checks as a pretext to cut open and spoil British cargoes as well as advance Dutch trading interests all along the frontier.[20] For their own part, the Dutch counterclaimed that British law enforcement agents charged with implementing the stipulations of the ban showed absolutely no zeal in carrying out these instructions and indeed bent over backward to allow arms smugglers into the Indies.[21] There seems to have been some truth to both of these assertions. Certainly there were many British officials who saw no benefit at all to the Straits Settlements in enforcing Batavia's arms bans and who lobbied for lower fines on apprehended individuals and less stringent controls throughout the late nineteenth century.[22] The Dutch were also often on their own when it came to serious patrolling against arms smugglers in Indies waters, a fact which seems to have been understood by Batavia, especially in the border residencies.[23]

Yet two factors put teeth in the Dutch bans and made the pursuit of illegal arms in the Indies more of a challenge to contrabanders than what they ordinarily might have faced. The first of these was the quality of the Dutch diplomatic presence in the Straits, epitomized by two men in particular, William H. Read and George Lavino. Read, who was British but became an official agent of the Dutch government in the Straits in 1847 and their consul in 1854, manned the Singapore diplomatic station until his retirement in 1885. During his forty years of service in the colony, he was a relentless advocate for Dutch concerns in the Straits, especially enforcement of the arms bans. He was so well placed in the superstructure of Straits political and economic power that his efforts on Batavia's behalf were often very effective, despite the foot-dragging of various British parties.[24] George Lavino, who started out as the Dutch agent for Acehnese affairs in Penang in the 1870s, later became the Dutch vice-consul in that port and in the mid-1880s replaced Read in Singapore upon his retirement. Lavino, who was Dutch, was also supremely energetic on behalf of the Dutch cause and was Batavia's point man in Penang, the port of origin for most of Aceh's incoming smuggled weapons.[25] The letters and dispatches of these two men provide much of the backbone of remaining documentation on arms transit into the Indies, as they reported back to their superiors both in Batavia and The Hague.

The other factor which helped advance the efficacy of the arms bans was the "European common cause" sentiment the Dutch tried to push on their English neighbors. A missive from the governor-general of the Indies to his counterpart in Singapore, dated June 22, 1881, lays out the parameters of this argument in its entirety. Not only rampant piracy and slave trading were caused by the free and unchecked flow of arms out of the British colonies, the Dutch governor said, but such munitions flows also raised the dangerous specter of Pan-Islam. Batavia played on this anxiety not only in the waters of the archipelago, which was shared with the administration in Singapore, but also in a wider context, mentioning British India as another domino which could fall if arms movements were not sufficiently controlled.[26] There is no direct evidence to prove these suggestive arguments are what carried the day in English policy-making sessions, but in the 1880s and 1890s there were more and more complaints in Straits circles about the dangers of arms to regional trade. Some of these were oblique. Newspaper articles such as one in the *Pinang Gazette* and another in the *Straits Observer* pointed to murders of merchants off the Aceh coast that could have been avoided had the Dutch been doing a better job of disarming the local populace.[27] Other dispatches were more direct in their criticism, referencing cases in which even gun smugglers themselves were caught unawares by armed assailants and relieved of their cargoes, also off the coast of North Sumatra.[28] The important trend to note is that over time, colonial administrations—and colonial opinion—on both sides of the Straits came to the conclusion that it would be better for everyone if local Southeast Asians had as few firearms as possible. Ensuring this state of affairs was another matter, however.

ARMS TO THE "CENTER": JAVA, 1870

An examination of the illegal arms transit into the Indies at this time can begin not on the border, but at the center of Dutch authority, in Java, in the year 1870.

Table 9. Official NEI Firearms Statistics for the North Java Coast, 1864–70

Numbers of Firearms in the Possession of Javanese in Semarang Area, 1868–70:

	1868	1869	1870
Semarang	687	655	607
Ambarawa	421	172	607
Salatiga	269	273	280
Kendal	920	920	931
Grobogan	371	359	390
Demak	588	880	769
Total	3256	3259	3167

Official NEI Statistics on Weapons Imports Into Java, 1864–69 (in guilders [f]):

Year	Batavia	Cirebon	Cilacap	Semarang	Surabaya	Pasuruan	Total
1864	20323	200	–	6940	13170	200	40833 f
1865	24425	–	–	5510	5175	–	35110 f
1866	30273	2219	–	6986	6697	310	46485 f
1867	24982	1904	1680	11849	9103	430	49948 f
1868	10341	5377	255	18108	13862	515	48458 f
1869	18977	1005	250	*82790*	12688	596	*116306 f*

Source: ARA, Collector of Import/Export Rights, Semarang: "Opgave van Ingevoerde Vuurwapenen van Weelde Gedurende het Jaar 1869", in (MvK, Verbaal 31 Oct 1870, La Z14 N41 Kab).

Two years previously an article in the newspaper *Locomotief had* claimed that firearms were continually falling into the hands of the Javanese; worse, (from the standpoint of the state), by 1870 the numbers seemed to be increasing. Various levels of the Indies government started to debate the matter, and administrators began to assemble statistics to keep a more accurate tab on the movements of such weapons into the Indies.[29] In Pasuruan, the numbers on imports seemed to have gone up considerably, while in Demak, a regional Islamic center of great importance because of its old mosque, the numbers had also risen. Indeed, in Semarang, a major port city on the north coast of the island, the net worth of firearms imports had shot up from 18,108 guilders in 1868 to 82,790 only one year later.[30] It had become apparent that arms imports into Java as a whole, which had hovered around 40,000–50,000 guilders per year for most of the second half of the 1860s, were now worth two and a half times this amount, and the rise occurred in the space of only twelve months (table 9).

In September 1870, an order went out to all residencies in Java that firearms transit and possession on the local level was to be strictly watched and the results reported on back to Batavia. As discussed earlier in this book, violence in the countryside in Java was still widespread in 1870; the director of the Justice Department in Batavia pointed out that bandits and robbers involved in this violence almost always possessed guns.[31] Worse still, from the perspective of the state, it was clear to policy planners and officials in the capital that a large percentage of the arms coming into the Indies was disappearing from the state's view almost as soon as they landed. In Java, many of these guns found their way into the "Vorstenlanden," the small pockets of territory still formally under indigenous rule.[32] Despite the fact that the Dutch administrative presence was stronger in Java than anywhere else in the Indies, the existence of these semi-independent dominions provided a crucial exit to firearms hidden from the vision of government. The resident of Semarang, where so many of these guns seemed to have been landing (especially after 1869), sent in his import/export duty statistics to Batavia but conceded he did not know how many arms simply entered his residency from the port and then disappeared into the countryside before anyone was aware of their transit. Though the official import statistics on firearms had more than quadrupled between 1868 and 1869, counts on the number of firearms in Javanese possession locally showed no increase whatsoever. Furthermore, he intimated that firearms not only bled into the countryside from Semarang, but also to the rest of the Indies, leaving his port by sea to other parts of the archipelago.[33]

Changes in the Indies tariffs seem to have been largely responsible for these trends. By Staatsblad no. 2/43, 1837, the import of firearms into the Indies, except for hunting guns, fine-worked pistols, and other collectors' pieces, was banned; even the exceptions were heavily taxed, usually at the rate of thirty guilders per piece, with a further fifteen guilders necessary to obtain a certificate of ownership. Changes in the tariffs in 1865 and 1866 ended this system, however, and took away some of the "weapons of wealth" standards that had placed firearms out of the reach of most people, except for the very rich. Starting in the beginning of 1866, there was no longer a value-minimum on arms imports; a flat 6 percent tariff was assessed on any incoming weapons, regardless of their value or the cases in which they came. Old rules about a one-hundred-guilder minimum on arms imports and special stipulations about packaging were discarded in an effort to make more revenue for the state.[34] Arms exporters, sensing a vast new market open to their products, seized this opportunity almost immediately. Cheap guns began to flow into the Indies from nearby in the Straits Settlements but also from further afield, even from factories as far away as Europe.[35]

Who marketed these guns to Java on an ever-increasing scale? Belgian weapons manufacturers seem to have been one of the foremost sources, especially as these concerns already had good contacts with Dutch distributors in Europe. German and Prussian factories also sent large numbers of guns, filling a niche at the upper end of the market for some of the most technologically sophisticated armaments.[36] Dutch manufacturers struggled to get in on the action, too, sending shipments through their own well-established networks into various parts of the outstretched Indies. Confidential reports coming into Batavia declared that the sale of firearms in Singapore was so brisk for merchants crossing into the Indies that prices were little different than in Europe, so much closer to the actual centers of production.[37] Some merchants did not even have to sell their wares in Singapore, however, but were granted dispensation to auction their arms in Java itself, so long as Batavia received a cut on the profits. This experiment, conducted in 1865, made the government some money. Yet as we have seen, it also put more weapons into circulation, only some of which Batavia was able to track.[38] A data-composition chart from 1869 shows how many arms—including carbines, rifles, pistols, and revolvers—were coming into the Indies legally in this way, acquired by customers who were allowed to buy them. The figures are very high and were rising all the time until the Dutch administration decided to severely limit the trade in the early 1870s.[39]

Yet it was the flow of arms to Asian populations, not so much to Europeans living in the Indies and the few non-Europeans who were allowed to possess such goods, that most worried Batavia. The significant trade in arms to these latter groups could be controlled much more easily than the commerce to the population at large, and it was this realization that came to the administration only slowly over the years. In 1870, a statistical survey was taken on how many guns were in the possession of various ethnic groups in Semarang, calculated back for the last several years. Anywhere between six and nine hundred Javanese were calculated to own firearms during this time (with the permission of the state), while three Chinese held this privilege, and no Arabs or other Vreemde Oosterlingen.[40] These government sources were plainly far off the mark and held no correlation at all with the reality of the situation. The realization that the illegal possession of arms in the Indies, with all of its attendant consequences, was a far larger problem than anyone had previously thought began to sink in at even the highest levels of government. In May the minister for the colonies in The Hague took the governor-general to task about why he was receiving so little information on the clandestine transit of arms into Java; a vague reply from Batavia was brusquely ignored and met with a further reprimand.[41] Holland itself had begun to become aware of the magnitude of the problem. Several months later suggestions that much more serious checks should again be instituted began to creep back into official Dutch discourse on the matter.[42] If the state could barely keep track of the movement of arms in the very center of its domain, how could Batavia hope to detect anything at all along the outstretched lands of the Anglo/Dutch frontier?

BUILDING A LEGAL STRUCTURE

One way to solve the firearms problem was to erect a vast, comprehensive system of laws. I have sketched a brief chronology of arms legislation earlier in this chapter, but it is useful here to delve deeper into the legal mechanisms imposed by both sides of the Straits to deal with the challenge of illegal arms smuggling. An imposing juridical edifice was constructed by both Singapore and Batavia to deal with the transit of unregistered weapons across the border, but the degree of energy with which these stipulations were enforced was not equal in both Dutch and English spheres. Nor did the state have the means to carry out its legal agenda: Dutch technology and the vast extent of Dutch Indies territory both militated against successful enforcement of arms laws. This combination of British ambivalence and Dutch inability allowed arms to pour over the frontier for several decades at the end of the nineteenth century.

Taken purely at face value, English laws in the Straits by the 1860s had started to provide everything Batavia could ask for in terms of tracking and then stopping the illegal export of weaponry. India Act no. 31 of 1860, which was in force in the Straits, stipulated several years' hard labor and enormous fines for the sale or manufacture of firearms without a license, though loopholes in the law allowed private citizens to sometimes import guns in small quantities for their own use. Similar restrictions were on the books for gunpowder, a license being necessary for anyone storing more than five pounds of the material; even dealers were unable to hoard more than fifty pounds of powder in their magazines at any one time.[43] Act 13 of 1867 allowed the governor of the Straits to ban the export of arms and ammunition to any place he desired (in conjunction with the Legislative Council of the colony), while the following year saw legislation enacted which forced the masters of incoming vessels to immediately declare their arms cargoes, with further stipulations on the storage of gunpowder within city limits.[44] The massive trade in arms described by earlier travelers still existed in the Straits, therefore, but many controls were in place to regulate and channel this commerce as the authorities saw fit.

With the outbreak of the Aceh War in 1873, Straits arms legislation progressively became tougher and tougher against smugglers, at least on paper. As we have seen, in that year the first Straits ban on arms exports to Aceh was promulgated by Sir Harry Ord, and this was followed in the decades after with a gradual tightening on all arms laws, for those pieces coming into the colony itself and also for any that might be transiting secretly into neighboring states like the Netherlands Indies. This culminated in the 1879 Straits ban on any arms shipments to the Indies as a whole (a similar ban from Labuan followed a year later), but the workings of these measures can be seen in many other acts as well. Ordinance no. 18 of 1887, for example, gave expanded new powers of search for firearms on board vessels within Straits harbors, while Ordinance no. 8 of 1894 presented broad new stipulations on bookkeeping and fees, broadening the surveillance powers of the state. Later acts, such as Ordinance no. 1 of 1899, dealt with a new threat to security in Straits waters, outlining the substances now being used to fabricate dynamite and other explosives (nitroglycerides, fulminates of mercury, etc.), which were also being traded across the frontier.[45] These questions were also taken up in British legislation outside of the Straits Settlements, as in the Federated Malay States, which passed its own careful stipulations like Ordinance no.13 of 1915.[46]

As impressive as all of this jurisprudence was on the books, in reality the vast compendium of British arms legislation was rarely exercised to the full extent of the law, as was pointed out by both British and Dutch observers of the time. The British representative in Uleelheue, Aceh, complained to his superiors in Singapore that no copies of the various ordinances and arms acts were available to him on a visit to Penang: the British magistrate there had no copies and neither did the police or the government store. No arms dealers he visited kept the government arms regulations posted in their shops, he complained, while to his knowledge none of the rules had been translated into the local Asian languages, (Telegu, Malay, and Chinese.)[47] It was difficult to see how traders could be expected to know the details of the government's policies when such information was difficult to uncover even by one of the servants of the state. George Lavino was even more forceful in his criticism of the prevailing state of affairs. He complained that loopholes in Straits laws—such as one which allowed arms smugglers to essentially go free if they could not pay the fines imposed for their smuggling—made a mockery of British interdiction efforts. The consul worked to get these loopholes plugged and periodically sent the British colonial secretary copies of Straits laws to show how certain provisions were routinely being ignored.[48] In one 1887 letter Lavino complained bitterly that many clauses on the books—which included stipulations that seized arms cargoes had to be directly proven to belong to a specific person on a ship for the vessel to be held accountable—seemed purposely constructed to evade the laws, if not in practice, then certainly in spirit.[49]

The realization that this indeed was the case prompted Batavia to try to enact its own corpus of import laws into as formidable a barrier as possible to incoming shipments of arms. We can see this all along the Dutch frontier residencies facing the British possessions. In Aceh, especially stringent stipulations remained on the possession and sale of firearms even into the twentieth century, while in Bangka, also near the British border, extra care was taken to ensure that powder was not being secreted in and hidden just across the frontier. A gunpowder magazine was installed in Belitung, not on the main island itself, but rather (for safety and surveillance reasons) on the small offshore atoll of Kalmoa. In West Borneo, discussions were put into motion by the regional administration about the banning of saltpeter entirely, as this compound was one of the primary components of gunpowder.[50] And all across the border residencies, from Sumatra's East Coast to Palembang to southeastern Borneo, special arms laws were enacted which differentiated between cities along the frontier and the much wider and more homogeneous hinterlands. These last enactments reveal some of the state anxieties discussed earlier in this book, as these cities—Medan, Palembang, and Banjarmasin among them—were usually the sites of large Foreign Asian populations, such as Arabs and Chinese.[51]

The Dutch effort to staunch the flow of arms into the Indies through legal devices was not only based on a geographic calculus, however, in drawing a legalistic ring around the frontier, but was also pursued topically, as conditions in the border residencies changed. For this reason, harbormasters (*shahbandars*) of Dutch ports were given special printed versions of the prevailing arms laws, so that they would have the full compendium of Dutch jurisprudence right at their fingertips.[52] Other civil servants were given instructions and arms decisions not just in Dutch, but in Rumi (Romanized Malay) versions as well, so that indigenous functionaries could be sure of what they were reading, as many of these men could not comprehend Dutch very well. One of these pamphlets reads in part as follows:

Ketentoean
A. Membawa Masoek dan Membawa Keloewar
Pasal 8.2: Membinasakan sendjata-api jang diserahkan.
B. Kepoenjaan, Pembawaan dan Pernijaganaan
Pasal 6.2: Banjaknja obat-bedil jang boleh dipoenjai tidak dengan soerat-izin.

Pasal 6.3: Kekoewasaan Sjahbandar akan menjimpan obat-bedil dan bekal pemasang jang tidak masoek bilangan kelengkapan perahoe atau kapal.

Psal 17.1: Ketentoean hoekoeman tentang melanggar peratoeran tentang mempoenjai dan membawa sendjata-api, obat-bedil atau bekal pemasang.

[Regulations

A. Imports and Exports

Article 8.2: Destruction of confiscated firearms

B. Possession, Transport, and Trade

Article 6.2: Amounts of gunpowder and munitions that may be possessed without proof of allowance.

Article 6.3: Competency of the harbormaster to confiscate gunpowder or munitions not belonging to the equipping of a vessel.

Article 17.1: Penalties against transgressions of the regulations on possession of firearms, gunpowder, or munitions and the transport of these goods.][53]

Specialized laws also made clear what steps were to be taken in certain specific circumstances, such as when ships came into the roads of a port with arms or ammunition on board, or when these materials were transported along government-owned railroad lines. As with British restrictions, Dutch laws paid suitable attention to the new transit in "explosive substances" such as dynamite in the years around the turn of the twentieth century.[54] Batavia, in other words, tried to create a legislative atmosphere that would make the passage of smuggled arms into the Indies an increasingly difficult matter over time. Attention was paid to new developments in technology and industry, and cooperation was sought in the corridors of power in London and Singapore. Yet how effective were all of these measures in checking or controlling the contraband trade in arms into the Netherlands Indies?

GEOGRAPHIES, RADIALS, SHIPMENTS

Judging from the vast ranges of territory smugglers traversed to get contraband weapons into the Indies, these proscriptions were not very effective at all. Arms did not cross at one point or even two or three, but at many junctures along the frontier, stretching from Aceh in North Sumatra all the way east to the tip of northern Borneo. When one compiles the available notices and statistics on seizures, however, certain patterns start to make themselves clear. Not all locations along the border were used equally as transiting points; some environments lent themselves better than others to the movement of these cargoes across the international divide. In general, the dispersion pattern seems to have followed a recognizable logic: Penang was the major distribution center in the Strait of Melaka for the market to Sumatra, while Labuan served the same function in Borneo and Sulu waters. Other ports, such as Melaka, for example, fulfilled tertiary functions, funneling arms in certain cases but in smaller volume than the former two harbors.[55] Yet Singapore was certainly the central locus of these operations, situated as it was at the terminus of the South China Sea, with access to Sumatra, Borneo, and the many other scattered islands of the Netherlands Indies. In Singapore, too, the manic chaos of Free Trade commerce was at its height, and the opportunities for smuggling arms or anything else for that matter were far larger. The port of Singapore, therefore, despite being the seat of British power in Southeast Asia, seems to have been the main location for breaking the standing arms laws of both sides of the Straits. This became apparent to the Dutch in Batavia and to the British themselves, though few administrators seemed to know what to do about it.

Arms crossed the shallow ribbon of the Strait of Melaka and diffused into Sumatra from the British possessions at many points. Though the Dutch tried to control the flow of weapons into the Outer Islands territories under their control, the sources show these attempts were not succeeding. In Palembang in 1870 shootings in the countryside were not uncommon, while in Jambi only two years later Dutch soldiers were periodically attacked by locals armed with firearms.[56] The following year (1873), the Straits ban on arms exports to North Sumatra finally went into effect, though this seems to have affected only the official statistics, not the overall trade.[57] Muskets, rifles, pistols, and revolvers continued to pour into Sumatra, especially now as their illegality raised the potential profits on transactions. Many of these weapons were on their way to Aceh, landed either directly on the Acehnese coast or at points south of the conflict, and then transshipped further north.[58] Yet firearms were also in demand in other parts of Sumatra, where local struggles against authority (and those also of a more internecine quality) were taking place on a less grand scale than in the north. This was the case in Siak, where men such as Haji Usman and various steamers like the *Tjang Wat Seng* and the *Pakan* were caught contrabanding, all in the early 1880s.[59] Indies perahus were also caught en route from Singapore to the outstretched shoreline of Sumatra's East Coast residency with arms on board, prompting the resident of that territory to complain that the arms bans were worth nothing in his dominion. Guns traveled as well across the Straits to Bagan Si Api-Api, the burgeoning Chinese fishing settlement nestled on Sumatra's Straits of Melaka coast.[60] Even in the distant south of Sumatra, well away from the Aceh conflagration and closer to the main sea routes and even Batavia, the arms continued to flow. In Palembang and Jambi, arms smuggling attempts were extremely common, both in the last two decades of the nineteenth and even into the early twentieth centuries.[61]

The situation in Borneo was little better from the vantage point of the state. Contemporary descriptions from the British side of the border show that arms trafficking on the coasts and in the large bays of North Borneo was still going on in the 1880s, even as the company was starting to stiffen its control over its territory.[62] On the Dutch side of the frontier matters were even more difficult to police. In southeastern Borneo, arms were being smuggled from some of the small independent sultanates such as Kutei into Dutch Sulawesi, while guns were also transiting into Batavia's sphere to Amuntai, Pasir, and Balikpapan, towns under direct Dutch control.[63] On the western side of the island, the calculus involving arms shipments grew increasingly more complicated, mostly as a result of the close proximity of Singapore and other British ports. The Ngee Hin Kongsi, so active in Penang and Singapore, had branches in West Borneo as well that were involved in a significant scale of arms trafficking across the Sarawak frontier.[64] These tentacles of Chinese commercial activity would give rise in the early twentieth century to increasing Dutch anxieties vis-à-vis the arms question, especially in West Borneo stretches along the border.[65] Yet on a much lower-level basis, firearms seem to have been entering West Borneo for decades as well, not in massive quantities but in a slow trickle that nevertheless seeped throughout the residency. Dutch reports of smuggling ships sailing to Sukadana, Sambas, and Pontianak are fairly common in the 1870s and 1880s, cataloging a steady stream of contraband pouring into one of the most unstable Dutch residencies anywhere on the frontier.[66] Occasionally muskets seem to have gone the other way too, as the *Sarawak Gazette* makes clear.[67]

Though Borneo and Sumatra girded the Anglo/Dutch frontier geographically, providing a necklace of Dutch-controlled territory thousands of kilometers long for smugglers to use, arms were also transited *through* the frontier and into other parts of the Netherlands Indies. We have already seen this in the Java of the late 1860s. This "puncture effect" can be observed in many places, however, as contrabanders sought to deposit firearms in any part of the archipelago where significant profits could be made. Sulawesi is a prime example of this phenomenon, and in fact received a high share of illegal weapons exports from the Straits over the entirety of the fifty years examined in this book. The 1873 Straits ban which cordoned off North Sumatra as an off-limits area for arms trading did so for parts of Sulawesi as well; all arms which were moved to the large ports of the island after this point were done so against the laws of the two colonial powers. Nevertheless, Pare Pare, Kaili, Makassar, and other ports were frequent destinations for perahus and junks running arms, as a voluminous correspondence in both Dutch and English makes clear.[68] Sulawesi was not the only end-destination for these cargoes, however. The scattered notices of arms seizures and intelligence reports read like a veritable spreadsheet of Indies geography where arms were frequently trafficked, usually via the Straits Settlements. Included in this cordon of ports and islands are Bali, Lombok, Riau, Sumbawa, Banda, New Guinea, and again Java, in addition to all of the Sumatra and Borneo ports listed above.[69] The diversity and geographic distance of these harbors show how big a business arms smuggling had become in the decades around the turn of the twentieth century.

Yet perhaps no single document shows these characteristics of the trade better than a single missive from the Dutch vice-consul in Singapore to the Dutch minister for foreign affairs in The Hague, dated January 30, 1888. This twelve-page letter on the patterns and dispersion of the commerce, written in microscopic detail, is a fascinating snapshot of arms smuggling along the Anglo/Dutch frontier in a single year, 1887. The great value of this document is in the cross-sectional view it gives of the arms trade for a discrete period of time; it is almost like examining the rings in a tree stump for clues to the life history of the larger entity. The vice-consul notes the spread of Dutch Indies ports which Singapore attempted to supply with weapons during the course of that year: Batavia, Surabaya, Cirebon, and Rembang are represented in Java; Kaili is mentioned for Sulawesi; Pontianak stands out in Borneo; Bali in the islands east of Java, and Jambi, Siak, and Bengkalis are all present for Sumatra. The ethnic actors involved in getting these firearms across the frontier are also diverse: Chinese, Boyanese, Arab, and European names are all mentioned in the various cases. The cargoes themselves merit interest as well, as not only large quantities of gunpowder and percussion caps were making the trip, but breach-loading muskets, revolvers, and even Winchester repeating rifles also went across. Finally, perhaps the most telling aspect of the letter altogether is the section marked *Resultaat* (Result) to the attempt to stop the contraband from getting into the Indies. In almost every single case for 1887, the two colonial states involved managed no result at all.[70]

Given the huge expanse of geography, the diffuse cast of concerned parties, and the open spectrum of products and wares, it is not surprising to find even after the turn of the twentieth century, therefore, continued references to guns making their way across the frontier. Legislation and technologies of enforcement may have changed over this fifty-year period, but neither the British nor the Dutch were ever able to completely stop the trade in arms spilling across the border. Dutch documents make this very clear. In the Gayo lands just south of Aceh proper, hauls of weapons were still being made in the early twentieth century, while in Lampung local populations sometimes fought off Dutch corvée details with arms, refusing state labor inductions.[71] In certain Batak areas of north-central Sumatra local chiefs were still procuring Winchester and Beaumont rifles on order in 1904, sometimes through Malay aristocrats, sometimes through Chinese from the lowlands, but almost always in exchange for mountain horses.[72] Dutch patrols in Jambi were periodically ambushed and killed by men with such weapons in the early twentieth century too; here the raison d'etre for resistance was Sultan Taha's rebellion, which still had not been vanquished after almost fifty years.[73] In Borneo, conditions were much the same. Fines were promulgated for indigenes who did not hand in their firearms at the request of the state, while marauding bands of men still managed to expropriate marginalized territories for short periods, using their weapons to harass local populations.[74] The geography of arms contraband did not shrink very much over the period 1865–1915. What did happen was that this trade was pushed further and further underground, as the state strove to cut off tendrils of supply that constantly adapted and changed.

ETHNICITY AND THE WEAPONS TRADE

Who was involved in these transactions? Which ethnic groups were concerned with arms smuggling as an ongoing economic enterprise? The short answer to both of these questions seems to have been "almost everyone," as an enormous cross-section of ethnic actors in the region dealt with arms trafficking in one way or another. Contemporary descriptions of trading populations passing through the archipelago show how international the Southeast Asian marketplace was around the turn of the century: Joseph Conrad, who traveled in these seas in the 1880s, mentioned Portuguese, Dutch, Chinese, Bugis, Malay, Bajau, Dayak, British, American, Spanish, "Sulu" (Taosug and/or Balangingi Samal), and Arab merchants all involved in trade.[75] The American, Bugis, and Chinese traders at different times seem particularly to have been involved in the widespread commerce in arms. Batavia understood this very well and promulgated arms edicts not just in Dutch, but in local languages as well. Some of these bans were published and posted in Chinese; others were printed in Jawi, the older, Arabic-alphabet language in which classical Malay was written.[76] Other promulgations were translated into Buginese or Javanese. The Dutch administration wanted to leave none of the interpretation of these bans to chance: the consequences of local populations not understanding the arms laws were simply too severe for the state. Whether indigenes took any notice of the bans or cared about their existence as anything but a hindrance to profitable free trade is another matter entirely.

Local Southeast Asian peoples of non-Chinese, Indian, or Arab descent were heavily involved in these transactions. Even in the years preceding 1865, Singapore was already a great center for arms trading, attracting perahus from all over the archipelago and trafficking in weaponry as one of its most significant items of export.[77] By the later decades of the nineteenth century, such dealings were illegal, but this did not stop local Southeast Asians of various ethnic groups from staying involved in this commerce. In Borneo, river-mouth *datus* stockpiled arms as a precaution against their aggressive neighbors, while the British North Borneo Company as late as 1896 was arresting local peoples for possessing firearms without a license.[78] This did not stop local Bajaus from killing Sikh policemen with guns, while in Brunei the scattered populace also was able to procure firearms at will, sometimes through their sultan and other times through Malay, Chinese, or European traders.[79] Outside of Borneo, the ability of indigenous Southeast Asians to procure guns was much the same. Bataks in Sumatra tried to get firearms from across the Straits to Deli, and from there to the highlands, by using small fishing boats as couriers.[80] Envoys from various chiefs in Jambi also made the trip to Singapore and "intrigued" there, according to Dutch spies, in their search for weapons.[81] Yet there are more notices of Bugis attempts to procure these cargoes than of any other indigenous group. Bugis merchants were known to be prime carriers of arms shipments into the Indies, distributing weapons to a wide spectrum of Dutch-controlled territories.[82] One captured letter from January 1879 contains a request from the Bugis raja of Wajo at Pare Pare to a Chinese arms merchant in Singapore; the missive was translated and caused a great stir, as the raja had ordered one hundred cases of muskets in addition to large quantities of powder and raw lead.[83]

Arabs and Muslim Indians in Southeast Asia, as well as indigenous peoples descending from these two groups, were also involved in the illegal commerce in arms. As we have seen, members of these groups were particularly feared by the Dutch state when it came to arms cargoes, often because of their wider Islamic connections. Because much of the financing of trade voyages in the Straits was underwritten by Chettiar money-lending houses, Muslim Indian communities were often involved behind the scenes in raising capital for such ventures.[84] Yet these communities were much more directly involved as well.

Indians in Singapore were sometimes caught secreting tins of gunpowder into the colony, as in the case of Mohamed Eusope and Meydinsah in 1896.[85] Arabs were also singled out in Penang as being among those who were most responsible for gun running to the resistance forces in Aceh. Even such men as the British envoy to Uleelheue in North Sumatra pointed this out, showing that this state of affairs was common knowledge and not just paranoia of the Dutch in the Indies.[86] The historical ship *Vidar*, immortalized in the tales of Conrad, was also an Arab-owned vessel with a reputation for arms running, as several documents many years apart make clear. Both in the early 1870s and later in the 1880s, the *Vidar* was known to be shipping firearms to Borneo and Sulawesi in the possession of Arab passengers transiting on board.[87] After the turn of the twentieth century Arabs in the Indies still seem to have been involved in these voyages, as in the case of one Arab who imported guns to hunt for slaves in Upland Toraja.[88]

Yet as was true of many of the other lines of contraband commerce already examined, Chinese populations seem to have had more than their numerical share of representatives in the seizure records. In North Borneo, the company had its hands full trying to stop the arms smuggling of various Chinese there, handing out fines and making significant seizures of rifles and gunpowder in the early 1880s.[89] Chinese secret societies in Labuan and also across the border in Dutch West Borneo seem to have been among the prime movers of these materials, usually for protection against one another's depredations.[90] Large-scale revolts of Borneo Chinese against the state were also feared, however, as in one case in particular in 1915 which almost set off an international incident.[91] In the Straits of Melaka Chinese were also heavily involved in this commerce. The Dutch envoy in the Straits railed against the Chinese in this context, reporting to The Hague that Chinese smuggled huge quantities of arms under the very noses of the British authorities, while earlier letters indicted them for fueling the Aceh war by supplying the resistance with arms from a range of offshore boats.[92] Yet even in Singapore itself, the seat of British power in Southeast Asia, Chinese were being arrested for arms running throughout the period 1865–1915. Companies like Lim Yem Eng and Chop Kaij Moi of Canal Road were periodically pinpointed as weapons traffickers, acting as agents for indigenous contacts across the Dutch border.[93] Individual Chinese are also described in the records as being caught with firearms in contravention of the laws of the state; among the many examples are a Teochew man in 1894 and a Straits Chinese woman in 1908[94] (fig. 13).

Even Europeans, who might have been thought to have patriotic reasons

Fig. 13. Chinese woman arrested, arms possession in Singapore, 1908. (*Source: Utusan Malayu*, 30 Jan. 1908, p. 3)

not to traffic in arms, did so all along the length of the Anglo/Dutch frontier. The lure of great profits was too great for many. Some of these voyages seem to have been isolated instances, such as the British schooner *Josef* landing arms in Aceh in 1873 and a Hong Kong trader (named White) illegally selling rifles in North Borneo in late 1880.[95] Similarly, an Australian named Strachan smuggled firearms into Portuguese Timor for eventual sale in the Indies, and another plot was uncovered to get two thousand rifles into Aceh via Penang, also through a network of Europeans.[96] Yet there were also more organized, systematic attempts by Westerners to get weapons into the Dutch sphere. A celebrated case in 1894 revealed a corps of Europeans, chief among whom were three characters named Paige, Niel, and Danielson, who tried to land crates of guns in Bali, weapons which were then to be brought via horse convoys into the interior of that island.[97] The Behn Meyer Company, a Hamburg firm that had its main Southeast Asia branch in Singapore, also was involved in arms trafficking on a large scale. European managers of the concern were indicted for weapons smuggling into the Indies in the 1880s and then again after the turn of the twentieth century.[98] Even many Dutchmen themselves were active in these trades, proving that profit was a stronger inducement than national-ism, at least for some. A Dutch family firm named van Delden attempted to get thirty-nine cases of firearms to Bali via Surabaya in 1873, while the Nether-lands concern de Lange was also known to be smuggling arms to Aceh almost ten years later.[99]

The Indo-Portuguese community of the Straits, long resident in the area and thoroughly intermarried into local society in these ports, also was involved in these trades. Indo-Portuguese merchants had all of the structural conditions in place to act as brokers in these transactions. Many in the community owned trading ships or captained those of other men; language was also usually not a problem, as a dialect of Malay was commonly spoken among its members, and long-standing contacts were maintained on both sides of the Melaka Straits. It is not surprising to read, therefore, that ship captains like a Mr. de Souza and a Mr. Jeremiah ran afoul of the Dutch arms laws in these shallow waters. Jere-miah, the supercargo of the *Phya Pakeht,* in 1872, was charged in conjunction with an Acehnese accomplice of selling arms all along the Aceh coast. Captain de Souza, who owned and commanded the schooner J*anus* operating out of Penang, was caught by the Dutch cruiser *Siak* in 1883 and accused of landing arms in Sumatra. De Souza wrote a lengthy letter of protest to the British con-sul at Uleelheue professing his innocence, though he acknowledged it was pos-sible that someone may have secreted the arms on board his vessel. The British consul in Aceh was unconvinced of his innocence, though he tried to intercede on de Souza's behalf with the Dutch. The consul informed Penang that he had heard there was a clique of Straits Portuguese actively trading in arms and that de Souza easily could be a member.[100] While these matters were being settled, however, de Souza was in custody and losing money, while his wife and chil-dren remained unprotected on Sumatra's east coast.[101] Gun running, obvi-ously, was a lucrative but dangerous business: its practitioners could make huge profits if all went well with the voyage, but the price of failure was high, both in professional and personal terms.

How much cooperation or competition was there between members of different ethnic groups in arms trafficking, as these weapons quietly transited across the border against the wishes of the two colonial states? Were language, class, or ethnic solidarity important factors in deciding who collaborated with whom in these ventures, and who did not? The historian John Furnivall has maintained that Southeast Asians of various ethnicities have only really ever met each other in the market, eschewing other "deeper" contacts to remain in their own separate groups.[102] That conclusion seems to be borne out to some degree here, though perhaps in a more nuanced form than Furnivall was ready to admit. The British thought that any commercial bonds of this nature would certainly be very thin; "for a pecuniary object," wrote the British consul in Aceh, "a Malay will inform against any Chinese, and a Chinese against any Malay."[103] Southeast Asians seem to have understood that their colonial over-lords felt this way and used this knowledge to their advantage. In a revealing ad-mission in a court case against arms smugglers, a Chinese coolie stated he had been told by his Chinese sponsors to say, in the event he was caught and forced to testify, that he had been paid by Arabs, not Chinese, to run weapons across the frontier:

> I am a coolie residing at Amoy Street. . . . About a week ago . . . the towkay of Chop Heng Guan Chan sent for me and asked me to go to Behr Co.'s godown to sew some gunny bags round five boxes. I went with the towkay's clerk named Goh Seng Lye. On arriving there the coolies in Mr. Behr's godown were putting rifles into a box and nailing up. I sewed the gunny bag around it, four other men assisted me. There were three other boxes already nailed up and covered with gunny bags. . . . The towkay and the clerk told me that if I was detected on my way to the steamer to leave the boxes behind and run away. If I was asked any questions by anyone to say that an Arab had hired me to take the boxes on board and not to mention the towkay's name. On the morning of the 4th I met Goh Seng Lye in the street. He told me the arms had been seized by the police. He gave me $2 and told me to go and hide myself and never to mention anything of the case. The arms are now in the possession of the po-lice.[104]

Such feints make sense when seen against the backdrop of colonial attitudes and perceptions. It was only natural that local Asian populations would try to use these prejudices against their masters in order to subvert the limitations that had been placed on free trade.

The majority of evidence, however, suggests that cross-ethnic alliances in gun smuggling were exceedingly common, as traders threw out their own eth-nic business preferences and trust networks (if necessary) in order to make po-tential profits. This is apparent in many contexts and across many groups between 1865 and 1915 but is particularly evident with Chinese traders, who seem to have been able to ally themselves with just about anyone in order to move these cargoes abroad. In western Borneo, resistance forces outside of Pontianak relied on Chinese connections in Singapore to supply them with guns, sending small perahus to the port to be filled with muskets and powder for eventual transit back to the island.[105] In Melaka, Chinese, Indians, Malays, and Acehnese were all involved together in getting arms to Sumatra, while in Penang, groups of Chinese and local Muslims collaborated, running guns via Perak.[106] The conflict in Aceh seems to have engendered some of the most sophisticated operations across ethnic lines, involving ships under British colors with Chinese skippers and Acehnese or Malay crews.[107] In correspondence kept in the Straits on the nature of weapons smuggling into North Sumatra, names of almost every ethnicity appear, indicating the wide spectrum of people who were involved in these transactions over the course of several decades.[108] This willingness to cooperate across boundaries both actual and metaphorical is not surprising, as resistance to colonial strictures—and profit opportunities—were inducements common to most of these groups. Many merchants, shippers, captains, and ordinary subjects seized these opportunities and transited arms whenever and wherever they could.

NOTES

1. Reid, "Europe and Southeast Asia: The Military Balance" (1982), 90–96.
2. For an introduction to military capacities during this early period, see Reid, *Southeast Asia in the Age of Commerce* (1993), 219 passim.
3. Artifacts in various museum collections, anthropological writings of the twentieth century, and period literature of European travelers all attest to the widespread transit of firearms in Southeast Asia.
4. See Manuscript Add. 12358 in the British Library, and Manuscript Malay 142, V, at the Royal Asiatic Society, both of which are described in Ricklefs and Voorhoeve, *Indonesian Manuscripts in Great Britain* (1977).
5. See the bone carving described in Museum of Mankind, 1933.3.7.33, also in Ricklefs and Voohoeve's manuscript catalogue (under Batak Manuscripts). Other protections described in other surviving carvings include those against rainstorms, inimical magic, and dangers while traveling.
6. Gov Labuan to CO, 22 April 1865, no. 6, in CO 144/24.
7. Chew, *Chinese Pioneers* (1990), 108; Gov Labuan to CO, 30 Nov. 1881, no. 86, in CO 144/55. They were also fired off at the planting and gathering times of the rice crop, at the arrival of a party which had been away gutta-percha collecting, and upon the arrival of friends or relatives from other river systems.
8. Kruijt, *Atjeh en de Atjehers,* 22; Swettenham *The Real Malay* (1900), 24–25.

9. Kruijt, op. cit., 28; Pramoedya, *Bumi Manusia* (1981), 46–47.

10. Warren, *The Sulu Zone,* 44, 8–9, 11–13, 24–26, 51–52; see also Resident West Borneo, Verslag April 1906 (West Borneo fiche no. 395) (MvK, PVBB).

11. Onreat, *Singapore: A Police Background,* 101.

12. ARA, Dutch Consul Singapore to GGNEI, 26 Aug. 1863, and GGNEI to MK, 1 Nov. 1863, Kab no. 318 La M11, both in (MvK, Verbaal 14 Jan. 1864, no. 1). Hundreds of thousands of dollars worth of firearms were sold each year from the Straits Settlements.

13. CO to Gov Lab, 10 Jan. 1865, in CO 144/23; Gov Lab to CO, 1 April 1865, no. 5, and Gov Lab to CO, 22 April 1865, no. 6, both in CO 144/24.

14. See "Proclamation, 31 March 1873," and "Government Notification, 13 June 1873, no. 125," both in *SSGG,* 1873.

15. See the Export Statistics on Arms and Ammunition from Singapore in *SSBB,* 1873, and 1874.

16. ARA, "Verbod op den Uitvoer van Wapenen . . ." (n.d), 4, in (MvK, Verbaal 16 July 1900, Kab. Litt T9.); ARA, Col Sec, SS to Dutch Consul, Singapore, 4 Jan. 1877, no. 7370/76, in 1877, MR no. 23; W. G. Hemson to GGNEI, 19 Nov. 1879, no. 7319/79, in 1879, MR no. 730; and 1880, MR no. 140.

17. Gov BNB to Gov Labuan, 29 Nov. 1881, Gov Labuan to Gov BNB, 30 Nov. 1881, both in CO 144/55; Gov Lab to CO, 4 Sept. 1882, no. 56, in CO 144/56; CO Jacket, 8 Aug. 1885, no. 45, in CO 144/59.

18. British Envoy, Madrid to FO, 30 March 1897, Jolo Protocol, 30 March 1897 Supplemental, and CO to FO, 10 April 1897, all in CO 144/71; ARA, Gov Aceh to GGNEI, 8 April 1900, no. 17 Secret, and First Gov't Secretary, Batavia, to Gov Aceh, 26 March 1900, no. 93a, both in MvK, Verbaal 16 July 1900, Kab. Litt. T9, 7826; GGNEI to Gov SS, 4 Aug. 1900, no. 1, and Gov SS, to GGNEI, 25 Aug. 1900, no. 6893/00, both in MvK, Verbaal 4 Dec. 1900, Kab. Litt. C16, 13119.

19. See Memo by W. H. Read, under CO Jacket 1 Feb. 1911, in CO 537/360. This general feeling did not stop individual imperial governments such as France from using international arms agreements as bargaining chips to procure other diplomatic aims.

20. ARA, "Sumatra Affairs: Letter by 'A Merchant,'" *Penang Gazette and Straits Chronicle,* 19 April 1882, 3; Penang Traders' Memorial enclosed under cover of Lavino to GGNEI, 24 March 1885, no. 187, both in (MvBZ/A Dossiers/box 111/A.49SS/"Uitvoerverbod . . .").

21. ARA, Dutch Consul, Singapore to MvBZ, Hague, 18 Dec. 1882, no. 729, in (MvBZ/A Dossiers/box 111/A.49SS/"Uitvoerverbod . . .").

22. See the debate over the Arms Exportation Bill in *SSLCP,* 21 Dec. 1887, B199–200.

23. ARA, 1st Gov Sec, Batavia to Chiefs of Regional Administration, Outer Islands, 13 Nov. 1881, no. 124, in (MvK, Verbaal 7 Aug 1894, no. 20).

24. See Read's autobiography, *Play and Politics, Recollections* (1901); see also Reid, "Merchant Imperialist" (1997), 34 passim.

25. For a short biography, see Reid, *The Contest for North Sumatra,* 133.

26. ARA, GGNEI to Gov SS, 22 June 1881, no. 1 Confidential, in (MvK, Verbaal 18 Oct 1881, A3/no. 15; 8594); see also ARA, Dutch Consul, Singapore to Dutch Ambassador, London, 22 Nov. 1879, no. 858, in 1879, MR no. 759, and GGNEI to Gov Labuan 11 Dec. 1882, no. 41, in 1882, MR no. 1222.

27. See the *Pinang Gazette,* 14 July 1882, 4; and the *Straits Observer* (Penang), 13 July 1897, 4.

28. "Memorandum on the Alleged Smuggling of War into Acheen by the British Consul in Oleh Oleh," 6 Aug. 1883, and Gov Aceh to British Consul, Oleh Oleh, 20 May 1883, no. 953, both in PRO/FO/220 /Oleh Oleh Consulate/1882–85/vol. 11.

29. ARA, MK to GGNEI, 6 Oct. 1868, A3, no. 2/1256, in (MvK, Verbaal 6 Oct 1868, no. 2/ 1256); ARA, Exh. S13 Kab Vertr, MK, 7 Oct. 1870, in (MvK, Verbaal 31 Oct. 1870, La Z14 N41 Kab); ARA, 1870, MR no. 398.

30. ARA, Director of Finance to GGNEI, 17 Aug. 1872, no. 13606, in 1872, MR no. 588; ARA, Resident Semarang to Directeur van Financien, Batavia, 20 July 1870, no. 6755i, in (MvK, Verbaal 31 Oct. 1870, La Z14 N41 Kab); ARA, Gov't Secretary, Batavia "Opgave van de Invoer van Wapenen Gedurende de Jaren 1864 t/m 1869" in (MvK, Verbaal 31 Oct. 1870, La Z14 N41 Kab).

31. ARA, Dir. Justitie Batavia to GGNEI, 9 Sept. 1870, no. 1140/2161, in (MvK, Verbaal 21 March 1871, La D6 N21 Kab Geh).

32. ARA, Director of Finances to Gov't Secretary, 5 Aug. 1870, no. 11501/M, in (MvK, Verbaal 31 Oct. 1870, La Z14 N41 Kab).

33. ARA, Resident Semarang to Director of Finances, Batavia, 5 July 1870, no. 6240/i, in (MvK, Verbaal 31 Oct. 1870, La Z14 N41 Kab); ARA, Resident Semarang to Director of Finances, Batavia, 20 July 1870, no. 6755i, in (MvK, Verbaal 31 Oct. 1870, La Z14 N41 Kab).

34. ARA, MK, 14 Oct. 1870, Exh. S16 Kab. Vertr, in (MvK, Verbaal 31 Oct. 1870, La Z14 N41 Kab.); ARA, Director of Finances to Gov't Sec, Batavia, 5 Aug. 1870, no. 11501/M, in (MvK, Verbaal 31 Oct. 1870, La Z14 N41 Kab).

35. ARA, Resident Djokdjakarta to Director of Finances, Batavia, 12 July 1870 Telegram, and Collector of Import/Export Rights, Batavia, to Director of Finances, 16 Nov. 1869, no. 195, both in (MvK, Verbaal 31 Oct. 1870, La Z14 N41 Kab).

36. ARA, Resident Djokdjakarta to Director of Finances, Batavia, 12 July 1870 Telegram, in (MvK, Verbaal 31 Oct. 1870, La Z14 N41 Kab); ARA, Director of Finances to Gov't Sec, Batavia, 5 Aug. 1870, no. 11501/M, in (MvK, Verbaal 31 Oct. 1870, La Z14 N41 Kab).

37. ARA, MK to Gov Gen NEI, 12 Aug. 1869, La V12/W Kab Vertr., in (MvK, Verbaal 12 Aug. 1869, La V12/W Kab Vertr.); and ARA, Collector of Import/Export Rights, Batavia, to Director of Finances, 16 Nov. 1869, no. 195, in (MvK, Verbaal 31 Oct. 1870, La Z14 N41 Kab).

38. Ibid.

39. ARA, Collector of Import/Export Rights, Semarang: "Opgave van Ingevoerde Vuurwapenen van Weelde Gedurende het Jaar 1869," in (MvK, Verbaal 31 Oct. 1870, La Z14 N41 Kab).

40. ARA, Resident of Semarang "Opgave van het Aantal Vuurwapenen te Semarang in het Bezit van Inlanders en met Gelijkgestelden in 1868, 1869, 1870" in (MvK, Verbaal 31 Oct. 1870, La Z14 N41 Kab).

41. ARA, MK to GGNEI, 5 May 1870, no. 40/634, in (MvK, 5 May 1870, no. 40/634).

42. ARA, Director of Finances to Gov't Sec, Batavia, 5 Aug. 1870, no. 11501/M, in (MvK, Verbaal 31 Oct. 1870, La Z14 N41 Kab).

43. "Memorandum on the Alleged Smuggling of War into Acheen by the British Consul in Oleh Oleh," 6 Aug. 1883, in PRO/FO/220 /Oleh Oleh Consulate/1882–85/vol. ii.

44. See Straits Ord. no. 13, 1867 and Ord. no. 8, 1868 in the *SSGG* of those two years.

45. See Straits Ord. no. 18, 1887, and Ord. no. 8, 1894; and Straits Ord. no. 1, 1899.

46. See Federated Malay States Ord. no. 13, 1915; the ordinance addresses dealers' licenses, penalties for unlawful import or export, concealment penalties, warrants, and the fate of ships used for arms trafficking into the Malay States.

47. "Memorandum on the Alleged Smuggling of War into Acheen by the British Consul in Oleh Oleh," 6 Aug. 1883, in PRO/FO/220 /Oleh Oleh Consulate/1882–85/vol. ii.

48. ARA, Dutch Consul, Singapore to Col. Sec., SS, 28 May 1887, no. 465; Gov, SS to Dutch Consul, Singapore, 7 Nov. 1887; Dutch Consul, Singapore, to GGNEI, 21 Dec. 1887, no. 1097, all in (MvBZ/A Dossiers/box iii/A.49SS/"Uitvoerverbod . . .").

49. ARA, Dutch Consul, Singapore to Col Sec, SS, 24 Feb. 1887, no. 194 in MvBZ/A Dossiers/box iii/A.49ss.

50. See Staatsblad 1900, no. 179, and 1866, no. 96; 1907, no. 319; Staatsblad 1873, no. 41; and Staatsblad 1913, no. 408.

51. See *Surat Surat Riau* (1970), contract of 18 May 1905, 253; Staatsblad 1907, no. 464; 1914, no. 454; 1873, no. 158; 1907, no. 319; 1897, no. 262; 1907 no. 319.

52. *Verzameling van Voorschriften ten Dienste van Havenmeesters* (1906).

53. *Pemimpin Bagi Prijaji Boemipoetera* (1919).

54. See, respectively, Staatsblad 1864, nos. 39, 40; 1907, no. 501; 1910, no. 487; and Staatsblad 1893, no. 234; 1894, no. 224; 1902, no. 206; 1904, no. 3; 1907, no. 318; 1908, no. 308.

55. See "Rex v. Mabot and Others," *SLJ* 3 (1890): 65 passim; this is only one of many examples of this phenomenon.

56. ANRI, Maandrapport Residentie Palembang 1871, 1872 (no. 74/9, no. 74/10: November, March).

57. ARA, 1873, MR no. 279.

58. Gov Aceh to British Consul, Oleh Oleh, 4 Aug. 1883, no. 1382, in PRO/FO/Oleh Oleh Consulate/1882–85/vol. ii.

59. ARA, Dutch Consul, Singapore to Algemeen Secretaris, Buitenzorg, 18 May 1883, no. 353 Secret, in 1883, MR no. 448; see also the various papers on the *Pakan* in ARA, MvBZ/A Dossiers/box iii/A.49ss.

60. ARA, Dutch Consul, Singapore, to GGNEI, 20 April 1888, no. 249, in (MvBZ/A Dossiers/box iii/A.49SS/"Uitvoerverbod . . ."); ARA, Resident Sumatra East Coast to GGNEI, 22 Sept. 183, La R7 Secret, in 1883, MR no. 888; also see ARA, Dutch Consul to GGNEI, 9 Oct. 1891, in MvBZ/A Dossiers/box iii/A.49ss.

61. ARA, Dutch Consul, Singapore, to GGNEI, 8 Dec. 1886, and Dutch Consul, Singapore to Col. Sec., SS, 2 Dec. 1886, no. 1308, both in (MvBZ/A Dossiers/box iii/A.49SS/ "Uitvoerverbod . . ."); see also ARA, Dutch Consul, Singapore to MvBZ, 19 May 1892, in MvBZ/A Dossiers/box iii/A.49ss; see also "Invoer van Kruit," *IWvhR,* no. 2075, 6 April 1903, 53–54.

62. Gov BNB to CO, 8 Aug. 1885, no. 45, and CO Jacket, 25 Nov. 1885, no. 67, both in CO 144/59.

63. ARA, Asst. Res. Koetei to Resident SE Borneo, 15 Feb. 1874, no. 11, in 1874, MR no. 248; Gov't Secretary to Commander of NEI Navy, 2 Oct. 1883, no. 1584, in 1883, MR no. 927.

64. ANRI, Algemeene Verslag Residentie West Borneo 1889 (no. 5/20).

65. See ARA, Resident West Borneo to Rajah of Sarawak, 13 Feb. 1915, no. 29, and Controleur of Sambas to Civil and Military Asst. Res., Singkawang, 29 Jan. 1915, no. 3, both in (MvBZ/A Dossiers/box 44/A.29 bisOK).

66. ARA, Dutch Consul, Singapore, to Col. Sec., SS, 2 Dec. 1886, no. 1308; Dutch Consul, Singapore to GGNEI, 23 Nov. 1886; and Dutch Consul, Singapore, to GGNEI, 13 April 1888, no. 378, all in (MvBZ/A Dossiers/box 111/A.49SS/"Uitvoerverbod . . ."); ARA, Dutch Consul, Singapore to MvBZ, 16 Feb. 1892, in MvBZ/A Dossiers/box 111/A.49ss; ARNAS, Vice-Consul Singapore to GGNEI, 19 April 1875, no. 1 Geheim, in Kommissoriaal 20 May 1875, no. 490az, in Aceh no. 5 "Stukken aan de Kommissie . . ."; ARA, Dutch Consul, Singapore to GGNEI, 21 Nov. 1884, no. 732, in 1884, MR no. 738.

67. See the brief notices in the *Sarawak Gazette*, 1 Aug. 1885 and 2 Jan. 1886.

68. ANRI, Dutch Consul Singapore to Col. Sec, SS, 10 Jan. 1876, no. 16; Col. Sec. SS to Dutch Consul, Singapore, 1 Feb. 1876, no. 216/76, both in Kommissoriaal 10 March 1876, no. 183az in Aceh no. 13, "Stukken Betreffende Atjehsche Oorlog, no. 235–469, 1876; ARA, Station Commander, Celebes to Naval Commander, NEI, 7 Aug. 1879, no. 1113, in 1879, MR no. 501; ARA, "Translation of a Bugis Letter from Rajah of Wajah at Pare Pare," 24 Jan. 1879, in (MvK, Verbaal 17 Feb. 1881, no. 33/298); ARA, H. P. Fenton, British Legation, Hague, to MvBZ, Hague, 1 Feb. 1881, and Dutch Consul, Singapore, to GGNEI, 13 April 1888, no. 378, both in (MvBZ/A Dossiers/box 111/A.49SS/"Uitvoerverbod . . .").

69. See, for example, ARA, 1876, MR no. 992, 261, 300; ARA, GGNEI to Gov SS, 30 March 1883, no. 10 Confidential, and Dutch Consul, Singapore, to Acting Col. Sec., SS, 30 Aug. 1888, no. 873, both in (MvBZ/A Dossiers/box 111/A.49SS/"Uitvoerverbod . . ."); ARA, Dutch Consul, Singapore to MvBZ, 5 May 1892, and 16 Feb. 1897, both in MvBZ/A Dossiers/box 111/A.49ss; "Regina on the Prosecution of E.H. Bell, Respondent, v. John Burnett Paige, Appellant, in *SSLR* (1894), 2:84 passim.

70. ARA, Dutch Vice-Consul, Singapore, to MvBZ, 30 Jan. 1888, no. 106, in (MvBZ/A Dossiers/box 111/A.49ss.)

71. *Java Courant,* 12 Dec. 1905, in (Atjeh, fiche no. 1) (MvK, PVBB), and Residentie Lampongsche Districten, Mailrapport 1906/7 no. 1054, in (Lampongs, fiche no. 386) (MvK, PVBB).

72. Asst. Resident Bataksche Aangelegenheden (Medan) to GGNEI, 14 April 1904, no. 1656/4, in (Sumatra Oostkust, fiche no. 156) (MvK, PVBB).

73. Gov. Heckler to GGNEI, 27 Sept. 1905, telegram no. 554, in (Riouw, fiche no. 296) (MvK, PVBB); First Gov't Sec to Commander NEI Army, 18 April 1900, Secret no. 120, in (Djambi, no. 324–25) (MvK, PVBB).

74. Resident West Borneo to Dienst Landvoegd, Buitenzorg, 22 June 1908, no. 273 telegram, in (West Borneo, fiche no. 395) (MvK, PVBB).

75. See, for example, Conrad, *An Outcaste of the Islands* (1992 reprint).

76. Both Chinese and Jawi notices forbid the import of arms into the Indies, except through

the use of permits, which had to be procured from the state. Batavia could therefore keep a close eye on who brought firearms into its territory and where, when, and why. See the verbatim copies of the Dutch Indies regulations found in Staatsblad 1875, no. 100, enclosed in ANRI, Resident Batavia to Algemeene Secretarie, 24 April 1875, no. 2474, and 29 April 1875, no. 2550, both in Aceh no. 8, "Atjehsche Verslagen 1874–75."

77. ARA/ Dutch Consul, Singapore to GGNEI, 26 Aug. 1863, in (MvK, Verbaal 14 Jan. 1864, no. 1).

78. See the diary of Mr. Everett at Papar (26 April 1880, vol. 73) in CO 874/Resident's Diaries; see also the *British North Borneo Herald,* 16 July 1896, 221.

79. Gov BNB to CO, 8 Aug. 1885, no. 45, in CO 144/59; FO to CO, 12 March 1897; British Acting Consul, Brunei to High Commissioner, Borneo, 27 Nov. 1896; and Extract from Report dated 4 Jan. 1897, from F. O. Maxwell, Acting Resident, Province Dent, all in CO 144/71; *Sarawak Gazette,* 1 May 1894.

80. See the *Deli Courant,* 4 July 1888, for example.

81. ARA, 1888, MR no. 516, 646, 683; ANRI, Dutch Consul, Singapore to GGNEI, 25 Jan. 1876, Confidential in Kommissoriaal 10 February 1876, no. 118az, in Aceh no. 12, "Stukken Betreffende Atjehsche Oorlog," no. 4–234, 1876.

82. ANRI, Dutch Consul, Singapore to GGNEI, 25 Jan. 1876, Confidential in Kommissoriaal 10 February 1876, no. 118az, in Aceh no. 12, "Stukken Betreffende Atjehsche Oorlog," no. 4–234, 1876; ARA, Dutch Consul, Singapore to Sec. Gen. Buitenzorg, 5 Jan. 1877, no. 5, in 1877, MR no. 287.

83. ARA, "Translation of a Bugis Letter from Rajah of Wajah at Pare Pare," 24 Jan. 1879, in (MvK, Verbaal 17 Feb. 1881, no. 33/298).

84. See ARA, Dutch Consul, Penang to Dutch Consul, Singapore, 30 Dec 1879, in (MvBZ/A Dossiers/box 111/A.49SS/"Uitvoerverbod . . .").

85. See "Meydinsah and Mohamed Eusope, Appellants, v. Regina, on the Prosecution of John Little, Respondent," *SSLR,* 1897, 4: 17 passim.

86. British Consul, Oleh Oleh to First Gov't Sec, Batavia, 20 Aug. 1883, no. 437, in PRO/ FO/220/Oleh Oleh Consulate (1882–85), vol. 11.

87. ARA, Asst. Resident Koetei to Resident SE Borneo, 15 Feb. 1874, no. 11, in 1874, MR no. 248; ARA, Dutch Consul, Singapore to GGNEI, 21 Dec. 1887, no. 1097, in (MvBZ/A Dossiers/box 111/A.49SS/"Uitvoerverbod . . ."); Sherry, *Conrad's Eastern World* (1966), 105.

88. ARA, Government Secretary to Regional Government Chiefs, Buitenbezittingen, 21 Aug. 1902, no. 2821, Circulaire, in 1902, MR no. 728.

89. Mr. Everett's Journal, Papar, 22 April and 5 June 1880, in CO/874/vol. 73/Resident's Diaries.

90. Gov. Labuan to CO, 29 June 1866, no. 16, in CO 144/25; ANRI, Algemeen Verslag Residentie West Borneo, 1889 (no. 5/20).

91. Chinese in Sarawak and Sambas were said to be ready to revolt in 1915. They had already hidden eight thousand rifles underground. Though there were eventual disturbances and some houses were burned on the Dutch side of the border, the movement was contained by European foreknowledge. This did not stop some Dutch officials from panick-

ing, however, and a request even seems to have gone out to the British for help, though this was quickly withdrawn (and explained away) later. See ARA, Resident West Borneo to Rajah of Sarawak, 13 Feb. 1915, no. 29; Controleur, Sambas to Civil and Military Asst. Res., Singkawang, 29 Jan. 1915, no. 3, and the surrounding documents, all in (MvBZ/A Dossiers/box 44/A.29 bisOK).

92. ARA, Dutch Consul, Singapore to General Secretary, Buitenzorg, 25 Oct. 1881, no. 646 Secret in (MvK, Verbaal 7 Aug. 1894, no. 20); ANRI, Dutch Consul, Singapore to GGNEI, 28 April 1876, Confidential, in Kommissoriaal 17 May 1876, no. 372az, in Aceh no. 13, "Stukken Betreffende Atjehsche Oorlog," no. 235–469, 1876; "Memorandum on the Alleged Smuggling of War into Acheen by the British Consul in Oleh Oleh," 6 Aug. 1883, in PRO/FO/220 /Oleh Oleh Consulate/1882–85/vol. 11.

93. ARA, Dutch Consul, Singapore to Acting Col. Sec., SS, 21 Nov. 1884, no. 731, in 1884, MR no. 738.

94. See *Bintang Timor,* 12 Dec 1894, 2; the article detailing the seizure of the Chinese woman's pistol is from *Utusan Malayu,* 30 Jan. 1908, 3. The woman's pistol, for which she had no permit, was found in her dwelling on Pasir Panjang Road. She was fined by the Straits magistrate.

95. ARA, Shiplog of the *Den Briel,* Logbook no. 712, 30 June 1873, 27–28, in Ministerie van Marine, 2.12.03; see also William Pretyman's Diary at Tempasuk, 7 Oct. 1878, in CO/874/vol. 72/Resident's Diaries.

96. ARA, 1893, MR no. 86, 714, 942; ARA, 1888, MR no. 74, 96, 119, 144, 153, 164, 185.

97. "Regina on the Prosecution of E. H. Bell, Respondent, v. John Burnett Paige, Appellant" in *SSLR,* 1894, 2:84 passim.

98. Gov Aceh to British Consul, Oleh Oleh, 15 Oct. 1883, no. 1915, in PRO/FO/220/Oleh Oleh Consulate (1882–5)/vol. 11; see also "Alexander von Roessing v. Regina" *SSLR,* 1905, 9:21.

99. "De Officier van Justitie, Soerabaya, contra F. W. de Rijk, Chef de te Soerabaya Gevestigde Firma Gebroeders van Delden," in *IWvhR,* 1873, no. 538, 20 Oct. 1873, 166–67; "A List of Cases of Smuggling Compiled in August 1882 by Mr. van Langen, then Assistent Resident on the West Coast of Acheen," in PRO/FO/220/Oleh Oleh Consulate/vol. 11.

100. De Souza to British Consul, Oleh Oleh, 18 Sept. 1883, in PRO/FO/220/Oleh Oleh Consulate/vol. 11; British Consul, Oleh Oleh, to Major McNair, Penang, 24 Sept. 1883, no. 530, in PRO/FO/220/Oleh Oleh/vol. 11.

101. Mr. de Souza to British Consul, Oleh Oleh, 10 Oct. 1883, in PRO/FO/220/Oleh Oleh Consulate/vol. 11.

102. See Furnivall, *Netherlands India: A Study of Plural Economy* (1939), 446 passim.

103. "Memorandum on the Alleged Smuggling of War into Acheen by the British Consul in Oleh Oleh," 6 Aug 1883, in PRO/FO/220 /Oleh Oleh Consulate/1882–85/vol. 11.

104. Testimony of Koh Lay, 7 Dec. 1891, Singapore, in ARA, Dutch Consul Singapore to MvBZ, 17 Dec. 1891, in MvBZ/A Dossiers/box 111/A.49ss.

105. ARA, Dutch Consul, Singapore, to Acting Col. Sec, SS, 21 Nov. 1884, no. 731, in 1884, MR no. 738.

106. See "Rex v. Mabot, 1890" *SLJ* 3 (1890): 65 passim; see also "Regina v. Khoo Kong Peh (1889)" *Kyshe* 4 (1885–90): 515.

107. ANRI, Dutch Consul, Singapore to GGNEI, 25 Jan. 1876, Confidential, in Kommis-soriaal 10 Feb. 1876, no. 118az, in Aceh no. 12 "Stukken Betreffende Atjehsche Oorlog, no. 4–234, 1876; Captain, "Citadel van Antwerpen" to Dutch Consul, Penang, 15 July 1873, no. 37, in PRO/FO/220/Oleh Oleh Consulate/vol. 11.

108. "Return for the Period 1873 to 1882 of the Cases in Which Ships Have Been Charged with Attempts to Smuggle Contraband of War into Sumatra, Compiled Out of the Records of the Dutch Consulate at Penang, 1883" in PRO/FO/220/Oleh Oleh Con-sulate/vol. 11.

Chapter 12 Praxis and Evasion:

Arms in Motion

The long history of arms trading in Southeast Asia shows that a wide variety of munitions, guns, and other matériel of war were trafficked through the region for many centuries. The identities of people moving these commodities were equally varied and changed through different periods. These two aspects of the arms trade—the guns themselves and the people trading them—were in constant flux. What did not change was the extremely high value attached to munitions as a category of commodities. This was true in regard to the appearance of the Portuguese and their cannons in the contact period, and later to the arrival of Americans and their muskets on Sumatra's pepper coasts in the first half of the nineteenth century. Southeast Asians knew that such commodities were necessary for survival, as the balance of power in the region quickly shifted to those populations that could most effectively make us of guns. It is for this reason that "commodities" of the most traditional wealth and power, such as slaves or ceremonial gongs, were exchanged for gunpowder and muskets in the Indies' Outer Islands even toward the end of the nineteenth century.[1] Firearms may have fit into the massive swirl of goods already in transit in commercial Southeast Asia, but these commodities also acquired a value of *primus inter pares,* as they seeped into the border geographies of the region. How was this diffusion accomplished? Which kinds of armaments traveled? How were they moved? What were the options available to smugglers in the face of the tightening boundary strictures of area states?

THE EVOLUTION OF MUNITIONS CARGOES

One of the easiest ways, initially, to transit firearms was through simple advertising. Prior to the 1873 ban to various parts of the Netherlands Indies (and even after this until 1879, for other parts of this outstretched territory), arms could simply be bought by answering advertisements in the local Straits newspapers. A notice in the January 6, 1870, issue of the *Penang Argus and Mercantile Advertiser* shows this plainly: the title of the advertisement was "Elley's Ammunition: Boxer Cartridges," and the notice went on to describe in great detail which armaments could be purchased from the company and at what prices. These included the firm's own cartridges, which were "waterproof, and imperishable in any climate," while "copper-rim-fire cartridges" were also available, for use in Smith and Wessons and other pocket revolvers. Caps and waddings for breach- and muzzle-loading rifles were also available from the company.[2] Almost twenty years later, during the height of the arms bans in the neighboring Dutch Indies, advertisements in newspapers like the *Straits Times* continued these sales pitches, informing customers that arms were available, though they could not be shipped south of the Straits. John Little and Company noted in the July 6, 1888, issue of that newspaper that a new shipment had arrived and that Martini-Henry rifles, Winchester Expresses, Sniders, and gunpowder were now available.[3] Many of these firms advertised the whole range of their goods in the Malay-language press as well, this same concern, John, Little and Company, also buying space in newspapers like Singapore's *Bintang Timor.*[4] Finding arms was not tremendously complicated, therefore, as suppliers of the items made sure any potential customers would certainly know where to look.

The various arms bans, ongoing conflicts, and resistance movements against colonial encroachment provided the necessary substrate for making this commodity line a success. Firearms and weapons of war flooded across the border into the Indies. Percussion caps were among the most commonly smuggled items. Tiny and easy to conceal—a box containing 62,500 caps (250 small tin boxes of 250 caps each) measured only about one cubic foot—these miniature explosives transited in huge numbers across the border.[5] Seizures of 10,000 caps or even 30,000 caps caught in a single raid were not unusual.[6] Tins of percussion caps lifted off dead Acehnese soldiers were shipped by the British envoy in Uleelheue across the Straits to his superiors; one of the tins is preserved in a documents box in the Public Records Office in London (fig. 14).[7] The caps were produced in Birmingham by the Kynoch Company and were imprinted on the obverse side with Chinese characters. Some of the Chinese characters represent Malay words, however, showing that the European firms who manufactured the items did so in the knowledge of who would be using them.[8] Other common items that passed across the frontier were muskets and donderbusses, older-style rifles that had been used for a very long time by various peoples in the region. Shipments of 400, 500, or even 600 muskets at a time are also not unusual in the records, though the numbers in single seizures were usually lower. Yet even such materials as bags of steel for making bullets or traditional krisses or knives also made these journeys. Pistols, spears, sabres, and bayonets all traveled together, an eclectic mix of armaments that found buyers in many ports.[9]

The illegal commerce in arms also included much more modern firearms, however, as many of the most technologically sophisticated European weapons found their way down to the Straits. The resident of Sumatra's East Coast complained to the Dutch governor-general that Enfields and other modern firearms could be had at "spot-prices" in Singapore by local peoples, which certainly seems to have been true, as these rifles were turning up all over Southeast Asia at the time, even in the interior of Borneo. The advanced Beaumont rifles being handed out to crew members aboard Dutch blockade ships off Aceh in the 1870s were also appearing, however, in enemy hands, the barrels modified to fit local needs, as Dutch patrols found out.[10] American Winchesters were also being used against the two colonial regimes by indigenous populations as well, in Aceh and in the Batak highlands in Sumatra, but also by Bugis crews coasting between Singapore and Sulawesi.[11] Even German Mausers were available in the region, as witnessed by the seizure of 500 of these guns and 500,000 Mauser cartridges that had left Singapore for Luzon in early 1899.[12] Not all of these shipments were of the small-bore variety, however: cannon were being fairly widely distributed around the region as well. The Dutch marine commander A. J. Kruijt spoke of impounding hundreds of cannon in his years patrolling off the Aceh coast, while other ships, including the *Zeeland*, the *Citadel van Antwerpen*, and the *Metalen Kruis* reported similar seizures.[13]

Perhaps the most commonly seized item in these waters was gunpowder, as it could be stored and transported so easily. Small barrels of powder that fetched

Fig. 14. Percussion caps found in Aceh, 1883. (Courtesy PRO, London)

around two dollars a keg in Aceh before the hostilities started went for ten dollars a keg in 1876 (three years later), the price jumping to levels near twenty dollars a keg by the early 1880s, depending on how far into the interior it needed to travel.[14] With high profit ratios such as these, it is little wonder that so much powder made its way illegally across the Straits. Yet intelligence reports from the days right before the war started showed that the Acehnese were in little need of powder, as they already possessed a great deal of their own. Much of Aceh's gunpowder at this point was probably stockpiled, but the local populace was skilled at fabricating a kind of low-grade, coarse powder on their own, which could be used for artillery.[15] Some of this was used in loose form, as in several of the Batak districts, while other Acehnese knew how to fashion cartridges filled with powder, such as one famed practitioner known to the Dutch as Tunku Mahmoed.[16] Around the turn of the century, however, this became more difficult, as the sophisticated new rifles needed fine machine-made powder and would not work with village-made composites.[17] Still, huge quantities of gunpowder managed to cross the Straits into the Dutch sphere for decades, sometimes coming a thousand kegs at a time. Court cases tried in Singapore show that these attempts took place often, from 1870 well toward the turn of the twentieth century.[18]

Sometimes it was uncertain what exactly was and what was not contraband of war, as many of these weapons were made up of several component parts.

The homemade powder available to the Acehnese, for example, came from varied sources: some was bought from Straits Settlements smugglers, but sulfur and charcoal were locally available, and saltpeter was obtainable by evaporating animal manure. (It was rumored there were Chinese in the interior of Aceh, alongside several deserters from the Dutch Indies army, who helped manufacture powder for the Acehnese side.)[19] When the Spanish in the southern Philippines declared sulfur to be contraband in 1898, protests were immediately lodged by several European powers. By the time of this declaration, sulfur was no longer one of the primary ingredients in machine-made gunpowder, and many Western firms saw potential profit losses for its nonmilitary purposes if the commerce in this item were to be strictly controlled.[20] Glycerin was another commodity that caused confusion. It was indeed used as a component in dynamite fabrication, but by the turn of the century it was utilized for predominantly nonmilitary purposes. It too was removed from the lists of banned substances in colonial Southeast Asia, as technology quickly passed it by.[21] Yet perhaps coal is the best example of how difficult it had become around the turn of the twentieth century to decide what was indeed contraband of war and what was not. Here again the context of the shipment was always at issue, as several important cases in the years 1904 and 1905 make clear.[22]

By this same time, however, one category of weapons running had become increasingly important from both geopolitical and technological perspectives: the passage of explosives. Dynamite and other explosive substances had been around for some time in 1865, but such goods began to become more commercially available only in the last decades of the nineteenth century. As early as 1879 in the Straits and 1884 in Labuan, rules were being promulgated about the carriage and sale of explosives. These instructions were woefully inadequate to stop the burgeoning commerce in such goods, however, as dynamite was used for a variety of functions to help open the frontier. Dynamite sometimes slipped into indigenous hands via private European enterprises; the consequences of such diffusion were so great to colonial governments that much more sophisticated legal structures were soon enacted. In the Straits, Ordinance no. 23 of 1899 saw to this. Classes of explosives, including nitrate-mixtures, nitro-compounds, chlorate-mixtures, and fulminates, were specifically laid out, while the explosives themselves, including blasting gelatins, ammonite, picric powders, and teutonite, were all listed and regulated, in all manner of their movement through the colony.[23] Dutch amendments to their own existing laws on explosives and their carriage through the Indies also mushroomed after 1893, when the first serious stipulations on explosives were pushed through.[24] Colonial sensibilities about the dangers these substances potentially represented seem to have far outstripped concern back in Europe, where enforcement of laws on the shipping of such cargoes was far less severe.[25] This appears to be fairly understandable, however. Both Batavia and Singapore saw their subject populations as eager consumers of such products, if the items themselves were put within local reach. Each colonial administration did its best to disallow this possibility, therefore, and tried to make the passage of explosives as insulated and as regulated a commerce as possible.

OUTFOXING THE STATE

The abilities of various actors in Southeast Asia to evade these proscriptions, both on explosives and on the trade in arms generally, were ingenious and sophisticated. The facility with which contrabanders were able to procure weapons cargoes always seemed to keep pace with the state's designs to improve its own interdiction capabilities. This dialectic is apparent even in the mid-1860s, when local populations were able to get arms from whaling ships, from China's open ports, and even through subterfuge, for example, pirates sailing as peaceful "traders" into harbors where arms were sold.[26] As the British and Dutch colonial states matured, however, around the turn of the twentieth century, many of the strategies employed to get hold of firearms had to evolve in sophistication as well. Syndicates used fall men, usually indigent coolies, to take the blame if an operation went sour; these men would go to prison sometimes, but their families miraculously would wind up much richer by the time they got out of jail.[27] Other strategies were also employed. Yet even after 1900, when the mechanics of smuggling had been worked out to grand designs to outwit the assembled forces of the state, simple ruses of hide-and-seek were also still employed. One of the most lyrical descriptions of an attempt to smuggle arms into Singapore can be found around 1915, when a Straits policeman noticed a coolie disembarking from a docking steamer. Something about the lilt or cadence of the coolie under his load was wrong; the object seemed too light for the way the man was straining. The detective asked the man to stop, but he dropped his burden and sprinted off into the crowd and was lost. When the policeman disassembled the wooden folding table the man had been carrying, a dozen pistols and several hundred rounds of ammunition spilled out of the hollowed-out legs of the table, falling onto the ground.[28]

Firearms not only transited to the difficult-to-police border residencies of the frontier, but also came in large numbers to the very core of the Dutch Indies state, as we have seen. In 1869 and 1870, colonial officials caught onto the fact that large caches of guns were being shipped illegally to Java from Holland disguised in piano cases. Pianos were perfect commodities in which to hide this illicit passage; as big-ticket items, their import duties were paid in Europe, meaning they were sealed into cases in ports like Rotterdam and went uninspected on the long journey out to the Indies. Dutch smugglers took advantage of this fact and hid sizable numbers of guns in the large shipping crates that stored these objects, bargaining that they would not be opened until they had reached their eventual buyers. This ruse seems to have worked for some time until the authorities became aware of it. Eventually, however, letters went out from the highest levels of Dutch government to the ship captains, dock loaders, and agents of certain steamers, informing them that such a commerce was strictly illegal.[29] Ships like the 's Gravenhage, the Dalwijk, the Huijdehopper, Albrecht's Beijling, and the Alblaserdam, which were all known to be transporting pianos, were watched and searched. Although many of the inspections turned up no solid evidence, one surprise examination did indeed find arms in the incoming piano shipments, pinpointing Rotterdam as the port of origin.[30] Rotterdam was the perfect center for contraband cargoes such as this one, as it was one of Europe's largest ports and was the scene of an enormous amount of activity (and a huge changeover in ships) every day. These structural conditions have allowed Rotterdam to fulfill this same smuggling role in the early twenty-first century, with the port's contraband still largely en route to Asia.

Piano cases were not the only place to hide illegal shipments of arms. Almost any other possible space was used as well, with limitations being exercised only be the ingenuity of the traffickers. Flasks were used to hide gunpowder, while other armaments were camouflaged as candles, soap, textiles, or dried fruit.[31] Kerosene oil tins were used to conceal gunpowder, while excess steel for making bullets was hidden away in large bags of onions.[32] Tobacco sacks and rice bales were utilized as well, while ships' ballast was also a popular choice for concealment.[33] Smuggling was aided even by structural adjustments to the design of ships, such as using false bottoms and pulling up the floor planks of craft, storing the contraband inside, and then nailing the beams back into place.[34] Fishing boats coasting along the Sumatra and Borneo seaboard and pepper-trading craft heading toward shore to pick up agricultural cargoes for shipment across the Straits were also notorious traffickers of illegal arms.[35] The range and ingenuity of contrabanders in their use of ships to smuggle arms into Aceh during the height of the conflict there became so broad that Batavia tried to limit its army-supply contracts only to Dutch-registered ships, though even this did not seem to ever actually help matters.[36] The fact that all ships, regardless of their country of origin, were allowed to carry small stores of powder for their own protection nearly ruined the Dutch blockade. It soon became clear that these stores were being sold for profit on many voyages under the pretense of use during an attack, with other powder then routinely repurchased in the next port of call.[37]

Evasion of the weapons strictures also came through other means, such as using loopholes in the standing corpus of Straits arms laws. As has been shown previously, the British authorities in Singapore were often in little hurry to enforce the Dutch arms bans, as many felt doing so would only hurt the free trade principles of the colony, not to mention the port's overall profitability. Straits court decisions reflected this ambivalence and often let smugglers off easily. The Chinese crew of tope no. 385 escaped punishment for their arms transgression into the Indies in 1875, for example, while several Bugis shippers also avoided incarceration simply because they were unable to pay the required fines.[38] Even European arms traffickers were exonerated on occasion, as Straits courts were often unwilling to convict unless the most damning of evidence was presented.[39] Yet there were also some in the British sphere who saw these allowances as getting too far out of hand. In 1887, the governor of the Straits asked his fellow policymakers on the Legislative Council whether they really desired a state of affairs in which just about any arms smuggler, no matter how blatant his actions, could eventually go free. Four years later, bills seeking to close some of the loopholes started appearing before the council, as even some of the colony's most Free Trade–oriented statesmen realized that such liberties might eventually come back to haunt them.[40] Yet only after the turn of the century were these legal lacunae truly being filled all along the length of the border, as in Perak in 1902, where new enactments stipulated careful procedures to be followed in the search and seizure of firearms.[41]

Besides using (and abusing) the existing legal codes, arms smugglers used local geography and local cultural configurations to get their cargoes across the border. As we have seen, saltpeter was indigenous to parts of North Sumatra, though it could be found in places in Borneo as well.[42] It was easily collected and used by various indigenous peoples to manufacture gunpowder and then sell it out of the reach of the two colonial states. Yet the very nature of the border as well, comprised as it was of huge, relatively unguarded coastlines and thousands of tiny islands, also made arms smuggling a tempting proposition. Dutchmen along various points of the boundary knew this and commented on how adept locals seemed to be in using Southeast Asia's geography for exactly this purpose.[43] The fact that many local chiefs maintained strong cultural ties with their neighboring potentates, regardless of whether their relationship with Batavia was weak or strong, also allowed arms to diffuse to various resistance forces. Steadfast allies of the Dutch, like Idi on Aceh's east coast, often double-dealt Batavia, therefore, signing arms agreements with one hand and dealing contraband weaponry to the "enemy" with the other.[44] A further way in which local culture was bent in this direction can be seen in Brunei, where the sultan told the British he needed ten piculs of gunpowder (1,333 lbs.) for ceremonial "saluting purposes" in 1897. Three salutes were fired, and the rest of the powder promptly disappeared.[45]

Sophisticated use of geography extended further than just the local domain, however. One of the most interesting aspects of smugglers' avoidance mechanisms can be found in the fact that extremely distant places were also used to outwit state authorities, often as third-country transshipment centers. Contra-banders made use of lands that had no arms-trafficking agreements with the Dutch at all, thereby outwitting the arms laws by utilizing these countries as the technical sources of cargoes that were en route to the Indies. French Vietnam, Cambodia, and British Burma were all used in this capacity, until colonial legislators in all three of these dominions eventually closed these avenues, at least on paper.[46] Parts of China, including Hainan island in the far south, were also used.[47] Sometimes these shipments actually traveled all the way to these places and were then re-exported. At other times, the listing of such destinations from Straits ports seems to have been only a ruse, as the cargoes were eventually transshipped into waiting craft out of harbor on the high seas or taken in the original vessel directly to the Indies. Places as far east in the Indies archipelago as Portuguese Timor and even New Guinea were utilized in this fashion.[48] The spread of destinations used as feints, if plotted on a graph with the Straits Settlements as the origin of cargoes, would shoot off in almost every direction.

A disproportionate amount of contraband weaponry seems to have gone through Siam, however. In 1885, the Siamese throne, under heavy pressure from several European powers, enacted much more rigorous legislation banning the import of arms into the kingdom (fig. 15).[49] Prior to this date, Siam seems to have been a clearinghouse for regional arms traffickers, especially for shipments south to the Netherlands Indies. There is a huge correspondence still in existence on this transit trade, much of it originating from the office of the Dutch consul in Bangkok during that time.[50] Steamers under the Siamese flag were involved in this commerce, but the ships of many other nations were certainly also complicit.[51] Siamese authorities knew very well this illicit trade was taking place from Siam's shores, but there seems to have been no energy expended to attempt to stop it. Even if arms exports from Siam were legal under some circumstances until 1885, they were still known to be illegal to the Dutch Indies. The minister for foreign affairs in Bangkok, in fact, acknowledged that arms cargoes were leaving his country's shores but blamed much of the traffic on governors in outlying principalities like Patani and Trengganu.[52] Many of these shipments found their way, eventually, down to the Dutch Indies in small boats, with the Dutch envoy in Bangkok given only evasive promises that matters would be examined.[53] This state of affairs existed far after the 1885 Siamese arms ban, though, with the Malay-language press in Singapore reporting seizures in Bangkok even after the turn of the century.[54]

Firearms were obtained in the Netherlands Indies through much less organized and more haphazard channels as well. Indigenous soldiers in the Dutch East Indies army (KNIL) were sometimes bribed to report their weapons lost, when they were really handed over to resistance forces for a cash fee.[55] Other firearms were dropped overboard "accidentally" by Dutch sailors into shallow water and were then picked up by waiting local boats, to be sold for a profit.[56] Such smuggling and corruption could be replaced by the seizing of perfect moments of opportunity, however. Attacks on solitary public servants like policemen, who were robbed of their weapons, or on remote outposts where the forces of "law and order" were far outnumbered also took place on occasion.[57] Yet sometimes indigenous populations could even make off with large numbers of firearms without having to directly fight for them, as in one incident in Jambi in the early 1880s. A controleur's house there was broken into one night in November 1880, and the unit's full complement of twenty rifles and ten swords was stolen by thieves. In the ensuing investigation, it became apparent the firearms had found their way all the way to Jambi's resistance forces in the distant up-country, who were still fighting a decades-old war of resistance against the Dutch occupying army in the lowlands. Batavia was furious over the ineptitude shown in this incident. Though the Dutch found out exactly who eventually came to possess the weapons in question, only two of the twenty rifles were ever retrieved, the rest residing with the "rebels" until after the twentieth century.[58]

Firearms were also procurable from other simple sources, sources which were common channels used in everyday economic life. Although manufactured iron and brass objects were subject to duties, as with the right tools they could

ประกาศ

ด้วย พระยา ภาสกรวงศวรราชานุกินนุปรักนสุปรีย   ผู้ บัญชา การ โรง ภาษี
ชาเข้าชา ออก - รับ พระยรมราชโองการใส่เกล้า ๆ   สั่งว่า   ให้ประกาศแก่ บรรทา
ผู้ที่บรรทุกสิน ค้าเข้า มาใน กรุงเทพ ๆ ให้ ทราย ทั่ว กัน ว่า   เพราะ เหตุที่ มีผู้บรรทุก
เครื่อง สาคราวุธ กระสุนคิน ค่า   ๆ ถ ๆ   นั้น เข้า มาใน กรุง สยาม   แล หัว เมือง ประ
เทศ ราชในเมื่อเร็ว ๆ นี้เปน ชัน มาก   คอเวอนมนต์ผู้ ปก ครอง แผ่นกิน   ของ พระบาท
สมเก็ร พระเจ้า อยู่ หัวใน กรุง สยาม   ได้ คิด จัด การ ที่ จะให้ การ เปน ไป ตาม พระราช กำ
หนก กฎหมาย   ตาม หนังสือ สัญญา ทาง พระราชไมตรี ทั้งปวง   จึ่ง ประกาศให้ ทราย
ว่า ตั้ง แต่ นี้ สืบ ไป   บรรทา การ บรรทุกเครื่อง สาคราวุธ กระสุน กิน ก๋า แล เครื่อง ระเบิด
ท่าง ๆ นั้น   จะไม่ อนุญากให้ มี เข้า มา   เว้นไว้ แต่ที่ได้ มีใบ อนุญาค วิเสศ ทาก คอเวอ
รเมนต์ ผู้ ปก ครอง นั้น   ได้ มา ก่อน เวฆาบรรทุกเข้า มา จึ่ง จะ อนุญาคให้

ศุลก สถาน กรุงเทพ ๆ วัน ประทัยยดึชัน เจ็ด ค่ำ เกือน สาม ข้ำ วอก ฉอศก ศักราช ๑๒๔๖

('TRANSLATION.)
NOTIFICATION

Phya Bhaskarawongse Wararajouat Nriparatnasupery, the Superintendant
of the Customs, has been directed by Royal Mandate to give notice to
all Importers, that in consequence of the large Importation of arms, ammunition &c. into Siam and its dependencies of late, His Siamese Majesty's
Government are taking means to enforce the laws according to the terms of
the Treaties; and that henceforth all such importation of arms, ammunition
and other explosive substances will not be permitted, unless the special permission of the Government shall have been previously obtained.

Custom House, Bangkok, 22nd January 1885.

Fig. 15. Siamese arms ban, 1885. (Courtesy ARA, The Hague)

be transformed into guns, the rules on their transit do not seem to have been widely enforced.[59] Smuggling vessels, too, constantly changed names and flags or gave false shipping numbers to the different port authorities they encountered in their journeys, further complicating state attempts to keep track of the flow of trade.[60] The fact that Straits Settlements ports contained no customs houses allowed these irregularities plenty of room. There were few existing mechanisms to check on cargoes, so that statistics, such as those on arms, often did not match those of nearby corroborating sources at all.[61] Even in the Dutch sphere, where the desire for enforcement was strongest, this proved to be the case. At Surabaya, the customs officers routinely (but inadvertently) allowed revolvers under the twenty-five-guilder minimum worth to slip past the port patrols, as such pistols were sold for only a third of that price in auctions inside the city.[62]

The particular nature of shipping and blockade surveillance in the waters of the Anglo/Dutch frontier also allowed many guns to slip through the frontier net. The British consul in Uleelheue, Aceh's main northern port, provided a long commentary on this subject to his superiors back in Singapore in 1883. He criticized the Dutch for complaining about English inactivity against arms smugglers when, as he said, the Dutch themselves had not done enough to stop arms from leaking across their own frontier. Dutch warships, he noted, were on average slower than indigenous junks or sloops and could not catch them if they chose to run; further, they often did not even have the inclination to try. Many of the naval officers did not like the work of smuggling prevention; they found it demeaning and outside of their "true" job description and therefore did the work only reluctantly. These men would indeed search vessels within the three-mile limit of the Dutch coasts, but outside of these limits,

> they can only look down [into] a hold that is full of various bags and packages; but even if they had the necessary labor at hand, there would be no room on the ships' decks to bring up all the cargo, and if nothing were found a steamer might put in a troublesome claim for detention and demurrage. They say themselves that they don't know the commercial usages regarding packing and so forth. They don't know the cases and bags in which different products are usually packed—they have no experience of sizes, quantities, marks and so forth. A lieutenant from a man of war is not an expert, he does not know whether a particular case is a chest of opium or a case of piece goods; and having no spirit for a work which they think is unfairly placed on their shoulders they do not feel disposed to make any study of the question.[63]

Many of Batavia's accounts of the same period privately seem to agree with this appraisal. The Dutch knew smuggling was always finding new channels into the Indies, they just didn't know how to stop it.[64] References abound in Dutch missives explicating previous tricks used by contrabanders to get arms south, including the methods and sometimes even locations of high-seas transshipments.[65]

The ruses involving the transit of gunpowder illustrate some of these processes in miniature. Here again, the British consul to Uleeheue detailed the strategies involved down to minute detail. He told the Straits authorities that the Acehnese could get their powder from across the frontier in a number of ways. Deli and Langkat perahus transshipped some on the high seas for profit, after taking supplies on in Singapore. Supposedly friendly chiefs who got the powder from the Dutch in the first place also sold some on the side to the resistance forces. Even the firm supplying the Dutch army, Katz Brothers and Co., seemed to be involved, as they had every interest in prolonging the war for their own financial well-being. Other avenues existed in the nonchalant attitude of the Singapore surveillance system. The inspector of powder, for example, was really only a clerk in the harbor master's office and had little time for powder supervision at all. Craft which were supposedly taking powder to Siam legally did so in the wrong monsoon, as the winds would actually take them not north, but south, straight into the Indies. An intricate system whereby crews visiting Singapore could buy two pounds of powder at a time in the city or ten pounds at a time outside of the city limits for self-protection allowed large quantities of the material to slip out of the Straits.[66] Dutch representatives found other loopholes too, however, such as blasting powder used for engineering and construction being misplaced and small-scale manufacturing of powder taking place deep in the Malayan jungle.[67]

Some of the issues surrounding smugglers' avoidance of the arms laws can also be found in two specific cases, the first one involving the ship *Batara Bayon Sree*, which was accused of gun running in the Makassar Strait between eastern Borneo and western Sulawesi in 1879. The story told by the master of that ship, William Cann, was that he had put into the roads of Pare Pare, a port in Sulawesi, for repairs of a broken propeller during that year. On the ship's manifest were crates of arms and ammunition, which were off-loaded to the local raja, who had ordered them; the ship was then slated to sail to Ampenan, a free port in Lombok. While Cann was waiting for his vessel to be attended to in Pare Pare, the Dutch harbormaster of Makassar arrived and, noticing arms among the list of cargo, seized the ship as a prize in violation of the Indies arms ban. Cann protested this action as utterly fraudulent; he had landed at Pare Pare in broad daylight and believing the raja of the place to be independent, had delivered up the weapons. No Dutch flag was flying in the roadstead; only the colors of the raja were present. The Dutch harbormaster didn't care and informed Cann he was under arrest for arms smuggling to a Dutch Indies vassal. Only after the part owner of the steamer, Gwee Kim Soon, and the British authorities, including men all the way up to metropolitan decision-making circles in London and The Hague, intervened with letters and diplomacy was the case settled. The British had to admit that Pare Pare was Dutch; in exchange, the *Batara Bayon Sree* eventually went free and was exempted from a one-thousand-guilder fine. The judgment of the Makassar court, however, shows clearly many of the issues we have seen elsewhere: the importance of diplomacy in deciding when smuggling was smuggling, the role of selective ignorance in acknowledging local border potentates, and everyday mechanisms of evasion.[68] To this day it is uncertain whether Cann really knew that gun running to Pare Pare was strictly off-limits.

A second interesting case deals with the flight of indigenous trading perahus from Singapore to West Borneo five years later. Here again Dutch frustrations with the supposed assistance they were receiving from across the Straits are in evidence. Batavia's consul in Singapore, W. H. Read, had received intelligence that four perahus would be heading for Borneo with arms and powder purchased in the Straits; he had informed the British colonial secretary about the imminent attempt, but "by some extraordinary chance [the letter] did not reach him" until after the ships had sailed. Read was furious about what he considered to be a quiet conspiracy to thwart his efforts at interdiction; he tried to get a steamer to go after the ships himself, but was told by the British governor this would be unfeasible, as such a pursuit would be technically illegal. The men involved, Mecijah, Ismail, Hadjie Allee, and Hadjee Saleh, had received clearance to sail to Trengganu on the Malay Peninsula, yet all concerned knew this was impossible, as the monsoon winds were blowing in the wrong direction.[69] The four indigenous perahus headed for Dutch Borneo laden with several hundred muskets each, gunpowder, opium, rice, and silver dollars. After great exertions and travail, the Dutch managed to catch one of the four perahus, as it was island hopping through the Riau archipelago. Because the ship was under British colors, however, the trial took place in Singapore courts, and the case was dismissed for lack of witnesses. "As I anticipated," Read wrote to his superiors, "the prosecution had no fair chance. The result is unfortunate as it will give the smugglers fresh courage."[70]

TWO THEATERS: NORTH SUMATRA AND
NORTH BORNEO

The patterns and mechanics of arms smuggling in turn-of-the-century South-east Asia can be rounded off here with brief glimpses into two arenas on this outstretched border: North Sumatra, including Aceh and the Straits Settle-ments, and North Borneo, including the company's lands and the wider Sulu Sea. These two theaters delineate the opposite ends of the three-thousand-kilometer Anglo/Dutch frontier, and both the populations in these two places and the kinds of smuggling carried out often were quite different from one an-other. In North Sumatra, the ongoing struggle between the Dutch and Aceh-nese dominated events in the northern waters of the Straits of Melaka for al-most the entirety of the period 1865–1915. Gun running in this space was seen as a direct threat to the military capabilities (not to mention the military honor) of the Dutch colonial state and therefore had to be stamped out merci-lessly by the forces at Batavia's disposal. Northern Borneo and the Sulu Sea were not as immediately important to European planning but were neverthe-less seen as trouble spots which needed to be controlled, especially vis-à-vis the commerce in arms. At the outset of the Aceh War in 1873, the Dutch had every reason to believe they had a solid ally in the fight against arms smuggling in the Singapore administration. Governor Ord, after all, had told Batavia it was his intention to publish a Straits arms ban as soon as Dutch hostilities had com-menced against the Acehnese.[71] Ord's stand was a personal one; he felt that "law and order" were needed in the waters of the Straits and that the sooner the Dutch had conquered any vestige of independent, non-European con-trolled authority in the region, the better it would be for everyone concerned. London did not concur entirely in this opinion, however, and consistently warned—and later berated—the governor for leaning too heavily on the side of the Dutch.[72] Ord's tenure in the Straits was short, though, and the policies of his immediate successors were much less favorable to the Dutch arms bans. Although an initial order was passed stipulating that trade ships would no longer be able to take armaments along for their own protection, this was quickly reversed when Straits merchants almost rioted, saying they would be at the total mercy of pirates.[73] Straits traders continued to take along arma-ments for their self-protection, and arms continued to bleed into the Acehnese countryside, in small but steady quantities.[74] When Dutch naval officers in-terviewed even allied Acehnese on the coast at this time, they were surprised by how well armed the local populations seemed to be. Local chiefs said their men needed the guns to kill wild animals that often raided their pepper gardens at night.[75]

Both the British and the Dutch tried to keep statistics on the flow of arms across the Straits, especially after the Aceh War began. Yet even where the two states could count the same relatively above-board figures, the numbers never seemed to agree. The British and the Dutch both tabulated how many arms went to Sumatra to supply friendly chiefs who were allied with Batavia against the resistance forces in Aceh. Yet the statistics here seem hardly credible. Both the British and the Dutch ledgers are scribbled down to careful, exact figures, but the totals which the Dutch saw coming to their allies were about twice what the British were able to count.[76] A period chart which purported to display the number of maritime smuggling attempts of arms into the Indies certainly falls short of any kind of accuracy. Between 1873 and 1882, only fifteen cases are listed, though any research through the corpus of archival materials on this subject finds many times this number.[77] What emerges from these statistical attempts to "count" smuggling on the frontier is how difficult, indeed, any such exercise must have been, if indeed it was possible at all. The smuggling of arms on the North Sumatra frontier was a huge, far-reaching enterprise, and was for all intents and purposes out of reach of the vision of the state.

Certain individuals in Batavia and Singapore seemed to understand this fact and faced the problem with an attitude of near resignation. Though some administrators on both sides of the Straits continued to put faith in the surveillance and interdiction efforts of colonial government, the more realistic voices of concern saw that the battle against weapons contraband was gradually being lost.[78] In Singapore, notices of seizures and the huge fines that sometimes resulted did not convince the press any progress was being made; the *Straits Times* said the profits involved were simply too high and the seizures too few to make any real difference.[79] Across the international divide in the Dutch sphere the attitude of many of the more perspicacious administrators was much the same. A dispirited letter from the commander of the Dutch naval forces in the Indies to the governor-general in Batavia acknowledges that the North Sumatra blockade was not working and that firearms continued to seep across the border.[80] Even the Dutch vice-consul in Penang, George Lavino, who did more to try to stop these voyages than any other single man (and whose job largely depended on his having at least some kind of success in doing so), was often pessimistic. Lavino saw the very structural elements of trade in the Straits as being against Batavia's efforts at control: the British free ports, the insufficiency of the police forces assembled, and the fact that most of the traders involved were

Asian all militated against government success. Still worse, wrote Lavino, was the fact that many in the English settlements actually had far stronger sympathies for the Acehnese than the Dutch, including not a few Britons themselves.[81]

These frustrations lasted for the duration of the long and costly Aceh War. Arms always seemed to be able to enter Aceh, even after 1900 when the conflict had become an almost entirely guerrilla affair with no more pitched battles of real consequence. These frustrations are evident in the writings of men like the resident of Sumatra's East Coast, who declared in 1883 that any attempts by local chiefs to procure weapons for themselves would be severely punished, but endeavors to spirit arms to the Acehnese would receive the far stiffer sentence of high treason.[82] This attitude of impatient severity did not entirely work, however. Although the conflict in Aceh did, eventually, sink to a low-level resistance movement only, the resolve and hatred of the Acehnese populace was too strong to overcome entirely (and it remains so today, even against the centralized Indonesian state in Jakarta). Firearms continued to trickle into North Sumatra and were used by all members of the population. One can see this best, perhaps, in the Outer Island Political Reports from Aceh (*Politieke Verslagen Buitengewesten*), which chart in daily, local detail the continued passage of weapons into the countryside and the resistance that accompanied this transit. In the mountains of the Gayo districts, firefights killed KNIL soldiers; in Leumbang, rifles and revolvers were continually seized, while in Pidie and Teunom the same pattern held sway.[83] Even the aging mothers of resistance leaders fought, and sometimes died, while scurrying into mountain hiding places where caches of arms had been stored.[84] The value of these firearms was simply too high to the local populace to just surrender stockpiles of them upon discovery; sometimes their owners perished with them. The arms trade into Aceh during the decades around the turn of the twentieth century was a commerce of major moral and economic consequence, therefore, to both sides of the conflict, though obviously for different reasons.

The context of arms trading in North Borneo and the Sulu Sea was somewhat different from the evolution of this commerce in the Straits of Melaka. In the former space, gun running had been an important part of everyday economic life for quite a long time and was acknowledged as such even by Europeans in the area. Important British officials in Labuan, for example, often said overtly that the trade in firearms should not be interfered with on the part of the administration because the results were inevitably so profitable to the colony.[85] The fact that an increasingly active weapons trade was conducted in

Brunei only a few nautical miles away and that the numbers of guns in circulation seemed to be rising appreciably in the mid–1860s, however, gave the
British cause for concern and started a rethinking of the Free Trade policy in
these goods. One of the principal reasons for this was that Labuan simply had
no idea where most of the arms were heading. No statistics were kept on where
the guns ended up, only that they had left the colony and were no longer within
the British avenue of vision.[86] As time went on, however, it became increasingly plain that large quantities of these cargoes were heading north, mostly to
regional datus in Sulu and the southern Philippines who were engaged in active
resistance against Spanish expansion.[87] Though arms were technically allowed,
like all other goods, to be traded openly in the Sulu Sea, ships caught running
guns to the "rebels" were liable to be impounded or destroyed by Spanish cruis-
ers. The specter of smuggling was already being raised in the regional context,
therefore, even before the transit of such items had become technically illegal in
this area.

In the interior of Borneo, similar attempts to begin controlling the long-
standing commerce in arms were also taking place. Yet as with the situation in
the maritime sphere, interdiction efforts at controlling this traffic were difficult
to enforce. For one thing, a certain degree of trade was simply reckoned in values equivalent to brass guns: thus there are reports of slaves being sold for the
weight of three of these objects (or seventy-five dollars), while old gongs were
also calculated into an appropriate value of guns. Limiting the commerce in
arms was difficult, then, as they were so widely used as a measurement of value
by peoples all over the island. State fines were also initially calculated by punishments in guns, however, so that even the government's own control of supposed wrongdoing was calculated by this scheme.[88] Yet it was the widespread
use of cannons, gunpowder, and muskets in warfare as well as for cultural celebrations such as Dusun burials and marriages which also made any ban on
these items particularly problematic.[89] This did not stop certain administrators
from trying to do exactly that, though officials with longer experience in Borneo cautioned against attempting too much at once. When Acting Governor
L. P. Beaufort tried to enact a flat ban on gun sales everywhere in North Borneo
in 1892, some saw his proposal as ridiculous and unrealizable. This opinion was
held by many, including Beaufort's predecessor, who said, "No law that we can
invent will prevent the natives of the interior from getting arms and ammunition."[90]

The fractured nature of British authority in Borneo, as we have seen in earlier chapters of this book, also made attempts at arms control exceedingly diffi-

cult. Each administrative polity under the larger British umbrella—Labuan, the North Borneo Company, Sarawak, and even London from a distance—had different aims to achieve in regard to the transit of guns. Much of the time, these aims were at cross-purposes. Ironically, more of a commitment existed by the 1880s to stop firearms from leaking into the Dutch sphere than could be found between British spheres themselves; diplomacy was taking care of the former, while internal rivalries still marred full cooperation in the latter. Though firearms were indeed trickling into the Netherlands Indies from British Borneo's waters, at least some of this cargo seems to have been smuggled across internal British divisions as well, also for profit. Officials in the Colonial Office in London hotly debated whether arms should be banned from transiting into the North Borneo Company's domains; the company persistently begged for such legislation to be enacted in the Crown Colonies, only to be rebuffed for many years. London felt the issue could be used as a lever against the company's directors, when issues more important to the Crown came up that needed negotiation.[91] Finally, in 1884, the Colonial Office assented to banning the flow of arms from Labuan to British North Borneo, though initially the move was instituted on a temporary basis.[92] London was trying to milk the profits of free trade for as long as it could and cared little for the related problems of this commerce when they spilled across the company's borders. Firearms poured into North Borneo from several directions up until this time, from Sulu in the north, from Sarawak in the south, and even on a smaller scale from the Netherlands Indies, the traditional recipient of the bulk of the illegal arms trade.[93]

The wider maritime spaces of Sulu continued to be the main locus of weapons trading in this region, however, up until the years of the turn of the twentieth century. The Sulu Protocol of 1885 had guaranteed the free commerce of all goods in the area, regardless of their nature; Spain periodically ignored this treaty with regard to the arms trade, but many firearms still managed to get through the Spanish patrols.[94] By 1897, however, new diplomatic initiatives between the major European powers were reversing laissez-faire free trade in the region, and the passage of arms was banned, as a cooperative move between all expanding imperial projects in the area.[95] This state of affairs lasted for less than a year. In 1898, the Spanish-American conflict erupted, and gun running once again became big business in the Sulu Sea. Although both the British and Dutch in Southeast Asia (among other interested parties, including the Chinese government) issued proclamations forbidding their subjects to run weapons to the region, arms trading picked up because of the lively profits to be made.[96] Local chiefs and autonomous movements saw the colonial struggle in the Philippines as a time to push programs for their own local expansion. The fact that coast lights and beacons had been shut down all over the islands by the Spanish as a defensive move against the American fleet surely helped the fluidity of this silent commerce. The state's "eyes in the dark" were literally extinguished, creating a zone of free interaction for the entrepreneurs of many nations.[97] A variety of armaments from a variety of places were indeed pushed across the maritime frontier and into the Sulu Sea at this time.[98] Batavia's naval command warned its servants in the Outer Islands to be especially vigilant for arms traffickers attempting to get arms out of the Indies.[99] By the end of the nineteenth century, there was little irony in this reversal of directions. Firearms were just another commodity to be bought and sold for profit, no matter whose frontiers they crossed in their quiet journeys in the dark.

It is clear that munitions transited across the Anglo/Dutch border for the entire period 1865–1915. Southeast Asia was a regional arms bazaar through much of the nineteenth century, until colonial enterprises thought better about selling such weapons indiscriminately and started to focus on controlling these enormous flows. Yet the dynamics of the imperial state-making project in this region also encouraged the traffic in firearms; new borders meant new opportunities for profit, as a host of entrepreneurs and local resistance leaders quickly realized. The tightening of the Anglo/Dutch boundary over this period made such freewheeling commodity trades more difficult, but neither Batavia nor Singapore was ever fully successful in stopping the transit of these items. By 1914, at the very end of this period, however, these patterns were about to change. The eve of World War I took the commerce in munitions in new directions, transiting arms flows not only across the Anglo/Dutch frontier but also *through* all of Southeast Asia as a conduit to larger struggles being played out on a global stage. The traffic of arms in this region became much larger after this date, as the scope of its radials widened. That particular history, however, is outside the parameters of this book.

NOTES

1. ARA, Resident Timor to GGNEI, 1 Dec. 1877, no. 1276, in 1878, MR no. 78; Frank Hatton's Expedition Diary up the Labuk River, and Overland to Kudat; and Mineral Investigations, 4–5/1882, in CO/874/vol. 75/Resident's Diaries.
2. *Penang Argus and Mercantile Advertiser,* 6 Jan 1870, 4.
3. *Straits Times,* 6 July 1888, 2.
4. *Bintang Timor,* 29 Nov 1894, 3.

5. ANRI, Lavino to GGNEI, 19 March 1873, no. 58/G Confidential in Kommissoriaal 3 April 1875, no. 358az, in Aceh no. 8, "Atjehsche Verslagen, 1874–75."

6. Ibid.; ANRI, Koo Eng Tin to J. A. Fox, Penang Harbor Master, 25 Feb. 1875, in Kommissoriaal 13 April 1875, no. 358az, in Aceh no. 8, "Atjehsche Verslagen 1874–75."

7. Gov Aceh to British Consul Oleh Oleh, 15 Oct. 1883, no. 1915, in PRO/FO/220/Oleh Oleh Consulate/vol. 11.

8. According to the protector of Chinese in Penang, E. Karl, the Chinese characters on one of the tins translated to "Real Tukang (A Malay phrase meaning "First-Rate Mechanic"). See British Consul, Oleh Oleh, to Gov SS, 15 May 1883, no. 238; British Consul, Oleh Oleh to Gov Aceh, 3 Nov. 1883, no. 628; and McNair, Honorary Resident Councilor, Penang, to British Consul, Oleh Oleh, 26 Oct. 1883, no. 6108/85, all in PRO/FO/220/Oleh Oleh/vol. 11.

9. ARA, Dutch Consul, Singapore to Acting Col. Sec. SS, 21 Nov. 1884, no. 731, in 1884, MR no. 738; ARA, "Translation of a Bugis Letter from Rajah of Wajah at Pare Pare," 24 Jan. 1879, in (MvK, Verbaal 17 Feb. 1881, no. 33/298); see also Gov Aceh to GGNEI, 20 Nov. 1905, telegram no. 909, in (Atjeh, fiche no. 1) (MvK, PvBB); ARA, Dutch Consul, Singapore to GGNEI, 20 April 1888, no. 249, in (MvBZ/A Dossiers/box 111/A.49SS/ "Uitvoerverbod . . ."); Captain, *Metalen Kruis,* to Dutch Consul, Penang, 4 Jan. 1875, no. 1264, and same to same, 4 July 1876, no. 1932, both in PRO/FO/220/Oleh Oleh Consulate/vol. 11.

10. ARA, Resident Sumatra East Coast to GGNEI, 22 Sept. 1883, La R7, Secret, in 1883, MR no. 888; William Pretyman's Diary at Tempasuk, 7 Oct. 1878, in CO/874/vol. 72/Resident's Diaries; ARA, Lt. Kommandant van Oordt (of the *Zeeland*) to Kommandant der Maritieme Middelen in de Wateren van Atjeh, 14 Aug. 1873, in no. 92, Verbaal Geheim Kabinet 17 Dec. 1873, D33; Gov Aceh to British Consul, Oleh Oleh, 4 Aug. 1883, no. 1382, in PRO/FO/220/Oleh Oleh Consulate/vol. 11.

11. *Java Courant,* 12 Dec. 1905 in (Atjeh, fiche no. 1) (MvK, PVBB); Resident Schaap telegram no. 353 (to Medan, 20 July 1904), in (Sumatra Oostkust, fiche no. 159) (MvK, PVBB); ARA, Dutch Consul, Singapore to Col Sec, SS, 24 Feb. 1887, no. 194, in MvBZ/A Dossiers/box 111/A.49ss.

12. ARA, *Manila Times,* 4 April 1899, in (MvBZ/A Dossiers/box 426/A.186).

13. J. A. Kruijt, *Atjeh en de Atjehers,* 97; Captain, *Citadel van Antwerpen,* to Dutch Consul, Penang, 15 June 1873, no. 37, and Captain *Metalen Kruis,* to Dutch Consul, Penang, 4 July 1874, no. 1932, both in PRO/FO/220/Oleh Oleh Consulate/vol. 11.

14. "Memorandum on the Alleged Smuggling of War into Acheen by the British Consul in Oleh Oleh," 6 Aug. 1883, in PRO/FO/220 /Oleh Oleh Consulate/1882–85/vol. 11; ANRI, Lavino to GGNEI, 20 June 1876, no. 98/G Confidential, in Aceh no. 14, "Stukken Betreffende Atjehsche Oorlog" no. 475–754, 1876.

15. ARA, Dutch Consul Penang to Dutch Consul Singapore, 19 Sept. 1873, no. 16, in MvK, Verbaal Geheim Kabinet 17 Dec. 1873, D33.

16. Asst. Res. Bataksche Aangelegenheden (Medan) to GGNEI, 14 April 1904, no. 1656/4, in (Sumatra Oostkust, fiche no. 157) (MvK, PVBB); ARNAS, Lavino to GGNEI, 9 Dec. 1875, no. 81/G, Confidential, in Kommissoriaal 4 Jan. 1876, no. 10az, in Aceh no. 12 "Stukken Betreffende Atjehsche Oorlog," 1876, no. 4–234.

17. Personal communication, Dr. Peter Boomgaard, former director, Koninklijke Instituut voor Taal-, Land-, en Volkenkunde (KITLV), Leiden, The Netherlands.

18. ARA, Dutch Consul Penang to Dutch Consul Singapore, 19 Sept. 1873, no. 16, in MvK, Verbaal Geheim Kabinet 17 Dec. 1873, D33; see "Buchanan v. Kirby (1870)," *Kyshe* 1 (1808–84): 230 passim; and "Attorney General v. Seven Barrels of Gunpowder (1890)," *Kyshe* 4 (1885–90): 688 passim.

19. "Memorandum on the Alleged Smuggling of War into Acheen by the British Consul in Oleh Oleh," 6 Aug. 1883, in PRO/FO/220 /Oleh Oleh Consulate/1882–85/vol. 11.

20. ARA, Dutch Consul, Madrid, to MvBZ, 30 May 1898, no. 198/86, and "The Rights of Belligerents and Neutrals," in *The Times of London,* 19 May 1898, both in (MvBZ/A Dossiers/box 426/A.186).

21. ARA, MvBZ to Hudig en Blokhuijzen, Rotterdam, 24 May 1898, A/186, in (MvBZ/A Dossiers/box 426/A.186).

22. The use of coal as fuel for warships made it a highly problematic article, especially around the time of the Russo-Japanese War in 1904–05. The vagaries of the matter led to some ships being attacked because they had coal cargoes on board, while in other places seamen sometimes refused to serve on freighters carrying coal cargoes, for fear of losing their lives. These trends took place all over the Asian sea lanes, from Japan to the Philippines and down to Singapore. See Gov HK to Col Sec, 9 Sept. 1904, no. 4915/34; British Consul, Tokyo to FO, 20 July 1904, no. 44; HK Harbor Master to Col Sec, 23 Nov. 1904, no. 39378/45; Gov HK to Col Sec, 7 Nov. 1904, no. 41763/49; Gov HK to Col Sec, 20 April 1905, no. 13272/54 telegram, and Gov SS to Col Sec, 26 May 1905, no. 17927/58, all in CO 882/Eastern Print, no. 94, HK/Straits.

23. Dynamite was also used for railway construction, road building, mineral exploration, and other purposes. See *SSLCP,* "Papers Laid Before the Legislative Council, Thursday 24 July 1879: Regulations Under the 'Gunpowder Ordinance, 1868', no. 8, for the Safe Landing, Storage, and Removal of Dynamite"; Gov Labuan to CO, 10 Oct. 1884, no. 83, in CO 144/58; see also "Rules Made by the Governor in Council to Regulate the Manufacture, Use, Sale, Storage, Transport, Importation, and Exportation of Explosive Substances," in *SSLCP,* 13 June 1899, C231 passim.

24. Staatsblad 1893, no. 234; 1894, no. 224; 1902, no. 206; 1904, no. 3; 1907, no. 318; 1908, no. 308. See also ""Reglement op den Invoer, het Bezit den Aanmaak, het Vervoer en het Gebruik van Ontplofbare Stoffen," 13–23, in *Verzameling van Voorschriften ten Dienste van Havenmeesters* (1906).

25. Shire Line Steamer Company to Marine Dept, Board of Trade, 2 Dec. 1907, in PRO/ Board of Trade/MT Series/MT 10: Harbour Department, Correspondence and Papers (1864–1919).

26. "Copy of Minutes Relating to the Arms Act, Labuan Session no. 1 of 1866, Tuesday, May 8th, Statement of the Colonial Treasurer," in CO 144/25; Gov Labuan to CO, 22 April 1865, no. 6, in CO 144/24.

27. ARA, "Regina v. Mahabod," Criminal Assizes 1887, 14 March, in *Straits Times,* 15 March 1887, all in (MvBZ/A Dossiers/box 111/A.49SS/"Uitvoerverbod . . .").

28. See Onreat, *Singapore: A Police Background,* 145.

29. ARA, Director of Finances to GGNEI, 2 Aug. 1870, Secret H, in (MvK, Verbaal 7 Oct.

1870, La Q13 Kab.); ARA, GGNEI to MK, 13 Aug. 1870, no. 1006/8, in (MvK, Verbaal 7 Oct. 1870, La Q13 Kab.)

30. ARA, MK to GGNEI, 29 Aug. 1869, La D13/Y Kab Vertr., in (MvK, Verbaal 20 Aug. 1869, La D13/Y Kab Vertr.); ARA, MK to GGNEI, 25 Aug. 1869, La M13/A1 Vertr., and Minister of Finance to MK, 20 Aug. 1869, no. 84 Secret, both in (MvK, Verbaal 25 Aug. 1869, La M13/A1 Vertr.)

31. *Straits Times,* 14 July 1888, 3; Dutch Consul, Singapore to British Consul, Oleh Oleh, 17 Feb. 1883, in PRO/FO/220/Oleh Oleh Consulate/vol. 11.

32. Leys (Administrator, Labuan) to CO, 25 Nov. 1885, no. 67, in CO 144/59; Gov Aceh to British Consul Oleh Oleh, 4 Aug. 1883, no. 1382, in PRO/FO/220/Oleh Oleh Consulate/vol. 11.

33. ARA, Dutch Consul, Singapore to MvBZ, Hague, 18 Dec. 1882, no. 729, and Dutch Consul, Penang, to GGNEI, 29 Dec. 1881, both in (MvBZ/A Dossiers/box 111/A.49SS/ "Uitvoerverbod . . ."); ARA, Kapt. Bogaart, *Timor,* to Military Commander in Aceh, 1 Aug. 1873, no. 4, in MvK, Verbaal 17 Dec. 1873, D33; ARA, 1897 MR no. 146.

34. ANRI, Dutch Consul Singapore to GGNEI, 18 May 1876, Confidential, in 20 June 1876, no. 469az, in Aceh no. 13, "Stukken Betreffende Atjehsche Oorlog," 1876, no. 235–469, 1876; Captain, *Metalen Kruis,* to Dutch Consul, Penang, 14 Feb. 1875, no. 1456, in PRO/ FO/220/Oleh Oleh/vol. 11.

35. *Straits Times,* 17 July 1888, 3; British Consul, Oleh Oleh to Gov Aceh, 21 Aug. 1883, no. 444, and First Gov't Secretary Batavia to British Consul, Oleh-Oleh, 17 Sept. 1883, no. 1494, both in PRO/FO/220/Oleh Oleh Consulate/vol. 11.

36. British Consul Oleh Oleh to Gov SS, 15 May 1883, no. 238, in PRO/FO/220/Oleh Oleh Consulate/vol. 11.

37. ANRI, Lavino to GGNEI, 2 Aug. 1876, no. 102/G, in Kommissoriaal 1 Sept. 1876, no. 635az, in Aceh no. 14 "Stukken Betreffende Atjehsche Oorlog," no. 475–734, 1876.

38. ANRI, Lavino to Sec. Gen. NEI, 2 April 1875, no. 166 Confidential, in Aceh no. 8, Atjehsche Verslagen 1874–75; ARA, Dutch Consul, Singapore to Col. Sec., SS, 24 Feb. 1887, no. 194, and Dutch Consul, Singapore to Col Sec SS, 18 March 1887, no. 249, both in (MvBZ/A Dossiers/box 111/A.49SS/"Uitvoerverbod . . .").

39. See "Alexander von Roessing v. Regina" *SSLR,* 1905, 9: 21, 24.

40. See the debate over the Arms Exportation Bill in *SSLCP,* 21 Dec. 1887, B199–200; "Arms Exportation Ordinance Amendment Bill," *SSLCP,* 1891, B79.

41. See FMS Enactment no. 4, 1902, which deals with permits, licenses, informers, rewards, and even compulsory markings on firearms so that they could be identified and tracked. *Perak Gov't Gazette,* 1902, 616–22.

42. See W. B. Pryer's Diary at Sandakan, 31 March 1878, in CO/874/vol. 67/Resident's Diaries.

43. Kruijt, *Atjeh en de Atjehers,* 98–99; ARA, GGNEI to Gov Labuan, 11 Dec. 1882, no. 41, in 1882, MR no. 1222, and ARA, Resident Sumatra East Coast to GGNEI, 22 Sept. 1883, La R7, Secret, in 1883, MR no. 888; ARA, GGNEI to Gov SS, 22 June 1881, no. 1 Confidential, in (MvK, Verbaal 18 Oct. 1881, A3/no. 15; 8594).

44. ARA, Kapt. Bogaart, *Timor,* to Military Commander in Aceh, 1 Aug. 1873, no. 4, and 26 April 1873, no. 21, both in MvK, Verbaal 17 Dec. 1873, D33; Captain of the *Zeeland* to

Dutch Consul, Penang, 20 April 1874, no. 732, and "Memorandum on the Alleged Smuggling of War into Acheen by the British Consul in Oleh Oleh," 6 Aug. 1883, both in PRO/FO/220 /Oleh Oleh Consulate/1882–85/vol. 11.

45. Memorandum of Pangeran Shahbandar, Muara Damit, 11 Jan. 1897, in CO 144/71.

46. ARA, Dutch Consul Singapore to General Secretary, Buitenzorg, 25 Oct. 1881, no. 646 Secret, in (MvK, Verbaal 7 Aug. 1894, no. 20); ARA, 1886, MR no. 608; ANRI, Dutch Consul Singapore to GGNEI, 18 May Confidential, in Kommissoriaal 20 June 1876, no. 469az, in Aceh no. 13, "Stukken Betreffende Atjehsche Oorlog," no. 235–469, 1876; ARA, 1891, MR no. 972; ARA, Dutch Consul, Bangkok to MvBZ, 27 Nov. 1882, in MvBZ/A Dossiers/box 111/A.49ss.

47. ANRI, Dutch Consul Singapore to GGNEI, 18 May Confidential, in Kommissoriaal 20 June 1876, no. 469az, in Aceh no. 13, "Stukken Betreffende Atjehsche Oorlog," no. 235–469, 1876; ARA, Dutch Consul Singapore to General Secretary, Buitenzorg, 25 Oct. 1881, no. 646 Secret, in (MvK, Verbaal 7 Aug. 1894, no. 20).

48. See ARA, Resident Sumatra East Coast to GGNEI, 22 Sept. 1883, La R7, Secret, in 1883, MR no. 888; many other sources show these activities being carried out. Also see ARA, Dutch Consul, Singapore to GGNEI, 12 Feb. 1887; Dutch Consul, Singapore to Acting Gov, Labuan, 18 July 1879, no. 531; same to same, 24 Oct. 1879, no. 792, all in (MvBZ/A Dossiers/box 111/A.49SS/"Uitvoerverbod . . ."); ARA, 1877, MR no. 287; ARA, 1886, MR no. 487, 568, 72A, 166; "Regina on the Prosecution of E. H. Bell, Respondent, v. John Burnett Paige, Appellant," in *SSLR,* 1894, 2:84 passim.

49. This proclamation, dated 22 Jan. 1885, is under cover of ARA, Siamese Minister of Foreign Affairs to Dutch Consul, Bangkok, 28 Jan. 1885, in MvBZ/A Dossiers/box 111/A.49ss.

50. See, for example, MvBZ to MK, 8 Jan. 1883, Afd 1, no. 113; Dutch Consul, Bangkok, to Dutch Consul, Singapore, 21 Oct. 1882, no. 356 and Siamese Private Secretary to Dutch Consul, Bangkok, 1 Nov. 1882, all in MvBZ/A Dossiers/box 111/A.49ss.

51. See, for example, ARA, Dutch Consul, Penang to GGNEI, 29 Dec. 1881, in (MvBZ/A Dossiers/box 111/A.49SS/"Uitvoerverbod . . .").

52. ARA, Siamese Minister for Foreign Affairs to Dutch Consul, Bangkok, 2 March 1882; Dutch Consul, Singapore to General Secretary, Buitenzorg, 25 Oct. 1881, no. 646 Secret; Dutch Consul, Bangkok to GGNEI, 12 Sept. 1882, no. 291, all in (MvK, Verbaal 7 Aug. 1894, no. 20).

53. ARA, GGNEI to Dutch Consul, Bangkok, 6 Jan. 1882, no. 7; Dutch Consul, Bangkok to GGNEI, 12 Sept. 1882, no. 292, both in (MvK, Verbaal 7 Aug. 1894, no. 20).

54. "Kapitan kapal api yang bernama Singapura itu khabarnya telah didenda $10 oleh hakim mahkamah wakil kerajaan Inggeris di Bangkok Siam karna membawa masok kasitu lima laras senapang dan obat bedil." *Utusan Malayu,* 1 Feb. 1908, 1.

55. "Memorandum on the Alleged Smuggling of War into Acheen by the British Consul in Oleh Oleh," 6 Aug. 1883, in PRO/FO/220 /Oleh Oleh Consulate/1882–85/vol. 11.

56. ARA, Loose sheet in front of the logbooks of the *Metalen Kruis,* no. 3108–09, reading "Process Verbaal," 17 August 1875, signed by Capt. and Quartermaster, telling that rifle no. 2988 of sailor 3rd class C. Koetelink fell overboard. (Ministerie van Marine, 2.12.03.)

57. ARNAS, Algemeene en Administratieve Verslag der Residentie Palembang 1886 (Palembang no. 65/6); ARA, telegram to Gov Gen NEI, sent via Penang 9/6/1885 (MvK); Res-

ident Deli to Gov Gen NEI, 12 March 1904, telegram no. 117, in (Sumatra Oostkust, fiche no. 156) (MvK, PVBB).

58. ARA, Controleur Djambi to Resident Palembang, 13 Nov. 1880, Ltt. W, in 1880, MR no. 999; ARA, 1881, MR no. 86, 169, 281; and ARA, Resident Palembang to Gov Gen NEI, 3 Jan. 1881, Ltt.B, in 1881, MR no. 33.

59. "Remarks by C. V. Creagh on the Proposed Customs Excise and Inland Revenue Consolidating Proclamation," 11 Jan. 1892, in CO/874/box 207.

60. ARA, "Nota ter Beantwoording van Sommige Punten . . ." in (MvK, Verbaal 16 Feb. 1880, A3/no. 2; 1299).

61. Dutch Consul, Singapore to British Consul, Oleh Oleh, 17 Feb. 1883, in PRO/FO/220/ Oleh Oleh Consulate/vol. 11; see also Melaka's arms imports, *SSBB*, 1873, 463.

62. *Straits Times,* 6 July 1888, 3.

63. "Memorandum on the Alleged Smuggling of War into Acheen by the British Consul in Oleh Oleh," 6 Aug. 1883, in PRO/FO/220 /Oleh Oleh Consulate/1882–85/vol. 11.

64. ARA, "Nota aan de Gouverneur van Atjeh," (n.d) in (MvK, Verbaal 24 Jan. 1884, A3/no. 28; 929).

65. ANRI, Extract of Lavino to GGNEI, 5 Sept. 1873, no. 15, in Kommissoriaal 15 April 1875, no. 374az, in Aceh no. 8, "Atjehsche Verslagen 1874–75."

66. "Memorandum on the Alleged Smuggling of War into Acheen by the British Consul in Oleh Oleh," 6 Aug. 1883, in PRO/FO/220 /Oleh Oleh Consulate/1882–85/vol. 11.

67. ANRI, Lavino to GGNEI, 5 July 1876, no. 100/G, in Kommissoriaal 21 August no. 607az, in Aceh no. 14, "Stukken Betreffende Atjehsche Oorlog," no. 475–754, 1876; ANRI, Dutch Consul Singapore to GGNEI, 8 June 1876, Confidential, in Kommissoriaal 10 Oct. 1876, no. 459az, in Aceh no. 13, "Stukken Betreffende Atjehsche Oorlog," 1876, no. 235–469, 1876.

68. ARA, GGNEI to MvK, 18 Aug. 1881, no. 1494/9, in (MvK, Verbaal 30 Sept. 1881, A3/no. 4, 8028); ARA, MvBZ to MvK, 5 Feb. 1881, no. 965; British Consul, Hague to MvBZ, 1 Feb. 1881; William Cann, Master of the "Batara Bayon Sree" to Col Sec, Singapore, 3 Nov. 1880; Decision of High Court of Justice, Makassar, 15 Sept. 1880; Petition of Gwee Kim Soon, Part Owner of the *Batara Bayon Sree,* to Gov SS, 6 Aug. 1880; GGNEI to Gov SS, 12 July 1880, no. 22, all in (MvK, Verbaal 17 Feb. 1881, no. 33/298); ARA, Station-Commandant, Celebes, to Commander NEI Navy, 7 Aug. 1879, no. 1113, in 1879, MR no. 501; and ARA, Captain of the *Batara Baijan Sree* to Singapore Master Attendant, 18 Aug. 1879, in 1879, MR no. 725.

69. ARA, Dutch Consul, Singapore, to GGNEI, 21 Nov. 1884, no. 732, in 1884, no. 732, in 1884, MR no. 738; ARA, Dutch Consul, Singapore to Acting Col Sec, SS, 17 Nov. 1884, no. 722, in 1884, MR no. 722.

70. ARA, Dutch Consul, Singapore to Acting Col Sec, SS, 21 Nov. 1884, no. 731, in 1884, MR no. 738; ARA, Dutch Consul, Singapore, to Sec. Gen., Buitenzorg, 19 Dec. 1884, no. 805, in 1884, MR no. 817.

71. ARA, "Verbod op den Uitvoer van Wapenen . . ." (n.d) in (MvK, Verbaal 16 July 1900, Kab Litt. T9; 7826).

72. See CO to Gov SS, 16 May 1873, and CO to Gov SS, 23 Sept. 1873, both in PRO/Admiralty/125/China Station: Correspondence [no. 140: The Straits of Malacca and Siam].

73. ANRI, Lavino to GGNEI, 9 Dec. 1875, no. 81/G Confidential, in Kommissoriaal 4 Jan. 1876, no. 10az, in Aceh no. 12, "Stukken Betreffende Atjehsche Oorlog," no. 4–234, 1876.

74. ANRI, Lavino to GGNEI, 11 May 1876, no. 94G Confidential, in Kommissoriaal 15 June 1976, no. 458az, in Aceh no. 13, "Stukken Betreffende Atjehsche Oorlog," no. 235–469, 1876.

75. Kruijt, *Atjeh en de Atjehers*, 53.

76. "Statement Furnished by the Dutch Consul at Penang of Arms and Ammunition Exported From Penang to Sumatra During the Year 1882 [Principally—If Not Entirely—to Supply 'Friendly' Chiefs," 1883, and "Total of the Arms and Ammunition Exported From Penang to Sumatra During 1882, According to Statistics Compiled by the Harbor Master at Penang," 1883, both in PRO/FO/220/Oleh Oleh/vol. 11.

77. "A List of Cases of Smuggling Compiled in August 1882 by Mr. van Langen, then Assistant Resident on the West Coast of Acheen," Aug. 1882, in PRO/FO/220/Oleh Oleh Consulate/vol. 11.

78. British Consul, Oleh Oleh to Major McNair, Penang, 26 Sept. 1883, no. 541, in PRO/FO/220/Oleh Oleh/vol. 11.

79. "The contraband trade has, hitherto, been carried out with such impunity, that fitful seizures will only make the smugglers more cautious. They will devise fresh means to baulk the law, and defeat the ends of justice." *Straits Times,* 10 July 1888, 3.

80. ARA, Commander of NEI Marine to Gov Gen NEI, 29 April 1885, no. 4623, in (MvK, Verbaal 2 Oct. 1885, Kab. B11).

81. ANRI, Lavino to GGNEI, 30 March 1875, no. 165, in Kommissoriaal 15 April 1875, no. 374az, in Aceh no. 8 "Atjehsche Versagen 1874–75."

82. ARA, Resident Sumatra East Coast to GGNEI, 22 Sept. 1883, La R17, Secret, in 1883, MR no. 888.

83. Gov Aceh to GGNEI, 24 Nov. 1905, telegram no. 921, and same to same, 27 Nov. 1905, telegram no. 927, both in (Atjeh, fiche no. 1) (MvK, PVBB).

84. *Javasche Courant,* 12 Dec. 1905, no. 99, and Gov Aceh to GGNEI, 16 Dec. 1905, telegram no. 962, both in (Atjeh, fiche no. 1) (MvK, PVBB).

85. "Copy of Minutes Relating to the Arms Act, Labuan Session no. 1 of 1866, Tuesday May 8th," Colonial Surgeon's Testimony, in CO 144/25.

86. Gov Labuan to CO, 29 June 1866, no. 16 in CO 144/25; Gov Labuan to CO, 22 April 1865, no. 6; Gov Labuan to CO, 29 June 1866, no. 16, in CO 144/25.

87. Warren, *The Sulu Zone,* see 129 passim.

88. William Pretyman's Diary at Tempasuk, 12 Dec. and 28 Feb. 1879, in CO/874/vol. 72/Resident's Diaries.

89. Mr. Everett's Journal at Papar, 27 April 1880 and 6 Oct. 1879, both in CO/874/vol. 73/Resident's Diaries.

90. "Remarks by C. V. Creagh on the Proposed Customs Excise and Inland Revenue Consolidating Proclamation," 11 Jan. 1892, in CO/874/box 207.

91. Gov Labuan to CO, 16 June 1880, no. 53, in CO/144/53; CO Jacket, 30 Nov. 1881, no. 86, in CO 144/55; CO to BNB HQ, London, 28 March 1882, and CO Jacket, 6 July 1882, both in CO 144/56..

92. Gov BNB to CO, 31 1884, no. 92; CO Jacket, 23 Oct. 1884; and CO to Gov BNB, 31 Oct. 1884, all in CO 144/58.

93. Gov Labuan to CO, 4 Sept. 1882, no. 56.

94. "Protocol Relative to the Sulu Archipelago, Signed at Madrid by the Representatives of Great Britain, Germany, and Spain on 7 March 1885," Article 4, in CO 144/71.

95. British Envoy, Madrid to FO, 30 March 1897, in CO 144/71.

96. ARA, Chinese Neutrality Decree, Tsungli Yamen, 9 May 1898; Proclamation of Neutrality by Netherlands India (in *Javasche Courant,* 26 April 1898), and Proclamation of Neutrality by the Straits Settlements (in *SSGG,* 25 April 1898), all in (MvBZ/A Dossiers/box 426/A.186).

97. See *Javasche Courant,* 29 April 1898, in (MvBZ/A Dossiers/box 426/A.186).

98. ARA, Dutch Consul, Manila "Report over the Months March and April, 1902," in (MvBZ/A Dossiers/box 426/A.186); Warren, *The Sulu Zone,* 129–30; *New York Herald,* 27 Sept. 1898; *Manila Times,* 4 April 1899, all in (MvBZ/A Dossiers/box 426/A.186). Some of the arms were coming to Aguinaldo and the members of the Filipino independence movement from Hong Kong and other northern ports.

99. ARA, Dutch Minister, Navy to Directors and Commanders, Dutch Ministry, Marine, May 1898, Circulaire no. 261, in (MvBZ/A Dossiers/box 426/A.186).

Section V A Frontier Story: The Sorrows of Golam Merican

The Harbour Master assures me that little reliance can be placed in the accuracy of returns given by Chinese and Natives. They have the entire Acheen trade in their hands, and frequently have motives for not stating the actualities of the goods they ship or receive.
—Dutch Consul Lavino, Penang, to Governor-General, Netherlands East Indies, 21 June 1876, #991G, ANRI

Chapter 13 Contraband and
the Junk *Kim Ban An*

The final two chapters in this book examine smuggling across colonial borders on an intimate scale, but from a vantage that is dependent on macrohistorical processes already discussed. Many of the issues encountered earlier in this book reappear here: the role of ethnicity in contrabanding, for example; the mechanisms of avoidance utilized by smugglers; and how legal structures were used by both smugglers and colonial states. But these phenomena resurface now within the confines of a single case. Sailing out of Penang in June 1873, the Chinese junk *Kim Ban An* was caught off the Acehnese coast two months later by a steamship of the gathering Dutch blockade. The court case which followed the *Kim Ban An*'s seizure gives an unparalleled glimpse into the lives and contexts of smugglers and their enemies, as the matter of this little ship wound its way through judicial, political, and personal circumstances for over twenty-five years. In doing so, the case left an abundance of records, some in the smugglers' own voices, giving various sides of an intricate story. Contrabanding, alliance, diplomacy, and the law all played a part in the eventual outcome of the case. These last two chapters examine smuggling and the crossing of colonial borders from ground-level, therefore. The trial of the *Kim Ban An* sheds light on how smuggling was defined and how that definition changed in the decades leading up to the turn of the twentieth century.

A MARITIME FRONTIER

The broad, shallow Straits of Melaka separated the historical Sultanate of Aceh on the northern tip of Sumatra from Penang and its adjacent coasts on the western littoral of Malaysia. Aceh had been for some time, by the late nineteenth century, one of the strongest polities in the Malay world. Two centuries earlier, the sultanate had been known as the "verandah of Mecca" for its close ties with the Arabian Peninsula, to which many Acehnese and other archipelago pilgrims sailed every year.[1] Aceh imported armaments from Ottoman Turkey and had emissaries in many other parts of Southeast Asia (and even in India, for a time), making it one of the most international powers in Southeast Asia's Age of Commerce. Yet the sultanate was also vital internally as well, boasting stone observatories to watch the movements of stars and other astral phenomena and a system of advancement in politics and the military which allowed women to assume distinguished roles in the state.[2] A rugged, mountainous interior gave way on the coasts to long stretches of beach, which were often calm and suitable for trade in the Straits and hit by thunderous surf from the open Indian Ocean on the western shoreline of the realm.

Penang, a British trade outpost established off the coast of the Malay Peninsula in 1786, was situated on the opposite end of this huge waterway (map 7). Originally a naval and trade/watering base for British ships on their way to China, Penang by the late nineteenth century had already seen its heyday and was dwarfed by Singapore as a metropolis in the region. Nevertheless, the port had adapted well as a feeder entrepôt for the northern part of the Straits, connecting coasting and even some longer-distance trade between Siam, Sumatra, India, and the shores of the Malay Peninsula. Its population was extremely multiethnic, Bengalis, Boyanese, Bugis, Burmese, Javanese, Chinese, and many other "races" all interacting in the port.[3] Agricultural laborers, seamen, carpenters, merchants, and administrators worked side by side in the harbor and the neighboring plantations, so that the city had a degree of multifunctionality somewhat out of proportion to its small size.[4] A huge range of currencies was in active circulation in the port, rendering commerce accessible and desirable, even to merchants and traders from far afield. Penang was a crossroads for the eastern Indian Ocean: sophisticated and well managed, it knew its strengths in

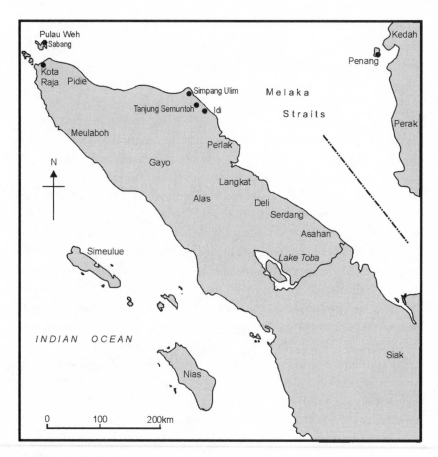

Aceh, the Straits of Melaka, and Penang

the functioning of the regional economy and marketed these to area peoples very successfully. The local Course of Exchange listed pounds sterling, Dutch guilders, and Mexican dollars daily, plugging the port into the markets of places even further outside of the region.[5]

The mainstay of Penang's trade, however, was North Sumatra, with the coasts of Aceh being most important of all. Here too the commerce was international, with several currencies being accepted for shipments of local agricultural produce, even in very small ports.[6] In the first few months of the year, most of the European cargoes, such as textiles, iron, brass, glassware, and manufactured goods, were landed in the Acehnese harbors.[7] Later in the year, starting in April but especially in May, June, and July, much of Aceh's pepper and betel cargoes would be ready for transshipment, often via Penang, to the wider

markets of the world.[8] Salina Binti Haji Zainol has provided an in-depth discussion of the history of this trade across the Straits in the first two-thirds of
the nineteenth century, showing the dimensions and mechanics of contacts
since the founding of Singapore. Although her narrative harkens back to the
seventeenth-century Acehnese Golden Age, providing descriptions of Iskandar
Muda's prosperous reign, the real value of this work is its attention to nineteenth-
century trade patterns, when Penang and Aceh became integrated into one
system. Her study shows clearly how pepper, tobacco, cloth, and coolies were
pressed into a single commercial orbit, linked by cash advances and steamships
and driven by fierce competition.[9] By the 1860s, actors of many ethnicities were
involved in this trade, plying back and forth between Aceh and Penang with the
regularity of the tides.[10]

As in other parts of the archipelago, however, certain groups drove commerce more relentlessly than others. In the northern waters of the Straits of
Melaka, two ethnic networks, Chinese traders and Muslim Indians, were most
visible. Period accounts of the Acehnese coasts paint a picture of Chinese
traders being nearly omnipresent in all commercial dealings; the Chinese community, mainly from the Straits Settlements, but some resident in Aceh itself,
were involved as merchants, chandlers, middlemen, and shippers, dotting the
length of the shore in significant numbers. There was a large Chinese community at Idi, one of Batavia's principal allies in Aceh; many of the traders here had
warehouses and shops, while others, such as a local revenue farming syndicate,
made large sums of money running trade across the Straits.[11] At times, the Chinese appear to have lost sizable amounts of money too, however, as happened
with the Penang firm Tek Wat, which was nearly $250,000 in debt in 1876,
partly as a result of the Aceh war.[12] Many Dutchmen looked askance at the
Chinese communities on these coasts, seeing them as parasites who essentially
made a living cheating the Acehnese pepper growers through the vagaries of an
advance-payment system.[13] Local Chinese also were used by the Dutch, however, for Batavia's own purposes: Toh Thing Hi of Penang, who had long experience as a trader in Aceh, was brought along by the Dutch fleet on surveying
missions of the coasts.[14] In December 1875, some Chinese even offered to help
the Dutch by providing troops in the fight against the Acehnese, though there
is no record the offer was ever accepted.[15]

South Indian Muslims were also very active in cross-Straits trade. Like the
Chinese, South Indians had been migrating and conducting commerce in these
shallow waters since the early centuries of the first millennium A.D. Muslims
from the Coromandel coasts of southeastern India had long since intermarried

into local Malay families on both sides of the frontier, though there were still distinct communities of more direct migratory Indian origin in certain places such as Penang. In much of the European literature on these trading minorities, the communities were called "Chulias" or "Klings," though the segments of the population who intermarried with local Malays usually called themselves Jawi Peranakan. Members of the original emigrating merchant families from South India as well as the mixed population of Jawi Peranakan seem to have been important players in the earliest community in Penang in the late eighteenth century. They provided a crucial connective function both to South India, where a fair portion of Penang's immigration and trade was centered, and to the local Malay communities on the Malay Peninsula and Sumatra coasts, where even more of this economic activity could be found. One founding member of the original South Indian migration of Penang, Kader Mydin Merican, was particularly important in establishing this community as an important component of Penang's economic society. He arrived with Francis Light at the colony's founding in 1786, and his descendants were trading extensively in the region by the late nineteenth century.[16]

The normal system of trade in this entire arena, between regions long accustomed to seasonal patterns of commerce and among groups such as the Chinese and South Indian Muslims long accustomed to facilitating these transactions, was massively disrupted in early 1873. Batavia's slow imperial crawl up the length of Sumatra had finally reached Aceh by this time; as the last major sultanate on the island not yet under Dutch sway, Aceh's days of independence were now clearly numbered.[17] Yet the first assault on Aceh, in March of that year, was beaten back by ferocious resistance.[18] The Dutch lost many men to Acehnese bravery and the intensity of the defense, but they also lost soldiers to rampant sickness (especially beriberi), and because of their overconfidence and disorganization.[19] The Acehnese had no navy capable of vying with the Dutch for control of regional seas, but the sultanate's fishing boats and trade ships were converted into a "guerrilla fleet," and these small ships harassed the Dutch ships in the early days of the war. Furthermore, Acehnese batteries near Kota Raja, the capital, and on the eastern coast interfered with Dutch capabilities of supply, forcing Batavia's fleet to stay well clear of the shoreline, thereby giving the Acehnese a large advantage.[20] The British sent ships to observe the conduct of hostilities, but after only a short while it had become clear that something almost unthinkable had happened. The massed forces of the Dutch East Indies army had lost the initial engagement against the Acehnese.[21] As word of the defeat spread throughout the Malay world and back to the Dutch public in Java and the Netherlands, Batavia's planners took a deep breath and pondered their next move.

Why had the Dutch not done better in the initial assault upon Aceh? How could a traditional sultanate manage to hold off the armed might of a Western power, even if Holland was by this time one of the lesser European nations? Perhaps most important, why had the Dutch not been better prepared for what turned out to be a bloody and remorseless battle on as island they had already known for centuries? These are questions that have occupied Dutch and Indonesian historians for decades, though different scholars have put forward different causal explanations for what was certainly seen as an unmitigated disaster in the Netherlands and an epic success in North Sumatra.[22] The first major victory of an Asian power over a European one in battle has traditionally been ascribed to the Russo-Japanese War of 1904–05, yet historiography concerned with imperialism would do well to predate this achievement to Aceh, some thirty years before the North Pacific conflict. Aceh's victory is even more impressive if it is acknowledged that the Acehnese accomplished what the Japanese also managed in the early twentieth century, but without the benefit of a modernizing, well-equipped military. The vast majority of Aceh's resources were completely outdated when compared to the martial capabilities of the Netherlands: none of their equipment was standardized, and few of their soldiers had any training in the warfare tactics of the day. Yet the Acehnese fought with a tenacity and a conviction that surprised the Dutch, though it would become a hallmark of this region's resistance to any kind of colonial rule—by Europeans or others—for at least a century to come.

For the Dutch, the defeat of early 1873 was a psychological blow as well as a challenge to their armed might in the archipelago. The Netherlands Indies had been slowly growing outside of its core islands, Java and Madura, for some decades by 1873, but this advancing tide of European influence had never come up against an enemy like the Acehnese. The sultanate was larger and more populous than previous victims of Batavia's expansion, and it had a longer history of martial prowess and large-scale organizational endeavor than any other indigenous polity in the region. Moreover, as I noted earlier in this book, Aceh was seen as a test case by many of the autochthonous sultans and rajas who still enjoyed their independence or semi-independence throughout the Malay world. The Acehnese knew they were being watched by others who would soon be in their position, and seem to have fought not only for themselves but also under a banner of Islam which was regional in orientation. Stumbling at this juncture, in full view not only of regional Asian kingdoms, but also before the increasingly aggressive powers of Europe, was not an option for most military planners in The Hague, therefore. Something would have to be done, and done quickly, to maintain the Netherlands' prestige both in Southeast Asia and before Holland's voracious neighbors at home.[23]

A new fleet would have to be raised and significantly more manpower assembled in order to defeat the Acehnese. This would take time, however, and the necessary forces did not arrive in Aceh for the second great assault until the end of the year. In the meantime, however, a window had opened, a period during which the two sides drew up strategies and plans. For the Acehnese, it was imperative to get as many war supplies as soon as possible, as it was evident to everyone that a second, much more concerted attack was certainly on the way. For Batavia, the hiatus would be needed to mass the new invasion force, but this was also a pause in which the Dutch needed to deny Aceh as many of the above supplies as possible. A blockade along the entire Aceh coast was instituted soon after the failed assault. From the very beginning of the blockade, though, the smuggling of arms, opium, pepper, and just about anything else that could either help in the war effort or provide cash to buy weapons was rampant.[24] The Dutch knew this through their system of spies in the Straits Settlements, and they also knew the carefully tabulated trade statistics that monitored these movements were very often wrong. The laissez-faire free trade policies of the British settlements ensured this, but the fact there was so much profit to be made now in running contraband across the Straits also contributed to this state of affairs.[25] The Dutch needed to staunch the flow of smuggling, and they needed to do so quickly. Yet how could this be done when Batavia as yet possessed no toehold on the Aceh coasts? What means could be utilized to prevent contraband cargoes from arriving? Perhaps most important of all, how could the Dutch draw a net around the Acehnese state and then suffocate it by denying the population the means to carry out resistance?

SETTING SAIL (JUNE 1873)

On June 26 and 27, 1873, several weeks after the Dutch blockade of Aceh had first been proclaimed, a group of traders in Penang agreed on a joint-venture voyage to pick up pepper on the Acehnese coast. The people involved in the journey mirrored the complicated ethnic mosaic of the Straits already discussed; the ship's crew and primary and secondary charterers were all from different groups, but had come together for the purpose of this voyage. Yeo Eng, a Chinese ship owner and British subject from Penang, provided the vessel, the *Kim Ban An,* a junk (or wangkang, depending on the description) of 85 tons. The firm of Lorrain Gillespie and Co., also based in Penang but with offices in Batavia and other harbors, was involved as well. This Anglo/Dutch concern signed onto the charter party for 360 piculs of Acehnese pepper to be delivered from the Aceh coast. Finally, the primary wholesaler of the voyage, a South Indian Muslim trader named Golam Meydinsah Merican, was also Penang-based and put in capital to procure an additional 700 piculs of Acehnese black pepper from the coast. The actual charterer of the ship was a man named George Tolson, a Dutchman from Lorrain Gillespie's Penang office who performed the negotiations for the vessel with Yeo Eng. The *Kim Ban An* was to sail for Tanjung Semuntoh on the Acehnese coast, stay up to ten days for loading, and then return home to Penang. Any duties, port, or other marine charges Yeo Eng was to pay; the tariffs on pepper or other agricultural cargoes were to be paid by the charterers. On Friday, June 27, the *Kim Ban An* pulled out of the Penang roads, setting sail for Sumatra.[26]

The eastern part of the Aceh coastline where the *Kim Ban An* was headed had a fairly long history of pepper production by this time. Pepper had been planted there starting in the early part of the nineteenth century; the proceeds generated by this product accrued to the local *uleebalang,* or princes, who in turn were taxed through a complicated system by the sultan of Aceh in Kota Raja. The reality of power, distance, and communications on the ground, however, made matters such that the local uleebalang enjoyed considerable independence from the sultan, even during the best of times. The twelve thousand square kilometers of this part of the coast was producing approximately one hundred thousand piculs of pepper annually by 1873, most of which went in small boats across the Straits to Penang. These cargo revenues made the *uleebalang* along this stretch of coast quite wealthy by the 1870s, so that the beginning of the conflict, and especially the blockade, was a matter of no small importance to them. The princes stood to lose most of their income if trade was interrupted too seriously or for too long, in amounts that approached one hundred thousand guilders per year for some of them. Local economic interests, therefore, were inimical to the blockade from the beginning. Penang was the feeder entrepôt for East Aceh's pepper, and most uleebalang sought to get their cargoes there one way or another.[27]

Tanjung Semuntoh, the specific destination of the *Kim Ban An,* was one of the pepper-producing petty vassals of the Acehnese Sultanate on this stretch of coast. Though a considerable amount of pepper was produced on this shoreline by the local raja and his populace, a large store of enmity toward the Dutch also seems to have been manufactured, if contemporary accounts are any guide. When Teuku Paya, one of the leaders of the Acehnese war party, returned to Sumatra after traveling abroad, he often slipped into Tanjung Semuntoh, which was considered to be one of the more radically anti-Dutch of Aceh's small polities.[28] Vessels of the Dutch blockade patrolled the coastline of this region as often as possible, often anchoring offshore in the middle of the night in order to maintain a kind of permanent, concerted presence.[29] Despite this pressure, three years after the initial Dutch attack on Aceh, Tanjung Semuntoh was still flying its own flag and had not submitted to Batavia.[30] Indeed, some of the population of the nearby inland areas was busy digging canals to try to connect their river to other river systems so that their pepper could be slipped past the blockade.[31] When the Acehnese resistance wanted to mislead the Dutch as to where their war supplies were entering Aceh, in fact, Tanjung Semuntoh's capitulation was sometimes dangled as bait: several times the polity pretended to submit to Batavia, only to appear again as members of the war party shortly thereafter.[32]

It was into this arena that the *Kim Ban An* was sailing in June 1873. The Merican family, as noted, had a long and illustrious presence in the South Indian Muslim community in Penang. In addition to Kyder Mydin Merican, who had been present at the colony's founding in 1786, the large, multibranched Merican clan claimed Mohamad Merican Noordin as an ancestor. One of Penang's chief merchants in the 1830s, Noordin owned ships that traded salt, pepper, chandu, and cloth throughout the eastern Indian Ocean. The community ethos within the Chulia commercial network in Penang was very strong. Nevertheless, by the latter part of the nineteenth century, the Mericans were no longer solely merchants but had spread out into various other occupations as well.[33] They were involved in the building of mosques and in religious education in Penang; the first mosque on the island had been built by Kyder Mydin Merican in 1801, while the most famous (and still extant) mosque, the Kapitan Kling, was also constructed with heavy Merican involvement. Other Mericans were less fortunate and subsisted on charities dispensed by the religious trusts set up by other members of the family. By the early twentieth century, some Mericans were in provincial government, mining, and the state judiciary, while others continued to function as Islamic teachers and as merchants.[34]

One of the best ways to glimpse the Merican community in the period 1865–1915 is through Straits courts records, where the Mericans are abundantly represented. Members of the Merican clan seem to have constantly been entangled with the law, either as accusers or defendants or in disputes and arbitrations among themselves. Many of these filings were financial or commercial in nature: Mericans suing companies over damaged goods, other Mericans involved in excise transgressions, still others embroiled in cases of fraud on repayments.[35] At other times, members of the clan were involved in potentially more serious matters, such as poisonings of rivals and even large-scale brawls within the community.[36] The extended family was large enough and competition sometimes fierce enough that members of the clan even engaged in suits against each other, which happened on several occasions in the 1880s.[37] Yet the focus of the Merican lineage was not limited to internal, Penang-based matters. Members of the family also were involved in helping the Acehnese with their struggle against the Dutch, including transporting diplomatic pleas for help from the Aceh coast to the American envoy in Singapore. A Merican sent one of these letters through paid-off stewards on a German steamer, while others were secreted in butter tins aboard other vessels.[38] Golam Meydinsah Merican does not appear in any of these particular sources himself, as he seems to have been only a middle-level merchant within the community. He does not appear on the genealogy charts of the major family tree of Mericans of Penang.[39]

The trade situation when the *Kim Ban An* departed was already becoming highly unstable. Commerce across the Straits in ordinary times was massive and freewheeling: almost every kind of commodity was sold or bartered, down to many obscure items. Hides, woven mats, rattans for building furniture, and other plant fibers were routinely exported from Aceh, along with cotton, tobacco, and large quantities of livestock, principally goats but also smaller breeds of coastal ponies.[40] In the reverse direction, Straits Settlements merchants carried a wide range of goods to the Acehnese, including shoes, hats, umbrellas, roofing tiles, and paint. Metals like zinc, brass, copper, and iron were always in demand, while specialty products like gold leaf and even quicksilver, which was thought to have medicinal purposes and was often ingested as an invulnerability potion by the Acehnese, also made the trip.[41] These trading voyages were undertaken in the vessels of many nations, including Chinese junks, Malay perahus, square-rigged sailing craft, and European steamers. Penang's shipping statistics from 1873 show how channeled and directed the radials of commerce truly were: that year Penang received most of its incoming vessels from Singapore and Sumatra, while these two places were also the primary destinations of Penang's own trading ships[42] (table 10).

Yet the most important exports from the Acehnese coasts were pepper and to a lesser extent betel nut. Betel nut was sold in large quantities to traders from Penang but attracted coasting craft from as far away as southeastern India,

Table 10. Straits of Melaka Official Trade Statistics at the Time of the Kim Ban An's Voyage

I. *Shipping Statistics, Penang with Singapore and Sumatra, 1873*

Number, Tonnage, and Crews of Vessels Entering Penang, 1873:

Provenance	Tonnage	# of Crewmen	Number of Ships
Singapore	136,778	9,856	238
Sumatra	47,623	7,388	233

Number, Tonnage, and Crews of Vessels Leaving Penang, 1873:

Provenance	Tonnage	# of Crewmen	Number of Ships
Singapore	189,691	12,103	258
Sumatra	29,811	4,808	185

II. *Stated Trade Values, Penang to Sumatra, 1873–75*

Item (worth in $)	1873	1874	1875
Firearms	5,357	170	485
Gunpowder	6,145	0	48
Cartridges	210	65	112
Benares Opium	284,012	351,039	328,243
Persian Opium	8,444	16,434	17,295
Turkish Opium	3,300	3,500	31,125

*** The figures for the two tables above are for Sumatra as a whole. The blockade of Aceh greatly affected the geographies of export.

III. *Common Export Trade Items, Penang to Aceh, 1874–75*

Cloth, cotton goods, gold and silver thread, shoes, hats, belts, umbrellas, indigo, quicksilver, iron nails, zinc, brass wares, copper wares, matches, glassware, roofing tiles, Chinese stores, bricks, lime, paint, padlocks, Arabic books, Chinese paper, betel boxes, snuff boxes, kerosene oil, salt, sugarcane, tea, Chinese medicinals, perfume, soap, sundries, etc.

Sources: Adapted from ANRI, "Comparative Table of Exports From Penang to Acheen in 1874 and 1875", in Kommissoriaal 14 July 1876, #522az, in Aceh #14 "Stukken Betreffende Atjehsche Oorlog (1876)", #475–734; also *SBB* 1874, p. 493–6.

where it was used, as in many other places in South and Southeast Asia, as a mild narcotic. Acehnese betel fetched prices of $14 to $17 per three picul's weight in the mid–1870s and attracted about twenty vessels of 150–300 tons each annually to pick up the cargo.[43] Malay language letters from the 1870s show how important these cargoes were for area potentates; the raja of Pasangan asked the Dutch how they could be considered allies or friends as their contract stated if the Dutch would not return several of his impounded betel boats.[44] Yet pepper was the true mainstay of the northern Melaka Straits economy: it brought more ships and more merchants to the region than any other commodity. American clippers from New England had long been accustomed to sail to Sumatra for these pepper stores, and merchants from as far away as Italy also came, sometimes transporting 8,000 piculs a year to Mediterranean ports.[45] By the time the *Kim Ban An* sailed, Simpang Ulim, one of the most violently anti-Dutch states on the Aceh coast, was making more than a million guilders a year on pepper sales. Once the blockade started, however, the majority of these profits had to be earned by nighttime voyages. Dutch commanders of the blockade marveled at how Acehnese chiefs treated the smuggling of pepper almost as a game. Outwitting the patrol vessels became a test of one's cunning, and a chief's status went up commensurably with the success of these voyages.[46]

Bulk rice cargoes were another important item in the regional trade orbit. Rice export statistics from Penang to Aceh in the years around the *Kim Ban An*'s sailing show how massive this transit was: the numbers were always in the 1,000-*coyan* range from 1872 to 1875, though these figures were sometimes cut short during the most active months of the blockade, when rice could travel only to "open" ports.[47] Most of this rice was of Rangoon no. 1 quality, which fetched over $100 per coyan in the mid–1870s.[48] The bulk rice trade also underwent large changes as a result of the war, though rice had always been imported into Aceh, even before the outbreak of hostilities. The blockade doubled the price of rice in Aceh as opposed to Penang, while also giving rise to a range of new smuggling routes to get rice to the resistance.[49] Reports reached the Dutch that considerable quantities of rice were reaching the war party through various coastal polities, eventually transiting overland to Tanjung Semuntoh and Simpang Ulim. The raja of Pidië also seems to have been involved in these transactions, as shortly after he concluded an agreement with the Dutch to open his port, rice was being sent to members of the war party from that harbor as well.[50] Indeed, the passage of rice became a contentious issue in the Straits, as it would be elsewhere, including China in the 1880s, as many parties complained it was unfair to consider it "contraband of war." Fair or not, the Acehnese needed rice to survive and fight, a state of affairs the Dutch command knew very well. Other actors, including the charterers of the *Kim Ban An,* also seem to have understood this perfectly.

The final commodities of importance in this arena were opium and arms, each of which commanded large sums of money in these waters, even during normal times. Persian, Turkish, and Indian opium all traveled through the Straits Settlements and into the Indies; British and Dutch statistics of exactly how much opium was transiting though Penang and into Sumatra differ for the early 1870s, but each shows the amounts in the hundreds of chests every year.[51] Opium was a highly desired item in Aceh for several reasons: dispensing it often bonded retainers to uleebalangs or other princes, while it could also be sold for large profits, especially during wartime.

Yet it was the trafficking of arms to the Acehnese that truly distressed Batavia for the long term. This too was a normal commerce of ancient pedigree in the Straits, and it also underwent profound changes with the start of the conflict in early 1873. On March 31, 1873, as we have seen, Governor Harry Ord in Singapore had seen fit to ban all arms shipments to North Sumatra. This was done despite the misgivings of the Colonial Office, which advised Ord to be friendly to the Dutch but not to really help them against the Acehnese.[52] Ord's decree only strengthened the cat-and-mouse seizure game the Dutch marine forces would play with arms smugglers in the region. Reading captains' reports of the Dutch blockade vessels in the 1870s is an exercise in repetition: over and over again, in various locations along the shore, vessels were stopped and seized and found to have clandestine armaments on board.[53] This state of affairs was part of the context of the *Kim Ban An*'s voyage too, as merchants who had been crossing the Straits for years often found themselves boarded and then hauled by force toward the shore.

On June 4, 1873, Governor-General James Loudon officially announced the blockade of Aceh's shores in a proclamation from Buitenzorg, the summer seat of Dutch government just outside Batavia[54] (fig. 16) The proclamation was published in London the next day and was officially printed in Singapore on June 13 and in Penang shortly after that.[55] The Dutch consuls and vice-consuls in Singapore and Penang were informed and given detailed instructions on how they were to help the blockade from their diplomatic posts. Extremely meticulous instructions were also sent out to other high-ranking Dutch Indies bodies, including the commander of the fleet, on how Batavia wanted the blockade to be arranged.[56] At the same time, the Indies administration was also asking for continual feedback from the field, and received detailed advice from the Raad van Indie (Council of the Indies) and from the chief admiral of the fleet on what measures should be adopted to make the cordon most effective.[57] Straits traders were already reporting difficulties with the Aceh trade in March 1873, months before the blockade was formally declared. By June, the evolving net around Aceh was making this commerce more and more difficult.[58] When

PROCLAMATIE.

De Gouverneur-Generaal van **Nederlandsch-Indie**, Opperbevelhebber der land- en zeemagt van Zijne Majesteit den Koning der **Nederlanden** beoosten de Kaap de Goede Hoop,

Brengt ter kennisse van een iegelijk wien zulks mogt aangaan, dat, naar aanleiding van den toestand van oorlog, waarin het Gouvernement van **Nederlandsch-Indie** met het rijk van **Atjeh** verkeert, de havens en landingsplaatsen, kusten, rivieren, baaijen en kreeken van genoemd rijk en zijne onderhoorigheden worden verklaard te zijn **in staat van blokkade**, met al de gevolgen daaraan verbonden, en dat met de uitvoering van dezen maatregel is belast de Kommandant der in de wateren van **Atjeh** gestationeerde Zeemagt.

Gedaan te **Buitenzorg**, den 4 Junij 1873.

LOUDON.

Fig. 16. Dutch proclamation of the Aceh blockade, 1873. (Courtesy ARA, The Hague)

the *Kim Ban An* was ready to set sail from Penang on June 27, 1873, Dutch naval officers already had been put aboard Indies coast guard ships participating in the blockade, and an extensive Dutch spy system was being organized in Penang, recruited among local traders.[59]

Despite all of this activity, life in the Straits Settlements in the days leading

Table 11. Meteorological Returns: Straits of Melaka Weather Patterns Around the Time of the Kim Ban An's Sailing

Mean Rainfall for the Five Years Up to and Including 1873				
1869	1870	1871	1872	1873
Yearly Rainfall In Inches				
90.63	123.24	109.45	75.30	75.30

		Weather Indications in Singapore, 1873			
Month	Rain (Inches)	Barometer (Inches)	Thermometer Dry	Wet	Wind
Jan	7.16	29.831	80.1	74.7	NW
Feb	9.57	29.845	78.5	74.4	NW
Mar	9.74	29.832	80.9	75.8	NE/NW
Apr	10.54	29.806	81.4	77.2	NE/NW
May	5.50	29.786	83.5	78.0	NE
Jun	4.81	29.807	83.5	77.7	SE
Jul	3.55	29.820	82.8	77.1	SE/SW
Aug	6.08	29.828	81.7	77.0	SE
Sep	3.00	29.847	82.7	77.4	SE
Oct	7.93	29.833	81.8	76.8	SE
Nov	12.56	29.864	79.8	76.1	NW/NE
Dec	5.16	29.850	79.0	74.9	NW/NE
Mean	7.13	29.829	81.3	76.4	n/a

Source: SSBB for 1873 (1874), p. 557.

up to the *Kim Ban An*'s departure was more or less normal. In Singapore, the Legislative Council was deliberating the pension of the late chief justice of the settlements as well as the overcrowding of passenger ships and a report from the inspector of schools.[60] Cheap real estate was becoming available for rent, while a shipment of new books had landed in the colony, including *Siamese Harem Life* by Mrs. Leonowens and *Alice in Wonderland,* both available at John Little and Co.'s store.[61] The Straits presses were blaring news of the blockade, and the opinion columns consistently berated Governor Ord for not taking steps to ensure the safety of the colony's trade.[62] In Penang itself, on the morning the *Kim Ban An* sailed, news reached the public that the geography of Penang's port had been freshly delineated and that some new rules had been promulgated to ensure better functioning of the harbor. J. B. Hewick, acting assistant superintendent of police, was sworn in as the coroner for all of Province Wellesley district the day before. A Captain Speedy, the superintendent of

Table 12. Positioning of Selected Ships of the Dutch Blockade Fleet Around Aceh

Ship Name	Week Around 27 June 1873 (Date *Kim Ban An* Departs)	Week Around 23 Aug 1873 (Date *Kim Ban An* Seized)
Den Briel	cruising around Idi	cruising around Idi
Coehoorn	cruising off Deli River	cruising off Tng. Semuntoh
Timor	in the Straits of Melaka	off Aceh East coast
Banda	Aceh roads to Idi roads	cruising around Idi
Bommelerwaard	[in the Red Sea]	cruising Aceh East Coast
Watergeus	Banda Aceh to Pulau Weh	cruising around Idi
Metalen Kruis	off Aceh roads	[off Padang, W. Sumatra]
Maas en Waal	[off Sibolga roads, W. Sumatra]	off Belawan River, E. Sumatra
Zeeland	off Aceh roads	off Aceh roads
Sumatra	[in Riau Straits]	off Idi roads
Siak	n/d/a	off Aceh East Coast
Adm. van King	[Banjarmasin to Riau]	off Aceh North Coast
Citadel van Ant	off Aceh East Coast	off Aceh roads

Sources: ARA, "Positie de Schepen en Vaartuigen in de Wateren van Atjeh op den 28 Augustus, 1873", in (MvK, Verbaal 17 Dec 1873, D33); various blockading ships' logs, all in Ministerie van Marine 2.12.03/ Scheeps-Journalen.

police for all of Penang, was giving notice that any stray dogs found in the street would summarily be destroyed.[63]

The *Kim Ban An* quietly slipped out of Penang's harbor on June 27, 1873. By piecing together the logbook journal entries of the Dutch blockade fleet, one can get an idea of what the weather and seas looked like on that particular day. Most of the handwritten logs that survive show there were heavy winds on the twenty-seventh in the northern part of the Straits, blowing primarily from the southwest. The day seems to have started out fairly clear but then became progressively cloudier, until rain and squall set in toward evening. Seas were high, and the blockading ships were able to make three knots under sail; ships powered by steam demanded between 1200 and 3700 kilograms of coal per four-hour watch. According to Dutch records, the barometer hung between .757 and .764; the temperature seems to have been between 25 and 28 degrees centigrade (78 to 88 degrees Fahrenheit).[64] Eighteen seventy-three was not a particularly rainy year in the Straits, but the month of June was always a time of bad weather in the area.[65] The southwest monsoon was at its height at this time, with roiling seas and frequent Sumatras, or high-speed winds, always in evidence. In a report on lighthouse construction in the Straits during 1873, the

Legislative Council in Singapore noted that it is a "notorious fact, known to every shipmaster plying in these waters, that the weather in the Straits of Malacca in the Southwest monsoon is proverbially bad"[66] (table 11). The *Kim Ban An* set out in this weather and in these seas. June through August was the time Acehnese pepper cargoes were ready for shipment, so the foul weather would have to be borne.

Across the Straits off the coast of Sumatra, the newly formed Dutch blockade fleet was waiting. A document in the Ministry of Colonies archive in The Hague reveals the spread of the blockading ships, their locations, crew compositions, and armaments for the middle of June. This chart also indicates where these ships were heading and where they had come from.[67] Yet the logs of the vessels themselves are an even more accurate record, registering down to tiny detail what the activities of these ships were on the day the *Kim Ban An* sailed (table 12). From these two sources one can piece together that the blockade ships were in constant motion in front of the Acehnese coast. Boiler and other repairs were being undertaken on many of the vessels, and rations were low on some, while discipline problems were rife on still others.[68] Additional sources, such as A. J. Kruijt's published memoirs of his time aboard the *Timor,* relate that beriberi was starting to make inroads among the indigenous sailors of the crews. Coal shortages were debilitating the range of the fleet, and the lack of storeships was also a hindrance, as vessels of the blockade had to sail all the way to Idi to take on new provisions.[69] An imperfect blockade, imperfect weather, and a small junk sailing southwest for pepper: this was the scenario in the Straits of Melaka at the end of June. Almost two months later, the *Kim Ban An* would appear again in the records, this time sailing off the shrouded coasts of Sumatra.

NOTES

1. Lombard, *Kerajaan Aceh Jaman Sultan Iskandar Muda* (1986).
2. See Hurgronje, *De Atjehers* (1893–94); L. Andaya, "Interactions with the Outside World" (1992), 383; and B. Andaya, "Political Development" (1992), 439; Hasjmy, *Kebudayaan Aceh Dalam Sejarah* (1983).
3. See the census statistics supplied in SSBB, 1873, 258.
4. Ibid., 261–62.
5. The course of exchange information is also provided; see ibid., 292. For further reading on Penang at this time, see City Council of Georgetown, *Penang Past and Present* (1993), and Low, *The British Settlement of Penang* (1972).
6. ANRI, Dutch Consul, Penang to GGNEI, 21 June 1876, no. 991G Confidential, in Kommissoriaal 14 July 1876, no. 522az, in Aceh no. 14 "Stukken Betreffende Atjehsche Oorlog (1876)"/no. 475–734.

7. ANRI, "Comparative Table of Exports from Penang to Acheen in 1874 and 1875," in Kommissoriaal 14 July 1876, no. 522az, in Aceh no. 14 "Stukken Betreffende Atjehsche Oorlog (1876)"/no. 475–734.

8. ANRI, Dutch Consul Penang to GGNEI, 9 Dec. 1875, no. 81/G Confidential, in Kommissoriaal 4 Jan. 1876, no. 10az, in Aceh no. 12 "Stukken Betreffende Atjehsche Oorlog (1876)"/no. 4–234.

9. Zainol, "Aceh, Sumatera Timur dan Pulau Pinang" (1995).

10. ANRI, Dutch Consul, Penang to GGNEI, 24 May 1876, no. 96G, Confidential, in Kommissoriaal 24 June 1876, no. 479az, in Aceh no. 14 "Stukken Betreffende Atjehsche Oorlog (1876)"/no. 475–734.

11. The Penang Chinese firm of Ang Pi Ouw, Lim Thik Soei and Co. had received the revenue farm for most of the import and export of Idi from the raja there. See Kruijt, *Atjeh en de Atjehers,* 186.

12. ANRI, Dutch Consul, Penang to GGNEI, 24 May 1876, no. 96G, Confidential, in Kommissoriaal 24 June 1876, no. 479az, in Aceh no. 14 "Stukken Betreffende Atjehsche Oorlog (1876)"/no. 475–734.

13. Kruijt, *Atjeh en de Atjehers,* 55.

14. "Men said that this Chinese was on board toward eventual action against Simpang Olim, to serve as a guide; he had traded along these coasts for years, and was current on many places . . ." See ibid., 54.

15. ANRI, Petition of Wong Shi Bing and Yeung Iin Ying, Dec. 1875, inside Asst. Resident Semarang to General Secretary, Batavia, 14 Jan. 1876, no. 402, in Aceh no. 12, "Stukken Betreffende Atjehsche Oorlog (1876)"/no. 4–234.

16. Sandhu, "The Coming of the Indians to Malaysia" (1993), 151–89; Mani, "The Indians in North Sumatra" (1993), 46–97; Sandhu, *Indians in Malaya* (1969); Bhattacharya, "The Chulia Merchants of Southern Coromandel" (1994); Khatchikiam, "The Chulia Muslim Merchants in Southeast Asia, 1650–1800" (1996); Fujimoto, *The South Indian Muslim Community* (1988); and Rudner, *Caste and Capitalism* (1994).

17. See Kielstra, "De Uitbreiding van het Nederlandsch Gezag op Sumatra" (1887), 256 passim.

18. Gerlach, "De Eerste Expeditie Tegen Atjeh" (1874), 73–76.

19. Van der Stok, "Wetenschappelijk Verslag" (1874/5), 577–91.

20. Kruijt, *Atjeh en de Atjehers,* 25, 28.

21. British Admiralty to Vice-Admiral Shadwell, China Station, 27 June 1873, no. 194, in PRO/Admiralty/125/China Station/box 140/Correspondence.

22. For two views from opposite sides, see van't Veer, *De Atjeh Oorlog* (1969), and *Perang Kolonial Belanda di Aceh* (1990).

23. The prestige argument is discussed in Locher-Scholten, "Dutch Expansion" (1994): 91–111.

24. ANRI, Dutch Consul, Penang to GGNEI, 24 May 1876, no. 96G, Confidential, in Kommissoriaal 24 June 1876, no. 479az, in Aceh no. 14 "Stukken Betreffende Atjehsche Oorlog (1876)"/no. 475–734.

25. Janssen, "De Statistiek van den Handel" (1892), 161–78; ARA, Dutch Vice-Consul Penang to Dutch Vice Consul Singapore, 2 May 1874, in (MvK, Verbaal 25 Aug. 1874,

E24, Kabinet); ANRI, Dutch Consul Penang to GGNEI, 10 May 1876, no. 95G, Confidential, in Kommissoriaal 15 June 1876, no. 458az, in Aceh no. 13: "Stukken Betreffende Atjehsche Oorlog (1876)"/no. 235–469.

26. ARA, Golam Meydinsah's Statement, 7 Feb. 1874, and Kim Ban An Charter Party, 27 June 1873, both in (MvK, Verbaal 10 Dec. 1899, no. 21.)

27. This information can be found in Ismail's article, "The Economic Position of the Uleebalang" (1994), 79–83.

28. ANRI, Dutch Consul, Penang to GGNEI, 24 May 1876, no. 96G, Confidential, in Kommissoriaal 24 June 1876, no. 479az, in Aceh no. 14 "Stukken Betreffende Atjehsche Oorlog (1876)"/no. 475–734. Simpang Ulim was also considered to be implacably anti-Dutch.

29. Kruijt, *Atjeh en de Atjehers,* 42.

30. ANRI, Dutch Consul, Penang to GGNEI, 13 April 1876, no. 921G Confidential, in Kommissoriaal 3 May 1876, no. 332az, in Aceh no. 13: "Stukken Betreffende Atjehsche Oorlog (1876)"/no. 235–469.

31. ANRI, Dutch Consul Penang to GGNEI, 11 May 1876, no. 94G Confidential, in Kommissoriaal 15 June 1876, no. 458az, in Aceh no. 13: "Stukken Betreffende Atjehsche Oorlog (1876)"/no. 235–469.

32. Ibid.

33. See Zainol, "Aceh, Sumatera Timur, dan Pulau Pinang," 249–51; Eusoff, *The Merican Clan* (1997), 29–51.

34. Helen Fujimoto, *The South Indian Muslim Community,* chaps. 1–3.

35. See, for example, "Noorsah Bawasah Merican v. William Hall and Co." in *Kyshe* 1:640 passim; "Palaniapah Chetty v. Hashim Nina Merican" *Kyshe* 4:559 passim; and "Ahamed Meah and Anor. v. Nacodah Merican" *Kyshe* 4:583 passim.

36. See "Mushroodin Merican Noordin v. Shaik Eusoof" *Kyshe* 1:390 passim; "Merican and Ors. v. Mahomed" *Kyshe* 3:138 passim.

37. "In the Goods of Muckdoom Nina Merican" *Kyshe* 4:119; "Noor Mahomed Merican and Anor., v. Nacodah Merican and Anor," *Kyshe* 4:88 passim.

38. See ARA, "Translation of a Letter from Omar Kattab Merican to Seenat Powlay Merican," 9 Sept. 1973, and same to same, 21 June 1873, both in (MvK, Verbaal 25 Aug. 1874, E24, Kabinet).

39. Fujimoto, *The South Indian Muslim Community,* genealogical indexes.

40. ANRI, Dutch Consul Penang to GGNEI, 10 May 1876, no. 95G, Confidential, in Kommissoriaal 15 June 1876, no. 458az, in Aceh no. 13: "Stukken Betreffende Atjehsche Oorlog (1876)"/no. 235–469.

41. ANRI, "Comparative Table of Exports from Penang to Acheen in 1874 and 1875," in Kommissoriaal 14 July 1876, no. 522az, in Aceh no. 14 "Stukken Betreffende Atjehsche Oorlog (1876)"/no. 475–734; ANRI, Dutch Consul, Penang to GGNEI, 21 June 1876, no. 991G Confidential, in Kommissoriaal 14 July 1876, no. 522az, in Aceh no. 14 "Stukken Betreffende Atjehsche Oorlog (1876)"/no. 475–734.

42. The statistics for these two places far outstrip any other provenances or destinations; see *SSBB,* 1873, 493–96.

43. ANRI, Dutch Consul Penang to GGNEI, 10 May 1876, no. 95G, Confidential, in Kom-

missoriaal 15 June 1876, no. 458az, in Aceh no. 13: "Stukken Betreffende Atjehsche Oorlog (1876)"/no. 235–469.

44. See the three Malay letters enclosed in ANRI, Civil and Military Commander, Aceh, to GGNEI, 12 Aug. 1876, no. 484, in Aceh no. 14 "Stukken Betreffende Atjehsche Oorlog (1876)"/no. 475–734.

45. ANRI, Dutch Consul, Penang to GGNEI, 21 June 1876, no. 991G Confidential, in Kommissoriaal 14 July 1876, no. 522az, in Aceh no. 14 "Stukken Betreffende Atjehsche Oorlog (1876)"/no. 475–734.

46. Kruijt, *Atjeh en de Atjehers,* 167, 143, 168.

47. ANRI, Comparative Table of Rice Exported from Penang to Acheen, in Kommissoriaal 14 July 1876, no. 522az, in Aceh no. 14 "Stukken Betreffende Atjehsche Oorlog (1876)"/no. 475–734.

48. ANRI, Dutch Consul, Penang to GGNEI, 21 June 1876, no. 991G Confidential, in Kommissoriaal 14 July 1876, no. 522az, in Aceh no. 14 "Stukken Betreffende Atjehsche Oorlog (1876)"/no. 475–734; ANRI, Dutch Consul, Penang to GGNEI, 19 July 1876, no. 101/G, in Kommissoriaal 21 Aug. 1876, no. 608az, in Aceh no. 14 "Stukken Betreffende Atjehsche Oorlog (1876)"/no. 475–734.

49. ANRI, Dutch Consul Penang to GGNEI, 7 Jan. 1876, no. 83G Confidential, in Department van Oorlog VII Afdeeling Generale Staf, in Aceh no. 12: "Stukken Betreffende Atjehsche Oorlog (1876)"/no. 4–234.

50. ANRI, Dutch Consul Penang to GGNEI, 9 Dec. 1875, no. 81/G, Confidential, in Kommissoriaal 4 Jan. 1876, no. 10az, in Aceh no. 12: "Stukken Betreffende Atjehsche Oorlog (1876)"/no. 4–234; ANRI, Dutch Consul, Penang to GGNEI, 19 July 1876, no. 101/G, in Kommissoriaal 21 Aug. 1876, no. 608az, in Aceh no. 14 "Stukken Betreffende Atjehsche Oorlog (1876)"/no. 475–734.

51. For the British side of the strait, see *SSBB,* 1873, 444; ANRI, Comparative Table of Opium Exported from Penang to Acheen, in Kommissoriaal 14 July 1876, no. 522az, in Aceh no. 14 "Stukken Betreffende Atjehsche Oorlog (1876)"/no. 475–734.

52. ANRI, "Proclamation of Col. Sec. Birch, 31 March 1873," in Aceh no. 5: "Stukken aan de Kommissie"; also see CO to Gov, SS, 23 Sept. 1873, no. 206, in PRO/Admiralty/125/China Station/box 140/Correspondence.

53. See, for example, Captain, Citadel van Antwerpen, to Dutch Consul, Penang, 9 May 1873, no. 283, and 15 June 1873, no. 37; Captain Vice-Admiral Koopman to Dutch Consul, Penang, 27 Jan. 1874, no. 251; Captain of the Zeeland to Dutch Consul, Penang, 20 April 1874, no. 732; Captain of the Metalen Kruis to Dutch Consul, Penang, 4 Jan. 1875, no. 1264; 14 Feb. 1875, no. 1456; 12 March 1875, no. 1293; and 4 July 1876, no. 1932, all in PRO/FO/220/Oleh Oleh Consulate/vol. 11/1882–85.

54. This proclamation, which states that the coasts, rivers, bays, and ports of Aceh are now to be considered under blockade, can be found in ARA, MvK, Verbaal 24 July 1873, B21.

55. See British Admiralty to Vice-Admiral Shadwell, China Station, 21 Aug. 1873, no. 239, in PRO/Admiralty/125/China Station/box 140; also see Government Notification no. 125, as published in the SSGG, 13 June 1873.

56. ARA, General Secretary, Buitenzorg, to Dutch Consuls Singapore and Penang, 21 June 1873, La H1 Secret; Extract Uit het Register der Besluiten aan den Gouverneur Generaal

van Nederlandsch Indië, 21 June 1873, La C3; and "Instructie voor de Kommandant der Maritieme Middelen Belast met de Blokkade van de Kusten van het Atjehsche Rijk" (n.d.), all in (MvK, Verbaal 16 Aug. 1873, J23 Secret.)

57. ARA, Advies van den Raad van NI Uitgebragt in de Vergadering van den 17 Junij, 1873; and Commander Dutch NEI Navy to GGNEI, 10 June 1873, no. 239 Secret, both in (MvK, Verbaal 16 Aug. 1873, J23 Secret.)

58. See ANRI, Dutch Consul, Singapore to Col Sec, Straits, 8 March 1873, no. 1a; Col. Sec, Straits, to Dutch Consul, Singapore, 11 March 1873; and Dutch Commissioner Niewenhuijzen to Col Sec, Straits, 13 March 1873, all in Aceh no. 5: "Stukken aan de Kommissie."

59. Backer-Dirks, *De Gouvernements Marine,* 170; Kruijt, *Atjeh en de Atjehers,* 34.

60. See *SSLCP,* meeting of 23 June 1873, 69.

61. *Singapore Daily Times,* 25 June 1873, 2. Leonowens was the famous English governess in the Bangkok court who would later be immortalized in *The King and I.*

62. The governor was "popularly supposed to be protector of trade in these parts" but had turned out to be "very much the reverse." See the *Singapore Daily Times,* 24 June 1873, 2.

63. See the day's events as reported in *SSGG,* 27 June 1873, 858, 877, 880, 883.

64. ARA, Logbook of the Den Briel, no. 712, 27 June 1873, 24–25; Logbook of the Coehoorn, no. 932, 27 June 1873, 144; Logbook of the Watergeus, no. 4887, 27 June 1873, 185–87; Logbook of the Metalen Kruis, no. 3108, 27 June 1873, 151–52; Logbook of the Citadel van Antwerpen, no. 908, 27 June 1873, 175–77; Logbook of the Maas en Waal, no. 2755, 27 June 1873, 60–61; Logbook of the Zeeland, no. 5157–58, 27 June 1873, 151–52, all in (Ministerie van Marine/2.12.03/Scheeps-Journalen.) These data are from the Dutch records; the meteorological information provided in the chart above is from British records and reflects the differing systems.

65. See the meteorological returns in *SSBB,* 1873, 557, which give the mean total rainfall for Singapore in the years around 1873.

66. The quote is Shelford's, in reference to the troubles building the North Sands lighthouse during this time of year. See *SSLCP,* 1873, 3.

67. ARA, "Atjehsche Eskader, Wateren van Atjeh 16 Junij 1873," in (MvK, Verbaal 24 July 1873, B21.)

68. ARA, Logbook of the Coehoorn, no. 932, 27 June 1873, 144; Logbook of the Metalen Kruis, no. 3108, 27 June 1873, 151–52; Logbook of the Citadel van Antwerpen, no. 908, 27 June 1873, 175–77; Logbook of the Maas en Waal, no. 2755, 27 June 1873, 60–61; Logbook of the Zeeland, no. 5157–58, 27 June 1873, 151–52, all in (Ministerie van Marine/2.12.03/Scheeps-Journalen.)

69. Kruijt, *Atjeh en de Atjehers,* 29, 30, 44.

Chapter 14 Worlds of Illegality, 1873–99

On August 23, 1873, the *Kim Ban An,* its holds full of Acehnese black pepper, was seized by the Dutch ship *Coehoorn* off the coast of Tanjung Semuntoh. As with June 27, the date of the *Kim Ban An*'s departure, August 23 was an uneventful day in the Straits of Melaka. True, there were noisy religious processions going on in Singapore ("There was never a town in the whole world more like Pandemonium than this place during the last six weeks," reported one observer), but on the whole the local atmosphere was rather quiet.[1] A shipment of harmonicas and concertinas had come into town, while black pepper that day was fetching fourteen dollars per *catty* in the Singapore markets.[2] Newspapers were reporting that more Dutch troops were on their way to Aceh from Java via Padang and that Acehnese emissaries were traveling afield in search of allies, even as far as Pontianak.[3] In Penang, a small earthquake had been recorded a few days previously, which shook some of the houses on Leith Street in particular; the Victoria Circus was in town, performing novel equestrian, gymnastic, and acrobatic displays.[4] Further off in the rest of the world, life seemed almost as prosaic. In Holland the entire Dutch cabinet was (again) threatening to resign, while in England the duke of Edinburgh was planning his impending marriage. In British India, an officer of the 10th Regiment was glumly preparing to be tried for bigamy in Lahore.[5]

THE SEIZURE, AUGUST 1873

August 23 was considerably more eventful off the Aceh coast, however. As the pepper harvest was in full swing, there were many ships in Idi's harbor, one of the only ports not yet under the Dutch blockade because of the raja's relationship with Batavia.[6] The rest of the extended shoreline, however, was off-limits to traders, and the Dutch fleet was kept very busy trying to prevent ships from reaching the coast. Seizures took place every day: the logs of the blockade squadron are full of references to junks, perahus, and even small steamers being impounded, as contraband was found on board these ships in a bewildering variety of places.[7] At the end of July the entire Acehnese littoral had been divided into three Dutch stations, from which Batavia's ships patrolled night and day in the hunt for transgressors of the blockade. The *Timor* reported having the entirety of its officers and crew busy at any one moment, chasing after vessels that were either leaving or approaching the Acehnese coast. A dozen or more craft could be seen from the deck of the ship sometimes, pulling mightily in different directions to evade the black smoke plume of the steamship.[8] On the eastern coast of Aceh at this time, the station ships were the *Timor, Siak, Den Briel,* and the *Coehoorn,* all of which criss-crossed the waters near the mouth of Tanjung Semuntoh's river.[9]

The weather conditions in August, as a rule, made chasing and catching ships very difficult work. This was a time when the winds in the northern waters of the Straits of Melaka often turned; some of the blockade ship journals listed the winds as coming from the northwest during the days around the seizure of the *Kim Ban An,* while others reported winds from the southwest, or even the southeast.[10] Because of this frontogenesis, baric pressures were often very high at this time. The seas were also fairly rough during this month, making pursuit difficult because of the choppiness of the water. Mean temperatures were high, with 77 to 81 degrees Fahrenheit normal for the month as a whole, though on August 23 the mercury reached 86 degrees.[11] This particular day dawned cloudy, with light drizzle off parts of the Aceh coast. Then there was a break in the weather, with substantial clearing, before the clouds began to roll in again from out over the sea. By the next day, the weather was starting to turn again, a full-scale storm hitting the area on August 25.[12] The *Kim Ban An* seems to have had the bad luck of hitting a small window of good weather when it left the Acehnese coast and tried to sail back to Penang. Had it sailed forty-eight hours earlier or later than it did, it probably would have slipped past the blockade unnoticed and disappeared into the fog, squalls, and seasonal rains of the Straits.

When the *Kim Ban An,* laden down with its full load of pepper, was about one mile off the coast of Tanjung Semuntoh, the blockade ship *Coehoorn* saw it and bore down with increasing speed. The junk may have turned tail and tried to make it back to the coast, but it is known that the *Coehoorn* reached the vessel before it was three miles offshore, that is, firmly in international waters.[13] The *Coehoorn's* logbook entries for August 23 no longer survive, but a subsequent report written by the captain, a man named C. de Klopper, indicates that the *Coehoorn* managed to pull alongside the *Kim Ban An* and eventually board her. The *Kim Ban An* and its captain, Chiulo Po, were accused by Captain de Klopper of running contraband across the blockade.[14] The logs of other blockade ships tell what happened next: the *Coehoorn* gave the junk over to the Gouvernements Marine steamer *Siak,* which took it in tow and brought it down to Idi. Two days later, the *Siak* steamed off to take on a load of coal in order to be able to tow the *Kim Ban An* further down the Sumatra coast. Four men were put on watch aboard the junk; the crew of the ship was held as prisoners. The vessel was hauled down to Deli, then to Riau, and finally all the way to the seat of Dutch power in distant Batavia.[15]

The *Kim Ban An* was not the first Straits-based trade ship to be caught running the blockade, and it wouldn't be the last. The seizure of the *Mariner's Hope* in July of the same year had sparked a huge reaction in the Straits, including widespread newspaper coverage. The ship's crew was put on trial in Batavia, and the vessel declared a fair prize.[16] The *Girbee,* also seized around this time, was brought to court in Java as well, though the crew ultimately managed to escape punishment as the action was deemed illegal.[17] Many other craft flying the British flag met the same fate during the initial months of the blockade, including the *Soon Chin Lee,* the *Kimon Thaij,* and the *Bintang Timor* as well as unnamed ships simply dubbed "perahu # 2, 3, 4, 5, and 6" in the Dutch marine records.[18] Sometimes the vessels were pronounced guilty of running the blockade, while at other times they were let off, depending on the evidence, context, and the circumstances of the seizure. Dutch policymakers at the highest levels knew the rights of prize taking in the Aceh theater were complex and often vague; depending on the ports or the nature of the cargoes, different decisions were sometimes handed down in rather similar cases.[19] When the Penang-based *Ningpo* was caught off the coast of Aceh in July 1873, it took over a year for the ship's case to be heard in court, prompting diplomacy and some angry exchanges of letters between Dutch and British statesmen.[20]

The ships of the blockade which caught the *Kim Ban An* were more or less typical of the Dutch marine forces in Aceh. The logs and letters of these vessels show what daily life was like aboard these ships during the height of the blockade: reveille, inspections, and cleaning of the ship were normal, patterned activities, as were more ceremonial tasks, such as the hoisting of flags and the firing of salutes. The ships were also constantly attending to and repairing their senescent boilers, the "hearts" of the vessels, which provided propulsion and navigation regardless of the weather. Provisioning with coal from barges that had been dragged all the way up to Aceh and the provisioning of food as well (potatoes, rice, salted meats, and especially fresh water) also took up much of the ship's time. Discipline in the ranks was also a large part of service in the blockade, especially in a theater of war. The log records of the fleet are full of notations about sailors being punished for a variety of offenses: theft, fighting, or falling asleep during the watch as well as the occasional attempted desertion. The larger picture imparted is that the ships of the blockade were often unprepared for their duties: coal was perpetually low, discipline was slack, and there were never enough vessels to maintain a comprehensive watch. Though the *Kim Ban An* was caught, along with many other craft in these initial months of the blockade, it is undoubtedly true that a significant number of other vessels must have pierced the blockading squadrons with their contraband cargoes intact.[21]

Acknowledging these deficiencies does not trivialize the real difficulties the blockading fleet faced, though trying to catch the legions of smugglers involved in this theater often must have seemed futile. Some of the most lyrical descriptions of the challenges and obstacles have been provided by J. A. Kruijt, the officer of administration aboard the *Timor*. Kruijt described the innumerable creeks in which smuggling craft could hide, pulling so close to the shore that the Dutch steamers often could not follow. Many of these voyages were by night, with contrabanders taking flight upon the appearance of a Dutch ship and then disappearing into the forest. Sometimes the blockade vessels would ascend the larger rivers in search of prey, keeping a close watch out on either side of the craft for silhouettes of people against the jungle. Huge, creeping vines often grew languorously on both sides of the rivers, hemming the Dutch ships in and nearly suffocating the oxygen out of the air. High grass grew along the banks, and occasionally the ship crews could make out footpaths or huts, though often they would see nothing for miles. The ridged backs of crocodiles were visible in the water. These narratives often have a Kurtzian feel to them, as if Conrad's *Heart of Darkness* has been transposed to Sumatra. Very infrequently, boats laden down with pepper or resiniferous woods would be found and seized, although the Dutch were more likely to encounter musket balls flying out of the dark than any evidence of contrabanders. Still, these patrols did net seizures sometimes, though seemingly never as much pepper as the blockading officers had hoped.[22]

Accounts of personnel aboard the Dutch fleet off Aceh are not limited to Kruijt's published narrative, however. Reports of the action various Dutchmen saw in this theater are published in the *Mededeelingen Zeewezen* (Seamen's Statements), in the form of narratives of individual actions or skirmishes all along the Aceh coast. These accounts from people who actually lived through the experience give an immediacy and first-person feel to events and tell the reader what everyday life was like in the blockade.[23] Even more valuable, perhaps, are the seamen's records preserved in the *Stamboeken* Personnel Records of the Ministry of Marine, The Hague. Here, in huge leather volumes, one can find information about many of the participants in the blockade, including their class backgrounds, stationing records, and dates of service. Captain de Klopper of the *Coehoorn*, the ship which seized the *Kim Ban An,* for example, was only thirty-four years old at the time of the seizure, though he had been serving aboard Indies ships from the tender age of twenty. De Klopper had been captain of the *Coehoorn* for only three months when the *Kim Ban An* was seized off of Tanjung Semuntoh and would end up serving on more than twenty ships over the course of his career.[24] Similarly, Captains Charles Bogaart and Hendrik van Broekhuizen of the *Coehoorn*'s fellow-station ships *Timor* and *Den Briel* were also young men in their thirties at the time the *Kim Ban An* was captured. They also had long experience in Indies waters and seem to have risen through the ranks at the same time as de Klopper.[25]

Yet one can delve even deeper than this and get down to the kinds of men the *Kim Ban An* would actually have seen jumping over the gunwales as they boarded the junk on August 23. Marines from the fleet like Lambertus Everaard of the *Watergeus* and Gerriet Nekeman of the *Timor* were typical. Everaard, twenty-one years old at the time of the seizure, had signed on as a marine for a 150-guilder advance; he received a pension and the Aceh Medal for his service, and left the Indies in 1875.[26] Nekeman was older, almost forty at the time the *Kim Ban An* was captured, and had signed on for a mere twenty-guilder advance when Everaard was only three years old. Like Everaard, he was from a small town in Holland and would eventually leave the service with a full pension.[27] Records of even the most basic servants of the blockading fleet survive, too, such as those of the *scheepelingen,* or sailors, who were also aboard these ships. The men of the *Kim Ban An* may have interacted with seaman second class Cornelis Sukkel of the *Timor* or with third-class sailor Jan Ostenbrug of the *Den Briel.* Sukkel had dark blue eyes, a long nose, and a pointed chin beneath light brown hair; he had been to Japan in the 1860s and had traveled even to Egypt.[28] Ostenbrug, blonde and blue-eyed, was only twenty-one at the time of the *Kim Ban An*'s seizure. He would eventually serve on no fewer than forty-seven different ships in the far-flung Dutch Indies navy.[29] Both of these men were on the eastern coast of Aceh in August 1873 and probably saw the *Kim Ban An* as she was towed into Idi harbor sometime that day. It is conceivable that both men's blue eyes—barely visible over the protective railings of their ships—were seen by the men of the *Kim Ban An* as well, as they began their long journey south to be judged.

LEGAL MACHINATIONS (1874–75)

Charged with an attempt to break the Dutch blockade, the *Kim Ban An* stood trial in the second half of 1874 and the first few months of 1875. The arena of conflict in Aceh had changed substantially by this time. In June 1873, when the *Kim Ban An* had sailed, and August of that same year, when she was caught off Tanjung Semuntoh, the Dutch military in North Sumatra was limited to a maritime presence, the vessels of the blockade cruising off the coast and occasionally bombarding the mainland. By December 1873, however, a much larger fleet and landing force had been assembled, and the invasion of the sultanate began again, this time in earnest. The Dutch were no longer overconfident or underprepared; a lesson had been learned by the catastrophe of the first attack, and this time Batavia's armed might came back with overwhelming force.[30] Over the course of December and January 1873/74, the capital of Kota Raja was taken in fierce fighting, and the main body of the Acehnese resistance fled to the hills.[31] Eighteen seventy-four and 1875 became a time of bloody skirmishes and guerrilla war in North Sumatra, as the Dutch tried to expand their beachhead around the capital and the Acehnese endeavored to pin the Europeans into the northern corner of the island[32] (fig 17). Casualties were heavy on both sides, and disease claimed many more victims as well. The Dutch sick and wounded were transported out of Aceh on ships of the blockade.

Despite the war and destruction, trade across the Straits along the entirety of

Fig. 17. Acehnese chiefs on the Aceh coast, 1880. (Photo Courtesy KITLV, Leiden)

Sumatra remained strong in 1874 and 1875. In Singapore, the Dutch consul there reported, trade statistics had increased for 1874, and no European trading houses had succumbed to bankruptcy because of the war, though several Chinese firms had gone under. The situation in 1875 was similar, as much of the Straits' commercial patterns got back to normal, and other matters, such as the developing civil war in Perak, attracted attention that was formerly laid upon Aceh.[33] In Penang, pepper prices actually fell from $12.50 per pikul in 1874 to $10 per pikul in 1875, and even to $8 per pikul in 1876, as more and more pepper was freed from the Aceh coast after large parts of the blockade were lifted. Tanjung Semuntoh, the site of the *Kim Ban An*'s seizure, and certain other Acehnese polities such as Simpang Ulim were still under blockade, but the pepper stuck in many other parts of the coast was now freed for export, and this ultimately brought prices down because of the enormous quantities being shipped.[34] Plenty of ships were still being seized by the blockade as prizes off various parts of the Aceh coast, however, a Dutch chart showing twenty-nine such vessels impounded for the second half of 1874 alone.[35]

One reason so many vessels continued to come across the Straits to pick up pepper despite the blockade was that the Dutch had instituted a "pass system" in the summer of 1873. The pass system, created under heavy pressure from Straits merchants, was developed to allow British traders to land on the Aceh coast and collect pepper they had already paid for in the form of last season's advances. Traders paid these sums to Acehnese chiefs to tide them over until the pepper harvest would be ready the following year. But with the setting of the blockade in June 1873, much pepper that was already paid for and promised to market had been trapped behind the Dutch fleet. This fact would become a crucial matter in the case of the *Kim Ban An*. Straits traders clamored to their government that the blockade was ruining their livelihoods; they at least should be allowed to pick up the cargoes already owed them. After much pressure, Batavia finally agreed, though it took considerable prodding from Singapore to bring this about.[36] A few copies of these passes, given out by the Dutch vice-consul in Penang to various ships, survive in the Central Archives in The Hague. The terms of these passes were that traders were not to bring any cash or cargoes to the Acehnese coast and only take on ballast until they had filled their holds with pepper. It was well known to Dutch naval officers, however, that vessels possessing these passes often brought cargoes with them, whether opium, cash, rice, or arms.[37] Any of these commodities, if found, were considered to be smuggled goods, and the cargo and the vessel transporting it were likely to be seized.

It was under these circumstances that the *Kim Ban An* was caught. The particulars of the case, including the personalities involved in the ship's trial and its surrounding diplomacy, are revealing. Though the *Kim Ban An* was a junk of only eighty-five tons berthen and had no Europeans on board when seized, the interested parties in the case stretched all the way up into the highest reaches of Dutch government. Two ministers of the colonies wrote letters on the affair at this time, including I. D. Franssen van de Putte, a famous reformer of colonial government who held the portfolio from 1872 until 1874, and his replacement, W. Baron van Goltstein, who was serving the first of two terms in his capacity as colonial minister.[38] Two Dutch ministers for foreign affairs were also involved in the case as it went to trial, including J. L. H. A. Baron Gericke van Herwijnen, one of Holland's top negotiators with Britain during his time, and his eventual successor for the portfolio, P. J. A. M. van der Does de Willebois, who served twice as foreign minister as well.[39] The governor-generals at the time of the trial and eventual decision were Governor Loudon, under whose watch the war with Aceh started, and Governor van Lansberge, who, like Gericke van Herwijnen, was something of a diplomatic expert in dealing with the

British.[40] Several ministers of the marine (navy) were also involved, but in a less concerted way.[41]

In the Straits themselves, the cast of concerned parties was much less august. The trader Golam Meydinsah Merican was a lesser member of the famous Merican clan of Penang, while the owner of the *Kim Ban An,* Yeo Eng, and the captain of the vessel, Chiulo Po, seem to have left no trace, other than their names. Lorrain Gillespie and Company, which had chartered 360 piculs of black pepper aboard the vessel, was an Anglo-Dutch concern with offices in Penang and Batavia. William Lorrain Hill seems to have frequently represented the firm in Penang, while G. P. Tolson was often involved in its dealings in the Dutch Indies, though he was also sometimes to be found in Penang as well. J. E. Henny was a Dutch lawyer and solicitor eventually hired to help represent the case of the *Kim Ban An* in the Batavia courts; he was a member of a famous juridical family in the Netherlands and had become a barrister in Batavia in 1866. Henny would eventually become a fairly important man: a decorated member of the Council of State in Holland, his family stayed involved with the case for over twenty-five years.[42] Finally, the Dutch special envoy for Acehnese affairs in Penang, George Lavino, and the Dutch vice-consul in that port, William Padday, also had a role in the case. Lavino, though unpopular with many Straits merchants because of the nature of his job, was by nearly all accounts a very good agent and worked tirelessly to advance Dutch interests in that harbor.[43] Padday was a different story. He seems to have used his position to advance his own interests first and made money out of the Aceh War by linking his own commercial fortunes to the supply of the Dutch military. The Dutch were quite aware of this after a time, however, and Padday was eventually forced to explain his actions, mostly in the abject terms of an apology.[44]

All of these various personages played a part in the continuing saga of the *Kim Ban An.* After its seizure on August 23, 1873, the ship was towed to Idi, the regional headquarters of the Dutch fleet on the eastern Acehnese coast. After deliberations and the fetching of more coal to be used in towing the craft further south, the *Kim Ban An* was eventually dragged to Deli, and then to Riau, and finally to Batavia in search of a court to hear the case. This process took months and seems to have imparted considerable wear and tear to the vessel and its cargo. By late 1874, more than a year after the actual capture of the craft, the *Kim Ban An* was described as being in a "sinking state." Though the merits of the junk's case had yet to be considered, the condition of the seized vessel and its vitiated cargo now demanded some sort of action. First, before they became further waterlogged and spoiled, its stocks of Acehnese pepper were taken out of the craft and sold at public auction. After expert opinions were taken, among others from an official of the harbor department of Batavia and members of the judiciary, it was decided to sell the ship itself for whatever price could be salvaged.[45] On October 24, 1874, in accordance with Dutch Indies prize law of much earlier in the century, the *Kim Ban An,* stripped of its pepper cargo and as yet unjudged, was also sold at auction in Batavia. The eighty-five-ton vessel went for just over 1,050 guilders, when the consignment cost of 62 guilders had been subtracted.[46]

Across the Straits in Penang, the various interested parties in the *Kim Ban An* and her cargo were not sitting idle during these long months of delay. Golam Meydinsah Merican had 700 piculs of pepper invested in the seized vessel, the members of Lorrain Gillespie had 360 piculs, while Yeo Eng had the loss of the ship itself to worry about. As soon as Golam Merican heard of the vessel's fate, he sent a message to Lorrain Gillespie and Co. and eventually to the Batavia branch of the firm as well. Intercessions with the authorities in Java did not seem to be working, so legal action was decided upon by the concerned merchants. On February 7, 1874, members of the Gillespie family met with William Lorrain Hill and legally appointed him their attorney in the matter. Their sworn statement on that day was solemnized by a public notary in Penang, Charles Williamson Rodyk.[47] Padday was also in attendance and stated for the record as well that both Rodyk and William Lorrain Hill were bona fide British subjects.[48] This seems to have been an attempt on the part of the merchants to draw an official Dutch presence into their legal claim. On the same day, Golam Merican also took sworn testimony for the suit, appointing Hill as his representative as well.[49] Merican's actions were also supervised by the Dutch vice-consul, who duly swore that both the notary public and Merican were also British subjects.[50]

The case came before the High Court in Batavia and was ruled upon on January 15, 1875. A thirty-five-page longhand version of the *Vonnis Definitief* (Definitive judgment) of the court, which survives in the Central Archives in The Hague, gives the parameters of the case in its many details, although it does not tell the entirety of the story of the *Kim Ban An.* The judgment of the court was a surprise to the high-level Batavian policymakers who had instituted the blockade. The *Kim Ban An* was found to be innocent of the charges of running the Dutch cordon. The crew of the junk had denied knowing anything about the blockade of Aceh. They had met no blockading vessels on their incoming voyage to the Aceh coasts and had come into Tanjung Semuntoh's river completely unaware of the maritime state of siege. As proof of this the court evi-

denced the statement of Captain de Klopper of the *Coehoorn*, which it took literally: he had deposed that Tanjung Semuntoh had been under blockade for six
weeks at the time of the *Kim Ban An*'s capture. Subtracting six weeks from the
August 23 seizure date, the court came up with July 12 as the time when the
blockade around Tanjung Semuntoh began. The *Kim Ban An* had already
sailed from Penang by this time, and as there were no warnings or notifications
in the ship's papers, as was required by international law if she had been met by
a vessel of the blockade, it must not have seen any blockading vessels. It was
therefore unaware of the cordon around that state. The court ruled that the
seizure and detention of the *Kim Ban An* were therefore illegal. The junk and its
cargo were to be returned to the defendants, along with any "expenses, damages, and interests incurred."[51]

Many in the Dutch Indies government were outraged by this decision. The
Kim Ban An had been caught red-handed trying to slip out of Tanjung Semuntoh's river quietly into the sea; it was stuffed to overflowing with pepper and
was making for the port of Penang. An appeal came before the High Court for
judgment on May 13, 1875. Lawyers for the Crown pushed their arguments
again, while the lawyers appointed by the men of the *Kim Ban An* tried to hold
the ground they had won. The decision this time was more ambiguous. The defendants were able to uphold the initial judgment, and the *Kim Ban An* was
again declared to be clear of the major charge of conspiring to break the blockade with contraband. The state also gained, however, in earning a reversal of
part of the judgment, namely the order for Batavia to pay "expenses, damages,
and interests incurred." The court decided it had overstepped its powers in this
matter: the ruling in Staatsblad no. 54 of 1829 on prizes said nothing about
awarding these extra costs to the defendant. By the powers given in Staatsblad
no. 28, 1819, therefore, the court partially reversed itself but still awarded the
majority of the victory to the *Kim Ban An*. The parties implicated in the voyage
to Sumatra would get their investments in cargo and the vessel itself back, but
any costs of the trial or its resulting dislocations were theirs to bear alone.[52]

During the course of the trial and its aftermath, differing advice on how to
proceed had been circulated through Dutch policy circles by the Justice Department, the Council of the Indies, and by the men of other influential bodies.[53] The *Kim Ban An*'s fate as a vessel accused of contrabanding across the international frontier was known to many people, yet much of the restitution
ordered by the court, ultimately, was alleged not to have ever been paid.
William Lorrain authorized George Tolson to represent him (again) in his dealings with Batavia.[54] Tolson wrote a letter to the governor-general himself, ex-

plaining that a large sum of money was still owed to the defendants. The *Kim Ban An* had possessed 50 sacks of 22 piculs' Acehnese pepper each, totaling 1,100 piculs in all; this translated to 1,356 Penang piculs weight, with pepper fetching $14.50 per picul at the time of seizure. This amount of pepper would have been worth $19,662 dollars, or, at an exchange rate of 1 dollar to 2.5 guilders, $49,155 guilders in 1873. With interest, Tolson explained, another 10,322 guilders had accrued from 1873 to 1875, giving a grand total of 59,477 guilders that needed to be paid. Tolson stated that 26,349 guilders of this sum was still owed the defendants.[55] As more time went by without payment, it was alleged, the Batavia branch of Lorrain Gillespie and Co. was eventually forced to shut its doors and subsequently went out of business. The headquarters of the firm in Penang soon followed suit. Finally, Golam Merican himself, pressed by creditors for his stake in the cargo, was confined to bed "with a very severe attack of paralysis."[56] "He did not improve physically," one of his descendants tells us, "but daily grew worse" under the strain of this case of purported smuggling.[57] Golam Merican would die shortly afterward, the troubles of the *Kim Ban An* leading him down a sad but inexorable path straight into his grave.

REPRISE (1898–99)

These complicated legal proceedings involving contraband, interethnic allegations of arms smuggling, and quiet border crossings over a troubled span of water seemed to have been finished by 1875. The details of this matter are known because the son of Golam Meydinsah Merican, Omar Nina Merican, took up the case almost twenty-five years later, in the late 1890s. The total amount of money promised to the defendants in the *Kim Ban An* smuggling case, according to Omar Merican, had never been paid. When he became an adult, therefore, almost a quarter of a century later, he tried to open the matter once again and recoup the family's losses from the Dutch. He wrote to C. M. Henny, the brother of J. E. Henny, who had helped represent the defendants' interests in the case in 1875. Omar Merican later went to see C. M. Henny in Batavia, where he was apprenticing in the family's law firm; the younger Henny then wrote to his brother, who was now back in the Netherlands for good, asking for the appropriate papers.[58] Though these strands of continuity still existed in the defendants and in the legal team representing them, the pantheon of Dutch politicians and administrators had completely changed. The new minister for the colonies was J. T. Cremer, a big planter of some fame who was known for his business talents, not his adroitness in diplomacy.[59] Cremer had appointed his friend W. Rooseboom to the governor-generalship in the Indies; he was the first military man in almost sixty years to be offered the post.[60] Finally, the minister for foreign affairs, who would eventually be negotiating the merits of the case with the British again, was W. H. de Beaufort, a man who eventually was the honorable chairman of the First Hague Peace Conference of 1899. His tenure was also marked, however, by rising anti-British sentiment in the Netherlands over the conduct of the Boer War, which had recently begun to rage in southern Africa.[61]

Trade and commercial security between the Straits Settlements and Sumatra had generally become much better by the time of Omar Merican's actions at the end of the century. The trade statistics on cross-Straits imports and exports were steadily rising, and figures prepared by the Dutch consuls in Singapore and Penang showed this to be a solid overall trend.[62] Construction was also being carried out on a large scale in the ports of the region, such as Penang, which was undergoing extensive surveying, wharf building, and viaduct building to enhance the port.[63] Yet perhaps the best indication of the gradual slide toward stability which had overtaken the region was the emergence of Sabang, a new port off the tip of Aceh on the island of Weh, as a major new harbor in the region. No longer content with having Singapore as the region's feeder entrepôt, Batavia decided to try to build her own modern roadstead for the vast traffic patterns of Straits shipping. Drydocks, coal stations, and mail services were all installed to service the port, and Sabang grew as a magnet for trade in the region. The harbor would never supplant Singapore (or Penang) as the major attraction for commerce in the northern waters of the Straits, but the mere building of the port signaled that some amount of enforced "order" had finally come to the region.[64]

There were still serious problems, however, and Omar Merican's reopening of the *Kim Ban An* question came at a time when analyses and complaints of the trading system were still very much in the air. Newspaper articles in the Straits from as far back as the late 1870s had decried the injustices of the Dutch blockade on British traders, howling that English trade was still being needlessly harmed by the functioning of the blockade's mechanics. Some merchants asked if Batavia was perpetrating these actions intentionally, as a way to harm another flag's commerce; others gave the Dutch the benefit of the doubt on rationale and simply asked how trade conditions could be ameliorated.[65] Even some Dutch authors questioned the conduct of the so-called *scheepvaartregeling* (shipping regulations), though these men were more likely to object to the use of these means as tactics against the Acehnese, rather than as potential thorns in the side of the British.[66] In the 1890s, therefore, despite the growth of trade and peace in large parts of the Straits as mentioned above, English complaints against Dutch treatment of merchant shipping were still very much a part of cross-Straits discourse. Indeed, much of the diplomatic contact between the two colonial governments at this time was occupied with this question, and how to ensure the needs of one administration without injuring the programs of the other.[67]

Omar Merican submitted his petition, an elegant twenty-three-page hand-written memorial, on October 13, 1898. In it he submitted to the British government that his father had been in the Sumatra pepper business with Yeo Eng and his ship, the *Kim Ban An,* since 1868; the operation had been running smoothly for five years, until the troubles of 1873. That year, he informed London, the blockade started, and Golam Merican obtained a pass from the Dutch vice-consul in Penang to head to the Aceh coasts. When the *Kim Ban An* was intercepted on its way home, it was searched for arms or ammunition but this proved fruitless, according to Omar Merican. She was towed to Batavia anyway. There, again according to Omar Merican, the "crew was put in prison." When the ship's case was finally judged by the High Court in Batavia, the *Kim Ban An* won the trial; the crew was to be released, Omar Merican said, and the contents as well as the junk itself returned to his father. The claim of damages was only partly paid, however, when the Dutch administration stopped payment. On August 31, 1875, Omar Merican said, the governor-general informed the defendants he would be unable to sanction the release of any more money in the case. As seen earlier in Tolson's memorial to Batavia, the firm of Lorrain Gillespie was eventually dissolved. J. E. Henny, their solicitor for part of the trial, sailed back to Holland shortly afterward, making any follow-up difficult or impossible. Golam Merican himself ultimately succumbed to paralysis as a result of the troubles and died thereafter. Omar Merican's plea was accompanied by letters from the governor of the Straits and the British envoy in The Hague, both of whom sought help on his behalf.[68]

The Dutch administration was very careful in its handling of the endgame of the *Kim Ban An* story. Much was at stake, and government officials in Batavia and The Hague realized this only too well. The minister for the colonies, the minister for foreign affairs, the governor-general in Batavia, the Raad van Indie (Council of the Indies), and the director of the Justice Department all weighed in on the matter. Cases were referenced in Mexico, Portugal, and China to check the international dimensions of the jurisprudence, while a variety of parties tried to decide whether civil or international law should be used to decide the case.[69] Though the junk had been seized inside the three-mile territorial water limit, its foreign provenance and changing laws of the sea complicated matters enormously. One Dutch source acknowledged that the Dutch might be at fault and conceivably might have to pay sizable damages in the case. It also queried whether the best course of action might not be to enact an emergency law (*noodwet*) to plug any loopholes in the eventual Dutch position.[70] The main reason for all of this anxiety was simple: the case's outcome, according to an admission by the minister for the colonies, could set a precedent.[71] The financial losses of the case could be very substantial in the long term. The very nature of contraband and the dynamics of smuggling and its definition, therefore, were all at stake.

The Dutch eventually decided to deal with the *Kim Ban An* matter through diplomacy, as it was felt this course provided the best chance of a favorable outcome. The British were told, in sparse but clear language, that they had been duped by Omar Merican's claims.[72] The exact wording of the reply to be sent across the Straits was a matter of considerable debate in Dutch policy circles; several drafts of the response were examined before a suitable rejoinder was settled upon. The minister for the colonies advised extreme caution in answering the British missives and sternly stated that only as much information on the case as was necessary (and asked for by the British themselves) should be handed over to their representatives.[73] The minister for foreign affairs also signaled that the reply was to minimize the chances that the British could interfere in any way in what was essentially seen as an internal matter of state.[74] The Council of the Indies concurred and drafted a short note to be sent to the British, with much longer analyses enclosed for the Dutch government itself.[75] The strategy seems to have worked. After August 1899, nothing more was heard from the English side of the Straits on the matter of the *Kim Ban An*.[76] Singapore and Whitehall seem to have accepted they were misled on the case by one of their own subjects. Omar Merican, his long-dead father, Golam Merican, and all of the other actors involved in the case simply vanished from history after this, twenty-five years after they had initially appeared.

But was the *Kim Ban An* smuggling when it was caught by the *Coehoorn* on August 23, 1873? What part of the cargo, if any, was considered to be contraband when the vessel was hauled toward Idi by the men of the blockade? How much truth and how much fiction had the Merican family told the two colonial administrations in reporting the facts of the case over the course of twenty-five years? The longer, internal analyses drawn up by the Dutch seem to provide some solid answers to these questions. For one thing, it is clear Omar Merican tried to throw both European governments off by saying the ship had been boarded because of contraband weapons. Weapons were never mentioned as the cause of the Dutch seizure, either in the court case or in any of the surrounding documents. Omar Merican seems to have lied or been misinformed on other counts as well. The ship was never chartered by his father, Golam Merican, as Omar says, but by Tolson; nor did the judge in 1875 say that the whole worth of the ship was to be given to Golam Merican, as he was never the owner of the craft (the Chinese shipper Yeo Eng was). The crew of the *Kim Ban An* was never imprisoned in Batavia either. J. E. Henny did not leave the Indies shortly after the court's decision, rendering any further appeals impossible; he left almost ten years later, returning to Holland. Golam, as well as the other men involved in the investment on the cargo, all seem to have received money back as well. Omar Merican knew the facts of the case would be vague twenty-five years later and seems to have relied on this gap in time to try to milk the colonial administrations for as much money as he possibly could.[77]

Perhaps more important, however, were the corpus delicti, or facts of the case, around the actual date of the *Kim Ban An*'s sailing. The junk left Penang on June 27, 1873, but news of the Aceh blockade, we know, reached Singapore on June 13, and Penang only two days after that. There is no possible way, as the men of the crew said upon their capture, that they did not know of the existence of the blockade, therefore. It was not only front page news in Penang for ten days before their sailing, but also a central fact of life for merchants in the colony (even if they did not read the newspapers), as it crucially affected all of their livelihoods. It is also highly unlikely the *Kim Ban An* had a pass to make the voyage to Tanjung Semuntoh, as no record of such a document survives, and it would certainly have been presented as evidence in Batavia's High Court. Yet the most crucial bit of evidence the Mericans failed to declare was that the ship left Penang with a small cargo on board, rather than only in ballast as the rules of the blockade required. The *Kim Ban An* had one hundred sacks of rice stowed away to sell to the Acehnese, which was definitely considered to be contraband by the ships of the blockade. Rice, though not a weapon of war, fed enemy troops; the debate on rice as an item of contraband was well known to both the British and Dutch, as there had been significant debates on the topic on the China coast in 1885. Copies of these debates are to be found in the Dutch archives with the papers of the *Kim Ban An,* showing that the Dutch certainly considered the incoming cargo of rice to be in violation of the blockade. The pepper stocks leaving from Tanjung Semuntoh, the *Kim Ban An*'s lack of a valid sea pass, the surreptitious possession of sacks of rice, and the ship's departure for Penang by cover of night—all of these were the reasons that led the ship to be seized for smuggling across the Straits.[78]

The case of the *Kim Ban An,* in occupying as it did numerous defendants and their lawyers as well as two generations of colonial civil servants for over twenty-five years, imparts some powerful lessons about the nature and dynamics of smuggling at this time. The business of contraband, first of all, seems to have been a multiethnic one: merchants, shippers, wholesalers, and growers, all of different races, were unafraid to combine to carry out these ventures, if enough profit was on the line. We see this very clearly in the Chinese captain and crew of the *Kim Ban An,* in the Indian Muslim and Anglo/Dutch traders who chartered the vessel, and in the Acehnese pepper farmers of Tanjung Semuntoh, all of whom were involved in the voyage. Smugglers also knew how to maneuver and use the existing legal system to their advantage as well, though in this particular case it took more than a quarter of a century before all of the legal options open to smugglers were foiled. The pursuit of gain through these channels seems to have been attempted as naturally as the use of local geographies: smugglers did not hesitate to use the colonial state's own structures and apparatus against it, if the proper avenues could be found.

Yet the most powerful lesson the *Kim Ban An* teaches may be learned through the smugglers' appraisal of context, and how it could always be used to the contrabanders' advantage. Straits merchants like the Mericans and Lorrain Gillespie knew there would be a surfeit of Acehnese pepper on the coasts following the declaration of the blockade; they also knew these same Acehnese would be eager to sell these cargoes, as it was in their financial interest to do so. Trouble in Straits waters also meant that less and less pepper would reach Penang, with the supplies that did end up in the port fetching higher and higher prices. In the early months of the blockade, this was certainly so. There was a great inducement on both sides to ignore the Dutch proclamation and take a risk on contraband ventures that presented themselves. Arms were the primary commodities that worried Batavia at this time, but rice, pepper, and other sundry goods also became contraband at this juncture, based on the context of the situation. None of these goods were ontologically off-limits to start with, in other words: they became so only as ports opened and closed, haphazardly and at different times. Participants at various levels of the food chain of Straits commerce understood this and moved cargoes from place to place, trying to outwit the Dutch blockade. Moreover, some smugglers even tried to use the psychology of the Europeans against them, drawing feints and dead-ends with the arms trade, when the real prizes to be shipped were other goods entirely. In this, Straits contrabanders showed a sophisticated knowledge not only of market conditions and local geographies, but also of the anxieties and preoccupations of the Dutch themselves. This calculus ultimately failed, however, in the case of the *Kim Ban An,* though the failure took almost three decades to make itself apparent.

The legacy of this junk of eighty-five tons was larger than its trial and the case's eventual denouement, however. The questions about contraband, international legality, and blockade the *Kim Ban An* raised survived in the problems and day-to-day realities of the two colonial states for many years. The immediate result of the trial in 1875 was to make the Dutch much more careful with their cordon around Aceh: new instructions were issued by the Raad van Indie to the commanders of the fleet on how to better seal off the coast from smugglers coming across the Straits.[79] The longer-term effects were considerably more profound, however. Instructions on how to visit and board merchant ships which might be carrying contraband were fine-tuned down to minute detail, so that such vessels—if they were indeed smuggling—no longer had any legal leg to stand upon.[80] For the British, the experience of the *Kim Ban An* also was instructive. The convolutions of the case induced London to procure a definitive statement from the Dutch about the operation of their prize courts, which were considered by Whitehall to be out of step with evolving international law.[81] It also helped pave the way for the Declaration of London in the early twentieth century, whereby the rights and obligations of ships carrying items deemed to be "contraband" were finally more clearly defined.[82] This was a fitting epitaph for the smugglers concerned with the *Kim Ban An.* For such a little ship, it embodied the troubles and opportunities of its times in a grand and fitting way.

NOTES

1. Descriptions of the religious processions, which appear to have been both Chinese and Indian, can be found in *SSLCP,* 1873, 126–27.
2. *Singapore Daily Times,* 23 Aug. 1873, 4.
3. *Singapore Daily Times,* 21 Aug. 1873, 2.
4. See the *Penang Guardian and Mercantile Advertiser,* 20 Aug. 1873, 2.
5. The assistant government astronomer in Madras had also committed suicide because his fiancée had broken off their engagement; in Ireland, murders and other violent crimes were on the rise. See the *Penang Guardian and Mercantile Advertiser,* 27 Aug. 1873, 3.
6. Even Idi was eventually blockaded, however. See Kruijt, *Atjeh en de Atjehers,* 39, 48.
7. See, for example, the letters tendered by the captains of the blockading ships (including the *Timor,* the *Coehoorn,* the *Siak,* the *Den Briel,* the *Watergeus,* and others) to the com-

mander of the Dutch Marine forces, all of which can be found in ARA, (MvK, Verbaal 17 Dec. 1873, D33).

8. Kruijt, *Atjeh en de Atjehers,* 83, 40.

9. ARA, "Positie de Schepen en Vaartuigen in de Wateren van Atjeh op den 28 Augustus, 1873," in (MvK, Verbaal 17 Dec. 1873, D33.)

10. ARA, Shiplog of the *Den Briel,* no. 712, 22 Aug. 1873, 76; Shiplog of the *Watergeus,* no. 4887, 23 Aug. 1873, 57; Shiplog of the *Bommelerwaard,* no. 585, 21 Aug. 1873, 91, all in (Ministerie van Marine/2.12.03/Scheeps-Journalen).

11. The actual Dutch reading was thirty degrees Centigrade, which converts to eighty-six degrees Fahrenheit. See the weather indications as provided in *SSBB,* 1873, 559−60; also ARA, Logbook of the *Citadel van Antwerpen,* no. 908, 914, 23 Aug. 1873, 118−19, in (Ministerie van Marine/2.12.03/Scheeps-Journalen).

12. ARA, Logbook of the *Banda,* no. 383, 23 Aug. 1873, 103−04; Logbook of the *Sumatra,* no. 4267, 23 Aug. 1873, 56, both in (Ministerie van Marine/2.12.03/Scheeps-Journalen).

13. ARA, Nota, Minister van Koloniën, 16 March 1899, in (MvK, Verbaal, 16 March 1899, U4 Kabinet.)

14. ARA, Commander of the *Coehoorn* to Station Commander, East Coast of Aceh, 25 Aug. 1873, no. 1006, entry for 23 Aug. 1873, in (MvK, Verbaal 17 Dec. 1873, D33).

15. ARA, Commander of the *Timor* to Commander of the Marine, Aceh, 26 Aug. 1873, no. 21, in (MvK, Verbaal 17 Dec. 1873, D33); ARA, Logbook of the *Den Briel,* no. 712, 23 Aug. 1873, 77; Logbook of the *Sumatra,* no. 4267, 23 Aug. 1873, 56, both logbooks in (Ministerie van Marine/2.12.03/Scheeps-Journalen).

16. See the details of the case in "Verbeurdverklaring van Prijzen. Blokkade, Mariners Hope," in *IWvhR,* 3 Aug. 1874, no. 579, 121−24.

17. The *Girbee*'s trial can be found in "Verbeurdverklaring van Prijzen. Blokkade, Girbee," in *IWvhR,* 19 Oct. 1874, no. 590, 165−66.

18. ARA, "Staat Aantoonende den Stand van de voor het Prijsgericht Aangangige Gedingen" 16 June 1874, in (MvK, Verbaal 24 Sept. 1874, no. 40); see also "Prijs en Buit. Blokkade. Schoener Ningpo," in *IWvhR,* 15 March 1875, no. 611, 42−44; "Prijs en Buit. Blokkade. Bintang Timor," in *IWvhR,* no. 632, 9 Aug. 1875, 126−27; "Prijs en Buit. Blokkade. Schending. Kim Soon Chin Lee," in *IWvhR,* 16 Aug. 1875, no. 633, 130−31.

19. ARA, MvBZ to MvK, 6 Aug. 1873, no. 3, in (MvK, Verbaal 7 Aug. 1873, N22).

20. ARA, British Envoy, Hague, to MvBZ, 8 Jan.1875; Gov. Straits to CO, 1 Sept. 1874, Col. Sec., Straits, to Sec. of Gov't, Batavia, 17 March 1874; Sec. of Gov't, Batavia, to Col. Sec., Straits, 17 April 1874; Col. Sec., Straits, to Gov't Sec., Batavia, 9 July 1874; and Gov't Sec., Batavia, to Col. Sec., Straits, 2 Aug. 1874, all in (MvBZ/A Dossiers/Box 199/A.105).

21. ARA, Commander of the *Siak* to Station Commander, East Coast Aceh, 18 Aug. 1873, no. 11; Commander of the *Coehoorn* to Station Commander, East Coast Aceh, 25 Aug. 1873, no. 1006; Commander of the *Den Briel* to Station Commander, East Coast Aceh, 12 Aug. 1873, no. 386; Commander of the *Timor* to Station Commander, East Coast Aceh, 26 Aug. 1873, no. 494, all in (MvK, Verbaal 17 Dec. 1873, D33); ARA, Shiplog of the *Coehoorn,* Logbook no. 932, 27 June 1873, 144; Logbook of the *Timor,* no. 4413, 25− 26 June 1873, 198−99, both logbooks in (Ministerie van Marine/2.12.03/Scheeps-Journalen).

22. See Kruijt, *Atjeh en de Atjehers,* 153, 157, 206.

23. See, for example, "Verslag over de Krijgsverrigtingen in Atjeh" (1875), 1–22; Verheij, "Rapport van den 1sten Luitenant" (1877), 103 passim.

24. ARA, "Cornelis de Klopper, Kapt. t/z 1st Klasse," Inventaris no. 3, Stamboek no. 218, in (Ministerie van Marine/2.12.06/Stamboeken).

25. Bogaert became a vice-admiral in 1892; van Broekhuijzen received distinction for service off of southwest Sulawesi and southeast Borneo. See ARA, "Charles Henri Bogaert, Lt. t/z 1st Klasse," Inventaris no. 2, Stamboek no. 158, and "Hendrik Jan.van Broekhuijzen, Lt. t/z 1st Klasse," Inventaris no. 2, Stamboek no. 197, both in (Ministerie van Marine/2.12.06/Stamboeken).

26. ARA, "Lambertus Jacobus Everaard, 2nd Klasse," Stamboek no. 12914, part 39, in (Ministerie van Marine/2.12.08/Stamboeken Mariniers).

27. Nekeman had served in the Dutch West Indies before shipping out to Batavia. See ARA, "Gerriet Nekeman, 1st Klasse," Stamboek no. 9053, part 36, in (Ministerie van Marine/2.12.08/Stamboeken Mariniers).

28. ARA, "Cornelis Sukkel, 2de Klasse," Stamboek no. 7569, part 11, in (Ministerie van Marine/2.12.07/Stamboek Scheepelingen).

29. Ostenbrug had also served in the Atlantic Ocean and at the Dutch station at the Cape of Good Hope. ARA, "Jan.Ostenbrug, 3de Klasse," Stamboek no. 11807, part 19, in (Ministerie van Marine/2.12.07/Stamboek Scheepelingen).

30. Alfian, *Perang di Jalan Allah* (1987), and Said, *Aceh Sepanjang Abad* (1981).

31. See "Kort Overzicht der Tweede Expeditie" (1875), 92 passim, 121 passim.

32. Ibid., 58 passim, 100 passim. See also van 't Veer, *De Atjeh Oorlog* (1969); *Perang Kolonial Belanda di Aceh* (1977); and Alfian, "Sejarah Singkat Perang de Aceh" (1973), 237–66. This photo is from 1880, a few years after the worst of the fighting.

33. "Jaarlijksch Verslag, Singapore" (1874), 490–92; (1875), 113.

34. Lavino, "Aanteekeningen Betreffende het Handelsverkeer in Atjeh" (1877), 751 passim.

35. ARA, "Opgave der Prijs en Buitgelden Gamaakt door de Schepen Behoorende tot het Station Oostkust van Atjeh, Gedurende het Jaar 1874," in (MvK, Verbaal 31 Aug. 1875, V20.)

36. See the discussion in the Legislative Council meeting, in *SSLCP,* 22 July 1873, 102–03.

37. Kruijt describes these cargoes as being hidden in mainsails, masts, and other places. See Kruijt, *Atjeh en de Atjehers,* 56–57.

38. "Putte, Isaac Dignus Fransen van de," in *Biografische Woordenboek van Nederland,* (1994), 4:1100; "Goltstein, Willem Baron van," in *Biografische Woordenboek van Nederland,* (1994), 1:954.

39. "Joseph Louis Heinrich Alfred Baron Gericke van Herwijnen," in *De Nederlandse Ministers van Buitenlandse Zaken, 1813–1900* (1974), 235; "Gericke van Herwijnen, Joseph L.," in Molhuysen and Kossmann, *Nieuwe Nederlandsch Biografisch Woordenboek,* (1937), 1:928; "Pieter Joseph August Marie van der Does de Willebois," in *De Nederlandse Ministers van Buitenlandse Zaken,* 251; and "Willebois, Pieter Joseph August Maria van der Does de," in *Nieuwe Nederlandsch Biografisch Woordenboek,* 10:1209–10.

40. Reid, *Contest for North Sumatra,* 28, n. 1; "Loudon, James" and "Lansberge, Johan Wilhelm van," in *Biografische Woordenboek van Nederland,* 3:792, 739.

41. The ministers were L. G. Brocx, I. D. Fransen van de Putte, and W. F. van Erp Taalman Kip; see Van Ette, *Onze Ministers Sinds 1798,* (1948), 28.

42. See "Johannes Eugenius Henny," in Van't Hoff, *Bijdrage tot de Genealogie van het Geslacht Henny* (1939), 21.

43. ANRI, Dutch Consul Singapore to Secretary General Buitenzorg, 11 Jan.1876, no. 18, in Aceh no. 12: "Stukken Betreffende Atjehsche Oorlog (1876)"/no. 4–234.

44. ANRI, Dutch Consul Singapore to Naval Commander, Batavia, 20 Dec. 1875, in Kommandant der Zeemagt en Department van Marine, 18 Aug. 1876, no. 122, in Aceh no. 14: "Stukken Betreffende Atjehsche Oorlog (1876)"/no. 475–734; ANRI, Dutch Vice Consul, Penang to Dutch Consul, Singapore, 23 Feb.1876, in Kommandant der Zeemagt, 7 July 1876, no. 6942, in Aceh no. 12: "Stukken Betreffende Atjehsche Oorlog (1876)"/no. 4–234.

45. ARA, Waterschout W. G. Lorreij to Asst. Resident for Police, Batavia, 7 Oct. 1874; "Requisitoir," 13 Oct. 1874; no. 12 of the Griffier van den Raad van Justitie te Batavia, 17 Nov. 1874, all in (MvK, Verbaal, 23 Aug. 1873, no. 21.)

46. ARA, Procureur-Generaal to GGNEI, 11 July 1899, no. 1258, in (MvK, Verbaal, 23 Aug.ust 1873, no. 21.)

47. ARA, Statement of William Lorrain Hill and Walter Gillespie, 7 Feb. 1874, and Notarizing of the Document by William Rodyk, 7 Feb. 1874, both in (MvK, Verbaal 10 Dec. 1875, Kab R30.)

48. ARA, Statements of W. C. S. Padday, 7 Feb.1874, on Rodyk and Lorrain Hill, both in (MvK, Verbaal 10 Dec. 1875, Kab R30.)

49. ARA, Statement of Golam Meydinsah Merican, 7 Feb.1874, in (MvK, 10 Dec. 1875, Kab R30.)

50. ARA, Statements of W. C. S. Padday, 7 Feb.1874, on Rodyk and Golam Meydinsah Merican, in (MvK, Verbaal 10 Dec. 1875, Kab 30.)

51. ARA, "Vonnis Definitief in de Zaak . . . *Kim Ban An,*" and "Sententie Definitief in de Zaak . . . *Kim Ban An,*" both in (MvK, Verbaal 10 Dec. 1875, Kab 30); also ARA, "Translation Extract," in (MvBZ/A Dossiers/Box 199/A.105).

52. See "Verbeurdverklaring. Prizen en Buit. *Kim Ban An*" in *IWvhR,* 21 June 1875, no. 625, 1875; and "Translation Extract," in (MvBZ/A Dossiers/Box 199/A.105).

53. ARA, "Konsideration en Advies van den Directeur van Justitie," 9 Aug. 1875; "Advies van de Raad van NI, Uitgebragt in de Vergadering van den 20 Augustus 1875"; and GGNEI to MvK, 31 Aug. 1875, no. 1289/3, all in (MvK, Verbaal, 10 Dec. 1875, Kab R30).

54. ARA, Statement of William Lorrain, 28 May 1875, in (MvK, Verbaal 10 Dec. 1875, Kab R30).

55. ARA, G. P. Tolson to GGNEI, 24 July 1875, in (MvBZ/A Dossiers/Box 199/A.105).

56. ARA, Memorial of Omar Nina Merican, 13 Oct. 1898, 17, in (MvBZ/A Dossiers/Box 199/A.105).

57. Ibid., 17.

58. Ibid, 19–20; see also "Christiaan Henny," in Van't Hoff, *Bijdrage tot de Genealogie van het Geslacht Henny* (1939), 25.

59. "Cremere, Jacob Theodoor," in *Biografische Woordenboek van Nederland,* 1:124.

60. The fact that Japan had just fought and won a war against China, and that Spain was los-

ing the Philippines to an imperial United States caused great anxiety in Dutch policy circles. This may have been one of the reasons for appointing a soldier to lead the government in Batavia. See "Rooseboom, Willem," in *Biografische Woordenboek van Nederland,* 1:500.

61. "Beaufort, Willem Hendrik de," in *Biografische Woordenboek van Nederland,* 1:28.

62. See "Consulaat Generaal der Nederlanden in de Straits-Settlements te Singapore," *Consulaire Verslagen en Berichten* (1899) no. 2, 798 passim; (1901), no. 1, 77 passim; (1902), no. 1, 17 passim; also "Consulaat der Nederlanden te Penang," *Consulaire Verslagen en Berigten* (1899), no. 2, 841 passim; (1900) no. 1, 121 passim; (1901), no. 2, 795 passim.

63. "Improvements to the Port of Penang" *SSLCP,* 15 Oct. 1891, C113–17.

64. See "Sabang Baai" (1903), 238; "Sabang als Kolenstation" (1904), 94; "Suikerpremie, Renteloos Voorschot en de Maildienst naar Poeloe Weh" (1903), 224–25; Cohen Stuart, "Sabang, Penang" (1905), 115 passim.

65. See the extracts clipped from the *Penang Gazette* of 13 Sept. 1879, 20 Sept. 1879, and 28 Sept. 1879, all in ARA, (MvBZ/A Dossiers/Box 199/A.105).

66. Kempe "De Scheepvaartregeling" (1893), 410–19.

67. See the letters by A. M. Skinner, 22 Aug. 1893, no. 6584/16i; the Penang Chamber of Commerce, 18 Aug. 1893, no. 6584/16i; the Earl of Rosebery, 4 Nov. 1893, no. 6584/17; and J. A. de Vicq, 16 Dec. 1897, no. 7243/111, all published in Nish, ed., *British Documents on Foreign Affairs* (1995).

68. ARA, Memorial of Omar Nina Merican to the Secretary of State for Foreign Affairs, 13 Oct. 1898; Dutch Envoy, Hague, to MvBZ, 4 Jan. 1899, no. 319; Gov Straits Settlements to Joseph Chamberlain, 17 Nov. 1898, no. 362, all in (MvBZ/A Dossiers/Box 199/A.105).

69. ARA, Minister van Koloniën, "Nota," 16 March 1899, in (MvK, Verbaal 16 March 1899, U4 Kabinet).

70. ARA, MvK to MvBZ, 16 March 1899, no. 3417, and MvK to MvBZ (draft), 16 Feb. 1899, both in (MvBZ/A Dossiers/Box 199/A.105).

71. ARA, MvK to MvBZ, 16 March 1899, no. 3417 (p. 9), in (MvBZ/A Dossiers/box 199/A.105).

72. See ARA, "Ontwerp, Aan de Britschen Gezant" (n.d.), in (MvK, Verbaal 25 May 1899, no. 1).

73. ARA, MvK to MvBZ, 25 May 1899, and MvK to MvBZ, 7 July 1899, both in (MvBZ/A Dossiers/box 199/A.105)

74. ARA, MvBZ to MvK, 3 June 1899, in (MvBZ/A Dossiers/box 199/A.105).

75. ARA, 1st Afdeeling, Raad van Staat to MvBZ, 25 April 1899, no. 30, in (MvBZ/A Dossiers/Box 199/A.105).

76. ARA, Minister van Koloniën, "Nota," 23 Aug. 1899, in (MvK, Verbaal 23 Aug. 1899, no. 21).

77. Of all of Omar Merican's false assertions, the one about the crew of the *Kim Ban An* being imprisoned in Batavia was the only one that the Dutch saw as a possible misunderstanding—and not as an outright lie—on the part of the younger Merican. The minister of the colonies hypothesized that Omar Merican had misunderstood the Dutch verb "bevrijd" (literally, freed) in the original Dutch court documents to mean that the crew

of the junk had been imprisoned and then let go. The actual meaning of "bevrijd" in the context of the case, however, was "absolved," as in "freed from suspicion." This was the only allowance the Dutch made for the entirety of Omar Merican's statements; a possible error in translation. For refutations of all of the above, see ARA, "Aantekeningen," inside MvK to MvBZ, 25 May 1899, in (MvBZ/A Dossiers/Box 199/A.105).

78. ARA, "Nota" and "Aantekeningen," both inside MvK to MvBZ, 25 Aug. 1899; "Correspondence with the French Government in 1885 Respecting the Treatment of Rice as Contraband," London, His Majesty's Stationery Office, 1911; and MvK to MvBZ, 16 March 1899, no. 3417, all in (MvBZ/A Dossiers/box 199/A.105).

79. ARA, "Advies van den Raad van Nederlandsch Indië, Uitgebragt in de Vergadering van den 14 Mei 1875," in (MvK, Verbaal 31 Aug. 1875, V20).

80. See the typed booklet "Handleiding in Tijd van Oorlog voor Eskader en Divisie-Commandanten en Commandeerende Officieren, Hr. Ms. Zeemacht" (Instructions in time of war for squadron and division commanders and commanding officers of the Royal Dutch navy, n.d.), which laid out extremely detailed instructions on these matters. These included the rights of visitation to neutral merchant ships, warnings to these ships, blockade installation, etc. The booklet is found inside (MvBZ/A Dossiers/Box 199/A.105). These procedures became matters of special importance to the Dutch off Venezuela in the early twentieth century, as The Hague once again had to deal with questions of smugglers and maritime contraband, this time in another arena. ARA, Minister van Marine to MvBZ, 6 Nov. 1908, no. 715A Secret, in (MvBZ/A Dossiers/box 199/A.105).

81. ARA, British Envoy, Hague to MvBZ, 19 Feb. 1908, in (MvBZ/A Dossiers/box 199/A.105).

82. See "The Declaration of London," The Times (London) 9 March 1911, 6–7.

Chapter 15 Conclusion

It is possible to lay a piece of tracing paper over the historical map of the world and draw a rough outline of the world economies to be found during any given period. Since these economies changed slowly, we have all the time in the world to study them, to watch them in action, and to weigh their influence. Slow to change contours, they reveal the presence of an underlying history of the world.
—Fernand Braudel, *Afterthoughts on Material Civilization and Capitalism* (1984), 84

I have argued in this book that smuggling and processes of border formation were inherently linked along a three-thousand-kilometer stretch of land and sea in colonial Southeast Asia. Imperial regimes governed from Batavia and Singapore looked out over the spaces separating them and slowly demarcated the territories they saw. This never was done in a completely premeditated way but rather was accomplished over several decades of encounters, negotiations, and events that decided factors on the ground.[1] Local peoples often were given little say in the politics of these developments, yet they made their voices heard through their activities in newly evolving geographies. Where boundaries now existed, cross-border smuggling took root. Contraband running had always been part of the region's geopolitical past, but now smuggling took place on an unparalleled scale.[2] Ships left by the hundreds to cross this arena's shallow seas; quiet forest paths were walked in the middle of the night. The processes of claiming a "legitimate" border and the crossing of new boundaries happened at the same time in the decades around the turn of the twentieth century.

In 1865, the British and Dutch colonial spheres in Insular Southeast Asia were largely limited to Java, Singapore, and a few far-flung island outposts scattered throughout the rest of the Indies archipelago. By 1915, this picture had changed dramatically: instead of having a piecemeal presence, local imperial projects now rubbed up against each other all along the length of this frontier.[3] The emergence and evolution of such a political boundary gave way to complicated new realities in Southeast Asia. Commerce, which had always been brisk in this part of the world, was suddenly ruled by new sets of conditions that were decided far away in London and The Hague. The Dutch, in particular, saw the maintenance of a firm grip on trade as a prerequisite for strong rule, an ideology that collided with many long-standing patterns in this region. The monopolistic regimes of the Dutch Indies state and even the freer, laissez-faire policies of the British (which nevertheless often had their own proscriptive qualities) were met in a variety of ways by local populations. Some trading communities subsumed themselves into the evolving economic order, scurrying to find niches in the permitted structures of trade. Other regional actors, however, resisted the new order and smuggled a variety of commodities in a variety of contexts for their own complicated reasons. This happened all along the Anglo/Dutch frontier in Southeast Asia and is evidenced in the sources in 1865 as well as in 1915.

European state-making resources were stretched to the limit during this half century of territorial growth, especially in the decades leading up to the turn of the twentieth century. Neither colonial regime was able to control vast stretches of their frontiers. Local peoples in Southeast Asia, facing the creation of these powerful states, continually challenged this emerging hegemony. Contrabanding was only one possible response open to the indigenous inhabitants of this region, yet it was an increasingly important one as armed resistance on a large scale became more and more unrealistic. As Singapore and Batavia expanded their power in the region, therefore, perhaps the one aspect of life Europeans most sought to influence was the nature of trade. The calculus here was fairly straightforward. States survive by skimming profits off their citizens' (or subjects') commerce: governments need revenues, and one of the main ways to raise such funds is through the taxation of goods in transit. Yet states also monitor which commodities move across their borders, where they travel, and who brings them—issues that can be matters of life and death for the survival of any government. All commodities may be taxed by the state, but it is more important for the state to monitor some goods than others. Prevailing moralities and instincts of self-preservation, financial and otherwise, dictate these hierarchies.

The changing structures of trade in this Southeast Asian locale permit a historical examination of several crucial questions about the nature of commerce and power. Some of the most important of these questions focus on the character of commodities themselves, namely, how they are defined by different actors in different contexts, and how culture comes to bear on their movement in an arena of power inequality.[4] There was, in fact, no ontology whatsoever to the category of contraband along this colonial Southeast Asian frontier: contraband was whatever those in power said it was, and these designations sometimes changed very quickly. In the Straits of Melaka in the nineteenth century, many specific commodities phased in and out of this category almost overnight, as certain ports or certain products were declared off-limits by European governments in the region. Rice, pepper, betel nuts, newspapers, and porcelain all fit this description at one time or another, as did a host of other items, all of which were considered to be contraband commodities in some contexts but not in others. Narcotics, counterfeit currency, human traffic, and arms were designated as smuggled goods often, as these particular commodities threatened state projects of consolidation more regularly than other items. Yet even these "products" were judged to be illegal only in context, as is witnessed by the massive commerce in opium run by these states for their own revenues, or the tolerated trade in prostitutes of many nations, so long as their passage was regulated and controlled.

This appraisal of commodities crossing frontiers as containers of shifting values seems to agree with much of the new literature on objects generally. Arjun Appadurai has spoken famously of the "social lives of things," tracing what he calls the "paths and diversions" of objects through time, space, and various social meanings.[5] The passage of contraband commodities across the Anglo/Dutch frontier very much fits into this formulation, showing how physical things could leave with one value and arrive on the other side of an arbitrary (but enforced) boundary with another one entirely. Though theorists have been talking about these kinds of transvaluations of things for some time now, the notion of objects changing values as they cross different kinds of space has been somewhat new in Southeast Asia.[6] The anthropologist Janet Hoskins recently has attempted this kind of analysis with drums, shrouds, and woven cloth, and she has also led inquiries into how more "debatable" objects—such as shrunken heads—have traveled in the region.[7] Patricia Spyer also has begun to probe such movements in the region, especially where these commodities may be moving across various kinds of "frontiers."[8] An examination of the emerging Anglo/Dutch boundary in the decades around the turn of the century, however, shows that these transits of both things and values are of long standing. The relationship of physical space to coercion and commodities was a complex one that continually changed in different contexts and places.[9]

This binding of the material and spatial seems to have been no less true in the global historical arena as well. The theorist Julian Thomas has remarked that "societies should be thought of as being composed of both people and artifacts. This allows us to consider the relationships between people and things as dialogical."[10] Certainly this has been a theme in anthropology for many years; pioneering researchers such as Malinowski long understood the crucial importance of commodities in motion (in his case, shells of the *kula* networks he described in the Pacific) for the functioning of regional societies.[11] The histories of many places are now being reimagined with these circuits in mind, to show how previous historiographical interpretations have missed the salience of goods in transit for the development of area cultures. The case of Japan is interesting in this light, for example, as new analyses of the supposedly "sealed" Tokugawa economy make clear. Though historians had long pointed to the relative isolation of Japan from the outside world from the mid-seventeenth to the mid-nineteenth centuries, these new studies have shown how a range of commodities—many of them smuggled—trickled into Japan alongside the very few goods that were tolerated entry into the islands by the Tokugawa *Bakufu*. These goods could be anything from tobacco to clocks or tableware to guns, each appreciated and sought after for different reasons. Contraband commodities crossed large oceanic spaces for centuries in this manner, as Dutch traders in particular learned how to funnel their cargoes across vast maritime geographies before depositing them in southern Japan.[12]

On the Anglo/Dutch frontier in Southeast Asia, smugglers particularly learned to operate in three zones of activity, as these spaces were found to give them both more reasonable chances at success and more protection from the searching eyes and reach of the colonial state. Frontiers were one of these spaces, as they were physically often—though not always—furthest from the apparatus of state power. Choke points such as the Straits of Melaka and the many mountain passes and valleys in the interior of Borneo were also often utilized, as commerce was channeled into avenues in these places where traders found many advantages. Even cities, however, were favored as a space for contrabanding, as the chaos and complexity of urban centers were ideal for covering illegal activities. Singapore was without peer in this respect. Sitting on the maritime border but adjacent to a maze of poorly patrolled Dutch islands, the port emerged as a center of smuggling, despite being the seat of British power in the region. Smaller, more localized entrepôts also took on these functions, however, among them Labuan off the coast of western Borneo and Melaka, Penang, and other ports in the Straits of Melaka. Each of these places built up a regional reputation for smuggling, specializing in certain goods, such as pepper in Penang, or certain geographies, such as the vast Borneo mainland for Labuan. Contrabanding and the many sidelight trades that swirled around it helped these ports survive and prosper in competitive seas, though tabulating the breadth and depth of these trades is an extremely difficult proposal.[13]

Much of the structure of smuggling in this vast arena was shaped by the particular growth and development of these two colonial states. Starting in the 1860s and 1870s, both the British and Dutch colonial regimes began programs of expansion that both caused and directly influenced smuggling patterns on the evolving boundary between them. There had always been a certain amount of trade which passed outside of the bounds of European control; the illegal passage of nonfarmed opium, for example, or the movement of certain spices outside of the Dutch spice monopoly had taken place for centuries by 1865. Yet the unleashed forces of exploration, mapping, technology, and state expansion in the late nineteenth century were of an entirely different order than at any previous time.[14] Armed infantry, naval patrols, and police units were all assembled to concretize European advances; laws and treaties made sure they had the stamp of legality, even if this was one-sided and coerced. Batavia and Singapore also laid out an impressive array of institutions to solidify the evolving border, such as coast lights, beacons, telegraph lines, and shipping services. Agents of the state, such as missionaries, anthropologists, and government civil servants, enhanced the European presence in these liminal spaces as well. With the renegotiation of treaties, the deaths of local chiefs, and population fluctuations and movements in certain areas the border undulated and changed on a micro level over time. Yet it also was quickly hardening, with dire consequences for politics, trade, and movement for a wide range of local actors.

Not all peoples along this three-thousand-kilometer ribbon allowed such solidification to happen quietly. Resistance to state formation in the periphery and the laying of hard and fast boundaries was determined and swift. Many nomadic and seminomadic peoples, both on land and on the sea, refused to be co-opted into the new political geography, preferring to maintain their wandering lifestyles for as long as they could. Some merchant syndicates also challenged the emerging boundaries by trading across the frontier in items now formally forbidden. This has been shown in some detail with the commerce in narcotics, counterfeit currency, and human beings, as well as in the trafficking of arms and ammunition. Counterfeiters largely lost this battle; by the turn of the twentieth century, Batavia was bringing this particular contraband trade more or less under control. The sale of human cargoes outside of state supervision, such as underage or unwilling prostitutes or unsupervised coolie labor, was only pushed further underground, however. Narcotics smuggling was never se-riously challenged by the processes of state formation and remains alive, vi-brant, and extremely profitable even today. Contrabanding, therefore, never was fully vanquished by state-making projects in this region and often man-aged to survive in spaces and places the state could not reach. The willingness of many actors within the human fabric of these same states helped these trades to adapt and thrive in a variety of circumstances.[15]

Even the attempt to stamp out smuggling and unrestricted movement along the frontier required processes of imagination and identification on the part of colonial Europeans. Blame had to be assigned to culprits, and certain popula-tions were suspected of these crimes more readily than others. *Vreemde Ooster-lingen,* or Foreign Asians, was one of the categories of people suspected in this regard, as Chinese, Japanese, and Arabs in the Indies were thought to have their own programs and agendas, often ones inimical to the state. Batavia's anxiety also was directed against the indigenous populations of the Indies themselves, as Islam and the sheer numbers of autochthonous peoples, who collectively dwarfed the Dutch presence in the region, were both thought to be dangerous to the ruling regime.[16] Yet there were often Europeans among the smuggling populations in the Indies as well, some of them English or Spanish or French, but still others among them Dutch, contrabanding against their own colony and flag. This was known to policy planners in Batavia, but the reality of these movements only seldom fit into the larger mental image about smuggling that was under the process of construction. Smuggling most often was conjured up as resistance, and Dutchmen, so the thinking went, did not resist their own ad-ministration. For this reason the piracy and violence present in large tracts of the Outer Islands were also imagined to be part of the narrative of smuggling. Various shadowy groups were thought to be conspiring to bring down the In-dies state, a notion that rarely, if ever, was true.

The massive contraband transit in arms across the Anglo/Dutch frontier to various populations either living, traveling, or trading across this arc shows why this colonial imaginary existed. Almost all of the peoples who bought arms illegally along the length of the border did so for their own protection, often against the advances of the state itself.[17] This was not insurrection, but rather a self-interested program of survival that had little to do with any organized political resistance against the state. Many actors also bought arms to compete with other Asians, such as factions of Chinese miners or secret societies in West Borneo or Bugis merchants and sailors who competed for the same stocks of valuable products of the sea. In the case of Aceh, however, the trade in guns from across the Anglo/Dutch frontier was indeed a concerted, political attempt at rebellion. The full fury of the Dutch Indies state was loosed upon Aceh after an initial failure in early 1873; Aceh became a rallying point for Dutch self-esteem and self-confidence, a fight which had to be won to maintain the state's image of itself. Firearms leaked across the frontier to the Acehnese over the course of fifty years, keeping alive a guerrilla war that nevertheless ultimately failed in its aims. Smuggling in this arena, therefore, took on meanings that were muted elsewhere in the archipelago. The traffic in guns to the resistance became a contraband commerce that needed to be stopped because it was a direct threat, at least in many Dutch minds, to the survival and legitimacy of Batavia itself. Given that its outlines and dynamics were so crucial to the Dutch Indies state, the arms trade has been given a particularly detailed place in this book.

A final glimpse of the relationship between smuggling and state formation has been provided in the narrative of the *Kim Ban An,* a Chinese junk from Penang that was caught smuggling off the Aceh coast in 1873. In the discourse around the seizure and trial of this vessel, many of the themes in this book play themselves out in miniature. A collaboration among diverse ethnic actors—Chinese, Indian, Acehnese, and European—frightened Batavia enormously, as did the possibility that this smuggling craft was only one among many, all of which were transgressing the frontier. The *Kim Ban An* was indeed only one among many other ships, and its capture and trial reveal the issues which caused the Dutch such anxiety. Arms were coming across the Straits in these craft, as were opium, silver cash, and other useful supplies like raw metals. Yet the *Kim Ban An* was only carrying rice to Aceh, and when it was stopped on a hot August day the only cargo aboard was pepper, destined for the return journey to Penang. The ensuing trial and the deliberations by the various actors involved, including the charterers of the ship and European officials at the highest levels of metropolitan government in Europe, show why any and all of these cargoes were so problematic. The case of the *Kim Ban An* also opens a window on the lives and minds of contrabanders themselves, as the memorials of the men involved survive amidst the much more numerous papers of the two colonial states. The affair illuminates for a brief moment the opaque world of smuggling in the Straits and beckons the modern reader to peer into spaces that usually are vague and dark.

CONTRABAND AND FRONTIERS: THE MARGINS OF DISSENT

The development of the modern manifestation of borders and economic acts that states have often sanctioned as "crime" seem to have gone hand in hand in world history. Thomas Wilson and Hastings Donnan have noted that in most premodern polities, it was the control over people, not land, which really mattered to ruling regimes.[18] People could go where they wanted, so long as they paid obeisance (and taxes, daughters, or corvée labor) to regional elites. Yet the imposition of boundaries in global space changed the nature of the relationships between rulers and ruled in important ways. Territoriality started to assume paramount importance for ruling regimes, and the voyages of subjects who now crossed lines in space had to be monitored both for what they brought in and what they took out of local polities. This happened in places like Tibet, where the "Great Game" was being played between England, China, and Russia in the late nineteenth century, and it also happened in Peru and Mexico as well as in other parts of the disintegrated Spanish Empire.[19] Indeed, a glance around the globe reveals evidence of these processes unfolding just about anywhere modern borders were coming into being.

Yet even if the nineteenth century was a watershed period globally for the unfolding of these processes, several theorists have conjectured that state or protostate polities, space, and illegality have been uncomfortable bedfellows for a very, very long time. Josiah Heyman has seen this relationship as almost necessarily dialectical when he wrote that the development of "state law inevitably creates its counterparts, zones of ambiguity and outright illegality."[20] This process of creation and countercreation can be found in political systems going back to the Ancient Mediterranean and to the Andean Altiplano, according to several scholars of the premodern world.[21] Yet if this phenomenon, already in existence, was concretized by the development of modern states and colonies in the nineteenth century, as David Herbert has asserted was true as a general principle, then it also became clear that patterns of crime were unevenly spread across cities and regions. This observation necessitates a spatial dimension to the examination of any modern political economy, regardless of its national or regional manifestation. The spaces where "illegality" happens matter, and these spaces can be tracked whether they are urban or semirural in nature.[22] The emargination of state authority happened in both of these rubrics. Crimes against authority, such as contrabanding in Insular Southeast Asia during the heyday of the European imperial advance, need to be analyzed with these historical structures in mind, therefore.

The Anglo/Dutch frontier was not the only site of colonial smuggling and contestation during the last several centuries of Southeast Asian history. The Spanish Philippines, a vast island archipelago ruled, like the Indies, with limited interdiction resources, also saw its fair share of illegally moved goods. Much of this commerce took place in the islands outside Luzon, the Spanish center, with Chinese junks in particular cruising far and wide in search of business opportunities unsanctioned by the Spanish Crown.[23] Yet even directly outside the walls of Intramuros, the Spanish center of colonial Manila, contraband often managed to flow freely, even if it was heading thousands of miles away. The annual run of the Manila galleon, the great treasure ship which sailed from the Philippines to Mexico laden with Spain's Asian booty, provided a yearly opportunity for the colonial smugglers of Manila to make significant fortunes. Likewise, the British colonial advance through Burma during the nineteenth century never realized a completely concomitant amount of revenue based on actual territorial conquest. Much of the commerce in high-value goods of the northern hill regions, such as jade, serpentine, rubies, and emeralds, drained silently north into Chinese Yunnan instead of into British coffers.[24] The French dealt with similar problems in Vietnam, Cambodia, and Laos, as did the Americans and the Germans in their limited imperial adventures in the greater Southeast Asian orbit.[25]

By the late nineteenth and early twentieth centuries, bustling, polyglot metropolises and huge plantation peripheries dotted Southeast Asia. European policies and infrastructural development, enforced both economically and politically, had finally affected the region in a way that several centuries of colonial trade had not. Yet the fact that these "high colonial" societies now existed with altered engines of growth did not mean that Europeans were able to stop, or even really curb, widespread smuggling. This was far from the case. Rather, the new cities became hotbeds of contraband activity, silently moving illegal commodities in many different directions. The concentration of colonial resources and attention on the profit-making engines of empire (ie: cities and plantations) also freed up "liminal" spaces not being used for such purposes for other functions. Drug-running became a hugely profitable commerce in large parts of Southeast Asia, encompassing portions of the mainland as well as wide swaths of the Austronesian world. The maritime frontier between the Spanish (and later American) Philippines, and the dominions of the British North Borneo Company in Sabah, was one of these spaces: European coast guards and navies fought a decades-long losing battle to stop the passage of opium here, which had already seeped into the life-styles and cultures of people on both sides of the maritime boundary.[26] The natural resources of remote areas (remote, at least, from the standpoint of European regional centers) also became items to be traded after dark, when colonial border-guards and provincial officials were asleep in their district houses. Huge tracts of Burmese forest were secreted out of ostensibly British territory in this way, finally ending up in the sawmills of Anglo/Siamese merchants across the frontier.[27]

The fact that these processes took place across a wide stretch of geography, and also involved many different Southeast Asian peoples (as well as different colonizing European powers), suggests some conceptual unity to the dynamics of smuggling on these frontiers. Similar projects of state-formation were happening all over Southeast Asia at this time, which demanded programs and responses that were often broadly analogous.[28] Telegraphs, naval presences, and rural administrations were built into the border landscapes of all of these colonies, for example, around this time. These were the ways in which European imperiums expanded their control, and brought their respective frontiers closer to the will of the "center." Yet smugglers seem to have had a strong say in these processes as well. Along some of these borders, contrabanders actively contested the expansion of these states, refusing to relinquish older trading patterns, or more insistent still, establishing new ones based on new political realities on the ground. Smuggling, therefore, was not only a mode of resistance to geographic and political changes brought about by growing states. It was also highly entrepreneurial in tilting these changes to local peoples' advantage. This dynamic is borne out over an over again in the records, among nomads and big businessmen, on the calm, shallow seas of Southeast Asia and overland in the forest. The contrabander's calculus, therefore, was one that was continually retallied, as local configurations of power, morality, and profit were calibrated and then weighed.

Studying the actions and interactions of smugglers on the Anglo/Dutch boundary enables a critique of some of the more important literature on how subaltern populations deal with the imposition of power. Albert Memmi has famously said that "revolt is the only way out of the colonial situation, and the colonizer realizes it sooner or later," yet this appears to be untrue. [29] Many contrabanders found that the colonial situation was a malleable reality, one that could be managed and manipulated to local ends, even if it was dangerous to do so. Partha Chatterjee already has suggested this in a colonial South Asian context, and Eric Wolf has demonstrated how the channeling of commodities—by both Europeans and non-Europeans—was intimately linked with new formations of power in the global political economy. [30] Yet it remains extremely difficult to see how these dynamics were viewed by those who did the actual smuggling themselves. Laurie Sears has talked about how these perspectives "keep gliding away from centers of elite power," but paradoxically it is in the colonial archives that most recorded vestiges of these century-old thoughts remain. [31] The "prose of counter-insurgency," is a very muted one in the case of smugglers, therefore. [32] It is known that there were literally thousands of smugglers crossing this frontier in the five decades surrounding the turn of the twentieth century, and that many of them undertook contrabanding as one possible form of resistance against the strictures of modernizing states. Yet it is not often known how they discerned these cross-border journeys in their own minds, except when their voices were recorded by these same colonial regimes.

The cross-border "crimes" of smuggling and illegal movement described in this book seem to have been part of a large milieu of transgressive measures against evolving states in colonial Asian societies. In *fin de siecle* China these challenges to imperial control consisted of secret societies and smuggling networks, not to mention the more "outright" forms of rebellion and revolt that typified parts of China's coasts at the turn of the century. [33] In India the range of transgressions against colonial authority may have been even larger, spanning "dacoity" and strikes, as well as what the British authorities termed "poaching," "street crime," and "banditry." [34] It hardly should be surprising that echoes of these indigenous forms of dealing with impressed authority should make themselves heard in Southeast Asia. In this region attempts at the deepening of state control consisted of panoptic colonial prisons and fingerprints, anthropometry and the institution of forest police. [35] Local manifestations of coercion as enunciated by Michel Foucault and local programs of evasion as put forward by Eric Hobsbawm and E. P. Thompson are everywhere: local historians from the region have begun chronicling the murmur and counterechoes of these processes as well.[36] Faced with the expanding reach and technological powers of colonial states on both sides of the Anglo/Dutch frontier, it makes intuitive sense that local peoples (including some transplanted Europeans) would try to challenge these regimes with profit and resistance schemes of their own.

Indeed, the problem is not in identifying transgression as a (perhaps) natural obverse of increased government colonial control and oppression, in colonial societies or elsewhere. A more difficult task has been asking how such systems work: when, where, how, and why, in a large spectrum of contexts and situations. Eric Monkonnen has volunteered that "counting is the major means of understanding crime and criminal justice in the past," yet I am less sanguine in this respect.[37] The study of smuggling shows clearly that not all compendia of statistics are the same, and that some of these numbers can be trusted more than others. Some, in fact, are not worth the paper they are printed on. Several theorists of crime have started to move in this conceptual direction, while others are now asking if analyses on how "criminals" make decisions—including spatial ones, such as those involving border-crossings—might not be more important.[38] These were the kinds of decisions that were very important on the Anglo/Dutch frontier at the turn of the century, precisely because of the complexity of factors that went into such considerations. This state of affairs remained true in 1865 as it was in 1915, though whole worlds in the region had changed in between.

The calculations of power, morality, and profit are still the determinations that make smuggling across the Malay/Indonesian frontier such a large part of border reality today. Many of these same "commodities" are still in motion across this divide: agricultural cargoes, human traffic (such as workmen, but also prostitutes, who often transit to Malaysia, where the currency is stronger), and arms, to name just a few. The border is still far too long to be adequately surveyed by the available resources of the state, and corruption still riddles the safeguards that are in place, at various points along the frontier. There also is still a waltz being danced by both interested parties, state and smuggler, as each learns from the other how to strengthen their own positions. Technology is "borrowed" and adapted by contrabanders, who know they must learn quickly to survive against the state's often superior resources; Kuala Lumpur and Jakarta continue to map the frontier down to smaller and smaller detail, so as to try to remove the advantage of "local knowledge" from those who would smuggle across it. Yet this is a contest, if history is any judge, which will not be won by either of the two parties. The history of smuggling across this particular border seems to show this definitively, especially in the decades around the turn of the twentieth century. In 1865, as in 1915, the frontier remained elusive: measurable, and sometimes enforceable, but more often permeable on both sides. It is likely to remain this way for quite some time to come.

NOTES

1. See Locher-Scholten, "Dutch Expansion and the Indonesian Archipelago" (1994), where this argument is laid out best for Insular Southeast Asia.
2. A provocative appraisal of "illegality" along the premodern Asian maritime routes can be found in Scammell, "European Exiles, Renegades, and Outlaws" (1992), 641–62.
3. For an interesting comparison of these geopolitical changes in Southeast Asia and South Asia, see Houben, "Native States" (1987), 107–35.
4. Marshall Sahlins has asked analogous questions about the transit of commodities throughout Asia and Oceania in the last several centuries; see his "Cosmologies of Capitalism" (1994). For the Indian Ocean, see Tagliacozzo, "Trade, Production, and Incorporation" (2002), 75–106.
5. See Appadurai, "Introduction: Commodities and the Politics of Value" (1986), 236–57.
6. There is a large and sophisticated literature on this subject; see, for example, Berger, *Reading Matter: Multidisciplinary Perspectives* (1992), 37–48; Dant, *Material Culture in the Social World* (1999), 40–59; Miller, "Why Some Things Matter" (1998), 3–24; and Bolton, "Classifying the Material" (2001), 251–68.
7. See Hoskins, *Biographical Objects* (1998), 83–114, 137–60, 25–58.
8. Spyer, ed., *Border Fetishisms: Material Objects in Unstable Spaces* (1998).
9. For a discussion of material culture and historiography in Southeast Asia, see Tagliacozzo, "Amphora, Whisper, Text (2002), 128–58.
10. See Thomas, "The Socio-Semiotics of Culture" (1998), 98.
11. Malinowski, *Argonauts of the Western Pacific* (1922).
12. For one of the best of these books, see Chaiklin, *Cultural Commerce* (2003).
13. See Hughes, "The Prahu and Unrecorded Inter-Island Trade" (1986), 103–13, and Richter, "Problems of Assessing Unrecorded Trade" (1970), 45–61.
14. For elegant arguments of how this happened in the Indies, see Mrazek, *Engineers of Happy Land* (2002), and Pyenson, *Empire of Reason* (1989). For meditations on how and why this transpired in global spaces, see Adas, *Machines as the Measure of Men* (1989), and Headrick, *The Tools of Empire* (1981).
15. See Onghokam, "Korupsi dan Pengawasan" (1986), 3–11, and Onghokam, "Tradisi dan Korupsi" (1983), 3–13.
16. For the ways in which Islam, politics, and commerce could be entwined in the region and often seen as dangerous by the colonial state, see Sutherland, "Power, Trade, and Islam" (1988), 145–65.
17. See the arguments as put forth by Abdullah in "Reaksi Terhadap Perluasan Kuasa Kolonial" (1984), and in Kartodirdjo, ed., *Sejarah Perlawan-Perlawan Terhadap Kolonialisme* (1973).
18. Wilson and Donnan, "Nation, State, and Identity" (1998), 8–9.

19. See Hopkirk, *Trespassers on the Roof of the World* (1995), 159–61; Nugent, "State and Shadow-State in Northern Peru" (1999), 63–89; Deeds, "Colonial Chihuahua" (1998), 21–40; and Kearney, "Transnationalism in California and Mexico" (1998), 117–41.

20. Heyman, "States and Illegal Practices" (1999), 1.

21. Fisher, "Workshop of Villains" (1999), 56; Berdan, "Crime and Control in Aztec Society" (1999), 263.

22. See Day, *Fluid Iron* (2002), for an exegesis of this argument.

23. Chu, *The Triads as Business* (2000), Chapters 10, 11, 12; Sidel, *Capital, Coercion, and Crime* (1999).

24. See Wickberg, *The Chinese in Philippine Life 1850–1898* (1965), 80–93. Also see Bankoff, "Bandits, Banditry, and Landscapes of Crime" (1988), 319–39.

25. Sardesai, *British Trade and Expansion in Southeast Asia* (1977), 136 passim.

26. The United States dealt with "trade leakages" and smuggling in the Philippines after the turn of the twentieth century, while the Germans experienced similar problems in their colony of New Guinea. For the situation in French Indochina, see Walker, *The Legend of the Golden Boat* (1999), 25–50.

27. See Warren, *The Sulu Zone* (1981), 109, for a discussion on this subject.

28. Ingram, *Economic Change in Thailand Since 1850* (1955); see table 10 in the appendix for a larger view.

29. Memmi, *The Colonizer and the Colonized* (1965), 127.

30. Chatterjee, "More on Modes of Power" (1983), 317; Wolf, *Europe and the People Without History* (1982), 310–50, esp. 343–46.

31. Sears, "The Contingency of Autonomous History" (1993), 18; see also Spivak, "Subaltern Studies: Deconstructing Historiography" (1988), 10.

32. The term, of course, is Ranajit Guha's; see his "The Prose of Counter-Insurgency" (1988), 45–88.

33. Wakeman, *Policing Shanghai* (1995), 60–78.

34. Mukherjee, *Crime and Public Disorder* (1995), appendix 2; Chakrabarti, *Authority and Violence in Colonial Bengal* (1997), 1–132; and Arnold, "Crime and Control in Madras" (1985), 62–82.

35. Zinoman, *The Colonial Bastille* (2001), chap. 7; Mrazek, "From Darkness to Light" (1999), 23–46; Barker, "The Tattoo and the Fingerprint" (1999), 129 passim; and Peluso, *Rich Forests, Poor People,* (1992), 44–90.

36. For the theorists, see Foucault, *Discipline and Punish* (1977), 169–170; Hobsbawm, *Primitive Rebels* (1959), 5, and Thompson, "The Crime of Anonymity" (1975), 272. For two differing Indonesian exegeses of resistance, see Suhartono, *Bandit-Bandit Pedesaan* (1995) generally, and Soeroto, "Perang Banjar", (1973), 163–202.

37. Eric Monkonnen, "The Quantitative Historical Study of Crime" (1980), 53.

38. See Louwman, "The Geography of Social Control" (1989), 241, and Rengert, "Behavioural Geography and Criminal Behaviour" (1989), 161–75. Also see Knafla, "Structure, Conjuncture, and Event" (1996), 34–64; Ruggiero, *Crime and Markets* (2000), 44–64; and Spitzer, "The Political Economy of Policing" (1993), 569 passim.

Bibliography

I. ARCHIVAL SOURCES

I. Indonesia

A. Arsip Nasional Republik Indonesia, Jakarta (ANRI)

I. Residentie Archiven, Buitengewesten (Residency Archives, Outer Islands)

A. ATJEH (1873 –1909)

Atjeh no. 3: Rapport der Commissie Onderzoek met Opzigt over Expeditie Tegen het Rijk van Atjeh.
Atjeh no. 4: Algemeen Verslag der 2de Expeditie Tegen het Rijk van Atjeh.
Atjeh no. 5: Stukken aan de Kommissie, Over de Expeditie, 1873.
Atjeh no. 8: Atjehsche Verslagen, 1874–75.
Atjeh no. 12: Stukken Betreffende Atjehsche Oorlog, no. 4–234: (1892) [1876].
Atjeh no. 13: Stukken Betreffende Atjehsche Oorlog, no. 235–469: (1875) [1876].
Atjeh no. 14: Stukken Betreffende Atjehsche Oorlog, no. 475–734: (1873) [1876].

B. BANKA (1803 – 90)

Banka no. 5: Maandrapporten no. 96–107 (1870–81).
Banka no. 5: Politiek Verslagen no. 123–6 (1870–73).
Banka no. 6a: Algmeen Verslagen no. 61–81 (1870–90).

C. BILLITON (1795 – 1890)

Billiton no. 2: Algemeen Verslagen no. 8–24 (1874–90).
Billiton no. 4a: Maandrapporten no. 41–52 (1870–81).
Billiton no. 4a: Politiek Verslagen no. 67–80 (1870–73).
Billiton no. 4a: Algemeen Administrative Verslagen no. 83–86 (1870–73).

D. LAMPONG (1739 – 1891)

Lampong no. 14: Algemeen Verslagen no. 14 (1868–73); no. 15 (1874–77); no. 16 (1878–84); no. 17 (1885–90).
Lampong no. 21: Maandrapporten (1866–73); no. 22 (1874–91).
Lampong no. 24: Politiek Verslagen (1863–72).

E. PALEMBANG (1683 – 1890)

Palembang no. 64–65: Algemeen Administrative Verslagen (1870–90).
Palembang no. 74: Maandrapporten (1870–81).

F. RIOUW (1621 – 1913)

Riouw no. 64/1–2: Algemeen Verslagen (1878–90).
Riouw no. 63/2: Algemeen Administratieve Verslagen (1871–73).
Riouw no. 66/2: Maandrapporten (1866–81).
Riouw: Selected Other Materials from the Riouw Files.

G. BORNEO, WESTERAFDEELING (1787 – 1890)

Borneo W. no. 22–36: Algemeen Verslagen (1874–90).
Borneo W. no. 49–52: Algemeen Administratieve Verslagen (1870–73).
Borneo W. no. 228–31: Politieke Verslagen (1870–73).

H. BORNEO, ZUID EN OOSTERAFDEELING (1664 – 1890)

Borneo Z.O. no. 120–43: Algemeen Verslagen (1870–90).
Borneo Z.O. no. 156–60: Politieke Verslagen (1871–73).
Borneo Z.O. no. 177–88: Maandrapporten (1870–82).

II. Netherlands

A. Algemeen Rijksarchief, den Haag (ARA)

I. Ministerie van Kolonien (Ministry for the Colonies)

2.10.02	Openbaar Verbalen	(1850–1900) [Various Verbalen].
2.10.02	Kabinetsverbalen	(1850–1900) [Various Verbalen].
2.10.02	Koninklijke Besluiten	(1850–1900) [Various Besluiten].

2.10.02	Oost-Indische Besluiten	(1850–1932) [Various Besluiten].
2.10.36.04	Openbaar Verbalen	(1901–19) [Various Verbalen].
2.10.36.051	Geheim Archief	(1901–1940) [Various Verbalen]
2.10.39	Memories van Overgave	(1849–1962).

43. Atjeh

KIT   1900   619   Steinbuch, W. (Asst. Resident) Beschrijving Zelfbesturend Landschap Djoelo Rajeu, 18 pp., 1900.

46. Oostkust van Sumatra

MMK   1910   182   Ballot, J. (Resident) Memorie van Overgave van de Residentie Oostkust van Sumatra, 71 pp., 1910.

48. Palembang

MMK   1906   206   Rijn van Alkemade, I.A. van (Resident) Memorie van Overgave van de Residentie Palembang. 50 pp. + appx., 1906.

49. Djambi

MMK   1908   216   Helfrich, O.L. (Resident) Memorie van Overgave van de Residentie Djambi, 73 pp. + appx., 1908.

50. Lampongse Districten

MMK   1913   229   Stuurman, J. R. (Resident) Memorie van Overgaven van de Lampongse Districten, 111 pp., 1913.

51. Riouw

MMK   1908   236   Kanter, W. A. de (Resident) Memorie van Overgave van de Residentie Riouw, 27 pp., 1908.

52. Banka

MMK   1906   243   Wolk, H. van der (Resident) Memorie van Overgave van de Residentie Banka, 45 pp., 1906.

53. Billiton

MMK   1907   250   Lesueur, P. L. Ch. (Asst. Resident) Memorie van Overgave van de Residentie Billiton, 49 pp., 1907.

54. Westerafdeeling Borneo

MMK   1912   260   Driessche, Th. J. H. van (Resident) Memorie van Overgave van de Residentie Westerafdeling Borneo, 63 pp., 1912.

55. Zuider- en Oosterafdeeling Borneo

MMK   1906   270   Swart, H. N. A. (Resident) Memorie van Overgave van de Residentie Oosterafdeeling Borneo, 39 pp. + appx., 1906.

2.10.52 Politieke Verslagen en Berichten Uit de Buitengewesten van Nederlandsch-Indie (1898–1940)

Atjeh	(1905–11)	Fiche nos. 1–42.
Sumatra Oostkust	(1898–1911)	Fiche nos. 155–72.
Riouw	(1899–1910)	Fiche nos. 294–304.
Djambi	(1900–10)	Fiche nos. 324–56.
Lampongs	(1906–33)	Fiche no. 386.
Banka/Billiton	(1908–13)	Fiche no. 389.
Borneo, West	(1898–1910)	Fiche nos. 393–401.
Borneo, Z.O.	(1898–1910)	Fiche nos. 443–82.

2.10.10; 2.10.36.02 Mailrapporten (1869–1900; 1900–53)
Openbaar, 1869–1910.

II. Ministerie van Buitenlandse Zaken (Ministry for Foreign Affairs)

2.05.03 "A" Dossiers (Political Affairs) (1871–1918)

Box 40:	A.29 bis OK	[various files].
Box 43:	A.29 bis OK	[various files].
Box 44:	A.29 bis OK	[various files].
Box 110:	A.49	[various files].
Box 111:	A.49SS	[various files].
Box 112:	A.49QU	[various files].
Box 199:	A.105	[various files].
Box 223:	A.111	[various files].
Box 277:	A.134	[various files].
Box 245:	A.119	[various files].
Box 246:	A.119	[various files].
Box 421:	A.182	[various files].
Box 426:	A.186	[various files].
Box 589:	A.209	[various files].

III. Ministerie van Marine (Ministry of Marine)

2.12.03 Scheepsjournalen [Ship Journals] (1813–1968)

Den Briel	(Logbook no. 712).
Coehoorn	(Logbook no. 932).
Timor	(Logbook no. 4413).
Banda	(Logbook no. 383).
Bommelerwaard	(Logbook no. 585).
Admiraal van Kingsbergen	(Logbook no. 2303).
Watergeus	(Logbook no. 4887).
Metalen Kruis	(Logbooks no. 3108/09/27).
Citadel van Antwerpen	(Logbooks no. 908/914).

Maas en Waal	(Logbook no. 2755).
Zeeland	(Logbooks no. 5157/58).
Sumatra	(Logbook no. 4267).
Schouwen	(Logbooks no. 3997/98).

2.12.06 Stamboeken van Zee-Officieren (Post-1850).
2.12.06 Stamboeken van Scheepelingen (19th Century).
2.12.07 Stamboeken van Mariniers (19th Century).
2.12.20 Archief Hydrografie (1812–1980)

Box 7:   Brievenboek A.R. Bloemendal, 1869–74.

Box 9:   Brievenboek, 1891–95 (no. 9).

Box 12:   Brievenboek, 1909–11 (no. 19).

Box 65:   Triangulatie Register Riouw en Lingga Archipel: Melville van Carnbee, 1894–99 (III B 1a).

Box 65:   Journaal van Hoekmetingen en peilingen Opname Straat Banka en N. Kust Banka, 1860–63 (III E 1c).

B. Koninklijk Instituut voor Taal-, Land-, en Volkenkunde (KITLV)

Map Collection, Period Maps.
Reading Room, Early Periodicals.

C. Court Cases, Indische Weekblad van het Recht

"Bevoegdheid. Arabier of Europeaan?" *IWvhR,* no. 2323, 6 January 1908, 3.

"In en Uitvoerregten," *IWvhR,* no. 1280, 9 January 1888, 5–6.

"In Omloop Brengen van Valsch Geld," *IWvhR,* no. 609, 1 March 1875, 35.

"Invoer van Kruit," *IWvhR,* no. 2075, 6 April 1903, 53–54.

"Koopmansboeken," *IWvhR,* no. 2005, 2 December 1901, 189–91.

"Medepligtigheid aan het Maken van Valsch Zilvergeld," *IWvhR,* no. 306, 10 May 1869, 84.

"Namaker van Zilveren Muntspecieen, Wettig Gangbaar in Nederlandsch-Indie," *IWvhR,* no. 291, 25 Januuary 1869, 17.

"Nog Eenige Opmerkingen over Amfioen-Overtredingzaken" *IWvhR,* no. 520, 16 June 1873, 96.

"Opium Reglement. Openbaar Ambtenaar. Omkooping," *IWvhR,* no. 846, 1879, 147–48.

"Opium, Praktijken van Deskundigen," *IWvhR,* no. 879, 3 May 1880, 71–72.

"Opium. Invoer van Opium," *IWvhR,* no. 1946, 15 October 1900, 166–67.

"Opiumovertreding. Acte van Beschuldiging," *IWvhR,* no. 752, 1877, 192.

"Opiumovertreding," *IwvhR,* no. 657, 31 January 1876, 19–20.

"Opiumreglement. Getuigenbewijs," *IWvhR,* no. 658, 1876, 22–24.

"Overtreding van Art. 20 Amfioenpacht-Reglement. Vrijspraak," *IwvhR,* no. 613, 30 March 1875, 613.

"Poging tot Omkooping van een Openbaar Ambtenaar van de Rechterlijke Macht," *IWvhR,* no. 835, 1879, 103.

"Prijs en Buit. Blokkade. Bintang Timor," *IWvhR,* no. 632, 9 August 1875, 126–27.

"Prijs en Buit. Blokkade. Kim Ban An," *IWvhR*, no. 606, 8 February 1875, 22–24.

"Prijs en Buit. Blokkade. Schending. Kim Soon Chin Lee," *IWvhR*, no. 633, 16 August 1875, 130–31.

"Prijs en Buit. Blokkade. Schoener Ningpo," *IWvhR*, no. 611, 15 March 1875, 42–44.

"Regeling van Rechtsgebied: Zeerof," *IWvhR*, no. 2030, 26 May 1902, 81–83.

"Reglement op het Rechtswezen in de Westerafdeeling van Borneo," *IWvhR*, no. 1376, 11 November 1889, 178–79.

"Slavenhandel. Slavernij," *IWvhR*, no. 1655, 18 March 1895, 42.

"Strafzaken," *IWvhR*, no. 569, 25 May 1874, 83–84.

"Verbeurdverklaring van Clandestine Opium, Waarvan de Eigenaars of Bezitters Ondbekend Zijn," *IWvhR*, no. 533, 15 September 1873, 146–47.

"Verbeurdverklaring van Prijzen. Blokkade, Girbee," *IWvhR*, no. 590, 19 October 1874, 165–66.

"Verbeurdverklaring van Prijzen. Blokkade, Mariners Hope," *IWvhR*, no. 579, 3 August 1874, 121.

"Vonnis in Zake Urbanus de Sha," *IwvhR*, no. 491, 2 December 1872, 492–93.

"Vreemde Oosterlingen. Bevoegdheid," *IWvhR*, no. 1561, 29 May 1893, 86–87.

"Zeerof," *IWvhR*, no. 1609, 30 April 1894, 70–71.

"Zeerof," *IWvhR*, no. 1800, 27 December 1897, 208.

"Zeerof," *IWvhR*, no. 1056, 24 September 1883, 155–56.

III. Singapore

A. Singapore National Archives

Colonial Office Document Series

C.O. 144:	Labuan (1846–1906).
C.O. 273:	Straits Settlements (1838–1919).
C.O. 531:	British North Borneo (1907–51).
C.O. 537:	Colonies, General (1759–1955).
C.O. 874:	British North Borneo Company (1865–1952).
C.O. 882:	Eastern Confidential Print (1847–1952).

B. National University of Singapore Law Library Court Cases

"Ahamed Meah and Anor. v. Nacodah Merican," *Kyshe*, 4:583.

"Ahvena Ravena Mana Aroomoogim Chitty v. Lim Ah Hang, Ah Gee, and Chop Lee Whatt" *SSLR*, 1894, 2:80.

"Alexander von Roessing v. Regina" *SSLR*, 1905, 9:21.

"Apolingam v. E.A.B. Brown," *SSLR*, 1893, 69.

"Attorney General v. Lim Ho Puah," *SSLR*, 1905, 9:13.

"Attorney General v. Seven Barrels of Gunpowder (1890)," *Kyshe*, 1885–90, 4:688.

"Attorney General v. Wong Yew," *SSLR*, 1908, 10:44.

"Brown v. Vengadashellum" *Kyshe*, 1889, 4:524.

"Buchanan v. Kirby (1870)," *Kyshe*, 1808–84, 1:230.

"Chua Ah Tong, Appellant, vs. Opium Farmers, Malacca, Respondents," *SLJ,* 1890, 2:92.

"In re Lam Tai Ying," *Kyshe,* Straits Settlements, 4:685.

"In the Goods of Muckdoom Nina Merican" *Kyshe,* 4:119.

"In the Matter of the Estate of Choo Eng Choon, Deceased, and Choo Ang Chee vs. Neo Chan Neo (et al.), Singapore" *SSLR,* 1911, 12:120.

"Ing Ah Meng v. The Opium Farmer," *Kyshe,* 1890, 4:627.

"Joseph Scher, Appelant, v. Regina, On the Prosecution of Henry Perrett, Respondent," *SSLR,* 1900–01, 4:84.

"Kim Seng vs. The Opium Farmer," *SSLR,* 1892, 66, and 1893, 115.

"Martin Mosesko, Appellant, v. the Queen. On the Prosecution of William Evans, Respondent," *SSLR,* 1900–01, 6:69.

"Merican and Ors. v. Mahomed," *Kyshe,* 3:138.

"Meydinsah and Mohamed Eusope, Appellants, v. Regina, on the Prosecution of John Little, Respondent," *SSLR,* 1897, 4:17.

"Moothoo Raman Chetty v. Aik Kah Pay and Another" *SSLR,* 1905, 9:115.

"Mushroodin Merican Noordin v. Shaik Eusoof," *Kyshe,* 1:390.

"Noor Mahomed Merican and Anor., v. Nacodah Merican and Anor," *Kyshe,* 4:88.

"Noorsah Bawasah Merican v. William Hall and Co.," *Kyshe,* vol. 1.

"Palaniapah Chetty v. Hashim Nina Merican," *Kyshe,* 4:559.

"Ramsamy v. Lowe," *Kyshe,* 1888, 4:396.

"Regina on the Prosecution of E. H. Bell, Respondent, v. John Burnett Paige, Appellant," *SSLR,* 1894, 2:84.

"Regina v. Khoo Kong Peh (1889)," *Kyshe,* 1885–90, 4:515.

"Regina v. Rajaya and Anor," *Kyshe,* 2:112.

"Regina vs. Tan Seang Leng," *SLJ,* 1889, 2:69.

"Regina vs. Wee Kim Chuan and Pong Yow Kiat," *SLJ,* 1890, 3:69.

"Rex v. Koh Chin, Ang Tap, and Ang Chuan," *SSLR,* 1908, 10:48.

"Rex v. Mabot and Others," *SLJ,* 1890, 3:65.

"Rex v. Mabot, 1890," *SLJ,* 1890, 3:65.

"Sultan Meidin and Meidin v. Regina," *SSLR,* 1898–99, 5:67–70.

"The Crown on Complaint of the Opium Farmers v. Lim Chiat," *SSLR,* 1904.

"The Opium Farm Respondent vs. Chin Ah Quee-Appellant," *SLJ,* 1891, vol. 4.

"Tio Ang Boi v. Hia Ma Lai," *Kyshe,* 1887, 4:230.

IV. United Kingdom

A. Public Records Office (PRO)

I. Admiralty

Admiralty no. 125: Station Records; China, Correspondence

nos. 19–21:   General (1870–74).

no. 140:   The Straits of Malacca, Siam (1873–76).

no. 148:   Piracy, Including Straits of Malacca (1828–74).

Admiralty no. 127: Station Records: East Indies

    nos. 1–7:   General (1865–1902).

II. Board of Trade

M.T. 9: Mercantile Marine Dept., Correspondence (1865–1902)

    Mno. 712/93:   Articles of Agreement: Clauses in Agreements of Indian Seamen Respecting Fines Imposed for Smuggling (1893).

M.T. 10: Harbour Department: Correspondence (1864–1919).

    Hno. 3910:   Foreshores (1905).
    Hno. 6457:   Lights (1897).

III. Foreign Office

Embassy and Consular Archives

    F.O: 220:   Holland and Netherlands: Oleh-Oleh (1882–85).
    F.O: 221:   Holland and Netherlands: Balikpapan (1897–1909).

OFFICIAL SOURCES AND NEWSPAPERS

A. Official Publications

Bijblad Indische Staatsblad.
British North Borneo Official Gazette.
Federated Malay States Annual Reports.
Indische Staatsblad.
Johore Annual Reports.
Kedah Annual Reports.
Kelantan Annual Reports.
Koloniaal Verslag.
Labuan Annual Reports.
Perak Government Gazette.
Perlis Annual Reports.
Sarawak Gazette.
Straits Settlements Blue Books.
Straits Settlements Government Gazette.
Straits Settlements Legislative Council Proceedings.
Straits Settlements Municipal Administrative Reports.

B. Newspapers

Algemeen Handelsblad.
Avondpost, De.

Batavia Niewsblad.
Bintang Timor.
British North Borneo Herald.
Chung Kwo Jih Pao (transl.).
Deli Courant.
Han Boen Sin Po (transl.).
Hoa Tok Po (transl.).
Indo-Chinese Patriot.
Japan Times.
Javasche Courant.
Kobe Herald.
Manila Times.
Melbourne Herald.
Nanyang Chung Wei Pao.
Nieuwe Rotterdamsche Courant.
Osaka Mainichi (transl.).
Pei Ching Jih Pao (transl.).
Penang Argus.
Penang Gazette.
Penang Guardian.
Sai Kai Kung Yik Po.
Singapore Daily Times.
Singapore Free Press.
Straits Maritime Journal.
Straits Observer.
Straits Times.
Straits Times Overland Journal.
Sun Chung Wa Po (transl.).
Times (London).
Tokyo Asahi (transl.).
Tokyo Nichi Nichi (transl.).
Utusan Malayu.

SOURCES CITED

"Aankondiging door De Hollander van het 'Hollandsch-Maleisch Technisch Marine-Zak-woordenboek' van M. J. E. Kriens, 's Gravenhage, De Gebroeders van Cleef, 1880." *IG,* no. 2 (1881): 810–11.

"Aanslagbijletten." *TBB* 10 (1894): 151–52.

Abalahin, Andrew. "Prostitution Policy and the Project of Modernity: A Comparative Study of Colonial Indonesia and the Philippines, 1850–1940." Ph.D. diss., Cornell University, 2003.

Abdullah, Taufik. "Dari Sejarah Lokal ke Kesadaran Nasional: Beberapa Problematik Metodologis." In *Dari Babad dan Hikayat Sampai Sejarah Kritis,* edited by Alfian T. Ibrahim et al., 232–55. Yogyakarta: Gadjah Mada University Press, 1987.

———. "Reaksi Terhadap Perluasan Kuasa Kolonial: Jambi Dalam Perbandingan." *Prisma* 13, no. 11 (1984): 12–27.

Achmad, Ya', et al., eds. *Sejarah Perlawanan Terhadap Kolonialisme dan Imperialisme di Daerah Kalimantan Barat.* Jakarta: Departmen Pendidikan dan Kebudayaan Direktorat Sejarah dan Nilai Tradisional, 1984.

Adas, Michael. *Machines as the Measure of Men: Science, Technology, and Ideas of Western Dominance.* Ithaca: Cornell University Press, 1989.

Adelante, H. A. "Concubinaat bij de Ambtenaren van het Binnenlandsch Bestuur in Nederlandsch-Indië." *TNI* 2 (1898): 304–14, 610–17.

Adhyatman, Sumarah. *Keramik Kuna Yang Diketemukan di Indonesia, Berbagai Bengunaan dan Tempat Asal.* Jakarta: Himpunan Keramik Indonesia, 1981.

"Adres in zake de Boekhouding van Vreemde Oosterlingen." *IG,* no. 2 (1881): 948–63.

Airriess, Christopher. "Port-Centered Transport Development in Colonial North Sumatra." *Indonesia* 59 (1995): 65–92.

Alfian, Ibrahim. *Perang di Jalan Allah: Perang Aceh 1873–1912.* Jakarta: Pustaka Sinar Harapan, 1987.

———. "Sejarah Singkat Perang de Aceh." In *Sejarah Perlawanan-perlawanan Terhadap,* edited by Sartono Kartodirdjo, 237–66. Jakarta: Pusat Sejarah ABRI, 1973.

Algadri, Hamid C. *Snouck Hurgronje: Politik Belanda Terhadap Islam dan Keturunan Arab.* Jakarta: Penerbit Sinar Harapan, 1984.

Algadri, Hamid. *Islam dan Keturunan Arab Dalam Pemberontakan Melawan Belanda.* Bandung: Penerbit Mizan, 1996.

Ali al-Haji Riau, Raja. *The Precious Gift (Tuhfat al-Nafis).* Translated by Virginia Matheson and Barbara Watson Andaya. Kuala Lumpur: Oxford University Press, 1982.

Alting von Geusau, J. "De Tocht van Overste Van Daalen door de Gajo-Alas- en Bataklanden (1904)." *IMT* 70, no. 2 (1939): 593–613.

Andaya, Barbara Watson. "From Rum to Tokyo: The Search for Anti-colonial Allies by the Rulers of Riau, 1899–1914." *Indonesia* 24 (October 1977): 123–56.

———. "Political Development Between the Sixteenth and Eighteenth Centuries." In *The Cambridge History of Southeast Asia.* Vol. 1, Part 2, 402–55, edited by Nicholas Tarling. Cambridge: Cambridge University Press, 1992.

———. "Recreating a Vision: Daratan and Kepulauan in Historical Context." *BKI* 153, no. 4 (1997): 483–508.

———. *To Live as Brothers: Southeast Sumatra in the Seventeenth and Eighteenth Centuries.* Honolulu: University of Hawaii Press, 1993.

Andaya, Leonard. "Interactions with the Outside World and Adaptation in Southeast Asian Society, 1500–1800." In *The Cambridge History of Southeast Asia.* Vol. 1, Part 2, edited by Nicholas Tarling. Cambridge: Cambridge University Press, 1992. 345–95.

Anderson, J. L. "Piracy in the Eastern Seas, 1750–1856: Some Economic Implications." In *Pirates and Privateers: New Perspectives on the War on Trade in the Eighteenth and Nineteenth Centuries,* edited by David Starkey, E. S. van Eyck van Heslinga, and J. A. de Moor, 87–105. Exeter: University of Exeter Press, 1997.

"Annexatie's in Centraal Sumatra. I." *TNI* 1 (1880): 57–80; 2 (1880): 161–94.

Anonymous. *Beschouwingen over de Zeemagt in Nederlandsch-Indië.* Nieuwe Diep: L. A. Laureij, 1875.

Anonymous. *De Rechtspraak in Nederlandsch-Indië en Speciaal die over den Inlander—Een Voorlopig Program door een Nederlandsch-Indië Ambtenaar.* Leiden: A. H. Adriani, 1896.

"Antwoord Namens de Soeltan van Sambas aan de Heer J. L. Swart." *Koloniaal Weekblad,* no. 20 (16 May 1907): 2–4.

Arendt, Hannah. *The Origins of Totalitarianism.* 2d enlarged edition. New York: Meridian Books, 1958.

"Argus en de Cyclops." *IMT* 2 (1893): 382–83.

Arnold, David. *Colonizing the Body: State Medicine and Epidemic Disease in Nineteenth- Century India.* Berkeley: University of California Press, 1993.

———. *The Problem of Nature: Environment, Culture, and European Expansion.* Oxford: Blackwell, 1996.

———. "Crime and Control in Madras, 1858–1947." In *Crime and Criminality in British India,* edited by Anand Yang, 62–88. Tucson: University of Arizona Press, 1985.

"Atavisme der O.I. Compagnie en van het Kultuurstelsel." *TNI* 13, no. 2 (1884): 401–37.

"Automobiel in Dienst van het Leger." *IMT* 1 (1906): 125–40, 179–97.

Backer-Dirks, F. C. *De Gouvernements Marine in het Voormalige Nederlands-Indië in Haar Verschillende Tijdsperioden Geschetst 1861–1949.* Weesp: De Boer Maritiem, 1985.

Bakker, Alexander. "Van Paradijs tot Plantage: Beeldvorming van Nederlands-Indië in Reisverslagen, 1816–1900." *Indische Letteren* 13, no. 2 (1998): 75–85.

Bakker, H. P. A. "Het Rijk Sanggau." *TBG* 29 (1884): 353–463.

Bakker, Petrus. *Eenige Beschouwingen over het Geldverkeer in de Inheemsche Samenleving van Nederlandsch-Indië.* Groningen: J. B. Wolters, 1936.

"Balakang Padang, Een Concurrent van Singapore." *IG,* no. 2 (1902): 1295.

Balen, A. van. "De Afschaffing van Slavenhandel en Slavernij in Nederlands Oost Indië (1986)." *Jambatan* 5, no. 2 (1987): 83–96.

Bankoff, Greg. *Crime, Society, and the State in the 19th-Century Philippines.* Manila: Ateneo de Manila Press, 1998.

———. "Bandits, Banditry and Landscapes of Crime in the Nineteenth-Century Philippines." *JSEAS* 29, no. 2 (1998): 319–39.

Barker, Joshua. "The Tattoo and the Fingerprint: Crime and Security in an Indonesian City." Ph.D. diss., Cornell University, 1999.

Bas, F. de. "Het Kadaster in Nederlandsch-Indië." *TAG* 2, no. 2 (1884): 252–70.

———. *De Triangulatie van Sumatra.* Aardrijkskundig Genootschap, Bijblad no. 10. Amsterdam, 1882.

Basu, Dilip, ed. *The Rise and Growth of the Colonial Port Cities of Asia.* Berkeley: University of California Press, 1985.

Baud, J. C. "Proeve van een eene Geschiedenis van den Handel en het Verbruik van Opium in het Nederlandsch-Indië." *BKI* 1(1853): 79–220.

"Bedevaart naar Mekka, 1909/1910." *IG,* no. 2 (1910): 1637–41.

"Belangrijke Wijzigingen in de Rechtsbedeeling van Inlanders." *IG,* no. 1 (1898): 431–41.

"Belastingen" *EvNI* 1 (1917): 222–64.

"Beoordeling van het werk van Dr. H. Blink Nederlandsch Oost- en West-Indië, Geographisch, Ethnographisch, en Economisch Beschreven, Leiden, EJ Brill, 1905 (I), 1907 (II)." *IG*, no. 2 (1907): 1102–06.

Berckel, H. E. van. "De Bebakening en Kustverlichting in de Koloniën." *Gedenkboek uitgegeven ter gelegenheid van het vijftigjarig bestaan van het Koninklijk Instituut van Ingenieurs (1847–1897)*, 308–11 's-Gravenhage: Van Langenhuysen.

Berdan, Frances. "Crime and Control in Aztec Society." In *Organised Crime in Antiquity*, edited by Hopwood, Keith, 255–270. Swansea: Classical Press of Wales, 1999.

Berg, L. W. C. van den. *Hadramaut dan Koloni Arab di Nusantara*. Jakarta: INIS, 1989.

———. "Het Kruis Tegenover de Halve Maan." *De Gids* 4 (1890): 68–101.

———. "Het Pan-Islamisme." *De Gids* 4 (1900): 228–69.

Berg, N. P. van den. *Currency and the Economy of Netherlands India, 1870–1895*. 1895. Reprint, Canberra: Economic History of Southeast Asia Project, ANU, 1996.

———. *De Muntquaestie met Betrekking tot Indië*. Batavia: Bruining and Wijt, 1874.

Berge, Tom van den. "Indië, en de Panislamitische Pers (1897–1909)." *Jambatan* 5, no. 1 (1987): 15–24.

Berger, Arthur Asa. *Reading Matter: Multidisciplinary Perspectives on Material Culture*. London: Transaction Publishers, 1992.

Beschouwingen over de Zeemagt in Nederlandsch-Indië. Nieuwe Diep: L. A. Laureij, 1875.

Bezemer, T. J. "Van Vrijen en Trouwen in den Indischen Archipel." *Tijdspiegel* 2, no. 1 (1903): 3–19, 138–60.

Bhattacharya, Bhaswati. "The Chulia Merchants of Southern Coromandel in the 18th Century: A Case for Continuity." Paper presented at meeting of "International History on the Bay of Bengal in the Asian Maritime Trade and Cultural Network, 1500–1800," Delhi, December 16–20, 1994.

"Bij de Kaart van het Boven-Mahakam Gebied." *TAG* 19 (1902): 414–16.

Biografische Woordenboek van Nederland. The Hague: J. Charite Instituut voor Nederlandse Geschiedenis, 1994.

Blok, Anton. *The Mafia of a Sicilian Village, 1860–1960: A Study of Violent Peasant Entrepreneurs*. New York: Harper and Row, 1975.

Blunt, Wilfred Scawen. *The Future of Islam*. London: Kegan Paul Trench, 1882.

Blusse, Leonard. "China Overzee: Aard en Omvang van de Chinese Migratie." In *Het Paradijs is Aan de Overzijde*, edited by Piet Emmer and Herman Obdeijn, 34–50. Utrecht: Van Arkel, 1998.

Boeke, J. H. *Economics and Economic Policy of Dual Societies*. Haarlem: H. D. Tjeenk Willink and Zoon, 1953.

———. *The Evolution of the Netherlands Indies Economy*. New York: Netherlands and Netherlands Indies Council, 1946.

———. *The Structure of the Netherlands Indies Economy*. New York: Institute of Pacific Relations, 1942.

"Boekhouding der Vreemde Oosterlingen." *Het Recht in NI* 37 (1881): 1–9.

Bogaars, G. "The Effect of the Opening of the Suez Canal on the Trade and Development of Singapore." *JMBRAS* 28, no. 1, 1955: 99–143.

Bolton, Lissant. "Classifying the Material." *Journal of Material Culture* 6, no. 3 (2001): 251–68.

Bombardier, J. "Een Nieuwe Vuurmond voor Expeditien in Moeijelijke Terreinen." *IMT* 2 (1895): 103

Boomgaard, Peter, et al. eds. *God in Indië: Bekeringsverhalen uit de Negentiende Eeuw.* Leiden: KITLV, 1997.

Booth, Anne, ed. *Indonesian Economic History in the Dutch Colonial Era.* New Haven: Yale University Southeast Asia Studies 35, 1990.

———. *The Indonesian Economy in the Nineteenth and Twentieth Centuries: A History of Missed Opportunities.* London: Macmillan, 1998.

Borrel, P. J. *Mededeelingen Betreffende de Gewone Wegen in Nederlandsch-Indië en Meer in het Bijzonder Omtrent den Aanleg Daarvan in de Buitenbezittingen.* The Hague: F. J. Belinfante, 1915.

Bossenbroek, Martin. "Volk voor Indië: De Werving van Europese Militairen voor de Nederlandse Koloniale Dienst 1814–1909." Ph.D. diss., Leiden University, 1992.

Braudel, Fernand. *On History.* Translated by P. M. Ranum. Baltimore: Johns Hopkins University Press, 1977.

———. *Afterthoughts on Material Civilization and Capitalism.* Baltimore: Johns Hopkins University Press, 1984.

Breman, Jan. *Koelies, Planters, en Koloniale Politiek: Het Arbeidsregime op de Grootlandbouwondernemingen aan Sumatra's Oostkust in het Begin van de Twintigste Eeuw.* Leiden: KITLV, 1992.

———. *Labour Migration and Rural Transformation in Colonial Asia.* Amsterdam: Free University Press, 1990.

———. *Taming the Coolie Beast: Plantation Society and the Colonial Order in Southeast Asia.* Delhi: Oxford University Press, 1989.

Brewer, Anthony. *Marxist Theories of Imperialism: A Critical Survey.* London: Routledge, 1989.

Broeze, Frank, ed. *Brides of the Sea: Port Cities of Asia from the 16th to the 20th Centuries.* Kensington: New South Wales University Press, 1989.

Brooke, Sir James. *Narrative of Events in Borneo and Celebes, Down to the Occupation of Labuan.* London: John Murray, 1848.

Brook, Timothy, and Bob Tadashi Wakabayashi. "Introduction." In *Opium Regimes: China, Britain and Japan 1839–1952.* Berkeley: University of California Press, 2000.

Brown, Ian. *Economic Change in South-East Asia.* Oxford: Oxford University Press, 1997.

Burns, Peter. "The Netherlands East Indies: Colonial Legal Policy and the Definitions of Law." In *The Laws of South-East Asia: Vol. 2 European Laws in South-East Asia,* edited by M. B. Hooker, 147–297. Singapore: Butterworth, 1987.

Burns, P. L., ed. *The Journal of J. W. W. Birch, First British Resident to Perak, 1874–75.* Kuala Lumpur: Oxford University Press, 1976.

Butcher, John, and Howard Dick. *The Rise and Fall of Revenue Farming: Business Elites and the Emergence of the Modern State in Southeast Asia.* New York: St. Martin's Press, 1993.

Campo, J. a. *Koninklijke Paketvaart Maatschappij: Stoomvaart en Staatsvorming in de Indonesische Archipel 1888–1914.* Hilversum: Verloren, 1992.

———."Orde, Rust, en Welvaart: Over de Nederlandse Expansie in de Indische Archipel Omstreeks 1900." *Acta Politica* 15 (1980): 145–89.

————. "Steam Navigation and State Formation." In *The Late Colonial State in Indonesia: Political and Economic Foundations of the Netherlands Indies 1880–1942,* edited by Robert Cribb, 11–29. Leiden, KITLV, 1994.

————. *Koninklijke Paketvaart Maatschappij: Stoomvaart en Staatsvorming in de Indonesische Archipel 1888–1914.* Hilversum: Verloren, 1992.

Cayaux, H. B. "Gerechtelijk-Scheikundige Onderzoekingen in Nederlandsch-Indië." *Het Recht in NI* 90 (1908): 1–26.

————. "Voorschriften voor de Watervoorziening." *IMT* 37 (1906): 80–83.

Chaiklin, Martha. *Cultural Commerce and Dutch Commercial Culture: The Influence of European Material Culture on Japan, 1700–1850.* Leiden: CNWS, 2003.

Chakrabarti, Ranjan. *Authority and Violence in Colonial Bengal, 1800–1860.* Calcutta: Bookland Private Ltd., 1997.

Chapelle, H. M. La. "Bijdrage tot de Kennis van het Stoomvaartverkeer in den Indischen Archipel." *De Economist* 2 (1885): 675–702.

Chatterjee, Partha. "More on Modes of Power and the Peasantry." In *Subaltern Studies II: Writings on South Asian History and Society,* edited by Ranajit Guha, 311–50. Delhi: Oxford University Press, 1983.

Cheah, Boon Kheng. *The Peasant Robbers of Kedah 1900–1929: Historical and Folk Perceptions.* Singapore: Oxford University Press, 1988.

Chew, Daniel. *Chinese Pioneers on the Sarawak Frontier 1841–1941.* Singapore: Oxford University Press, 1990.

Chew, Emrys. "Militarized Cultures in Collision: The Arms Trade and War in the Indian Ocean During the Nineteenth Century." *Royal United Services Institute Journal* (October 2003): 90–96.

Chew, Ernest, and Edwin Lee. *A History of Singapore.* Singapore: Oxford University Press, 1991.

Chiang, Hai Ding. *Straits Settlements Foreign Trade 1870–1915.* Singapore: Memoirs of the National Museum, 1978.

"Chineesche Zee. Enkele Mededeelingen Omtrent de Anambas, Natoena, en Tembelan-Eilanden." *Mededeelingen op Zeevaartkundig Gebied over Nederlandsch Oost-Indië,* no. 4 (1 August 1896): 1–2.

Christanty, Linda. "Nyai dan Masyarakat Kolonial Hindia Belanda" *Prisma* 23, no.10 (1994): 21–36.

Chu, Yiu Kong. *The Triads as Business.* London: Routledge, 2000.

"Circulaires van het Raadslid Mr. T.H. der Kinderen aan de Betrokken Ambtenaren aangaande de Invoering van het Nieuwe Regtswezen in de Residentiën Benkoelen en Borneo's Z.O. Afdeeling." *Regt in NI* 34 (1880): 305–28.

City Council of Georgetown. *Penang Past and Present, 1786–1963: A Historical Account of the City of Georgetown Since 1786.* Penang, 1993.

Clarence-Smith, William Gervase. "Hadhrami Entrepreneurs in the Malay World, 1750 to 1940." In *Hadhrami Traders, Scholars, and Statesmen in the Indian Ocean, 1750s–1960s,* edited by Ulrieke Freitag, and William G. Clarence-Smith, 297–314. Leiden: Brill, 1997.

Cleary, M. C. "Indigenous Trade and European Economic Intervention in North-West Borneo, 1860–1930." *MAS* 30, no. 2 (1996): 301–24.

Cobb, Richard. *The Police and the People: French Popular Protest 1789–1820.* London: Oxford University Press, 1970.

Cohen, Joanna Waley. *Exile in Mid-Qing China: Banishment to Xinjiang 1758–1820.* New Haven: Yale University Press, 1991.

Cohen Stuart, J. H. "Sabang, Penang en Onze Handelsbetrekkingen met Britsch-Indië." *Tijdschrift voor Nijverheid en Landbouw in Nederlandsch-Indië* 71 (1905): 115–203.

Colijn, H., ed. *Nederlands Indië, Land en Volk / Geschiedenis en Bestuur / Bedrijf en Samenleving,* 2 vols., 2d ed. Amsterdam, 1913–14.

Columbijn, Freek. "Van dik hout en Magere Verdiensten: Houtkap op Sumatra (1600–1942)." *Spiegel Historiael* 32, nos. 10–11 (1997): 431–37.

Comaroff, John. "Colonialism, Culture, and the Law: A Foreword." *Law and Social Inquiry* 26 (2001): 305–11.

"Controle op Inlandsche Hoofden in zake Geldelijke Varantwoordingen." *TBB* 17 (1899): 218–20.

"Controleur op de Buitenbezittingen." *Koloniaal Weekblad* (19 May 1910): 2–3.

Conrad, Joseph. "Because of the Dollars." In *Within the Tides: Tales,* 172–73. London: Dent's Collected Edition, 1950.

———. *Lord Jim.* New York: Norton, 1968.

———. *An Outcaste of the Islands.* Oxford: Oxford University Press, 1992.

Cooper, Fred, and Ann Stoler. "Tensions of Empire: Colonial Control and Visions of Empire." *American Ethnologist* 16, no. 4 (2001): 609–21.

Coops, P. C. "Nederlandsch-Indische Zeekaarten." *Het Nederlandsche Zeewezen* 3 (1904): 129–30.

Cornelis, W. "Een Poging tot Verbetering der Kaarten van Noord-Sumatra." *TAG* 24 (1907): 1030–47.

"Corps Ambtenaren bij het Binnenlandsch Bestuur op de Buitenbezittingen." *TBB* 1 (1887/1888): 286–300.

Craandijk, C. "Het Werk Onzer Opnemingsvaartuigen in den Nederlandsch-Indischen Archipel." *TAG* 27 (1910): 75–76.

Cremer, J. T. "Per Automobiel naar de Battakvlakte." *Eigen Haard* 16 (1907): 245–53.

Courtenay, P. P. *A Geography of Trade and Development in Malaya.* London: G. Bell and Sons, 1972.

Cribb, Robert, ed. *The Late Colonial State in Indonesia: Political and Economic Foundations of the Netherlands Indies 1880–1942.* Leiden: KITLV, 1994.

Daalen, H. B. van. "Spoorwegen in Nederlandsch-Indië." *Indische Mail* 1 (1886): 633–45, 697–711, 769–80.

Dant, Tim. *Material Culture in the Social World: Values, Activities, Lifestyles.* Philadelphia: Open University Press, 1999.

Day, Tony. *Fluid Iron: State Formation in Southeast Asia.* Honolulu: University of Hawaii Press, 2002.

Deeds, Susan. "Colonial Chihuahua: Peoples and Frontiers in Flux." In Robert Jackson,

New Views of Borderlands History, edited by Robert Jackson, 21–40. Albuquerque: University of New Mexico Press, 1998.

Dekker, P. *De Politie in Nederlandsch-Indië: Hare Beknopte Geschiedenis, Haar Taak, Bevoegdheid, Organisatie, en Optreden.* Soekaboemi: Drukkerij Insulinde, 1938.

"Deli-Spoorwegmaatschappij." *IG* 2 (1884): 682–85.

Dery, Luis. "Prostitution in Colonial Manila." *Philippine Studies* 39, no. 4 (1991): 475–89.

Dest, P. van. *Banka Beschreven in Reistochten.* Amsterdam, 1865.

Dick, Howard. "Indonesian Economic History Inside Out." *RIMA* 27, nos. 1–2 (1993): 1–12.

———. *The Indonesian Inter-Island Shipping Industry.* Singapore: ISEAS, 1987.

———. "Interisland Trade, Economic Integration, and the Emergence of the National Economy." In *Indonesian Economic History in the Dutch Colonial Era,* edited by Anne Booth et al. New Haven: Yale University Southeast Asian Studies, 1990.

Dijk, C. van. "Java, Indonesia and Southeast Asia: How Important is the Java Sea?" In *Looking in Odd Mirrors: The Java Sea,* edited by Vincent Houben et al. Leiden: Vakgroep Talen en Culturen van Zuidoost-Azie en Oceanie, 1992.

Djoko. "Si Singa Mangaraja Berjuang Melawan Penjajah Belanda." In *Sejarah Perlawanan-perlawanan Terhadap Kolonialisme,* edited by Sartono Kartodirdjo, 267–99. Jakarta: Pusat Sejarah ABRI, 1973.

Doel, H. W. van den. "Military Rule in the Netherlands Indies." In *The Late Colonial State in Indonesia: Political and Economic Foundations of the Netherlands Indies 1880–1942,* edited by Robert Cribb, 60–67. Leiden: KITLV, 1994.

Dongen, J. van. "Gerechtelijk Scheikundige Onderzoekingen in Nederlandsch-Indië." *TBB* 33 (1907): 714–19.

Douglas, R. S. "A Journey into the Interior of Borneo to Visit the Kalabit Tribes." *JSBRAS* 49 (1907): 53–62.

"Dr. Nieuwenhuis' Derde Tocht." *Indische Mercuur* 24, no. 4 (1901): 63–64.

"Draadlooze Telegraphie." *Indische Mercuur* 26, no. 16 (1903): 259.

Drabble, John. *An Economic History of Malaysia, 1800–1990.* London: Macmillan, 2000.

"Dutch Government, and Mahommedan Law in the Dutch East Indies." *Law Magazine and Review* 20, no. 295 (February 1895): 183–85.

Drakard, Jane. *A Malay Frontier: Unity and Duality in a Sumatran Kingdom.* Ithaca: Cornell University Southeast Asia Program, 1990.

Dyserinck, H. de. "De Roeping van Zr. Ms. Zeemacht, en Een Blik op Haren Tegenwoordigen Toestand." *Militaire Gids* 5, no. 2 (1886): 65–106.

Eccles, W. J. *The Canadian Frontier 1534–1760.* Albuquerque: University of New Mexico Press, 1983.

Eekhout, R. A. "Aanleg van Staatsspoorwegen in Nederlandsch Borneo en Zuid-Sumatra." *TAG,* 2d ser., 8 (1891): 955–83.

"Eenige Mededeelingen van de Zending in de Battaklanden." *Berichten uit de Zendingswereld* (15 August 1905): 1–8.

"Eenige Opmerkingen over de Reorganisatie van het Rechtswezen in de Bezittingen Buiten Java en Madura." *IG,* no. 1 (1882): 340–46.

Eerde, J. C. van. "De Adat Volgens Menangkabausche Bronnen." *Wet en Adat* (1896–98) 1/2, no. 3, 1, pp. 209–20.

"Eerste Kamer over de Brandstof voor de Indische Vloot." *Het Nederlandsche Zeewezen* 9 (1910): 93–94.

"Eigendinkelijke van Onze Behandeling der Inlandsche Vorsten" *IG*, no. 1 (1891).

Ellen, Roy. "The Development of Anthropology and Colonial Policy in the Netherlands, 1800–1967." *Journal of the History of Behavioral Sciences* 12, no. 4 (1976): 303–24.

Elson, R. E. *Village Java Under the Cultivation System, 1830–1870.* Sydney: Allen and Unwin, 1994.

"Emigratie naar de Lampongsche Districten" *IG*, no. 2 (1906): 1734–35.

Emmer, P. C. "Mortality and the Javanese Diaspora." *Itinerario* 21, no. 1 (1997): 125–36.

"Engelands Hydrographische Opnemingen in Onze *Koloniën.*" *IG*, no. 2 (1891): 2013–15.

Engelbregt, J. H. "De Ontwikkeling van Japan met het Oog op het Gele Gevaar." *TNI* (1897): 800–15.

"Enkel Woord Over de Voeding van den Soldaat te Velde." *IMT* 2 (1883): 160–70.

Enthoven, J. J. K. *Bijdragen tot de Geographie van Borneo's Westerafdeeling,* 2 vols. Leiden: Brill, 1903.

———. *De Militaire Cartographie in Nederlandsch-Indië.* Indisch Militair Tijdschrift, 1905.

Erman, Erwiza. "Tauke, Kuli dan Penguasa: Ekspolitasi Hutan Pangalong di Riau." *Sejarah, Pemikiran, Rekonstruksi, Persepsi* 5 (1994): 20–33.

Ette, A. J. H. van. *Onze Ministers Sinds 1798.* Alphen aan de Rijn: N. Sansom N. V., 1948.

"Europeesche Industrie in Borneo's Westerafdeeling" *IG*, no. 2 (1891): 2011–12.

Eusoff, Datin Ragayah. *The Merican Clan.* Singapore: Times Books, 1997.

Faes, J. "Het Rijk Pelalawan." *TBG* 27 (1881): 489–537.

Faragher, John. *Rereading Frederick Jackson Turner: "The Significance of the Frontier in American History" and Other Essays.* New York: Henry Holt and Co., 1994.

Fasseur, C. "Cornerstone and Stumbling Block: Racial Classification and the Late Colonial State in Indonesia." In *The Late Colonial State in Indonesia: Political and Economic Foundations of the Netherlands Indies 1880–1942,* edited by Robert Cribb. Leiden: KITLV, 1994.

———. "Een Koloniale Paradox. De Nederlandse Expansie in de Indonesische Archipel in het Midden van de Negentiende Eeuw (1830–1870)." *Tijdschrift voor Geschiedenis* 92 (1979): 162–86.

Fisher, Nick. "Workshop of Villains: Was There Much Organised Crime in Classical Athens?" In *Organised Crime in Antiquity,* edited by Keith Hopwood, 53–96. Swansea: Classical Press of Wales, 1999.

Fong, Mak Lau. *The Sociology of Secret Societies: A Study of Chinese Secret Societies in Singapore and the Malay Peninsula.* Kuala Lumpur: Oxford University Press, 1981.

Foucault, Michel. *Discipline and Punish: The Birth of the Prison.* Harmondsworth: Penguin, 1977.

Fremery, H. de. "Militaire Luchtscheepvaart." *Orgaan Indische Krijgskundige Vereeniging* 9, no. 17 (1907).

Fujimoto, Helen. *The South Indian Muslim Community and the Evolution of the Jawi Peranakan in Penang up to 1948.* Tokyo: Gaigokugo daigaku, 1988.

Furnivall, John. *Netherlands India: A Study of Plural Economy.* Cambridge: Cambridge University Press, 1939.

Gallagher, J., and R. Robinson. "The Imperialism of Free Trade." *Economic History Review* 6, no. 1 (1953): 1–15.

Gallant, Thomas. "Brigandage, Piracy, Capitalism, and State-Formation: Transnational Crime from a Historical Word-Systems Point of View." In *States and Illegal Practices,* edited by Josiah Heyman, 25–62. Oxford: Berg Publishers, 1999.

Gayo, M. H. *Perang Gayo Alas Melawan Kolonialis Belanda.* Jakarta: PN Balai Pustaka, 1983.

"Geheimzinnige Werving van Neger Soldaten in Liberia" *IG,* no. 1 (1892): 505–10.

George, Kenneth. *Showing Signs of Violence: The Cultural Politics of a Twentieth-Century Headhunting Ritual.* Berkeley: University of California Press, 1996.

Gerlach, A. J. A. "De Eerste Expeditie Tegen Atjih. Eene bijdrage tot de Indische krijgsgeschiedenis." *Tijdspiegel* 1 (1874): 73–120.

Gerlach, L. W. C. "Reis naar het Meergebied van de Kapoeas in Borneo's Westerafdeeling." *BITLV* (1881): 285–322

Gersen, G. J. "Oendang-Oendang of Verzameling van Voorschriften in de Lematang-Oeloe en Ilir en de Pasemah Landen van Oudsher gevolgd, en door langdurig Gebruik Hadat of Wet geworden." *TITLV* 20 (1873): 108–50.

Goor, J. van. "Imperialisme in de Marge?" In *Imperialisme in de Marge: De Afronding van Nederlands-Indië.* Utrecht: HES Uitgevers, 1986.

Gouda, Frances. *Dutch Culture Overseas: Colonial Practice in the Netherlands Indies, 1900–1942.* Amsterdam: Amsterdam University Press, 1995.

Graves, Elizabeth. *The Minangkabau Response to Dutch Colonial Rule in the Nineteenth Century.* Ithaca: Cornell Modern Indonesia Project, Monograph no. 60, 1981.

Groot, Cornelis de. *Herinneringen aan Blitong: Historisch, Lithologisch, Mineralogisch, Geographisch, Geologisch, en Mijnbouwkundig.* The Hague, 1887.

Groot, Jan J. M. de. *Het Kongsiwezen van Borneo: Eene Verhandeling over den Grondslag en den Aard der Chineesche Politieke Vereenigengen in de Koloniën met eene Chineesche Geschiedenis van de Kongsi Lanfong.* The Hague: Nijhoff, 1885.

Gueritz, E. P. "British Borneo." *Proceedings of the Royal Colonial Institute, Royal Commonwealth Society* 29 (1897/98): 61–67.

Guha, Ranajit. "The Prose of Counter-Insurgency." In *Selected Subaltern Studies,* edited by Ranajit Guha, and Gayatri Spivak, 45–88. New York: Oxford University Press, 1988.

Gullick, John. "The Kuala Langat Piracy Trial." *JMBRAS* 69, no. 2 (1996): 101–14.

Haas, W. H. van der. "Belasting op het Vervoer van Djatihout." *IG* 1 (1897): 416–18.

Haeften, F. W. van. "Voorkoming van Darmziekten te Velde." *IMT* 2 (1895): 80–87.

Haeften, J. van. "Voorkomen van Darmziekten Bij het Leger te Velde." *IMT* 2 (1895): 80.

"Handel en Scheepvaart." *EvNI* 2 (1918): 10–47.

Hane, Mikiso. *Peasants, Rebels, and Outcastes: The Underside of Modern Japan.* New York: Pantheon, 1982.

Harfield, Alan. *British and Indian Armies in the East Indies, 1685–1935.* Chippenham: Picton Publishing, 1984.

Harper, T. N. "The Orang Asli and the Politics of the Forest in Colonial Malaya." In *Nature and the Orient: The Environmental History of South and Southeast Asia,* edited by Richard Grove, 936–66. Delhi: Oxford University Press, 1998.

Hart Everett, A. "Notes on the Distribution of the Useful Minerals in Sarawak." *JSBRAS* 1 (1878): 13–30.

Harrison, Barbara. *Pusaka: Heirloom Jars of Borneo.* Singapore: Oxford University Press, 1986.

Hashim, Muhammad Yusoff. *Kesultanan Melayu Melaka: Kajian Beberapa Aspek Tentang Melaka pada Abad Ke-15 dan Abad Ke-16 Dalam Sejarah Malaysia.* Kuala Lumpur: Dewan Bahasa dan Pustaka Kementerian Pendidikan Malaysia, 1990.

Hashiya, Hiroshi. "The Pattern of Japanese Economic Penetration of the Prewar Netherlands East Indies." In *The Japanese in Colonial Southeast Asia,* edited by Saya Shiraishi, and Takashi Shiraishi, 89–112. Ithaca: Cornell University Southeast Asia Program, 1993.

Hasjmy, A. *Kebudayaan Aceh Dalam Sejarah.* Jakarta: Penerbit Beuna, 1983.

Hasselt, A. L. van, and H. J. E. F. Schwartz. "De Poelau Toedjoeh in het Zuidelijk Gedeelte der Chineesche Zee." *TAG* 15 (1898): 21–45.

Hasselt, M. A. L. "The Object and Results of a Dutch Expedition into the Interior of Sumatra in the Years 1877, 1878, and 1879." *JSBRAS* 15 (1885): 39–59.

"Havens- en Scheepvaartregeling op Atjeh." *IG* 2 (1907): 1079–80.

Headrick, Daniel. *The Tools of Empire: Technology and European Imperialism in the Nineteenth Century.* Oxford: Oxford University Press, 1981.

Heidhues, Mary Somers. *Bangka Tin and Mentok Pepper: Chinese Settlement on an Indonesian Island.* Singapore: ISEAS, 1992.

———. *Golddiggers, Farmers, and Traders in the Chinese Districts of West Kalimantan, Indonesia.* Ithaca: Cornell University Southeast Asia Program, 2003.

Hekmeijer, F. C. *De Rechtstoestand der Inlandsche Christengemeenten in Nederlandsch-Indië.* Utrecht: Utrechtse Stoomdrukkerij P. den Boer, 1892.

Heldring, E. "Poeloe Weh. Zijne Topographische Beschrijving en Eenige Opmerkingen met Betrekking tot de Beteekenis van het Eiland." *TAG,* 2d ser., 17 (1900): 622–39.

Hellfrich, O. L. "Bijdrage tot de Kennis van Boven-Djambi, Ontleend aan eene Nota van den Assistent-Resident." *TAG* 21 (1904): 973–97.

Herbert, David. "Crime and Place: An Introduction." In *The Geography of Crime,* edited by David Evans and David Herbert, 1–15. London: Routledge, 1989.

Hershatter, Gail. "The Hierarchy of Shanghai Prostitution 1870–1914." *Modern China* 15, no. 4 (1989): 471

———. "Modernizing Sex, Sexing Modernity: Prostitution in Early Twentieth-Century Shanghai." In *Engendering China: Women, Culture, and the State,* edited by Christina Gilmartin et al., 147–74. Cambridge: Harvard University Press, 1994.

"Herziening van de Areaal-Opgaven Betreffende de Buitenbezittingen." *IG,* no. 2 (1894): 1734–38

Heshusius, C. A. *Het KNIL van Tempo Doeloe.* Amsterdam: Bataafsche Leeuw, 1988.

Heslinga, Marcus. "Colonial Geography in the Netherlands." In *Geography and Professional Practice,* edited by V. Berdoulay, and J. A. van Ginkel, 173–93. Utrecht: Faculteit Ruimtelijke Wetenschappen Universiteit Utrecht, 1996.

Hesselink, Liesbeth. "Prostitution: A Necessary Evil, Particularly in the Colonies." In *Indonesian Women in Focus,* edited by Elsbeth Locher Scholten, and Anke Niehof. Leiden: KITLV, no. 127, 1987.

Heyman, Josiah, and Smart, Alan. "States and Illegal Practices: An Overview." In *States and Illegal Practices,* edited by Josiah Heyman, 1–24. Oxford: Berg Publishers, 1999.

Hickson, S. *A Naturalist in North Celebes.* London: John Murray, 1889.

"Hindoe-Strafrecht op Lombok" *TNI* 1(1896): 166–68.

Hirosue, Masashi. "The Batak Millenarian Response to the Colonial Order." *JSEAS* 25, no. 2 (1994): 331–43.

Hobsbawm, Eric. *Primitive Rebels: Studies in Archaic Forms of Social Movement in the Nineteenth and Twentieth Centuries.* Manchester: Manchester University Press, 1959.

———. *Bandits.* London: Weidenfield and Nicholson, 1969.

Hoff, B. van't. *Bijdrage tot de Genealogie van het Geslacht Henny.* Zutphen, 1939.

Holleman, J. F. *Van Vollenhoven on Indonesian Adat Law.* The Hague: Martinus Nijhoff, 1981.

Hooker, M. B. "Dutch Colonial Law and the Legal Systems of Indonesia." In *Legal Pluralism: An Introduction to Colonial and Neo-colonial Laws,* 250–300. Oxford: Clarendon Press, 1975.

Hopkirk, Peter. *Trespassers on the Roof of the World: The Secret Exploration of Tibet.* New York: Kodansha, 1995.

Hose, Bishop. "The Contents of a Dyak Medicine Chest." *JSBRAS* 39 (1902): 65–70.

Hoskins, Janet, ed. *Headhunting and the Social Imagination in Southeast Asia.* Stanford: Stanford University Press, 1996.

Hoskins, Janet. *Biographical Objects: How Things Tell the Stories of People's Lives.* New York: Routledge, 1998.

Houben, Vincent. "Native States in India and Indonesia: The Nineteenth Century." *Itinerario* 11, no. 1 (1987): 107–35.

———. "Nyabrang/'Overzee Gaan': Javaanse Emigratie Tussen 1880 en 1940." In *Het Paradijs is Aan de Overzijde,* edited by Piet Emmer, and Herman Obdeijn, 51–65. Utrecht: Van Arkel, 1998.

Hughes, David. "The Prahu and Unrecorded Inter-Island Trade." *Bulletin of Indonesian Economic Studies* 22, no. 2 (August, 1986): 103–13.

Huijts, J. "De Veranderende Scheepvaart Tussen 1870 en 1930 end de Gevolgen voor de Handel op Nederlands-Indië." In *Katoen voor Indië,* edited by J. Huijts, and S. Tils, 57–73. Amsterdam: NEHA, 1994.

Huizer, H. D. P. "De Opium-Regie in Nederlandsch-Indië." *IG,* no. 1 (1906): 360–80.

Hulshoff, B. "Het Kaartsysteem. Een Middel tot Vereenvoudiging van Publiekrechtelijke Administratiën en Meer Speciaal van die der Belastingen." *TBB* 38 (1910): 262–73.

Hurgronje, C. Snouck. *De Atjehers.* Leiden: E. J. Brill, 1893–94. (I)

———. *Mekka in the Latter Part of the 19th Century: Daily Life, Customs and Learning, the Moslims of the East-Indian Archipelago.* Leiden: E. J. Brill, 1931.

Hyam, Ronald. "Concubinage and the Colonial Service: The Crewe Circular (1909)." *Journal of Imperial and Commonwealth History* 14, no. 3 (May 1986): 170–86.

"Hydrographie." *EvNI* 2 (1918): 125–27.

"Hydrographische Opname in Oost-Indië." *Eigen Haard* 48 (1907): 756–59.

"Iets over de Organisatie van het Politiewezen op de Buiten-Bezittingen." *TBB* 2 (1888): 183–85.

"Iets over het Kadaster op de Buitenbezittingen." *IG,* no. 2 (1885): 1582–85.

"Indisch Concubinaat en Prostitutie, besproken door den Schrijver van 'Politieke Vragen'." *IG,* no. 2 (1899): 1378–85.

"Indische Hydrografie." *TAG* 6 (1882): 122–40.

Ingleson, John. "Prostitution in Colonial Java." In *Nineteenth and Twentieth Century Indonesia,* edited by David Chandler, and M. C. Ricklefs, 123–40. Melbourne: Monash Southeast Asian Studies, 1986.

Ingram, James. *Economic Change in Thailand Since 1850.* Stanford: Stanford University Press, 1955.

"Inlanders bij de Rechtelijke Macht." *IG,* no. 1 (1906): 432–34.

"Inlandsche Christenen." *Wet en Adat* 1/2, no. 1 (1896–98): 321–30.

Innes, E. *The Chersonese with the Gilding Off.* 1885. Vol. 1. Kuala Lumpur: Oxford University Reprints, 1974.

"Invloed der Vreemdelingschap op het Rechtswezen in NI." *Wet en Adat* 1/2, no. 1 (1896–98): 159–97.

"Invoering van het Nieuwe Strafwetboek." *IG,* no. 2 (1902): 1235–36.

Irfan, Nia Kurnia Sholihat. *Kerajaan Sriwijaya: Pusat Pemirintahan dan Perkambangannya.* Jakarta: Grimukti Pusaka, 1983.

Irschick, Eugene. "Order and Disorder in Colonial South India." *MAS* 23, no. 3 (1989): 459–92.

Irwin, Graham. *Nineteenth-Century Borneo: A Study in Diplomatic Rivalry.* Singapore: Donald Moore Books, 1967.

Ismail, Muhammad Gade. "The Economic Position of the Uleebalang in the Late Colonial State: Eastern Aceh, 1900–1942." In *The Late Colonial State in Indonesia: Political and Economic Foundations of the Netherlands Indies 1880–1942,* edited by Robert Cribb. Leiden: KITLV, 1994.

———. "Seuneubok Lada, Uleebalang, dan Kumpeni Perkembangan Sosial Ekonomi di Daerah Batas Aceh Timur, 1840–1942." Ph.D. diss., Leiden University, 1991.

"Jaarlijksch Verslag. Singapore." *Consulaire Berichten en Verslagen* (1874): 544–48; (1875): 490–92.

Jackson, James. *Chinese in the West Borneo Goldfields: A Study in Cultural Geography.* Hull: University of Hull Occasional Papers, 1970.

Janssen, C. W. "De Statistiek van den Handel, de Scheepvaart en de In- en Uitvoerrechten in Nederlandsch Indië." *Bijdragen Statistisch Instituut* 8 (1892): 161–78.

Jaschok, Maria. *Concubines and Bondservants.* Hong Kong: Oxford University Press, 1988.

"Javaansche 'Hadat'." *De Economist* (1869): 1222

Jennings, John. *The Opium Empire: Japanese Imperialism and Drug Trafficking in Asia, 1895–1945.* Westport: Praeger, 1997.

Jones, David. *Crime, Protest, Community, and Police in Nineteenth-Century Britain.* London: Routledge and Kegan Paul, 1982.

Jonge, Huub de, and Nico Kaptein, eds. *Transcending Borders: Arabs, Politics, Trade, and Islam in Southeast Asia.* Leiden: KITLV, 2002.

Juriaanse, Maria. *De Nederlandse Ministers van Buitenlandse Zaken, 1813–1900.* The Hague: Leopold, 1974.

Juynboll, H. H. "Mededeelingen omtrent Maskers in den Indischen Archipel." *Internationales Archiv für Ethnographie* 15 (1902): 28–29.

"Kaartbeschrijving: Zeekaarten." *EvNI* 2 (1918): 240–41.

Kan C. M. "De Belangrijkste Reizen der Nederlanders in de 19e Eeuw Ondernomen. De Voornaamste Werken, in dat Tijdperk op Geographisch Gebied Verschenen." *TAG*, 2d ser., 6 (1889): 510–81.

———. "Geographical Progress in the Dutch East Indies 1883–1903." *Report of the Eighth International Geographic Congress. Held in the United States 1904–1905*, 715–23. Washington, D.C.: Government Printing Office, 1905.

Kaptein, Nico. "Meccan Fatwas from the End of the Nineteenth Century on Indonesian Affairs." *Studia Islamika* 2, no. 2 (1995): 141–60.

Kater, C. "De Dajaks van Sidin. Uittreksel uit eene Reisbeschrijving van Pontianak naar Sidin in April 1865." *TBG* 16 (1867): 183–88

———. "Iets over het Pandelingschap in de Westerafdeeling van Borneo en de Boegineesche Vestiging aan het Zuider-Zeestrand te Pontianak." *TNI* 2 (1871): 296–305.

Karl, Rebecca. "Creating Asia: China in the World at the Beginning of the Twentieth Century." *American Historical Review* 103, no. 4 (October 1998): 1096–1117.

Kartodirdjo, A. Sartono, ed. *Sejarah Perlawan-Perlawan Terhadap Kolonialisme.* Jakarta: Departemen Pertahanan Keamanan, 1973.

Katayama, Kunio. "The Japanese Maritime Surveys of Southeast Asian Waters before the First World War." *Institute of Economic Research Working Paper*, no. 85. Kobe: Kobe University of Commerce, 1985.

"Katholieke Propaganda." *IG*, no. 1 (1889): 69.

Kaur, Amarjit. *Economic Change in East Malaysia: Sabah and Sarawak Since 1850.* London: Macmillan, 1998.

———. "'Hantu' and Highway: Transport in Sabah 1881–1963." *MAS* 28, no. 1 (1994): 1–50.

———. "Tin Miners and Tin Mining in Indonesia, 1850–1950." *Asian Studies Review* 20, no. 2 (1996): 95–120.

Kearney, Michael. "Transnationalism in California and Mexico at the End of Empire." In *Border Identities: Nation and State at International Frontiers,* edited by Thomas Wilson and Hastings Donnan, 117–41. Cambridge: Cambridge University Press, 1998.

Kempe, E. "De Scheepvaartregeling." *De Militaire Spectator* 62 (1893): 410–19.

Kennedy, R. H. *A Brief Geographical and Hydrographical Study of Straits Which Constitute Routes for International Traffic.* United Nations Document A/Conference 13/6, 23 October 1957.

Kerckhoff, Ch. E. P. "Eenige Mededeelingen en Opmerkingen Betreffende de Slavernij in Nederlandsch-Indië en Hare Afschaffing." *IG*, no. 1 (1891): 743–69.

Kern, R. A. "De Controleurs en 't Concubinaat." *TBB* 28 (1905): 250–52.

Keuchenius, L. W. C. *Handelingen van Regering en der Staten-Generaal Betreffende het Reglement op het Beleid der Regering van Nederlandsch-Indië.* Utrecht: Kemink, 1857, II.

Khatchikiam, Levon. "The Chulia Muslim Merchants in Southeast Asia, 1650–1800." In *Merchant Networks in the Early Modern World, 1450–1800,* edited by Sanjay Subrahmanyam. Aldershot (U.K.): Variorum, 1996.

Kielstra, E. B. "De Uitbreiding van het Nederlandsch Gezag op Sumatra." *De Gids* 4 (1887): 256–96.

———. "Steenkolen en Spoorwegen ter Westkust van Sumatra." *De Gids* 4 (1884): 1–41.

Kielstra, J. C. "De Rechtspraak over de Inlandsche Bevolking in het Gouvernement Celebes en Onderhoorigheden en de Residentie Timor." *IG*, no. 1 (1907): 165–93.

"Klassen der Bevolking van Nederlandsch-Indië." *Wet en Adat* 1/2, no. 1 (1896–98): 79–81.

Klavaren, Marieke van. "Death Among Coolies: Mortality and Javanese Labourers on Sumatra in the Early Years of Recruitment, 1882–1909." *Itinerario* 21, no. 1 (1997): 111–25.

Klerks, E. A. "Geographisch en Etnographisch Opstel over de Landschappen Korintji, Serampas, en Soengai Tenang." *TITLV* 39 (1897): 1–117.

Knafla, Louis. "Structure, Conjuncture, and Event in the Historiography of Modern Criminal Justice History." In *Crime History and Histories of Crime: Studies in the Historiography of Crime and Criminal Justice in Modern History,* edited by Clive Emsley, and Louis Knafla, 33–46. Westport: Greenwood Press, 1996.

Kniphorst, H. P. E. *Tijdschrift voor het Zeewezen.* "Historische Schets van den Zeeroof in den Oost-Indischen Archipel" (1876) 6, pp. 3–84; (1876) 6, pp. 159–224; (1876) 6, pp. 283–318; (1876) 6, pp. 353–452; (1877) 7, pp. 1–64; (1877) 7, pp. 135–210; (1877) 7, pp. 237–316; (1878) 8, pp. 1–48; (1878) 8, pp. 107–64; (1878) 8, pp. 213–306; (1879) 9, pp. 1–67; (1879) 9, pp. 85–146; (1879) 9, pp. 173–227; (1879) 9, pp. 1–67; (1880) 10, pp. 1–64; (1880) 10, pp. 89–204; (1880) 10, pp. 235–358.

Kohlbrugge, J. "Prostitutie in Nederlandsch-Indië." *Verslagen der Indisch Genootschap* (1901): 17–36.

Kol, H. van. *De Bestuurstelsels der Hedendaagsche Koloniën.* Leiden, 1905.

———. "Het Lot der Vrouw in Onze Oost-Indische Koloniën." *Koloniaal Weekblad* (25 Dec 1902): 5.

"Koninklijk Besluit van den 15den Sept 1909, Houdende Vaststelling van de Gewijzigde Samenstelling en Sterkte der Scheepsmacht voor Nederlandsch-Indië Benoodigd." *Marineblad* 24 (1909/1910): 401–402.

"Kontroleurs op de Bezittingen Buiten Java en Madura." *IG* 1 (1884): 14–20.

Kort, Marcel de. "Doctors, Diplomats, and Businessmen: Conflicting Interests in the Netherlands and Dutch East Indies, 1860–1950." In *Cocaine: Global Histories,* edited by Clive Emsley, and Louis Knafla, 123–45. London: Routledge, 1999.

Kort Overzicht der Tweede Expeditie naar Atjeh, Getrokken uit de Officieele Verslagen." *IMT* (1875): 92–119; (1876): 58–87, 100–122.

"Kort Overzicht van de Ongeregeldheden op Halmahera." *IMT* 38, no. 1 (1907): 328–31.

"Kort Overzigt van den Stand van Zaken op het Eiland Ceram." *IMT* 37, no. 1 (1906): 167–69.

Kossmann, K. *Nieuwe Nederlandsch Biografisch Woordenboek.* Leiden: Sijthoff's Uitgevers, 1937.

Koster, J. L. "Een Stem over de Drankquestie in het Nederlandsch-Indisch Leger." *TNI* (1902): 21–41.

"Kraing Bonto-Bonto; Verhaal van den Opstand in de Noorder-districten van Celebes in 1868 en van het Dempen van dien Opstand." *IMT* 3 (1872): 198–233.

Kratoska, Paul. *Index to British Colonial Files Pertaining to British Malaya.* Kuala Lumpur: Arkib Negara Malaysia, 1990.

Kreemer, J. J. "Bijdrage tot de Volksgeneeskunde bij de Maleiers der Padangsche Beneden-landen." *BTLV* 60 (1908): 438–87.

Kroesen, R. C. "Aanteekeningen over de Anambas-, Natoena-, en Tambelan-Eilanden." *TBG* 21 (1875): 235–47.

Kruijt, J. A. *Atjeh en de Atjehers: Twee Jaren Blokkade op Sumatra's Noord-Oost Kust.* Leiden: Gualth Koff, 1877.

Kruseman, J. W. G. "Beschouwingen over het Ontwerp-Wetboek van Strafrecht voor Inlanders in Nederlandsch-Indië." Ph.D. diss., University of Amsterdam, Haarlem, 1902.

Kuitenbrouwer, M. *The Netherlands and the Rise of Modern Imperialism: Colonies and Foreign Policy, 1870–1902.* New York: Berg Publishers, 1991.

Kustverlichting in Nederlandsch-Indië. Uitgegeven door het Hoofdbureau van Scheepvaart (Dept. van Marine), naar Aanleiding der Eerste Nederlandsche Tentoonstelling op Scheepvaartgebied te Amsterdam, 1913.

"Kustverlichting in Ned.-Indië." *IG,* no. 1 (1906): 80–81.

Labour Commission: Glossary of Words and Names in the Report of the Commissioners; Index to Evidence and Analysis of Evidence Taken by the Commission. Singapore: Government Press, 1891.

Laffan, Michael. *Islamic Nationhood and Colonial Indonesia: The Umma Below the Winds.* London: Routledge, 2003.

Lange, H. M. *Het Eiland Banka en Zijn Aangelegenheden.* 's Bosch: Muller, 1850.

Lapian, Adrian. "The Sealords of Berau and Mindanao: Two Responses to the Colonial Challenge." *Masyarakat Indonesia* 1, no. 2 (1974): 143–54.

Lavino, G. "Aanteekeningen Betreffende het Handelsverkeer in Atjeh, in 1874–1876, Ontleend aan Berigten van den Waarnemenden Consul der Nederlanden te Penang." *Consulaire en Andere Berigten en Verslagen over Nijverheid, Handel en Scheepvaart* (1877): 751–52.

League of Nations: Commission of Inquiry into the Traffic in Women and Children in the East; Report to the Council, IV, Social 1932, Official no. C.849.M 393, p. 81.

Leeuwen, F. H. G. J. van. "Een Voorstel tot hervorming van desa-instellingen en district-politie." *TBB* 31 (1906): 193–210, 321–23.

"Legerbelang." *IMT* 1 (1897): 44–51.

Lindblad, J. Thomas. "Between Singapore and Batavia: The Outer Islands in the Southeast Asian Economy in the Nineteenth Century." In *Kapitaal, Ondernemerschap en Beleid: Studies over Economie en Politiek in Nederland, Europa en Azie van 1500 tot Heden.* C. A. Davids et. al., eds. Amsterdam: NEHA, 1996.

———. "Economic Growth in the Outer Islands, 1910 to 1940." In *New Challenges in the Modern Economic History of Indonesia.* Leiden: Program in Indonesian Studies, 1993.

———. "Economische Aspecten van de Nederlandse Expansie in de Indonesische Archipel, 1870–1914." In *Imperialisme in de Marge: De Afronding van Nederlands-Indië,* edited by J. van Goor. Utrecht: HES, 1986.

———. "The Outer Islands in the 19th Century: Contest for the Periphery." In *The Emergence of a National Economy: An Economic History of Indonesia, 1800–2000,* edited by Howard Dick et al. Honolulu: University of Hawaii Press, 2002.

———, et al., eds. *Het Belang van de Buitengewesten: Economische Expansie en Koloniale Staatsvorming in de Buitengewesten van Nederlands Indië 1870–1942.* Amsterdam: NEHA, 1989.

Locher-Scholten, Elsbeth, "Dutch Expansion in the Indonesian Archipelago Around 1900 and the Imperialism Debate." *JSEAS* 25, no. 1 (1994): 91–111.

———. "National Boundaries as Colonial Legacy: Dutch Ethical Imperialism in the Indonesian Archipelago Around 1900." In *Indonesia and the Dutch Colonial Legacy*, edited by Frances Gouda and Elsbeth Locher-Scholten. Washington, D.C.: Woodrow Wilson Center Asia Program Occasional Paper no. 44, 1991.

———. *Sumatraans Sultanaat en Koloniale Staat: De Relatie Djambi-Batavia (1830–1907) en het Nederlandse Imperialisme*. Leiden: KITLV, 1994.

Lockhard, Craig. "Charles Brooke and the Foundations of the Modern Chinese Community in Sarawak, 1863–1917." *Sarawak Museum Journal* 19, no. 39 (1971): 77–108.

Loh, Francis. *Beyond the Tin Mines: Coolies, Squatters and New Villagers in the Kinta Valley, Malaysia, 1880–1980*. Singapore: Oxford University Press, 1988.

Lombard, Denys. *Kerajaan Aceh: Jaman Sultan Iskandar Muda*. Jakarta: Balai Pustaka, 1986.

Lontaan, J. U. *Sejarah Hukum Adat dan Adat Istiadat Kalimantan Barat*. Jakarta: C. V. Pilindo, 1975.

Low, James. *The British Settlement of Penang*. Singapore: Oxford University Press, 1972.

Lowman, John. "The Geography of Social Control: Clarifying Some Themes." In *The Geography of Crime*, edited by David Evans and David Herbert, 228–59. London: Routledge, 1989.

Lulofs, C. *Onze Politiek Tegenover de Buitenbezittingen*. Batavia, H. M, van Dorp & Co, 1908.

———. "Wegen-Onderhoud op Java en op de Buitenbezittingen." *TBB* 26 (1904): 31–39.

Mac-Leod. Norman "Het Behoud Onzer Oost-Indische Bezittingen. I" *TNI* (1898): 755–71, 871–92.

Maddison, Angus, ed. *Economic Growth in Indonesia 1820–1940*. Dordrecht: Foris Publishers, 1989.

"Makassaarsche Scheepvaart-Overeenkomsten (Tripangvangst)." *Wet en Adat* 1/2, no. 3 (1896–98): 48–54.

Malinowski, Bronislaw. *Argonauts of the Western Pacific: An Account of Native Enterprise and Adventure in the Archipelagoes of Melanesian New Guinea*. 1922; reprint, Prospect Heights, Ill.: Waveland Press, 1984.

Margadant, C. W. "Beoordeling van het Geschrift "De Rechtspraak in Nederlandsch-Indië en Speciaal die over den Inlander. Een Voorloopig Program door een N.-I. Rechterlijk Ambtenaar." *Recht in NI, Het* 68 (1897): 1–10.

———. *Verklaring van de Nederlandsch-Indische Strafwetboeken*. Batavia, 1895.

"Marine Militaire du Japon," "La Marine Militiare de la Chine," and "La Station Anglaise de l'Inde." *Revue Maritime et Coloniale* 50 (1876): 536–42.

Mani, A. "Indians in North Sumatra." In *Indian Communities in Southeast Asia*, edited by K. S. Sandhu and A. Mani, 46–97. Singapore: ISAES, 1993.

Marx, Karl. "Theories of Surplus Value." In *Karl Marx: Selected Writings in Sociology and Social Philosophy*, edited by Thomas Bottomore and Maximilien Rubel, 158–60. New York: McGraw-Hill, 1964.

McKeown, Adam. "Conceptualizing Chinese Diasporas, 1842 to 1949." *Journal of Asian Studies* 58, no. 2 (May, 1999): 306–37.

Means, Gordon. "Human Sacrifice and Slavery in the 'Unadministered' Areas of Upper Burma During the Colonial Era." *SOJOURN* 15, no. 2 (2000): 184–221.

Meerwaldt, J. H. "Per Motorboot 'Tole' het Tobameer Rond." *Rijnsche Zending* (1911): 63–69, 83–87, 113–16.

Meijier, J. E. de. "Zeehavens en Kustverlichting in Nederlansch-Indië" *Gedenkboek uitgegeven ter gelegenheid van het vijftigjarig bestaan van het Koninklijk Instituut van Ingenieurs (1847–1897)*, 303–05. 's-Gravenhage: Van Langenhuysen (1847–97).

Memmi, Albert. *The Colonizer and the Colonized*. Boston: Beacon Press, 1965.

"Metalen in Borneo's Westerafdeeling." *TAG* 7 (1883): 12–13.

Mevius, Johan. *Catalogue of Paper Money of the VOC, Netherlands East Indies, and Indonesia*. Vriezenveen: Mevieus Numisbooks, 1981.

Meyer, Kathryn, and Terry Parssinen. *Webs of Smoke: Smugglers, Warlords, Spies, and the History of the International Drug Trade*. Lanham: Rowman and Littlefield, 1998.

Mihalopoulos, Bill. "The Making of Prostitutes: The Karayuki-san." *Bulletin of Concerned Asian Scholars* 25, no. 1 (1993): 41–57.

"Militaire Administratie in Indië." *IG* 2 (1887): 1883–84.

Miller, Daniel. "Why Some Things Matter." In *Material Cultures: Why Some Things Matter*, edited by Daniel Miller, 3–24. Chicago: University of Chicago Press, 1998.

Ming, Hanneke. "Barracks-Concubinage in the Indies, 1887–1920." *Indonesia*, no. 35 (April 1983): 65–93.

"Missive van Z.Exc. den Minister van Koloniën, d.d. 8 Mei 1888, Gericht tot het Nederl. Zendelinggenootschap." *Mededeelingen Nederlandsche Zendings Genootschap* 33 (1889): 336–50.

Mobini-Keseh, Natalie. *The Hadrami Awakening: Community and Identity in the Netherlands East Indies, 1900–1942*. Ithaca: Cornell University Southeast Asia Program, 1999.

"Mohammedaansche Broederschappen in Nederlandsch Indië." *TNI* 2 (1889): 15–20.

"Mohammedaansch-Godsdienstige Broederschappen, door een oud O.-I. Ambtenaar." *TNI* 2 (1891): 187–205.

Molenaar, T. J. A. "Het Aluminium en de Waarde van dat Metaal voor Militair Gebruik." *IMT* 1 (1895): 509–17.

Molengraaf, G. A. F. *Geologische Verkenningstochten in Centraal Borneo (1893–94): Atlas in 22 Bladen*. Leiden: Brill, 1900.

Molewijk, G. C. "De Telegraafverbinding Nederland-Indië." *Jambatan* 8, no. 3 (1990): 138–55.

Monkonnen, Eric. "The Quantitative Historical Study of Crime and Criminal Justice." In *History and Crime*, edited by James Inciardi and Charles Faupel, 53–74. London: Sage Publications, 1980.

Mrazek, Rudolf. *Engineers of Happy Land: Technology and Nationalism in a Colony* Princeton: Princeton University Press, 2002.

———. "From Darkness to Light: The Optics of Policing in Late-Colonial Netherlands East-Indies." In *Figures of Criminality in Indonesia, the Philippines, and Colonial Vietnam*, edited by Vicente Rafael, 23–46. Ithaca: Cornell University Southeast Asia Program, 1999.

Mukherjee, Arun. *Crime and Public Disorder in Colonial Bengal, 1861–1912*. Calcutta: KP Bagchi, 1995.

Multavidi. "Een Nieuwe Staatsinkomst van fl. 10,000,000 per Jaar." *TBB* 30 (1906): 338–52.

Murphy, Robert. *Headhunter's Heritage: Social and Economic Change Among the Mundurucu Indians.* Berkeley: University of California Press, 1960.

Murray, Dian. "Living and Working Conditions in Chinese Pirate Communities 1750–1850." In *Pirates and Privateers: New Perspectives on the War on Trade in the Eighteenth and Nineteenth Centuries,* edited by David Starkey, E. S. van Eyck van Heslinga, and J. A. de Moor. Exeter: University of Exeter Press, 1997.

———. *Pirates of the South China Coast, 1790–1810.* Stanford: Stanford University Press, 1987.

Naim, Mochtar. *Merantau: Pola Migrasi Suku Minangkabau.* Yogyakarta: Gadjah Mada University Press, 1979.

Napitupulu, S. H. *Perang Batak: Perang Sisingamangaradja.* Jakarta: Jajasan Pahlawan Nasional Sisingamangaradja, 1971.

Nederburgh, J. A. "Wijziging in Art. 109 Regeeringsregelement (Japansche Europeanen)." *Wet en Adat* 1/2, no. 3, vol. 2 (1896–98): 287.

Neumann, J. B. "Reis Naar de Onafhankelijk Landschappen Mapat Toenggoel en Moeara Soengei Lolo VI Kota." *TBG* 29 (1884): 1–37, 38–87.

Niermeyer, J. F. "Barrière-Riffen en Atollen in de Oost Indiese Archipel." *TAG* (1911): 877–94.

"Nieuwe Kaart van Sumatra." *Indische Mercuur* 31, no. 38 (1908): 680–81.

"Nieuwe Kabelverbindingen in Ned. Oost-Indië." *Marineblad* 18 (1903/1904): 784–802.

"Nieuwe Tarieven van Invoer- en Uitvoerrechten in Nederl.-Indië." *Indische Mercuur* 9, no. 17 (1886): 213–14.

Nieuwenhuis, A. W. *In Centraal Borneo: Reis van Pontianak naar Samarinda.* 2 vols. Leiden, 1900.

Nieuwenhuyzen, W. C. "De Beoefening der Inlandsche Talen in het Indische Leger." *IG,* no. 1 (1884): 335–62.

———. "Het Negerelement bij het Indische Leger." *IG,* no. 1 (1899): 525–46.

Nijland, J. C. C. "Rapport Betreffende de Proef met 10 Verlichte Geweren, met Drie Bijlagen, gemerkt A, B, en C." *IMT* extra bijlage no. 6, ser. 2 (1903): 1–9.

Nish, Ian, ed. *British Documents on Foreign Affairs: Reports and Papers From the Foreign Office Confidential Print,* Part 1, Series E (Asia, 1860–1914), Vol. 29. University Publications of America, 1995.

Nonini, Donald. *British Colonial Rule and the Resistance of the Malay Peasantry.* New Haven: Yale University Southeast Asia Program, 1992.

"Noordoostkust Borneo: Van Hoek Mangkalihat tot de Berouwrivier." *Mededeelingen op Zeevaartkundig Gebied over Nederlandsch Oost Indië* 28 (July 1902): 1–12.

Nordholt, Henk Schulte. "The Jago in the Shadow: Crime and 'Order' in the Colonial State in Java." *RIMA* 25, no. 1 (1991): 74–91.

Nota over de Uitoeffening van Staatstoezicht op de Werving en Emigratie van Inlanders op Java en Madoera Bestemd voor de Buitenbezittingen of voor Plaatsen Buiten Nederlandsch-Indië. Batavia: Landsdrukkerij, 1907.

Nugent, David. "State and Shadow-State in Northern Peru Circa 1900: Illegal Political Networks and the Problem of State Boundaries." In *States and Illegal Practices,* edited by Josiah Heyman, 63–98. Oxford: Berg Publishers, 1999.

"Numerieke Opgave van Militairen Die Zijn Gedegradeerd en van Die, welke in de 2e Klasse van Discipline Zijn Geplaatst, Zoomede Omtrent de Toepassing van de Straf van Rietslagen (1867–1875)." *IMT* 2 (1881): 286–325.

O'Connor, Richard. *A Theory of Indigenous Southeast Asian Urbanism.* Singapore: ISEAS Monograph no. 38, 1983.

Ockerse. "Emigratie van Javanen naar de Buitenbezittingen." *IG,* no. 2 (1903): 1221–23.

"Officiëel Relaas Omtrent Samenzweringen in Midden- en Oost- Java." *IG,* no. 2 (1888): 1992.

"Officiëel Relaas van de Ongeregeldheden in Solo" *IG,* no. 1 (1889): 216–21.

"Officiëel Relaas van de Onlusten te Tjilegon en Pogingen tot Oproer in Midden- en Oost-Java" *IG,* no. 2 (1889): 1768–76.

"Officier van Justitie te Soerabaya, contra F. W. de Rijk, Chef der te Soerabaya Gevestigde Firma Gebroeders van Delden." *Indisch Weekblad van het Recht* no. 538 (20 October 1873): 166–67.

"Olifanten voor het Transportwezen bij de Troepenmacht in Atjeh." *IMT* 2 (1880): 517–19.

"Onafhankelijke Bataks Benoorden het Tobameer." *IG,* no. 1 (1902): 246–48.

Onghokam. "Korupsi dan Pengawasan dalam Perspektif Sejarah." *Prisma* 15, no. 3 (1986): 3–11.

———. "Tradisi dan Korupsi." *Prisma* 12, no. 2 (February 1983): 3–13.

"Onlusten in Bantam." *IG,* no. 2 (1888): 1122–23.

Onreat, Rene. *Singapore: A Police Background.* London: Dorothy Crisp, n.d.

"Onze Opium Politiek." *TNI,* no. 1 (1884): 401–12.

Opium-Aanhalingen." *IG,* no. 1 (1888): 474–75.

"Opium-smokkelhandel ter Zee." *TNI,* no. 1 (1884): 29–45.

"Opmerkingen en Mededeelingen: Circulaires van de Commissaris Mr. T.H. der Kinderen tot Toelichting op het Nieuwe Reglement Betreffende het Regtswezen in de Residentie Riouw." *Regt in NI* 38 (1882): 333–54.

Ooi, Keat Gin. *Of Free Trade and Native Interests: The Brookes and the Economic Development of Sarawak, 1841–1941.* Kuala Lumpur: Oxford University Press, 1997.

Oort, W. B. "Hoe een Groote Kaart tot Stand Komt." *Onze Eeuw* 9, no. 4 (1909): 363–85.

"Overeenkomsten met Inlandsche Vorsten: Djambi." *IG,* no. 1 (1882): 540–42.

"Overeenkomsten met Inlandsche Vorsten: Lingga/Riouw." *IG,* no. 1 (1907): 233–42.

"Overeenkomsten met Inlandsche Vorsten: Pontianak." *IG,* no. 1 (1882): 543–54.

"Overeenkomsten met Inlandsche Vorsten: Suppletoir Contract met Lingga, Riouw, en On-derhoorigheden." *IG,* no. 1 (1888): 163–64.

"Overzicht van Artikelen van Notaris Vellema, in het Bataviasch Nieuwsblad en het "Vader-land," over de Circulatie van Valsche Munt in Indië." *IG,* no. 2 (1896): 1252–55.

"Overzicht van eene Voordracht van J.J. de Groot over dat Gedeelte van China Waar Emi-gratie naar de Koloniën Plaats Hebben." *TAG* 8, no. 1 (1891): 305–11.

"Overzigt van een in het Berlijnsche Tijdschrift 'Der Kulturkaempffer' Heft 64 van 1882 Opgenomen Artikel over de Hollanders en hun Werfdepot te Harderwijk en over het Sol-daten Leven in de Hollandsche Koloniën." *IG,* no. 2 (1882): 480–85, 681–85.

Ownby, David, and Mary Somers Heidhues. *"Secret Societies" Reconsidered: Perspectives on the Social History of Early Modern South China and Southeast Asia.* Armonk, N.Y.: M. E. Sharpe, 1993.

Paine, S. C. M. *Imperial Rivals: China, Russia, and Their Disputed Frontier.* Armonk, N.Y.: M. E. Sharpe, 1996.

Pan, Lynn. *Sons of the Yellow Emperor: A History of the Chinese Diaspora.* New York: Little, Brown, 1992.

Panäri, Mäti. "Krijgstucht in het Indische Leger" *IMT* 2 (1881): 225–35.

Pekelharing, C. A. "De Loop der Beri-Beri in Atjeh in de Jaren 1886 en 1887." *TNI* 1 (1888): 305–11.

Pelly, Usman, et al., eds. *Sejarah Sosial Daerah Sumatra Utara Kotamadya Medan.* Jakarta: Departmen Pendidikan dan Kebudayaan Direktorat Sejarah dan Nilai Tradisional, 1984.

Peluso, Nancy. *Rich Forests, Poor People: Resource Control and Resistance in Java.* Berkeley: University of California Press, 1992.

Pemimpin Bagi Prijaji Boemipoetera di Tanah Djawa dan Madoera, no. 24/B.B.: Sendjata-api, Obat-Bedil dan Bekal Pemasang; A. Pembawaan Masoek dan Bembawaan Keloewar; B. Kepoenjaan, Pembawaan, dan Pernijagaan. Batavia: Drukkerij Ruygrok Co., 1919.

Perang Kolonial Belanda di Aceh. Banda Aceh: Pusat Dokumentasi dan Informasi Aceh, 1990.

Perelaer, E. "De Rechtspraak over de Inlandsche Bevolking in Nederlandsch-Indië." *TBB* 32 (1907): 418–22.

Perelaer, M. T. H. "Recensie over 'Jottings Made During a Tour Amongst the Land Dyaks of Upper Sarawak, Borneo, During the Year 1874, by Noel Denison, Formerly of the Sarawak Service, Singapore, Mission Press, 1879.'" *IG* (1881) 1, pp. 514–15

Philips, W. J. "De Transportdienst te Velde bij het Nederlandsch-Indische Leger." *IMT* 1 (1891): 46–49.

Piepers, M. C. "De Rechtspraak in Ned. Indië en Speciaal die over den Inlander." *TNI* 1 (1897): 293–309.

Pleyte Wzn., C. M. "Eene Bijdrage tot de Geschiedenis der Ontdekking van het Toba-Meer." *TAG* 7 (1895): 71–96, 727–40.

"Poeloong-Zaak, een ernstige Vingerwijzing." *IG* 1 (1886): 231–38.

"Politie." *TBB* 1 (1887–88): 379–82.

Pluvier, J. M. "Internationale Aspekten van de Nederlandse Expansie." *Bijdragen en Mededeelingen Betreffende de Geschiedenis der Nederlanden* 86, no.1 (1971): 26–31.

Pope, Andrew. "The P & O and the Asian Specie Network, 1850–1920." *MAS* 30, no. 1 (1996): 145–72.

Popkin, Samuel. *The Rational Peasant: The Political Economy of Rural Society in Vietnam.* Berkeley: University of California Press, 1979.

Post, Peter. "Japan and the Integration of the Netherlands East Indies into the World Economy, 1868–1942." *RIMA* 27, nos. 1–2 (1993): 134–65.

———. "Japanse Bedrijvigheid in Indonesie, 1868–1942: Structurele Elementen van Japans Vooroorlogse Economische Expansion in Zuidoost-Azie." Ph.D. diss., Vrije Universiteit, Amsterdam, 1991.

Potting, C. J. M. "De Ontwikkeling van het Geldverkeer in een Koloniale Samenleving Oostkust van Sumatra, 1875–1938." Ph.D. diss., Leiden University, 1997.

Pramoedya Ananta Toer. *Bumi Manusia.* Melaka: Wira Karya, 1981.

Prescott, J. R. V. *Political Frontiers and Political Boundaries.* London: Allen and Unwin, 1987.

Pridmore, F. *Coins and Coinages of the Straits Settlements and British Malaya, 1786 to 1951.* Singapore: Memoirs of the Raffles Museum, 1955.

Pringle, Robert. *Rajahs and Rebels: The Ibans of Sarawak Under Brooke Rule, 1841–1941.* Ithaca: Cornell University Press, 1970.

"Privaatrechtelijke Toestand der Chineezen in Nederlandsch-Indië." *TNI* (1898): 210–32.

Pyenson, Lewis. *Empire of Reason: Exact Sciences in Indonesia, 1840–1940.* Leiden: E. J. Brill, 1989.

Quahe, Yvonne. *We Remember: Cameos of Pioneer Life.* Singapore: Landmark Books, 1986.

Quarles van Ufford, J. K. W. "Koloniale Kroniek. Koloniale Literatuur: Ontginning van het Ombilin-Kolenveld en Spoorwegaanleg in Midden-Sumatra." *De Economist* 1 (1882): 260–72.

Rabinow, Paul. *French Modern: Norms and Forms of the Social Environment.* Cambridge: MIT Press, 1989.

Raffles, Sir Thomas Stamford. *Memoir of the Life and Public Services of Sir Thomas Stamford Raffles.* London: James Duncan, 1835.

Read, W. H. *Play and Politics, Recollections of Malaya by an Old Resident.* London: Wells Gardner, Darton, 1901.

"Recensie van 'De Draadlooze Telegrafie en hare Toepassing in Oost-Indië' door M. F. Onnen, Leiden E. J. Brill, 1906." *IG* 1 (1906): 936–39

Reelfs, J. C. T. "Consulaat Generaal der Nederlanden in de Straits-Settlements te Singapore. Jaarverslagen over 1899, 1900, 1901." *Consulaire Verslagen en Berichten,* no. 41 (1899): 798–814; no. 6 (1901): 77–94; no. 2 (1902): 17–42.

Rees, R. P. A. van. "Verslag over de Krijgsverrigtingen in Atjeh, door den 2den Luitenant bij het Korps Mariniers, R.P.A. van Rees, Kommandant van het Detachement Mariniers, aan boord van Zr. Ms. Stoomschip Metalen Kruis." *Mededeelingen Zeewezen* 7, no. 18 (1875): 1–22.

Reid, Anthony. *The Contest for North Sumatra: Atjeh, the Netherlands, and Britain, 1858–1898.* Kuala Lumpur: Oxford University Press, 1969.

———. "The Decline of Slavery in Nineteenth-Century Indonesia." In *Breaking the Chains: Slavery, Bondage, and Emancipation in Modern Africa and Asia,* edited by Martin Klein, 64–82. Madison: University of Wisconsin Press, 1993.

———. "Europe and Southeast Asia: The Military Balance." James Cook University of North Queensland, Occasional Paper 16. Townsville, Queensland, 1982.

———. "Flows and Seepages in the Long-Term Chinese Interaction with Southeast Asia." In *Sojourners and Settlers,* 15–49. St. Leonards, NSW: Allen and Unwin, 1996.

———. "Introduction: Slavery and Bondage in Southeast Asian History." In *Slavery, Bondage, and Dependency in Southeast Asia,* 1–43. St. Lucia: University of Queensland Press, 1983.

———. "Merchant Imperialist: W. H. Read and the Dutch Consulate in the Straits Settlements." In *Empires, Imperialism, and Southeast Asia,* edited by Brook Barrington, 34–59. Clayton, Australia. Monash Asia Institute, 1997.

———. "Nineteenth-Century Pan-Islam in Indonesia and Malaysia." *JAS* 26, no. 2 (1967): 267–83.

————, ed. *Slavery, Bondage, and Dependency in Southeast Asia.* New York: St. Martin's Press, 1983.

————. *Southeast Asia in the Age of Commerce: The Lands Beneath the Winds.* Vol. 1. New Haven: Yale University Press, 1988.

Rengert, George. "Behavioural Geography and Criminal Behaviour." In *The Geography of Crime,* edited by David Evans and David Herbert, 161–75. London: Routledge, 1989.

"Reorganisatie der Geneeskundige Dienst in het Indische Leger." *IMT* 2 (1880): 449–66, 596–608.

Report of the International Opium Commission, Shanghai, China, February 1–26, 1909. Shanghai: North-China Daily News and Herald, 1909.

Resink, G. J. "Conflichtenrecht van de Nederlands-Indische Staat in Internationaalrechtelijke Zetting." *BTLV,* no. 1 (1959): 1–39.

————. "De Archipel voor Joseph Conrad." *BTLV,* no. 2 (1959): 192–208.

————. "Onafhankelijke Vorsten, Rijken, en Landen in Indonesie Tussen 1850 en 1910." *Indonesie* 9, no. 4 (August 1956): 265–96.

"Resumé van Artikelen in de Turksche Bladen te Constantinopel over de Beweerde Slechte Behandeling van de Arabieren in Ned. -Indië en van de Beschermingen ter Zake van de Ned. Pers." *IG* 2 (1898): 1096–1108.

Review of the Netherlands Indian Tariff Law: Tariffs of Import and Export Duties Up to 1 July 1921 (Government Edition). The Hague: Official Printing Office, 1921.

Richter, H. V. "Problems of Assessing Unrecorded Trade." *Bulletin of Indonesian Economic Studies* 6, no. 1 (March 1970): 45–61.

Ricklefs, M. C. *A History of Modern Indonesia Since c. 1200.* Hampshire: Palgrave, 2001.

Ricklefs, M. C., and P. Voorhoeve. *Indonesian Manuscripts in Great Britain: A Catalogue of Manuscripts in Indonesian Languages in British Public Collections.* Oxford: Oxford University Press, 1977.

Riddell, Peter. "Arab Migrants and Islamization in the Malay World During the Colonial Period." *Indonesia and the Malay World* 29, no. 84 (2001): 113–28.

Rijn, P. H. van. "Jenevermisbruik doer de Europeesche Fusiliers van het NI Leger." *Milit. Spectator* (1902): 744.

Robinson, Geoffrey. *The Dark Side of Paradise: Political Violence in Bali.* Ithaca: Cornell University Press, 1995.

Roff, W. R. "The Malayo-Muslim World of Singapore at the Close of the Nineteenth Century." *JAS* 24, no. 1 (1964): 75–90.

Römer, G. A. "Chineezenvrees in Indië." *Vragen des Tijds* 2, no. 23 (1897): 193–223.

Rookmaaker, H. R. "Heerendiensten in de Buitenbezittingen." *TBB* 23 (1902): 312–20.

————. "Is de officiele waarheid in Indië plotseling overleden?" *TBB* 24 (1903): 278–82

"Roomsch-Katholieke Propaganda in de Minahasa." *IG* 2 (1902): 1407–08.

Rooseboom, J. W. "Valsche Rijksdaalders in Nederlandsch-Indië." *IG* 1 (1899): 393–99.

Rossum, J. P. van. "Bezuiniging bij de Zeemacht Tevens Verbetering." *De Gids* 2 (1907): 47–66, 474–91; 3 (1907): 287–305.

Rouffaer, G. P. "Foutieve Vermelding van Berghoogten op Schetskaarten der Buitenbezittingen." *TAG* 27 (1910): 787–90.

Rouffaer, G. P. "Uitzwerming van Javanen Buiten Java." *TAG*, 2d ser., 23 (1906): 1187–90.

Roy, J. J. le. "Een Eigen Telegraafkabel." *IMT* 1 (1900): 287–95.

Rudner, David West. *Caste and Capitalism in Colonial India: The Nattukottai Chettiars.* Berkeley: University of California Press, 1994.

Ruggiero, Vincenzo. *Crime and Markets.* Oxford: Oxford University Press, 2000.

"Ruilhandel bij de Bahau's van Midden-Borneo." *Katholieke Missiën* 35 (1909/1910): 185–86.

Ruitenbach, D. J. "Eenige Beschouwingen in Verband met het Huidige Politie-Vraagstuk." *IG* 2 (1905): 985–1014.

Rush, James. *Opium to Java: Revenue Farming and Chinese Enterprise in Colonial Indonesia, 1860–1910.* Ithaca: Cornell University Press, 1990.

Rütte, J. M. Ch. F. le. "Is Gelijkstelling van den Christen-Inlander met den Europeaan Wenschelijk?" *Recht in NI, Het* 72 (1899): 45–57.

Rutter, Owen. *The Pirate Wind: Tales of the Sea-Robbers of Malaya.* Singapore: Oxford University Press, 1986.

"Sabang als Kolenstation." *Het Nederlandsche Zeewezen* 3 (1904): 94.

"Sabang Baai." *Het Nederlandsche Zeewezen* 2 (1903): 236–47.

Sahlins, Marshall. "Cosmologies of Capitalism: The Trans-Pacific Sector of the World System." In *Culture, Power, and History: A Reader in Contemporary Theory,* edited by Nicholas Dirks et al., 412–58. Princeton: Princeton University Press, 1994.

Sahlins, Peter. *Boundaries: The Making of France and Spain in the Pyrenees.* Berkeley: University of California Press, 1989.

Said, H. Mohammad. *Aceh Sepanjang Abad.* Medan: P. T. Harian Waspada Medan, 1981.

Salmon, Claudine. "Taoke or Coolies? Chinese Versions of the Chinese Diaspora." *Archipel* 26 (1983): 179–210.

Sandhu, Kernial. "The Coming of the Indians to Malaysia." In *Indian Communities in Southeast Asia,* edited by K. S. Sandhu and A. Mani, 151–89. Singapore: ISEAS, 1993.

———. *Indians in Malaya: Some Aspects of Their Immigration and Settlement.* Cambridge: Cambridge University Press, 1969.

Sardesai, D. S. *British Trade and Expansion in Southeast Asia (1830–1914).* Bombay: Allied Publishers, 1977.

Saw, S. H. *Singapore Population in Transition.* Philadelphia: University of Pennsylvania Press, 1970.

Scammell, G. V. "European Exiles, Renegades and Outlaws and the Maritime Economy of Asia, 1500–1750." *MAS* 26, no. 4 (1992): 641–62.

Schaalje, M. "Bijdrage tot de Kennis der Chinesche Geheime Genootschappen." *TITLV* 20 (1873): 1–6.

Schelle, C. J. van. "De Geologisch-Mijnbouwkundige Opneming van een Gedeelte van Borneo's-Westkust: Verslag no. 1: Opmerkingen Omtrent het Winnen van Delfstoffen in een Gedeelte der Residentie Wester-Afdeeling van Borneo." *Jaarboek Mijnwezen* 1 (1881): 263–88.

———. "De Geologisch-Mijnbouwkundige Opneming van een Gedeelte van Borneo's Westkust: Verslag no. 6: Onderzoek naar Cinnaber en Antimoniumglans in het Bovenstroomgebied der Sikajam Rivier, met twee Kaarten." *Jaarboek Mijnwezen* 2 (1884): 123–49.

Scheltema, J. F. "The Opium Trade in the Dutch East Indies." *American Journal of Sociology* 13, no. 1 (1907): 79–112; no. 2 (1907): 224–51.

Schendel, Willem van, and Michiel Baud. "Towards a Comparative History of Borderlands." *Journal of World History* 8, no. 2 (1997): 211–42.

Schich, C. F. "De Rechtstoestand der Inlandsche Christenen." *IG* 2 (1892): 1532–45.

Schmidhamer, P.G. "De Expeditie naar Zuid Flores." *IMT* 24, no. 2 (1893): 101–15, 197–212.

Schoffer, I. "Dutch 'Expansion' and Indonesian Reactions: Some Dilemmas of Modern Colonial Rule (1900–1942)." In *Expansion and Reaction: Essays on European Expansion and Reactions in Asia and Africa,* edited by H. L. Wesseling, 78–99. Leiden: E. J. Brill, 1978.

Schoemaker, J. P. "Het Mohammedaansche Fanatisme." *IG* 2 (1898): 1517–37.

Scholten, C. *De Munten van de Nederlandsche Gebiedsdeelen Overzee, 1601–1948.* Amsterdam: J. Schulman, 1951.

Schöttler, P. "The Rhine as an Object of Historical Controversy in the Inter-War Years: Towards a History of Frontier Mentalities." *History Workshop Journal* 39 (1995): 1–21.

"Schroefstoomschepen Vierde Klasse." *IG* 2 (1880): 161–62.

Schumpeter, Joseph. *Imperialism and Social Classes.* New York: Augustus Kelley, 1951.

Scott, James. *Domination and the Arts of Resistance.* New Haven: Yale University Press, 1990.

———. *The Moral Economy of the Peasant.* New Haven: Yale University Press, 1976

———. *Seeing Like a State: How Certain Schemes to Improve the Human Condition Have Failed.* New Haven: Yale University Press, 1998.

———. *Weapons of the Weak: Everyday Forms of Peasant Resistance.* New Haven: Yale University Press, 1985.

Scwalbenberg, Henry. "The Economics of Pre-Hispanic Visayan Slave Raiding." *Philippine Studies* 42, no. 3 (1994): 376–84.

Sears, Laurie. "The Contingency of Autonomous History." In *Autonomous Histories, Particular Truths: Essay in Honor of John Smail,* 3–38. Madison: University of Wisconsin Southeast Asian Studies Monograph 11, 1993.

Senn van Basel, W. H. "De Chineezen op Borneo's Westkust." *TNI* 1 (1875): 59–75.

———. "De Maleiers van Borneo's Westkust." *TNI* 2 (1874): 196–208.

"Serawak en Noord-Borneo, Volgens de Jongste Mededeelingen." *TNI* 2 (1881): 1–25.

Shaw, K. E., and George Thomson. *The Straits of Malacca in Relation to the Problems of the Indian and Pacific Oceans.* Singapore: University Education Press, 1979.

Sherry, Norman. *Conrad's Eastern World.* Cambridge: Cambridge University Press, 1966.

Shimizu, Hiroshi. "Evolution of the Japanese Commercial Community in the Netherlands Indies in the Pre-War Period" (from Karayukî-san to Sôgô Shôsha) *Japan Forum* 3, no. 1 (1991): 37–56.

———. "The Rise and Fall of the Karayuki-san in the Netherlands Indies from the Late 19th Century to the 1930's." *RIMA* 26, no. 2 (1992): 20

Shimizu, Hiroshi, and Hitoshi Hirakawa. *Japan and Singapore in the World Economy: Japan's Economic Advance into Singapore, 1870–1965.* London: Routledge, 1999.

Shiraishi, Takashi. *An Age in Motion.* Ithaca: Cornell University Press, 1990.

Sidel, John. *Capital, Coercion, and Crime: Bossism in the Philippines.* Stanford: Stanford University Press, 1999.

Siebelhoff, M. W. "Gewapende Politiedienaren in Verband met Expeditiën, Afschaffing Schutterij en Legerreserve." *IMT* 2 (1907): 864–67.

Skeat, W. W. "The Orang Laut of Singapore." *JSBRAS* 33 (1900): 247–50.

Skinner, William. "Creolized Chinese Societies in Southeast Asia." In *Sojourners and Settlers,* edited by Anthony Reid, 51–93. St. Leonards, NSW: Allen and Unwin, 1996.

"Slaverij in Nederlandsch-Indië." *IG* 1 (1907): 425–26.

Sluijs, A. G. H. van. "Heerendiensten in de Buitenbezittingen." *TBB,* 24, 1903, pp. 282–87.

"Smokkelen van Opium Tusschen Singapore en Nederlandsch-Indië." *IG* 2 (1891): 2015–16.

Snelleman, J. F. "Tabakspijpen van de Koeboe's aan de Boven-Moesi-Rivier (Sumatra)." *Aarde en Haar Volken,* no. 24 (12 May 1906): 151.

Snow, Capt. Parker. "Colonization and the Utilisation of Ocean and Waste Spaces Throughout the World." In *Proceedings of the Royal Colonial Institute, Royal Commonwealth Society* 2 (1870–71): 117–21.

Soeroto, Soeri. "Perang Banjar." In *Sejarah Perlawanan-perlawanan Terhadap Kolonialisme,* edited by Sartono Kartodirdjo, 163–202. Jakarta: Pusat Sejarah ABRI, 1973.

Sone, Sachiko. "The Karayuki-san of Asia 1868–1938: The Role of Prostitutes Overseas in Japanese Economic and Social Development." *RIMA* 26, no. 2 (1992): 44–62.

Spakler, H. "Consulaat der Nederlanden te Penang. Jaarverslagen over 1898, 1899, 1900." *Consulaire Verslagen en Berigten* 43 (1899): 841–53; 7 (1900): 121–25; 47 (1901): 795–810.

Spat, C. "Welke Resultaten Mogen Verwacht Worden van het Onderwijs in de Maleische Taal aan de Kon. Mil. Academie?" *IMT* 1 (1899): 30–34.

Spitzer, Steven. "The Political Economy of Policing." In *Crime and Capitalism: Readings in Marxist Criminology,* edited by David Greenberg, 568–94. Philadelphia: Temple University Press, 1993.

Spivak, Gayatri. "Subaltern Studies: Deconstructing Historiography." In *Selected Subaltern Studies,* edited by Ranajit Guha and Gayatri Spivak, 3–32. New York: Oxford University Press, 1988.

"Spoor- en Tramwegen." *EvNI* 4 (1921): 68–85.

"Spoorwegaanleg op Noord-Sumatra." *TNI* (1899): 817–20.

St. John, Spenser. *The Life of Sir James Brooke: Rajah of Sarawak from His Personal Papers and Correspondence.* Edinburgh and London: William Blackwood and Sons, 1879.

Star, J. A. van der. "De Noodzakelijkheid voor de Inlandsche Scheepsonderofficieren om Nederlandsch te Leeren." *Marineblad* 18 (1903/1904): 191.

"Steenkolen en Brandstoffen in Oost-Indië." *Het Nederlandsche Zeewezen* 9 (1910): 66–71.

Steffens, W. "De Bouw van den Lichttoren op de van Diamontpunt Afstekende Zandbank. N.O. Hoek van Sumatra." *Het Nederlandsche Zeewezen* 5 (1906): 89–92.

Stok, N. P. van der "Wetenschappelijk Verslag over de Voorgekomen Verwondingen bij de 1e Expeditie Tegen het Rijk van Atjeh." *Geneeskundig Tijdschrift voor Nederlandsch-Indië* 16 (1874/1875): 577–720.

Stoler, Ann. *Capitalism and Confrontation in Sumatra's Plantation Belt 1870–1979.* New Haven: Yale University Press, 1986.

Struijk, N. J. "De Toekomst der Inlandsche Vorsten op de Buitenbezittingen." *IG* 1 (1883): 449–61.

Sugihara, Kaoru. "Japan as an Engine of the Asian International Economy, 1880–1936." *Japan Forum* 2, no. 1 (1990): 127–45.

Suhartono. "Cina Klonthong: Rural Peddlers in the Residency of Surakarta, 1850–1920." In *State and Trade in the Indonesian Archipelago,* edited by G. J. Schutte. Leiden: KITLV, 1994.

Suhartono. *Bandit-Bandit Pedesaan di Jawa: Studi Historis, 1850–1942.* Yogyakarta: Aditya Media, 1995.

"Suikerpremie, Renteloos Voorschot en de Maildienst naar Poeloe Weh." *Het Nederlandsche Zeewezen* 2 (1903): 224–25.

Sulistinyono, Singgih. "The Java Sea Network: Patterns in the Development of Interregional Shipping and Trade in the Process of National Economic Integration in Indonesia, 1870s–1970s." Ph.D. diss., Leiden University, 2003.

Surat-Surat Perdjandjian Antara Kesultanan Bandjarmasin dengan Pemerintahan Pemerintahan V.O.C, Bataafse Republik, Inggeris dan Hindia-Belanda 1635–1860. Jakarta: Arsip Nasional Republik Indonesia, 1965.

Surat-Surat Perdjandjian Antara Kesultanan Riau dengan Pemerintahan (2) V.O.C. dan Hindia-Belanda 1784–1909. Jakarta: Arsip Nasional Indonesia, 1970.

Sutherland, Heather. "Power, Trade, and Islam in the Eastern Archipelago, 1700–1850." In *Religion and Development: An Integrated Approach,* edited by Philip Quarles van Ufford, et al., 145–65. Amsterdam: Free University Press, 1988.

Sutherland, W. "Rapport Betreffende de Verrigtingen der Expeditionaire Mariniers op Sumatra van Julij 1874 tot Februarij 1876." *Mededeelingen Zeewezen* 19 (1877): 89–102.

Swettenham, F. A. *The Real Malay: Pen Pictures.* London: John Lane Bodley Head, 1900.

Tagliacozzo, Eric. "Ambiguous Commodities, Unstable Frontiers: The Case of Burma, Siam, and Imperial Britain, 1800–1900." *Comparative Studies in Society and History* 46, no. 2 (2004): 354–77.

———. "Amphora, Whisper, Text: Ways of Writing Southeast Asian History." *Crossroads: Interdisciplinary Journal of Southeast Asian Studies* 16, no. 1 (2002): 128–58.

———. "Finding Captivity Among the Peasantry: The Malay/Indonesian World, 1850–1925." *South East Asia Research* 11, no. 2 (2003): 203–32.

———. "Hydrography, Technology, Coercion: Mapping the Sea in Southeast Asian Imperialism, 1850–1900." *Archipel* 65 (2003): 89–107.

———. "Kettle on a Slow Boil: Batavia's Threat Perceptions in the Indies' Outer Islands, 1870–1910." *Journal of Southeast Asian Studies* 31, no. 1 (2000): 70–100.

———. "A Necklace of Fins: Marine Goods Trading in Maritime Southeast Asia, 1780–1860." *International Journal of Asian Studies* 1, no. 1 (2004): 23–48.

———. "Smuggling in Southeast Asia: History and Its Contemporary Vectors in an Unbounded Region." *Critical Asian Studies* 34, no. 2 (2002): 193–220.

———. "Trade, Production, and Incorporation: The Indian Ocean in Flux, 1600–1900." *Itinerario: European Journal of Overseas History* 26, no. 1 (2002): 75–106.

Tarling, Nicholas. *Imperialism in Southeast Asia: A Fleeting, Passing Phase.* London: Routledge, 2001.

———. *Piracy and Politics in the Malay World: A Study of British Imperialism in Nineteenth-Century Southeast Asia.* Singapore: Donald Moore, 1963.

Teitler, G. *Ambivalentie en Aarzeling: Het Beleid van Nederland en Nederlands-Indië ten Aanzien van Hun Kustwateren, 1870–1962.* Assen: Van Gorcum, 1994.

———. "Een 'Nieuw' en een 'Oude Richting': Militair Denken in Nederland en Nederlands-Indië Rond de Eeuwisseling." *Mededelingen van de Sectie Krijgsgeschiedenis* 1, no. 2 (1978): 165–86.

Terwiel, B. J. "Bondage and Slavery in Early Nineteenth-Century Siam." In *Slavery, Bondage, and Dependency in Southeast Asia,* edited by Anthony Reid, 118–39. St. Lucia: University of Queensland Press, 1983.

Thio, Eunice. "The Chinese Protectorate: Events and Conditions Leading to its Establishment 1823–77." *Journal of the South Seas* 16, 1/2 (1960): 40–80.

Thomas, Julian. "The Socio-Semiotics of Material Culture." *Journal of Material Culture* 3, no. 1 (1998): 97–108.

Thompson, E. P. "The Crime of Anonymity." In *Albion's Fatal Tree: Crime and Society in Eighteenth-Century England,* edited by Douglas Hay et al., 255–308. New York: Pantheon Books, 1975.

Thomson, Janice. *Mercenaries, Pirates, and Sovereigns: State-Building and Extraterritorial Violence in Early Modern Europe.* Princeton: Princeton University Press, 1994.

Thongchai, Winichakul. *Siam Mapped.* Honolulu: University of Hawaii Press, 1994.

Tirtosudarno, Riwanto. "Dari Emigratie ke Transmigratie: Meninjau Kembali Latar Belakang Kebijaksanaan Pemindahah Penunduk di Indonesia." *Sejarah, Pemikiran, Rekonstruksi, Persepsi* 6 (1996): 111–21.

Tissot van Patot, A. "Kort Overzicht van de Gebeurtenissen op Flores en Eenige Gegevens Betreffende dat Eiland" *IMT* 38, no. 2 (1907): 762–72.

"Toekomst van Groot-Atjeh." *TNI* 1 (1880): 241–55.

"Topographische Opneming van Borneo's Westerafdeeling." *IG* 1 (1892): 1148–50.

Touwen, Jeroen. *Extremes in the Archipelago: Trade and Economic Development in the Outer Islands of Indonesia, 1900–1942.* Leiden: KITLV Press, 2001.

"Tractaat van Handel en Scheepvaart Tusschen Nederland en Japan." *IG* 1 (1897): 351–54.

Tractaat van Londen 1824; Tractaat van Sumatra 1872; Bepalingen Inzake Kustvaart Doorschoten, met Aantekeningen in Handschrift. Indische Staatsblad no. 477, 479, 1912.

"Transportschepen voor het Indische Leger." *IMT* 1 (1880): 36–55.

Trocki, Carl. "Drugs, Taxes, and Chinese Capitalism in Southeast Asia." In *Opium Regimes: China, Britain, and Japan, 1839–1952,* edited by Timothy Brook and Bob Tadashi Wakabayashi, 79–104. Berkeley: University of California Press, 2000.

———. *Opium, Empire, and the Global Political Economy: A Study of the Asian Opium Trade, 1750–1950.* London: Routledge, 1999.

———. *Opium and Empire: Chinese Society in Colonial Singapore 1800–1910.* Ithaca: Cornell University Press, 1990.

———. *Prince of Pirates: The Temenggongs and the Development of Johor and Singapore 1784–1885.* Singapore: Singapore University Press, 1979.

Troupier, P. S. "Borneo. Een Goed Gelukte Overvalling" *IMT* 40, no. 2 (1909): 1046–51.

"Uitbreiding der Indische Kustverlichting." *IG* 2 (1903): 1172.

Tsuchiya, Kenji. "The Colonial State as a 'Glass House': Some Observations on Confidential Documents Concerning Japanese Activities in the Dutch East Indies, 1900–1942." *Journal of the Japan-Netherlands Institute* 2 (1990): 67–76.

Turnbull, C. Mary. *A History of Singapore*. Singapore: Oxford University Press, 1981.

Turner, F. S. *British Opium Policy and Its Results in India and China*. London: Sampson Low, Marston, Searle and Rivington, 1876.

Turner, Frederick Jackson. *The Frontier in American History*. New York: Henry Holt, 1920.

"Upper-Sarawak, Borneo, During the Year 1874, by Noel Denison, Formerly of the Sarawak Service, Singapore, Mission Press, 1879." *IG* 1 (1881): 514–17.

"Valsche Rijksdaalders in Indië." *IG* 2 (1899): 952.

Vanvugt, Ewald. *Wettig Opium: 350 Jaar Nederlandse Opium Handel in de Indische Archipel*. Haarlem: In de Knipscheer, 1985.

"Varia." *TNI* 2 (1880): 481–83.

Veer, Paul van't. *De Atjeh Oorlog*. Amsterdam: Uitgeverij De Arbeiderspers, 1969.

Velde, PGEIJ van der. "Van Koloniale Lobby naar Koloniale Hobby: Het Koninklijk Nederlands Aardrijkskundig Genootschap en Nederlands-Indië, 1873–1914." *Geografisch Tijdschrift* 22, no. 3 (1988): 211–21.

Velden, Arn. J. H. van der. *De Roomsch-Katholieke Missie in Nederlandsch Oost-Indië 1808–1908: Eene Historische Schets*. Nijmegen: Malmberg, 1908.

Velders, J. A., and A. J. du Pon. *Practisch Handboekje ten dienste van het Personeel der Stoomschepen van de Gouvernments-Marine, en de Ambtenaren, Belast met het Beheer of de Administratie der Gouvernements Gewapende en Adviesbooten*. Batavia: H. M. van Dorp, 1868.

"Verdeeling van het Zendingsveld in Indië Tusschen Katholieken en Protestanten." *IG* 1 (1889): 596–99.

"Verduurzaamde Levensmiddelen." *IMT* 1 (1896): 482–90.

Verheij, J. B. "Rapport van den 1sten Luitenant der Mariniers J.B. Verheij, Betreffende de Krijgsverrigtingen op Atjeh vanaf 26 December 1875 tot en met 7 Februarij 1876, Hoofdzakelijk ten Opzigte van het Detachement Mariniers, dat aan die Krijgsverrigtingen Heeft Deelgenomen." *Mededeelingen Zeewezen* 19 (1877): 103–55.

Verkerk Pistorius, A. W. P. "Het Maleische Dorp." *TNI* 2 (1869): 97–119

———. "Palembangsche Schetsen. Een Dag bij de Wilden." *TNI* 1 (1874): 150–60.

"Verschillende Zendelinggenootschappen in NI." *IG* 2 (1887): 1922.

"Verslag Omtrent den Zeeroof over het Jaar 1876." *TITLV* 24 (1877): 475–79.

"Versterking van het Indische Kadastrale Personeel met Ambtenaren uit het Moederland." *Tijdschrift voor Kadaster en Landmeetkunde* 20 (1904): 187–89.

Verzameling van Voorschriften ten Dienste van Havenmeesters en als Zoodanig Fungeerende Ambtenaren: Buskruijt en Wapenen, Ontplofbare Stoffen, Ontvlombare Olien, Steenkolen, Koperen Duiten, Opium, Hoofdstuk F. Batavia: Landsdrukkerij, 1906.

Veth, P. J. *Atchin en Zijn Betrekkingen tot Nederland: Topographisch-Historische Beschrijving, met een Schetskaart van het Rijk Atchin en de naastbij gelegen Nederlandsche Nederzettingen op Sumatra, naar de nieuwste bronnen te zamen gesteld door W.F. Versteeg*. Leiden: Gualtherus Kolff, 1873.

———. "De Heilige Oorlog in den Indischen Archipel." *TNI* 1 (1870): 167–76.

———. *Java: Geographisch, Ethnologisch, Historisch*. Vol. 4. Haarlem: De Erven F. Bohn, 1907.

Villiers, John, and J. Kathirithamby-Wells. *The Southeast Asian Port and Polity: Rise and Demise*. Singapore: Singapore University Press, 1990.

Vink, J. A. "Sprokkelingen Uit den Vreemde op het Gebied der Hygiène voor een Leger in de Tropen." *IMT* 2 (1899): 676–86.

Viraphol, Sarasin. *Tribute and Profit: Sino/Siamese Trade 1652–1853.* Cambridge: Harvard University Press, 1977.

Vissering, G. *Muntwezen en Ciculatie-Banken in Nederlandsch-Indië.* Amsterdam: J. H. De Bussy, 1920.

Vollenhoven, C. van. *Het Adatrecht van Nederlandsch-Indië.* 3 vols. Leiden: E. J. Brill, 1918–33.

"Voor de Practijk." *IMT* 2 (1906): 669.

"Voorheen. Rietslagen en Discipline." *IMT* 2 (1883): 342–52.

Voorhoeve, J. J. C. *Peace, Profits, and Principles: A Study of Dutch Foreign Policy.* Leiden: Nijhoff, 1985.

"Voorstel tot Beteugeling der Twee Hoofdzonden in het Leger." *IMT* 1 (1895): 540–42.

"Voorstel tot Opheffing van het Verbod dat de Vreemde Vlag Uitsluit van de Kustvaart in Nederlandsch Indië." *IG* 1 (1887): 938–42.

Voûte, W. "Goud-, Diamant-, en Tin-Houdende Alluviale Gronden in de Nederl. Oost- en West-Indische Koloniën." *Indische Mercuur* 24, no. 7 (1901): 116–17.

Vredenbregt, Jacob. "The Hadj: Some of its Features and Functions in Indonesia." *Bijdragen tot de Taal-, Land-, en Volkenkunde* 118 (1962): 91–154.

Waerden, J. van der. "Spoorwegaanleg in Zuid-Sumatra." *Indisch Bouwkundig Tijdschrift* 7, no. 9 (1904): 173–82.

Wagner, Ulla. *Colonialism and Iban Warfare.* Stockholm: OBE-Tryck, 1972.

Wakeman, Frederic. *Policing Shanghai, 1927–1937.* Berkeley: University of California Press, 1995.

Wal, S. L. van der. "De Nederlandse Expansie in Indonesie in de Tijd van het Modern Imperialisme: de Houding van de Nederlandse Regering en de Politieke Partijen." *Bijdragen en Mededeelingen Betreffende de Geschiedenis der Nederlanden* 86, no. 1 (1971): 47–54.

Walker, Andrew. *The Legend of the Golden Boat: Regulation, Trade and Traders in the Borderlands of Laos, Thailand, China, and Burma.* London: Curzon, 1999.

Walker, J. H. *Power and Prowess: The Origins of Brooke Kingship in Sarawak.* Honolulu: University of Hawaii Press, 2002.

Wang Gungwu. *China and the Chinese Overseas.* Singapore: Times Academic Press, 1991.

Warren, James. *Ah Ku and Karayuki-san: Prostitution in Singapore 1880–1940.* Singapore: Oxford University Press, 1993.

———. "Joseph Conrad's Fiction as Southeast Asian History." In *At the Edge of Southeast Asian History,* 12. Quezon City: New Day Publishers, 1987.

———. *Rickshaw Coolie: A People's History of Singapore 1880–1940.* Singapore: Oxford University Press, 1986.

———. *The Sulu Zone: The Dynamics of External Trade, Slavery, and Ethnicity in the Transformation of a Southeast Asian Maritime State.* Singapore: Singapore University Press, 1981.

Water, J. van de. "Doelmatige Kleeding. Algemeene Eischen aan Kleeding te stellen." *IMT* 1 (1902): 230–46; 2 (1902): 212–27.

"Waterdichte Kleedingstukken." *IMT* 1 (1897): 224–25.

Waterschoot van der Gracht, W. A. J. M. van. *Rapport over de Opsporing van Delfstoffen in Nederlandsch Indië. Krachtens Opdracht bij Koninklijk Besluit van 9 Juni 1913 no 54.* 's-Gravenhage: Algemeene Landsdrukkerij, 1915.

"Waterval van Mansalar." *TAG* 28 (1911): 109.

Webster, Anthony. *Gentlemen Capitalists: British Imperialism in Southeast Asia, 1770–1890.* New York: St. Martin's Press, 1998.

"Wegen op Sumatra." *IG* 1 (1881): 921–24.

"Wenk voor de Ontwikkeling van de Buitenbezittingen." *TNI* 1 (1881): 318.

Wertheim, W. F. *Indonesie van Vorstenrijk tot Neo-Kolonie.* Amsterdam: Boom Meppel, 1978

Wesseling, H. L. "The Giant That Was a Dwarf, or the Strange History of Dutch Imperialism." In *Theory and Practice of European Expansion Overseas: Essays in Honor of Ronald Robinson,* edited by A. Porter and R. Holland. London: Frank Cass, 1989.

Wheatley, Paul, ed. *Melaka: Transformation of a Malay Capital 1400–1980.* Kuala Lumpur: Oxford University Press, 1983

White, Richard. *The Middle Ground: Indians, Empires, and Republics in the Great Lakes Region, 1650–1815.* New York: Cambridge University Press, 1991.

Wickberg, Edgar. *The Chinese in Philippine Life, 1850–1898.* New Haven: Yale University Press, 1965.

Wilson, Thomas, and Hastings Donnan. "Nation, State, and Identity at International Borders." In *Border Identities: Nation and State at International Frontiers,* 1–30. Cambridge: Cambridge University Press, 1998.

Wilson, Thomas, and Hastings Donnan, eds. *Border Identities: Nation and State at International Frontiers.* Cambridge: Cambridge University Press, 1998.

Witlox, Marcel. "Met Gevaar voor Lijf en Goed: Mekkagangers uit Nederlands-Indië in de 19de Eeuw" in Willy Jansen en Huub de Jonge (redac). In *Islamitische Pelgrimstochten,* 24–26. Muiderberg: Coutinho, 1991.

Wolf, Eric. *Europe and the People Without History.* Berkeley: University of California Press, 1982.

———. *Peasant Wars of the Twentieth Century.* New York: Harper and Row, 1973.

Wollaston, A. N. "The Pilgrimage to Mecca." *Asiatic Quarterly Review* 1 (1886): 390–409.

Wolters, O. W. *Early Indonesian Commerce.* Ithaca: Cornell University Press, 1967.

Wray, Leonard. "Settlements of the Straits of Malacca." *Proceedings of the Royal Colonial Institute, Royal Commonwealth Society* 5 (1873/74): 103–26.

Young, J. W. "A. Liang-Ko: Opiumsluiken en Weldoen." *TNI* 23, no. 1 (1894): 1–29.

———. "Bijdrage tot de Kennis der Chineesche Geheime Genootschappen." *TITLV* 28 (1883): 546–77.

Young, Kenneth. *Islamic Peasants and the State: The 1908 Anti-Tax Rebellion in West Sumatra.* New Haven: Yale University Southeast Asia Monograph Series, 1994.

Yuan Bingling. *Chinese Democracies: A Study of the Kongsis of West Borneo, 1776–1884.* Leiden: CNWS, 2000.

Zainol, Binti Haji Salina. "Hubungan Perdagangan Antara Aceh, Sumatera Timur dan Pulau Pinang, 1819–1871." MA thesis, Universiti Malaya, 1995.

"Ziekenbehandeling onder de Dayaks (Midden Borneo) Door een Missionaris Capucijn." *Katholieke Missiën* 33 (1908): 99–101.

Zinoman, Peter. *The Colonial Bastille: A History of Imprisonment in Vietnam, 1862–1940.* Berkeley: University of California Press, 2001.

Zondervan, H. "Bijdrage tot de Kennis der Eilanden Bangka en Blitong." *TAG* 17 (1900): 519–27.

Index